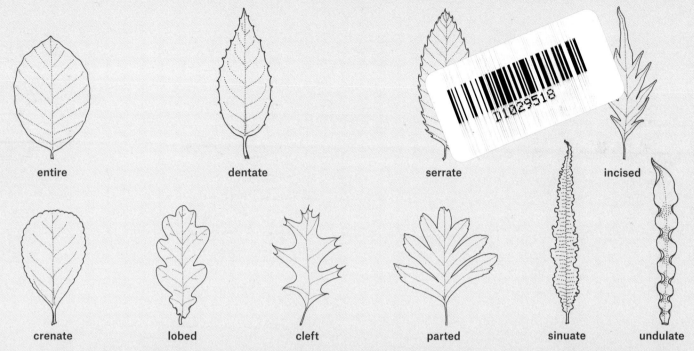

entire   dentate   serrate   incised

crenate   lobed   cleft   parted   sinuate   undulate

LEAF MARGINS

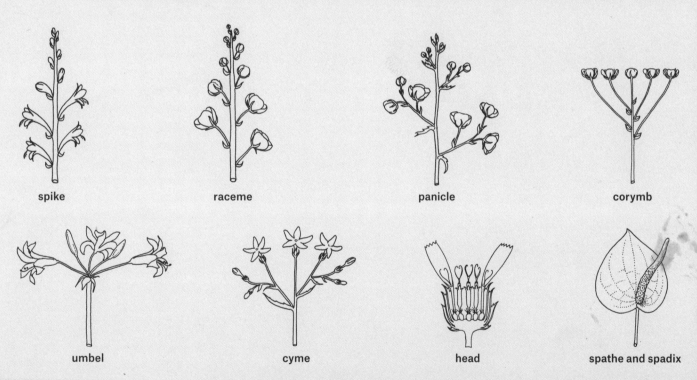

spike   raceme   panicle   corymb

umbel   cyme   head   spathe and spadix

INFLORESCENCE TYPES

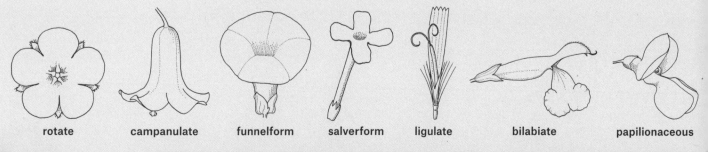

rotate   campanulate   funnelform   salverform   ligulate   bilabiate   papilionaceous

COROLLA SHAPES

Essential Perennials

Essential Perennials

The Complete Reference to 2700 Perennials for the Home Garden

**RUTH ROGERS CLAUSEN
and THOMAS CHRISTOPHER**

photographs by Alan L. Detrick & Linda Detrick

Timber Press
Portland | London

Acknowledgments

We owe a great debt to all the nursery
professionals who generously shared plants
and knowledge with us during the writing of
this book. Gardeners are a passionate group;
many have shared with us their opinions about
the superiority or otherwise of recent plant
introductions, and we thank them for that. We
thank our editor, Tom Fischer of Timber Press,
an extraordinary gardener in his own right,
who kept us abreast of changes in botanical
nomenclature and showed exceptional
patience in helping us to bring this project to
completion. Thanks go to Michael Dempsey
for his invaluable editorial assistance. Finally,
we thank Alan and Linda Detrick for their
friendship, encouragement, perseverance, and
most of all for their superb photography.

The Haseltine Building
133 S.W. Second Avenue, Suite 450
Portland, Oregon 97204-3527
timberpress.com

6a Lonsdale Road
London NW6 6RD
timberpress.co.uk

Printed in China
Cover and text design by Laken Wright

Library of Congress Cataloging-in-Publication Data
Clausen, Ruth Rogers, 1938-
  Essential perennials: the complete reference to 2700 perennials for the
home garden/Ruth Rogers
Clausen and Thomas Christopher; photographs by Alan L. Detrick and
Linda Detrick.—First edition.
     pages cm
  Includes index.
  ISBN 978-1-60469-316-4
  1. Perennials—Handbooks, manuals, etc. I. Christopher, Thomas. II. Title.
  SB434.C57 2015
  635.9'32—dc23
                    2014020896

A catalog record for this book is also available from the British Library.

For passionate, experienced gardeners, and those who are just discovering the joy of gardening with perennials.

In memory of Nicolas H. Ekstrom, our friend and colleague.

Contents

Ornamental grasses and asters extend the fall season at Chanticleer Garden in Pennsylvania.

Introduction

ANY EXPERIENCED GARDENER KNOWS that perennials—herbaceous (more or less non-woody) plants that go dormant in the fall and then return in the spring—are the main fabric of an ornamental garden. Trees and shrubs provide architecture, annuals may embroider the design, but it's the perennials that supply the enduring keynotes of texture, the calculated sequences and rhythms of colors and forms. Perennials dominate through persistence. If you've chosen your plants well, once you lay down a theme in perennials, it returns year after year, becoming the framework around which you arrange other plants and furnishings.

This is why selecting your perennials wisely is such an important process—the decisions you make can and should have long-lasting repercussions. The process of selection is challenging. Indeed, because of our good fortune, it's more challenging, or at least more complicated, than ever before. In the last 30 years the American gardener has moved from a situation of perennial famine to one of feast. A generation ago we had access to only a relative handful of old standbys. Since then, however, enterprising breeders, growers, nurseries, and plant hunters have introduced tens of thousands of new species and cultivars to the North American market. What's more, thanks to the Internet, virtually all these introductions are available for a click and some cash, no matter where you live.

There are obvious advantages to this opening of the horticultural floodgates. Plant collectors can satisfy their lust for novelty without ever leaving their own homes, and designers seeking just the right shade of iris or delphinium to perfect a color scheme can find it almost instantly and have it delivered to their mailbox within days. Yet this multiplicity of choices brings its own challenges: confronting a menu so extensive can be daunting. Hostas, for example, are a mainstay of shade gardens: who could imagine such a display without them? There are at least 3000 distinct cultivars of hosta registered with the American Hosta Society and an equal number of unregistered cultivars are in circulation. Which one is best for your situation and tastes? How do you choose? And the multiplicity of hostas actually seems manageable when compared to the selection of daylilies. There are some 60,000 or so daylily selections in cultivation now, with 2000 or more being added every year.

The glut of new material, each element of which is advertised in glowing terms, creates a dilemma. No gardener wants to miss out on the best of the new introductions, the plants that combine exceptional beauty with hardiness, easy care, and reliability. But at the same time, no one wants to cope with what amounts to horticultural spam.

A new kind of guide is needed to confront this wealth of plants, and that's just what you'll find here: a focus on 348 genera that in our opinion furnish a core group of the most reliable and rewarding herbaceous perennials—a toolbox of the truly *essential* perennials that are outstanding not only for the foliage, flowers, and forms they contribute to the garden, but which also are reliable and robust performers in the landscape. Many of the plants included are commonly seen in garden centers and catalogs, but in an effort to collect the very best, most useful, and most interesting perennials, this book also describes lesser-known species and cultivars. All are commercially available locally or by mail order.

Not all the plants included in this guide are equally exceptional in all categories, of course. A culturally demanding plant may be indispensable because of its unique look, its fragrance, or the glorious hue of its blooms. Similarly, a less aesthetically extraordinary plant may earn its place here because of its exceptional ability to cope with difficult conditions such as drought, summer humidity, or extreme winter cold. Some plants are essential because of their excellence as *supporting* actors: they may not be brilliant themselves, but they offer the benefit of reinforcing and heightening the effect of those around them.

Nomenclature

The most basic step in selecting and obtaining a particular perennial is getting the name correct. That involves becoming comfortable with botanical nomenclature. It's true that many of us use common (or English) names to identify individual plants when we discuss gardens among ourselves, but in communicating with nurseries and garden centers—and especially online—we are better advised to use the botanical (or Latin)

Gaura, purple coneflowers, and other perennials decorate the beds of a formal garden at the Indianapolis Museum of Art, Indiana.

nomenclature. Often the common name for a plant varies regionally or even within the same region: your beebalm may be someone else's bergamot. These differences in common names lead to misunderstandings, so that what you receive in a shipment from a nursery is not always what you had anticipated. As a resident of a prairie state, for example, you may wish to plant the lavender flowers with aromatic leaves known locally as beebalm or bergamot; if you order it by that name, however, you are more likely to get a scarlet-flowered eastern wildflower. Order *Monarda fistulosa*, which is the botanical name for that prairie wildflower, and the nursery should *not* send you its eastern relative, *Monarda didyma*. And unlike common names that derive from folk tradition, the botanical names are assigned according to very definite sets of rules. These are the International Code of Botanical Nomenclature and the International Code of Nomenclature for Cultivated Plants, and they are regularly updated to ensure accuracy.

The use of botanical nomenclature offers another advantage to the gardener—it indicates the relationships between plants. Each plant's botanical name, usually printed in italics, consists of two parts. The first part (*Monarda*, for example) is the genus name or generic epithet; this corresponds roughly to your family name, indicating the small group of immediate relatives to which the plant belongs. The second part of the botanical name (e.g., *fistulosa*), the species' name or specific epithet, is similar to a personal name in that it establishes exactly which member of the group is under discussion. Plant species of the same genus share characteristics such as the structure and appearance of their flowers as well as adaptations to environmental conditions such as soil type and climate. For this reason, when you have determined that one species is suited to your garden, you may assume that other members of the same genus are probably good prospects, too.

Often a perennial will have a cultivar (or cultivated variety) name attached to its botanical name, as with *Monarda didyma* 'Cambridge Scarlet'. This cultivar is a selection that has some desirable characteristic such as flower color or disease resistance, and so has been propagated and preserved intact. Some such selections "come true" from seed— seeds collected from a plant produce seedlings with the same desirable characteristic. More often, however, cultivars must be propagated vegetatively (asexually) by some method of cloning, such as division of the parent rootstock, root cuttings, or soft or hardwood cuttings taken from the original.

Many of the perennials listed in the following pages are hybrids—that is, they are the offspring of crossbreeding or the hybridizing of two distinct populations of a species or of two different species (*Salvia* ×*sylvestris*, for example, is the result of crossing *S. nemerosa* and *S. pratensis*). Occasionally, as in the case of ×*Heucherella*, the hybrids are crosses between two different genera (*Heuchera* and *Tiarella*). The goal of the plant breeder or hybridizer is to create a plant with the best qualities of both parents, and often hybrids exhibit advantages such as larger, more colorful, or more numerous flowers than either of the parents. Hybrids may possess a quality known as "hybrid vigor"—their mixed genetic parentage causes them to be extra vigorous, more adaptable, and often disease resistant, too. Many hybrids are also sterile and must be propagated vegetatively; these tend to be more consistent and uniform both in their appearance and their garden performance than species plants. On the down side, hybrid perennials may be more expensive than species perennials due to the extra work involved in producing them at the nursery. Increasing stock involves time-consuming and more laborious division or rooting cuttings.

Using this Book

The format of this book is focused on taking the reader step by step through the process of successful perennial selection. It begins, as any gardener should, with a broader survey designed to identify groups of plants that are both adapted to the conditions in the readers' gardens and suited to their design goals. Accordingly, the individual perennials here are grouped together by genus. Note, too, that each genus is listed with its botanical family, a more inclusive category that indicates other genera to which a genus is related. If you find the plants of some genus particularly appealing or successful in your garden, you'll surely want to explore their relatives.

Under each genus heading in this book, readers will find a succinct description of its attractions and benefits. Also included here are notes about any serious liabilities associated with that particular genus—even the most essential plant genus may suffer from susceptibility to insect pests and diseases, for example. Browsing these notes and scanning the photographs of the various perennials will allow you to identify quickly those that appeal to you. Occasionally this preamble may include a warning as well. Some genera, for example, may have proved too hardy and vigorous, becoming invasive in certain areas. If so, this fact is prominently noted. Historically, gardeners have been responsible for introducing many foreign (exotic) plants into their own countries. Japanese barberry (*Berberis japonica*) and purple loosestrife (*Lythrum salicaria*), for instance, have escaped from cultivation and proliferated freely, displacing natives and becoming threats to regional ecosystems. One of the missions of this book is to help gardeners ensure that this sort of mistake is not repeated. If in doubt about a particular perennial, contact your local Cooperative Extension Office (you can find the number in your phonebook, or at www.csrees. usda.gov/Extension).

PLANT ATTRIBUTES

A number of characteristics play a central role in determining whether a particular perennial is likely to perform well in your garden; to simplify your selection process this book addresses these key characteristics at the beginning of each species description.

- Flower color and season of bloom. If a flower won't please your eye or provide color when you

This patio garden at Plant Delights Nursery in North Carolina is created with assorted succulents planted in terra cotta pots for unified impact.

A partially enclosed garden creates a romantic setting for lavenders, artemisias, and other hardy perennials in the Laking Garden at the Royal Botanical Gardens in Ontario, Canada.

want it to, then you will not want to grow it. The season of bloom is expressed as a range, from the season when you can expect flowering to begin to the season when you can expect it to end.

- Height and width are expressed as ranges of inches or feet, such as 1.5–2 ft. × 18–30 in., which describes a plant that grows to a height of 1.5 to 2 feet and a width or spread of 18 to 30 inches. If the perennial won't fit in the space you can give it, you don't want to plant it.

- The amount of light a perennial requires for healthy growth. *Sun* means that this particular plant requires exposure to at least six hours of direct sunlight a day, preferably from mid-morning to midafternoon, when sunlight is most intense. *Part shade* means it will flourish with exposure to less than six hours of sun daily, but that it requires some direct sunlight or, alternatively, day-long dappled sunlight filtered through an intermittent canopy of high tree branches. *Shade* means that this species can subsist without any direct sunlight, just light reflected off trees, pavement, or buildings. By observing the conditions found in different parts of your garden, you can use these notes on light to determine if a particular plant is suited to the available location.

- Winter hardiness is expressed as a range of zones, such as Z4–9; the zones correspond to geographical areas outlined on the USDA Plant Hardiness Zone Map (http://planthardiness.ars.usda.gov/PHZMWeb). This map uses the average

coldest winter temperature experienced in each region to divide the United States into 13 zones (zone maps based on the USDA system are also available for other countries; for directions on obtaining these, turn to the resources section of this book). If a perennial is listed as hardy from zones 4 through 9, that means that if given an adequate site and care, typically it will persist from year to year within the area from the northern border of zone 4 to the southern border of zone 9. Snow cover acts as insulating mulch; plants growing in areas where snowfall is infrequent are more vulnerable to extreme cold and bitter winds. Winter temperatures also vary locally in response to altitude, proximity of large bodies of water, and garden microclimates. Treat hardiness ratings only as a guide.

In some instances you will find the letters *HS* (heat sensitive) following the zone description. This indicates that the perennial in question is sensitive to the combination of summer heat and humidity found throughout much of the southeastern United States. This plant may thrive in the warmer zones specified for it when grown in arid western climates, but it is a poor choice for regions with warm and humid summers. Alternatively, a plant may be exceptionally well adapted to regions of heat and humidity, in which case, the hardiness description will be followed with the letters *HT* (heat tolerant).

An additional consideration to keep in mind when considering a plant's hardiness description is that when the USDA revised the Plant Hardiness Zone Map in 2012, it chose to use data that

At Chicago Botanic Garden, sweeps of late summer–blooming native perennials are planted right down to the water so they are reflected in the lake.

In the New Jersey Colonial Park Gardens, copious plantings of bluebeards, black-eyed Susans, and Shasta daisies make fall gardens as exuberant as they are in spring.

understates the recent warming of the US climate. While the zone map is the standard reference of the nursery industry and as such is indispensable when making decisions about plant selection, it is also worth consulting the National Arbor Day Foundation hardiness map (www.arborday.org/media/zones.cfm). The latter uses the same winter temperature zone system as the USDA map, but it reflects more accurately recent changes in the North American climate.

OTHER INFORMATION
Following each species name, you will also find listed any obsolete or alternative botanical names (e.g., syn. *Acanthus balcanicus, A. longifolius*). Botanists are constantly revising and correcting the nomenclature—a plant known as one thing today may overnight become something else. Sometimes this is a mere updating or a consolidation of species names; in other cases plants may be assigned to new genera. For example, the huge *Chrysanthemum* genus has been split several times, so that many former members are now classified in *Dendranthema, Argyranthemum, Tanacetum*, and *Leucanthemum*. We have used the most up-to-date botanical nomenclature, but we include also the former names as some nurseries still sell the plants under those labels. In a few cases where the nursery industry as a whole has continued to use the obsolete name, this book lists the species under that name while noting the update. To eliminate any

potential for confusion, we have included an index of such synonyms at the end of the book. At the start of each species description, you will also find the most widely used common names for that plant.

NATIVE RANGES
A good way to determine whether a perennial is likely to thrive for you is to check its native climate and habitat. Clearly, if you are planning a garden in a groomed woodland area, where you have cleared the brush and weed trees to let in more light, it would be wise to select plants native to open woodlands in climates similar to your own. Perennials for a meadow garden should be grassland or prairie plants; dryland perennials are the obvious choice for arid or semi-arid gardens. That's why we have included (following the common names) information in each plant entry about the habitat and geographical area in which that species is found in the wild. Many gardeners choose to focus their attention only on plants native to their region. This greatly reduces the chance of introducing exotic invasive species into the local ecosystem, and can be a means of restoring natural biodiversity.

PLANT DESCRIPTION AND CULTURAL TIPS
After common names and native ranges, foliage is generally addressed next in each plant description because it has the most persistent influence on a plant's visual impact—the flowers may be spectacular, but their season is limited, whereas the foliage

Low-growing sedums are the predominant plants in this green roof garden at the Oregon Garden in Silverton, Oregon.

is mostly a garden presence throughout the growing season; that of evergreen perennials shines through the winter, too. Floral descriptions may include technical terminology such as *umbel* or *cyme* that may not be familiar to the reader; they are easy to interpret with the illustrated endpapers that open and close the book.

Cultural information is critical and includes the type of soil the plant prefers, and its need (if any) for irrigation. Although the soil type recommended may vary from sandy to organic-enriched, and from dry to moist, in most instances the cultural tips call for one that is "well drained." Soil drainage denotes the ease with which water passes through the soil, and that depends on how porous the soil is. Clay soil, composed of very fine particles, is naturally dense with small pores; any water deposited on it will pass through only very slowly—a soil of this kind is "poorly drained." Soil with coarser particles, such as loam or a sandy soil, has larger pore spaces that allow water to pass through more quickly. The novice may wonder how a soil that is moist can also drain well. Particles of decomposed organic material (compost or rotted leaves, for example) in the soil act like sponges absorbing and retaining moisture. The addition of organic matter creates a soil that is both well drained and consistently moist. Such a soil will satisfy the needs of peonies and other perennials and also remain sufficiently moist to satisfy moisture-loving Japanese iris and hostas.

Additional information included in the genus

descriptions includes usual propagation methods, tips about where to site the plants, and which plants are compatible companions. Notes on drought resistance, and deer and critter resistance are also included, along with any problems or pests. Below the species description, outstanding cultivars or hybrids are included. These are by no means comprehensive, but rather focus on noting the very best, a pool of selections that will provide the gardener with the most outstanding options.

Some plants included in this book, including colocasias (elephant ears), dahlias, and impatiens, have been regarded traditionally as annuals in chillier zones due to their sensitivity to cold. However, in mild zones where not subjected to significant winter cold, these plants perform as perennials. As American gardening has become less parochial over the last generation, these plants have reclaimed their true identity. Gardeners in cold-winter regions have come to value the perennial character of these tender plants as the fashion has arisen for using them as dramatic additions to summertime container displays (some refer to them as temperennials).

One further note: most of the plants included in this book are commonly seen in garden centers and catalogs, but in an effort to collect the very best and most useful perennials, this book also describes many lesser-known species and cultivars. All those described, however, are commercially available, at least in the form of seed on the Internet.

Perennial Basics

IN MANY RESPECTS, garden plants constitute what an investment adviser would describe as "fungible assets"—that is, they are interchangeable, at least in the sense that if you can grow one successfully, you can apply those same techniques to others. You can, for example, use the skills you perfected in growing tomatoes to grow other annuals such as petunias (which are, in fact, close relatives of tomatoes). But when you move on to more dissimilar plants, you do have to make adjustments. Cultivating orchids with exactly the same techniques you perfected with cacti will result in disappointment.

That may seem obvious, but many gardeners who have developed their skills on annuals and food crops don't bother to inform themselves about the special needs of perennials before they begin to invest in them, and the results can be painful. What follows is a rundown of special points that gardeners new to perennials—or even those with more experience—should keep in mind when embarking on perennial gardening.

From the Ground Up

When cultivating annuals or vegetables, you have the opportunity to refresh and redig the soil (if necessary) every growing season. With perennials, however, this is not possible, so extra care must be taken to prepare the soil well and thoroughly before planting.

The details of soil preparation will depend partly on what sorts of perennials you plan to grow. A soil test is the first step in designing any perennial planting (this can be done at nominal cost from your state's Cooperative Extension Service or from the agricultural division of your state's land-grant university). It will tell you your soil's pH (it's relative acidity) and type (loam, clay, silt, or sand, or any combination of these)—both will determine which types of perennials will grow there successfully. Some gardeners insist on trying to modify their soil to suit their favorite plants, but typically this involves a great deal of work and expense, and rarely produces results as good as selecting plants that are adapted to the kind of soil you already have.

One requirement that is common for the vast majority of perennials is the need for a well-drained soil. There are exceptions, and these have been noted in this book's plant descriptions, but they are few. A definition of what constitutes a well-drained soil has been included in the introduction to this book. You'll know that the soil in your garden or prospective border doesn't qualify if it puddles up or remains waterlogged overnight or even longer after at least an inch of rain has fallen.

If necessary, there are several ways to improve the drainage of your soil:

- Apply a layer of decomposed organic material, such as compost or leaf mold, to a depth of several inches. Dig this in about 8 in. or more deep; it will help to increase the porosity of the soil. By increasing the soil's bulk, it helps to raise the surface of the treated area above its surroundings, allowing gravity to pull the water out of the soil more efficiently.

- If you are planting species that prefer a sandy or gritty soil—those recommended for rock gardens generally require such conditions—improve the existing drainage by digging in a fifty-fifty mixture of organic matter and coarse, sharp sand or grit. Coarse sand is sold by masonry supply companies, and turkey grit is available from feed stores. Avoid the sand sold in bags at the big-box home and garden stores as it is too fine to be effective and, if the existing soil is clayey, will turn it into something like concrete.

- The classic location for a rock garden is on a sunny slope. A sloping site enhances the drainage of the soil naturally by allowing excess water to run off.

- To improve the drainage of soils in a flat or low-lying area, installing raised beds is the most effective technique. To make a raised bed, heap up the soil so that it sits above the level of the surrounding ground, thus enabling excess water to drain away. In a formal design, raised beds may be edged and contained with timber, bricks, or stones; an informal effect can be achieved by grading the edges of the raised area into a stable slope. To be effective, soil in a raised bed should stand at least 6 in. higher than its surroundings; in really damp locations, 8 in. is better.

An additional advantage of a raised bed is that the soil warms up more quickly in spring. Thus the growing season is lengthened in chilly northern or high-altitude climates, which can be a significant advantage for perennials planted there. However, due to their enhanced drainage, raised beds are also more susceptible to drought, and require more frequent irrigation during dry seasons.

Shopping for Perennials

The prime key to success with perennials is to start out with healthy, pest- and disease-free stock. This is critical with perennials since you expect to grow them in the garden for several years; an underperforming weakling may dog you for a long time. Taking full advantage of the perennials described in this book means coming to terms with bare-root (no soil on the roots) nursery stock. This is a traditional but somewhat outdated method of raising perennials in which plants are field grown, dug when dormant, and kept in cold storage over the winter. In late winter or early spring, the still-dormant plants have the soil washed from their roots, and are packed and shipped to customers. These are not the most inspiring sight when you first remove them from their shipping containers. In fact, with their brown roots and withered remains of last year's leaves, new arrivals may appear lifeless to a novice. However, if the nursery has handled and packed the plants carefully, and if you plant them promptly upon receipt, the survival rate of bare-root plants is excellent. After recovery, they'll start into growth fast. Such plants do, however, require special treatment during transplanting into your garden:

Succulents can be used in a variety of garden locations. Here at the Thomas Hobbs residence in Vancouver, Canada, they present an unusual feature of the garden.

1. When a shipment arrives from the grower, open the box immediately and inspect the contents. If the plants inside seem dry, moisten them. Set the box in a cool place, such as a basement or garage, until you can find time to plant the contents. If the plants are moldy or decaying at the time of arrival, call the retailer and demand replacements.

2. Don't procrastinate. Ideally, bare-root plants should be planted within a day of their arrival on your doorstep. Kept moist and cool, bare-root plants will generally survive a few days without planting, but every day of delay decreases the odds of success. If the plants arrive when the garden soil is unsuitable (frozen or just thawed, or too cold and wet to be worked) pot them, water them, and hold them in a sheltered sunny spot until you can plant them. They will be fine for several weeks if kept moist.

3. Stand bare-root plants in a bucket of water for a couple of hours before planting to rehydrate the roots. They are likely to have become somewhat desiccated during storage and shipping.

4. To plant, dig a hole in a well-prepared bed, deep enough and wide enough to accommodate the roots of the plant. Mound soil into a cone in the center of the hole, and set the plant on top, draping the roots over the sides. Position the plant so that its crown—the point where the stem and roots connect—is at or just below the level of the surrounding bed. Refill the hole with soil, gently working it in, over, and among the roots with your fingertips. Firm all around gently with your foot.

5. Water well. If the soil settles as it absorbs the water, top up with more soil as necessary, and water again. In a sunny position, drape floating row cover material over the plant to protect it from sunburn and dehydration for the first week or so.

Today, however, most perennials are container grown—raised in pots rather than in the ground—which does offer some advantages. If properly cared for, they can sit for weeks in a nursery's yard without harm, which extends the shopping and planting season, and makes impulse purchases possible. Container-grown plants are sold while in active growth, so it is easier for an inexperienced shopper to tell whether they are healthy. Here are some easily observed clues that reveal the status of a plant's health:

A monochromatic scene becomes more interesting when the plants differ in shape and habit, as seen here at Chicago Botanic Garden.

- When shopping at the local garden center or retail nursery, fight the temptation to select the largest specimens. Extra-large plants, out of scale and too large for their containers, have been sitting in their pots too long; this neglect stunts the plant's growth and has long-term effects on their health and vigor. Roots emerging from the drainage holes in the bottom of a container are another sign that the plant has been in the container too long.

- Always inspect the roots of any plant you contemplate buying. With the nursery's permission, slip the plant out of its nursery pot—the roots should be crisp and white, reaching out over the exterior of the soil ball but not overly long so that they've wrapped themselves around it. That condition, known as being "pot bound," also indicates that the plant has been left too long in its container.

- Check the leaves—tops and bottoms—and along the stems for insects or insect eggs; flecks of discoloration on the leaves can also be a sign of insect infestation. Bringing home infested plants releases pests into your garden that may prove difficult to eradicate.

- Unless you are inspecting a cultivar that is supposed to feature variegated foliage, yellowing leaves or ones blotched with pale patches are signs of trouble. Such off-colored leaves may be a sign of disease or mistreatment by the retailer; in either case you don't want that plant in your garden.

In addition, container-grown plants forgive procrastination; if you leave them in the shade on the porch for a few days and keep them watered until you have time to get them in the ground, container-grown plants seldom suffer any significant harm—that said, make the time delay as short as possible.

Relying on container-grown perennials to stock your garden, however, entails a couple of serious disadvantages. They tend to be more expensive than their bare-root equivalents, and some mail-order nurseries prefer to ship plants bare root because it is much more economical to do so. Consequently, customers of container-grown plants are forced to rely mainly on local retail nurseries and garden centers that may stock only a small selection of top sellers. If you want not just a phlox, but a phlox that is mildew-resistant and has flowers of a particular shade of lavender or pink, you'll probably have to shop by mail order. Similarly, if you want not just the most popular perennials, but those best adapted to *your* conditions and needs, you may have to shop by mail order.

For a listing of a few reliable mail-order nurseries, see the book's resources section. Keep in mind, however, that this business is subject to constant change, and a large number of small specialist firms

Raised beds at Robinson York State Herb Garden at Cornell Plantations in Ithaca, NY, allow the viewer to get up close and personal with the plants, especially important in fragrance gardens or those designed for the sight impaired.

Here the beautiful fountain is the focal point of the scene, with assorted perennials playing second fiddle.

The dark foliage and tall vertical spires of *Actaea* 'James Compton' set off the rounded clumps of *Helianthus* 'Lemon Queen'.

Perennials nestled against rocks benefit from a cool root run.

have not been listed in this book. Be adventurous in your mail-order shopping, but keep track of the performance of the nurseries you patronize. Some do a better job of storing, packing, and shipping bare-root plants, which is reflected in the higher survival rate (and sometimes price) of their plants. The many gardening forums on the Internet are helpful with this kind of shopping; many include nursery reviews detailing other gardeners' experiences.

Maintenance

Because of their distinctive, cyclical pattern of growth, perennials require a somewhat different kind of care from annuals or woody plants.

WINTER VS. SUMMER HARDINESS

Because our gardening tradition came to us mostly from northern Europe, Americans have focused on tolerance for winter cold as the criterion of a plant's hardiness. This attitude is reflected in the USDA Plant Hardiness Zone Map, which defines its geographical zones by the average lowest winter temperatures experienced in each region. If a plant is rated as "hardy to zone 5," it will tolerate the coldest temperatures it will encounter, on average, in any region of the United States that the USDA (Department of Agriculture) has included in that zone. Similar maps have been developed for Canada and

Britain and may be found at www.plantmaps.com, and the Australian National Botanic Gardens have created a plant hardiness map for their continent. It defines zones by somewhat different criteria from those used by the USDA, but includes a tool for correlating the two systems.

This continues to be a useful guide to the likelihood of any perennial's survival in a given region. But as southern parts of our country have come to play a larger role in American gardening, summer hardiness has become an issue too. An inch-deep layer of some organic mulch, including pine needles or shredded bark, helps keep the soil moist and cool, protecting perennials against high summer temperatures; siting plants so they receive some afternoon shade from deciduous trees when sunlight is particularly intense is also beneficial—deciduous shade is preferable as it allows the plants to enjoy winter sun during short days.

The combination of heat and humidity experienced in the summer throughout much of the southeastern United States is particularly challenging to many perennials. It's best to select plants that are adapted to this sort of climate. In addition, provide protective afternoon shade, grow plants in raised beds to improve free-air circulation, thus reducing the effects of summer humidity, and top-dress humidity-sensitive plants with sand, gravel, or grit to enable surface moisture to drain quickly—this looks particularly appropriate in rock gardens.

IRRIGATION

Gardeners whose experience has been principally with annuals and vegetables will find that the styles of watering they used successfully with those plants are less beneficial when applied to perennials. Annuals and most vegetables complete their life cycle in a single growing season and so respond best to generous watering and fertilization. Perennials, on the other hand, aside from those recommended for xeriscapes and dry soils, need adequate and consistent moisture for satisfactory growth and flowering; too generous irrigation results in soft growth. This leaves plants susceptible to pests and diseases, and also prone to sprawl.

Fundamental to supplying your perennials the level of moisture they prefer is thorough preparation of the soil before planting. Dig and amend the soil to a depth of at least 10 in.—ideally twice the length of your spade—through double digging. In situations where shallow soil makes that impractical, deepen the layer of fertile, porous soil by spreading layers of amendments over the beds and forking them in—or create raised beds.

The amendments you add will depend on the preferences of the plants you intend to grow. For most rock-garden plants and those that prefer a gritty or sandy soil, the principal amendment should be coarse, sharp sand combined with a modest amount of poultry grit. For perennials that prefer a woodland-type soil (organic enriched and evenly moist), a fitting amendment is decomposed organic matter, such as compost, leaf mold, or sphagnum peat. In either case, the goal is to create soil that naturally retains the level of moisture preferred by the plants grown in it.

With a properly prepared soil, irrigation should be deep and infrequent. An inch of water administered once a week during periods of hot, dry weather is sufficient for perennials that require a moist soil; similarly, deep watering once every two weeks or even less during droughts should satisfy a xeriscape. An easy way to test if the irrigation has penetrated through the root zone is to poke a metal rod into the soil—it will slip with relatively little resistance through wet soils and stop penetrating when its tip encounters dry soil.

But it's not only how much water you apply, but how you apply it that's important. Soaker hoses or drip irrigation systems apply water directly to the soil surface. They not only minimize water lost to evaporation during irrigation but also avoid wetting plant foliage, reducing the danger of infection and spread of fungal diseases. When irrigating really dry soils, as in xeric conditions, it is most effective to apply water in two stages. Allow the first application to soak through the soil before applying the second. This deepens penetration and reduces water loss to surface runoff.

Astilbes and Russian sage appear to be growing at the feet of the magnificent *Aesculus parviflora* shrub. In fact they are at different planting levels separated by the wall.

Plants that prefer dry conditions such as lavender thrive in dry walls to dramatic effect at Powell Gardens in Kingsville, MO.

PINCHING AND DEADHEADING

The tasks of pinching and deadheading both involve narrowly targeted, low-impact pruning that requires very little labor. However, if completed in a timely fashion, these tactics greatly enhance the form and bloom of many perennials.

Pinching consists of removing the growing tip from a plant stem with your thumb and fingertip or with a pair of clippers. The result is to awaken dormant buds farther back along the stem and encourage branching, leading to more compact, bushier growth. This makes the plant stouter, reducing or even eliminating the need for staking, and often increases flowering.

Late-blooming perennials such as chrysanthemums, asters, and sedums are commonly treated this way. Otherwise they are likely to produce long, floppy stems rather than the more attractive cushion-like growth for which such plants are known.

These examples are pinched at 6 in. tall, and again as the stems add each new 6-in. increment, until early July when flower buds should be allowed to develop. Summer-blooming perennials that tend to flop, such as summer phlox and beebalms, benefit from a curtailed version of this treatment: shear stems back by half in midspring (known as the Chelsea chop) to encourage sturdier growth.

Perennial species that bear their leaves in basal rosettes and their flowers on long, upright spikes do not respond positively to pinching. Among these unpinchables are columbines, astilbes, delphiniums, daylilies, coral bells, hostas, irises, foxgloves, and dianthus.

Deadheading is more of an ad hoc process that is applicable to virtually all perennials—it just involves snipping or pinching off spent or aging flowers as they fade. Most plants stop producing flowers as they begin to set seed; by preventing

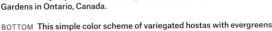

TOP Where there is plenty of room, break it up into more visually manageable spaces. Attractive trellises are dividers, and provide vertical accents to draw the eye upward at the Laking Garden at the Royal Botanical Gardens in Ontario, Canada.

BOTTOM This simple color scheme of variegated hostas with evergreens complements the white birch trunks to perfection.

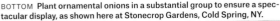

TOP Informal red poppies and billowy blue catmint add just enough color to this parkland setting at Chanticleer Garden in Pennsylvania.

BOTTOM Plant ornamental onions in a substantial group to ensure a spectacular display, as shown here at Stonecrop Gardens, Cold Spring, NY.

Massed plants make quite an impact.

them from reaching this point, deadheading helps extend bloom time. Spike-forming perennials—delphiniums, monkshood, and the like—are best deadheaded to the base of the spike to encourage later bloom on laterals; those that have solitary flowerheads on long stems, such as coreopsis and other daisies, are deadheaded to the base of the leafless stem—don't just pop off the heads, which leaves an ugly "porcupine" effect. On other perennials, look for shoots emerging lower down the stem, and cut the spent one just above it. In many cases (as noted in the species entries) the more drastic treatment of shearing a plant back by a third or a half after bloom time will provoke a burst of new growth and often a second round of flowering.

STAKING AND SUPPORT
Taller perennials, especially the more spectacular, spike-flowering types such as delphiniums, monkshood, and foxgloves, may require support to keep flower stems from toppling, especially on windy sites. Staking is also an effective way to keep heavy-headed flowers such as peonies from sprawling.

Staking is an art form. The secret of providing effective and unobtrusive support for your plants is to do your installations early in the season. Plants will then grow up, through, and around the stakes or other support, camouflaging them so that they provide an internal structural skeleton or corset while the plants preserve a natural appearance. Waiting until the plants are already sprawling or on the verge of collapse, and then cinching them with stakes and twine, yields a constricted, unnatural look.

The traditional means of supporting perennials is called brushing up. Find some brushy twigs—short and branching wild cherry and birch are favorites, but virtually any twiggy branches will work. Clip them to a length so that the tops stand a few inches below the expected height of the plant, adding perhaps an extra 10 in. to allow enough length to anchor them in the ground. Insert the branches around and among the stems of each perennial that needs support, pushing the bases firmly into the ground. This process, also known as pea-sticking, is effective for clump-forming and mounded perennials, including chrysanthemums, coreopsis, asters, and summer phlox. A less laborious, but more expensive, alternative is to encircle the plants with circular metal supports sold as peony rings. These wire rings with wire legs vary in diameter. Position the ring over the newly sprouted perennial in spring and push the legs into the soil so that the ring is about 6 in. or so above the soil surface. As the stems grow, the legs of the ring can be slipped up a bit with them. There are many other staking products on the market, as well; choose what works best for you.

Support spike-forming perennials, such as delphiniums, individually with bamboo or metal stakes pushed into the ground near the base of the plant in spring. As the flowering spikes emerge, tie them

TOP LEFT Large plant masses take on importance when delimited by short evergreen hedges at Sarah P. Duke Gardens, Durham, NC.

TOP RIGHT Native plants are valuable for more than their beauty, but also for their place in the ecosystem. Beautiful late-blooming smooth aster is a source of nectar for migrating butterflies.

BOTTOM Along a shaded path at Chicago Botanic Garden, white astilbes brighten the way. Blocks of plants not quite opposite each other entice the viewer to explore what lies ahead.

loosely to the stakes in a figure 8 with soft twine; as the spikes grow, retie every foot or so. Avoid tying too tightly and bruising—or worse, breaking the stems.

WINTER AND SUMMER MULCHES

The benefits of organic mulch to perennials in summertime has already been mentioned. It's worth noting that by insulating the soil and reducing evaporation of soil moisture into the atmosphere, an organic mulch can reduce the need for summertime irrigation by as much as half. As the mulch decomposes, it slowly adds humus to the surface soil. In a garden where chemicals are used with restraint, earthworms flourish and carry decomposing organic matter down to their burrows, thus adding to the organic content of the soil and improving soil drainage.

A winter mulch, applied in very late fall, is a lifesaver for perennials in cold-winter regions. Dormant perennials cope better with consistent cold than with rapid temperature fluctuations and the resulting cycle of freeze, thaw, and refreeze. Wait until the ground is frozen, then apply an insulating blanket of evergreen boughs or several inches of a loose, fast-draining mulch (straw, shredded leaves, etc.) and your borders will overwinter well with little damage. Remove the mulch in early spring as new growth begins.

Unsold Christmas trees, mostly available free and often in bulk the day after Christmas, are excellent and economical sources of winter mulch material. Watch for neighbors putting out their discarded trees for collection—a little tinsel here and there will not affect the plants (and it provides construction material for nesting birds).

COPING WITH PESTS AND DISEASES

The best defense against the twin threats of pests and diseases is to plant healthy specimens of resistant plants, and then provide good care. Insects can sense when a plant's natural defense system has been compromised by stressors such as drought or inadequate light, and predators will deliberately target these vulnerable victims. Weak plants are also more susceptible to diseases and less able to cope with them once infected. Weeds serve as hosts for insect pests, and compete for resources, starving adjacent desirable plants. Avoid overly generous fertilization and irrigation that encourages soft, lush growth that makes the garden a target for insect pests, deer, and other browsing animals.

Even the best-cultivated gardens, however, sometimes fall prey to such invaders. It is important that you deal promptly with any infestations before they become too general or entrenched. A good policy is to inspect the garden for pests and diseases daily. Information about possible pests and diseases is included in the species descriptions in this book to help the gardener identify incipient problems promptly.

Of all the garden perennials, peonies are among the most popular. 'Do Tell' is a winner.

Methods for controlling pests and diseases continue to evolve, often rapidly, as older pesticides lose their effectiveness or are taken off the market, and biological controls are developed and introduced. To secure the most up-to-date information about pest and disease control, contact your state's Cooperative Extension Service—most local offices keep a horticulturist on staff or can refer gardeners to an appropriate specialist with the state university system. Help with the diagnosis of what is troubling your plant and advice on recommended responses is usually free and, above all, reliable. Contact information has been included in the book's resources section.

Propagation

Having bought a plant that turns out to be a favorite, you will probably want to have more of the same. Of course you can always buy more, but it is more economical and fun to increase your own. This is known as propagation, and may be vegetative or asexual by several methods, or sexual by seed.

DIVIDING PERENNIALS

Division is a simple procedure that allows gardeners to increase their stock of perennials; it also reinvigorates some species, returning aging specimens to a younger, healthier type of growth. Division produces offspring that are genetically identical to the parent plant. This method is ideal to propagate cultivars or hybrids that do not reproduce true to type by seed, but isn't applicable to all perennials. Taprooted plants such as poppies, sea hollies, and hollyhocks typically resent any disturbance to their roots. When division is inappropriate, this fact has been noted in the individual entries in this book.

Divide fibrous-rooted perennials such as summer phlox by inserting a pair of garden forks, back to back, into the excavated root mass and prying it apart into two pieces; with a large clump, this process may be repeated one or more times to subdivide the root mass into a number of pieces. Save the healthiest divisions.

Some perennials, including anchusa and campions, prove short lived unless reinvigorated by division every three or four years. The plants die out in the center of the clump after a couple of years; remedy this by digging and separating the strongest outside pieces from the clump and discarding the dead center.

Timing is crucial to the success of this operation. In cold-winter regions, early spring, just as new growth is emerging, is usually the best time to divide perennials, as the leaves and stems are still small and less easily damaged, and the root systems are full of stored energy that helps the divisions recover and make new growth. Spring divisions have an entire growing season to reestablish, before facing the challenge of winter. In hot and dry climates, with mild winters and torrid, droughty summers, early fall can be a better season to divide perennials. Some perennials such as bearded and Siberian irises, Asiatic lilies, daylilies, summer phlox, Jacob's ladders, Oriental poppies, and herbaceous peonies prefer fall division, regardless of climate.

PROPAGATION BY CUTTINGS
Another method of increasing stock is by taking cuttings. These may be made from soft, young growth, from semi-ripe growth that is slightly hardened at the base, or from hardwood cuttings, which are reserved for woody plants. For a few perennials, Oriental poppies for example, root cuttings can be taken from fat roots, usually in winter.

Soft wood or stem cuttings and basal cuttings are pieces of stem or young shoots that are cut off the mother plant. Trim cuttings to about 3–6 in. long, depending upon the species, cutting preferably just below a node where leaves emerge. Remove the bottom leaves, dip the base in rooting compound (to stimulate root production) and tap off excess, then insert the cuttings into a container of seed mix, sand, or peat or perlite mix (this is called sticking). Gently firm the cuttings and water from below or lightly from on top. Place the containers in plastic bags, blow up, and seal. Place them in a shaded spot until rooting occurs. Most species take at least two to four weeks or more to root, although

chrysanthemums, for instance, root from 2- to 3-in. cuttings in a week if conditions are ideal.

Semi-ripe cuttings are taken much the same way, although the cuttings are probably longer. These are often taken with a heel—that is, with a piece of the mother stem attached. Strip the side branch from the mother, pulling downward to take a short spur of tissue with the cutting. Trim it up before sticking.

Root cuttings are taken from species such as anchusa, bleeding heart, and some peonies that have thick, fleshy roots. Look for roots that are about as thick as a pencil, sever a few pieces, and trim them up. Make a slanted cut at the end of the root that was closest to the plant and a horizontal cut at the other end. The roots can then be laid horizontally on top of a rooting soil mix and covered to about the depth of their thickness. Water carefully.

Layering is a method used to increase some perennials, especially dianthus. Bend the stem down if necessary, then nick no more than a third of the way through the underside of it with a sharp knife or razor blade. Open the wound and sprinkle a little rooting hormone on the cut, then peg it down to the soil (a hairpin or opened paperclip works well). Cover the wounded section with a mound of mixed soil, peat, and sand, and keep evenly moist until rooting occurs.

STARTING FROM SEEDS
Starting plants from seed is an economical and easy—albeit slow—way to furnish your perennial beds. The caveat is that sexual reproduction (seed production) results in some reshuffling of genetic material. Offspring will be variable and not always exact copies of their parents. Plant breeders, however, have created many desirable hybrid strains, which can be relied upon to come true and which are sold as seed. Propagation by seed is arguably the best way to secure a quantity of plants for a wild or meadow garden; by introducing genetic variability into your planting, it increases its resilience to pests, diseases, and extreme weather. No matter what the challenge, a less homogenous, seed-propagated population is likely to contain some individuals with natural resistance; conversely a garden planted with a handful of spectacular cloned (genetically uniform), named cultivars may be more susceptible.

As a rule, the instructions printed on the seed packet offer a good guide to the proper treatment of that particular perennial. The following tricks, however, may be helpful to ensure your success. Start the seeds indoors, in shallow containers (with drainage holes in the bottom, of course) filled with your favorite soilless seed-starting mix. Starting indoors produces the best results because you can protect the germinating seeds from fluctuations in temperature and moisture, as well as from insects and birds. These mixes are naturally sterile and greatly reduce the danger of fungi that might attack newly sprouted seedlings. A dressing of milled sphagnum or coarse grit also reduces the threat of damping off, a fungal disease. Fluorescent fixtures, outfitted with a combination of "warm-white" and "cool-white" tubes provides a nearly ideal light source.

The following are some ideas for pre-treatments that will help you get the most from your seeds:

- Some seeds, including baptisia, thermopsis, and hardy geraniums, have thick, hard seed coats that prevent water from penetrating, causing delayed germination. Scarify the seed coats by rubbing the seeds lightly over coarse sandpaper; then soak them in water overnight prior to sowing to increase both the speed and rate of germination.
- To delay germination until spring arrives, the seeds of perennials that evolved in very harsh climates often remain dormant and require a winter-like period of moisture and chilling (stratification) to break dormancy. To satisfy this requirement, after sowing the seeds enclose the containers in sealed plastic bags and store them in the refrigerator or outdoors for winter chill for a minimum of eight weeks. If germination doesn't occur when the containers are brought back into warmer temperatures, don't throw them out—they may simply need another chilling cycle.
- Gentle, even warmth enhances the germination rate of many perennial seeds. The best way to provide this is to set your seed-starting containers on a waterproof, thermostatically controlled heating mat—these devices are available from many nurseries and horticultural supply companies, as well as some mail-order seed catalogs. Failing that, you can put them on top of the refrigerator, but make sure to monitor them closely.

Perennials A-Z

Acanthus spinosus

Acanthus
Acanthaceae
bear's breech

One of the most architectural of perennials, bear's breech's bold leaves—variously lobed, cut, and divided, some tipped with spines—inspired the decorative foliage on Corinthian column capitals. The bracted, tubular flowers, borne in dramatic spikes above the foliage, are mostly white, often almost concealed by a purple or mauve hood, and are excellent for cut flowers, fresh or dried.

These are not plants for tight conditions or for the faint of heart. Bear's breech can take over a small space and is considered by some to be invasive, especially on favorable sites—its tenacious roots are almost impossible to eradicate. Established plants tolerate drought well, though good drainage is critical. In cold-winter climates, apply a protective winter mulch.

A fine subject for large containers for a deck or patio, bear's breech also stands out massed beside lightly shaded driveways or on the edge of woodlands, where it can spread freely. In flower borders, protect from intense sun. Garden phlox, upright milky campanula, and meadow rue are good back-of-the-border companions. Underplant with geranium 'Rozanne' or sweet woodruff. Seldom browsed by deer.

Propagate by division or by detaching young plants from the base in spring or fall. Sow seed in spring, or take root cuttings when the plants are dormant.

Acanthus hungaricus
syn. *A. balcanicus, A. longifolius*
- white, purple
- late spring to summer
- 3–4 ft. × 3 ft.
- sun, part shade
- Z6–10

Balkan bear's breech. Southeastern Europe. Clumps of deeply divided, dull green leaves are thistle like but lack spines. White flowers are hooded with plum bracts equipped with spines.

Acanthus mollis
- white, purple
- late spring to summer
- 4 ft. × 3 ft.
- sun, part shade
- Z7–10, HS

Bear's breech. Southeastern Europe, northwestern Africa. Deeply lobed, glossy leaves to 2 ft. long. Slow to establish, especially when grown from seed. Intolerant of heat coupled with humidity.

'Hollard's Gold' emerges with bright gold foliage in spring, which unfortunately matures to green. Can be used as a startling focal point to contrast with ostrich fern (*Matteuccia struthiopteris*) in light shade, or as a specimen or container plant. Spikes of white and wine-colored flowers rise to 5 ft. tall all summer long.

'Rue Ledan' thrives in hot, humid conditions. Clumps of handsome, shiny leaves may reach 3 ft. across. Spikes of pure white flowers rise to 3 ft. Not as heat tolerant. Z6–8.

'Whitewater' bears eye-catching, deeply cut leaves generously splashed and tipped with white, and white-and-pink snapdragon-like flowers in summer. Tough, excellent in difficult areas.

Acanthus spinosus
syn. *A. spinossissimus*
- white, purple
- summer
- 3–4 ft. × 2–3 ft.
- sun, part shade
- Z6–9

Bear's breech. Eastern Mediterranean. This species does not establish quickly but is worth the wait. The thistle-like, dark green leaves are glossy and variably spiny.

Other Notable Cultivars
'Holland Days', often listed under *Acanthus spinosus*, has deeply cut, sharply pointed (but not spiny) leaves, and purple-bracted, white flowers. Ideal for smaller gardens, but beware of its invasive tendencies. 1 ft. × 3 ft. Z6–10.

'Summer Beauty' sports huge, deeply cut, shiny, dark leaves; 4- to 6-foot flower stems with mauve-bracted, white flowers. Tolerates southern heat and humidity. Z6–10.

Achillea
Asteraceae
yarrow

Summer-blooming yarrows are major players in sunny ornamental gardens. Their ease of culture and sturdy constitution reward beginners and experienced gardeners alike. A few low-growing species, such as *Achillea ageratifolia* and *A. tomentosa* 'King Edward', are best suited to rock gardens, but

Achillea 'Coronation Gold' contrasts vibrantly with blue salvias and geraniums

the majority of yarrows are upright and suitable for mixed and perennial borders, and butterfly, wildlife, and cutting gardens.

Foliage is green or silvery gray-green, finely divided, and has an aromatic odor that deters browsing by deer and rabbits. Fibrous flower stems are crowned with flattened simple or compound heads of colorful, little daisy flowers, the outer all female and the inner bisexual and mostly yellow. Excellent as fresh or dried cut flowers; harvest in the cool of the day, taking flowers on which pollen is visible for longest vase life.

Yarrows thrive in most well-drained soils and tolerate drought when established. Also tolerant of salty winds, and excellent in coastal gardens. For best results, grow in full sun with lean soil; poor drainage and rich soil encourages soft, disease-prone growth that may need staking. After blooms are spent, deadhead to the ground. To maintain vigor, divide plants every two to three years.

Complement yellow-flowered achilleas with blue delphiniums, red hot pokers, monkshood, and bellflowers, or create a monochromatic design with yellow coreopsis, goldenrods, and yellow-toned daylilies. Pink and red yarrows are handsome planted with daylilies of similar hues; the habits and flower shapes contrast well.

Propagate named cultivars and hybrids by division or soft cuttings in spring; sow seed of species in spring.

Achillea filipendulina
syn. *A. eupatorium*
- yellow
- early summer to early fall
- 3–4 ft. × 2–3 ft.
- sun
- Z3–9

Fern-leaf yarrow. Caucasus. Rosettes of aromatic, deeply cut, greenish foliage give rise to strong stems topped with 4- to 5-in.-wide, golden flowerheads. Requires lean, very well-drained soil.

'Cloth of Gold' has brilliant yellow flowerheads. Tolerates very light shade. Comes true from seed. 4–5 ft. tall.

'Gold Plate' is one of the tallest yarrows, with 6-in.-wide heads of bright golden flowers. Tolerates heat and humidity well. Z3–8.

'Parker's Variety' is another fine selection with large, golden flowerheads. 4–5 ft. Z3–8.

Achillea grandifolia
- white
- summer to late summer
- 3–4 ft. × 2 ft.
- sun
- Z5–8

White yarrow. Turkey and the Balkans. An uncommon species worth seeking out. Large, fern-like, cut, gray-green leaves; strong stems bear 3-in.-wide heads of clean white flowers. Great companion for vibrant echinaceas, daylilies, and checker mallows.

Achillea millefolium
- white
- summer to early fall
- 2–2.5 ft. × 4 ft.
- sun
- Z3–9

Common yarrow, sneezeweed, soldier's friend. Temperate regions. Weedy, a poor garden plant but parent of many fine selections and hybrids. Divide every two to three years to maintain vigor.

'Apfelblute' ('Apple Blossom') has soft lilac to rose flowerheads, and green foliage. Excellent for massing.

'Apricot Delight', sometimes called 'Tutti Frutti', has salmon, deep and light pink heads of flowers above grayish foliage. Compact, suitable for containers. 15 in. tall.

'Oertels Rose' sports strong, non-fading pink flowers. 12–24 in tall.

'Paprika' has dusty red flowers in 2- to 3-in. heads. Mid-green foliage. Pinch to control height, especially in hot, humid climates. Deadhead for rebloom. 18–36 in tall.

Seduction Series is a strain bred for their stellar performance in the hot, humid climates of the Southeast. Sturdy, upright, and compact. 18–24 in. Z4–8.

Achillea ptarmica
- white
- early summer to fall
- 18–24 in. × 24 in.
- sun, part shade
- Z3–9

Sneezeweed, sneezewort, bridewort. Europe. With 2- to 3-in.-long, lanceolate, green leaves and branched stems, sneezeweed is not the average

Achillea millefolium 'Oertels Rose'

Achillea 'Terra Cotta'

yarrow. Loose clusters of button-like, single or double, white flowers top slender stems like a bouquet. The foliage has been chewed to quiet a toothache or dried for use as snuff. May spread in average soil; best where the soil is poor and dry. The double forms are most popular.

'Ballerina', a dwarf version of 2-ft.-tall 'Angel's Breath', is a baby's breath lookalike. Long blooming. Deadhead to prevent self-seeding. 12 in. tall.

'Perry's White'. Pure white, double flowers make this superior to rather dingy 'The Pearl'. Upright and vigorous but may become floppy; provide support. 30 in. tall.

'Stephanie Cohen' may be listed under *Achillea sibirica*. Pale pink flowers are carried in clusters 2–4 in. across. Named for American horticulturist Stephanie Cohen. 15–24 in. tall.

Achillea tomentosa

- yellow
- summer
- 8–15 in. × 18 in.
- sun
- Z3–9, HS

Woolly yarrow, dwarf yarrow. Western Asia, southern Europe. Evergreen mat-former with aromatic, gray foliage finely divided and covered with soft hairs. Clusters of bright yellow flowers attract birds and butterflies throughout the summer. Site in poor, free-draining soil. Excellent in rock gardens, but it has invasive tendencies. Drought tolerant; ideal for xeriscapes.

'Aurea', golden creeping yarrow, bears lemon-yellow flowers on 6- to 10-in. stems. 'Maynard's Gold' may be a synonym.

'Goldie' has bright golden flowers. 6–8 in. tall.

'King Edward'. An old cultivar, often listed as *Achillea ×lewisii*. Creamy-yellow flowers. 8 in. tall.

Other Notable Cultivars

Anthea ('Anblo') is a heat-tolerant, clump-forming British hybrid with summer to early fall bloom. Pale yellow flowerheads, 3 in. wide; soft silvery foliage. Deadhead or cut plants by half after the first flush. 18–28 in. × 36 in. Z3–9.

'Coronation Gold' (*Achillea clypeolata* hort. × *A. filipendulina*). Perhaps the most popular yarrow for long-lasting cut flowers. Plate-like, 3- to 4-in. inflorescences in late spring to late summer. Aromatic, gray-green, ferny foliage. Tolerates heat, humidity, and dry spells with aplomb. Divide every three to four years. Partner with mauve and purple asters. 2–3 ft. × 2 ft. Z3–9.

Galaxy Hybrids (*A. millefolium* × *A.* 'Taygetea'), a fine strain with heads of pink, red, or yellow flowers from late spring to midsummer. Select superior colors; colors may fade in intense sun. Propagate by division. 2–3 ft. × 2 ft. Z3–9.

'Moonshine', an Alan Bloom hybrid, has wide, long-lasting, bright yellow flowerheads from early summer to fall; finely dissected, fragrant, silvery foliage. Cut back after first floral flush for rebloom. Sensitive to heat and humidity. Partner with daylilies, speedwells, and bellflowers. 18–24 in. × 18 in. Z4–8, HS.

Summer Pastels strain has green foliage and flowerheads in pinks, purples, yellows, and white. Less aggressive than many yarrows. Blooms first year from seed. 24–30 in. tall.

'Terra Cotta' has silvery foliage and heads of flowers that range in color from peach and salmon to burnt orange. 3 ft. tall.

'Taygetea'. Rich gray, dissected leaves provide a fine foil for soft lemon flowerheads; summer to fall. Easy to grow, undemanding, perfect for smaller spaces. Not to be confused with weedy, white Greek yarrow, *A. taygetea*. 12–18 in. × 18 in. Z3–10.

Aconitum
Ranunculaceae
monkshood, aconite

This genus of 250 or more species has accumulated a wealth of common names, including wolf's bane, leopard's bane, helmet flower, and devil's helmet, most of which refer to the plants' poisonous qualities or the helmet-like shape of the flowers. All parts of the plants are toxic; the sap (containing the poison, aconitine) has found use as a poison to tip arrows for hunting and war. Even so, a number of species and hybrids are definitely garden worthy, though they should never be planted where children play or near vegetable or herb gardens. *Aconitum* nomenclature is very confused; locating a recommended species may involve searching under the synonyms included in the descriptions below.

Monkshoods usually have tuberous roots that give rise to upright stems clothed with attractive, alternate foliage, deeply cut, dissected, or lobed.

The 1- to 2-in. flowers are hooded or helmet shaped with a large sepal that protects the sexual parts. Blooms are borne in long racemes or panicles, up to 20 in. long, raised well above the mass of foliage.

Although they prefer part shade, monkshoods accept full sun where summers are temperate as long as the soil does not dry out. Ideally, soils should be fertile, cool, and moisture retentive but not waterlogged. Maintenance is minimal; deadhead spent flower spikes to their bases only, as lateral branches will bloom later. Some species may require staking. Always wear protective gloves when working with aconitum and avoid exposing open wounds or eyes to the sap. *Never* decorate a plate of food with the blooms. In beds and borders, summer phlox, assorted daisies, and daylilies are good companions; avoid placing the blue-flowered monkshoods against a dark background as the flowers tend to disappear.

Resistant to deer and rabbit browsing. Bumblebees pollinate the flowers and suck nectar from the end of spurs under the hood.

Divide the tuberous roots in fall or early spring every three years or so to maintain vigor and to increase. Start from seed in spring.

Aconitum ×cammarum

syn. *A. napellus* var. *bicolor, A. ×bicolor*
- various
- summer to fall
- 3–4 ft. × 2 ft.
- sun, part shade
- Z3–7, HS

Bicolor monkshood. Of garden origin. Probably a cross between *Aconitum napellus* and *A. variegatum.* Habit varies from stiffly erect to more relaxed. Lustrous, deeply five- to seven-fingered, dark green, 2- to 3-in. leaves.

'Bicolor' (syn. *A. ×bicolor*) bears wide, loosely branched panicles of 1.5-in., white, helmet-shaped flowers edged with blue; midsummer. May need staking. 4 ft. tall.

'Bressingham Spire' has narrow wands of violet-blue flowers on sturdy stems that seldom need staking. 2–3 ft. tall.

Aconitum carmichaelii

syn. *A. fischeri*
- deep blue
- late summer to early fall
- 2–5 ft. × 2 ft.
- sun, part shade
- Z3–7, HS

Azure monkshood, autumn-flowering monkshood. Central and western China, North America. Tuberous roots give rise to erect stems to 5 ft. tall under ideal conditions; more often 2–3 ft. Handsome leathery, dark-green foliage is deeply cut into three to five lobes. Dense, 8-in.-long panicles of large, violet or deep blue flowers. Prefers consistently moist soils; a fine choice for wet soil beside water features, in damp woods, and rain gardens.

'Arendsii' (syn. *Aconitum ×arendsii*). Branched

Aconitum carmichaelii 'Arendsii'

panicles of large, strong azure-blue helmet flowers in fall. Stout stems seldom need staking. Introduced by Georg Arends of Germany. 2–4 ft. tall.

'Barker's Variety' has loose spikes of deep violet flowers in fall. Start from seed. To 6 ft. tall.

'Cloudy', a mutation of 'Arendsii', is upright, with thick stems and lots of bicolored, light-blue-and-white flowers. 34 in.

Aconitum henryi

- indigo blue
- summer
- 4–5 ft. × 2 ft.
- sun, part shade
- Z3–7

Henry's monkshood. Western China. Sturdy lower stems, but upper ones are thin and may even semi-twine. Foliage is not as leathery as *Aconitum carmichaelii*'s, but is divided into three to five lobes almost to the leaf base. Loose clusters of flowers. Usually needs support.

'Spark's Variety' (syn. *A.* 'Spark', *A.* 'Spark's Variety', *A. ×cammarum* 'Spark's Variety'), autumn monkshood, is summer blooming with branched clusters of amethyst-blue flowers on slender stems. 4 ft. Z5.

Aconitum napellus

- blue
- mid- to late summer
- 2–4 ft. × 1 ft.
- sun, part shade
- Z3–8

Common or English monkshood, helmet flower. Europe. Variable, but leaves are usually divided into five to seven lobes, and further cut into lance-shaped segments. Terminal racemes of indigo-blue flowers.

'Album' (syn. *Aconitum napellus* var. *albidum*) has spires of white flowers in midsummer. 3–4 ft. Z5–8.

'Carneum' (syn. *A. compactum* 'Carneum') has

Aconogonum 'Johanniswolke'

blush-pink flowers that intensify in color in cool, damp climates. 4–5 ft. Z2–8.

'**Rubellum**'. Dark foliage shows off the spires of light pink flowers well. Best in part shade; may fade in intense sun. Good cut flower. 36 in. Z4–8.

Aconitum vulparia
syn. *A. lycoctonum* hort.

- yellow
- summer to early fall
- 3–5 ft. × 1.5 ft.
- sun, part shade
- Z3–6

Yellow wolfsbane, badger's bane. Central and southern Europe. Long-stalked basal leaves diminish in size as they ascend the stem. Foliage is dark green, paler beneath, rounded or kidney shaped and cleft into five to nine divisions, each toothed and three lobed. Pale yellow, 0.75-in. flowers crowd into terminal racemes; blossoms rounded at the top and narrowed at the middle.

Other Notable Cultivars

'**Blue Lagoon**' is compact with bright blue flowers that open from the bottom up. Excellent as cut flowers. Mid- to late summer bloom. 10–12 in. Z4–8.

'**Blue Scepter**' is excellent for cutting and adapts well to shaded borders. Branching spires of white flowers broadly edged with purplish blue. 28 in. Z4–8.

'**Ivorine**' is compact, bushy, and erect with short, dense spikes of small, creamy-white flowers in early to midsummer. Best in part shade. 36 in. Z4–8.

'**Newry Blue**' has navy-blue flowers on erect stems. Comes true from seed. 4–5 ft. Z3–7.

'**Pink Sensation**' is a Piet Oudolf introduction with silvery pink flowers accented with a dark throat. No staking required. Best in sun. 36–40 in. Z3–8.

'**Stainless Steel**' bears metallic-blue flowers from early to late summer, with complementary grayish foliage. 40 in. Z2–9.

Aconogonum
Polygonaceae

A genus in the making, *Aconogonum* includes a number of species that until recently were classified as *Persicaria* or *Polygonum*. Only one cultivar is garden worthy. See the entry for *Persicaria* for cultural notes.

Aconogonum 'Johanniswolke'
syn. *Persicaria polymorpha, Polygonum polymorphum*

- white
- late spring to late summer
- 4–6 ft. × 4 ft.
- sun
- Z4–8

White dragon fleece flower, giant fleeceflower. High altitudes, gravelly soils, China and Japan. Develops large, vase-shaped clumps of vigorous, fleshy stems, but is not aggressive. Terminal panicles of white flowers that elongate into creamy-white plumes are long lasting, flush pink with age. Very good for cutting and a show stopper in the garden. Do not confine to small spaces as these plants like to strut their stuff. Better in cooler climates than in the hot and humid South.

Acorus

Acoraceae
calamus, sweet flag

A handful of very ancient plants that were recently assigned their own family, sweet flags have traditionally been valued for the sweet smell produced when their leaves or rhizomatous roots were bruised or cut. Medieval housekeepers strewed sweet flag foliage on their floors as natural air fresheners; the leaves of some species were used as flavorings for beer.

These plants thrive in wet soils and even shallow water, making them invaluable for aquatic and bog gardens. Showier cultivars make attractive additions to damp beds, borders, and meadow plantings in areas where the soil remains reliably moist. The variegated cultivars are striking when grown in so-called miniature aquatic gardens— containers of soil topped with water. Effective as a substitute for ornamental grasses in shaded places where grasses fail. Sometimes attacked by rust and root rot. Seldom browsed by deer.

Propagate by division of the roots or start from seed.

Acorus americanus

- yellow
- late spring to summer
- 2–4 ft. high and wide
- sun, part shade
- Z4–7

Sweet flag. Northern half of North America. Vigorous and fast spreading, useful for stabilizing wet soils and as a groundcover in bog gardens and wet meadows. The lush sword-shaped leaves are green, though somewhat coarse; tiny, tawny-yellow flowers are borne in thumb-like spadices (dense flower spikes surrounded by a sheath or spathe), and are replaced in late summer and fall by dark berries. The foliage exudes a citrus fragrance when bruised. *Acorus calamus* is a closely similar European species sold by many nurseries, but it is invasive and should be avoided.

Acorus gramineus

- yellow
- late spring to early summer
- 0.5–1 ft. high and wide
- sun, part shade
- Z5–9

Japanese sweet flag. Eastern Asia. Semi-evergreen, produces tussocks of 0.25-in.-wide, grass-like leaves that smell of cinnamon; the tiny, yellow flowers are easily overlooked, though the red berries that follow are ornamental. A reliable but not-too-aggressive spreader, this species is most effective massed around the margins of ponds or along stream banks where it helps control erosion, or it can be used as an edging for moist borders. Japanese primulas, turtleheads, and cardinal flowers make fine

Acorus gramineus 'Ogon'

companions. Occasionally subject to fungal leaf spot or rust, but usually no serious pest or disease problems; deer resistant. Early afternoon shade is beneficial in regions where sun is intense.

'Minimus Aureus' makes 3–4 in. × 6–9 in. tufts of yellow, grass-like foliage; insignificant greenish yellow flowers appear in spring.

'Oborozuki' (10–12 in.) and 'Ogon' (8–10 in.) are closely similar, compact, variegated cultivars with showy, green-striped, golden-yellow leaves.

Actaea

Ranunculaceae
baneberry

In recent years botanists have expanded the genus *Actaea* to include all the plants formerly classified as species of *Cimicifuga* (*C. japonica*, *C. matsumurae*, *C. racemosa*, and *C. simplex*). Many nurseries still sell these plants under their old names, so these have been included here as synonyms.

Natives of temperate Northern Hemisphere woodlands, baneberries flourish in moist, well-drained, humus-rich soils in situations of partial shade, dappled sunlight, or even full shade. Their combination of attractive foliage, small but elegant flowerheads, and ornamental fruits make them

To propagate, sow seed in containers in fall and overwinter outdoors in a cold, but protected spot, or divide mature plants in early spring.

Actaea japonica
syn. *Cimicifuga japonica*
- white
- late summer
- 36–48 in. × 22 in.
- part shade, shade
- Z3–9

Japanese bugbane. Japan. Blooming later than most baneberries, this Japanese native has just three large leaflets per leaf and flowers borne in branching panicles. The best *Actaea* for the hot, humid southeastern United States.

'Cheju Island Form' is compact, making a mound of foliage just 12–14 in. high. Flower stems might reach 4–5 ft.; floriferous—a single mature plant may bear 12–15 flower spikes.

Actaea matsumurae
syn. *Cimicifuga matsumurae, C. simplex* var. *matsumurae*
- white
- late summer to early fall
- 3–4 ft. × 2–3 ft.
- part shade, shade
- Z4–9, HS

Bugbane. Central and eastern Asia. Chiefly available as the cultivar 'White Pearl' (syn. *Cimicifuga simplex* 'White Pearl'). Arching, bottlebrush-like racemes to 24 in. long with small, white flowers borne on slender stems; these rise well above the mound of dissected, fern-like, medium green leaves that emerge late in spring.

Actaea pachypoda
syn. *Cimicifuga pachypoda*
- white
- mid- to late spring
- 1.5–2.5 ft. × 2–3 ft.
- part shade, shade
- Z3–8

White baneberry, white cohosh, doll's eyes. Eastern North America. This low-key but charming woodland wildflower thrives under tree canopies and in clearings. Astilbe-like, compound leaves of three-toothed leaflets remain attractive all season. Sweetly scented, tiny, white flowers in oblong clusters are held aloft on long stems that turn red as the pea-sized, white berries, each with a single purple spot, develop. The berries do indeed resemble doll's eyes but are extremely poisonous, making white baneberry a poor choice for households with children. The toxicity deters wildlife, so the fruit display lasts typically until a killing autumn frost. Ideal in woodland or shade gardens, as well as in shady borders. Long lived, it often naturalizes and forms colonies. Ferns, blue sedge, bugbanes, and goldenseal are good companions.

'Misty Blue' has delicate blue-green foliage together with white springtime flowers. Poisonous white berries follow. 2–3 ft.

Actaea simplex 'James Compton'

good choices for a woodland or wild garden. Those formerly classified as *Cimicifuga* are stately, elegant perennials, with lacy foliage and fluffy spires of sweetly scented, small, star-like flowers borne atop soaring, erect, or arching stems. All are intolerant of dry conditions but otherwise easy to grow, with few serious pests or other problems. Deer appear to ignore them. Typically long lived if their basic needs are met, actaeas often naturalize in hospitable locations.

Be warned that many members of this genus are poisonous in some or all their parts, especially the fruits (which are, however, attractive fare for many birds).

Actaea racemosa

Adenophora bulleyana

Actaea racemosa

syn. *Cimicifuga racemosa*
- white
- late spring to early summer
- 4–6 ft. × 2–4 ft.
- part shade, shade
- Z3–8, HS

Black bugbane, black snakeroot, black cohosh. Rocky woods throughout most of the United States east of the Mississippi. Produces white-flowered spikes that may soar to 8 ft. in ideal conditions—humus-rich, evenly moist soil, and a sheltered, semi-shaded site. Astilbe-like foliage, three times divided, is an attractive deep green. Provide support for flower spikes, especially in windy spots.

Actaea rubra

- white
- mid- to late spring
- 1–3 ft. × 6–12 in.
- part shade, shade
- Z4–8, HS

Red baneberry. Cool, moist, nutrient-rich sites throughout the northeastern and midwestern United States, the Rocky Mountains, and Pacific Coast regions. Stems bear few coarsely toothed, deeply lobed leaves that emerge in a bushy clump. Clusters of lightly rose-scented, small, delicate, white flowers open above the foliage; conspicuous glossy red or occasionally white berries follow in late summer and fall. The fruits are favorites of many birds, including grouse, gray catbirds, and

robins. Best in woodland gardens where trilliums, meadow rues, gaultheria, and false Solomon's seal are appropriate native companions.

Actaea simplex

syn. *Cimicifuga simplex, C. ramosa*
- white
- late summer to early fall
- 3–4 ft. × 2–3 ft.
- part shade, shade
- Z4–8, HS

Bugbane, Kamchatka bugbane. Mongolia, eastern Russia, and Japan. Late in the season numerous, small, creamy-white, strongly scented flowers bloom in fluffy spires atop tall, upright, wiry stems. Attractive dark green, astilbe-like foliage, compound with deeply cut leaflets. Often self-seeds and naturalizes. Provide support for flowering stems; best where sheltered from strong winds. Bugbane is an asset in woodland gardens, among shrubs, in cottage gardens, and naturalized areas. Most attractive when planted in multiples; white spires show up well against dark backgrounds.

Atropurpurea Group (black bugbane) includes a number of dark-leaved cultivars that are still listed in many catalogs under *Cimicifuga ramosa*: 'Atropurpurea', 6 ft.; look for clones with darker-hued foliage. 'Black Negligee' is vigorous, with deeply cut, black-purple foliage on dark stems and bottlebrushes of purple-tinged, white flowers; to 5 ft. 'Brunette' has bronze-hued foliage to set off the white, sometimes pink-tinged wands of flowers, each about 8 in. in length. Fragrant 'Hillside Black Beauty' has black stems up to 7 ft. that bear white flowers; dark, coppery-purple foliage. 'James Compton' is compact with deep bronze foliage and white, sometimes pink-tinged flowers; its clumps are 2–3 ft. × 1.5–2 ft.

Adenophora
Campanulaceae
ladybells

Like other members of the bellflower family, ladybells are noted for their spikes of dangling, bell-shaped, blue or violet flowers that furnish long-lasting color to the middle and back of a border. Branched, upright stems bear mostly alternate stem leaves with toothed margins. The thick roots resent disturbance. Ladybells thrive in sun if their roots remain moist, or in partly shaded, damp places. Soil should be high in humus with good drainage. For neatness and to prevent self-seeding, remove spent blooms as they fade. Lovely in lightly shaded woodlands, in borders, or among shrubs. Appropriate companions for shaded spots include lady's mantle, hostas, and hellebores; in sun, tickseeds and beardtongues make attractive partners. In addition to the species described here, others, including *Adenophora pereskiifolia*, bear mention but are not readily available.

Not browsed by deer or rabbits, but slugs and snails may be a problem.

Propagate by seed sown indoors (do not cover) in late winter through early spring, by basal cuttings taken in early spring, or by root cuttings taken in winter.

Adenophora bulleyana
· pale blue
· late summer
· 3–4 ft. × 1–1.5 ft.
· sun, part shade
· Z3–8

Ladybells. Western China. Upright with lustrous, mostly basal leaves, serrated along the edges and wider than those of other species. Spires of dainty, 0.5-in., pendulous flowers are often grouped in threes on the stem; attractive light to medium blue, bell-shaped flowers. Valued not only for its charm, but also for its time of flowering with late garden phlox, agastaches, and lantanas.

Adenophora confusa
syn. *A. farreri*
· blue
· late spring
· 24–36 in. × 24 in.
· sun, part shade
· Z3–7

Common ladybells. China. This plant is similar to and often confused with creeping bellflower (*Campanula rapunculoides*), which is a roving thug and extremely difficult to eliminate. To ascertain whether you have the correct species before planting, tear a flower apart and look closely; ladybells have a noticeable thick basal disk at the base of the style. Deep blue, bell-shaped flowers about 0.75 in. long. Fleshy roots are difficult to divide, but pencil-thick ones may be used for root cuttings. Group in the border or naturalize in light woodlands. White or pale pink astilbes provide an attractive contrast in light shade; use yellow-foliaged evergreens or shrubs such as European elder (*Sambucus racemosa* 'Sutherland Gold') as a backdrop. Best planted in groups for impact.

Adenophora liliifolia
syn. *A. communis*
· blue
· summer
· 18–24 in. × 24 in.
· sun, part shade
· Z3–9

Lilyleaf ladybells. Europe. Not quite as tall as *Adenophora confusa*, but equally lovely. However, roving roots spread rapidly and must be contained unless in a naturalistic setting. The branched stems are hairy, clothed with lance-shaped leaves and topped with spikes of fragrant, nodding, lavender-blue bells. Tolerates heat and humidity well—the best species for warm southern gardens.

Other Notable Cultivars
'Amethyst' ('Amethyst Chimes'), possibly a hybrid of indeterminate parentage, is well behaved and produces erect, tall, leafy stems. From late spring to midsummer these are topped with loose spikes of lightly fragrant, pendulous, flaring, bell-shaped flowers of amethyst blue. In sun or part shade this clump former spreads only slowly and is best left undisturbed, especially where the plants can naturalize. A good cut flower. 18–36 in. × 12–24 in. Z3–8.

Adonis
Ranunculaceae
pheasant's eye

What a joy to see the bright yellow, buttercup-like flowers of pheasant's eye opening above its cluster of ferny leaves in late winter. Named for the god of beauty and desire in Greek mythology, *Adonis* flowers make outstanding additions to rock gardens, shaded woodland edges, under deciduous trees, or in raised beds and containers. Of the 20 or so species, several are annual and not covered here.

Cupped or spreading flowers, borne on branched or unbranched stems, are mostly yellow, terminal, and solitary, with petal-like sepals and up to 30 petals. Double forms are sterile and must be increased by division. The alternate, fern-like leaves are triangular in outline and three-times divided; each toothed lobe is lance shaped.

Pheasant's eyes prefer humus-rich, well-drained soil in a cool, partly or fully shaded spot (especially in hot southern gardens). Plant several together to make an impact; they bulk up slowly. Mulch with pine needles through the winter. Seldom browsed by deer, but often attacked by slugs and snails and should be protected from them.

Divide the rhizomatous roots of established plants in early to midsummer, or collect and sow fresh seed as soon as it ripens after bloom—usually when the foliage begins to die down into summer dormancy.

Adonis amurensis
syn. *A. dahurica*
- yellow
- late winter to early spring
- 6–9 in. × 12 in.
- part shade
- Z4–7

Pheasant's eye, Amur adonis. Manchuria, Korea, Japan. Perhaps the earliest species to bloom, it produces its cupped, 1- to 2-in., yellow flowers (brown in the bud) as soon as winter temperatures moderate. Clumps of dissected foliage appear when the flowers are open, going dormant by early summer. Mark the spot where they grow to avoid damage from cultivation through the season. Below are a few of the exciting cultivars on the market; for more, check Japanese nurseries, including the Rare Plant Nursery and Shikoku Garden.

'**Fuku Jukai**' is semi-double, with 2-in.-wide, yellow flowers. Early. 6 in.

'**Pleniflora**' ('Plena') has double, yellow buttercups, with raggedy petals flecked with green at the center. 6 in.

'**Sandan Zaki**' ("three-step blooming") is similar to 'Pleniflora' but has four alternating layers of frayed, yellow and green petals. Sterile and possibly hard to find, but quite a gem.

Adonis amurensis

Adonis vernalis
- yellow
- early spring
- 9–12 in. × 6 in.
- part shade
- Z4–7

Spring adonis, pheasant's eye. Europe. Somewhat later to bloom than *Adonis amurensis*, spring adonis is also slightly hardier. Stems are not branched and most of the finely dissected, 1- to 2-in.-long leaves lack petioles. The spreading, butter-yellow flowers, 2–2.5 in. across, flatten their petals to the sun. Dress with limestone chips if soil is strongly acid. Very slow to bulk up.

Aethionema
Brassicaceae
stonecress

Most of the 40 or so low-growing stonecresses are typically relegated to rock gardens or stone walls, although several are superb at the front of the border or along pathways where their abundant bloom sparkles.

These evergreen or semi-evergreen shrublets blanket themselves with clusters of four-petaled, 0.25-in. flowers in spring. They do best in full sun in very well-drained, preferably sweet soil. Add lime if necessary or provide a mulch of lime chips around the crown. Shear after bloom time to encourage vegetative growth. Pest and disease free, except for crown rot in damp soils.

White-blooming *Aethionema iberideum* grows to only 6–9 in., but blooms abundantly. It does not tolerate hot, humid weather; difficult to find outside of alpine specialists circles.

Increase by soft cuttings in late spring or from seed in spring.

Aethionema armenum
- pink, white
- spring to early summer
- 8–12 in. high and wide
- sun
- Z5–7

Turkish stonecress. Caucasus and Turkey. This short-lived evergreen or semi-evergreen subshrub bears linear, gray-green leaves to 0.5 in. long. Dense, terminal clusters of pale pink, cruciform flowers cover the plant for several weeks. Reseeds generously. Best in raised beds, tumbling over a wall, or in rock gardens where drainage is perfect. Small spring bulbs, including grape hyacinths, squills, and tulips, are good springtime companions, perhaps followed by dwarf bellflowers. Deer seem to avoid it, at least in the Sierras.

'**Warley Rose**'. Possibly a hybrid, this 4- to 6-in.-tall beauty may spread to 24 in. across, and looks best massed as a groundcover or as a specimen plant among other low-growing plants. Abundant clusters of dark pink flowers rise above the mass of blue-green leaves.

'**Warley Ruber**' has almost maroon flowers. Z6–8.

Aethionema armenum

Aethionema coridifolium
syn. *A. coridifolia*
- pink
- early summer
- 6–10 in. × 12–15 in.
- sun
- Z4–8

Lebanon stonecress. Lebanon. Upright grower that forms mounds of unbranched stems with slender, fleshy, bluish green leaves. Flower stems are crowned with 1-in. clusters of lavender or dusty pink flowers. May self-sow in good conditions especially when mulched with gravel or stone chips.

Aethionema grandiflorum
syn. *A. pulchellum*
- pink
- late spring to early summer
- 12–18 in. × 18 in.
- sun
- Z5–9, HS

Persian stonecress. Western Asia, Caucasus. Upright, shrubby, and evergreen with grayish, needle-like leaves; the largest of the genus, suitable for the front of flower borders. The loose clusters of delicately veined, pink blooms are showy, even suitable as cut flowers. Add lime especially to clay soils to raise the pH and break up the clay. A full-sun position with free drainage as found between pavers and surrounding patios is ideal. Drought tolerant and appropriate for xeriscapes. Shear lightly when blooms are spent to prevent abundant self-seeding, as well as to shape. Perennial candytuft (*Iberis sempervirens*) is an attractive companion requiring similar cultural conditions. Protect from browsing deer.

Agastache 'Blue Fortune'

Agastache
Lamiaceae
giant hyssop

An old-fashioned favorite, *Agastache* is ideally suited to modern gardens. The various species have much of the vigor and toughness of their mint relatives but with little of the invasiveness that make the mints so problematic. *Agastache* flowers are pretty and sweet scented but for the most part modest. Although they don't grab the eye like some of their more flamboyant fellows, they are borne over a long season, typically from midsummer to early fall when blooms of any kind are scarce in perennial gardens. They also attract a steady stream of hummingbirds, butterflies, and other pollinators. Foliage is usually aromatic on sturdy stems that rarely require staking. They fit easily into a wild or meadow garden.

Though occasionally subject to powdery mildew, agastaches are typically pest free and notably resistant to grazing deer and rabbits. They flourish in a wide range of well-drained soils, though are likely to live short lives on damp clays. Small wonder then that this traditional standby is receiving renewed attention from plant breeders, who have introduced a host of fine new cultivars in recent years.

A natural for butterfly gardens, agastaches also make good companions for roses—the fragrances are complementary and the well-furnished foliage of giant hyssops masks the rose's leggy stems. Likewise, their spires of blossoms make agastaches useful as visual punctuation for summertime mixed borders. The drought tolerance of the western US species makes these North American natives perfect for xeriscapes. Encourage rebloom by routine deadheading

Propagate by seed or division, or by taking semi-hardwood and softwood cuttings just as flowering is about to begin.

Agastache cana
- pink
- early summer to midfall
- 24–36 in. × 18 in.
- sun, part shade
- Z5–9, HS

Texas hummingbird mint. Texas and New Mexico. Long-blooming spikes of fragrant, raspberry-pink flowers borne above aromatic, gray-green foliage. Drought tolerant but will not stand wet feet or humidity.

Agastache foeniculum
- lavender, purple
- midsummer to early fall
- 2–4 ft. × 1.5–3 ft.
- sun, part shade
- Z4–8

Giant blue hyssop. Native to fields, prairies, and woodland openings throughout the upper half of North America. This perennial grows well on moist, well-drained soils, but once established also tolerates dry soils. Unlike most agastaches, giant blue hyssop copes well with humidity. The flowers are borne in whorls around the square stems, stacked one on top of the other in tall spikes. The anise-scented foliage may be dried for use in teas; flowering stems add color as well as fragrance to cut-flower arrangements.

'Golden Jubilee' bears young foliage that is yellow to chartreuse, maturing to lime green.

Agastache rugosum
- violet-blue
- midsummer to early fall
- 4 ft. × 1.5 ft.
- sun, part shade
- Z5–9

Korean hyssop. Introduced into the nursery trade by plant collector Dan Hinkley, this Asian native balances its long-blooming, violet-blue flowers with glossy, deep green, intensely mint-scented foliage. Like *Agastache foeniculum*, this species tolerates humidity.

'Honey Bee Blue' bears blue flowers with gray-green foliage.

Agastache rupestris
- orange
- midsummer to early fall
- 1–3 ft. high and wide
- sun
- Z5–9, HS

Rock anise hyssop. West Texas and Mexico. A combination of orange and yellow blooms edged with magenta and pink and licorice-scented, silvered foliage makes this species the showiest of the bunch. It is notably drought tolerant, but is likely to fall prey to fungal infections where summers combine heat with humidity.

Agastache foeniculum

Other Notable Cultivars

'Acapulco Salmon and Pink' bears mint-scented foliage and spikes of large, bicolored orange-and-pink flowers. 24–30 in. × 15 in. Z5–10.

'Black Adder' displays spikes with stacked whorls of smoky red-violet blossoms all summer and into early fall. 2–3 ft. × 1.5–2 ft. Z6–9.

'Blue Fortune' produces tall spikes of powder-blue flowers. 3–4 ft. × 1.5 ft. Z5–9.

'Firebird' has spikes of mixed copper, coral, and red flowers. 4 ft. × 2 ft. Z6–9.

'Heatwave' has plenty of deep hot-pink spikes on tight, clumping plants. Tolerates heat and humidity. 36 in. in bloom. Z5–10.

'Tutti Frutti' (*Agastache barberi* × *A. mexicana*) bears large, deep pink flowers over a mound of grayish foliage. 2–3 ft. × 1–2 ft. Z6–9 in the east, Z6–10 in the west.

Ageratina

Asteraceae
white snakeroot

Formerly classified with the eupatoriums, white snakeroot has been moved to its own genus. This native is excellent in wild or native plant gardens where it attracts bees and butterflies.

Ageratinas appreciate soil rich in organic matter, and require moderate but regular irrigation while young for the best bloom. However, plants tolerate drought once established. Staking is seldom necessary. A good cut flower. Seldom browsed by deer; combine with other deer-resistant natives, including goldenrods and asters.

Propagate by dividing mature clumps in late winter or spring, by seed, or by stem cuttings taken in spring.

Ageratina rugosus

syn. *Eupatorium rugosum*
- white
- midsummer to early fall
- 3–5 ft. × 2–3 ft.
- sun, part shade
- Z4–8

White snakeroot. Eastern half of North America. Large, coarsely toothed, heart-shaped leaves borne on strong, branching stems; the small, pure white flowers are carried in flat-topped, branching clusters. Tolerant of partial shade—the most shade tolerant of the genus, in fact. Leaf miner may cause unsightly, white-traced leaves. This plant is toxic if consumed in quantity.

'Chocolate' (syn. *Ageratina altissima* 'Chocolate'), an introduction of the Mt. Cuba Center, has striking maroon-brown foliage and chocolate stems.

Ajania

Asteraceae
silver-and-gold

This genus in the daisy family has only one species of interest to gardeners. It was formerly lumped with chrysanthemums and later dendranthemas, but due to the considerable rearranging of genera of that clan, it now has its own genus.

It is valuable as a fine specimen plant, and does well in containers.

Ajania pacifica

syn. *Chrysanthemum pacificum, Dendranthema pacificum*
- yellow
- fall
- 1–2 ft. × 1–3 ft.
- sun, part shade
- Z5–9

Silver-and-gold. Asia. A fine plant prized as much for its attractive foliage as for its branched clusters of showy, fall-blooming, bright yellow button flowers. Neat, rounded mounds of stems are clothed with lobed, light green, 1- to 2-in. leaves, each accented with a crisp silver edge, and hairy, silver undersides. Pinch young growth in early summer to encourage bushy plants. Best where soil is average to even poor, but drains well. Somewhat tolerant of drought, vulnerable to wet winter soils. Silver-and-gold is appropriate in the foreground of beds and borders, among low evergreens, even massed as a 1-ft.-tall groundcover or as an attractive skirt for specimen trees. Striking companions include colorful yellow tickseeds, trailing *Dichondra* 'Silver Falls', variegated ivies, or golden bidens. Seldom browsed by deer, but slugs and snails may be a problem. Occasionally attacked by white rust; locally

Ajania pacifica

prohibited in areas prone to that disease. Terminal cuttings root easily from new spring growth.

'Pink Ice' (pink ice daisy) is probably a hybrid with garden chrysanthemums. It has very short, pink ray flowers surrounding the central yellow disk.

'Yellow Splash' has yellow-variegated foliage and yellow flowers.

Ajuga
Lamiaceae
bugleweed

Bugleweeds have gotten a bad rap for being invasive. They certainly can be a nuisance when spreading into your lawn, but in a spot where their spread can be controlled, their vigorous growth makes them ideal groundcovers.

Bugleweed foliage is attractive—the undivided leaves are borne in opposite pairs on square stems, and superior cultivars offer evergreen, colored, sometimes textured leaves that provide interest all year. In late spring and early summer bugleweeds bear terminal spikes of small, two-lipped, brilliant blue, pink, or white flowers carried in tiered whorls (verticillasters) up the stem.

Tolerant of most moisture-retaining soils, bugleweeds benefit from the addition of organic material, such as compost or well-rotted leaves, at planting time. Shaded and partly shaded sites are ideal, although where sun is not intense they thrive in full sun. Maintain vigor by dividing in spring or fall every two to three years. Common bugleweed, in particular, is inclined to invade and overcome lawns; plant where their invasive tendencies are an asset on the edge of woodlands, along shaded pathways, and on difficult shaded banks to control erosion. Other species adapt well to planting at the front of beds and borders, under shrubs, and even

in containers. The flowers attract hummingbirds and butterflies. Sometimes susceptible to crown rot under hot, humid conditions; infected plants die out rapidly. Deer resistant.

Propagate named cultivars by division or detach the stolons in midsummer after blooming; start species from seed sown in late summer to Thanksgiving for germination the following spring.

Ajuga genevensis
syn. *A. alpina, A. rugosa*

- various
- early summer
- 6–15 in. × 9 in.
- sun, part shade, shade
- Z4–9

Geneva bugleweed, blue bugleweed, upright bugleweed. Southern Europe. The erect stems of brilliant blue flowers are especially eye-catching massed as a groundcover. The glossy dark green, 3- to 5-in.-long leaves are often hairy, toothed, or lobed along the edges. This species tolerates dryer soil conditions. Plant spring-blooming bulbs between the clumps in fall and enjoy a colorful vignette each spring.

'Alba' has white flowers.

'Pink Beauty' has pink flowers on 4- to 8-in. stems.

'Variegata' has white-mottled leaves. Not as vigorous as others of its kind.

Ajuga pyramidalis
syn. *A. metallica*

- blue
- spring to early summer
- 6–12 in. × 12 in.
- sun, part shade, shade
- Z5–9

Pyramidal bugleweed. Central Europe. The dense, pyramidal flower spikes give this species its name. Clumps of basal rosettes of slightly toothed leaves thrive in damp, moisture-retentive soil but seldom spread much due to the lack of stolons common to other species.

'Metallica-Crispa' ('Crispa', 'Metallica-crispa Purpurea', 'Min Crispa Red') has lustrous reddish brown leaves, crisped along the edges. Best leaf color is displayed in sun, where it is a fitting companion for low, silvery artemisia. Short spikes of blue flowers. 6 in. tall.

Ajuga reptans
syn. *A. repens*

- blue
- late spring to early summer
- 2–12 in. × 9–12 in.
- sun, part shade, shade
- Z3–9

Common bugleweed, carpet bugleweed. Europe, Japan. This sturdy evergreen perennial creeps rapidly by stolons to develop large patches, sometimes up to 36 in. across. It is excellent as a dense groundcover—a few cultivars even tolerate light foot traffic.

Ajuga reptans 'Catlin's Giant'

Spoon-shaped, dark green leaves, with 3.5-in.-long, spikes of dark blue flowers. Mow spent flower spikes after bloom time, or trim with a string trimmer or hedge shears. Slugs may be a problem, along with perhaps southern blight, fungal leaf spots, and crown rot. Tolerates deer and rabbits.

Cultivars abound; this is a brief selection:

'Black Scallop' ('Binblasca') has fast-spreading rosettes of glossy, crinkled dark maroon foliage, with best color in sunny spots. Brilliant rich blue flowers. Excellent weed-suppressing groundcover. Provide good air circulation in hot, humid regions. 4–6 in. Z4–9.

'Bronze Beauty' ('Atropurpurea', 'Purpurea') has deep bronzy purple foliage in sun; dark green in shade; deep blue flowers in late spring. Tough and drought tolerant. Spreads freely. 3 in. tall.

'Burgundy Glow' has eye-catching tricolored leaves of creamy white, rosy plum, and dark green. Not as aggressive as some, this cultivar is appropriate for rock gardens and as edgings. 'Multicolor' is darker-leaved. 6 in. tall.

'Catlin's Giant' is larger than other cultivars. Spikes of blue flowers to 8–12 in. above rosettes of bronzy, 6-in., spinach-like leaves. 3–12 in. Z4–8.

Chocolate Chip ('Valfredda') is extremely dwarf and less aggressive. Tight, 2-in.-high mats of narrow, crinkled, deep chocolate–colored leaves accented with maroon; best color in sun; spikes of blue flowers. Attractive planted between pavers and stepping stones. 3 in. Z4–9.

'Planet Zork'. Spoon-shaped, crinkled leaves

that are cupped to expose a light-colored rim from beneath. Tolerates heat and humidity. 2 in. tall.

'Silver Beauty' has rosettes of waxy, gray-green leaves, irregularly edged with cream. Withstands light foot traffic. Blue flowers. 4 in. tall.

Other Notable Cultivars

'Brockbankii' is a hybrid of *Ajuga genevensis* × *A. pyramidalis*. Almost a dwarf form.

Alcea

syn. *Althaea*
Malvaceae
hollyhock

No cottage garden is complete without hollyhocks, which are known for their graceful, stately spires of blossoms and are among the best loved and most evocative of flowers. The cup-shaped, sessile, or nearly stalkless flowers arrange themselves in racemes around a central stem that in ideal conditions—full sun, good air circulation, moist, well-drained soil, and a dry climate—may soar to a height of 10 ft.

In less than ideal conditions, however, especially in moist, humid climates, hollyhocks are likely to prove martyrs to rust, a fungal infection. Prevention of rust is easier and more effective than controlling an outbreak; buy only disease-free plants, or start rust-resistant types from seed. Clean up thoroughly in late fall to prevent rust spores from overwintering onsite.

Hollyhocks are also subject to attack by slugs, snails, and spider mites, as well as Japanese beetles, but they are seldom browsed by deer. Staking is necessary to support the taller cultivars. Though not long lived, hollyhocks are more persistent if cut to the base after blooming; leave a stalk or two to set seed to be assured of volunteer seedlings the next spring.

Ajuga reptans 'Burgundy Glow'

Alcea rosea is perfect for cottage gardens

The soft colors of mixed *Alcea rosea* blend well together

Alchemilla mollis

With this minimal care, hollyhocks provide a spectacular backdrop to shorter perennials and make dramatic cut flowers. One of the few plants that flourish in the root zone of black walnut trees. The blooms attract hummingbirds and butterflies.

Propagate by seed.

Alcea ficifolia

- various
- midsummer to early fall
- 6–8 ft. × 2–3 ft.
- sun
- Z3–9

Fig-leaf hollyhock, Russian hollyhock. Siberia. As the name indicates, the leaves of this species are deeply cut, "fingered" like the leaves of a fig. The white, yellow, copper, pink, or red flowers are single, to a diamater of 3 in. Rust resistant.

Happy Lights is a seed strain in the full range of flower colors; late-winter-sown seeds produce plants that bloom the first year.

Alcea rosea

syn. *Althaea rosea*

- various
- midsummer to early fall
- 6–8 ft. × 1–2 ft.
- sun
- Z3–10, HS

Hollyhock. Turkey, Asia. The classic hollyhock of Old World cottage gardens. Only those in dry, sunny climates should expect good results.

Countless strains and cultivars are available, including:

Chater's Double Hybrids include double powder-puff flowers in a full range of mixed or individual colors.

'Crème de Cassis' bears 3- to 4-in., single or semi-double, black currant–colored flowers edged with paler rose. 4–6 ft.

Majorette Mix is a dwarf strain. Double or semi-double flowers in whites, yellows, pinks, and reds. 24–30 in. × 12 in.

Powder Puffs Mix has white, yellow, rose, or red, fully double flowers to 4 in. across.

'Sunshine' has large, single flowers of sunny yellow. 5–6 ft. Z3–9.

Alcea rugosa

- yellow
- midsummer to early fall
- 6–8 ft. × 2–3 ft.
- sun
- Z3–9

Russian hollyhock. Ukraine. Furrowed, gray-green leaves are cleft into five lobes. Hairy stems carry single, 4-in., butter-yellow flowers. Rust resistant.

Alchemilla

Rosaceae
lady's mantle

Lady's mantles, particularly *Alchemilla mollis*, are among those cottage-garden perennials that people often remember with nostalgia from their childhood. Indeed, the softly hairy, lobed, and pleated leaves that hold a drop of rain or dew like a pearl, and the froth of tiny chartreuse flowers are irresistible. The name of the genus refers to the belief that the beads of water held by the leaves were "celestial water," pure enough to be used by alchemists trying to turn base metals into gold.

Only a few species are cultivated. Alchemillas do best in shade or part shade, especially when grown in warm regions. Avoid planting sites in intense sun. Soil should be humus rich and moisture retentive; leaves may burn if allowed to dry out. Low maintenance, except for deadheading to control promiscuous self-seeding. Cut back shabby foliage to the crown; fresh new growth will appear in a few weeks. The flowers can be enjoyed as fresh cuts or dried for later use; the leaves serve as attractive filler in flower arrangements. Air-dry flower sprays by hanging them upside down in bunches in a cool, well-ventilated place.

Lady's mantle is excellent as edging along pathways or massed as a groundcover, perhaps broken up with sweeps of hardy geraniums, hostas, or lilyturf. It is valued in partly shaded beds and borders; appropriate partners include grape hyacinths, daffodils and other spring bulbs, astilbes, toad lilies, and Japanese anemones. Partner smaller species in rock gardens with rock cress, perennial candytuft, and low-growing herbs such as thymes. Deer and rabbits seldom browse, but slugs and snails attack young seedlings; a light scattering of fish tankage or turkey gravel deters them.

Divide established or overgrown plants in early spring every three to five years as growth commences; discard worn out pieces. Sow seed in spring.

Alchemilla alpina

- green
- early summer
- 3–8 in. × 20 in.
- sun, part shade
- Z3–7

Mountain lady's mantle. Alpine regions of Europe. A diminutive plant with 2-in., deeply lobed, sharply toothed leaves, rimmed with silvery hairs that also blanket the underside. Loose sprays of frothy flowers rise on 3-in. stems. Excellent in rock gardens or between pavers. *Alchemilla conjecta* is similar but may reach 16 in.; *A. ellenbeckii* (Z5–7) rises only a few inches with deeply lobed, 1-in. leaves, hairy on both sides. Plant with creeping thymes and mazus.

Alchemilla erythropoda

- yellow green
- late spring to late summer
- 6–12 in. × 8 in.
- sun, part shade
- Z3–7

Red-stemmed lady's mantle. Mountains of Turkey and Russia. This "mini-mollis" gets a red tinge to its stems in full sun. The leaf stems or petioles are covered with fine hairs and both sides of the bluish green, shallowly lobed leaves are also velvety. Excellent for troughs, rock gardens, and where space is limited.

Alchemilla mollis

- green-yellow
- late spring to early summer
- 18–24 in. × 24 in.
- sun, part shade
- Z3–8

Lady's mantle. Turkey and Carpathian Mountains. This, the most widely grown of the lady's mantles, has light green, velvety leaves to 6 in. across, pleated into 7 to 11 lobes, and serrated along the rim. Airy sprays of 0.25-in., greenish yellow, petalless flowers in early summer. Deadhead routinely to prevent self-seeding; excessive self-seeding of lady's mantle has resulted in it becoming almost invasive in some places. Keep soil moist. Lady's mantle is charming as an underplanting for pink roses, and a fine companion for cottage garden flowers: foxgloves, hollyhocks, iris, and bellflowers.

Alchemilla mollis is possibly a synonym for common lady's mantle, *A. vulgaris*; reportedly *A. vulgaris* has a somewhat looser habit.

'Robusta' is an upright clumper, more full bodied and with larger leaves than the species. Yellowish green flowers in early summer, repeating later in the season. Tolerates heavy clay soil and drought when established. 15 in. × 36 in.

'Senior' grows to about 10 in. × 28 in.

'Thriller' is more compact. Green-flowered inflorescences to 9 in. across. 14 in. × 30 in.

Allium
Amaryllidaceae
onion

This enormous and cosmopolitan genus ranges throughout temperate regions of the Northern Hemisphere, with a handful of species from Central and South America, and also Africa. Within this range, alliums have adapted to habitats as diverse as sandy uplands and lowland swamps, though most prefer well-drained, even droughty sites.

Alliums include several staples of the kitchen garden, including onions, garlics, shallots, leeks, and chives. Their blooms may be less familiar in the flower garden, but they are, nonetheless, as essential in their own way as their edible relatives. Their ability to store energy in their bulbs makes alliums nearly invulnerable to seasonal drought—many species grow best where summers are hot and dry—and helps them weather all sorts of other adverse conditions. Furthermore, the sulfur-based chemicals that give alliums their pungent aroma act as repellents to deer, rabbits, and rodents, even many insect pests. Be alert for onion flies and thrips, however. Wet soils, especially during dormancy, may cause bulbs to rot.

Typically allium leaves are long and cylindrical (think chives) or strap shaped (think leeks), and though attractive enough when fresh and green, they grow tattered and flop as the season progresses. Accordingly, plant alliums in fall among bushy flowers or ornamental grasses that will hide the alliums' aging foliage; such neighbors will also help to support the alliums' naked scapes (flower stalks). Small individual flowers are borne in umbels, radiating clusters that collectively look like bright, botanical starbursts. Most bloom is in late spring or early summer, neatly bridging the June gap, the temporary dearth of bloom that afflicts perennial gardens after most spring bulbs are spent and before the summer perennials do their stuff.

Planted in groups along the length of a border, alliums' sculptural flowers add a visual rhythm to any design. Allium flowers attract nectar-foraging butterflies and bees; many ornamental onions make elegant cut flowers.

To propagate alliums, lift and divide the clumps of bulbs when dormant, or start from seed—many alliums are prolific seed producers and surround themselves with hosts of volunteer seedlings without any encouragement from the gardener.

Allium aflatuense
syn. *A. hollandicum*
- purple
- late spring
- 3–4 ft. × 6 in.
- sun
- Z3–8

Purple ornamental onion. Iran. Baseball-sized heads of brilliant purple, tiny, starry flowers rise on tall scapes. Typical bluish, strappy foliage that begins to die back at bloom time. Pastel-colored German irises, silvery catmints, and wormwoods are compatible bedfellows; a skirt of lady's mantle camouflages fading leaves.

'Purple Sensation' is more widely grown than the species; plant in groups of 10 to 12 for a real impact. Fortunately, the bulbs are not expensive.

Allium atropurpureum
- dark purple
- late spring
- 12–24 in. × 4 in.
- sun
- Z3–8

Ornamental onion. East Asia to northern India. So dark is the purple of this allium's star-shaped flowers, that the densely packed, tennis-ball-sized umbel looks almost black. They pose a dramatic contrast to the blossoms of lighter colored relatives such as hybrid 'Mont Blanc' and a complement in form as well as color to the simultaneous flowers of 'Sooty' sweet William.

Allium bulgaricum
syn. *Nectaroscordum siculum* subsp. *bulgaricum*
- cream, maroon
- late spring to early summer
- 24–36 in. × 6–8 in.
- sun, part shade
- Z5–10

Sicilian honey lily. This Mediterranean native requires regular irrigation through its period of growth until the end of bloom time, but thereafter prefers a drier soil. The parasol of pendulous, 0.5- to 1-in. flowers measures 4 in. or more across, with individual cream flowers, striped with maroon and touched with green. Baptisias and tall bearded irises, which bloom at the same time, make good companions.

Allium aflatuense 'Purple Sensation' makes a vibrant splash of color in a late spring border

Allium caeruleum

syn. *A. azureum*

- blue
- early summer to summer

- 12–36 in. × 6–12 in.
- sun
- Z3–9, HS

Blue globe onion. This Asian native blooms a couple of weeks later than *Allium atropurpureum* or *A. bulgaricum*, and provides one of the few true blues of the early summer perennial garden. The flowers are borne in 1-in., spherical clusters; the leaves die back before the flowers emerge. An asset to cottage, meadow, and rock gardens, this onion blooms simultaneously with herbaceous peonies; its exquisite flowers contrast handsomely with the peonies' lush blooms.

Allium cernuum

- pink
- early to late summer
- 12–18 in. × 6–8 in.

- sun, part shade
- Z3–9

Nodding onion, lady's leek. Dry clearings, rock outcroppings, and prairies in mountainous regions from Canada to Mexico. Nodding onion produces its loose umbels of drooping, pink or white flowers atop scapes that bend downward at the top, possibly to restrict the variety of pollinating insects. The strappy leaves are flattened and solid, with a small ridge along the length. Very easy to grow, nodding onion seeds about unless deadheaded, but never becomes aggressive. The bulbs sometimes produce offsets, creating clumps. Tolerates a wide range of well-drained soils; drought tolerant when established. Attractive with beebalms, black-eyed Susans, and milkweeds in native, meadow, or wild gardens.

Allium moly

- yellow
- late spring
- 9–18 in. × 6–9 in.

- sun, part shade
- Z3–9, HS

Lily leek. Southern Europe. Starry, greenish yellow flowers are borne in loose, 2-in.-wide clusters. In average, well-drained soil and full sun (avoid intensely sunny spots) this species naturalizes, forming extensive colonies readily, though it isn't an aggressive invasive.

'Jeannine' is a superior selection that bears two scapes per bulb, topped with golden yellow flowers.

Allium bulgaricum

Allium moly

Allium schubertii

- rose-purple
- late spring
- 12–36 in. × 12–18 in.
- sun
- Z7–9

Schubert onion. This native of the eastern Mediterranean and central Asia bears spherical, starburst heads of flowers, 1 ft. or more in diameter, which are guaranteed to stop traffic. One of the best alliums for hot southern regions, *Allium schubertii* overwinters successfully in zones 5–6 given well-drained soil and tucked in with an insulating mulch of straw or evergreen boughs in late fall. Enjoy the blooms in your garden, allow them to go to seed and dry, then bring them indoors to serve as focal points of dried arrangements.

Allium senescens

syn. *A. montanum*

- pink
- mid- to late summer
- 9–24 in. × 12 in.
- sun
- Z4–10

German garlic, broadleaf chives. Europe, northern Asia. Bulbous with short rhizomes that make vigorous, but not invasive, clumps. Strappy basal leaves, 2–12 in. long; dense, 0.75-in. umbels composed of 20 or more fragrant, cup-shaped flowers last for

Allium senescens

several weeks. Suitable for rock gardens and atop retaining walls.

'Blue Twister' was selected for its unusual bright blue, twisted leaves. Deadhead routinely to extend bloom. 12 in. Z3–8.

'Glaucum' (subsp. *glaucum*) has interesting clumps of twisted, bluish gray foliage. Lavender-pink heads of flowers rise above the foliage mass. Decorative even when not in bloom.

Allium thunbergii

- reddish violet, white
- fall
- 18–24 in. × 10 in.
- sun, part shade
- Z5–8

Japanese onion. Japan. This underused species deserves a wider audience, if only for its late bloom time. Through the season, slightly untidy tufts of mid-green, grassy foliage, triangular in cross section, mark their spot. In late summer, sturdy, 8- to 9-in. scapes are topped with small, green buds the shape of dunce caps; these enlarge and open to 1- to 2-in.-wide globes of numerous reddish violet flowers with slender exserted stamens and styles that produce a dainty appearance. Foliage takes on orange hues after the first hard frost. Flowers dry well and if left on the plant remain decorative as the flowers fade to deep pink. Drought tolerant. Divide in spring.

'Alba' is white flowered. Not as robust as 'Ozawa'. 12–15 in.

'Ozawa' sports heads of many reddish violet flowers. 12–20 in.

Allium tuberosum

- white
- late summer to early fall
- 12–30 in. × 12 in.
- sun, part shade
- Z4–8

Garlic chives, Chinese chives. Southeast Asia. Rhizomatous clumps of bulbs produce a mass of bluish green, flattened leaves, keeled at the base; these are edible and can serve as a substitute for garlic. In late summer, tall scapes topped with heads of small, starry, fragrant, white flowers appear that attract numerous pollinating insects. Deadhead to prevent widespread self-seeding, which may become a nuisance. Holds its own with white garden phlox 'David', spider plants, and panicle hydrangeas (*Hydrangea paniculata*) in white combinations in beds and borders. Seeds about too much for planting in rock gardens, but valuable in herb garden containers.

Alstroemeria

Alstroemeriaceae
Peruvian lily, princess lily

These South American perennials are best known to the wider public as particularly long-lasting cut flowers. Indeed, to satisfy the appetite of the floral industry, millions of alstroemerias are raised in the fields and greenhouses of South America, Holland, and Israel, as well as California. They are often seen as symbols of friendship and devotion and are quite common in gift bouquets.

The genus *Alstroemeria*, named by Swedish botanist Carl Linnaeus for his friend, Baron Klaus von Alstroemer, includes some 60 species, a few of which are appropriate as garden flowers. Some, such as *A. pygmaea*, are highly ornamental, but are so demanding to grow that they are confined mainly in alpine greenhouses.

Alstroemerias arise from fleshy rhizome-like tuberous roots (invasive in some species) that generally form clumps up to 2 ft. or so across. Their stems are well clothed with narrow, mid-green leaves, grayish beneath and 3–5 in. in length; the petioles (leaf stalks) are twisted so that they invert the leaves. Showy, even gaudy flowers are tubular and held in loose, simple or compound umbels at the stem tips. Each flower is six tepaled (petals and sepals are not differentiated) and grows from 1.5–4 in. long. Attracts hummingbirds and butterflies.

Plant Peruvian lilies carefully, avoiding damage to the tuberous roots, in moisture-retentive, fertile, well-drained soil. Add organic matter at planting time and mulch with compost or well-rotted

leaves annually to reduce water loss. The tuberous roots suffer if allowed to dry out. Evergreen in mild climates, alstroemerias go dormant in fall where winters are cold; protect clumps with evergreen boughs in winter. As alstroemerias brighten a floral arrangement, so too do they introduce more vivid hues into perennial and mixed borders. An obvious choice for cutting gardens, but a number of selections have been bred for planting in containers and at the front of borders. Tall selections look cheerful planted among evergreens such as rhododendrons, azaleas, and Japanese andromeda. Deadhead to extend bloom time.

Be alert for virus diseases and gray mold that mar the flowers and leaves. Slugs dine on young foliage and flowers, but deer and rabbits mostly ignore them. Those with sensitive skin may react to the sap of alstroemerias; protect hands with gloves when working with these plants.

Increase by division in spring or fall, or start seed in containers to avoid disturbing the tubers at transplanting time. Seed germinates readily.

Alstroemeria aurea
syn. *A. aurantiaca*
- orange
- summer
- 30–36 in. × 18 in.
- sun, part shade
- Z7–10

Peruvian lily. Chile. Clumps of running tuberous roots produce erect, well-foliaged stems. The tepals are bright orange, the upper pair freckled and splashed with red; exserted stamens are drooping.

'Luna' is clear yellow.

Alstroemeria huemulina
- orange
- summer to late summer
- 24 in. × 18 in.
- sun
- Z8–11

Peruvian lily. South America. Easy to grow, with clumps of non-running roots. Medium-size blooms are brown splashed, with brilliant deep orange tepals. First flush of bloom is repeated a few weeks later.

Alstroemeria psittacina
syn. *A. pulchella*
- red
- summer to fall
- 2–3 ft. × 3 ft.
- sun, part shade
- Z7–10

Parrot flower. Brazil. Clusters of exotic-looking brownish red flowers tipped with green. Mauve-spotted stems bear 3-in.-long, lance-shaped leaves. Roots spread widely and can become more than a nuisance. Best protected from intense afternoon sun. Very long-lasting as cut flowers.

'Variegata' has clean white–edged leaves. Red flowers are speckled with maroon and green. Summer dormant after bloom time. Z6–9.

Allium tuberosum

Alstroemeria 'Casablanca'

splotched with yellow and dashes of maroon. 10 in. Z7–8. Princess Ivana ('Staprivane') has 2-in.-wide, yellow-throated, cherry-red flowers. Mounding habit, great for containers and in the landscape. 12–15 in. Z8–11.

'The Third Harmonic' (*Alstroemeria* 'Peach Harmony' × *A. aurea*), introduced by George Hare, has large, orange flowers speckled with purple at the lip, and claret-flushed beneath. Tolerates warm, humid regions. 48 in. Z6–9.

Alyssum
Brassicaceae
madwort

Most madworts, including the summer-blooming *Alyssum alpestre*, silver madwort *A. argenteum*, and the pale yellow, spring-blooming *A. wulfenianum*, are candidates only for rock gardens, troughs, and between pavers. The larger species, however, can also fill spots at the front of sunny borders. Of some 150 species, few cope well with southern heat and humidity, although they may be grown in that region as colorful spring annuals.

Leaves of madworts are small, simple, and alternate, often grayish silver with hairs. Conspicuous, showy clusters of four-petaled, cross-shaped yellow or white flowers bloom in spring to early summer.

They are seldom bothered seriously by pests or diseases, but look out for aphids. Deer resistant.

Propagate by seed sown in spring or by softwood cuttings.

Other Notable Cultivars
Alstroemerias are bred for the cut-flower trade but perfect for residential gardens. Most are well-behaved hybrids with amazing, sparkling flowers borne over a long season. This is a tiny sampling of what is available:

'Casablanca' has pink-flushed, white flowers flecked with maroon. 40 in. Z6–9.

'Freedom' is clump forming with reddish peach flowers blotched with cherry-sprinkled white on the upper petals. An introduction from Mark Bridgen's Cornell breeding program. 30 in. Z5–8.

'Glory of the Andes' is a variegated selection derived from 'Sweet Laura'. 24–30 in. Z6.

Inca Series, from Dutch breeder Könst, includes several superior introductions for compact, non-invasive growth and long bloom (early summer to fall). Inca Adore ('Koadore') has red flowers accented with a wide band of yellow with brown freckles. Inca Ice ('Koice') has whitish flowers, yellow at the throat and speckled with deep maroon dashes. Mostly 24 in. × 36 in. Z6–9.

Princess Lilies Series, bred by Van Zanten Plants in Holland, is superior for window boxes and planters, and at the front of cottage garden borders. Though frost sensitive, they are especially heat tolerant. Princess Oxana ('Staprioxa') is deep rose

Alyssum montanum
syn. *A. pedemontanum*
- yellow
- mid- to late spring
- 8–12 in. × 12 in.
- sun
- Z2–7, HS

Mountain madwort. Northern Europe. Trailing mounds of silvery, evergreen foliage, above which rise clustered masses of bright mustard-yellow flowers.

'Berggold' (Mountain Gold) has a dense habit and abundant fragrant, bright lemon flowers. Combines well with other low spring bloomers, including rock cress and perennial candytuft.

Alyssum spinosum
syn. *Ptilotrichum spinosum*
- white
- late spring to early summer
- 6–12 in. × 18 in.
- sun
- Z6–9, HS

Spiny alyssum. Southern France, southeast Spain. Mounding with spatulate, evergreen, 2-in., silver-gray leaves and wiry stems clothed with prickly spines. Tiny, honey-scented, pink-tinged, white flowers crowd into terminal clusters. Appropriate for edging and rock gardens where drainage is good; drought tolerant. Rabbit resistant.

'Roseum' has white flowers tinged with lavender. Silvery foliage is interesting year-round. 8–12 in. tall.

Amsonia
Apocynaceae
bluestar

The underused bluestars are mostly native North American perennials that create floral displays in spring, often followed by amazing autumn foliage color.

The durable clumps are tough and easy to grow in ordinary garden soils that drain well; established plants tolerate short periods of drought. Clusters of starry flowers in various shades of pale blue top foliage-clad stems and provide nectar for early scavenging butterflies, especially mourning cloaks. After bloom time, slender seedpods remain on the plants.

Little maintenance is required: bluestars seldom need division and require staking only if grown in too much shade. If the plants begin to flop, encircle with wire rings or "pea sticks" (bushy, woody stems saved from shrub pruning); cut back by 6 in. after bloom time. Mostly disease free although susceptible to rust, bluestars are generally free of pests too, including deer and rabbits.

If used as cut flowers, sear the base of the stems with a flame to prevent the milky sap from bleeding and fouling the water. Some people report skin irritation from contact with the sap.

Propagate by division or softwood cuttings in spring. Species seeds germinate readily in spring or fall.

Amsonia ciliata
syn. *A. angustifolia*
- ice blue
- late spring
- 2–3 ft. high and wide
- sun, part shade
- Z5–9

Downy amsonia, fringed bluestar. Southeastern United States. Although it flourishes in the wild over a broad range, downy amsonia is not as popular for gardens as other species. However, it is an excellent plant, especially on sandy soils with pH above 7, amended with organic matter. Young growth is downy and silky soft. Showy clusters of flowers perch on erect but not very strong stems clothed with lanceolate, 1.5-in.-wide leaves. In sunny spots, fall foliage is brilliant yellow. If plants sprawl, prune gently into a rounded bush and support stems with pea sticks. Mass in native plant or wildlife gardens to attract butterflies and other insects. Astilbes and hardy geraniums are good border companions for spring; try goldenrods and blue leadwort for fall. Slow to establish.

'Spring Sky' has larger, longer-blooming flowers than the species. Fall color is yellow or bronze.

Amsonia hubrichtii

Autumn foliage of *Amsonia hubrichtii*

Amsonia hubrichtii
- steel blue
- late spring to early summer
- 3–4 ft. × 3 ft.
- sun, part shade
- Z5–9

Arkansas bluestar, Hubricht's amsonia, narrow-leaved bluestar. Arkansas, Oklahoma. Not as stiffly upright as other species, this easy-care Arkansan native has smooth, thread-like leaves that present unusual textural beauty. Provide acid soil and a sunny site; in too much shade, plants will open up and sprawl. The showy powder-blue, 0.5-in., starry flowers cluster at the tops of the stems, where they attract butterflies; needle-like fruits follow. Cut back by 6–10 in. after bloom time to groom the plants into a neat mound of feathery foliage; the fruits will be lost in this process, but fall color will be more dramatic. Plants grown in full sun produce the best fall color, an arresting banana yellow and orange. Arkansas bluestar is perfect for native, wild, and wildlife gardens; in flower borders, combine with peonies, Oriental poppies, and late-blooming perennials, or provide a dark-leaved shrub, such as ninebark (*Physocarpus*) or *Weigela* Wine and Roses ('Alexandra'), as a background. The brilliant fall foliage is eye-popping against tall sedums 'Matrona' and 'Autumn Joy'. Slow to establish. Named the Perennial Plant of the Year for 2011 by the Perennial Plant Association.

Amsonia montana

syn. *A. tabernaemontana* 'Montana'
- light blue
- sun, part shade
- spring
- Z3–9
- 12–24 in. × 9–12 in.

Dwarf bluestar. Massachussetts to Missouri. Now considered by some authorities to be a species in its own right, dwarf bluestar differs from *Amsonia tabernaemontana* in producing dense clusters of somewhat deeper blue flowers earlier in spring on more compact plants. Drought tolerant once established. In sun, the willowy leaves turn gold in fall.
    'Short Stack' is a 12-in.-tall dwarf selection. Z5–9.

Amsonia orientalis

syn. *Rhazya orientalis*
- lavender-blue
- sun, part shade
- spring
- Z6–9
- 18 in. high and wide

Bluestar. Greece, Turkey. A change in taxonomy has brought this European native into the *Amsonia* genus. Popular in the UK and Europe, this plant is quite similar to *A. tabernaemontana*, but with a more refined look. The flowers are larger and a stronger blue, best seen when plants are grown in part shade. Keep soil moist, especially in sunny places.

Amsonia tabernaemontana

syn. *Tabernaemontana amsonia*
- pale blue
- sun, part shade
- mid- to late spring
- Z3–9
- 2–3 ft. high and wide

Blue starflower, blue dogbane, eastern bluestar. Eastern and central United States. Upright with somewhat stiff stems, blue starflower is clothed with smooth, willow-like leaves. In sun, these turn brilliant yellow come fall, though its color is not as spectacular as that of Arkansas bluestar. Pale blue, starry flowers cluster at the ends of the stems; spindle-like fruiting pods follow. This tough plant tolerates less than ideal conditions, but prefers a moist, well-drained soil. Spectacular massed in rough meadows or native plant gardens as well as in butterfly gardens where it provides food for coral hairstreak caterpillars. In beds and borders or among shrubs, group several plants together. An excellent cut flower, sear the base of the stems before conditioning them to prevent sap bleed. Lovely in front of shrubby yellow potentillas or dark-leaved ninebark.

var. *salicifolia* (syn. *Amsonia salicifolia*), woodland or willow-leaved bluestar, has very slender leaves. 2–2.5 ft.

Other Notable Cultivars

'Blue Ice' is a hybrid selection from *Amsonia tabernaemontana*, possibly with *A. montana* or *A. orientalis*. Extremely long blooming, with terminal clusters of intense deep lavender flowers, good for cutting. Tolerates part shade, but in sun foliage turns vivid yellow and orange in fall. Provide consistently moist, humus-rich soil; drought tolerant and adapts to hot, humid summers. Compact, ideal for small gardens. 15 in. × 24 in. Z5–9.
    'Seaford Skies' (*A. hubrichtii* × *A. tabernaemontana*) displays hybrid vigor. Pyramidal clusters of star-like, sky-blue flowers from mid- to late spring. Vibrant yellow fall color. Bred by noted garden writer Pam Harper. 3 ft. × 5 ft. Z5–9.

Anacyclus

Asteraceae
Mt. Atlas daisy

Just one species in this genus of about 15 species is of interest to gardeners, especially those that have shallow, poor, but well-drained soil.

Anacyclus pyrethrum var. depressus

syn. *A. depressus*
- white
- sun
- early to midsummer
- Z5–8, HS
- 1–3 in. × 15 in.

Mt. Atlas daisy, mat daisy. Mountains of Morocco. Mat-like rosettes of finely dissected, crinkly, gray-green leaves, from the center of which sprawl prostrate and ascending flower stems. These bear red flower buds that on sunny days open to single,

Anacyclus pyrethrum var. *depressus*

yellow-centered, 1-in., white daisies borne above the foliage. The flowers close at night and during cloudy weather, revealing a charming red reverse. Provide very well-drained, poor soil for best results. Needs little water; will succumb to root rot if kept too wet. Apply a gravel mulch to improve water runoff from the foliage cushion. Easily grown as a groundcover for dry places, and a fine rock garden, trough, and crevice garden plant; effective along the edges of gravel paths where Mt. Atlas daisy will seed itself. Partners well with mossy saxifrages and low sedums. Best in cooler climates; the combination of high heat and humidity is likely to be fatal. Resistant to deer. Easily propagated by seed sown in spring.

'Garden Gnome' is reputedly more compact than the species.

'Silberkissen' ('Silver Kisses'). Silvery feathery leaves on compact, 3-in. plants. Flowers 1–2 in. across. Perfect for troughs.

Anaphalis
Asteraceae
pearly everlasting

The clustered white flowers of this genus are long blooming and even longer lasting; when cut and dried they are a staple of dried flower arrangements. In the garden, their white blossoms and gray-green foliage serve as cooling counterpoints to other, hotter-colored perennials. They add a subtle floral note to dry meadows or prairies, native plantings, and wildflower gardens; butterflies love them. The genus includes 110 or so species that grow wild in various types of habitats throughout the Northern Hemisphere. The diversity of their origins makes this a versatile group of perennials that flourishes in both moist and dry conditions. In general, pearly everlastings are trouble free, and require very little maintenance.

Propagate by seed started indoors or direct sown in spring, or divide in spring or fall.

Anaphalis margaritacea
- white
- mid- to late summer
- 1–3 ft. × 1–2 ft.
- sun, part shade
- Z3–8

Western pearly everlasting. Northern North America, northern and central Europe, northeast Asia. In the wild, this species grows on dry, sandy, or gravelly soils, but in gardens it thrives on any average, well-drained soil; tolerant of nutrient-poor soils and drought. The handsome foliage—narrow, woolly, and silvery gray—complements the flattened clusters (corymbs) of tiny, globular, yellow-centered, white flowers at stem tips. The stoloniferous roots may spread aggressively on favorable sites. Excellent for xeriscapes or where water is limited.

Anaphalis triplinervis
- white
- early summer to early fall
- 18–24 in. × 9–18 in.
- sun, part shade
- Z3–9

Pearly everlasting. Himalayas from Afghanistan to southwestern China. Less drought tolerant than *Anaphalis margaritacea*. Provide humus-rich soil that is well drained but consistently moist. Borne on zigzag stems, the very narrow, elliptic-obovate leaves to 5 in. long are gray on top and downy white beneath; they will degenerate rapidly if irrigation is neglected during dry spells. Individual flowerheads, 0.75 in. or so across, are surrounded by collars of papery white bracts; collectively, the flowerheads are borne in dense, domed corymbs. A good choice for cottage gardens and wild gardens.

'Summer Snow' ('Sommerschnee') has flowerheads of a purer white than the species, and the yellow centers are less visible.

Anchusa
Boraginaceae
alkanet

Usually short lived, perennial alkanets provide true-blue flowers, a rare color among garden plants whose "blue" flowers are more typically lavender- or purple-blue. Alkanet stems and leaves are coarsely

Anchusa azurea 'Dropmore'

hairy and the forget-me-not-like flowers are arranged at the tip of the stems, coiled in a bud like the tail of a scorpion (scorpioid). Stem leaves are alternate and clasping.

With their awkward, rather lax habit, alkanets are not the most elegant of plants but combine well with peonies, irises, and others in the midsection of flowerbeds and borders where their ungainliness is not obvious. They attract butterflies and bees, but are seldom browsed by deer or rabbits. Cutworms and vine weevil larvae may attack the roots.

Best propagated from pencil-thick root cuttings in late winter, or basal cuttings in spring. Sow seed in containers in spring.

Anchusa azurea
syn. *A. italica*
- blue
- early summer
- 3–5 ft. × 2 ft.
- sun
- Z3–8, HS

Italian alkanet, Italian bugloss. Mediterranean region. Italian alkanet thrives in rather dry, poor soils typical of its native region. The combination of southern heat and humidity is not to their liking, but plants thrive and are long lived in the dry heat of southern California. Winter wet causes root rot. In the garden, excess water or fertilizer promotes undesirable rank, floppy growth. Branching flower stems rise above clumps of mostly basal 4- to 12-in.-long, coarsely bristly leaves, and may need staking—best done with pea sticks or brush. The tubular and flaring, 0.5-in. flowers are abundant and provide glorious gentian-blue color for several weeks. Cut back to the basal leaves after blooming. The species is grown infrequently, but several superior cultivars are available. All make eye-catching combinations with tickseeds, blanket flowers, Shasta daisies, and silver-leaved artemisias, and in front of variegated shrubs.

'Dropmore' is a tried-and-true cultivar with deep blue flowers in mid- to late summer. At 4–5 ft. tall, it usually needs staking.

'Feltham Pride', sometimes listed as Feltham Pride strain, has medium blue flowers on multi-branched, 30- to 36-in.-tall stems.

'Little John' is dwarf, perfect for smaller gardens. The bright steel-blue flowers bloom from late spring into summer. Late daffodils make colorful companions. 16–20 in.

'Loddon Royalist' produces 0.75-in., gentian-blue flowers in late spring and early summer. 3 ft. tall.

Anemone
Ranunculaceae
windflower

When the breeze sets their long-stemmed clusters of silken-petaled flowers dancing, anemones truly earn their common name of windflower. On a more practical level, the many species of this hardy and

Anemone ×hybrida 'Whirlwind'

vigorous genus offer such a variety of blooming seasons that one could furnish a garden with flowers throughout the growing year with anemones alone. Wood anemones (*Anemone nemorosa*), for example, supply some of the first flowers of spring, while the fall-blooming Japanese anemone (*A. ×hybrida*) with its graceful, informal blossoms, provides the perfect counterpoint and companion to autumn's bombastic chrysanthemums.

Anemone blooms consist of single, or occasionally double, circles of petal-like tepals surrounding a central knot or boss of thread-like, usually golden stamens. The overall effect ranges from daisy-like in some species to looser, almost poppy-like flowers in others. Typically, anemone leaves emerge from the base of the plant on long stems. They may be divided palmately like fingers, lobed and toothed, or sometimes palmately compound; the lush but neat mounds of leaves furnish a handsome complement to other, showier foliage plants such as hostas, grasses, and ferns.

Though best adapted to partial shade, anemones tolerate full sun in cool climates, and flourish on most well-drained soils other than heavy clays. The

Anemone blanda 'Blue Shades'

'Radar' has magenta-pink flowers with contrasting white eyes.

'Violet Star' has white-eyed, amethyst flowers and yellow stamens.

'White Splendour' has pure white, daisy-like flowers accented with yellow stamens.

Anemone coronaria

- blue, red, white
- midspring to early summer
- 9–18 in. × 6–9 in.
- sun, part shade
- Z7–10

Poppy anemone. Native throughout the Mediterranean basin and considered by some to be the Biblical "lilies of the field." Tuberous roots bear solitary, showy, poppy-like, single flowers to a diameter of 2.5 in. with six to eight colorful tepals and black centers, borne on 10- to 12-in. stems. May be grown in containers; popular and long-lasting cut flower.

De Caen Hybrids is an heirloom strain that has poppy-like, single flowers of scarlet, violet-blue, white, or mauve.

'Mr. Fokker' bears single, violet-blue flowers.

St. Brigid Hybrids is another heirloom strain with semi-double or double, dahlia-like flowers of scarlet, violet-blue, white, and mauve.

Anemone hupehensis

- pink
- mid- to late summer
- 18–24 in. × 12–18 in.
- sun, part shade
- Z4–8

Japanese anemone, Japanese thimbleweed. Actually native to central China, this misnamed perennial bears 2- to 3-in.-wide, slightly cupped flowers; typically these have five rose-pink tepals surrounding a prominent central ring of yellow stamens. Prefers a moderately fertile soil; ideal for partially shaded woodland gardens or borders. Seeds about and may become aggressive in ideal conditions. No serious pests.

'Praecox' is an exceptionally robust cultivar, blooming early in midsummer. To 50 in. tall.

var. *japonica* 'Bressingham Glow' (syn. *Anemone* 'Bressingham Glow') bears deep pink, semi-double or double flowers with a silvery sheen.

'Pretty Lady Diana' belongs to a line of dwarf cultivars. Masses of single, 2-in.-wide, pink flowers. 'Pretty Lady Emily' has semi-double, silver-pink flowers. Ideal in containers. 16 in. × 24 in. Z5–9.

Anemone ×hybrida

- white, pink
- late summer to fall
- 24–48 in. × 12–18 in.
- sun, part shade
- Z4–8

Japanese anemone. A collection of garden hybrids similar to *Anemone hupehensis*; some authorities treat these as a subdivision of that species.

'Andrea Atkinson' has white, single or semi-double flowers, to 3–5 ft. 'Whirlwind' is similar. 2–4 ft.

spring- and summer-blooming species are tuberous rooted or rhizomatous, and these roots should be planted in fall like spring bulbs. The fall bloomers are more commonly fibrous rooted, best planted in spring or fall along with other perennials.

Include anemones in beds and borders, though they are also appropriate in woodland gardens. Spring-blooming species partner well with lungworts, woodland phlox, and foamflowers; the fall bloomers do well with Japanese toad lilies, *Allium thunbergii* 'Ozawa', and asters. The tuberous-rooted species (including *Anemone blanda*) can be forced in containers like spring bulbs. Seldom browsed by deer but need protection from slugs; anemones provide long-lasting cut flowers.

Propagate and reinvigorate named cultivars by division every two to three years, ideally in early spring; species may be started from seed sown as soon as it ripens.

Anemone blanda

- blue, pink, red, white
- early spring
- 6–9 in. × 4–6 in.
- sun, part shade
- Z5–8

Grecian windflower. Southeastern Europe and Middle East. This tuberous-rooted species naturalizes readily in well-drained soils. It spreads by seed or by root to form expansive mats of foliage and, in season, brightly colored, daisy-like flowers. Especially attractive under spring-flowering trees. Soak tubers overnight before planting. Prone to a variety of fungal diseases, though rarely seriously affected. Slugs and snails may be a problem. Deer damage is rare.

'Blue Shades' produces blooms in a range of blues.

'Charmer' is deep lilac accented with a white ring around the stamens.

Anemone ×hybrida 'Prinz Heinrich'

Anemone vulgaris

'Honorine Jobert' flowers are pure white and single. The benchmark for white-flowered introductions.

'Konigin Charlotte' ('Queen Charlotte') is vigorous; 4-in.-wide, semi-double, pink flowers with purple backs.

'Pamina' is double with deep rosy tepals.

'Prinz Heinrich' ('Prince Henry') resembles 'Bressingham Glow' but spreads more quickly.

'September Charm' is silvery pale purple, single.

Anemone nemorosa

- pink, purple, white
- late winter to midspring
- 6–12 in. × 6–9 in.
- sun, part shade
- Z5–8

Wood anemone. Northern Europe to western Asia. Naturalizes well in moist woodlands, expanding by rhizomes into large colonies; can become a pest if allowed to spread unchecked. Flowers about 1 in. across with six to eight tepals. Foliage is similar to that of *Anemone blanda*; it dies back right after bloom.

'Allenii' has large, lavender-blue flowers.

'Bowles' Purple' has purple flowers.

'Bracteata Pleniflora' is semi-double with green-tipped, double, white flowers.

'Vestal' is double, with pompon-like white flowers.

A. ×lipsiensis 'Pallida' (*A. nemorosa × A. ranunculoide*), has pale yellow flowers.

Anemone patens

syn. *Pulsatilla patens*
- blue-violet
- early spring
- 3–12 in. × 3–6 in.
- sun
- Z3–7

Eastern Pasque flower. Northern Europe, Russia, North America (Alaska south to Washington, New Mexico, Texas, and Illinois). State flower of North Dakota. One of the first spring wildflowers of the northern Great Plains, with flowers opening while foliage is still emerging, often amid patches of snow. Basal foliage deeply divided, fern-like, and covered with silvery hairs. Flowers, usually blue-violet but occasionally white or yellow, are bell shaped and open, borne on 4- to 5-in.-tall stems that stretch to 8–12 in. as blossoms mature. Followed by plume-like, ornamental seedheads. Best in gritty, well-drained, dry to moderately moist soils in cool climates; tolerates light shade. Somewhat difficult from seed. No serious pests or diseases, welcome harbinger of spring in rock gardens, prairie plantings, and border fronts.

Anemonella thalictroides 'Schoaff's Double Pink'

Anemone sylvestris

- white
- spring
- 12–18 in. × 9–12 in.
- part shade, shade
- Z4–8

Snowdrop anemone. Central and eastern Europe. A reliable and undemanding plant that prefers sandy, organic-rich soils. Naturalizes in hospitable sites and can be aggressive on loose soils; spreads less in clay. Nodding, fragrant, cupped, five-tepaled, white flowers with yellow anthers. The 1.5- to 2-in.-wide flowers are borne on 18-in. stems above medium green, deeply lobed foliage. White, woolly seedheads follow the flowers. Excellent for woodland gardens or meadows.

Anemone tomentosa
syn. *A. vitifolia*

- pale pink
- late summer to fall
- 2–3 ft. × 15–18 in.
- sun, part shade
- Z4–8

Grape-leaf anemone. This native of northern China prefers a moist site, but rots on persistently wet soils. A source of spectacular late-season color, *Anemone tomentosa* is robust—indeed, it is most often available as the cultivar 'Robustissima'. It forms dense mounds of deep green, attractively cut foliage, above which rise branching stems topped with clusters of cupped, pinkish mauve flowers. Naturalizes readily, but it can be aggressive, overwhelming neighbors in the border. Impressive among shrubs.

Anemone vulgaris
syn. *Pulsatilla vulgaris*

- purple, white
- early spring
- 9–12 in. high and wide
- sun, part shade
- Z4–8

Pasque flower. Northern Europe. Flowers are five sepaled, goblet like, and solitary, 2–4 in. across. They range in color from blue to reddish purple, with a central knot of golden stamens; blooms appear before leaves, borne on stout stems. Pasque flower forms low clumps of silky, fern-like, deeply cut basal leaves, 3–6 in. long and gray-green. Flowers give way to showy, feathery seedheads. Prefers rich, humusy soil but tolerates most average, well-drained, moderately moist ones. No serious pests or diseases. Provides early color and texture for rock gardens and border fronts.

'Rote Glocke' ('Red Bells') has bright crimson flowers.

Anemonella
Ranunculaceae
rue anemone

This is another single-species genus, and not to be missed. A charming native woodlander that sparkles in late winter sun.

Anemonella thalictroides
syn. *Syndesmon thalictroides, Thalictrum thalictroides*

- white
- spring to early summer
- 4–6 in. × 6–12 in.
- part shade
- Z4–8

Rue anemone. Eastern states, west to Oklahoma and Texas. With foliage that resembles that of meadow rue, rue anemones are among the most charming of our spring ephemerals. Growing from underground tubers, delicate slender stems carry blue-green, thrice-divided (ternate) leaves, the terminal leaflet scallop toothed. Grouped in clusters, the 0.5-in.-wide, sparkling white or pale pink flowers each have up to ten petal-like sepals, surrounding a central knob or boss of stamens; true petals are absent. Small, ribbed fruits, similar to those of related buttercups, follow. Easy to grow in average, well-drained soil amended with humus. Rue anemones do not tolerate drought, and become dormant as summer heat settles in after bloom. Plants bulk up slowly, but are worth the wait. Suitable to line woodland paths, among shrubs, in shaded rock gardens and native plant gardens, or even in troughs or containers with other shade lovers. Any of the cultivars makes an attractive partner for diminutive anemones, primroses, or green 'n golds. They are seldom browsed by deer; pest and disease free.

Propagate by seed sown in fall and overwintered outdoors, or by division. Sensitive-skinned gardeners may have an adverse reaction to the sap, so wear gloves if dividing the clumps.

'Cameo' has double, rose-pink to white flowers.

'Eco-Pink', selected by Don Jacobs, from Decatur, GA, is a single-flowered pink.

'Just Precious' ('Jade Feather', 'Green Hurricane', 'Green Dragon'). This novelty, probably only for collectors, has unique double, green flowers.

Anemonopsis macrophylla

'Schoaff's Double Pink' ('Schoaf's Pink', 'Schoaf's Double Pink') is widely grown. It is similar to 'Cameo', but with only pink flowers.

Anemonopsis
Ranunculaceae
false anemone

A single species is all this genus has to offer, but it is a prize. A Japanese woodland native, false anemone is similar to but smaller and daintier than a Japanese anemone. A natural for woodland gardens and shady borders, false anemone mixes easily with other shade lovers such as ferns, hostas, hellebores, and lungworts. Pests and diseases are seldom a problem. Resistant to deer.

Propagate by division in early spring or fall, or sow seed as soon as it ripens either in a nursery bed or in containers overwintered outside—a period of chilling is required to break dormancy.

Anemonopsis macrophylla
- lavender-pink
- midsummer to early fall
- 2–3 ft. × 1.5 ft.
- part shade, shade
- Z5–8

False anemone. Japan. Airy fern-like foliage provides an attractive backdrop for exquisite 1-in., nodding, bowl-shaped, waxy blossoms. Plant in acid, well-drained soil in a sheltered spot away from dehydrating summer winds. Provide moist soil conditions during the growing season; it will not tolerate wet feet during winter dormancy. Tolerates full sun only in moist, cool regions such as the Pacific Northwest.

Angelica
Apiaceae
angelica

Angelicas are familiar as dramatic features of medicinal herb gardens, but their stately architectural presence makes them an asset in ornamental plantings as well. The strong stems are hollow; each petiole (leaf stem) sheaths the stem at the node. The leaves are twice divided into three. Provide rich soil amended with plenty of humus to retain soil moisture. Sometimes attacked by aphids. Ignored by deer.

To propagate, sow seeds as soon as they are ripe, leaving them uncovered, as light is required for germination. Transplant seedlings promptly to avoid trauma to their sensitive root systems.

Angelica archangelica
- white
- early summer
- 5–7 ft. × 4 ft.
- sun, part shade
- Z4–8

Archangel, wild parsnip. Native to Scandinavia and Greenland. Strongly vertical and statuesque, archangel is a short-lived perennial or biennial. Its

Angelica gigas

divided leaves may reach 2 ft. in length, the leaflets toothed along the edges. Countless, small, greenish white flowers are held in large, domed umbels, sometimes 8 to 10 in. across; these make intriguing additions to floral arrangements. Deadheading before seed set may promote a longer lifespan for individual specimens. However, as this species comes so easily from seed, it is prudent to keep a supply of young plants that can serve as understudies. Archangel makes an excellent focal point in damp or even wet places, or at the back of large borders. Partner in herb and vegetable gardens with rhubarb for dramatic impact; ornamental rhubarb, *Rheum palmatum* 'Atrosanguineum', makes a stunning companion at the back of ornamental borders. Dark-leaved cultivars of weigela, smokebush, and ninebark, and variegated red-stemmed dogwoods are reliably memorable companions in shrub collections.

Young leaves and stems of archangel are edible and were formerly used as natural sweeteners; bright green, candied angelica tastes of anise and can be used to decorate cakes and cookies.

Angelica gigas

- purple
- late summer to early fall
- 3–6 ft. × 4 ft.
- sun, part shade
- Z4–9

Purple parsnip, Korean angelica. Native to damp woodlands of Japan, northern China, and Korea. This vigorous plant is a good conversation piece in any garden, especially when it blooms in its second year. Light green leaves that may reach 12 in. or more in length, borne on purplish stems; where leaves meet stems, the nodes are covered with inflated burgundy sheaths. Purple clusters of buds open to domed, 8-in.-wide heads of deep plum flowers. Best in full sun in cool regions, but shield from intense sun elsewhere. Partner with dark-leaved shrubs or perennials, or create an eye-catching vignette with Joe-Pye weed, or tall willow-leaf sunflowers. Self-seeds but not reliably. Assist this process by putting a paper bag over the ripening seedhead to collect the seeds as they dry; sow fresh seed outdoors in fall, or chill and sow indoors in an unheated structure.

Antennaria

Asteraceae
pussy-toes, cat's-ears

Don't let the common name mislead you—these small, furry plants may have a cuddly appeal, but they are tough, resilient groundcovers, thriving on dry and poor soils in sun-drenched, drought-prone locations. They tend to be enthusiastic spreaders; select one of the many native North American species to avoid turning your garden into a beachhead for an exotic invasive.

Though there is variation from species to species (there are 45 of them), in general pussy-toes share silver, furry, fine-textured foliage and a mat-forming pattern of growth. The everlasting flowers, borne in dense heads on furry, upright stems, do suggest the upthrust foot of some botanical feline; white or pink, the flowerheads individually are insignificant but massed they have a certain charm. The generic name, *Antennaria*, refers to thread-like stamens that sometimes protrude from the flowers, resembling the antennae of insects.

Antennaria dioica

As a group, pussy-toes attract insect pollinators. Some native species play a crucial role in the life cycle of some native moths, including white-spotted midget moth, whose larvae feed exclusively on these plants. Not a favorite of deer.

Though they adapt to a wide range of soils, good drainage is essential, especially in winter. They compete most effectively in dry, sunny situations. In rock gardens they are valuable as groundcovers, especially interplanted with small bulbs and dwarf conifers, and they flourish when tucked into the joints of a flagstone pavement or path. Here, they may complement other herbs, such as creeping thymes, with elegance. They will tolerate heat, but not humidity, and are therefore unsuitable for southeastern US gardens.

Propagate by dividing established clumps in early spring, or sow seed in fall for spring germination.

Antennaria dioica

- white, pink
- late spring to early summer
- 2–5 in. × 18 in.
- sun
- Z5–9, HS

Pussy-toes. North America, Europe, northern Asia. Handsome, fine-textured foliage, excellent for xeriscapes as well as dry spots in ordinary landscapes.

'Nyewoods' is compact with deep rosy pink flowers.

'Rubra' has deep pink flowers.

Antennaria rosea

- pink, white
- early to late spring
- 4–6 in. × 6–9 in.
- sun
- Z3–8, HS

Rosy pussy-toes. Open woods and meadows of western North America. Forms dense mats of fine, velvety, silver-green foliage, with light pink or white flowerheads. Drought tolerant once established. Reseeds and spreads readily in hospitable environments.

Anthemis
Asteraceae
chamomile

Summer-long bloom and aromatic, divided leaves make this genus valuable for sunny, well-drained borders and rock gardens. Average or even poor soil is fine; overly rich soil produces soft, disease-prone growth. The white or yellow daisy flowers are carried atop long stems; they are often fragrant and make good cut flowers, as well as attracting butterflies to the garden. Chamomile does best in cooler climates and may melt in the heat and humidity of southern gardens. Seldom browsed by deer, but protect young plants from slugs.

Propagate by seed sown in spring, by division in spring, or by rooting basal cuttings in late spring to early summer.

Anthemis tinctoria 'Kelwayi'

Anthemis ×hybrida 'Susanna Mitchell'

Anthemis ×hybrida
- yellow, white
- summer
- 24–30 in. × 24 in.
- sun
- Z3–8

Hybrid chamomile. Of hybrid origin. Several of the named cultivars in this genus are probably hybrids of *Anthemis tinctoria* and either *A. sancti-johannis* or *A. punctata* subsp. *cupiana*, but may still be listed under *A. tinctoria* in some catalogs. They are fine long-blooming border plants that mix well with speedwells, yarrows, phlox, and lupines. Keep soil moist; stake if necessary. Excellent cut flowers.

'E. C. Buxton' has lemon-centered, cream daisies.

'Grallagh Gold' produces bright golden flower-heads on 24-in. stems.

'Kelwayi' has bright yellow flowers.

'Moonlight' is pale yellow with deeper yellow centers. Flowers may bleach out in full sun.

'Susanna Mitchell' has yellow-centered, creamy-white daisies and silver-green, feathery leaves. It is drought tolerant and appropriate for xeriscapes. Combine with blue bellflowers or salvias. 18–24 in. tall.

Anthemis marshalliana
syn. *A. biebersteiniana, A. rudolphiana*
- yellow
- late spring to early fall
- 10–18 in. × 12–24 in.
- sun
- Z5–8, HS

Marshall's chamomile. Caucasus. Bright yellow daisy flowers, 1–2 in. across, rise above low mats of silky, silver foliage. Routine deadheading extends the bloom period. Not recommended for hot, humid gardens.

Anthemis punctata subsp. cupiana
syn. *A. cupiana*
- white
- early summer
- 8–12 in. × 36 in.
- sun
- Z5–8, HS

Sicilian chamomile. Italy. Beautiful lacy, gray-green leaves spread out in delicate mats of foliage. In early summer, stems are topped with solitary, yellow-eyed, white daisy flowers, 1–2 in. across. Superb in rock gardens or at the front of the border, perhaps with Dalmatian bellflower and woolly speedwell. Does poorly in heat and humidity.

Anthemis sancti-johannis
- orange
- summer
- 24–36 in. × 24 in.
- sun
- Z3–8

Golden marguerite, St. John's chamomile. South-western Bulgaria. This bushy clumper has ferny, grayish, 2-in. leaves covered with soft hairs. Its 2-in.-wide, very short-rayed, bright orange daisy flowers are deep yellow in the center. Excellent, long-lasting cut flowers. Keep soil moist, and dead-head routinely to extend bloom time. May need staking. Attracts bees and butterflies. Self-seeds gently, or collect seed and direct sow in fall.

Anthemis tinctoria
- yellow
- summer to fall
- 24–36 in. × 24 in.
- sun
- Z3–7, HS

Golden marguerite. Europe, Caucasus, Turkey. A clumping perennial with green, ferny leaves, gray with soft hairs beneath. Yellow to cream daisies, 1 in. or more across, bloom atop branched stems for several weeks. Do not allow to completely dry out in hot weather; stake if necessary. Tends to melt in the heat and humidity of southern summers. This species is a parent of several excellent hybrids.

Anthericum
Asparagaceae
St. Bernard's lily

Though not particularly showy in themselves, the two species of St. Bernard's lily commonly culti-vated as garden perennials have the valuable abil-ity to serve as foils for other, more visually assertive plants. Charming and easy to grow, they deserve wider use in American gardens. Both of the garden species form tussocks of grass-like leaves and bear white, six-tepaled flowers on tall, slender stalks.

The two are also alike in their adaptability: if given a rich, well-drained soil and a sunny site, they'll thrive in southern New England and the Pacific Northwest, as well as in the humidity of a Florida summer and the drier heat of southern California.

Wherever you grow them, they make a dramatic contrast when set against dark-foliaged shrubs such as 'Black Lace' or 'Black Beauty' elderberries, and the hybrid ninebark 'Summer Wine'. The grassy foliage of St. Bernard's lilies also integrates easily with plantings of compact ornamental grasses. In combinations of this kind, the flowers serve as a delightful surprise. Try a combination with spike speedwells and hardy geraniums, or peonies.

Propagate by seed direct sown in fall or started indoors in early spring—seedling anthericums take a couple of years to reach blooming size. Established clumps may be divided in spring. Guard against slugs and snails.

Anthericum liliago
- white
- late spring to early summer
- 24–36 in. × 12–16 in.
- sun
- Z5–9

St. Bernard's lily, grass lily. Dry pastures, open woods, and stony soils in Europe and Turkey. Rhizomatous-rooted clumps bear airy spikes of fragrant, 1-in.-long, white flowers that open sequentially from the bottom of the spike to the top, prolonging the period of bloom. This unbranched species is particularly attractive when naturalized in a meadow with grassland bulbs such as *Narcissus*, *Camassia*, and *Allium*. Good for cutting.

'Major' (syn. *Anthericum algeriense*) has larger flowers than the species, snowy white on 2.5-ft. stems. Midsummer bloom.

Anthericum ramosum
- white
- early to midsummer
- 16–32 in. × 12 in.
- sun, part shade
- Z5–9

St. Bernard's lily. Western Europe to central Asia. Forms a trim, compact clump of grassy leaves, 20 in. long and 0.2 in. wide. Beginning in midsummer, erect, branched stems emerge to bear clouds of 1-in., starry, white flowers, each with a yellow ovary and sporting yellow anthers; bloom is repeated periodically throughout the summer.

Aquilegia
Ranunculaceae
columbine

Both the scientific and common names celebrate this plant's intriguing flower structure. *Aquilegia* derives from the Latin for "eagle," and refers to the five long, hollow spurs sweeping back from the flower's face, supposedly resembling the talons of a bird of prey; columbine (Latin for "dove") offers

Aquilegia 'Origami Red-and-White'

a gentler vision—turn the flower over and look for the resemblance to five doves perched around a fountain. In addition to the flowers, aquilegias offer daintily divided or lobed, rich green or blue-green foliage.

Easy to grow, columbines thrive in most soils as long as they drain well. To promote the best growth and bloom, water regularly but avoid soaking; overwatering is generally fatal. Full sun is fine in cooler, northern regions; morning sun with afternoon shade is preferable in warmer ones.

The most common pest is leaf miner, which disfigures the foliage by burrowing beneath the leaf surface, marking it with pale, winding tracks; cut back to the ground and destroy foliage of infested plants immediately after bloom time. This promotes healthy new growth. The seeds and roots of columbines are toxic, and should not be ingested. Resistant to deer and rabbits, but attractive to hummingbirds and butterflies.

Plant larger-flowered species and hybrids in borders with spring bulbs and perennials: perennial flax, dame's rocket, and spurges for example. Less showy types adapt well to rock gardens and at woodland edges. Well suited to cottage gardens and excellent in containers and as cut flowers.

Easily started from seed; propagate named cultivars by dividing mature clumps carefully; columbines resent root disturbance and are slow to recover from such treatment.

Aquilegia alpina
syn. *A. montana*
- blue
- late spring
- 1–2 ft. × 6–12 in.
- sun, part shade
- Z4–8

Alpine columbine. European Alps. Flowers are cobalt blue, 2–3 in. across. Well-drained soil is essential; prefers partial shade in warmer, sunnier regions. Reseeds freely in hospitable locations.

var. *alba* bears white flowers on slightly shorter plants.

Aquilegia caerulea
- blue, white
- spring to early summer
- 8–24 in. × 18–24 in.
- sun, part shade
- Z3–8, HS

Rocky Mountain columbine. Rocky Mountain states. Large flowers to 3 in. across, white and pale to cerulean blue. Provide protection from afternoon sun in the warmer part of its range. Self-seeds in hospitable locations.

'Florida' has bicolored flowers of pale and golden yellow.

'Georgia' has extra-large, red flowers with white corollas.

'Kristall' is pure white.

'Red Hobbit' is dwarf with carmine flowers with white corollas. 12–15 in.

Aquilegia canadensis 'Corbett'

Aquilegia canadensis
- pink, red-yellow
- mid- to late spring
- 2–3 ft. × 1–1.5 ft.
- sun, part shade
- Z3–8

Canadian columbine. Rocky woods, slopes, and open areas throughout North America, east of the Rockies. Bright red flowers with yellow corollas dance in the slightest breeze. Adapts to a wide range of soils, including dry ones. Attractive to hummingbirds, well suited to wildlife gardens as well as native plant collections. Tolerates drought, deer, and rabbits. Self-seeds and naturalizes in hospitable locations. Reportedly resistant to leaf miners.

'Corbett' has pale yellow flowers on 8- to 10-in.-tall plants. May lack vigor.

'Little Lanterns' is a dwarf that bears brilliant red flowers with yellow corollas. 8–10 in.

Aquilegia chrysantha
- yellow
- late spring to early summer
- 1–3 ft. × 1–3 ft.
- part shade, shade
- Z3–8

Golden columbine. Southwestern North America. Delicate flowers have gently curving spurs to 3 in. long. Fast growing and successful on a wide range of well-drained soils; keep well watered in full sun in cool climates; prefers partial shade elsewhere. Self-seeds in hospitable locations. Rust and powdery mildew may attack in dry summers; be alert for fungal leaf spots and the occasional southern blight.

'Yellow Queen' bears especially bright yellow-and-gold flowers.

Aquilegia ecalcarata
syn. *Semiaquilegia ecalcarata*
- red, purple
- spring
- 15–18 in. × 12 in.
- sun, part shade
- Z4–7

Spurless columbine. Japan, China, Korea. This short-lived perennial has ternate, 10- to 12-in. basal leaves on long petioles. The leaflets are sometimes further divided. Starry burgundy to purple flowers nod in loose clusters atop branched stems; in this species, the floral spurs of other aquilegias are replaced by small pouches at the base of the flowers. *Semiaquilegia adoxoides* is similar but has pale pink flowers.

Aquilegia flabellata
syn. *A. atkinensis*
- purple, white
- spring to early summer
- 1–3 ft. × 0.5–1 ft.
- sun, part shade
- Z4–8

Fan columbine. Japan and Korea. Flowers are bicolored, bluish purple with white tips and centers. Self-seeds in hospitable locations.

'Blackcurrant Ice' has a dark purple corolla with yellow sepals and spurs.

'Cameo Blue-and-White' is extra compact with blue and white flowers. 6 in.

var. *pumila* is very dwarf, just 3–5 in., with blue-and-white flowers.

Aquilegia vulgaris

- blue, pink, white
- early to late spring
- 12–36 in. × 6–12 in.
- sun, part shade
- Z3–8

European columbine, Granny's bonnet. Europe. The wild species has blue or purple-and-white flowers, but cultivars offer many other hues. Nodding flowers appear congested, with short, hooked spurs. Prefers humus-rich, moist but well-drained soils.

'Leprechaun Gold' has gold-marbled, bright green foliage and large, deep violet flowers borne on reddish pink stems.

'Nora Barlow' has tightly double flowers of red and white with very short spurs. Named for Charles Darwin's granddaughter.

'Ruby Port' has wine-red flowers; 'Variegated Ruby Port' bears similar flowers with yellow-specked foliage.

'William Guiness' ('Magpie') bears double flowers of black-purple, with white corollas, blooming from late spring through early summer.

Other Notable Cultivars

Biedermeier Mix has single and double, upward-facing blooms in violet, cream, lilac, pink, and deep red. 12–18 in. Z3–9.

Dragonfly Hybrids strain is dwarf with blue, pink, red, salmon, white, or yellow flowers. 12–18 in. Z3–9.

McKana Hybrids grow up to 24 in. tall and bear large, long-spurred flowers in a wide range of pastel colors.

Origami Series (or Butterfly Series) is a hybrid mix with bicolored flowers with slender spurs. Often listed as *Aquilegia caerulea*, which is a prime parent. Superior named cultivars include 'Origami Red-and-White' and 'Origami Yellow-and-White'.

Arabis
Brassicaceae
rock cress

Even though rock cresses are often confined to the rock garden, a number of species and hybrids are also suited to dry banks and walls, for use as groundcovers, or at the front of beds and borders to provide early spring color.

Rock cresses form mats or tufts of evergreen, sometimes hairy leaves, above which rise short stems topped with clusters of four-petaled flowers in white, pink, or rosy purple. Grow in full sun

Aquilegia vulgaris 'Nora Barlow'

Arabis caucasica

where drainage is very good to prevent winter root rot; drought is seldom a problem. Shear spent flowers after bloom time to keep a neat appearance and avoid straggly stems. Rock cress combines well with small, spring-blooming bulbs such as squills, mini-daffodils, and compact species tulips. Basket-of-gold and yellow corydalis also make attractive companions. Seldom browsed by deer.

Propagate by seed sown in spring, by softwood cuttings taken in early summer, or by division.

Arabis ×arendsii

- pink
- spring
- 4–8 in. × 12 in.
- sun
- Z4–8

Hybrid rock cress. *Arabis caucasica* × *A. aubretioides*. Evergreen mats of gray-green, hairy leaves arranged in rosettes. These can be detached and rooted after bloom time.

'Rosabella' has deep rose flowers, 0.5 in. across.

Arabis blepharophylla

- pink
- spring
- 4–8 in. × 15 in.
- sun
- Z5–8

Rose rock cress, fringed rock cress, coast rock cress. Coastal hills of California. Sweetly fragrant, 0.5-in., purplish pink flowers cluster atop slender

Arisaema sikokianum

hairy stems. Fuzzy leaves form basal rosettes. Tolerant of xeric conditions.

'Frühlingszauber' ('Spring Charm') is the most widely available selection. It has brilliant magenta flowers. Easy from seed; for best germination do not cover. May be listed under *Arabis* ×*arendsii*. 10 in. × 8–10 in.

Arabis caucasica

syn. *A. albida*, *A. alpina* subsp. *caucasica*, *A. billardieri*

- white
- spring
- 8–12 in. × 12–20 in.
- sun
- Z3–8, HS

Wall rock cress, Caucasian rock cress. Caucasus mountains. Grayish, 1- to 2-in. leaves form loose, low mats of foliage. In spring these are blanketed with 0.5-in., white flowers clustered at the tips of wiry stems. Shear after flowering to maintain compact growth and prevent straggliness. Short lived in warm climates; best in cooler regions.

'Compinkie'. Bright pink flowers above compact mounds of leaves. Appropriate for troughs. 6 in.

'Flore Plena' ('Plena') has double, chalk-white flowers.

'Snowcap' has fragrant, pure white flowers for several weeks. Excellent as groundcover or as a skirt for spring-blooming and dark-foliaged shrubs.

'Variegata'. White flowers and gray-green leaves rimmed with white. Striking in winter.

Arabis procurrens

- white
- spring
- 6–12 in. × 12 in.
- sun, part shade
- Z3–7, HS

Alpine wall cress, running rock cress. Southern Europe. This species has oblong, dark green, 1-in. leaves with a glossy surface. The small, white flowers are typical of the genus. Good for containers and between pavers.

'Glacier' has bright white flowers that cover deep green foliage mats for several weeks. 2–4 in. *Arabis sturri* is very similar.

'Variegata' (syn. *A. ferdinandi-coburgi* 'Variegata') develops mats of broadly cream-rimmed, gray-green and pinkish leaves. Trim after bloom and check to remove any shoots that have reverted to green. Grown for its foliage. Excellent tumbling over a wall.

Arisaema

Araceae
Jack-in-the-pulpit, cobra lily

In recent years Jack-in-the-pulpits have become trendy, much sought after for woodland and partly shaded gardens. Anyone who has spent time in the spring woodlands of eastern North America undoubtedly remembers our native species,

Arisaema triphyllum, with its curious hooded flower. This, however, has largely (except in native plant gardens) been supplanted in gardens by exciting exotic species that modern plant explorers have been discovering in Asia. These new introductions are often larger and more dramatically colored than the familiar native, but the plants' general characteristics remain the same. The leaves, appearing with or just after the flowers, are divided into leaflets; the inflorescence consists of a slender spadix or "Jack" that bears tiny male and female flowers at the base, and is surrounded by a showy hood-like spathe or "pulpit." The hood, often decorated with colorful stripes, is the source of these plants' other common name, cobra lily. If the flies do their work as pollinators, *Arisaema* flowers are followed by dense clusters of glossy red or orange berries reputedly dispersed by ants. Remarkably, arisaemas are able to change their sex: male plants may transform into females or hermaphrodites as they increase in size and age.

Plant the fleshy tubers or rhizomes of arisaemas in neutral to acid, moisture-retaining soil rich in humus. Asian species prefer drier, well-drained soil. Although Jack-in-the-pulpits are reportedly deer resistant, others have observed heavy browsing of the berries, which are also food for birds and rodents. Protect from slugs.

Propagate by division or seed in fall or spring.

Arisaema candidissimum

- white
- early summer
- 12 in. high and wide
- part shade
- Z5–7

White Jack. Rocky banks in western China. This species produces a beautiful translucent inflorescence with a showy 5- to 6-in.-long, pink-and-white-striped spathe, pink within, and a fragrant, yellow-green spadix. A pair of three-lobed leaves, with leaflets to 2 in. wide, appears at bloom time. Clumps expand in well-drained sites.

Arisaema ringens

- purple, green
- early spring
- 10–20 in. × 20 in.
- part shade
- Z5–9

Cobra Jack. Korea, China, Taiwan, Japan. This popular species may be the easiest of the cobra lilies to grow. Each tuber produces a pair of large, glossy, trifoliate leaves, above which rises the inflorescence. The striped purple-and-green (sometimes green-and-white) spathe bends over the spadix covering it like a hood. It is further twisted, revealing its purple inside. Plant groups of tubers in soil amended with plenty of moisture-retaining organic material.

Arisaema sikokianum

- purple, white
- early spring
- 12–20 in. × 20 in.
- part shade
- Z4–9

Gaudy Jack. Japan. True to its common name, this species produces a stunningly beautiful inflorescence. The upright spathe is purplish black, surrounding a pure white, club-shaped spadix. The green or sometimes mottled leaves emerge at the same time. Plant in a sheltered spot where frost damage is unlikely to harm this early bloomer.

Arisaema triphyllum

- purple, green
- spring
- 12–24 in. × 12 in.
- part shade, shade
- Z3–9

Jack-in-the-pulpit, Indian turnip, three-leaf Jack-in-the-pulpit. Damp woodlands of eastern North America. This native Jack produces a pair of trifoliate leaves below a purple, green, or striped hooded pulpit that droops at the top. The spadix may also be purple or greenish white. Round, red berries follow. Goes dormant in summer heat. Combine with other natives such as wild sweet William, green 'n gold, and blue cohosh. The tuberous roots were a staple starchy food for Native Americans.

'Black Jack' has green-veined, black leaves and black pulpits in late spring. 1 ft. Z6–9.

Armeria
Plumbaginacae
sea pink, thrift

In the wild, sea pinks flourish in coastal areas, often growing among rocks at the high-tide mark, where they are flooded with salt water by the higher tides of spring and fall. These tough plants are tolerant of seaside gales and mountain cold, and ideal for coastal gardens. They develop rounded evergreen tufts of fine grassy leaves, green or bluish green, from which rise naked stems topped with tight globes of small pink, red, or white flowers. The foliage tufts expand slowly but not aggressively enough to make a large-scale, weed-controlling groundcover. Sea pinks thrive in very well-drained, rather poor soil; avoid fertilizing these plants, as overly rich soil promotes crown rot.

Plant sea pinks in rock gardens, as edgings, or on walls, or plant closely as a groundcover in small spaces. They also do well on green roofs, and in troughs and containers. Appropriate low-growing companions include basket-of-gold, rock cress, thymes, lavenders, and creeping bellflowers, as well as larger Russian sage, wormwoods, and fine-leaved ornamental grasses. Deadhead to encourage rebloom.

Attractive to birds and butterflies, but seldom browsed by deer. Rarely bothered by pests and diseases, although the centers of the plants may die

Armeria maritima 'Nifty Thrifty'

narrow green leaves rimmed with a slender cream band, beneath pink flowers. Interesting in winter. 4–6 in. Z2–9.

'Vindictive' has dark green foliage and strong pink flowers from late spring to early summer. 6–10 in. Z4–8.

Armeria pseudoarmeria

syn. *A. cephalotes, A. latifolia*
- pink or white
- summer
- 12–18 in. × 12 in.
- sun
- Z5–9

False sea pink, plantain thrift, wide-leaf thrift. Coastal west Portugal. Lance-shaped, green leaves to 8 in. long. Large heads of pale pink or white flowers to 1.5 in. across.

Ballerina Series blooms from seed its first year and comes with flowers in red, white, and lilac (so far). Flowerheads 1 in. across are borne on 8-in. stems from early summer to early fall. The broad green leaves are similar to those of narrow-leaf plantain. Heat tolerant and good in hot, humid climates. Z6–9.

Joystick Series produces golf ball–sized flowers in red, white, lilac, and pink on 1-ft.-tall scapes. Seed started in midwinter blooms that summer. Grow as annuals in cold zones. Especially good for cutting and drying. Z7–8.

Other Notable Cultivars

'Bees Ruby' is a hybrid involving *Armeria pseudoarmeria* with broader, greener foliage than most other sea pinks. Cerise flowers in late spring to early summer. 12–16 in. × 9–12 in. Z3–8.

Artemisia
Asteraceae
mugwort, wormwood

This is a huge genus of herbs and shrubs, a number of which are popular, if occasionally troublesome, residents of perennial gardens, valued not only for their lacy and aromatic, silver foliage but also their toughness. Once established, they are almost drought proof, flourishing in exposed, sun-drenched spots with poor soils; in a hospitable site they are notably vigorous. This last characteristic can create problems in cultivated landscapes, because many species are prone to become invasive and gardeners are likely to find them extremely difficult to eradicate. In particular, gardeners should avoid the attractive, variegated cultivars of common mugwort, *Artemisia vulgaris*, such as 'Oriental Limelight' and 'Variegata'; this native Alaskan species has proven tenaciously invasive throughout much of the lower 48 states.

Carefully selected and controlled, however, artemisias can make a powerful contribution. An obvious choice for dry and xeriscape sites, they also

out with age or rot; lift and separate healthy pieces from the perimeter of the clumps for replanting; discard the center. Flowers are good for small arrangements.

Divide in spring before bloom time or start seed in late winter.

Armeria maritima

- pink
- early summer
- 6–12 in. × 10 in.
- sun
- Z3–9

Sea pink, thrift. Mountains and coastal regions of the Northern Hemisphere. Foliage is mostly dark green, less than 0.75 in. wide and to 5 in. long, and forms dense evergreen tufts. Lots of stiff, 8-in. flower scapes topped with globes of pink, white, or purplish flowers emerge in summer.

'Bloodstone' bears large, very deep pink flowers for several weeks. Possibly a hybrid. 8–10 in. Z4–8.

'Blue Mound' blooms into midsummer, extending the season. Pink flowers above a mound of bluish foliage. Z4–9.

'Cotton Tail' is similar to 'Alba', but the dark green mats of foliage spread more widely. Z4–8.

'Dusseldorf Pride' ('Dusseldorf Stolz') has rosy pink flowers. 6–8 in.

'Nifty Thrifty' is a British introduction. It has

Artemisia absinthium 'Lambrook Silver'

Artemisia absinthium

- yellow
- midsummer to midfall
- 24–30 in. × 30 in.
- sun
- Z4–8, HS

Wormwood, absinth. Europe, northern Africa, and western Asia. Formerly a key ingredient of the potent liqueur absinthe. Handsome finely cut, silvery gray foliage is covered in silky hairs. A popular garden plant in its native Europe, but an aggressive seeder considered invasive in some of the US western states. May melt out.

'Lambrook Mist' has finely divided foliage. 20 in.

'Lambrook Silver' has brilliant, silver foliage on arching stems. One of the best of the artemisias. To 40 in.

'Silver Frost' (syn. *Artemisia ludoviciana* 'Silver Frost') has compact, silvery foliage; wider than it is tall. 24 in.

Artemisia arborescens

- yellow
- spring
- 4–6 ft. high and wide
- sun, part shade
- Z9–10

Tree wormwood. Eastern Mediterranean native that flourishes in milder regions of the US Southwest. Silvery, fern-like foliage with a strong odor. Good for the back of the border, perhaps against a wall or fence in cooler regions. Inconsequential small, yellow flowers.

Artemisia californica

- yellow-green, pink
- summer to fall
- 1.5–4 ft. high and wide
- sun
- Z7–10

California wormwood. Coastal California. Woody stems and deeply divided, almost thread-like, evergreen, gray-green foliage with sweet, aromatic fragrance.

'Canyon Gray' is a prostrate cultivar that reaches a height of only 12–18 in. and spreads to 36–48 in.

Artemisia lactiflora

- white
- late summer to midfall
- 4–6 ft. × 4 ft.
- summer
- Z4–9

White mugwort. This Asian native develops clumps of stems with green, divided leaves and tiny, creamy-white flowers borne in attractive plumes. Rabbits can be a problem. Attractive as a border plant and cut flower, fresh for the house or dried for winter arrangements.

'Guizhou' has striking red-purple, almost black stems, which contrast well with the widely branched flower plumes. Sometimes granted specific status as *Artemisia kitadakensis*.

thrive in ordinary garden conditions. Keep the soil dry and avoid additional nitrogen that promotes overly lush, floppy growth. The silver foliage contrasts splendidly with scarlets, purples, and blues, and can create a sophisticated counterpoint to sun-loving shrubs and grasses. Artemisias work well in containers and their clean, astringent smell is a welcome addition to a sunny terrace or court. Though the silver foliage lends itself to use in flower arrangements, some find the fragrance overpowering indoors.

Plant artemisias in a sunny spot with well-drained, ideally sandy soil; water when dry, but avoid overwatering. The usually small flowers are not particularly attractive. Shear plants back in spring but be sure to leave enough buds on the stems to enable dense regrowth, and never cut back to the ground. Pests or diseases (except root rot in persistently damp soils) seldom trouble these plants; their bitter foliage is rarely browsed by deer or rabbits. Some species melt out in high heat and humidity, with portions of the crown rotting.

Propagate by division of established plants in early spring or by softwood cuttings taken in early summer.

Artemisia abrotanum

- yellow
- mid- to late summer
- 3–5 ft. × 2 ft.
- sun
- Z4–10

Southernwood, lad's love, old man. Southern Europe. This Old World native is grown as a shrub in cottage gardens and mixed borders. Thread-like, grayish green foliage has a pleasant, citrus fragrance.

'Tangerine' produces mounds of feathery, deep olive-green foliage. To 3 ft. high and wide.

Artemisia ludoviciana 'Valerie Finnis'

Artemisia 'Powis Castle'

Artemisia ludoviciana
syn. *A. palmeri, A. purshiana*
- yellow
- midsummer to early fall
- 2–3 ft. high and wide
- sun
- Z4–9

White sagebrush, western mugwort. All the lower 48 states, except Florida and Alabama. Gray-white, downy, aromatic leaves are lance shaped, to 4 in. long; flowers inconspicuous. Upright clumps spread rapidly by rhizomes to colonize adjacent areas if not checked. Useful as a groundcover for sunny, droughty areas—shear such plantings in spring with a lawn mower.

'Silver King' is less aggressive than the species but nevertheless spreads unless kept in check. Upright grower; 0.75-in., white, woolly leaves.

'Silver Queen' forms a compact, well-clothed mound 2 ft. tall and 4 ft. wide. Spreading. Tends to melt out.

'Valerie Finnis' is the best cultivar of this species with broader, showier leaves than the species. Not as rampant. 18–24 in. × 24–30 in.

Artemisia schmidtiana
- white
- summer to early fall
- 10–12 in. × 1.5–3 ft.
- sun
- Z3–7, HS

Silvermound. Japan. Forms a low, neat, symmetrical mound of silver-green, silky haired foliage. Melts out in the US South. One of the rare, non-invasive artemisias.

'Silver Mound' ('Nana') seems to be the only type available in the nursery trade. 6 in. × 12 in.

Artemisia stelleriana
- grown for foliage
- early to midsummer
- 6–12 in. × 12–15 in.
- sun
- Z2–9, HS

Beach wormwood, dusty miller, old woman. Alaska; naturalized in the northeastern United States and the Pacific Northwest. Thrives in cultivation in all but the hottest regions.

'Silver Brocade' ('Boughton Silver', 'Mori') forms a spreading mat of bright silvery-white, scallop-edged, 1- to 2-in. leaves; inconsequential yellow flowers. Demands excellent drainage. Use for edging, as a groundcover, or in containers and hanging baskets; effective in sloping rock gardens and coastal gardens. Snip off any upright shoots to maintain procumbent habit.

Other Notable Cultivars
'Huntington' ('Huntington Gardens') is a hybrid with soft, filigreed, silver-frosted leaves. Fairly heat tolerant. 3 ft. high and wide. Z5–8.

'Powis Castle'. Mostly sterile, a probable hybrid (*Artemisia arborescens* × *A. absinthium*). Dense mounds of finely divided, feathery, silver foliage 2–3 ft. tall and 1–2 ft. across. Rarely blooms. If necessary, prune to shape during active growth. Tends to spread by rhizomes into adjacent plants. An introduction from Powis Castle, Wales. Z6–9.

Arum italicum 'Marmoratum'

Arum
Araceae
arum, lords-and-ladies

Perfect to add pizzazz to the off-season garden, arums produce their often showy, undivided leaves (related *Arisaema* has divided leaves) from tubers in fall and retain them all winter long; they are arrow shaped and often decorated with contrasting marbling. Flowers typical of the Araceae, composed of a hood-like spathe surrounding the erect spadix, appear in spring. If pollinated, bright red berries (favorite food for wildlife) appear on the spadix above the leaves. Berry production appears to be best where summer heat is moderate. Provide well-drained but moisture-retaining soil, high in humus. The plants avoid the summer heat, becoming dormant till fall. Other perennials with attractive winter foliage, such as bigroot geranium, coral bells, pigsqueak, and sedges, make good companions in partly shaded borders. Resistant to deer.

Divide large clumps when they break dormancy, and replant the tubers at once. Seed can be collected, cleaned of its fleshy fruits, and sown in fall, but it is slow to germinate and benefits from a period of moist cold (stratification).

Arum creticum
- creamy yellow
- spring
- 18 in. high and wide
- sun, part shade
- Z8–10

Cretan arum. Crete, Greece, and Turkey. The arrow-shaped, 8- to 10-in. leaves of this species are single hued, but hold their bright green color well. The yellow or cream spathe is erect; as it matures it droops backward to reveal the surprisingly lemon-scented, school bus–yellow spadix. Selections slightly hardier than the species are available.

Arum italicum
- greenish white
- late spring
- 12–20 in. × 18 in.
- part shade, shade
- Z6–9

Italian arum. Southern Europe, Italy, Mediterranean Africa, western Asia. This woodland species is at home in shaded beds and borders, and among shrubs and trees. Bright green, arrow-shaped, 12-in. leaves boldly marked with white along the veins; greenish spathes, surrounding the bright cream spadix, appear as the foliage is withering prior to summer dormancy. A sturdy column of decorative, round, reddish orange berries follows. May self-seed but the resulting seedlings are variable, and their leaves may even be plain green. The sap can cause skin and eye irritation.

'Marmoratum' has large, cream-veined foliage, and 12-in.-tall, whitish flowers in spring. The leaves are striking additions to floral arrangements. Often confused with 'Pictum', which is similar and even considered synonymous by some. 12 in. Z4–9.

'Winter White' has dramatic, brightly marbled-in-white leaves, eye-catching in arrangements. The white, late-spring flowers give way to a column of bright orange berries by late summer. Blooms best in sun. 8–12 in. Z5–9.

Aruncus
Rosaceae
goat's beard

Often confused with similar astilbes, goat's beards are vigorous, clump-forming perennials with airy, plume-like blooms that inject a note of lightness into the garden. The loose, feathery, branched wands of tiny blossoms rise high above the leaves and are valued as cut flowers. Masses of dark green, divided foliage are handsome and sometimes display fall color.

Grow in partly shaded spots where the soil does not dry out readily—drought may cause leaves to become crispy and brown. The sides of streams and ponds and similarly damp places are ideal locations if the soil is rich in humus. The taller of the two species, *Aruncus dioicus*, is effective under trees and shrubs or as a backdrop at the back of the border. Partner with foxgloves, columbines, and late-blooming bulbs, including camassias. In native plant gardens woodland phlox, blue cohosh, wild geranium, and trilliums are appropriate companions. Pest and disease free; seldom browsed by deer.

Propagate by division in early spring or fall, or by seed sown in fall and overwintered in a protected spot.

Aruncus hybrid 'Misty Lace'

This bold clumping perennial prefers high-humus woodland soils and should not be allowed to dry out. Tolerant of sun, but intense sun burns the foliage even with extra irrigation. Erect and shrub-like, the branching stems bear an abundance of two- or three-times divided leaves with oval leaflets, doubly serrated along their edges. Tall, feathery plumes of creamy-white flowers, up to 20 in. long, rise well above the foliage mass. Male and female flowers are borne on separate plants; the male flowers tend to be showier and fluffier. Appropriate for native plant, wild, and meadow gardens, along stream banks, and around ponds. Mass, group, or grow as a specimen. The rootstock becomes very tough and woody with age—if you plan to increase stock by division, you may need a machete.

'Kneiffii' has much more deeply cut, almost thread-like foliage. Good for smaller spaces in moist soil. 2–3 ft.

Other Notable Cultivars

'Guinea Fowl' (*Aruncus dioicus* × *A. aethusifolius*). Neat, compact clumps of leaves, more dissected than those of *A. aethusifolius*. Inflorescence a delicate spray of tiny white flowers. Best in light shade. 12–18 in. Z5–7.

'Misty Lace', also a hybrid of *A. dioicus* × *A. aethusifolius*, tolerates full sun and is somewhat hardier that 'Guinea Fowl'. This hybrid displays intermediate characteristics of its parents. Better than others for hot and humid gardens. An Allan Armitage introduction. 18–24 in. Z4–7.

Asarum
syn. *Hexastylis, Heterotropa*
Aristolochiaceae
wild ginger

Rhizomes of the wild gingers have a spicy fragrance that recalls the culinary spice, but the two groups of plants are not related. Despite the advice offered by some wild food enthusiasts, do *not* use wild ginger to flavor your cuisine, as some species in this genus contain aristolochic acid, which according to the US Food and Drug Administration can cause serious and permanent kidney damage. Instead, enjoy these woodland perennials in the garden, where their large, kidney-shaped leaves furnish an elegant and shade-tolerant groundcover. Most species are evergreen or nearly so (some botanists have split the genus, moving the evergreen species into *Hexastylis*). The foliage is more of a presence in the garden than the calabash pipe- or cup-shaped flowers, which, though intriguing, are modest in size and commonly hidden beneath the leaves.

Most wild gingers prefer moist but well-drained, humus-rich soils with a neutral to acid pH. Typically they flourish on woodland sites, and though they appreciate regular irrigation during hot, dry weather, most are reasonably drought resistant once well established. They spread by creeping,

Aruncus aethusifolius
- white
- early to midsummer
- 10–16 in. × 12 in.
- sun, part shade, shade
- Z3–9

Dwarf goat's beard. This Korean species develops clumps of very finely divided, dark green leaves that in sunny spots become reddish in fall. Astilbe-like, creamy-white flowers bloom above the leaves. Great as a foliar contrast for small hostas in rock gardens, troughs, or at the front of partly shaded borders. Carefree and cute.

Aruncus dioicus
syn. *A. sylvestris, Spiraea aruncus*
- cream
- late spring to early summer
- 4–6 ft. × 2–4 ft.
- sun, part shade
- Z3–7

Goat's beard, white goat's beard, bride's feathers. Europe to eastern Siberia, eastern North America.

Asarum europaeum

fleshy roots or rhizomes, slowly forming expanding clumps or patches. Because even the deciduous wild gingers keep their foliage throughout the growing season, they make good companions for spring ephemerals such as spring beauties, trilliums, and trout lilies. The evergreen species are excellent as container plantings year-round.

Deer resistant; the only serious pests are slugs or snails.

Beyond the species featured here, the Asian *Asarum splendens* and its large-leaved cultivar 'Quicksilver', *A. maximum* and its selections 'Green Panda' and variegated 'Ling Ling', and our western US native *A. hartwegii* (syn. *A. marmoratum*) are also interesting and worth seeking.

To propagate, collect seeds in summer as soon as they ripen and sow in pots to overwinter in a cold frame or sheltered spot; or divide mature clumps into well-rooted pieces 6–8 in. across in early spring or fall. Alternatively, wash the soil from rhizomes and use a sharp knife to slice them into pieces, each including two leaves or a node; plant rhizome cuttings shallowly, with leaf-bearing end exposed; mulch to keep moist.

Asarum arifolium
- brown
- late spring
- 6–8 in. × 12 in.
- part shade, shade
- Z4–8

Arrow-leaf ginger. Southeastern United States. Evergreen with smooth, variably mottled, triangular or arrow-shaped leaves to 8 in. long. Beige-brown flower buds are visible among last year's leaves in early spring; they open to little brown jugs usually with spreading lobes. Handles heat and humidity with aplomb.

'Beaver Creek' may have more vigor. A Mt. Cuba Center, Delaware, introduction.

Asarum asaroides
- purple-brown
- spring
- 4 in. × 15 in.
- part shade
- Z5–9

Asarum leaf, perennial wild ginger. Reliable and vigorous Japanese native that quickly forms 15-in.-wide clumps of evergreen, heart-shaped leaves marked with silver, to 6 in. long. At the base of the plant, 2-in., dark purple-brown flowers emerge in spring. Very easy to grow.

Asarum canadense
- purple-brown
- midspring
- 6–12 in. × 1–1.5 ft.
- part shade, shade
- Z3–8

Canadian wild ginger. Eastern half of North America, from Manitoba to North Carolina. An undemanding, deciduous species with downy, heart- to kidney-shaped, matte dark green leaves to 6 in. across; cup-shaped, purplish brown flowers are 1 in. wide.

'Eco Choice' has somewhat denser foliage.

Asarum caudatum
- maroon, white
- late spring to early summer
- 2–8 in. × 3 ft.
- part shade, shade
- Z5–10, HS

Western wild ginger, long-tailed wild ginger. Moist forests from British Columbia through southern California and eastward into Montana. Shiny, evergreen, heart-shaped leaves, 2–5 in. across; drought tolerant once established. Cup-shaped, three-lobed flowers end in long, graceful tails. The form *album* has creamy-white flowers.

Asarum europaeum
- purple-brown
- midspring
- 6 in. × 8–12 in.
- part shade, shade
- Z5–9

European wild ginger. Finland to Macedonia, France, and Italy. Slow to spread but perhaps the most elegant of the wild gingers with its dense cover of glossy dark green leaves. Excellent for woodland gardens but also for edging shady borders. Self-sows sparingly in hospitable locations. Protect from slugs. Avoid planting too deeply.

Asarum shuttleworthii

- purple-brown
- part shade, shade
- midspring
- Z6–9
- 6–9 in. × 6–12 in.

Shuttleworth ginger. Moist woodlands in the Appalachian mountains. This species may offer the most beautiful foliage of all: silver mottling on the leaves creates a pattern almost like fish scales. Slow to spread, but lovely as an edging plant in a shady border, a groundcover, or container specimen.

'Callaway' is tighter than the species, with good-looking mottled leaves. Very slow to bulk up. Introduced by Fred Galle at Callaway Gardens, Georgia.

'Velvet Queen' has the same distinguished leaves as 'Callaway' but is larger and bulks up more quickly.

Asclepias
Apocynaceae
milkweed

It may seem counterintuitive to include a plant in your garden because of its ability to attract insects, but for many, that is the most persuasive argument for planting milkweeds. Several species do bear attractive, even showy flowers, and most are hardy and reliably perennial given an appropriate site. But what makes them really special is that they serve as nurseries for the caterpillars that metamorphose into monarch butterflies.

The common name for this genus refers to the milky appearance of its sap, which in many species is toxic. By feeding on milkweed leaves, monarch butterfly larvae (caterpillars) make themselves poisonous, thus protecting themselves against birds and other predators. The toxicity of asclepias plants makes them resistant to deer, rabbits, and squirrels. Some species have been esteemed as medicinal, although all parts of the plant are toxic in quantity unless cooked. Gardeners with sensitive skin should protect themselves with gloves when working around these plants.

Milkweeds form clumps of sturdy, fibrous stems with ovate to blade-shaped, generally leathery, green leaves, and dense, rounded, or flat-topped clusters of flowers at stem tips and leaf axils. The flowers attract many different butterflies in addition to monarchs. Prolong bloom time of individual plants by deadheading before seed set; to encourage a second crop of flowers, cut plants back after the first flush of bloom. The fat or skinny, spindle-shaped seedpods that follow split when ripe to release seeds equipped with gossamer parachutes that aid dispersal by wind.

With the exception of a few species adapted to wetland habitats, milkweeds thrive in full sun in almost any well-drained garden soil, even nutrient-poor ones. Pinch off the tips of new shoots when they are 5 in. tall to encourage bushiness. Fungal and bacterial leaf spots may attack milkweeds in hot and humid conditions.

An obvious choice for butterfly and wildlife gardens, milkweeds are also at home in meadow gardens, while the more refined cultivars hold their own in mixed borders. They make bright and long-lasting cut flowers; sear the base of the stem with a flame to seal in the sap.

Propagate in containers to obviate root disturbance at planting time. Sow scarified seed outdoors in fall, or stratify and start indoors in early spring. Spring basal cuttings root readily in sand; milkweeds are taprooted and do not respond well to division.

Close-up of *Asclepias curassavica*

Asclepias curassavica

- scarlet, orange
- sun
- early summer to fall
- Z9–11
- 2–3 ft. × 1.5–2 ft.

Blood flower, Mexican butterfly weed. Tropical Central and South America. Often grown as an annual in colder climates. Showy flowers borne over a long season attract hummingbirds and bees as well as butterflies. Self-seeds prolifically in warmer southern areas of the United States, becoming invasive. A valuable cut flower.

Asclepias incarnata

- pink, white
- sun
- early to late summer
- Z3–6
- 4–5 ft. × 2–3 ft.

Swamp milkweed. Across the United States as far west as the Rocky Mountain States. A wetland species that is ideal for rain gardens, or pond and stream banks, but which also tolerates better-drained soils in garden borders. Clusters of small, fragrant flowers, usually pink to mauve but occasionally white, followed by interesting long pods. Attracts hummingbirds, butterflies, and bees.

'Cinderella' bears exceptionally large clusters of pink, vanilla-scented flowers from midsummer to early fall.

'Ice Ballet' has pure white flowers that contrast dramatically with butterfly visitors. 3- to 5-ft. tall.

Asclepias purpurascens
- pink, purple
- late spring to midsummer
- 2–3 ft. × 1–3 ft.
- sun, part shade
- Z3–9

Purple milkweed. Eastern North America from New Hampshire to North Carolina, west to Minnesota and Arkansas. Tolerates poor, dry, and rocky soils. A vigorous spreader, it often forms large colonies; not suitable for flower borders but an asset in native plantings, meadows, or open woodlands. Rose pink to purple flowers.

Asclepias tuberosa
- orange, yellow
- midsummer to early fall
- 1–2.5 ft. × 1–1.5 ft.
- sun
- Z3–9

Butterfly weed, pleurisy root. Eastern and southwestern North America. The showiest of the milkweeds, bears clusters of brilliant orange or yellow flowers from midsummer. Butterfly weed performs well in ordinary garden soils, but once established, this tough plant also thrives on poor, dryish soils that do not become waterlogged. Not an aggressive spreader.

Gay Butterflies is a hybrid mix with blooms in red, orange, or yellow. Especially good for cut flowers. 24–30 in.

'Hello Yellow' has lively yellow flowers. 24–30 in. tall.

Asphodeline
Asphodelaceae
Jacob's rod

These stately plants, which supposedly grew in the Elysian Fields, provide strong vertical accents in

Asclepias tuberosa

Asphodeline lutea

Asphodeline lutea
- yellow
- late spring to early summer
- 3–6 ft. × 1–2 ft.
- sun
- Z6–9, HS

King's spear, Jacob's rod, yellow asphodel. Grasslands of Eastern Mediterranean region, Turkey, and the Caucasus. Makes untidy clumps or rosettes of long, bluish leaves from which rise leafy unbranched stems topped with dense, 12- to 18-in. racemes of highly fragrant, yellow flowers. These are showy, star shaped, and 1 in. or so across, with prominent stamens. Plant in groups or drifts for best effect. In dry meadow plantings they assort well with little bluestem and other blue-foliaged grasses; in xeriscapes partner with lavenders, sages, and artemisias; dwarf blue spruce makes a stunning background. Protect from slugs, but otherwise pest and disease free; may be browsed by deer.

Asphodelus
Asphodelaceae
asphodel

Native to open meadows, rocky waste- and scrublands in central Europe, and Mediterranean regions and as far east as the Himalayan Mountain range. These plants bear their white or pale pink flowers in erect spikes on leafless, unbranched stems (scapes); the blossoms are accented by brown or pink veining on the reverse of each petaloid tepal. Asphodels perform best on moderately fertile soils. Note that 18-in.-tall *Asphodelus fistulosus* (syn. *A. tenuifolius*), onion grass, has become an invasive alien in the canyons and coastal ranges of California.

Susceptible to aphids, but otherwise free of pests and diseases including deer and rabbits.

Propagate by seed sown in spring (do not cover), or by division of plants while dormant.

Asphodelus albus
- white
- early summer
- 3–5 ft. × 1 ft.
- sun, part shade
- Z7–11, HS

White asphodel. Found in shallow soils around the Mediterranean, white asphodel produces showy spikes of white flowers on thick stems. Each tepal has a single brown stripe on the reverse that produces a slightly pink effect. The grassy, mid-green foliage is keeled and flattened; leaves sometimes reach a length of 24 in. Deadhead fading flowers unless seeds are wanted, as the spikes become shabby looking when left on the plant; if allowed to mature, they will throw countless seedlings the following season. Excellent in California and in dry soils elsewhere, but not in the hot, humid Southeast. Group in sunny spots among shrubs, or in wild gardens, meadows, and rough grass.

the garden. Jacob's rods increase in size slowly, the rhizomatous roots eventually forming large clumps. The triangular, grassy basal leaves and the spirally arranged stem foliage have a fresh green appearance and retain their good looks into fall. The flowers and, later, the fruiting spike may be cut and dried for use in winter arrangements. To harvest the seed, crack open the conspicuous round seedpods when they have ripened.

Average or even poor soil is fine as long as it drains freely; Jacob's rods tolerate drought conditions readily. Heavy clay soils that remain wet in winter, however, are likely to prove fatal. Protect dormant plants with a winter mulch in colder zones.

To propagate, divide large clumps after flowering has ended or harvest and sow seed, which germinates readily, in fall.

Asphodeline liburnica
syn. *Asphodelus liburnicus*
- pale yellow
- midsummer
- 24–30 in. × 12 in.
- sun
- Z6–10

Jacob's rod. Southeastern Europe. This upright, clump-forming perennial bears blue-green leaves on the lower part of the stems only. Flower stems arise in midsummer to support loose, 8-in. spires of starry, 2-in., pale yellow flowers striped on their backs with green. Interesting knobby seedpods follow. Suitable for dry meadows and large rock gardens, where yarrows and purple sages make fine companions.

Aspidistra

Asparagaceae
cast-iron plant

This genus illustrates one of today's most exciting trends in American gardening: over the past generation gardeners in the southern United States have built on their local traditions to make the region a horticultural hotspot, and in the process our national plant palette has broadened immensely. A couple of decades ago, aspidistras were known as little more than "cast-iron" parlor or houseplants; only ten or so species were recognized worldwide. As southeastern landscapers increasingly demanded aspidistras, plant explorers searched and discovered in excess of 80 previously unknown species in their Asian homeland. This genus is now among the most dynamic foliage plants in the nursery trade.

The attraction of aspidistras is not only their bold evergreen foliage, leathery and broad bladed, but also their extraordinary tolerance for difficult hot, humid summers. Aspidistras thrive in heat and humidity, yet tolerate significant cold—some species can survive a dip into the mid-teens (°F) or even lower. Such a cold snap may kill the foliage to the ground, but new leaves will emerge from the roots. Once established, aspidistras do well in dry shade too, ideal for regions such as central Texas, where summer often brings drought. Susceptible to mealybugs and spider mites, but infestations are rarely serious; deer resistant. Aspidistras' tolerance for neglect is legendary—these are the ultimate low-maintenance perennials.

Borne singly at ground level, and commonly hidden under the foliage, aspidistra flowers are intriguing with an odd, almost starfish or sea anemone–like form. Floral designers prize the long-lasting foliage.

Moist but well-drained soil produces the most vigorous growth. Avoid overwatering or overfeeding; a nutrient-poor soil encourages the best foliage color. Deeply dug, organic-enriched, acid loam suits these plants best, although they adapt to a wide range of soils, and are moderately salt tolerant. Partly or fully shaded sites are preferred; aspidistras tolerate direct sunlight if shaded at midday. Excessive sun results in yellowing leaves.

Interesting species not described below include slender-leaved *Aspidistra linearifolia*, yellow-spotted *A. crispa*, *A. hainanensis* and its cultivar 'Jade Ribbons', and yellow-flowered *A. attenuata* from Taiwan. Collectors will want to seek out these and others. Though tough and virtually foolproof, aspidistras are very slow growing. Propagate by division but expect offspring to require two or more years to bulk up. Start species from seed, but be prepared to wait a decade for maturation.

Aspidistra elatior

- cream
- late spring to early summer
- 2–3 ft. × 1–2 ft.
- part shade, shade
- Z7–11

Cast-iron plant, barroom plant. China and Japan. Evergreen, with lustrous, long-stemmed and arching, lanceolate, dark green leaves to 24 in. long by 4 in. wide. Insignificant purple-spotted, creamy flowers, deep red within, may appear at soil level. Overwinters outdoors in zone 7b with protection.

'Asahi' has bold green leaves, to 30 in. long and 5 in. wide; the tips mature to striking white.

'Fuji No Mine' boasts glossy, dark leaves, 3 ft. long and 5 in. wide, accented with a central creamy-yellow streak.

'Milky Way' ('Amanogawa') forms a dense clump of leaves, 18 in. tall and 2 in. wide, striped and freckled with white and yellow.

'Okame' has upright leaves with bold, vertical, white striping. 30 in.

'Spek-tacular' has 40-in.-long leaves abundantly flecked with yellow, and arched at the tips.

Aspidistra guangxiensis

- purple
- spring to summer
- 18 in. × 12 in.
- part shade, shade
- Z8–11

Cast-iron plant. Guangxi region of China, a new introduction available chiefly as the selection 'Stretch Marks'. It has medium green leaves, 3 in.

Aspidistra elatior

wide by 10 in. long, speckled heavily with oval, creamy-yellow spots. The flowers have an uncanny resemblance to sea urchins with grape-purple centers ringed by yellow-green tendrils. Overwinters outdoors in zone 7b, though the leaves die back.

Aster

Asteraceae
aster, Michaelmas daisy

Once a sprawling genus of some 600 species, recently asters have been reorganized by botanists so that all except one of the North American members have been assigned to other genera (*Eurybia, Symphyotrichum, Doellingeria*, etc.). For convenience sake, the reassigned species' former names are included in this book's index.

However you name them, this invaluable, colorful group of plants includes many tough and persistent species. Some, like the attractive Siberian *Aster tataricus*, can be too successful, even invasive, and need a large space in the landscape; others are well-behaved stalwarts of summer and fall displays in gardens of all kinds. Asters bear composite daisy flowers, typically in great abundance, with petals (ray flowers) in shades of blue, purple, white, and pink. The centers (disks) of each blossom (actually a head of flowers composed of countless individual flowers) are usually yellow. As a rule, asters and their kin prefer a well-drained, organic-rich soil, and struggle if planted in dense clays; they do well in coastal, sandy soils. Full sun is best for most species, though some tolerate part shade. Taller species benefit from being cut back by half before midsummer to promote branching and more compact growth that can forgo staking. Asters are prone to foliar diseases including powdery mildew and rust, as well as some insect pests including aphids, leafhoppers, and spider mites. Though such infestations rarely kill the plants,

they disfigure them and may affect garden neighbors. Search out disease- and pest-resistant cultivars. Deer seldom browse asters; butterflies flock to their flowers.

Propagate by division of mature clumps in spring or fall, or start seed indoors in late winter. Softwood stem cuttings taken in late spring root readily.

Aster ×frikartii

syn. *A. amellus* × *A. thompsonii*
- lavender
- early summer to fall
- 2–3 ft. × 1.5 ft.
- sun, part shade
- Z5–10, HS

Frickart's aster. This hybrid isn't as pest and disease resistant as some of the species, but it blooms early and long from late spring to midfall if deadheaded conscientiously. Vivid, fragrant flowers, 2.5 in. wide, top loose mounds of dark green, oval leaves. Protect dormant plants with mulch of evergreen boughs through winter in cold zones; well-drained soil is essential. Superb for containers.

'Flora's Delight', an introduction by Alan Bloom, is more compact (1.5–2 ft.) with 2-in., lilac-colored flowers. Somewhat less cold hardy than other members of this group.

'Monch' bears 2-in., lavender flowers with yellow centers. 2 ft. tall.

'Wonder of Staffa' has slightly paler lavender flowers but is hard to distinguish from 'Monch'. 2 ft.

Aster tataricus

- blue
- mid- to late fall
- 3–6 ft. × 3 ft.
- sun
- Z3–9

Tatarian daisy. Siberia. Among the latest to bloom, this species is notable for seldom needing staking. In late summer to fall, bristly flower stalks arise from a basal mass of thick, spinach-like, 2-ft. leaves. Sessile leaves clothe the stems that branch in their upper reaches. Numerous yellow-eyed, blue to purple daisies bloom until weather becomes too cold. Spreads freely. Divide every few years to control its invasive tendencies as well as for propagation.

'Jindai', a selection by plantsman Rick Darke, is similar but on shorter stems. 3–4 ft.

Aster tongolensis

- blue, purple
- early summer
- 1–1.5 ft. × 1 ft.
- sun
- Z3–9

East Indies aster. Western China. Stoloniferous and mat forming, with oval leaves in a slowly spreading cushion; in early summer, erect, thick, and hairy, almost leafless stems branch at the top, and bear solitary, 6-in.-wide, violet-blue flowers centered with orange-yellow. Ideal for rock gardens, troughs, and the front of borders.

Aster ×frikartii 'Monch'

'Berggarten' blooms prolifically with 2- to 3-in.-wide, orange-eyed, bright violet-blue flowers. 24 in. tall.

'Napsbury' has light violet-blue flowers with slender rays. 18 in.

'Wartburg Star' is 1.5–2 ft. high and wide, with long-blooming, 2-in., violet-blue flowers.

Astilbe

Saxifragaceae
astilbe, plume flower

A moist shaded garden without astilbes is like a cock without its crow! Their beautiful fluffy plumes of pink, red, purple, or white flowers and attractive fern-like leaves would earn them a place even were it not for their tolerance of shade and easy-care ways. And as a bonus, deer don't seem to find them tasty.

Astilbes are indigenous to damp woodlands and streamsides in China and Japan, as well as the United States (e.g., *Astilbe biternata*). The bulk of the named selections on the market are the result of extensive hybridization between species. Clumps of astilbe grow from a mass of rhizomes that becomes woody with age. Young foliage, two- or three-times divided into toothed leaflets, erupts in spring. Leaf color is variable, mostly dark or mid-green; red-flowered selections often display young, deep red foliage. Fluffy plumes of tiny flowers are borne mostly above the foliage mass in summer on leafless stems of varying heights. Bloom time runs from late spring (early) through to mid- to late summer (late). Catalogs may list selections as early, midseason, or late. Seedheads and leaves become an attractive rusty brown and can provide interest through the winter months. Allowed to remain intact, these provide unusual contrast to early-blooming stinking hellebores or Italian arum, for example, and are interesting in dried flower arrangements.

Provide rich, acid soil that remains moist but does not become waterlogged; be sure plants remain well watered in hot weather, as drying out results in crisping of the leaf margins. Amend the soil with plenty of organic matter as astilbes are greedy feeders; an annual dressing of rotted manure or compost is beneficial. Divide the woody root-stocks every three to four years in spring or fall to maintain vigor or to propagate.

Astilbes are often major players in moist, shaded beds and borders, and beside streams or ponds, where they may be massed to provide large drifts of color or grouped with other shade lovers. Among their most popular companions are bold-leaved hostas, hellebores, lungworts, hardy begonias, and ferns. The tall types look well among flowering shrubs, especially early- or late-blooming ones to extend the season of interest. Both compact and tall astilbes grace any container solo or mixed with others plants that like damp feet.

A partly shaded bed with cultivars of *Astilbe* ×*arendsii*

Astilbe 'Amethyst'

Astilbe 'Bridal Veil'

Astilbe 'Rhythm and Blues'

Pests and diseases are few, although leaf spots and mildew may damage the foliage. Ignored by deer and rabbits.

Increase by dividing the clumps in spring; pot up or replant at once.

Astilbe ×arendsii

- red, pink, white, purple
- late spring to midsummer
- 2–4 ft. × 2 ft.
- part shade
- Z3–8

Hybrid astilbe. This hybrid group displays amazing variety in all aspects, and includes the bulk of available cultivars. Flowering time varies from early to late, enabling gardeners to have color over many weeks.

'Amethyst' has robust lavender plumes. Early to late. 18–24 in.

'Bridal Veil' ('Brautschleier'). Thick plumes of white flowers. Midseason. 18–24 in.

'Deutschland' may be the whitest of whites, not turning ivory. A strong grower. Early.

'Fanal'. Dark red flowers bloom above bronzy foliage. Early. 24 in.

'Montgomery' has bright red plumes with green foliage. Midseason. 20–24 in.

Music Series blooms mid- to late season: 'Jump and Jive', bright pink with dark foliage, 12–16 in. 'Rhythm and Beat', fuchsia pink with medium green leaves, 14–18 in., reblooms. 'Rhythm and Blues', hot pink over dark leaves, 20–24 in. 'Rock and Roll', black-stemmed, white plumes above bronzy leaves; 18–24 in.; reblooms.

'Peach Blossom'. Light salmon-pink flowers. Reliable old variety, often listed under *Astilbe ×japonica* or *A. ×rosea*. 24 in. Z4–9.

'Prof. van der Wielan' has open plumes of white flowers. Late. 30–48 in. Z4–9.

'Straussenfeder' ('Ostrich Plume') has elegant branched, pendulous inflorescences of hot-pink flowers. Tolerates heat and humidity. Has *A. thunbergii* blood. 3 ft.

Astilbe chinensis

- white, pink
- mid- to late summer
- 10–36 in. × 24 in.
- sun, part shade
- Z3–8

Chinese astilbe. Siberia, China. Vigorous, with bronzy, softly hairy leaves divided into three rounded leaflets rimmed with double teeth. The species is seldom cultivated, but there are plenty of superior selections.

'Diamonds and Pearls' has dense plumes of pure white flowers above dark green foliage. Heat and humidity tolerant. 2 ft. tall.

'Finale'. Leaves are bronzy green and lacy. Lavender-pink flowers. Appropriately named, blooming into early fall. 15–18 in.

'Maggie Daley'. Bright fuchsia-pink plumes over green foliage. A strong grower. Midseason. 28 in.

'Pumila' has lilac-pink plumes on 10-in. stems. Good groundcover if kept damp, but often displays unattractive half-spent plumes. May be a hybrid. Fast spreader. Late.

'Visions' is compact with upright bright raspberry flower plumes. Bronze green foliage. Mid- to late season. 15 in. Others in the excellent Visions Series include pale 'Visions in Pink' (18 in., mid- to late season) with bluish green leaves, 'Visions in Red' (15 in., midseason), with bronze foliage, and 'Visions in White' (20–30 in., early) with soft white plumes.

Astilbe ×crispa

- pink
- early to midsummer
- 6–10 in. × 10 in.
- part shade, shade
- Z4–8

Crisp-leaved hybrid astilbe. This diminutive hybrid has crimped, deep green leaves below a full complement of fluffy flower plumes. Excellent for rock gardens, containers, or as edging along shaded pathways

'Lilliput' has light salmon flowers. 6–8 in.

'Perkeo' ('Peter Pan') has deep rose-salmon plumes. 8–10 in.

Astilbe simplicifolia

- pink, white, magenta
- early to midsummer
- 12–18 in. × 24 in.
- sun, part shade
- Z3–8

Star astilbe. Japan. This short species is best known for its contribution as a parent to many superior hybrid selections:

'Key West' has mounds of dark burgundy leaves, with feathery plumes of carmine red. Excellent for cutting and in containers. Midseason. 16–20 in.

'Pink Lightning'. Open, pale pink plumes over dark lustrous leaves. Early. 16–20 in.

'Sprite' is a favorite, with airy shell-pink flower plumes and bronzy leaves. Late. 12 in. An Alan Bloom selection. Perennial Plant of the Year 1994.

Astilbe simplicifolia 'Sprite'

Astilboides tabularis

'White Sensation' is particularly compact with 10-in. mounds of glossy green foliage. Dainty white flowers. Mid- to late season. 18 in.

Astilboides

Saxifragaceae
shieldleaf

This genus boasts just a single species, but for gardeners who love drama, it's a must-have plant. It has its limitations, however: it does not thrive in hot regions or where the soil dries out. Provide moist soil and at least a partially shaded site. Mulch in summer to retain soil moisture. Plant alongside a stream or in a low-lying wet spot, or use it to frame a pool or pond. Spectacular in a bed or border, or as a solo container specimen. Ferns, hostas, cardinal flowers, and astilbes are handsome companions.

Foliage may be affected by late spring frosts, but new leaves will develop. In fall, refrain from cutting back too early as there is often beautiful yellow fall color. Protect against slugs.

Propagate by sowing seed in fall or divide mature plants in early spring as the foliage emerges.

Astilboides tabularis
syn. *Rodgersia tabularis*
- white
- summer
- 3 ft. × 3–4 ft.
- part shade, shade
- Z5–7

Shieldleaf. Veteran gardeners may recognize this plant by its former name, *Rodgersia*, and once you've seen it you certainly won't forget it. A native of northeast China and Korea, it bears 2-ft.-wide, ruffle-edged, parasol-like leaves atop furry, 3-ft. stems, creating a dense, tropical-seeming canopy of vegetation. In midsummer it sprouts even taller plumes (even up to 5 ft.) of creamy-white flowers that could be mistaken for an astilbe on steroids.

Astrantia major 'Primadonna'

Astrantia
Apiaceae
masterwort

A border filled with all the usual floral suspects may be colorful, but also predictable; including a drift or even just a group of masterworts, with their quirky elegance, is a sure remedy. Though still uncommon in American gardens, these plants featured in British cottage gardens as early as the 17th century. The starburst-like heads of small, sweetly scented blossoms are backed by a ruff of bracts that would look quite at home around the neck of some Jacobean dandy. Attractive though not striking parsley-like foliage forms mounding basal rosettes that are handsome backdrops for the flowers. In temperate climates astrantias bloom from late spring into early fall; where summers are hot, bloom peters out in early summer.

Masterworts have earned their enduring popularity by the ease with which they are grown. Relatives of Queen Anne's lace, they have a similar ability to thrive in a wide range of soils, even fairly heavy clay; on such sites, dig in plenty of organic matter to ensure consistent moisture. Though masterworts perform best on well-drained soils, they tolerate wet ones well. They thrive in sun or part shade; where summers are hot, shelter from early afternoon sun. Best where night temperatures drop below 70°F in summer. No serious pests and resistant to deer; reputed to repel slugs, and so protect susceptible neighbors.

Aside from the dash of novelty their flowers add to a humdrum bed or border, masterworts are useful as authentic elements for a cottage garden, and they are a source of intriguing cut flowers for fresh or dried arrangements. Their leaves make an attractive contrast to bold-textured hostas and ligularias. In addition, the flowers entice insects and butterflies.

Propagate by division of established clumps in spring, or sow fresh seed into pots or trays in fall and allow to overwinter outdoors.

Astrantia major
- white
- summer
- 24–36 in. × 12–18 in.
- sun, part shade
- Z4–7

Great masterwort. Europe and western Asia. This is the most popular ornamental astrantia, offering many fine cultivars.

'**Claret**' bears dark red flowers on black stems. To 30 in. tall.

'**Hadspen Blood**'. Vigorous, with very dark red flowers. Introduced from Hadspen House, England. 30 in.

subsp. *involucrata* '**Shaggy**' ('Margery Fish') has pink-tinged, white-and-green flowers with fringed, green-tipped white bracts.

'**Moulin Rouge**' bears green-and-red flowers;

pointed, deep red bracts are tipped with purple-red. Sometimes reblooms in fall if cut back after first flush. 18–24 in.

'Primadonna' has 1.5-in., silvery rose flowers with maroon-tipped bracts. Long blooming. 24 in. Z6–9. A sport, 'Vanilla Gorilla', has bluish green leaves irregularly edged with white; soft pink flowers.

'Star of Beauty'. White-and-purple flowers, white bracts tipped deep dusty purple.

Aubrieta
Brassicaceae
false rock cress

No self-respecting spring rock garden should be without false rock cress—its evergreen, small, sometimes toothed, and often hairy leaves creep across the ground in a neat, compact carpet, and for several weeks each spring it is smothered with brightly colored, four-petaled, cross-shaped flowers. Moderately fertile, well-drained soil with a neutral to alkaline pH is ideal. When established, false rock cress handles drought well. Shear hard after bloom before seed set to restrain seed production, both for the sake of neatness and to preserve the plant's vigor. False rock cress is short lived and does not adapt well to summer heat. In hot climates it is often

Aubrieta deltoidea 'Whitewell Gem'

treated as a biennial. Watch for aphid infestations.

Outside the rock garden, false rock cress is excellent tumbling over walls, among paving stones, or at the front of sunny beds. It is colorful spilling from hanging baskets and containers in early spring, perhaps mixed with polyanthus primroses, forget-me-nots, pansies and violas, or English daisies. Basket-of-gold, white-flowered rock cress, and miniature spring bulbs including daffodils, grape hyacinths, and checkerboard lily are fine companions also. An attractive underplanting for spring bedding displays. Deer resistant.

Some selections come true from seed. Propagate those that don't from new growth that appears after deadheading, or divide in fall.

Aubrieta deltoidea
- various
- early spring to spring
- 2–6 in. × 12 in.
- sun, part shade
- Z5–7, HS

False rock cress, rock cress, aubrietia. Mediterranean to central Asia. This species has been used extensively in breeding, with the result that most selections on the market are hybrids. They may also be listed as *Aubrieta* ×*cultorum*.

'Aureovariegata'. Mauve-purple flowers above grayish leaves irregularly edged with yellow.

'Barker's Double' bears double, purplish blue flowers.

'Red Cascade' belongs to the Cascade strain. The flowers are magenta-red. 'Blue Cascade' is deep lilac-blue, 'Purple Cascade' is rich purple. Can be started from seed.

'Silver Edge' ('Silberrand'). Indigo-blue flowers over green foliage, crisply rimmed with white.

'Whitewell Gem' has purple to violet blooms. Comes true from seed.

'Variegata' has gold-variegated leaves and lavender-blue flowers. Not very robust.

Aurinia
Brassicaceae
basket-of-gold

Like its close relatives *Aubrieta* and *Arabis*, this genus provides a host of spring-blooming prizes for rock gardens, for spilling over walls, and for tucking into crevices. Woody at the base, basket-of-gold's upper growth forms loose clumps of evergreen, grayish, spoon-shaped leaves to 5 in. long. This superstructure bears masses of brilliant school bus–yellow flowers that bloom over several weeks from spring into early summer. Best in full sun, basket-of-gold thrives in well-drained, poor to average soil but is not fussy as long as the roots do not remain wet; rich soil promotes soft, leggy growth, susceptible to insects. Established plants are drought tolerant. Shear after bloom for neatness and to ensure vigor.

Sow seed in late fall outdoors or with protection in very early spring. Named cultivars must be

Aurinia saxatilis

Baptisia 'Solar Flare Prairieblues'

propagated vegetatively: summer cuttings usually root easily, but attempting division in fall is not reliable.

Aurinia saxatilis
syn. *Alyssum saxatile*

• yellow	• 8–12 in. × 12–18 in.
• spring to early summer	• sun
	• Z3–8, HS

Basket-of-gold, goldentuft, madwort. Southeastern and central Europe. This cheerful plant is easy to grow and provides dramatic spring color. Rather floppy foliage is mostly grayish, felted with hairs, and a perfect foil for the flowers. Replace old woody plants with young stock; plants may self-seed freely unless cut back before seed set. In hot, humid regions, it is best grown as an annual.

'Citrinum' ('Luteum', 'Sulphureum') has pale lemon-yellow flowers.

'Compactum' is a 4- to 8-in. miniature form. 'Compactum Flore-Pleno' ('Plena') has double flowers.

'Dudley Neville Variegated' has cream-edged foliage and is beautiful throughout the season, especially with yellow corydalis. Apricot buff flowers. In hot climates, provide midday shade, or treat as an annual.

'Golden Flourish' was bred for container cultivation. Masses of mustard-yellow flowers above green foliage. Eye-catching spilling over the edges of planters with tulips, pansies, daffodils, and other early bloomers.

'Sunny Border Apricot' has soft orange-yellow flowers. A Sunny Border Nursery introduction. Z6–9.

Baptisia
Fabaceae
false indigo, wild indigo

Although well known to Native Americans who used false indigo as a source of blue dyes, this genus has only recently found a major place in US gardens. Native to eastern and midwestern North America, baptisias vary in stature and flower color, but in general bear pea-like flowers in showy spikes in spring, and trifoliate, commonly blue-green leaves. The leaves are arranged alternately on stems that cluster in dense, shrub-like groups. Baptisias' naturally neat form and tolerance for poor soils, even clays and rocky ones, as well as drought, has made them staple plantings over the last decade. As their popularity has grown, they've attracted interest from plant hybridizers, especially at the Chicago Botanic Garden and North Carolina Botanical Garden. A steady stream of refined and floriferous cultivars and hybrids have appeared in recent years, with flowers in novel colors and bicolored combinations.

False indigos perform best on sunny sites, though they also tolerate partial shade. They are taprooted and difficult to transplant: container-grown specimens are easier to establish in the garden than bare-root stock. However, their long taproots equip baptisias to reach deeper than many plants, making them exceptionally drought tolerant. Shear and shape the plants after flowering (unless saving the seed pods) to encourage compact growth and eliminate the need for staking. Seldom attacked by pests and diseases; resistant to deer.

Baptisias are attractive in beds and borders as single specimens or in groups of several plants. The larger types can be imposing and are useful for adding structure to perennial or mixed plantings, or even planted among low shrubs. Their season of bloom coincides with Siberian irises and peonies, both of which make fine companions. A blue-flowered baptisia energizes a predominantly yellow planting; the blue-green foliage common to many harmonizes nicely with silver-foliaged artemisias and lavenders. These tough plants work well in prairie plantings, native gardens, and meadows, and their combination of striking flowers and handsome foliage makes them useful additions to cottage gardens. Baptisias attract butterflies. If left unsheared, the plants produce plump black seedpods that are popular elements of dried flower arrangements.

Propagate the species by seed; scarify seed to allow water to penetrate the hard seed coat. Sow in containers to avoid transplant shock when planting out later. Propagate named cultivars by stem cuttings taken in spring while still green and soft.

Baptisia albescens

syn. *B. alba*
- white
- early spring to midspring
- 2–4 ft. × 2–2.5 ft.
- sun, part shade
- Z5–8

White false indigo. Southeastern United States. Multiple small, white, pea-like flowers, to 0.5 in. long, carried in numerous 12-in. spikes or racemes atop charcoal-black flower stems; these rise above a mound of clover-like, trifoliate, bluish green leaves that remain attractive for most of the season.

var. *alba* (syn. *Baptisia pendula*) reaches a height of 3–4 ft., with pendent, large, black seed pods.

var. *macrophylla* (syn. *B. leucantha*, *B. lactea*) has white flowers on 5- to 7-ft. stems.

Baptisia australis

- indigo blue
- mid- to late spring
- 3–4 ft. high and wide
- sun, part shade
- Z3–9

Blue false indigo. Rich woods, thickets, and stream banks from Pennsylvania, south to North Carolina

and Tennessee. Upright bushes of leafy stems bear bold spires of blue pea flowers. May need support in less than full sun. Prune after bloom to shape as a shrub "wannabe," although this forfeits the rattling, black seedpods. Excellent naturalized in meadows or used to control erosion on difficult banks.

var. *minor* (syn. *Baptisia minor*) is more compact than the species, reaching half its height and spread. It grows naturally as far west as Kansas and Texas.

Baptisia sphaerocarpa

- yellow
- mid- to late spring
- 2–3 ft. × 2–3 ft.
- sun, part shade
- Z5–8

Missouri to Oklahoma, south to Louisiana and Texas. Yellow flowers (to 0.5 in. long) in abundant 12- to 15-in. spikes borne atop yellow-green stems above a mound of blue-green foliage. Spherical seedpods to 0.75 in. ripen to tan and then brown.

'Screamin' Yellow' may reach 5 ft. Bears a profuse crop of yellow flowers above mounds of yellow-tinged, green foliage. From Larry Lowman's program.

Other Notable Cultivars

Several of these were introduced by Jim Ault at Chicago Botanic Garden and Rob Gardner at the North Carolina Botanical Garden in Chapel Hill.

'Dutch Chocolate' bears chocolate-purple flowers over mounded, blue-green foliage. Late spring to early summer. 2.5–3 ft. × 2 ft. Z4–9.

'Midnight Prairieblues' bears 24-in.-long spikes of violet-blue flowers over three to four weeks in early summer. 48 in. × 48–54 in. Z4–9.

The Prairieblues Series, from the Chicagoland Grows program, was bred especially for regions with very cold winters and hot summers, although they thrive in most parts of the country: 'Solar Flare Prairieblues'is golden yellow. 36 in. × 36–48 in. 'Starlite Prairieblues' has soft blue flowers; 'Twilite Prairieblues'has bicolored burgundy-and-lemon flowers. 5 ft. high and wide. Z4–8.

'Purple Smoke' carries black stems with smoky violet flowers in midspring. 3–4 ft. Z4–9.

Beesia

Ranunculaceae
false bugbane, beesia

This outstanding genus of two species was introduced by Dan Hinkley, who brought specimens back from a Chinese plant exploration trip in the 1990s. Both have handsome evergreen foliage with rosettes of strikingly beautiful and long-lasting, heart-shaped leaves; they are welcome alternatives to the familiar run-of-the-mill groundcover plants.

False bugbanes prefer rich, organic soils, well-drained but slightly moist even during dry spells. They require little maintenance beyond removal of spent blooms. Slugs feast on the new growth but otherwise pests and diseases are seldom a problem. Reportedly, deer ignore the foliage.

Exceptional as groundcovers, false bugbanes are fine companions for woodland plants, including trilliums, hardy cyclamens, hostas, and ferns. Plant them at the feet of bugbanes for a floral echo. False bugbanes provide drama in front of 'Hummingbird' summersweet or other low, shade-loving shrubs, or mix with spring-blooming bulbs such as squills and winter aconites.

Propagate by dividing the rhizomes of established plants after bloom has ended, or sow seed in containers in fall and overwinter outdoors or in the refrigerator to enable seeds to break dormancy the following spring.

Beesia calthifolia

- white
- spring
- 8–10 in. × 12 in.
- part shade, shade
- Z6–8

Ginger-leaf false bugbane. Mountain meadows and open woodlands of eastern Asia. Dense, rhizomatous clumps of polished, bronzy green, cordate leaves (similar to wild ginger, *Asarum*) that turn dark red in winter. Leaves are accented with a network of lighter veins, edged with red, and rimmed with teeth. Short racemes of starry, white flowers rise on purple stems from late spring on.

Beesia deltophylla

- white
- early to late summer
- 10–18 in. × 24 in.
- part shade, shade
- Z6–9

False bugbane. Sichuan Province, China. Slowly expanding clumps of smooth, purple-tinted, deep green, glistening leaves. These are heart shaped, deeply veined, and with a puckered texture; the serrate margins undulate slightly. Winter foliage is edged irregularly with a wide, reddish brown band. Mature leaves may reach 10 in. across. Sparse sprays of small, white flowers rise on 20-in. stems.

Begonia
Begoniaceae
hardy begonia

This large genus mostly contains plants suited to tropical and subtropical regions, and these (Rex begonias, for example) are grown usually as houseplants or as annual bedding plants (wax begonias and others) in colder areas. However, a few begonias are hardy in temperate zones and are well worth inclusion in perennial gardens. These species thrive in partly shaded positions, where their tropical-looking foliage and lovely flowers add pizzazz from midsummer on. In particular, they make excellent partners for ferns, hostas, and astilbes, as well as low, shade-loving shrubs.

The easiest method of propagation is by collecting and sowing the pea-sized bulbils that form in the leaf axils; these frequently self-sow. Propagation by seed is also possible but offspring may not resemble their parents. Otherwise, take basal or stem cuttings in spring.

Begonia grandis subsp. evansiana
syn. *B. evansiana*

- pink
- summer to fall
- 12–48 in. × 12–18 in.
- part shade, shade
- Z5–9

Hardy begonia. Malaysia, China, Japan. In early spring it may seem like you've lost this wonderful plant, but don't despair: the new growth does not emerge until well after late spring. Thereafter, however, overwintered bulbils or tubers make rapid progress, throwing up fleshy pink stems with large angel-wing leaves that expand to 12 in. or more long and 6 in. across. The stems are somewhat brittle; the leaves are bright green with startling red veins and a red reverse.

Hardy begonias tolerate most conditions, even dry shade. In full sun keep the soil moist, as the plants are very shallow rooted. Average to rich soil amended with plenty of organic matter is ideal as long as it drains freely. Be alert for slug and snail damage, especially when foliage is young. Attractive

Begonia grandis subsp. *evansiana* 'Heronswood Pirouette'

pink flowers, good for cutting (harvest when just opening), are carried in nodding, 6- to 12-in. sprays above the leaves, followed by lingering triangular, deep pink seedheads. Bulbils dropping from leaf axils when ripe can create a colony in a few years' time. Site where the foliage will be backlit by the sun for a glowing picture.

'Alba' has white flowers with a slight pink blush. The angel-wing foliage is light green with no hint of red. Not as robust a grower as the species, but it brightens up dark places beautifully.

'Heronswood Pirouette' is more compact than the species but with longer sprays of hot-pink and lavender-pink flowers. 18 in. Z6–10.

'Wildwood Purity' is worth seeking. It has deep red undersides to the leaves in dramatic contrast to the pure white flowers, offset with red seedpods.

Belamcanda
Iridaceae
blackberry lily, leopard lily

By no means rare, these iris lookalikes are nevertheless too often neglected by gardeners. Blackberry lilies are reliable, generally trouble-free plants that contribute a steady supply of showy flowers to summer borders. They have many of the virtues of their iris relatives: hardy over a wide range of climates, blackberry lilies flourish in any average,

Belamcanda chinensis

well-drained soil, and are notably drought resistant once established.

The leaves, blade-like, flat, and borne in fans, are very similar to those of bearded iris; the roots are rhizomatous, creeping outward so that the plants form slowly increasing clumps. The flowers, composed of six petal-like perianth segments (sepals and petals are not delineated), are borne in branching sprays. The blooms are followed by beige, pear-shaped pods that in late summer split open to reveal blackberry-like clusters of shiny black fruits. These fruiting stems make interesting additions to dried flower arrangements. Blackberry lilies furnish an energizing contrast to purple or blue flowers such as purple coneflowers or early-blooming asters, and harmonize well with other hot-colored blossoms such as blanket flowers and daylilies.

Iris borers can be a problem, tunneling into and destroying the rhizomes. Destroy affected rhizomes and dress wounds with powdered sulfur. Propagation is by division of the rhizomes or by seed, which requires four to six weeks of moist chilling to germinate. On hospitable sites, blackberry lilies self-seed sparingly.

Belamcanda chinensis
- orange
- mid- to late summer
- 24–36 in. × 9–24 in.
- sun
- Z5–10

Blackberry lily, leopard flower. Central Asia to India, China, and Japan. The 1.5- to 2-in. flowers are tawny and freckled with red spots. Sword-shaped leaves may reach 8 in. long. Though drought tolerant, regular irrigation during dry spells promotes more abundant bloom and growth. Not a long-lived perennial, but commonly blooms in its first year when started from seed.

'Freckle Face' bears 2-in., golden-apricot flowers flecked with tiny spots of deeper orange-red.

Belamcanda flabellata
- yellow
- mid- to late summer
- 1.5–2 ft. × 1.5 ft.
- part shade
- Z5–10

Dwarf yellow blackberry lily. Asia. More compact than *Belamcanda chinensis*, this species is also more tolerant of shade and moist soils. Bears lemon-yellow flowers.

'Hello Yellow' has butter-yellow flowers; often listed as a cultivar of *B. chinensis*.

Bergenia
Saxifragaceae
heart-leaved bergenia, pigsqueak

A well-grown ground cover of bergenias is handsome indeed, though it can become shabby if neglected. These clumping perennials from rocky moors and meadows of Asia have large leaves like ping-pong paddles, often heart shaped at the base. Some are evergreen, and many of these turn red, purple, or bronze in cold weather. Clusters of pink, red, or white flowers, bell or funnel shaped, are borne atop thick succulent stems, sometimes pink tinged, branched or not.

Deadhead regularly to extend bloom time, and remove shabby foliage to the base as necessary. Foliage and flower buds of some are frost tender; flower buds brown and do not open, and leaves become black-brown and unsightly. This is not as prevalent where snow cover is reliable; elsewhere protect from searing winds and frost with a winter mulch applied in late fall.

In spite of the common recommendation to grow bergenias in shade, in temperate climes they do better in full sun. Part shade is also fine, but avoid deep shade. In general, bergenias are not well adapted to hot regions, and if attempted there they must be protected from midday sun. Soil should be average, deep, moist, and enriched with well-rotted compost or manure. Heavy clay that waterlogs easily is not satisfactory; amend with organic matter to improve drainage. Resistant to deer and rabbits, but protect from slugs, which otherwise promote that shabby appearance.

Mass bergenias as a groundcover along with meadowsweets, foxgloves, and Siberian iris to create contrasts in height and foliage texture. Planted as a skirt beneath white-barked birches or red-stemmed dogwoods, they can create a memorable winter-garden tableau. Use as edging plants along pathways or to delimit flowerbeds. British garden designer Gertrude Jekyll edged many a small bed with bergenias, often accompanied by our delicate native white wood asters (*Eurybia divaricata*) that tumbled over the cabbage-like leaves. Other appropriate companions include columbines, lungworts, and ferns.

Propagate by division in spring or fall. Otherwise, at the end of the growing season take 3-in. cuttings of the rhizomatous stems, making sure to include a bud. Propagate species by seed.

Bergenia ciliata
syn. *B. ligulata*
- white, pink
- early spring
- 6–12 in. × 12–24 in.
- part shade
- Z5–8

Winter begonia, frilly bergenia, winter bergenia. Nepal. Grown mainly for its hairy, deciduous, rounded, wavy-edged, bright green leaves that may reach 12 in. across. Clumping, spreads slowly by rhizomes. Clusters of rose-flushed white or pink flowers.

Bergenia cordifolia
- pink
- early spring
- 12–24 in. × 24–30 in.
- sun, part shade
- Z3–8

Heart-leaved bergenia, pigsqueak, winter begonia. Central Asia. Creeping rhizomes give rise to shiny, thick, cabbagey leaves, heart shaped at the base, about 12 in. long. These may turn purple and bronze as temperatures fall; some cultivars display better winter color than others. Evergreen or nearly so, in all but the coldest places. Tight clusters of deep pink flowers with rosy centers and calyces top branched pink stems.

Close-up of *Bergenia* 'Bressingham Ruby' flowers

Bergenia 'Bressingham Ruby'

'Purpurea' (syn. *Bergenia purpurea*) has bright purple-red flowers on red, 20-in. stems. Purple winter foliage.

'Rotblum' has red flowers and deep red winter foliage. 18 in.

Other Notable Cultivars

'Baby Doll' has maroon winter foliage color that contrasts well with the early spring clusters of pale pink flowers; these mature to hot pink over several weeks. Protect from intense sun. A heavy protective mulch in winter is beneficial. 8–10 in. Z6–8.

'Bressingham Ruby', a hybrid, is valued for its tolerance of dry shade. Large, cabbagey, dark green leaves become polished burgundy in cold weather. Clusters of rosy flowers above the leaves in spring. A great groundcover. 12–16 in. Z4–10.

'Cabernet'. Large, deep green leaves emerge early, closely followed by the bud clusters carried on pink stems, which open to deep pink bells. Bloom continues through late spring. Fall foliage turns deep red when temperatures drop. Semi-evergreen in zone 6 and warmer. 10–12 in. tall.

'Eroica'. A superior long-blooming selection, displays clusters of bright purple flowers held well above wine-flushed leaves. Requires moist soil. Considered by some to be an improvement on better-known 'Abendglocken'. 12–14 in. Z4–8.

'Herbstblute' (fall pigsqueak) tolerates heat and humidity well. Low basal rosettes of 6-in., rounded, dark green leaves. Light pink flowers in spring, and occasionally through the season. 6 in. Z2–7.

'Overture' makes tight mounds of lustrous dark foliage, purple in fall. Clusters of dramatic fuchsia flowers open in midspring on fleshy stems above the leaves. Stunning when planted in drifts or massed in semi-shade.

'Winterglow' ('Winterglut') has leathery, heart-shaped foliage with good substance. Fall color is ruby red. Clusters of deep pink flowers in spring, often with repeat bloom in fall. 12–15 in. Z3–8.

Berlandiera

Asteraceae
chocolate daisy

Sure to appeal to any gardener with a sweet tooth, this intriguing southwestern US native bears night-blooming, yellow daisy flowers that emit a fragrance of chocolate, most powerfully in early morning. Chocolate daisies thrive in full sun, tolerate drought well, and handle most soil types that drain freely. Avoid overwatering and fertilize sparingly, if at all. Add lime if soil is strongly acid.

Encourage a prolonged period of bloom by regular deadheading to the base of the individual flowerhead stem; cut plants back to the foliage mass after flowering is finished unless you are saving seed for yourself or as food for wildlife. Cut overly tall plants to ground level in midsummer. Otherwise, stake tall species or grow them among strong-stemmed perennials such as yarrows and goldenrods, or let them lollygag on sturdier neighbors; low shrubby bluebeards or silver-leaved Russian sage work well for this. Plant in drifts or patches for the strongest visual and olfactory impact. Excellent in fragrance gardens and wild or native plant gardens, as well as for edgings or grouped in flower borders. Seldom bothered by pests and diseases, and largely ignored by deer.

Propagate by direct seeding in spring after the danger of hard frost has passed, by tip cuttings in spring, or by division in spring or fall.

Berlandiera lyrata

- yellow
- summer to fall
- 12–36 in. × 12–24 in.
- sun
- Z4–9

Chocolate daisy, chocolate flower, green eyes. Open fields and grasslands of the southwestern United States and Mexico. Chocolate daisy makes loose clumps of grayish green, fiddle-shaped foliage. Light yellow daisies 1–2 in. across are accented with a central brown disk and chocolate-colored stamens. The reverse of the ray flowers (petals) is striped in red. The flowers close during the day, opening toward evening. After the ray flowers drop, a green cup (hence "green eyes") composed of multiple calyces remains. When dry it turns tan and the seeds drop. Excellent cut flower, both fresh and dry, and in containers.

Berlandiera lyrata

Bletilla striata

Bletilla

Orchidaceae
hardy ground orchid

The exotic beauty of orchids with none of the fuss—that's what the genus *Bletilla* offers gardeners in temperate regions of North America. Indeed, though they are natives of eastern Asia, hardy ground orchids take to garden cultivation much more easily than most North American species. In hospitable settings, individual bletillas expand into large, floriferous clumps, and have even been known to naturalize in Florida. Fortunately, they have shown no invasive tendencies.

Bletillas are ground dwelling; they grow from corm-like pseudobulbs that root right into the soil. Each pseudobulb sprouts several pleated leaves to 16 in. long in spring. Before the new growth has matured, a flower shoot emerges bearing a raceme of blossoms reminiscent of smaller versions of the cattleya orchid you wore to the senior prom. Healthy, established plants bear a number of such flowering shoots that continue to bloom for up to ten weeks.

Organic-rich, well-drained but evenly moist soil is essential; bletillas are winter hardy through zone 5, but won't tolerate a combination of cold and waterlogging. In cool, northern coastal gardens, full sun is fine; elsewhere, a lightly shaded site with dappled light (a woodland edge or tall meadow, for example) is ideal; a partly shaded border or container is also suitable. These plants are shallow rooted, so avoid cultivating around their bases. In zones 5 and 6, tuck bletillas in with 2 in. of straw or other loose organic mulch after the first hard fall freeze to insulate the roots and moderate midwinter temperature swings. Winter warm spells may induce the plants to emerge prematurely; provide more protective covering if a sudden frost should occur. They force readily indoors for early spring color.

Fertilize sparingly; apply a light dose of a balanced fertilizer in early spring only, none at all during first year after planting.

Good companions for hardy ground orchids include hostas, low ferns, hellebores, and other woodlanders. Bletillas bloom best when crowded, but the pseudobulbs of mature clumps may be divided in early spring to increase stock.

Bletilla ochracea

- yellow
- late spring to early summer
- 12 in. × 6–12 in.
- sun, part shade
- Z7–10

Yellow bletilla. Grasslands of China's Sichuan and Yunnan provinces. This species is slower growing and less robust than some others in the genus. Favors a moist, rich soil and morning sun, or light, filtered shade. Each flower stalk bears three to five pale yellow flowers sporting a purple, orange, and yellow-flecked lip.

Chinese Butterfly seed strain is reported to be extra vigorous. Introduced by Linda Guy. 18–24 in. Z6–9.

Bletilla striata

syn. *B. hyacinthina*

- purple
- mid- to late spring
- 1–1.5 ft. × 6–12 in.
- sun, part shade
- Z5–9

Hyacinth bletilla. China, Japan, Burma, and Tibet. This species has 1-in.-wide, pleated leaves that grow to 10 in. long; it bears pinkish purple flowers (to 1.5 in. long) in three- to seven-flowered racemes that reach 18 in. long. Withstands temporary drought. On a hospitable site, it may form a clump 2 ft. across in five years.

'Alba Variegata' has white-edged leaves and white flowers.

'Albostriata' has leaves edged with white, bright purple blooms.

'Big Bob' produces 2- to 3-ft. stalks with up to 20 blooms each. These are rose-lavender accented with purple and white.

'First Kiss' has white-edged leaves and white flowers with a purple blush on the lip.

'Soryu' bears mauve-blue flowers with a darker mauve-blue lip.

Other Notable Cultivars

'Kate' (*Bletilla striata* × *B. formosana*) bears 40-in.-long flower spikes with up to 35 lavender flowers on each. Z6–9.

Boltonia
Asteraceae
white doll's daisy, false aster

Excellent perennials for sunny, late-season gardens, boltonias flower when there is often little else in bloom. Bearing pink, lavender, or white aster-like flowers on tall branching stems, these natives are ideal for the back of the border, as well as in meadows, wildlife gardens, and in native plant gardens where butterflies flock to the blooms. The plants increase slowly by underground stems and naturalize if left alone.

Best sited in full sun, boltonias prefer soil of average fertility that drains well. In dry soils, growth is reduced and fewer flowers result, whereas in overly rich, moist soils and in part shade, growth is likely to be soft and lush, requiring staking. To promote shorter, stockier growth and heavier bloom, pinch out the tips of the stems periodically until midsummer. Deer resistant; may be susceptible to various foliage fungal problems.

Divide in early spring or start from seed (with protection where winters are very cold) in fall.

Boltonia asteroides

- white
- late summer to fall
- 24–60 in. × 18–36 in.
- sun, part shade
- Z3–9

White doll's daisy, false aster, false chamomile. Poorly drained meadows and marshes, wet thickets, and ditches of the eastern and midwestern United States. Upright plants with branching stems clothed with slender, blue-green leaves. Bears masses of 0.75- to 1-in., yellow-eyed, white daisies. Growth may get a little weedy, so false asters do best in informal settings such as meadows and native plant gardens, though cultivars are sufficiently refined for flowerbeds and borders. A great cut flower.

'Nana', a selection of var. *latisquama*, blooms in early to midfall with lavender-pink flowers. 36 in. × 24 in.

'Pink Beauty' (syn. *Boltonia rosea*), beloved of butterflies, bears abundant soft pink flowers. Has a more open, lax habit than 'Snowbank'. 4–5 ft. tall.

'Snowbank' is tough and more disease resistant than other cultivars. Bluish green foliage topped with clouds of white daisies on stems to at least 48 in. Plants may spread to 48 in., so allow plenty of space. For stronger stems and less height, cut back by about a third by midsummer. Mixes well with tender sages including Mexican sage, pitcher sage, and anise sage, and makes a statement backed with dark-foliaged shrubs.

Boltonia asteroides 'Snowbank'

Brunnera
Boraginaceae
perennial forget-me-not

This genus contributes one species with a number of notable selections to the garden. Since the foliage remains attractive throughout the growing season, plants are effective in flowerbeds as specimens or grouped as a foil for colorful summer perennials and annuals. Variegated cultivars—ideal for containers in light shade—are especially susceptible to leaf burn when exposed to intense sun.

Provide moisture-retaining fertile soil for best results; the leaf edges tend to crisp if allowed to dry out, especially where temperatures are higher. Brunneras contrast well with spring bulbs, including daffodils, grape hyacinths, and summer snowflakes. Barrenworts, lungworts, and ferns are good companions in light shade, massed under trees and shrubs, or in drifts. Deer resistant, but protect from slug damage. Pests and diseases are seldom serious. Foliage of variegated forms may revert to all green; remove such reversions at their base.

This low-maintenance perennial self-seeds freely, but propagate selections vegetatively by division in spring. Increase the species by root cuttings in winter.

Brunnera macrophylla
syn. *Anchusa myosotidiflora*

- blue
- late spring to early summer
- 1–2 ft. × 18 in.
- sun, part shade
- Z9–3, HS

Siberian bugloss, heart-leaved brunnera, perennial forget-me-not. Moist, open woodlands from eastern Europe to western Siberia. Rough-textured foliage held aloft on long petioles rises from the crown to form handsome clumps that mature after the plants bloom; young leaves expand into heart-shaped blades 6–8 in. across. The 0.25-in., yellow-eyed, blue flowers are carried in loose, terminal panicles atop slender, hairy stems.

'Dawson's White' has irregular cream margins to its leaves. Similar to 'Variegata' but reputed to be less susceptible to sunburn. Foliage may revert. To 18 in.

'Emerald Mist' bears mid-green leaves widely blotched with silver toward the edges. 18 in. tall.

'Hadspen Cream' has leaves irregularly bordered with cream. 12–15 in.

'Jack Frost' has predominantly silver leaves etched with emerald veins below blue flowers. 'Mr Morse' is similar but white flowered. 15–18 in.

'Langtrees' ('Aluminum Spot') sports pairs of large, silver ditto marks around the leaves. To 12 in.

'Looking Glass', a sport from 'Jack Frost', has more silvery leaves and less green veining. Not as hardy as other cultivars. 6–15 in.

Bulbinella
Asphodelaceae
Maori onion

Hailing from the grasslands of South Africa and New Zealand, Maori onions are likely to suffer frost damage in cold regions. However, they thrive in warmer, less humid areas, especially on the West Coast; where they can't overwinter outdoors safely, cultivate in pots and set outside in summer.

Maori onions have fleshy roots, from which sprout basal rosettes of glossy, grassy leaves. From late winter on toward summer, sturdy scapes rise from the foliage rosettes, bearing cone-shaped clusters of starry flowers at their tips; flowers may be yellow, orange, white, or pale pink. After flowering, the plants undergo a period of summer dormancy, and though Maori onions benefit from regular watering during their growing season, they should be kept dry during dormancy. When the plants retreat underground is also the best time to snip off the dead, grass-like debris that accumulates around the base. Excellent for cut flowers.

The species described here is the most commonly available, but specialist growers offer other species, too. Pests and diseases are insignificant; may be browsed by deer.

Propagate by seed as soon as it ripens, or divide in autumn.

Brunnera macrophylla 'Jack Frost' makes a charming skirt for weigela flowers

Buphthalmum salicifolium 'Alpengold'

Bulbinella hookeri

syn. *Anthericum hookeri, Chrysobactron hookeri*

- yellow
- late spring to early summer
- 1.5–3 ft. × 1–3 ft.
- sun, part shade
- Z8–9

Maori onion. New Zealand. This clumping perennial has succulent, grass-like leaves, 2 ft. long, with a longitudinal channel. They arch outward giving a vase-like effect. Strong scapes rise above each clump, topped with tight spikes of bright yellow, starry flowers tipped with a cone of green buds. Excellent beside ponds or in damp rock gardens, where they will not dry out during the growing season. Outside their range of hardiness, Maori onions provide good material for containers overwintered in a sunroom or porch, and put outdoors in summer.

Buphthalmum

Asteraceae
yellow oxeye daisy

A perky yellow daisy distinguished by its long bloom time and its excellence as a cut flower. This hardy, widely adapted genus flourishes even in poor, damp soils where so many other perennials fail. Rich soil causes soft growth that must be staked. Prefers sweet soils.

Pests and diseases are usually insignificant; seldom browsed by deer or rabbits.

Propagate by division prior to bloom time in spring or immediately afterward. Seed germinates readily in spring or fall.

Buphthalmum salicifolium

- yellow
- late summer to fall
- 1–2 ft. × 2 ft.
- sun
- Z5–8

Willowleaf oxeye, dwarf sunwheel. Central Europe. Slender, upright stems clothed with alternate, narrow, toothed, willow-like leaves to 4 in. long. Blooms are solitary and bright yellow, 2–3 in. wide, with a darker yellow disk; the ray flowers are squared off at the tips. Flowers open over a period of several weeks. Partners well with blue sage, Russian sage, and bluebeard, and also makes a fine show in meadows or wild gardens, especially when intermingled with mountain mint and grasses.

'Alpengold' has 2-in.-wide, golden flowers. 20 in. Z3–9.

'Dora' carries the yellow flowerheads atop dark purple stems. 24–30 in.

Calamintha

Lamiaceae
calamint

Calamintha is literally translated as "beautiful mint," which accurately summarizes the virtues of this genus. The calamints are close relatives of the mints and have strongly aromatic foliage—plant one beside a path and every time you brush against it the garden will be filled with a pleasant fruity, minty scent. The flowers are mint-like too, small but abundant, clustering in the leaf axils, tubular with a pair of lips framing the mouth. Calamints typically bloom for six weeks or more, attracting hosts of birds, butterflies, and hummingbirds. Calamints have the adaptability and persistence of mints, thriving in virtually any well-watered, well-drained soil, and in sun or part shade, but they lack mint's aggressive nature, and are not invasive or prone to weediness.

Though deer and insect resistant, calamints may be susceptible to powdery mildew; grow them in an open, airy location, especially where humidity is high. Propagate by seed or division in spring.

Calamintha grandiflora

syn. *Satureja grandiflora*

- pink
- late spring to early fall
- 18–24 in. × 12–15 in.
- sun, part shade
- Z5–9

Showy calamint. Southern Europe. This erect and bushy species bears bright pink flowers, 1–1.5 in. long, with a large, pouting, three-lobed lower lip.

Calamintha grandiflora

The ovate leaves are opposite, 2–3 in. long, and strongly toothed around the edges. Cut back by half after the first flush of bloom to encourage rebloom.

'Variegata' has light green leaves attractively marbled with white. Makes a fine, summer-long underplanting for hybrid teas and other roses. Less vigorous than the species.

Calamintha nepeta

- white, light blue
- summer
- 12–18 in. high and
- wide
- sun
- Z5–7

Lesser calamint. Central and southern Europe. Bushy, dense, and sometimes sprawling with ovate, gray-green leaves to 0.75 in. long, and tiny but abundant flowers. It is perfect for edging walks, patios, or herb gardens, or at the front of a border. Allow to spill over retaining walls or showcase in a container. Drought tolerance makes this species suitable for rock gardens too.

'Blue Cloud' is compact with light blue flowers and fine, gray-green foliage. To 15 in. high and wide. 'White Cloud' has white blooms.

subsp. *glandulosa* is more vigorous than the species, with 1.25-in. leaves and slightly larger flowers that bloom all up and down the stems.

Callirhoe

Malvaceae
poppy mallow

This genus of North American prairie plants is a boon to gardeners in dryer regions who want long-lasting floral color with little investment in irrigation: poppy mallows' deep taproots make these plants outstandingly drought tolerant, ideal subjects for xeriscapes and gardens where water is in short supply. Another common name for members of this genus is "wine cups," which provides a vivid picture of its flowering: the five-petaled, upward-facing flowers are shaped like bowls, and range in color from an almost burgundy reddish purple through shades of rosé to a limpid white. The blooms make a fine showing against the lacy foliage and are borne abundantly for a couple of months or even longer, depending on the species and the local climate—a very hot, dry summer can shorten the display.

Callirhoes prefer a sunny spot and well-drained, even sandy soil; a persistently damp soil, especially in winter, is likely to prove fatal. Sometimes attacked by aphids and red spider mites; seldom browsed by deer.

Other than the species described here, *Callirhoe alcaeoides* and its white cultivar 'Logan Calhoun', *C. digitata* with its fringed flowers, and clustered poppy mallow, *C. triangulata*, are also interesting.

The taproot makes dividing or even transplanting older plants difficult. Propagation by seed is

Callirhoe involucrata

better, whether sown directly in spring or started in containers, thus minimizing root disturbance when transplanting.

Callirhoe involucrata

- pink, purple
- midspring to early fall
- 0.5–1 ft. × 1–3 ft.
- sun
- Z4–8

Purple poppy mallow. Prairies, fields, and roadsides from North Dakota east to Missouri, south to New Mexico and Texas. This species forms low, spreading mounds of palmately divided leaves; magenta flowers to 2.5 in. across are borne on slender stems above the foliage. Delicately textured, excellent as a groundcover at the front of borders, in rock gardens, or meadows. Especially attractive spilling over stone walls.

Caltha

Ranunculaceae
marsh marigold

Just how this genus acquired the common name of marigold isn't clear, but it's a misnomer, for caltha flowers are clearly close relatives of buttercups. The most widely cultivated species is *Caltha palustris*, which the Royal Horticultural Society describes as "an essential plant to brighten up the margins of a pond or a boggy area with sunny yellow flowers." The only other species commercially available is *C. leptosepala*, a native of western US mountains, which shares *C. palustris*'s preference for wet or moist situations but blooms later, thus prolonging the marsh marigold show.

All parts of marsh marigolds are toxic—even the sap may raise a rash in sensitive individuals. This makes these perennials a poor choice for a landscape with children but endows the plants with resistance to deer. Marsh marigolds thrive in a wide range of soils, so long as they are rich in organic matter and consistently moist.

Propagate by dividing mature plants or by seed collected as soon as it is ripe; sow in late summer and overwinter in a cold frame or other cool but protected spot.

Caltha palustris

- yellow
- early to midspring
- 10–12 in. × 12–18 in.
- sun, part shade
- Z3–7

Yellow marsh marigold, kingcup. Bogs and other wet locations throughout the northern and coastal parts of North America, and northern temperate regions worldwide; flourishes inland if given sufficient moisture. Mounds of glossy, heart- or kidney-shaped leaves with stout, hollow, branching stems. Buttercup-like, waxy, bright golden-yellow flowers are 1.5 in. across, with five petal-like sepals, carried on upright stems 12–18 in. Sometimes reblooms in late summer or fall. May spread by seed on consistently damp soils.

var. *alba* bears single, white flowers.

'Flore Pleno' (possibly 'Multiplex', 'Monstruosa', 'Monstrosa-Plena'), sometimes known as May blob, bears double yellow pompon-like flowers with greeny-yellow centers, similar in appearance to a florist's ranunculus. Sterile and longer blooming.

Campanula
Campanulaceae
bellflower

This large and diverse genus of about 420 species includes plants of many different habits—from upright to creeping—whose diversity enables them to fill niches in plantings ranging from perennial borders to rock gardens. A large number of species is native to North America, with its western mountains being an especially rich source. Campanulas supply some of the finest, clearest blues in the garden, though the palette of floral colors found in this genus extends to a range of whites and pinks as well. It should be noted that the species *Campanula armena* was formerly sold under the name of *Symphyandra*, but since being reclassified, most nurseries are now advertising them under the new name.

As the common name indicates, campanula flowers are often bell shaped, although there are species with tubular, star-, or cup-and-saucer-shaped blossoms as well. Conscientious deadheading prolongs the season of bloom.

Note that several species described below tend to be invasive. Creeping or roving bellflower (*C. rapunculoides*—not described here) is one to avoid for all but the wildest, most informal and open spaces. Once introduced it is almost impossible to eradicate. Another hardy, though less aggressive

Caltha palustris

species worth investigating is *C. rotundifolia*, native to most of North America and northern Europe.

Though usually easy to grow, bellflowers are susceptible to snails, slugs, spider mites, and aphids. Powdery mildew and rust may also be problems. As a group, campanulas attract hummingbirds, but resist deer browsing. The longer-stemmed species are decorative as cut flowers; sear the base of the stems to avoid the milky sap fouling the vase water.

Sow seed in containers in spring or early fall (overwinter with protection), by division in spring or autumn, or by basal stem cuttings from new spring growth.

Campanula armena
syn. *Symphyandra armena*

- blue, white
- late spring to early summer
- 15 in. × 12 in.
- sun, part shade
- Z7–8

Ring bellflower. Caucasus, Turkey, Iran. Deeply toothed, heart-shaped, hairy leaves on domed networks of branching stems. Nodding, bell-shaped, lavender-blue or white flowers are borne prolifically. At home in any light, well-drained garden soil. Long-lived treasure for rock gardens or border foregrounds.

Campanula punctata 'Kent Belle'

Campanula carpatica

- blue, purple, white
- early to late summer
- 6–12 in. × 1–3 ft.
- sun, part shade
- Z4–7

Carpathian harebell. Mountains of eastern Europe. A species of modest vigor and stature best suited to the front of a border, rock, or cottage garden, or for display in a container. Heart-shaped, dark green leaves form neat tussocks that in summer are covered with bell-shaped flowers with a diameter of 2–3 in. Well-drained soil—regularly moistened but allowed to dry between waterings—promotes good growth.

'Blue Clips' is low growing and spreading with violet-blue flowers.

'Pearl Deep Blue' blooms heavily with large, bright blue flowers.

'White Clips' is compact, 6–8 in., with pure white flowers.

Campanula cochlearifolia

- blue, purple
- early to late summer
- 2–4 in. × 6–8 in.
- sun, part shade
- Z3–8

Fairies' thimbles. European mountains. This fast-growing, even aggressive, species has a low and spreading habit that makes it valuable for edgings or as an underplanting for taller perennials. The dense mat of diminutive leaves provides a pretty backdrop for the showy 0.5-in. bells.

'Bavaria Blue' has sky-blue flowers.

'Bavaria White' bears heavy crops of pure white flowers.

'Elizabeth Oliver' bears intricate double, pale lavender flowers.

Campanula glomerata

- blue, purple
- summer
- 12–24 in. × 15–24 in.
- sun, part shade
- Z3–8

Clustered bellflower. Europe, Asia. Free blooming; forms clumps of upright stems above basal rosettes of long-stemmed oval, toothed leaves 4–5 in. long. Lacking petioles, the stem leaves are sometimes clasping and smaller. Dense but rather ungainly clusters of funnel-shaped, 0.75- to 1-in., bright purple flowers clump at the stem tips and in leaf axils. Long lasting as cut flowers. Provide part shade in hot regions, full sun is preferable in cooler climates. Group with daylilies, tickseeds, Helen's flower, and summer phlox.

'Crown of Snow' ('Schneekrone') has pure white flowers. 18–24 in.

'Freya', named for the Norse goddess of love and fertility, produces starry, lilac-purple flowers on the top two-thirds of the stems. Late spring to summer. Non-invasive. 10–15 in. tall.

'Joan Elliot' blooms early with upward-facing, light purple-blue flowers. Good for cutting. Tolerates wet soils. 18 in.

'Superba' is a strong grower with bright purple-violet flowers. 24 in.

Campanula lactiflora

- blue, purple, white
- midsummer to early fall
- 3–5 ft. × 1–3 ft.
- sun, part shade
- Z4–10, HS

Milky bellflower. Caucasus. Long lived and imposing, milky bellflower forms a group of tall stems clothed with rounded leaves and topped with conical spires of sweet-scented, 1.5-in., bell-shaped flowers. Cut back to 1 ft. in midspring to encourage denser, sturdy growth that doesn't require staking. Performs best on rich, moist but well-drained soils. Self-seeds. Combine at the back of the border with hollyhocks.

'Alba' has white flowers, but is otherwise similar to the species.

'Dwarf Pink' is compact but floriferous, bearing an abundance of pink flowers. Late spring to early summer. 18–24 in.

'Lodden Anna' bears pale pink flowers.

'Pfouffe' is dwarf, with an abundance of pale blue flowers. 1–2 ft. tall.

'Pritchard's Variety' bears violet-blue flowers over an extended season. 3 ft.

Campanula persicifolia

- blue, purple, white
- late spring to early fall
- 1–3 ft. × 1–1.5 ft.
- sun, part shade
- Z3–8, HS

Peach-leaved bellflower. Mountainous areas of Europe, northern Africa, and northern and western Asia. Forms a rosette of narrow, glossy, bright green leaves. Cup-shaped flowers in shades of blue, lilac, or white borne along the full length of tall, slender stems. Prefers an evenly moist soil that drains well, and some afternoon shade in regions where sun is intense. Does not tolerate summer heat and humidity well. Self-seeds readily and also spreads by rhizomes. Appropriate in cottage gardens, borders, and open woodlands, and as a cut flower. Good companions include catmint, daylilies, hardy geraniums, and lilies.

'Alba' is white flowered.

'Chettle Charm' has flowers that are creamy white, edged with lavender-blue.

'Kelly's Gold' has bright golden foliage and white flowers tinged blue around the edges.

'La Belle' is compact, with small, double flowers, deep blue with a silver gloss, borne all summer. To 24 in.

'Telham Beauty' is extra vigorous (to 4 ft. tall) with porcelain-blue flowers.

Campanula glomerata 'Freya'

Campanula portenschlagiana

syn. *C. muralis*

- blue, purple
- late spring to midsummer
- 3–6 in. × 1–3 ft.
- sun, part shade
- Z4–8

Dalmatian bellflower. Rocky uplands of Dalmatia, Croatia. In favorable locations, this low, mat-forming plant spreads rapidly by rhizomes. Heart-shaped, dark-green leaves with toothed edges; abundant 1-in., funnel-shaped, blue to purple flowers. Protect from the early afternoon sun in hot climates. Suitable for rock gardens, edgings, and for containers.

var. *alba* is white flowered.

'Aurea' has golden foliage.

'Birch Hybrid' makes a neat cushion, 4–6 in. tall and 20 in. across, covered with cupped, blue-purple flowers from early summer into fall.

'Resholt Variety' bears intensely violet-blue flowers.

Campanula poscharskyana

- blue
- midspring to early summer
- 4–12 in. × 1–1.5 ft.
- sun, part shade
- Z3–8

Serbian bellflower, Dalmatian bellflower. Northern Balkans. A sprawling, prostrate species that forms a low, mounded groundcover of oval to cordate, medium green leaves to 1.5 in. long. Evergreen where winters are mild. Lilac-colored, star-shaped, 1-in. flowers borne in loose panicles along the

Campanula poscharskyana 'Blue Waterfall'

stems. Excellent as edgings along a path or around a patio, in containers, or spilling over the top of a retaining wall or down a bank.

'Blue Rivulet' is a similar but more compact form of 'Blue Waterfall'. Perfect for containers and small gardens. 6–7 in.

'Blue Waterfall' bears an abundance of lavender-blue flowers. 8–10 in.

'E. H. Frost' has white flowers. Excellent tumbling over walls and rocks. 8 in.

'Stella' has violet-blue flowers. 6–12 in.

Campanula punctata

- pink, white
- early to midsummer
- 1–2 ft. × 1–1.5 ft.
- sun, part shade
- Z5–7

Spotted bellflower. Siberia and Japan. Long blooming and easily grown; forms basal rosettes of rounded, toothed, green leaves to 5 in. long, from which rise arching stems. These sport racemes of nodding, tubular, white to pale pink flowers as much as 2 in. long, spotted purple inside to guide foraging bees. Spreads freely by rhizomes or self-sown seeds and can become thuggish; suitable for informal borders, cottage gardens, and lightly shaded woodland settings. Keep under control.

'Bowl of Cherries' has pink to dark purple-red bells on 15-in. plants. Remove spent flowers for later rebloom. Vigorous. Z5–9.

'Cherry Bells' has rose-red flowers. Tolerates heat and humidity well. 24 in.

'Hot Lips' is dwarf, with large, bell-shaped, pale pink flowers, speckled burgundy inside, above rich dark green foliage. 10–12 in.

'Kent Belle' has glossy violet-blue flowers on upright stems. Tolerates southern heat and humidity. Sterile. Striking with silver-leaved companions. 24 in. Z5–9.

'Pink Chimes' has nodding, pink flowers. 9–18 in. tall.

Cardamine pratensis

Campanula takesimana

- pink
- mid- to late summer
- 18–24 in. × 24 in.
- sun, part shade
- Z5–8

Korean bellflower. Korea. Rhizomatous roots produce basal rosettes of heart-shaped leaves, 3–4 in. long, above which rise winged flower stems. Branching sprays of nodding, tubular, pink-flushed, white flowers, 2–3 in. long, decorated inside with maroon spots and speckles. Deadhead routinely to keep neat. Spreads vigorously, valuable only in informal or very lightly shaded woodland, shrub, or wild gardens and for cutting.

'Elizabeth' blooms freely with plenty of purplish pink, speckled blooms. Vigorous.

Other Notable Cultivars

'Bumblebee' bears masses of small, upright, blue bellflowers in summer. Excellent in containers and crevices. 4 in. × 12 in. Z4–8.

'Sarastro' is upright and compact. Abundant large, purple flowers from early summer, repeating until fall. 18 in. × 24 in. Z3–8.

'Viking' displays tubular, light lavender flowers. Compact, excellent for the middle and front of borders, and cottage and cutting gardens. Spreads in a quiet, civilized way; sterile. Attracts hummingbirds and butterflies. 18 in. tall.

Cardamine
syn. *Dentaria*
Brassicaceae
bittercress, cardamine

The genus *Cardamine* now includes plants formerly known as *Dentaria*, although some nurseries still sell them under their former names. These modest plants are most effective in damp areas in wild gardens, under shrubs, or in the flower garden. They do best where winters are mild, and summers cool without too much humidity; the heat and humidity of the southeastern United States is not to their liking. Spikes of cruciform (petals arranged in a cross) flowers of white, pink, mauve, or lavender are carried above the leaves that may be entire or divided into leaflets. Several native American species, such as *C. diphylla* and *C. bulbosa*, are perfect for moist woodlands and native plant gardens but are difficult to find in the trade.

Propagate by seed or divide in spring or fall.

Cardamine pentaphyllos
syn. *Dentaria digitata, D. pentaphyllos*
- white, purple, lilac
- late spring
- 12–18 in. × 12 in.
- part shade
- Z5–9, HS

Showy toothwort, bittercress. Mountains of southern Europe. The mid-green, palmately divided leaves contrast well with loose clusters of 0.5- to

0.75-in., bright pink or purplish flowers. Lovely under spring shrubs or allowed to naturalize with bulbs.

Cardamine pratensis

- mauve, pink
- late spring
- 12–18 in. × 12 in.
- sun, part shade
- Z5–8, HS

Lady's smock, cuckoo flower, milkmaid's delight. Wet meadows and marshes of North America, Europe, and northern Asia. Short, scaly underground stems give rise to basal rosettes of glossy, dark leaves with several pairs of leaflets. Clusters of pale lavender or pink, 0.5- to 0.75-in flowers top unbranched stems. Leaf-tip cuttings and bulbils may also be removed for propagation. Allow to naturalize in rough grass around a pond or stream.

'Flore Pleno' has double, mauve flowers. 8 in. tall.

Cardamine trifolia

- white
- late spring
- 6–9 in. × 12 in.
- part shade
- Z6–8, HS

Trifoliate bittercress. Wooded areas in mountains of central and southern Europe. Dark green leaves with three leaflets may be reddish beneath. Cupped, white flowers crowd into short clusters, displaying bright yellow anthers, reminiscent of *Arabis*. Perfect for damp rock gardens or beside a pond or waterfall partnered with summer snowflakes and forget-me-nots.

Catananche caerulea

Catananche
Asteraceae
Cupid's dart

According to tradition, plants of this genus earned their common name through their former use as the principal ingredient for love potions; certainly, any gardener is likely to fall in love with such an easy, adaptable, and showy flower as Cupid's dart.

As natives of the lands bordering the western Mediterranean, Cupid's darts prefer well-drained soils; a consistently damp soil may prove fatal, especially in winter. Its drought tolerance makes this genus a good choice for xeriscapes, and its grayish foliage is an attractive companion for wormwoods (*Artemisia* spp.), lamb's ears, and other silver-leaved herbs. Cupid's dart harmonizes especially well with lavenders; its airy foliage is useful for adding texture to beds and borders. Excellent cut, fresh or dried. The old-fashioned look of the fringed flowerheads makes this a natural for cottage gardens too. Pests and diseases, except powdery mildew, are seldom a problem. Deer tolerant.

Propagate by seed started indoors or direct sown in spring, divide in spring, or take winter root cuttings.

Catananche caerulea

- blue
- early to late summer
- 18–24 in. × 10–12 in.
- sun
- Z4–9, HS

Cupid's dart. Clump forming, with wiry flower stems rising from a nest of narrow, grassy, gray-green leaves topped with 2-in., cornflower-like heads of blue to lavender-blue. The petal-like ray flowers are prettily fringed on the outer end; a darker-hued eye accentuates each flowerhead. Deadhead to extend bloom time. This species is mostly short lived but commonly self-sows.

'Alba' has white flowers accented with a blue eye.

'Armor White' has white flowers with a purple eye that bleeds a lavender tinge to the rays.

'Major' is deeper colored than the species, with a dark eye.

Caulophyllum
Berberidaceae
blue cohosh, squaw root

A gem for native woodland gardeners. Unlike many of the spring-blooming natives that are ephemeral, this species retains its handsome bluish, airily divided leaves through the summer and into fall. Not only do they make good filler plants, but in autumn they mount a striking display of conspicuous bright blue berries that hang on even after leaf drop or until eaten by mice or other wildlife.

Each plant produces one or two large leaves on tall, grayish stems; in blue cohosh (*Caulophyllum thalictroides*) these appear as the flowers open, but slightly later in giant or purple-flowered blue cohosh (*C. giganteum*). The two species overlap in range along the eastern US seaboard inland to Mississippi, with the latter species reaching well north into upper Canada. An Asian species, *C. robusta* is seldom cultivated in the United States.

Blue cohosh thrives in moist woodland soil high in organic matter. In cold climates protect the over-wintering crowns with dry leaves. Otherwise, maintenance is low; plants are seldom browsed by deer probably due to the bitter taste of the leaves, which are reputed to be poisonous to mammals. As suggested by the common names, blue cohosh has been used medicinally by generations of Native Americans. Today it is still widely used as a homeopathic remedy, especially for female complaints.

In woodland gardens or native plantings, group or mass with native ferns, Virginia bluebells, black snakeroot, and turtleheads.

Divide mature plants in spring and fall, when plantings become overcrowded; blue cohosh resents disturbance. Sow seed as soon as it ripens. Germination may be erratic and plants seldom flower until they are four to five years old.

Caulophyllum thalictroides

Caulophyllum thalictroides

- yellow green
- early to late spring
- 12–30 in. × 8–15 in.
- part shade, shade
- Z3–8

Blue cohosh, squaw root, papoose root. Rich, well-drained mixed woodlands from southeastern Canada and Maine to Alabama, Oklahoma, and Mississippi including the eastern seaboard. Emerging stems are purple and carry grayish purple leaves reminiscent of meadow rue foliage; later they turn an attractive blue-green. The variably yellow-green or purple-green, 0.5-in. flowers are arranged in flat-topped clusters, but they are not memorable except to nectar-collecting bees. The grape-like clusters of fleshy dark, blueberry-like seeds, however, are eye-catching. Look but don't eat, however, as these seeds cause gastrointestinal distress, especially in children; all parts of the plant can irritate the skin of sensitive individuals. Blue cohosh does not thrive in regions of intense heat.

Centaurea

Asteraceae
knapweed, cornflower

Although this is a large genus, only a few species are deemed worthy of ornamental gardens. These are most suitable for flower borders, but are also appropriate for less formal places, such as interplanted among grasses.

Their strong stems topped with showy flower-heads make the ornamental knapweeds ideal as long-lasting cut flowers, both dried or fresh. Butterflies, bees, and other insects enjoy the pollen and nectar, so they are excellent additions to wildlife gardens. Generally suitable for xeric gardens; wet feet in winter is often lethal. The soil should be sweet, preferably with a pH above 7. Deadhead almost to the ground after the first flush of bloom to encourage rebloom later. Be aware that some species have roaming roots and may become invasive. Staking is seldom necessary, and knapweeds usually require little maintenance. Deer generally ignore these plants, but rabbits find them tasty. The foliage is occasionally attacked by mildew, especially where air circulation is poor.

Propagate by seed sown in spring or by division in spring or fall.

Centaurea cineraria

syn. *C. candidissima*, *C. gymnocarpa*

- mauve
- late spring
- 36 in. × 12 in.
- sun, part shade
- Z7–11

Dusty miller. Italy. Commonly grown as an annual but perennial in milder climates. The common name, dusty miller, is also applied to a variety of other plants with silvery foliage, notably white- or yellow-flowered *Senecio cineraria*; beware of misidentifications in catalogs. *Centaurea cineraria* produces clumping mounds of velvety, lobed, white leaves that make an elegant foil for other, more brilliant colors in sunny beds or borders. The foliage seems to glow at night, making it perfect for moon gardens. Mauve, pincushion flowers on lanky 30-in. stems. Easy to grow in well-drained soils; tolerates drought but soon succumbs to wet feet; effective in coastal gardens.

'Cirrhus' is dwarf. 12 in.

'Colchester White' has intricately cut, filigreed foliage and lavender-blue flowers.

'Silver Dust' has lace-cut, white leaves. 14–24 in.

Centaurea dealbata

- pink
- late spring to summer
- 20–30 in. × 18 in.
- sun
- Z3–8

Persian cornflower, whitewash cornflower. Caucasus Mountains. Coarsely divided leaves, white with hairs below, and solitary, fluffy, pink or lavender 2- to 3-in. flowerheads; outer florets are deeply fringed. The plants tend to stretch and flop in hot, humid areas, requiring staking to be presentable. In cooler climes their strong stems remain upright.

'Steenbergii' is the most often grown selection. Full, white-centered, thistle-like, hot-pink heads grace this attractive plant. Bees and butterflies flock to the flowers that make excellent long-lasting cut flowers. This vigorous grower may become invasive. Tolerates drought well. 1–2 in. Z4–8.

Centaurea hypoleuca

- pink
- late spring to midsummer
- 15–24 in. × 18 in.
- sun
- Z3–7

Knapweed, Persian cornflower. Armenia, Iran, and Turkey in alkaline soils. Similar to *Centaurea dealbata*, but smaller. Dull green leaves with white-woolly undersides. The species is seldom cultivated but the following is popular:

'John Coutts' has 4-in.-wide, deep rosy-pink flowers enclosed in a "thistlehead" of white, papery bracts. Deeply cut stem leaves are white beneath. Deadhead hard to encourage a second flush of bloom. Sometimes listed under *C. dealbata*. 24 in. Z4–8.

Centaurea macrocephala

- yellow
- early to midsummer
- 3–4 ft. × 1.5–2 ft.
- sun
- Z3–8

Armenian basket flower, yellow hardhat, globe centaurea. Caucasus region. Armenian basket flower displays stiff-stemmed, egg-sized, toast-colored buds that burst into bright yellow, 3- to 4-in.-wide, thistle-like flowers. Long blooming and fine for cutting, both fresh and dried. Requires little

maintenance, and tolerates dry soil, even drought, when established. Excellent as specimen plants or grouped in flower borders where they provide vertical accents. Catmints and speedwells make good companions; effective massed with grasses in rough grass or meadows.

Centaurea montana

- blue
- early to midsummer
- 12–24 in. × 18–24 in.
- sun
- Z3–8

Mountain bluets, perennial cornflower, perennial bachelor's buttons. This European native bears showy, blue, 2-in. flowers on unbranched stems for several weeks. A second crop may bloom in late summer; cut back to the ground after the first flush. Drought tolerant, mountain bluets thrive where soil is moisture retentive but drains well. Maintain vigor by division of the rhizomatous rootstock every few years, which also helps control plant's roaming ways. Prefers slightly alkaline soils in cool-summer climates. Eye popping with *Euphorbia polychroma* 'Bonfire'.

Centaurea montana 'Gold Bullion'

'Alba' has delicate, sparsely rayed, white flower-heads flushed with lavender in the center. Drought tolerant. Z5–8.

'Amethyst Dream' has light amethyst-blue flowers on 1- to 2-ft.-tall stems. Z4–8.

'Amethyst in Snow' sports showy white ray flowers surrounding a small purplish blue central boss of flowers. Silvery foliage. 15 in. Z5–8.

'Black Sprite' has startling dark purple, spidery flowers, dramatic when grown with *Artemisia* 'Powis Castle' or other silver-leaved plants. A Skagit Gardens introduction. 14 in.

'Gold Bullion' is dramatic with its bright yellow foliage in contrast to black flower buds and cornflower blue flowers. Compact. 12–15 in. Z4–8.

Centranthus
Caprifoliaceae
Jupiter's beard, valerian

Though this genus includes a dozen or so species, only *Centranthus ruber* is popular with gardeners. Easy to grow and extremely undemanding, Jupiter's beard was a favorite of old-time cottage gardeners.

It is an ideal beginner's plant, very forgiving and flourishing even in poor, infertile, and droughty soils, and yet its rewards are sophisticated enough to please connoisseurs.

Jupiter's beard prefers a slightly alkaline pH, but succeeds in any average, well-drained garden soil; its tolerance for drought makes this an excellent choice for xeriscapes and coastal gardens. Unless saving seed, remove fading flowers to promote a second flush of bloom; Jupiter's beard tends to be short lived so it is wise to have replacement seedlings handy. Cut stems back to 6 in. in late summer to stimulate new vegetative growth for overwintering. Attractive to butterflies and bees; seldom browsed by deer, and mostly reported resistant to rabbits. A good groundcover for sunny banks; seeds itself into crevices between pavers or in walls. Commonly found seeded into the mortared walls of European castles and ruins.

A traditional choice for cottage gardens, Jupiter's beard partners well with other alkaline-loving, old-fashioned flowers such as baby's breath, pinks, and pin-cushion flower. Useful source of cut flowers.

Propagate by seed, by division of mature plants in early spring or fall, or by spring basal cuttings.

Centranthus ruber
syn. *Valeriana rubra, V. coccinea*
- red, pink, white
- late spring to late summer
- 1.5–3 ft. × 2–3 ft.
- sun, part shade
- Z5–8

Jupiter's beard, fox's brush, keys-of-heaven. Native of Europe, northern Africa, and the Middle East, this plant has naturalized in our Pacific Coast states, Arizona, Utah, and Hawaii. The fleshy leaves are bluish green and lance shaped, borne on ascending, often sprawling stems. Dense cymes of fragrant, small, star-shaped flowers.

'Albus' bears creamy-white flowers. Compact to 2 ft.

'Atrococcineus' flowers are deep brick red.

'Coccineus' has carmine flowers. To 2 ft.

'Roseus' has rosy-pink flowers.

Cephalaria
Dipsacaceae
yellow scabious

Few plants have the combination of bulk and grace to furnish the back of large borders better than yellow scabious. If space allows, mass for dramatic effect as a summer hedge or naturalize informally in meadows and wildlife gardens where the flowers attract butterflies. An asset for cottage and cutting gardens if space permits.

Start new plants from seed (stratify to aid germination), or divide mature clumps in spring.

Centranthus ruber

Cephalaria gigantea
syn. *C. tatarica*
- yellow
- early to midsummer
- 5–6 ft. × 3–4 ft.
- sun
- Z3–8

Yellow scabious, Tatarian cephalaria, giant scabious. Caucasus Mountains to Siberia. Grows naturally in moist, sweet soils that seldom dry out. Best in sheltered, full-sun sites; even part shade encourages the stems to flop. Vigorous with large bushes of dark green foliage to about 5 ft. Individual leaves are deeply cleft and may reach 15 in. long. Slender, striped flower stems topped with 2.5-in.-wide, pale yellow flowers rise above the mass of foliage. The blooms, similar to related scabious, consist of countless four-parted florets, the outer ones are enlarged. Deadhead to encourage further bloom but leave the late heads for winter interest.

Cerastium
Caryophyllaceae
snow-in-summer

Of this genus's 100 species, only *Cerastium tomentosum* is of interest to perennial gardeners. Other species, including the similar Taurus cerastium, *C. biebersteinii* from the Crimean region, differ in a few minor botanical details and some authorities include them with *C. tomentosum*, as the *C. tomentosum* Group.

Snow-in-summer prefers full sun in the northern regions, but requires midday shade where sun is intense. High heat and humidity cause plants to melt out, or rot at the crown. Well-drained, average to poor soil is satisfactory; neutral to sweet soil is preferable, typical of many members of the Caryophyllaceae. Aggressive and may become invasive under good conditions, spreading quickly by

Cephalaria gigantea

Cerastium tomentosum 'Columnae'

underground stems. Shear after bloom time to prevent seeding. Pests and diseases are seldom a problem; deer and rabbit resistant.

Provides a restful foil for speedwells, bellflowers, and spurges. Good as a groundcover, especially in sandy coastal gardens, rock gardens, or rough, dry banks where it tolerates drought; ideal tumbling over rocks or walls. Eye-catching in winter gardens combined with purple-leaved bergenias.

Propagate by division in spring or fall, or direct sow seed in spring or sow indoors in fall before the last frost.

Cerastium tomentosum

- white
- late spring to early summer
- 6 in. × 12–24 in.
- sun
- Z3–7, HS

Snow-in-summer, mouse-ear chickweed. Italy. A well-grown patch of snow-in-summer is a cool delight to the eyes. The softly hairy, silver leaves, each less than 1 in. long, form dense mats that are topped with short-stemmed clusters of glistening white, starry flowers. Individual blooms have five petals, notched at the tips.

'Columnae' is somewhat more refined and is hardy to zone 8. Possibly tolerates light foot traffic. Avoid all but poor soils to maintain habit. 'Silver Carpet' is similar and may be a synonym.

'Yo-Yo' is a compact cultivar, better suited for growing in limited space such as containers, or crevices between rocks. Not as aggressive as the species.

Ceratostigma
Plumbaginaceae
leadwort , plumbago

Some flowers charm not through sheer brilliance but through their timing. The leadworts, for example, cannot rival such stars as summer phlox in brilliance of floral display, but they open their blossoms during the late summer lull when the garden needs them most. Commonly, they continue blooming well into the fall, when their small but abundant flowers make a piquant contrast to the red, orange, and yellow hues of autumn foliage.

Moderately moist, well-drained garden soils are ideal, but plumbagos also thrive on poor soils. Extra fertilizer is unnecessary; drought tolerant once established. Protect from intense sun in hot regions. Cut back to the ground to promote fresh, vigorous regrowth in early spring.

Attractive to butterflies, deer resistant, and generally trouble free, the cultivated species of *Ceratostigma* are as undemanding as they are rewarding.

Propagate by cuttings taken in spring or layer stems in fall.

Ceratostigma plumbaginoides
syn. *Plumbago larpentiae*

- blue
- midsummer to fall
- 9–12 in. × 12–18 in.
- sun, part shade
- Z5–9, HS

Ceratostigma plumbaginoides

Blue leadwort, plumbago. Native to western China, this mat-forming, woody-based perennial spreads by rhizomes to form an attractive groundcover. Oval to obovate, shiny medium green leaves, 2–3.5 in. long, are bristly with wavy margins, and turn bronze-red in fall. Five-petaled flowers, to 0.75 in. across, cluster at the stem tips; spiky, red buds open to brilliant deep blue blossoms. Blue leadwort is outstanding as a groundcover, especially for slopes, with trees and shrubs, and in rock gardens. A perfect companion for spring bulbs: blue leadwort foliage emerges late as bulbs fade, camouflaging the bulbs' ripening leaves. Prone to powdery mildew. Not suitable where summers are hot and humid.

Ceratostigma willmottianum

- blue
- late summer to fall
- 24–36 in. × 3–4 ft.
- sun, part shade
- Z6–9, HS

Chinese plumbago. China and Tibet. This woody perennial is shrubby in mild regions, but dies back in cold-winter regions. Lanceolate, green leaves, often edged with purple, turn red in autumn. Five-petaled, 1-in., cobalt-blue flowers borne abundantly in dense clusters at stem tips. Attractive as a color echo and foil with russet ornamental grasses; Chinese plumbago's shrubby form hides the naked grass bases. Doesn't thrive in the southern United States.

'My Love' has golden-yellow foliage.

Chelone
Plantaginaceae
turtlehead

Never did a flower's common name do it such a disservice. In fact, chelones bear only the most notional resemblance to a reptile's head; instead, they rank among the most desirable, if underutilized, native North American wildflowers.

Chelones' unusual blooms have an intriguing form, and their foliage is bold and handsome. They are undemanding and require only humus-rich, consistently moist, or even wet soil. Pinch back stem tips at 6–9 in. during spring to encourage bushy, compact growth and eliminate the need for staking. Mildew may be a problem where air circulation is poor.

Use versatile turtleheads to serve as focal points in shade or woodland gardens, moist meadows, bog gardens, and the edge of ponds or slow-moving streams. Their tolerance for wet feet equips them to be stars in rain gardens, although they are sufficiently refined to also hold their own in formal settings. Attractive to butterflies. Partner them with other damp-loving plants: ligularias, rose mallows, blue lobelia, and cardinal flower, for example.

Propagate by seed or division in spring or fall.

Chelone lyonii 'Hot Lips'

Chelone glabra

- white, pink
- midsummer to early fall
- 2–3 ft. × 1.5–2.5 ft.
- sun, part shade, shade
- Z3–8

Turtlehead, snakeshead. United States east of the Mississippi, except for Florida and Louisiana. Clump forming, with stiff, erect stems well clothed with dark green, coarsely toothed, lance-shaped leaves, 3–6 in. long. The 1.5-in.-long, white, sometimes pink-tinged flowers are hooded, two-lipped, and snapdragon-like, borne in tight, spike-like, terminal racemes.

This plant is the main larval food source of the lovely and rare Baltimore checkerspot butterfly. Deer often browse these plants.

Chelone lyonii

- pink, purple
- midsummer to early fall
- 2–4 ft. × 1.5–2.5 ft.
- sun, part shade
- Z4–8

Shellflower. Southeastern United States. Similar to *Chelone glabra*, except with ovate, 6- to 7-in. leaves and rose-pink flowers; in general it is somewhat bolder and taller. Shellflower spreads by rhizomes and may self-seed to form a colony. Keep soil moist with a shredded leaf mulch in sunny sites. Reputedly, deer avoid this species.

'Hot Lips' has blooms of a richer pink than the species, red stems and purple-green foliage.

Chelone obliqua

- purple, pink, white
- midsummer to early fall
- 2–3 ft. × 1–2 ft.
- sun, part shade
- Z4–9

Red turtlehead. Throughout the United States east of the Mississippi. Dark green leaves are coarsely toothed and lance shaped. Flower color is variable, though most commonly a rich rose to rosy purple. Seldom browsed by deer.

Chiastophyllum
Crassulaceae
lamb's tail

This genus is prized for its succulent evergreen mats of foliage and "lamb's tails" of small, yellow flowers. Excellent in rock gardens or tucked into crevices between rocks or pavers, it is also useful as a neat groundcover, in raised beds, rock gardens, and containers with other succulents. A lovely and unusual companion for coral bells, rock cress, and creeping bellflowers.

Lamb's tail prefers average, well-drained soil, and tolerates drought when established. Thrives in full sun in the Pacific Northwest but elsewhere is best protected from intense summer sun. Adapts poorly to heat with humidity. Slugs may be a problem.

Start seed indoors in spring. Mix the dust-like seeds with fine sand to simplify even distribution; do not cover. Germination takes one to two months. Propagate by division in early summer or take soft cuttings from side shoots in summer.

Chiastophyllum oppositifolium
syn. *C. simplicifolium, Cotyledon simplicifolia*

- yellow
- late spring
- 2–4 in. × 6 in.
- sun, part shade
- Z6–9

Yellow lamb's tail, golden lamb's tail, golden drop. Native to areas of limestone rocks in the Caucasus Mountains. Plants expand slowly by rhizomes, but do not become aggressive; basal rosettes of waxy, evergreen, rounded, succulent leaves, scalloped along the margins. In late spring flowering stems rise to 6–8 in., adorned with dangling chains of small, bright yellow bells. Cut back after bloom time.

'Jim's Pride' ('Frosted Jade'). Waxy foliage is gray green, edged and variegated with cream and pink tones in cold weather. Pale yellow flowers.

Chrysanthemum
Asteraceae
chrysanthemum, mum

Cultivated chrysanthemums derive from an Asian tradition that focused on the development of spectacular blossoms, often at the expense of the vigor and hardiness of the plant. This trend has been perpetuated by many Western breeders who have

Chrysanthemum arcticum 'Red Chimo'

Chrysanthemum ×koreana 'Painted Lady'

created a wide variety of hybrids (often listed in catalogs as *Chrysanthemum ×morifolium*) whose magnificent blossoms make them the ultimate florist's flowers, but which generally will not flourish outside a greenhouse. As a rule, the plants sold in bloom by retailers in the fall belong to this category and should be regarded as annuals. However, a handful of perceptive horticulturists have focused on developing garden-hardy types that integrate readily into beds and borders, and overwinter reliably outdoors throughout much of North America and elsewhere. Typically, plants of this category are available only by mail order.

Hardy chrysanthemums have the virtue of timeliness, bearing their flowers of golds, russets, oranges, reds, pinks, and white in late summer and fall when most other perennials are winding down. The foliage—typically rich green and deeply lobed—is attractive and, when well grown, chrysanthemums have a bushy form that makes them desirable garden elements even when not in flower. Although not long lived, hardy mums are easily propagated.

For best results, give garden chrysanthemums a spot with at least six hours of direct sun daily and a well-drained, organic-enriched soil. Because they are shallow rooted, chrysanthemums need regular irrigation during dry spells to keep the soil consistently moist—these plants will survive some drought but their bloom will be severely diminished. Avoid setting chrysanthemums near a strong night-time light source, including street lamps, as this can prevent them from setting flower buds.

An early to midspring planting is best, although container-grown hardy chrysanthemums can be planted successfully in early summer. To keep plants compact and maximize bloom, pinch off the tip of each shoot every two to three weeks from the time when new growth reaches 4–6 in. until

early June. Deadhead for neatness in warm regions, where the foliage will remain green into winter. In colder climates, leave the fading flowers and withering stems intact to provide winter protection. Cover dormant plants with a protective winter mulch, such as evergreen boughs, where winters are cold.

Hardy chrysanthemums combine well with other fall bloomers such as sedums, goldenrods, and Russian sage, and provide an attractive counterpoint to the russet fall foliage of ornamental grasses. Little troubled by pests aside from occasional visits from slugs and infestations of aphids and mites. Susceptible to a variety of diseases, but usually only when plants are stressed by an overly shady spot or poorly drained soil.

Divide established plants every third year in spring to renew their vigor. Propagate by stem cuttings taken from new growth in mid- to late spring.

Chrysanthemum arcticum

syn. *Arctanthemum arcticum*
  - white, pink
  - late summer
  - 10–16 in. × 12–24 in.
  - sun
  - Z4–9

Arctic daisy. Native throughout the northern parts of the Northern Hemisphere, including most of Canada and Alaska. Forms cushions of medium green leaves, wedge shaped, semi-pinnatifid with three to five lobes or teeth; daisy-like flowerheads with up to a diameter of 2 in. with yellow disk centers are solitary, but often borne in great profusion. Suitable for the border, rock garden, edging paths, or in mixed containers.

'Red Chimo' bears lavish crops of bright pink flowers. Continues to bloom even after light frost. Canadian bred.

Chrysanthemum ×koreana

- yellow, orange, pink, red, white
- late summer to late fall
- 30–36 in. × 36 in.
- sun, part shade
- Z4–9

Korean hybrids. Originals bred by Alex Cumming of Bristol Nurseries in Connecticut, from a plant collected in Korea, *Chrysanthemum zawadskii* var. *sibiricum*, which is also the principal parent of the rubellum hybrids. Korean hybrids were originally shorter and bushier than their ×*rubellum* relatives, with double, semi-double, or single, daisy-like flowers, although interbreeding has blurred the distinction.

NYBG Series. Bred at the New York Botanical Garden; large, single flowerheads in a range of colors. Excellent cut flowers. Selections include 'Painted Lady', 'Cambodian Queen', and 'Arizona Sunset'.

Chrysanthemum ×rubellum

- yellow, pink, red
- late summer to fall
- 24–36 in. high and wide
- sun, part shade
- Z5–9

Korean mum, rubellum hybrids. This is the other major group of hardy garden hybrids, bred in Britain during the late nineteenth and early twentieth centuries. Several excellent examples are still commercially available.

'Clara Curtis' has pink, single, daisy-like flowers, with a diameter of 3 in. More shade tolerant than most chrysanthemums. 18–24 in. × 18 in.

'Emperor of China' has double, rose-pink flowers in midfall; foliage turns mahogany-red as weather cools. 3–4 ft. × 1.5 ft. Z4–9.

'Mary Stoker' has single, apricot-yellow flowers in early fall. 24–30 in. × 16 in.

Chrysanthemum weyrichii

syn. *Dendranthema zawadskii*

- white, pink
- late summer to late fall
- 6–12 in. × 18–24 in.
- sun, part shade
- Z4–8

Miyabe. Native from northern Japan to Alaska. Mat forming with toothed leaves and single flowers with yellow centers to 2 in. across, borne on short stems. Equally at home in rock gardens or the front of borders.

'Pink Bomb' has pale pink flowers.

'White Bomb' has white flowers, dark green leaves, and purplish stems.

Chrysanthemum yezoense

syn. *Dendranthema arcticum* subsp. *maekawanum*

- white, purple
- early fall to late fall
- 3–8 in. × 2 ft.
- sun, part shade
- Z5–9

Groundcover chrysanthemum. Ground-hugging Japanese coastal native, spreads slowly by rhizomes to an indefinite width. Long-stalked, evergreen, lobed and toothed leaves. Abundant display of 2-in., white or purplish flowers. Drought tolerant; handsome additions to rock gardens or cascading down a bank.

Other Notable Cultivars

'Autumn Moon'. Abundant 2.75-in., single flowers of pale yellow touched with pink. Late fall. 18–24 in. Z4–9.

'Glowing Ember' bears prolific crops of 2.5-in., semi-double, red flowers edged with gold. Late fall. 22–24 in. Z4–9.

'Mei Kyo' has small, double, lavender blooms in late fall; doesn't require the regular division needed to reinvigorate many other chrysanthemums. 36 in. high and wide. Z4–9.

'Ruby Mound' has burgundy-centered, double, deep red flowers. 16–24 in. × 16 in. Z5–9.

'Sheffield Pink'. Loose sprays of large, yellow-eyed, pale, single, salmon-pink flowers. Early to midfall. 24–36 in. high and wide. Z5–9.

'Single Apricot Korean' bears 2.5-in., pale apricot-pink flowers. Midfall. 2–3 ft. × 2 ft. Z4–9.

Chrysogonum

Asteraceae
goldenstar

This low, mat-forming native contributes a shot of bright early spring color to woodland gardens. Easy to grow, it spreads by leafy runners that create patches 2–3 ft. or so across. The leaves, 1–2 in. long and oval, are notched along their margins and are covered with soft hairs. Evergreen in mild climates. The single, 1-in.-wide daisy flowerheads consist of five showy golden ray flowers surrounding a central cluster of brownish stamens. Bloom time is long, especially in cool regions, and may last into summer with sporadic repeat bloom when nights become cool. Goldenstars are valued in the garden as groundcovers, especially in shaded places; in cool climates they tolerate sunny spots too. Soil must be well drained; enrich with organic matter to retain moisture. Goldenstars mix well with early spring bulbs including squills and mini-daffodils, and are good companions for ferns, wild blue phlox, may apples, polemonium, bleeding hearts, and other woodlanders. Pests and diseases are few; deer are seldom a problem.

Divide in spring, or start from seed.

Chrysogonum virginianum 'Norman Singer's Form'

Chrysogonum virginianum

- yellow
- early spring to summer
- 6–12 in. × 12 in.
- sun, part shade, shade
- Z5–9

Goldenstar, green-and-gold, gold star. Rich woodlands and open shade from Pennsylvania to Mississippi and Florida. A variable species. The type makes a thicker groundcover, spreading by underground stems. Flower stems are often branched, and lift the flowers well above the mat of leaves. Bloom extends into summer, especially in cool climates. Several named but similar cultivars are available.

'Allen Bush', a dense, fast grower to 8 in. Excellent along shaded pathways and as a groundcover.

var. *australe* spreads quickly by long aboveground runners that root at their tips. Flowering stems and bloom time are shorter than those of the species and the leaves are darker and glossier. Native to the southern part of the species' range; may be more susceptible to cold, wet winters.

'Eco Lacquered Spider' has shiny purple-tinged foliage. Golden ray flowers are prominently notched or "pinked" at the tips. Rapid spreader by purplish runners that can reach 3–4 ft. annually. 4 in.

'Norman Singer's Form' ('Superstar') is excellent in dry, partly shaded conditions. 4–6 in.

'Pierre' is more clumping and tolerates dryer soil conditions.

'Quinn's Gold' produces yellow flowers that mature to light yellow and cream so that differently colored flowers decorate the plant at any one time.

'Springbrook' is the most compact cultivar. 5 in.

Chrysopsis

Asteraceae
golden aster

Got a dry, sunny spot beyond the reach of a hose? Golden asters are just the plants to fill it. These wonderful but underused plants are tough sun lovers that tolerate droughty conditions well and thrive on average or even poor soils, as long as they drain well.

The leaves of golden aster are borne alternately on stems crowned with clusters of bright yellow daisies, each about 1.5 in. across. Deadheading encourages further bloom. Cut down after hard frost but allow a few stems to self-seed and feed seed-eating birds. All species cited here are suitable for native plant, meadow, or wildlife gardens where they make good companions for purple and mauve asters, grasses, blazing stars, and other drought-tolerant wildflowers.

Nomenclature of this genus has been unsettled in recent years. Formerly classified as *Chrysopsis villosa*, hairy golden aster is now known as *Heterotheca villosa*. It grows to 5 ft. tall and is native to our western states; hardy in zones 3 to 8. Sickle-leaved golden aster, formerly known as *C. falcata*, is now classified as *Pityopsis falcata*. Native to coastal areas from Massachusetts to New Jersey, this last species doesn't exceed a height of 1 ft. and is hardy in Z5–9. Both are found in catalogs under their old names as well as the new, so be forewarned.

These taprooted plants are best propagated by seed in containers and transplanted to the garden as seedlings. They self-seed on hospitable sites.

Chrysopsis mariana

syn. *Heterotheca mariana*

- yellow
- midsummer to midfall
- 1–2 ft. × 1.5 ft.
- sun, part shade
- Z5–9

Maryland golden aster, broad-leaved golden aster, shaggy golden aster. Open spaces and rocky woods in dry sandy soils from New York to Ohio, and south to Texas and Florida. Mounding clumps of erect silky stems are clothed with alternate, 6-in.-long, shiny, spatula-shaped leaves on short petioles. Branched stems are topped with golden, 1-in. flowerheads that crowd into tight showy clusters. They continue to bloom throughout hot weather. This species is the most drought tolerant of the clan.

Cirsium

Astereaceae
plumed thistle

Gardeners are far more accustomed to eradicating members of this genus than planting them, for the plumed thistles include 200 species and such wide-ranging noxious weeds as the bull thistle

(*Cirsium vulgare*), native to Europe, Asia, and northern Africa, and the so-called Canada thistle (*C. arvense*), a native, despite its common name, of Europe and northern Asia. There is, however, a pair of *Cirsium* species that do make rewarding garden perennials. These attract butterflies and make striking cut flowers; seedheads provide food for finches and other seed-eating birds. Although their spiny foliage and stems makes plume thistles hard to handle even with gloves, you must protect them from deer and rabbits.

Propagate by seed, or by division of mature clumps in spring.

Cirsium occidentale

- crimson
- early to late spring
- 3–4 ft. × 2 ft.
- sun, part shade
- Z9–10

Cobweb thistle. Deserts, mountains, and valleys of California, into western Nevada, southern Oregon, and southwestern Idaho. White, spiny foliage and stems. The crimson thistle flowers perch on spiny, globular, white bases wrapped in a cobweb-like net of hairs. Drought tolerant; not invasive. This hummingbird favorite may self-seed sparingly.

Cirsium rivulare

- pink-purple
- early summer to early fall
- 36–48 in. × 18–24 in.
- sun
- Z4–9

Brook thistle. Native to southern and central Europe, available only as the cultivar 'Atropurpureum'. This statuesque selection bears densely packed, dark crimson flowers on upright, branched, leafless stems. The prickly leaves—narrow and jaggedly scalloped along the edges—form a new rosette each year, making a slowly spreading colony. Requires a consistently moist soil. For drama, partner with other purple-flowered perennials with a similar bloom time such as *Papaver orientale* 'Patty's Plum', or contrast it with *Pennisetum setaceum* 'Rubrum' or other red-hued grasses.

Claytonia
Montiaceae
spring beauty

Most spring beauties are native to North America, though they also range south into Central America and across the Bering Straits into northeast Asia. Indigenous peoples valued these plants for their starchy, chestnut-like corms and edible, succulent greens. Contemporary gardeners seldom grow them outside of native plant or wild gardens despite their lovely delicate blooms and vigorous trouble-free nature. Only two species, *Claytonia virginica* and *C. sibirica*, are in cultivation and no cultivars or selections of either are presently available in the nursery trade.

Both species are woodland natives that prefer an organic-rich, moist but well-drained soil. In a hospitable site, both will spread, eventually forming a solid, often extensive groundcover. But whereas *C. sibirica*'s coverage lasts through the gardening season, that of *C. virginica* is more seasonal; this species is a spring ephemeral and goes dormant with the onset of summer heat. This makes it unsuitable for formal displays in beds and borders, where the sudden disappearance of a groundcover leaves an obvious gap. *Claytonia sibirica*, however, is useful in such a setting, due to its adaptability in a wide range of exposures. In general, the fragile delicacy of spring beauties makes them best suited for woodland gardens, rock gardens, and meadows, where larger, bolder neighbors won't outshine them.

Propagate by seed sown in fall and overwintered outdoors in a cold frame or protected spot. Clumps of *C. virginica* may also be divided in spring after flowering is finished and before the plant retreats underground.

Claytonia sibirica
syn. *Montia sibirica*
- pink-and-white
- early to late spring
- 12–18 in. × 12 in.
- sun, part shade, shade
- Z4–10

Peppermint candy flower. West Coast from southern California, north through coastal Alaska.

Claytonia virginica

Short-lived perennial best adapted to shady sites, although it also flourishes in full sun if the soil remains consistently moist. Individual plants form rosettes of fleshy stems with broadly lanceolate leaves borne in opposing pairs. The five-petaled, candy-striped, pink-and-white flowers measure no more than 0.75 in. across but make up in quantity what they lack in size. Blooms over a long season, sporadically through summer and even into fall in temperate locations. Individual plants rarely survive more than three years but reseed freely, typically forming a self-perpetuating colony.

Claytonia virginica
- pink, white
- late winter to midspring

- 6–9 in. high and wide
- sun, part shade
- Z3–8

Spring beauty. Rich, moist woodlands, valleys, and prairies throughout the eastern half of North America, except Florida. Narrow, grass-like leaves usually grow in pairs; the star-shaped flowers have five pink-veined, white or light pink petals, and are borne atop slender, 4- to 6-in. stems, usually as soon as the weather moderates at winter's end. The foliage persists for some weeks past bloom time, but retreats back to the fleshy roots with the onset of hot weather.

Clematis heracleifolia

Performs best in a moist, rich soil. Reseeds and spreads vigorously, so best planted in a spot that can accommodate this trait and where it won't over-run herbaceous neighbors. It naturalizes well in a lawn combining well with other early-blooming bulbs, such as crocuses and squills, for a charming spring tapestry.

Clematis
Ranunculaceae
clematis

Mention clematis and most gardeners think of tall vines sporting large open flowers in bright jewel tones, or clouds of small, white blossoms enveloping arbors. But there are also several non-climbing, upright weavers or sprawling species that deserve a place among herbaceous perennials. The weavers bring a sense of random informality in otherwise orderly beds; the sprawlers, supported by small shrubs, pea sticks, or rustic tepees, provide height in midborder.

Clematis have opposite leaves that are generally compound and composed of several leaflets. Instead of petals, flowers have four or five petaloid (petal-like) sepals that surround a central cluster or boss of yellow or white stamens. Some produce interesting plumed fruits. In chilly climates clematis do best in sun, but where sun is more intense they prefer lightly shaded spots. Averse to drought, they require evenly moist, average to rich soil, ideally amended with compost, and should never dry out. Stake as necessary. Blooms are borne on new growth; prune hard in spring. Slugs may damage young foliage; deer are seldom a problem. Clematis wilt is not as widespread on the herbaceous species as on the vining types, but gardeners should watch for the symptoms.

Propagate by cuttings taken from new shoots emerging from the base of the plant in spring, or by seed sown outdoors in fall, or stratified and sown indoors in containers in spring. Dividing non-climbing clematis is possible but risky, and best accomplished in late winter or early spring while the plant is still dormant.

Clematis heracleifolia
- blue
- late summer
- 2–3 ft. × 4 ft.

- sun, part shade
- Z3–7

Tube clematis, shrubby clematis, bush clematis. China. Tubular, variably fragrant, light blue flowers about 0.5 in. long are borne in dense clusters at the stem tips and leaf axils and are quite showy. Tips of the sepals reflex backward as with hyacinths. Bloom is more abundant in full sun, but the roots need cool, evenly moist conditions; mulch in spring. Large, three-parted leaves, with a larger middle leaflet. Mostly upright and bushy; plants can be staked if preferred. Attracts bees and butterflies. Tolerates deer and the toxic roots of black walnut trees. Rabbits dine on the young growth. Plants are reportedly poisonous. Most named selections are actually hybrids with other species.

'Blue Mood' is best planted among low shrubs such as fothergilla, bush cinquefoil, and Russian sage for support. True blue flowers. Z5–9.

'China Purple' has clusters of small, violet-blue flowers. Prefers full sun. 2 ft. Z5–9.

'Mrs. Robert Brydon' (*Clematis tubulosa* × *C. virginiana*) is a hybrid with bold dark leaves and a multitude of hyacinth-like, pale blue flowers. Excellent as a groundcover to suppress weeds.

'Rosea' has fragrant, pink flowers similar to the species.

Clematis integrifolia

- blue
- summer
- 1.5–3 ft. × 4 ft.

- sun, part shade, shade
- Z3–8

Solitary clematis. Southern Europe. Solitary, 2-in., nodding, blue-lavender flowers, each with four twisted sepals borne at the tips of wiry stems; attractive heads of silvery seeds follow. Pairs of dark green, lance-shaped leaves sparsely clothe the stems. This sprawling species is excellent in beds and borders where it benefits from being staked with twiggy branches or pea sticks. In cottage and meadow gardens allow it to ramble through other plants. Stems are less robust in shaded sites. Hardy geraniums, meadow sages, ornamental onions, and coreopsis are good companions.

'Hendersonii', often listed as a cultivar of solitary clematis but in fact a hybrid (*Clematis integrifolia* × *C. viticella*), is larger flowered and indigo-blue. Long blooming.

'Rooguchi' is a lax climber with non-woody stems. Fleshy plum-colored bell flowers.

Clematis recta

- white
- late spring to summer
- 2–4 ft. × 2.5 ft.

- sun, part shade, shade
- Z3–9

Ground clematis. Native to southern Europe. Scrambling or more erect, with up to nine pointed, oval leaflets per leaf. Silvery seedheads follow frothy clouds of fragrant, 1-in., starry, white flowers borne in large clusters. Provide obelisks, tepees, or other structures for support or plant alongside low shrubs through which the plants can ramble. Ground clematis may be confused with similar but vining sweet autumn clematis (*Clematis terniflora*).

'Purpurea' displays bronzy purple foliage. Variable; select a well-colored form.

'Purpurea Select' has more intensely purple foliage; best in full sun.

Clematis tubulosa

syn. *C. tubulosa* var. *davidiana*, *C. heracleifolia* var. *davidiana*

- blue
- midsummer
- 4 ft. high and wide

- sun, part shade
- Z3–7

Tube clematis. Central and northern China. Dense clusters of very fragrant, open, violet flowers that bloom a little earlier than most clematis. Leaves are also fragrant.

'Wyevale' is clump forming with fragrant, reflexed, mid-blue flowers. Attractive fluffy seedheads follow. Some authorities consider this to be a hybrid; others, a selection of *Clematis heracleifolia*.

Clintonia
Liliaceae
clintonia

Native to rich woods of the eastern United States, clintonias (also known as "Clinton's lilies") are increasingly difficult to find in the wild and should never be collected for transfer to the garden—look for them at native plant nurseries. The genus is named after New York's Governor DeWitt Clinton, a key promoter of the Erie Canal and keen amateur naturalist.

Clematis integrifolia 'Rooguchi'

Clintonias do best in moisture-retaining, rich to average, acid, damp soil. Amend with plenty of compost or rotted leaves, and apply a mulch of rotted leaves in summer to moderate soil temperatures. These delightful natives thrive in woodland gardens.

Young growth is a magnet for slugs and snails. Rust can also be a problem.

Clean and sow fresh seed in containers in fall; overwinter in a cold frame. Divide established plants in spring; recovery and reestablishment may be tediously slow.

Clintonia borealis

- yellow
- spring to midsummer
- 9–15 in. × 12 in.
- part shade, shade
- Z2–7

Blue-bead-lily, dogberry, snakeberry. Woodlands of eastern North America. Rhizomatous; produces two to four glossy, slightly succulent, light green leaves, 4–12 in. in length, with a conspicuously depressed central vein. Leaves clasp the stem, and curve outward. Open, bell-shaped, six-petaled flowers, each 0.5–0.75 in. across and with prominent stamens like sparklers, are borne in umbels; somewhat drooping blooms are a delicate greenish yellow. Shiny blue berries follow. Very slow growing; protect from deer.

Clintonia umbellulata

- white
- midspring
- 9–12 in. × 12 in.
- part shade, shade
- Z4–7

Speckled wood lily, Clinton's lily. Mountains of New York to Ohio, south to Georgia and Tennessee. Foliage of this species is very similar to that of *Clintonia borealis*, although not quite as tall. Tiny, white, starry flowers, sometimes green and purple dotted, cluster atop scapes in rounded umbels of five to thirty blooms, 6–10 in. above the leaves. Round, black berries, appreciated by wildlife, follow. Deer reportedly ignore this plant, but it is prudent to take precautions anyway. Easier to cultivate than *C. borealis*.

Codonopsis
Campanulaceae
bonnet bellflower

Herbalists have used these Asian relatives of campanulas to treat everything from memory loss to hypertension, but in the garden it is the exquisite beauty of the bell-shaped blossoms that earns them a place. Display these plants where the fine detail of the flowers' interiors can be appreciated. However, keep them away from paths or steps as the oval to lanceolate leaves emit a strong odor when bruised.

Humus-rich, moisture-retentive soil and full sun or light shade are ideal for these plants. Mulch in late fall where winters are cold to keep the plants from breaking dormancy early; the soft new growth is vulnerable to sharp winds and late frosts. These are twining, sprawling plants that, when not cascading, show to best advantage staked with twiggy branches or pea sticks, or where they can clamber up through small shrubs. Slugs, snails, and rabbits relish codonopsis, though the strong-smelling foliage deters deer.

Propagate by seed sown in spring or fall.

Codonopsis clematidea

- blue
- late summer
- 2–3 ft. × 2 ft.
- sun, part shade
- Z4–9

Asian bellflower. Rocky slopes of eastern Asia. This pubescent, delicate-looking, sprawling semi-vine is splendid for trailing over rocks and walls, especially where the intricate markings within the pendent blossoms can be appreciated from a lower vantage. Milky white tinged with blue, the solitary, 1-in. bells are etched within with yellow, blue, and black. Branched stems bear alternate, pointed, gray-green leaves about 1 in. long. Easy to grow and deserving of wider usage. Kashmir bellflower (*Codonopsis ovata*) is similar but not as easy to grow.

Colocasia
Araceae
elephant ear

The flowers are modest, with the hooded spathe and spadix blossoms typical of members of the aroid family. But colocasia leaves live up to the common name: they can be every bit as large as an elephant's ear. Foliage colors include near-black purples and chartreuses as well as green, and variegations in a host of patterns with black, silver, and

Codonopsis clematidea

gold veining, marbling, and splashes. Shade tolerant and fast growing, elephant ears invite flamboyance, turning a container into a statement, or a shady border into a tropical fantasy.

Such assertive foliage overwhelms understated partners, so match colocasias with hot reds, oranges, and yellows. Indeed, hues that would seem lurid or extravagant in other surroundings look perfect in such an association. The orange- and green-striped leaves of canna 'Phasion', for instance, look only exotic, not gaudy, when stirred into a pot of green-leaved *Colocasia esculenta*. Likewise, a knot of white-flowered calla lilies makes a most elegant counterpoint to the black-leaved *C. esculenta* 'Black Magic'.

The stoloniferous or rhizomatous roots, or corms of elephant ears tolerate ordinary garden soils if well irrigated, but grow most vigorously in organic-rich, moist, even wet ones. They flourish in semi-shade and shade, but tolerate full sun (except in hot, dry regions) if their roots remain moist.

These tropical plants can be surprisingly cold tolerant; some cultivars are reported to overwinter outdoors in zones 7 or 6 if the crowns are buried a foot deep with shredded leaves after the first killing frost. Alternatively, dig roots and overwinter indoors in moist peat moss or perlite. Move container plantings into a sunny, frost-free spot such as a sunroom or conservatory; water sparingly.

Propagate by fresh seed sown on moist, soilless mix. Propagate named cultivars by division, by removing and replanting offsets from the corms, or from new clumps sprouted at the ends of stolons.

Colocasia esculenta 'Tea Cup'

Colocasia esculenta

- yellow
- summer
- 2.5–5 ft. high and wide
- sun, part shade, shade
- Z8–11

Taro. Native to southeast Asia but distributed globally as a starchy food crop and widely naturalized in tropical and subtropical regions; an invasive weed in Florida. Tiny, yellow flowers and heart-shaped leaves to 3.5 ft. long and 2.5 ft. wide. Many ornamental cultivars, some reputedly hardy in mild parts of zone 7.

var. *antiquorum* 'Illustris' is compact, to 30 in.; black leaves with contrasting green veins. Z7–10.

'Black Magic' bears dusky purple-black leaves to 2 ft. long.

'Mojito' has medium green leaves flecked with dark purple. Z7.

'Pineapple Princess' forms a low 3 × 5 ft. clump of 18-in., matte gray-lavender leaves, each highlighted by dramatic purple veins. Flowers have a fruity scent. Z7.

'Tea Cup' has upright, bright green leaves that curve into a teacup shape. Dark purple stems and leaf veins. To 6 ft.

Colocasia fallax

- yellow
- summer
- 18 in. × 24 in.
- sun, part shade, shade
- Z7–10

Taro, silver-leaf elephant ears. Thailand and Vietnam. Dwarf with green leaves accented by a central silver midrib radiating silver veins. Small, yellow spathe-and-spadix flowers borne all summer long. Spreads vigorously by short, aboveground stolons on moist soils. Winter hardy into the warmer portions of zone 7.

Colocasia gigantea

- white
- summer
- 8–10 ft. high and wide
- sun, part shade, shade
- Z7–10

Giant elephant ear. Available chiefly as the Thailand Giant strain, this southeast Asian species is fast growing, producing leaves that may reach 5 ft. long and 4 ft. wide. These are an attractive glaucous-gray. Unlike most colocasias, the flowers of this species, though not in scale with the leaves, are large, sweetly scented, and borne in clusters.

Commelina

Commelinaceae
day flower, widow's tears

This large genus includes some notable weeds, such as *Commelina benghalensis* that is included in the federal noxious weeds list, but also a few garden-worthy perennials, mostly useful as groundcovers for sunny or partly shaded areas. Day flowers may be tuberous or fibrous rooted and mostly hail from tropical and subtropical forests where they inhabit the forest floor. They are easily grown—in some cases too easily—in dry or moist soil. Propagate by seed sown in spring or division in spring.

Commelina tuberosa

syn. *C. coelestis*
- blue
- late summer to midfall
- 1.5 ft. high and wide
- sun
- Z8–11

Blue spiderwort, Mexican dayflower. Mexico. This tender perennial grows from tuberous roots that can be lifted and stored in cold winters; it may also be grown as an annual in cold-winter regions. The dark, clear blue of the 1-in. flowers is the main attraction and although each blossom lasts only a single day, the bloom period is long, continuing well into fall. Flowers are similar to those of related *Tradescantia* but feature two large petals and one smaller one. Clusters of buds emerge one at a time from a sheathing bract. Clumps of erect, rather succulent, jointed stems root at the nodes and carry shiny, 6- to 7-in., lance-shaped leaves. Valuable as a camouflage plant for dying bulb foliage, or to fill holes left by bleeding hearts or Oriental poppies that have died back. May seed about.

Conradina

Lamiaceae
wild rosemary

The aromatic wild rosemarys are principally natives of southern United States. They have been used as a substitute for true rosemary in cooking, but harvesting from wild plants is discouraged as all seven species of *Conradina* are rare and threatened or endangered in the wild. Instead, raise your own supply of these low, shrubby plants with juniper-like, evergreen, gray-green needles. The two-lipped flowers, in contrast, more resemble mints.

Provide wild rosemarys with a very free-draining, poor, sandy, acid soil; they will even grow in deep pure sand. Root rot may be a problem in heavier soils. Tolerates heat and humidity well. Shear back lightly after bloom time. Best planted or transplanted in spring and watered sparingly until established.

Propagate by seed, by softwood cuttings taken during the growing season, or by division of mature clumps in autumn.

Conradina canescens

Conradina canescens

- lavender
- midspring
- 1–2 ft. × 2 ft.
- sun
- Z7–10, HT

False rosemary, gray-leaved conradina. Pine barrens of coastal Alabama and Florida. Wiry, branching, upright stems clothed with whorls of fuzzy, rosemary-like leaves. Lavender flowers.

Conradina verticillata

- lavender
- summer
- 12–15 in. × 36 in.
- sun
- Z5–8, HT

Cumberland rosemary, wild rosemary. Sandbars along the Cumberland River and its tributaries in Kentucky and Tennessee. This low, bristly plant bears clusters of rosemary-like needle leaves on peeling reddish stems. Abundant displays of two-lipped, 0.5-in., lavender-pink flowers appear in summer, with the blossoms borne singly or in small clusters in the leaf axils. Lovely in containers, along a path or retaining wall, or in rock gardens where the fragrant foliage may be bruised by passersby.

'Snowflake' is white flowered. 'Cumberland Snow' is also white flowered, possibly identical.

Convallaria majalis 'Rosea'

Convolvulus sabatius

Convallaria

Asparagaceae
lily-of-the-valley

Cherished for its delicious perfume—"Muguet de Bois"—lily-of-the-valley is an old-fashioned flower that remains a fine, if somewhat invasive, garden plant. Its expansive tendencies can be a virtue, for it makes an outstanding groundcover in cool, shady gardens, where its dense system of rhizomes suppresses weeds efficiently. In milder regions this plant is not as aggressive and may even struggle to bloom well.

Best grown in partial or full shade, in moist, fertile, well-drained soil. In cooler zones, lily-of-the-valley tolerates full sun if given midday shade. Plant the roots about 0.75 in. below soil surface with growing tips (pips) sticking through. Deer resistant. All parts of the plant are poisonous to humans (some advise wearing gloves while handling), but for centuries it has been used as a medicinal herb to treat heart problems, and the flowers are collected for posies and for their fragrant oils.

Lily-of-the-valley is excellent under tall trees, in shrub borders, or in fragrance and cutting gardens. Combine with spring bulbs, ferns, hellebores, or bold-leaved hostas. Avoid pairing with coral bells or other plants that could be swamped by the aggressive roots. Grow in containers to force early bloom indoors.

Propagate by seed (plants produce pea-sized, orange-red berries after bloom) in spring, or divide the roots in fall.

Convallaria majalis

- white
- spring
- 8–12 in. × 24 in.

- sun, part shade, shade
- Z2–7

Lily-of-the-valley. Northern temperate regions worldwide. Creeping rhizomes produce pairs of smooth basal leaves to 8 in. long. These are broadly oval on short petioles. Bell-like, 0.25-in. flowers, each on a short stem, are arranged along one side of smooth, arching stems. The cultivars tend to be less invasive than the species.

'Albostriata' has foliage beautifully striped longitudinally with creamy white.

'Flore-Plena' ('Pleniflora') has double flowers that persist longer than usual.

'Fortin's Giant' is vigorous with wider leaves and large flowers.

'Hardwick Hall' has foliage rimmed with yellow.

'Rosea' has pale pink flowers.

Convolvulus

Convolvulaceae
morning glory, bindweed

This genus is commonly overshadowed by *Ipomoea*, a related genus of showy-flowered annual vines that are also called morning glories. More often than not, the only *Convolvulus* that gardeners are likely to recognize is field bindweed, *C. arvensis*, an aggressive, troublesome, and invasive vine of European origin. Three species of *Convolvulus*, however, perform as more mannerly—though short lived—perennials that thrive in the milder regions of the United States and elsewhere. All offer appealing flower and foliage effects. The funnel-form flowers attract hummingbirds and a variety of butterflies. *Convolvulus cneorum* and *C. sabatius* are notably drought tolerant, fine additions to xeriscapes or water-conserving gardens.

Propagate by seed (scarified and soaked in water overnight) sown in spring or by softwood cuttings of young growth taken in late spring to early summer. Morning glory seeds are toxic; take care not to ingest them.

Convolvulus cneorum

- white
- late spring to early fall
- 2–3 ft. × 2–4 ft.
- sun
- Z8–10, HS

Bush morning glory, silverbush. Limestone hills in southern Europe. A woody perennial or subshrub with evergreen, lanceolate leaves, 1–2.5 in. long and 0.5–0.75 in. wide, that are covered with silky, gray hairs. In a sunny spot and trimmed annually in early spring, this plant makes a handsome, dense, and silvery mound; in partially shaded locations, *Convolvulus cneorum* tends to sprawl. Pink buds open into 1-in.-wide, white trumpets, centered with yellow. Requires a well-drained soil, prefers an alkaline pH, and tolerates sandy, nutrient-poor ones. Thanks to its reflective foliage, this species tolerates considerable dry heat, but not high humidity. Bush morning glory works well in rock gardens, containers, in the foreground of xeriscape plantings, and other exposed locations. Appropriate drought-tolerant companions include agastaches, prairie zinnias, and succulents.

'Snow Angel' has pink-flushed, white flowers on compact plants. Z7.

Convolvulus sabatius

syn. *C. mauritanicus*

- blue
- spring to fall
- 6–12 in. × 18–36 in.
- sun, part shade
- Z8–10, HS

Blue rock bindweed, ground morning glory. Italy and northern Africa. This trailing plant bears small, rounded, light gray-green, hairy leaves and light blue, funnel-shaped flowers. Sometimes requires periodic irrigation in arid climates. Excellent for rock gardens or edging, it also works well spilling over the edge of containers, window boxes, and hanging baskets. Prefers well-drained soils, tolerates a range of pH. Prune back stem tips at the beginning of the growing season to encourage new growth and more abundant bloom.

'Moroccan Beauty' ('Blue Casbah') forms a low blanket of silvery foliage with lavender flowers. 1–3 in. × 12–14 in.

Convolvulus tricolor

- blue, white, yellow, pink
- early summer to early fall
- 10–14 in. × 12–18 in.
- sun
- Z9–11

Dwarf morning glory. Mediterranean native commonly grown as an annual but perennial in mild-winter regions. It quickly forms a mound of stalkless, oval to elliptic, matte green leaves that bears a wealth of funnel-shaped flowers to 2.5 in. across. The blossoms are, as the species name suggests, typically tricolored; the wild type has a circle of blue surrounding one of white and a central eye of yellow, but horticultural cultivars offer other colors as well. Thrives in a range of moderately fertile, well-drained soils. Tolerant of heat and dry weather, dwarf morning glory is a colorful groundcover for sunny banks and rock gardens, an abundant source of color spilling over a retaining wall, edging a mixed border, or in containers and hanging baskets. Short lived but self-sows.

Enchantment Series offers compact selections with flowers in shades of blue, pink, red, white, and yellow. 16 in. × 12 in.

Ensign Series is a seed strain that includes 'Blue Ensign' (indigo blue with a white band and yellow eye), 'Red Ensign' (carmine red, white band, yellow eye), 'Rose Ensign' (rings of light pink, darker pink, and white ring, with a yellow eye), and 'White Ensign' (with a yellow eye).

'Light Blue Flash' has flowers of sky blue, white, and yellow

Coreopsis
Asteraceae
tickseed

Despite its unappealing common name, this genus has become a perennial garden standby, an easy-to-grow group of plants that tolerates a range of soils and climates and bears colorful, showy daisy blossoms through a prolonged season of bloom. Heights vary considerably: some may reach 4 ft. tall and are useful for the back of a border or for interplanting with ornamental grasses; others are mounded and more compact at 18–30 in., ideal for midborder; still others top out at 12–15 in. tall and are perfect for containers or for edging. Most species are native to North America. They attract pollinating insects and butterflies and resist deer browsing. Most also tolerate dry soils and hot, sun-drenched sites, though in droughty situations irrigation helps to increase and prolong bloom.

Coreopsis flowers are daisy-like, 1.5–2.5 in. or more across, and are commonly colored in warm hues of yellow and red, though pinks and whites are increasingly available. The leaves are lance shaped, oval, or thread-like; the small, flat seeds do indeed resemble ticks.

Many of the species and older cultivars are relatively short lived, flourishing for just a few years before succumbing to old age. This, however, is less of a problem than it might seem, as tickseeds commonly self-sow in hospitable sites, providing their own replacements. Newer hybrids—of which there are a host—are generally less fertile and persist longer.

Full sun and well-drained soil are essential for most tickseeds, though some types tolerate partial shade. They partner well with other drought-tolerant sun lovers such as salvias, yarrows, and daylilies, and with other grassland natives including echinaceas, baptisias, and the shorter native warm-season grasses. Tickseeds are naturals for native plant and butterfly gardens, meadow plantings, and cottage gardens; they furnish outstanding cut flowers.

Stake taller types with cut brush or pea sticks to prevent sprawl, and deadhead fading flowers to prolong bloom. Cut stems back by half after the first flush of bloom to encourage rebloom. Be sparing with fertilizer; to maintain vigor divide mature plants every few years in spring as new growth begins. Tickseeds are susceptible to powdery mildew—in cooler climates where this might be a problem, choose resistant cultivars.

Propagate by seed, or division in spring, or by basal softwood cuttings.

Coreopsis auriculata

- yellow
- midspring to summer
- 12–36 in. high and wide
- sun, part shade
- Z4–9

Mouse-ear tickseed, lobed tickseed. Woodland edges and openings throughout the southeastern United States. This hardy, low-growing species bears small, hairy, lobed leaves in lush basal rosettes and along stems; in mild climates the foliage persists through most of the winter. The 1- to 2-in. flowers are bright yellow, and appear through early summer and then sparsely until frost.

'Nana' is dwarf, forming a mat of foliage with bright yellow flowers. 2–4 in.

'Snowberry' is more cold tolerant than the species. It has creamy-white flowers with burgundy-red centers. 32 in. × 24 in. Z3–8.

Coreopsis grandiflora

- yellow
- late spring to early fall
- 1–3 ft. × 2–3 ft.
- summer
- Z4–9, HT

Bigflower tickseed. Meadows, grasslands, and roadsides throughout eastern North America and in the south as far west as New Mexico, and California. A short-lived perennial that reseeds to provide its own replacements. Spatulate to lanceolate leaves; lower basal leaves are mostly entire, smaller stem leaves are often pinnately lobed. Flowers are

Coreopsis rosea 'Sweet Dreams' nestles among lamb's ears

Coreopsis grandiflora 'Early Sunrise'

solitary; deadheading is essential to prolong season of bloom and control prolific reseeding. Thrives in a range of well-drained soils, including poor, sandy, or rocky ones. Tolerant of heat, humidity, and drought; resistant to rabbits and deer.

'**Domino**' bears single, 2-in., yellow daisies with maroon centers. Comes true from seed.

'**Early Sunrise**' bears semi-double, 2-in.-wide, bright yellow flowers. 18–24 in. high and wide.

'**Sunray**' produces prolific crops of large, bright yellow, double and semi-double flowers on 18-in. plants. Hardy to zone 3.

Coreopsis lanceolata

- yellow
- midspring to early summer
- 1–2 ft. × 1.5–2 ft.
- sun
- Z4–9

Lanceleaf coreopsis. Longer lived but similar to the preceding species. Prairies, fields, and roadsides in central and southeastern United States; another

Coreopsis verticillata 'Moonbeam'

tough, drought- and heat-tolerant species that flourishes on poor and rocky, well-drained soils. The 1- to 2-in., composite flowers have eight petal-like rays, toothed at the tips, borne singly atop slender erect stems. Self-seeds prolifically and can be a nuisance in formal settings; reserve for wild, native, and meadow gardens where it forms large, showy colonies. Conscientious deadheading prolongs bloom time.

'**Baby Sun**' has golden-yellow blooms. To 1.5 ft.

'**Brown Eyes**' has golden daisies marked with maroon-brown centers. To 2 ft.

'**Double Sunburst**' has semi-double, golden-yellow flowers with prominent centers. Comes true from seed. To 1.5 ft.

'**Goldfink**' is compact, to 10 in.; single, golden-yellow blooms.

'**Sterntaler**' produces double, golden blooms marked with showy brown centers. 1–1.5 ft.

Coreopsis rosea

- pink
- early summer to early fall
- 1–2 ft. × 1.5–2.5 ft.
- sun
- Z3–8, HS

Pink tickseed. Nova Scotia to Maryland; requires a consistently moist but well-drained soil. This rhizomatous perennial forms dense, bushy clumps. Light green, grassy, linear leaves are borne in whorls, giving the plants an attractive, airy texture. Daisy-like, 0.5- to 1-in. flowers have toothless pink rays and yellow central disks. They are borne profusely and singly on short stalks for a lengthy bloom time. Does not tolerate heat and humidity well. Winter hardiness is sometimes a problem in cold-winter regions.

'**American Dream**' bears abundant 1-in., golden-centered pink flowers on compact 18-in. plants.

'**Heaven's Gate**' has yellow-centered, pink flowers with a purple eye.

'**Sweet Dreams**' bears yellow-centered, white flowers with a raspberry eye.

Coreopsis verticillata

- yellow
- late spring to late summer
- 1–3 ft. high and wide
- sun
- Z3–9

Threadleaf coreopsis, whorled tickseed. Eastern North America. Another heat- and drought-tolerant species that flourishes even on poor, rocky soils. The dark green, thread-like leaves provide a beautiful setting for bright yellow, daisy-like flowers borne singly in loose clusters. It spreads by rhizomes as well as seed and sometimes can be aggressive.

'**Moonbeam**' is compact, with creamy-yellow, golden-centered, 1- to 2-in. flowers. These are sterile, eliminating the threat of reseeding, thus making this cultivar a superior choice for borders and beds. Deadheading is tedious but extends bloom time. Demands full sun. To 2 ft.

'Zagreb' is more compact, to 12–15 in. high and wide, with 1- to 2-in.-wide, bright yellow, golden-centered flowers.

Other Notable Cultivars

'Autumn Blush'. Pastel yellow blossoms with wine-red eyes. 32 in. × 24 in. Z4–9.

The Big Bang Series are exciting hybrids, bred by Darrell Probst, featuring well-branched plants that bear striking flowers from early summer into fall. Excellent for containers and edging or at the front of a border. 'Cosmic Eye' has yellow flowers with a wine-colored ring surrounding the orange center. Compact at 12–15 in. × 12 in. 'Full Moon' bears single, 3-in.-wide, canary-yellow flowers with orange centers. Foliage is glossy green. 24–30 in. × 30 in. 'Galaxy' produces double, yellow flowers on compact plants to 12 in. high and wide. 'Redshift' displays yellow flowers with crimson eyes in summer, turning all red as weather cools in fall. 12 in. high and wide. 'Sienna Sunset' flowers have soft-orange petals streaked with yellow and orange centers. 16–20 in. × 12–24 in.

'Crème Brulée' is similar to 'Moonbeam' but more vigorous, with larger, deeper yellow inflorescences, and brighter green leaves. Resistant to powdery mildew.

Limerock Series are grown as annuals in colder regions but perennial in zones 8–10, where they tolerate heat and humidity well. Extraordinarily floriferous, covering mounds of ferny green foliage with a solid sheet of flowers from early summer to mid-fall. Exceptional for containers or edging. Prefers moist soil. 'Limerock Dream' bears apricot-pink flowers in spring, turning coppery-orange in mid-summer. 12–16 in. × 24–30 in. 'Limerock Passion' flowers are pinkish lavender. 16 in. × 30 in. 'Limerock Ruby' has 1.5-in.-wide, ruby-red flowers. 12 in. tall.

'Little Sundial' is dwarf with bright yellow blooms with maroon centers. 10 in. high and wide.

'Pinwheel' has light yellow, petal-like ray flowers, curled like the vanes of a pinwheel. Sterile, does not reseed. Blue-green, mounded foliage. 24 in. × 30 in.

'Tequilla Sunrise' blooms with orange-centered, yellow daisies above variegated yellow-and-green foliage. 12–16 in. high and wide. Z5–9.

Coreopsis 'Limerock Ruby'

Cornus
Cornaceae
dogwood

This genus is known for woody trees and shrubs, but one species deserves recognition as a perennial. Bunchberry, *Cornus canadensis*, is valuable as a groundcover in woodlands and other shaded situations where its dark lustrous foliage and charming spring floral display are cherished. It spreads gently by rhizomes, producing short twiggy stems that bear whorls of oval, 1-in. leaves at their tips. These may turn slightly reddish in fall before leaf drop. In late spring appear what seem to be pale, 1-in. flowers; actually, these are clusters of small, greenish flowers framed by a circle of four 0.5-in., pointed, white bracts. If pollinated, usually by solitary bees or bumblebees, the flowers give rise to clusters of green, pea-sized berries that turn bright red at maturity. These serve as food for birds, moose, deer, and other wildlife—hence the alternate common names, including crowberry, pigeonberry, and squirrelberry.

Propagate by seed sown outdoors in fall; germination takes two to three years. Or divide clumps in spring or fall.

Cornus canadensis

Cornus canadensis
- white
- late spring to summer
- 4–6 in. × 15–24 in.
- part shade, shade
- Z2–7

Bunchberry, creeping dogwood, crackerberry. Greenland into Canada and Alaska, and south to Indiana, West Virginia, and Colorado; also northern Asia. In the wild, bunchberry favors damp, acid soils in bogs, seepage banks, and woodlands. Difficult to grow in warm climates, but thrives in cool summers in part shade. May be slow to establish. Excellent in wildlife gardens or with compatible groundcovers including partridgeberry, dwarf blueberries, heaths, and vinca under acid-loving flowering shrubs.

Corydalis
Fumariaceae
fumewort

This genus was almost unknown in American nurseries until the latter part of the 20th century, but in the years since it has assumed a prominent place in our gardens. It deserves even wider planting. The generic name means "crested lark," a reference to their exquisite spurred flowers; these can illuminate partially shaded parts of the landscape with an invaluable burst of color. Note that two popular species formerly included in this genus, *Corydalis lutea* and *C. ochroleuca*, have recently been reassigned to their own genus, *Pseudofumaria*.

Corydalis roots are fleshy or tuberous, and their leaves are finely divided; depending on the species

Corydalis cheilanthifolia

they may be yellowish, bronzy, or light green, often infused with a bluish cast. Flowers are tubular and spurred, usually held in dainty loose clusters at the tips of succulent stems. Corydalis requires a consistently cool, moist soil high in organic matter; in cold climates mulch the plants well in winter. Most species excel in cool-summer regions, whereas few tolerate muggy heat and humidity in summer. Where they flourish, they make excellent companions for small bulbs, ferns, epimediums, lungworts, lilyturf, and other shade lovers in woodlands, along pathways, and in rock gardens. Deer resistant; tubers are sometimes dug and devoured by squirrels and chipmunks.

Propagate by seeds sown outdoors in fall or indoors with stratification followed by bottom heat (65–75°F).

Corydalis cheilanthifolia

- yellow
- spring
- 6–18 in. × 6–12 in.
- sun, part shade
- Z3–8, HS

Fernleaf corydalis. China. Very finely divided foliage, bronzy green with stronger bronze hue when young. Flower clusters held above the leaves and on separate stems. Fleshy rooted. Seeds about;

Corydalis flexuosa 'China Blue'

collect seed when ripe (black) and sow in place. Resents transplanting. Beautiful with early miniature narcissus.

Corydalis elata

- blue
- late spring to early summer
- 16 in. × 12 in.
- part shade
- Z6–8, HS

Blue corydalis, blue false bleeding heart. Sichuan Province, China. Cobalt-blue flowers appear after the foliage has emerged. This species is easier to grow and more heat tolerant than most *Corydalis flexuosa* selections, and not as prone to going dormant in summer heat.

Self-seeds once established. Be alert for rust, slugs, and aphids.

Corydalis flexuosa

- blue
- late spring to summer
- 12–15 in. × 12 in.
- part shade
- Z5–8, HS

Blue corydalis. Western Sichuan Province, China. Summer dormant growing from small bulbs. Light green foliage, sometimes flushed with purple, is twice divided into three. Long-spurred, bright blue flowers, white at the throat, crowd into terminal and axillary racemes. Humus-rich soil that drains freely is ideal.

'Blue Panda'. Spurred, elongated, light blue flowers, pinkish and yellow tipped at the mouth. Summer dormant but fall rebloom. 10 in.

'China Blue'. Fragrant, dark blue flowers, purple at the mouth. Often summer dormant; mulch to cool soil and retain moisture. 16 in.

'Père David' has clear blue flowers and divided leaves touched with red or purple. 12 in.

Corydalis solida

syn. *C. halleri*

- red-purple
- spring
- 6–12 in. × 8 in.
- part shade
- Z4–8

Purple corydalis, fumewort. Eastern Europe. Gray-green, ferny, 3-in. leaves emerge early in the spring from tuberous roots. Spikes of as many as 20 narrow-spurred, 1-in., tubular blossoms cluster at stem tips. After a brief bloom time the foliage yellows and disappears tidily.

'Beth Evans'. Very floriferous with pink flowers accented with white throats. Z6–8.

'George Baker' has red flowers. Z6–8.

Other Notable Cultivars

'Berry Exciting' is well named with its bright purple-red flowers set against golden leaves. Summer dormant. 10 in. Z5–9.

'Blackberry Wine' has lacy, bluish green foliage

and fragrant, deep maroon flowers from late spring to early summer. 10 in. Z5–8.

'Canary Feathers' has upright spikes of bright yellow flowers set against bluish foliage. Blooms in spring into summer and sporadically as the temperatures cool. Great in rock gardens or along woodland paths. 7–8 in. Z6–9.

Cosmos
Asteraceae
cosmos

Come spring you'll find six-packs of annual cosmos, *Cosmos bipinnatus* and *C. sulphureus*, in every garden center; much harder to obtain, but just as rewarding, are their perennial relatives. In fact, only two of the perennial cosmos species are available commercially: *C. atrosanguineus* and *C. peucedanifolius*.

Provide a humus-enriched, well-drained, moist soil in a sunny spot—cosmos tolerate part shade but bloom may suffer. These perennials are tuberous-rooted; in cold-winter regions where they are not hardy (both species are vulnerable to temperatures below 5°F), the tubers should be dug in fall and stored indoors over the winter. Replant outdoors when soil has warmed the following spring.

Cosmos atrosanguineus and yellow *Berlandiera*

The flowers of both perennial species resemble those of the more familiar annuals: they have rounds of petal-like ray flowers surrounding a plush central button of golden disk flowers. They also have the same airy aspect, with the daisies perched atop long, wiry stems. Their somewhat sprawling habit can be disciplined by staking, but still appears casual and charming. Better choices for a cottage garden than a formal border, they are also effective to lighten the aspect of a formal floral display. Outstanding as cut flowers.

Pests and diseases are seldom serious although aphids may attack overly lush or unhealthy plants. Protect from deer.

Propagation is by seed or division of established clumps.

Cosmos atrosanguineus
- maroon
- midsummer to early fall
- 2–3 ft. × 1–2 ft.
- sun, part shade
- Z7–10

Chocolate cosmos. Mexico. Bushy plants with dark green, compound leaves, pinnately divided into ovate to lance-shaped segments. Flowers measure 1.5 in. in diameter, and are borne atop slender stems; they smell of chocolate mixed with vanilla. Flowering is more prolific in older plants. The flower color makes a good counterpoint to silver-foliaged plants including wormwoods and lavenders, and is especially outstanding in containers. Butterflies are drawn to the flowers.

'Chocamocha' is compact. 12 in. high and wide.

Cosmos peucedanifolius
- pink
- late spring to early fall
- 24–30 in. × 18–24 in.
- sun, part shade
- Z7–10

Perennial cosmos. This South African species is new to the garden scene and still of limited availability. Plants may straggle the first year but fill in to make more shapely mounds thereafter. Deep green foliage is topped with unscented, pink flowers borne over a long season.

'Flamingo' has lavender flowers.

Crambe
Brassicaceae
colewort

These wild relatives of cabbages have varied uses (for example, the seeds of Abyssinian mustard, *Crambe abyssinica*, are pressed to yield a superfine industrial lubricant, used as a substitute for sperm whale oil), but only two species earn their keep as ornamentals. Colewort, *C. cordifolia*, was a common feature of Victorian landscapes, but its imposing size, which appealed to that expansive era, caused downsizing gardeners in the 20th century to reject the plant. The current generation of designers, however, is turning once again to this gigantic flower to play with the sense of scale in smaller plots. Meanwhile, less impetuous gardeners are rediscovering its more modestly proportioned relative, sea kale (*C. maritima*), growing it both for its traditional use as an edible green and now for its visual appeal. Both species offer bold foliage and clouds of honey-scented small, white flowers. They work well in beds and borders with other perennials and shrubs, and are alike in preferring a rich, well-irrigated, well-drained soil. Pollinators flock to them, especially the cabbage white butterfly (*Pieris rapae*), whose caterpillars devour brassica crops. Deer may make a meal of them also.

Propagation is by seed; these plants form deep taproots and should not be disturbed once they have become established in a site.

Crambe cordifolia

- white
- late spring to early summer
- 4–7 ft. × 2–3 ft.
- sun
- Z5–8

Colewort. Caucasus Mountains of eastern Europe. Colewort forms a 2- to 3-ft. basal mound of crisp, lobed, wrinkled green leaves, each of which may measure 12–14 in. across. From this rises a tall, sometimes head-high stem that bears what seems

to be a hovering cloud of minute, four-petaled, white flowers, giving the effect of gypsophila (baby's breath) on steroids. Staking is recommended, as is vigilance in protecting the foliage from slugs and caterpillars. A striking specimen or accent within the border, allow sufficient room to achieve full development. Best seen backed by dark evergreens or a wall or solid fence. Interesting among dark-leaved shrubs, including *Weigela* Wine and Roses ('Alexandra').

Crambe maritima

- white
- early to midsummer
- 24–36 in. × 24–30 in.
- sun
- Z4–9

Sea kale. Coastal areas of northern Europe. The mound of kale-like large, leathery, powder-blue, ruffled-edged leaves make this an outstanding foliage and textural plant. A secondary benefit is the large clusters of small, sweet-scented flowers that hover over the leaf-cushion during flowering season. Tolerates sandy soils and salt spray; an excellent plant for seaside gardens. Can be used as an edging, massed, or as a specimen plant in containers and borders. Edible.

Crepis
Asteraceae
hawk's beard

Athough not in the top rank of ornamental flowering perennials, the dandelion-like flowers of hawk's beard provide a welcome splash of color in cottage garden borders, raised beds, or rock gardens. They require average, moisture-retentive, well-drained soil, and are not fussy about soil pH. Easy to grow from seed.

Crambe cordifolia

Crepis incana

Crepis aurea
syn. *C. kitaibelli*
- orange
- summer to fall
- 6–12 in. × 12 in.
- part shade
- Z5–7

Golden hawk's beard. Mountain meadows of the European Alps, Italy, and the Balkans. Upright with rosettes of shiny oval leaves to 4 in. in length, shallowly lobed or undulate along the edges. Solitary, 1-in.-wide, orange or fiery reddish orange daisy flowerheads top stems covered with black and white hairs. Self-seeds readily, especially in gravel.

Crepis incana
- pink
- early to midsummer
- 10–12 in. × 12 in.
- sun
- Z5–7, HS

Pink dandelion, pink hawk's beard. Greece. Clump forming with grayish, dandelion-like leaves to 5 in. long. Clear pink to magenta flowerheads are borne on erect, branched stems. Seldom self-seeds. Lovely in rock gardens against gray rocks. Received the Award of Garden Merit from the Royal Horticultural Society.

Crocosmia
Iridaceae
montbretia, coppertips

"All the world's a stage," and a sense of timing is just as important in the garden as on Broadway. Crocosmias earn star billing by blooming precisely when the perennial gardener needs flowers most, from midsummer into fall when many other standbys are waning. Crocosmia inflorescences are spectacular, too: 4 to 20 funnel-shaped or tubular blossoms in brilliant shades of red, orange, or yellow are borne in sprays along the tip of a wand-like stem. The long, blade-like leaves are also attractive and add structure to a border.

Most of the crocosmias in the nursery trade are hybrids, often resulting from crosses of several species. This diverse heritage makes them exceptionally adaptable. They thrive in well-drained, organic-enriched, moisture-retentive soil, but thanks to their cormous roots, crocosmias are able to withstand substantial drought. Hardy to zone 6, or in some instances to zone 5, especially when protected with a winter mulch. In colder regions, lift the corms after first frost and store over winter as for gladiolus.

Crocosmia 'Lucifer'

Crocosmia 'Bright Eyes'

Crocosmia aurea
- yellow, orange-red
- early to late summer
- 24–36 in. × 6–12 in.
- sun, part shade
- Z6–9

Falling stars, montbretia. Forests and river banks in South Africa. Spreads by stolons from corms, forming colonies in hospitable sites. Downward-facing flowers, to 1.5 in. in diameter, are carried on branched stems, as many as ten to a spike. These are followed by seedpods that take on an orange hue as they ripen, then split to reveal shiny black seeds with a bright orange covering. Cold sensitive; provide winter protection in cool-winter zones.

Crocosmia masoniorum
- orange
- mid- to late summer
- 24–36 in. × 4–18 in.
- sun
- Z6–10

South Africa. Frequently misspelled as "masonorum" in the nursery trade. Upfacing, brilliant orange or orange-red flowers, borne in profusion, 12 to 30 per stem. Proliferates rapidly and may even become invasive in hospitable sites.

Other Notable Cultivars
'Bright Eyes' ('Walbreyes') is compact, to 20 in., with red-eyed, orange blossoms. Z6–9.

'Emberglow' bears burnt orange-red flowers on 40-in. stems. Z5.

'Emily McKenzie' ('Lady McKenzie') carries large, maroon-splotched, orange blooms on 30-in. stems. Z6.

'Golden Fleece' ('George Davison', 'Citronella') is an heirloom from 1902. Small, lemon-colored flowers on 2- to 2.5-ft. stems. Z5–9.

'Little Redhead' ('Walrhead') is compact, to 20 in., bearing tomato-red flowers with yellow throats. Z6–9.

'Lucifer'. This popular hybrid has intense glowing scarlet-red flowers. 2–4 ft. × 18 in. Z5–9.

Crocosmias prefer full sun, except in hot climates where they appreciate partial shade. Bloom becomes less abundant as clumps become crowded, but division restores plants to vigor.

Most visually effective when planted in multiples, crocosmias are outstanding for summer beds and borders as well as among shrubs, and in meadows with grasses and wildflowers. In informal areas, especially close to water, they are spectacular combined with bold-leaved ligularias, large-leaved hostas, and tall ferns. They also make fine container plantings, perhaps with tall floss flower, bluebeard, or mountain mint. Enjoy them indoors as a source of elegant, eye-catching cut flowers.

Deer resistant, attracts hummingbirds. Spider mites may damage foliage and impair flowering unless controlled. Some of the most vigorous hybrids, which are sometimes called montbretias, have proven invasive in areas of the US Pacific Northwest.

Propagate by dividing older congested clumps in spring before growth commences. Offsets sprout at the base of the main corms; remove and replant to further increase stock. Species may be started from seed sown indoors in a warm location in late winter.

Cyclamen
Primulaceae
cyclamen

The most familiar of the cyclamens is *Cyclamen persicum*, the Persian, florist's, or greenhouse cyclamen that is often forced into flower for the holiday season and sold by the millions as decorative houseplants or to be planted out in frost-free areas. They have been hybridized extensively for compact growth, attractively marked foliage, diminutive size, jewel colors, and more attributes. However, as beautiful as they are with their attractive heart-shaped foliage and brightly colored, swept-back petals, few succeed outdoors year-round in colder gardens. Fortunately, the same beauty is also found in hardier species that also hail from the eastern Mediterranean.

Cyclamen coum

Cyclamen cilicum
- white, pink
- fall
- 2–3 in. × 6–8 in.
- sun, part shade
- Z6–9

Hardy cyclamen. Evergreen woodlands of the mountains of southern Turkey. Pale pink to rosy flowers blotched with purple on the nose. Deep green, rounded or heart-shaped leaves, boldly marked with silver, appear with or just after the flower buds in fall. Bloom lasts for several weeks; the foliage persists into spring. There is a white-flowered form. Add composted pine needles to the soil to raise acidity and increase drainage. Excellent in dry shade under deciduous trees and shrubs. Good for containers.

Cyclamen coum
- white, pink
- winter to early summer
- 2–3 in. × 6–8 in.
- part shade, shade
- Z4–9

Western Black Sea coast of Bulgaria, east to Iran, Turkey, Lebanon, and Israel. Rounded, deep green leaves patterned with silver, or plain but lustrous. After the leaves have appeared, flowers bloom in several shades of pink, rimmed with white at the snout and stained purple red. Provide a site with diffuse light, especially under tall deciduous trees where soil is humus rich and moisture retentive but not waterlogged. Tolerates drought well. Plant tubers shallowly, slightly above soil level; appreciates a winter mulch in cold regions. Sometimes catalogs separate clones with different leaf markings into groups such as the "Pewter Group."

'Album' (f. *albissimum*) has white flowers marked with carmine at the nose.

'Silver Leaf' bears exquisite heart-shaped, silvery leaves with a dark green center.

Cyclamen hederifolium
syn. *C. hederifolium* 'Rosenteppich', *C. neapolitanum*
- white, pink
- late summer to early fall
- 4–5 in. × 6–8 in.
- sun, part shade, shade
- Z4–8

Ivy-leaved cyclamen grows wild from southern France to the Balkans, and along the northern Mediterranean and Aegean Sea to western Turkey. The hardiest species, it does best in soil generously enriched with humus to improve soil tilth and moisture retention. Mulch in summer, and in regions with intense sunlight protect from midday rays. Excellent under high deciduous trees, where a colony may increase and thrive for many years; in time, the tubers may grow to 3 in. or more across. Nodding flowers and foliage appear at the same time, or the pointed flower buds may precede the foliage that then persists through the winter

Cyclamen grow from corm-like tubers that gradually expand with age. From these emerge plain or variously silver-marked, rounded or heart-shaped leaves borne on succulent stems, above which rise swept-back flowers in reds, pinks, and white, mostly blotched at the nose with deep red. Cyclamens grow best in a slightly alkaline, well-drained soil. They go dormant after blooming and should then be allowed to rest; ideally, keep the soil barely damp. All parts of the plants are mildly toxic if ingested, but are still acceptable to browsing deer. Sometimes known as sow bread, alluding to the fact that pigs root for the tubers in the wild.

If flowers are pollinated, seed capsules develop at the tips of spiraling stems and split when seed is mature. Sow as soon as ripe. Protect seedlings and young plants from digging squirrels.

months into the following spring. Gray-green leaf blades are usually marked with purplish silver, and held at an angle on long pedicels (stalks). Plant the tubers as soon as you receive them, less than 1 in. deep. Plants are very variable. Suitable for container culture.

'**Album**' ('Perlenteppich') has all-white flowers.

Cyclamen purpurascens
syn. *C. europaeum*
- red, purple
- summer to fall
- 4–5 in. × 6–8 in.
- part shade, shade
- Z5–9

Purple cyclamen. Central and southern Europe. This woodlander is happy in alkaline soil amended with plenty of composted leaf mold; less tolerant of summer drought than some other species. The dark reddish purple flowers are fragrant and start to bloom at the same time as the leaves emerge in mid- to late summer and into early fall. The foliage remains evergreen, sometimes for ten or so months. Not a great seed producer, except in very favorable conditions. A sugary coating envelops the seed coat to attract ants that serve as seed disseminators.

Cynara
Asteraceae
cardoon, artichoke

Only one species of this Old World genus finds a place in our gardens. It is most familiar in the form of subspecies *Cynara cardunculus* subsp. *flavescens*, the edible artichoke; unfortunately, relatively few gardeners know of the species itself, the highly ornamental, easily grown, and edible cardoon, *C. cardunculus*.

Propagate by seed, by the division of mature plants in spring, or by root cuttings taken in winter.

Cynara cardunculus
- purple, lavender
- late spring to early summer
- 3–6 ft. × 1–3 ft.
- sun
- Z7–9

Cardoon, artichoke thistle. Native to the lands surrounding the western and central Mediterranean, this plant has the appearance of a huge, spectacular, and unexpectedly elegant thistle. The foliage and form are bold, forming a highly sculptural, vase-shaped fountain of arching leaves, upright stems, and, in season, stately flowers. Lower leaves may measure 3 ft. long (this size decreases as the leaves ascend the stems), silver-gray on top, white and felted with hairs below, deeply lobed, and spiny. The 2- to 3-in. flowers, borne on branching gray stems, are composed of dense, symmetrical tufts of violet-purple filaments set into prickly spined, cup-shaped, purplish bases.

Cardoon requires a sunny site and well-drained soil. Though it prefers a rich soil, it tolerates poor

Cynara cardunculus in flower

ones and has escaped from the garden to become a troublesome weed in areas of California and the semi-arid West. At the northern end of its range (zone 7) it performs best in a sheltered site; a good subject for seaside gardens. A natural for xeriscapes or low-water gardens, cardoon's silvery foliage provides an attractive complement to shrubs or flowering plants with red or bronze foliage; try it with *Weigela* Wine and Roses ('Alexandra') or purple smokebush. It's blue-violet flowers harmonize well with other blues such as lungworts, monkshoods, and delphiniums, or make a stunning "color echo" combination with purple alliums. Its strong, sculptural form helps to create architectural and visual definition in a sunny border. It also makes a striking container planting and the flowers, when cut and dried, are outstanding in dried arrangements.

Normally trouble free, cardoons may be subject to root rot in moist climates in less than well-drained soils, and are also susceptible to slugs and aphids.

Cynoglossum
Boraginaceae
hound's tongue

True, vivid blue is a color rarely found in flowers and thus is much sought after by gardeners;

this makes hound's tongues real finds. Not all are suitable for perennial gardens; although attractive, *Cynoglossum amabile* is biennial, and common hound's tongue, *C. officinale*, whose burr-like seed clusters snag onto clothing and animal fur, is an unwelcome invasive weed. However, there is one species, described here, that is a well-behaved and desirable perennial.

Hound's tongues are rather coarse plants with bristly leaves and curled sprays of tubular forget-me-not flowers clustered like a scorpion. These expand and continue to bloom over several months. Provide a sunny or partly shaded spot where the soil remains moist but not waterlogged; it need not be too rich.

Propagate by seed sown in spring or fall or by division in spring.

Cynoglossum nervosum
- blue
- late spring to summer
- 18–24 in. × 24 in.
- sun, part shade
- Z5–8

Hairy hound's tongue. Himalayas. This is an upright, branched grower with a rosette of prominently veined, slender basal leaves. Cymes of brilliant blue flowers, each about 0.5 in. across, bloom over several weeks. Protect from intense southern sun; withhold fertilizer to avoid floppy growth, but do not allow dry out.

Other Notable Cultivars
Wild comfrey (*Cynoglossum virginianum*), a North American native, has very bristly stems and pale blue flowers over a shorter season. 1–2 ft. tall.

Cypripedium
Orchidaceae
ladyslipper orchids

This genus defies the common conception of orchids as tree-dwelling, tropical plants; ladyslipper orchids are not only ground dwelling, but many are remarkably cold hardy, with one species, *Cypripedium guttatum*, flourishing on the Alaskan tundra. A total of 11 species are native to North America.

Cypripediums have long, pubescent, pleated, green leaves; the flowers, either solitary or borne in sparse terminal racemes, have three sepals (the lower two often joined), two petals, and an inflated, pouched (slipper-like) lip. These are slow-growing plants, with some species requiring a decade or more to progress from seed to flowering age in the wild. In addition, some cypripediums, notably the pink ladyslipper (*C. acaule*), are extremely difficult to maintain in cultivation. Fortunately, several species adapt well to cultivation, and a host of new hybrids are more vigorous and tolerant than their wild parents.

If you decide to try your hand at these connoisseurs' flowers, *be sure* that the plants you purchase have been nursery propagated and grown—the

Silvery gray–leaved *Cynara cardunculus* shows off surrounded by *Nolina* and *Lorapetalum*

commercial collecting of cypripediums from the wild has had a disastrous impact on wild populations. One clue to a nursery-propagated plant is the price, which is typically substantial; bargain ladyslippers are almost certainly collected from the wild and seldom fare well in gardens. When they find a situation they like, cypripediums self-seed or spread by stolons to form large colonies. Gardeners, however, are far more likely to experience them as shy and solitary jewels to be displayed in a semi-shaded spot in woodland gardens among slower-growing ferns, epimediums, or, in the case of hybrids, among dwarf hostas. The preferences of the various species differ slightly, but generally a loose, well-drained, moist, organic-rich soil is adequate. A site that receives two to three hours of direct sunlight early or late in the day, with dappled light otherwise, is ideal. Do not dig in new plants; instead, stretch the roots out horizontally over the surface of the prepared soil and then cover with a thin layer of compost and a mulch of shredded leaves or conifer needles. Water attentively so that soil does not dry out, especially during the first growing season.

Propagate by division; seed propagation is best left to the experts and is very slow.

Cypripedium calceolus

- yellow-and-maroon
- part shade
- mid- to late spring
- Z3–8
- 9–30 in. × 12 in.

Yellow ladyslipper. Open woods with moist, calcareous soils across Europe and through Asia. Prefers neutral to mildly alkaline soil (pH 6.5–7.5). Pleated leaves to 8 in. long; large, yellow, slightly fragrant flowers are borne one or two to a stem. This is the easiest cypripedium to grow in the garden, succeeding on most neutral to slightly acid loams.

Cypripedium candidum

- white
- sun, part shade
- midspring
- Z3–6
- 4–14 in. × 9–12 in.

White ladyslipper, prairie ladyslipper. Moist grasslands and meadows in northeastern and north-central North America. More sun tolerant than other ladyslippers, this species prefers neutral to slightly alkaline (pH 6.6–8.5), consistently moist soils. Two to four pleated green leaves, to 2.5 in. wide and 6 in. long, are borne on the upper halves of stout, upright stems. Solitary flowers may reach 1 in. long with a white pouch and greenish yellow sepals and petals.

Cypripedium parviflorum

- yellow
- 12–24 in. × 9–12 in.
- midspring to early summer
- part shade
- Z4–7

Small yellow ladyslipper. Deciduous and hemlock woodlands from Alabama to Nebraska, and east to Massachusetts and North Carolina. Bears four to seven ovate leaves, 8 in. × 4 in., and one or two 1.5-in. flowers; pouch is dark yellow, sepals and petals are maroon or streaked with maroon. Prefers neutral to slightly acid (pH 6.0–7.0), consistently moist soils.

var. *pubescens* (greater yellow ladyslipper) is found in moist deciduous woods and swamps throughout North America, except in California, Oregon, and Nevada. It differs from the type by having flowers to 2.25 in. long and green sepals and petals streaked with maroon. This species is one of easiest cypripediums to transplant and establish. Z3–8.

Cypripedium reginae

- white-and-pink
- part shade
- early summer
- Z3–7
- 2–2.5 ft. × 1 ft.

Showy ladyslipper. Eastern and central North America. Clusters of sturdy, hairy stems bear one to two flowers each; 2- to 3-in. blossoms have white petals and sepals, deep rose pouch. Prefers neutral to slightly acid, consistently moist soil. One of the most spectacular species of the genus.

Other Notable Cultivars

There are numerous hybrids, and in general these are easier to grow than the species:

'Aki' has large, plum- to pink-striped flowers with twisted, pinkish sepals. 18 in. Z4–7.

'Gisela' bears flowers with a creamy-yellow pouch streaked with burgundy and backed by three large, dark burgundy sepals. 15 in. Z4–7.

'Hank Small' displays flowers with a deep yellow pouch backed by long, twisted, cinnamon-colored sepals. 18 in. Z4–7.

Cypripedium parviflorum var. *pubescens*

'Inge' flowers have a large, ivory pouch set against twisted, amber-purple sepals. Vigorous and fast growing. 16 in. Z4–7.

'Ulla Silkens' is vigorous and floriferous. A mature clump may bear 100 large burgundy and white slippers, each backed by three large, pure white sepals. 2 ft. Z3–7.

Dactylorhiza
Orchidaceae
marsh orchid

These wonderful tuberous terrestrial orchids deserve a broader use in North America; even the most modest European gardens frequently display a striking patch or two. Healthy specimens of marsh orchids produce spikes of as many as 60 or more bird-like, two-lipped flowers in dense, 6-in. racemes, with vibrant colors ranging from pink, lilac, purple, to white with contrasting spots on the lip.

A rich source of color for partly shaded woodlands, rock gardens, and meadows, marsh orchids prefer a damp but not waterlogged soil that is deep and rich in humus.

Flattened, finger-like tubers give rise to slender, lance-shaped leaves, usually mid-green and often covered with dark spots. Each tuber grows for a year and then is replaced by a new tuber sprouting from its tip. Plant in fall; a summertime topdressing of organic matter encourages marsh orchids to spread. Although these plants aren't the easiest to grow, the rewards for success are great.

Marsh orchid tubers resent disturbance, but may be divided in spring. Alternatively, sow seed in containers of soil obtained from a site where these plants are already growing—a symbiotic fungus must be present for the seeds to germinate.

Dactylorhiza foliosa
syn. *D. maderensis, Orchis maderensis*
- purple
- summer
- 1–2 ft. × 1 ft.
- part shade
- Z7–8

Madeiran marsh orchid. Madeira. Lustrous, broadly lance-shaped leaves, generally without spots. Bloom spikes may reach 6 in. long, crowded with intense purple flowers, with contrasting speckles on the lip. Perhaps the easiest species to grow. Broad-leaved or western marsh orchid (*Dactylorhiza majalis*) from western and central Europe is similar but blooms somewhat earlier with foliage usually heavily marked with chocolate-purple.

Dactylorhiza praetermissa
syn. *Orchis praetermissa*
- purple
- early summer
- 8–26 in. × 12 in.
- part shade
- Z6–8

Southern marsh orchid. Northern Europe. Robust spikes of light purple flowers, each daintily marked with darker purple on the lip. Leaves may be spotted as well but not always. Similar Algerian Marsh orchid (*Dactylorhiza elata*) produces its cylindrical blooms a little later. The spikes are robust and closely set with 0.75-in. flowers. Unmarked leaves.

Darmera
Saxifragaceae
umbrella plant

Another genus with but one species, *Darmera* offers a more-compact but visually stimulating alternative to giant-leaved *Gunnera*. Ideal for smaller gardens.

Spring blooms of *Darmera peltata*

Dactylorhiza foliosa

Propagate by seed sown in spring or fall or by division in spring.

Darmera peltata
syn. *Peltiphyllum peltatum*
- pink, white
- early to midspring
- 2–4 ft. × 3–4 ft.
- sun, part shade, shade
- Z5–9, HS

Umbrella plant. Streamsides in mountain wood-lands of southwestern Oregon and northern California. The five-petaled, white to bright pink flowers emerge in spring before the leaves, and are borne in spherical cymes or flat-topped clusters atop tall, bristly, branching stems that sprout from the rhizomatous roots. Becoming dense and matted, the roots provide effective erosion control on wet soils. The parasol-like, peltate leaves, lobed along the edges, measure 10–12 in. across, forming lush, dark green mounds that turn a spectacular shade of red in fall. Umbrella plant tolerates full sun when rooted in consistently damp soil but is more at home in partial shade. It makes a strong statement in water-side plantings or bog and rain gardens. Prefers cool summers and dislikes the combination of heat and humidity. Generally trouble free, but leaves may scorch if plants are subjected to drought. Deer resistant.

Propagation is by division, but the tough clumps are not for the fainthearted. Once established, they are difficult to eradicate.

'Nana' is a dwarf form that seldom tops 18 in. tall.

Delosperma
Aizoaceae
ice plant

These southern African succulent plants are easy to grow, requiring little care, and provide a convenient as well as attractive solution for troublesome hot and droughty areas of the landscape. They are also promiscuous: there are 100 or so species and they interbreed freely in the wild, causing considerable debate among botanists trying to sort out the ice plant family tree.

Ice plants provide vivid splashes of color in the landscape and their mats of jellybean-like foliage are often seen blanketing steep banks and hillsides beside highways where they generally flourish with-out any care. They actually prefer rocky, average to poor soil, as long as it drains well. The drainage is non-negotiable: ice plants will surely die in their first winter if planted in waterlogged clay or any other soil that remains persistently wet. Even where the drainage is good, a gravel topdressing or mulch is beneficial to facilitate water runoff around the crowns of the plants.

Although ice plants tolerate partial shade, their bloom is most abundant when grown in full sun. Partner them with other succulents such as sedums, sempervivums, opuntias, crassulas, and

Darmera peltata foliage

Delosperma cooperi

red hot poker aloes in crevices between rocks, in raised beds, on dry, nutrient-poor banks, or containers. Deer resistant.

Propagate from seed at about 70°F, or take stem cuttings in spring or summer. Increase cultivars vegetatively.

Delosperma cooperi

syn. *Mesembryanthemum cooperi*

· magenta	· 3–5 in. × 24–36 in.
· early summer to late fall	· sun, part shade
	· Z5–9, HS

Hardy ice plant, Cooper's ice plant, trailing ice plant. Native to rocky slopes of central southern Africa, hardy ice plants are adapted to very well-drained but average soils. This fleshy creeper has cylindrical, light green leaves 1–2 in. long; these may become red in cold temperatures. Showy solitary, daisy-like, 2-in., hot-pink flowers with white anthers cover the plants all summer until frost. Very tolerant of drought, and invaluable in xeric gardens; excellent as a groundcover on difficult dry, sunny banks, as well as being well suited to rock gardens, containers, and raised beds. Fast growing and considered an exotic invasive in some areas. Melts out in the humidity of the southeast United States, but excellent in coastal gardens.

Delosperma dyeri

· orange, coral	· sun
· spring to fall	· Z5–9
· 2–3 in. × 18–20 in.	

Red mountain ice plant. Native to the mountains of South Africa's Eastern Cape. A prolific bloomer, red mountain ice plant covers itself with shiny, white-eyed, coral- and watermelon-red starry flowers for a period of several months. Provide a sunny spot with very free drainage. Drought tolerant. Especially handsome in rock or raised gardens.

'Psdold' has scarlet flowers. 2007 Plant Select winner.

Delosperma nubigenum

· yellow	· sun
· spring	· Z6–9
· 4 in. × 24 in.	

Yellow ice plant. Found at high altitudes of the Lesotho Mountains of South Africa, this species tolerates more humidity than most. Low, succulent, evergreen mats of pointed, oval, bright green leaves that become watery green (like green grapes) in winter, sometimes tinged with red. They thrive in poor, rocky soil with little water, so are excellent for dry and even xeric gardens as ground cover, on walls, as edgings, or in rock gardens. Do not irrigate. In spring these easy-to-grow plants are covered with bright yellow, orange-eyed daisies that attract butterflies.

'Basutoland' produces masses of bright yellow flowers in late spring into summer. Oval, lettuce-green leaves. Tolerates bright shade as well as sun. Great for raised beds and containers. 2–4 in. Z5–9

Other Notable Cultivars

'Beaufort West' sports small, light pink daisies above cushions of fat, succulent, 1-in. leaves. Z5–7, HS.

'Eye Candy' belongs to a group of smaller-flowered, white-eyed ice plants bred in Japan. Carmine-red flowers, maturing to orange. Spring blooming. Z5–7, HS.

'Fire Spinner' is exceptionally hardy with white-eyed, brilliant orange-and-magenta flowers, 1.5 in. across. Plant Select winner in 2012. Z5–8.

'John Proffitt' (Table Mountain) is considered superior to similar *Delosperma cooperi*. Long-blooming, glistening, bright magenta daisies. Plant Select winner in 2002. Z6–8.

'Kelaidis' (Mesa Verde). Another Plant Select winner in 2002. Salmon-pink daisy flowers on compact plants from spring to fall. Tolerates light shade. Z4–8.

'Pink Ribbon' is bicolored pink-and-orange. All summer bloom. Z5–11.

Delphinium

Ranunculaceae
larkspur

The hybrid delphiniums that are cultivated to such perfection in English mixed borders, with their head-high, regal spires of vividly colored blossoms, are rightfully iconic. However, they are also finicky plants that in the United States perform well only in such cool, moist regions as the Pacific Northwest or coastal New England, and even there require plenty of nurturing. This has led too many American gardeners to dismiss delphiniums out of hand. In fact, this remarkably diverse genus offers hardy species adapted to almost every region of our country. Indeed, many are native to this continent. Additionally, in recent years breeders have introduced new strains of hybrids that offer many of the assets of their English relatives, but combine them with a more vigorous, self-sufficient constitution.

Few perennials are as effective as delphiniums in providing a vertical accent in beds or borders. Although the pattern of growth varies somewhat with the species, delphiniums typically produce clusters of upright, sometimes branching stems, crowned in season with flowers borne in spikes or racemes, sometimes in panicles. Each flower consists of five petal-like sepals surrounding a "bee" of two to four smaller true petals at the center, and commonly with a spur projecting from the back. Although blue is the color associated with delphinium flowers in the popular imagination, delphinium blossoms include pigments for red and yellow as well; depending upon the balance of pigments, flowers can range from pale cerulean to deep blues and violets to pinks, reds, yellows, and white. Delphinium leaves may be basal or alternate on the stem, and are palmately lobed or divided.

Delphiniums prefer a well-drained, humus-rich soil and thrive in full sun to light shade. Recommended care includes regular deep watering during spells of rainless weather, feeding in early spring and fall with a balanced (avoid high-nitrogen products) slow-release fertilizer, and staking to support the individual flower spikes of taller hybrids. Cut spent spikes back to their bases to encourage rebloom of laterals.

Pests and problems are legion, and include slugs and snails on succulent young growth, and black-spotted foliage caused by cyclamen mites; curled and distorted leaves are usually a symptom of aphids; yellow and stunted plants may indicate nematodes. Black, foul-smelling decay at the base of plants is caused by bacterial crown and root rot; powdery mildew can disfigure stems and foliage, and stunt growth. The flowers attract butterflies, bees, and hummingbirds, but they resist deer and rabbits.

Very few perennial delphiniums will tolerate the combined heat and humidity of southeastern US summers; in that region, they are more commonly treated as winter annuals.

Delphiniums are poisonous in all or some of their parts, and cause skin irritation in some people. Protect your hands with gloves. *Never* decorate food plates with these flowers.

Plants can be started from seed or propagated by dividing healthy plants. Cuttings of young shoots root readily in spring.

Delphinium ×*belladonna*

- various
- spring to summer
- 3–4 ft. × 2 ft.
- sun
- Z3–10, HS

Belladona delphinium. Of garden origin. A group of hybrids that derives principally from crosses between *Delphinium elatum* and *D. grandiflorum*. Characterized by finer foliage and somewhat smaller stature than the classic border delphiniums, the belladonna hybrids require less staking than their loftier relatives. They bear loose racemes of single or double, 1.5- to 2-in. flowers on branching stems over an extended season; deadheading promotes another flush in late summer. Mildew resistant.

'Belladonna' bears light blue, single flowers.

'Bellamosum' ('Bellamosa') has dark blue blossoms.

'Casa Blanca' has pure white, single flowers.

Connecticut Yankee Hybrids produce single flowers in shades of white, blue, lavender, and purple on numerous branched stems. Seldom need staking; ideal for small gardens. Compact at 24–30 in. × 10–14 in.

Delphinium cardinale

- red
- spring to summer
- 6 ft. × 2 ft.
- sun
- Z7–10, HS

Scarlet larkspur. This Californian thrives on well-drained soils in hot, dry regions, with occasional deep irrigation. Palmately divided leaves, with 1-in., vivid scarlet flowers with yellow bees. Plants become semi-dormant after bloom; withhold water until growth resumes. Propagate from seed.

Delphinium ×*elatum*

- various
- late spring to early summer
- 3–6 ft. × 2 ft.
- sun, part shade
- Z3–7, HS

Tall hybrid delphinium. Of garden origin. The quintessential English border delphiniums were bred by crossing Siberian *Delphinium elatum* with *D. exaltatum* and *D. cheilanthum*. This hybrid group comes with double and single flowers in shades of white, yellow, pink, blue, and purple.

Such tall, imposing flowers require adequate support. Install three stakes as tall as the ultimate projected height in a triangle around each plant, early in the growing season; tie in stems periodically as they extend upward. Propagate from soft cuttings or start from seed.

Blackmore and Langdon Strain, long a favorite from California, has exceptionally large flower

Delphinium ×*elatum* 'Pink Punch'

spikes that reach a height of 5 ft. or more; blossoms in hues ranging from creamy yellows through blues and purples to pink, often with a contrasting bee at the center of each flower. Usefulness in North American gardens is limited by sensitivity to humid heat.

Blue Fountains Strain is dwarf at 2.5–3 ft. tall in shades of blue. Available as seed.

New Millennium Series. A collection of 14 color-themed strains of delphiniums bred by Terry Dowdeswell of Dowdeswell's Delphiniums, Wanganui, NZ. Double or single flowers, often with a contrasting bee. They are winning popularity for their superior hybrid vigor and improved resistance to disease and environmental stress. Available as seed; each strain offers subtly different expressions of the basic type. 3–5 ft. 'Blue Lace' has light, sky-blue petals with a pinkish tinge. 'Innocence' sports fluffy, fully double, pure white flowers. 'Pink Punch' has frilled flowers in pink and purple shades, with striped bees. 'Royal Aspirations' is deep sapphire to navy blue with contrasting white bees.

Pacific Giant Strain is another favorite. True to their name, in perfect conditions these California-bred cultivars can reach a height of 8 ft. Semi-double, 3-in. blossoms in white, pink, lavender, and blue. Garden favorites since their introduction in the 1930s, the Pacific Giants have, according to experts, degenerated over the decades, losing vigor and the purity of their colors.

'Princess Caroline' has pink flowers. 24 in. tall.

'Red Caroline' represents a breeding color breakthrough, a border delphinium with double, true-red blossoms. Stems are 4- to 6-ft. Propagate vegetatively.

Delphinium grandiflorum

- blue
- spring to summer
- 1–2 ft. × 1–1.5 ft.
- sun
- Z3–8

Chinese or Siberian delphinium, Siberian larkspur. Russia and China. Forms compact, bushy mounds of deeply palmately divided, dark green leaves and loose, airy racemes of blue or white flowers. Typically short lived but self-seeds readily.

'Blue Mirror' bears gentian-blue flowers over a prolonged season.

Delphinium nudicaule

- red
- spring to summer
- 1–2 ft. × 1 ft.
- sun, part shade
- Z4–10, HS

Dwarf scarlet larkspur. California and Oregon. Single or double, long-spurred, orange-red flowers. Intolerant of winter damp as well as summer humidity, but appropriate in southern California. Often short lived.

'Laurin' has bright scarlet flowers.

Delphinium ×elatum 'Royal Aspirations'

Delphinium tatsienense

- blue, white
- spring to summer
- 1.5–2 ft. × 1–1.5 ft.
- sun
- Z6–10, HS

Chinese delphinium. Western China. This bushy, compact species is suited to the front of a bed or border, or containers. Hirsute leaves are divided into three segments; 1.25-in. flowers borne in branched racemes. Start from seed.

Sky Lights Strain bears white, pale blue, or deep blue flowers. Blooms the first year from seed. 10–12 in. tall.

Delphinium tricorne

- white, blue-purple
- early spring
- 18–24 in. × 9 in.
- sun, partial shade
- Z7–4

Dwarf larkspur. Native to eastern and midwestern North America, this species blooms for three weeks in early spring. It bears 0.75- to 1-in., lavender-blue to dark purple flowers with white bees, with occasional all-white-flowered specimens. Prefers average to moist, humus-rich soils; self-sows readily before going dormant with summer's onset. Attracts bees and butterflies, and ideal for wildlife or native plant gardens, and on the edge of light woods. Combine with wild sweet William seed.

Dianthus

Caryophyllaceae
pink

Although this genus of 350 species includes many with exquisitely beautiful and often sweetly scented flowers, until recently American gardeners have made little use of dianthus. Carnations (*Dianthus caryophyllus*) might be standbys in the cutting garden, and alpine gardeners have long prized the neat, cushion-forming species for their rock gardens, but the demanding nature of most cultivated dianthus—older types tolerated neither poor drainage nor summer heat and humidity—and their relatively short season of bloom made them infrequent choices for perennial gardens. Over the last couple of decades, however, plant breeders have successfully addressed these two limitations in their new introductions. As a result, dianthus is claiming increased space in our gardens, even in the muggy southeastern United States, where traditionally dianthus were grown almost solely as winter annuals.

The common name for these flowers—pinks—may seem to derive from the rosy hues so common among dianthus blossoms, but actually it is a reference to the petals' frilly edges, which look as if they've been cut or "pinked" with a tailor's pinking shears. Another old name is "clove pink"—the deliciously spicy scent common to these flowers formerly made them a popular ingredient for

potpourri, and for flavoring wines and ales. Modern cooks garnish salads and other cold dishes with edible dianthus petals. Scent, fortunately, is one of the qualities emphasized by contemporary dianthus breeders who have introduced a number of hybrids with outstanding perfumes.

Borne singly or in few or many-flowered panicles, cymes, or heads, dianthus flowers are usually colored in shades of white and pink to red, often with a contrasting central eye. Pairs of grassy, often glabrous, blue-gray or gray-green leaves form dense mats or cushions that are commonly evergreen or semi-evergreen.

Dianthus require a well-drained soil, ideally with a neutral to alkaline pH; mulch with limestone chips if soil is acid. Poor drainage promotes root rot and rust. They grow best in full sun, though light afternoon shade can be beneficial where the sun is intense. Many of the new hybrids can be raised from seed and often bloom their first year. Deadhead routinely for possible bloom later.

Deer resistant and generally pest free, dianthus may suffer from powdery mildew in humid weather, especially where air circulation is poor. Compact forms provide neat edgings for the front of a border or bed, and they flourish if tucked into a soil-backed stone wall; mat-forming cultivars thrive if set into the cracks of a dry-laid stone pavement. Taller species make long-lasting cut flowers.

Propagate named cultivars by taking 2- to 3-in.-long cuttings from side shoots stripped off with a bit of the main stem (a heel) or from "pipings," shoot tips snapped off at a node. Dianthus also layer easily.

Dianthus gratianopolitanus 'Bath's Pink'

Dianthus ×allwoodii

- various
- late spring to late summer
- 10–18 in. high and wide
- sun
- Z3–10

Cottage pink, border carnation, Allwood pink. Of hybrid origin: *Dianthus caryophyllus* × *D. plumarius*. Tufted plants with grass-like, grayish green foliage. Solitary, single, semi- or fully double, 1.5- to 2-in.-wide flowers with pinked petals are often bicolored.

'Agatha' is compact, long lived, and cold hardy; semi-double, pink flowers with darker eye, and outstanding fragrance. 10 in. high and wide.

'Alpinus'. Extra-compact plants form neat mounds of blue-green foliage beneath strongly perfumed, single flowers in shades of pink and red, often with contrasting darker eye. Early summer to frost. Available as seed. 6–9 in. tall.

'Aqua' has 12-in. stems bearing fragrant, double, white flowers.

'Doris' bears perfumed, semi-double, salmon-pink flowers with a deep rose eye.

'Frosty Fire' bears cherry red, double flowers flecked with white. Fragrant, drought and heat resistant. 12 in.

Dianthus amurensis

- lavender blue
- late spring to late summer
- 6–12 in. × 12–15 in.
- sun, part shade
- Z3–8

Amur pink. This compact species displays the toughness one would expect of a Siberian native. Long lived and drought tolerant once established.

'Siberian Blue' bears lavender-blue, 0.5- to 1-in.-wide blooms in small but abundant clusters over blue-green foliage; the flowers offer the closest to true blue found in this genus. Unscented, best in gritty soils, and ideal for rock gardens or containers.

Dianthus barbatus

- various
- late spring to early summer
- 1–3 ft. high and wide
- sun
- Z3–10

Sweet William. Southern Europe, Asia. A short-lived perennial or biennial that is often grown as an annual (especially in regions with hot summers). This cottage gardening favorite is useful for cutting and in sunny mixed borders. It bears dense, many-flowered, flat or domed clusters of single, semi-double, or double flowers in white through shades of pink to crimson; commonly multicolored. Often fragrant, individual flowers measure 0.5–1 in. in diameter. They attract bees, hummingbirds, and butterflies. Dark green, glossy, strap-shaped leaves. A source of long-lasting, strong-stemmed cut flowers; encourage prolonged bloom and preserve vigor of plants by cutting stems of fading flowers off at ground level to prevent seed set. Best in cool climates but tolerates heat where summers are dry.

'Dunnett's Dark Crimson' has deep crimson flowers with a white eye.

'Heart Attack', one of the best cultivars for hot, humid regions, bears dark red, almost black, carnation-like flowers on 12- to 18-in. stems from early spring through summer. May persist for many years; unusually long lived for this species. Z4–8.

Indian Carpet is a dwarf strain, with flowers in white through shades of pink to red, often with contrasting bands. Late spring to summer. 6–12 in. Z3–9.

'Newport Pink' produces fragrant, single, coral-pink flowers that bloom from late spring through early summer. 18–24 in. × 2 ft. Z4–11.

'Sooty' has mahogany foliage and maroon flowers from spring through early summer. Fragrant. 12–18 in. × 9–12 in.

Dianthus deltoides

- various
- late spring to early summer
- 6–18 in. × 12 in.
- sun, part shade
- Z3–10, HS

Maiden pink. Northern Europe. Among the cold-hardiest dianthus, maiden pinks are exceptional for this genus because they thrive in partial shade. Forming loose mats of evergreen, narrowly linear to lance-shaped leaves, these plants are covered with 0.75-in., slightly fragrant flowers. Blossoms of unimproved specimens are typically deep pink with a darker band at the base of the petals. Shear off fading flowers for neatness, to prevent seed set, and to encourage rebloom in fall. Cover with evergreen boughs through winter in cold climates; crown rot may afflict plants grown on poorly drained soils. Excellent for rock gardens, edgings, and containers.

'Confetti Cherry Red' bears a profusion of candy apple–red flowers. Deadhead for fall rebloom. 6 in. tall.

'Zing Rose' bears deep rose-red blossom in late spring and, if deadheaded, again in fall. 6–12 in. 'Zing Salmon' is similar but with bright salmon-pink flowers.

Dianthus gratianopolitanus

syn. *D. caesius*, *D. suavis*

- various
- spring to summer
- 6–12 in. × 12 in.
- sun
- Z3–10, HS

Cheddar pink. Western and central Europe. Another cold-hardy dianthus that is sensitive to summer humidity, though some cultivars are more tolerant than others. Grassy, gray-green to blue-gray, evergreen foliage spreads in dense mats, making this species an outstanding choice for border edging, tucking in between the stones of a wall, or spilling down a sunny bank. Bears an abundance of solitary,

Dianthus gratianopolitanus 'Feuerhexe'

single or double flowers in spring; shear off fading flowers and pinch back straggling foliage to promote dense growth and intermittent summer rebloom.

'Bath's Pink' bears clove-scented, single, pink flowers marked with magenta ring; heat and humidity tolerant, thriving as far south as Atlanta. 1994 Herbaceous Perennial Georgia Gold Medal Winner. 8 in.

'Feuerhexe' ('Firewitch') grows 3–6 in. tall and to 12 in. wide. Cold hardy, but tolerates heat and humidity. Bears heavy crops of single, clove-scented, hot-pink blossoms in late spring. 2005 Perennial Plant of the Year.

'Tiny Rubies'. Dense mats of deep green foliage, 10–12 in. across, covered with 4-in.-tall, tiny, double, unscented, deep pink blossoms. Tolerates heat and humidity. Beautiful as a groundcover or to edge a path.

'Wicked Witch' is a sport of 'Feuerhexe' that bears cherry-red flowers.

Dianthus knappii

- yellow
- late spring to midsummer
- 12–18 in. × 9–12 in.
- sun
- Z3–9

Hairy garden pink. Eastern and central Europe. The only yellow-blooming dianthus has 0.5- to 1-in.-wide flowers with no fragrance. Lanky stems, with an open growth habit, support fine-textured, pubescent, grayish foliage. Blooms during its first year from seed.

'Yellow Harmony' offers larger flowers and tidier, more upright growth than the species.

Dianthus plumarius

- various
- summer to fall
- 6–12 in. × 8–24 in.
- sun
- Z3–10, HS

Cottage pink, grass pink. This heirloom flower, brought to the United States from Europe in Colonial times, was a favorite of old-time cottage gardeners. Cottage pinks form loose tufts or mats of

Dianthus plumarius 'Cyclops'

evergreen, blue-green foliage; in season it bears clusters of single or double, usually fragrant flowers, elevated 12 in. above the leaves. Long blooming, especially if deadheaded. A nostalgic addition to bouquets, cottage pinks make fine edgings for beds and borders, and thrive in sunny rock gardens. Requires a moist, humus-rich soil.

'Birmingham' bears fragrant, double, white flowers. Heat and humidity tolerant, and well adapted to the southeastern US gardens where it blooms in spring. Z4–8.

'Cyclops' has single flowers in red, pinks, and white. 12 in.

'Mrs. Sinkins' has exquisitely perfumed, fully double, white flowers. Largely replaced by modern selections; the calyx tends to split causing the flower to "blow."

Romance Mix produces single flowers in a wide range of pinks, many bicolored.

Sweetness Mix blooms the first year from seed, bearing sweet-scented flowers in shades of rose, pink, carmine, and white. Compact, excellent for containers and bedding. 4–6 in.

Dianthus superbus

- various
- late spring to early summer
- 12–30 in. × 24 in.
- sun
- Z4–8, HS

Lilac pink. This Eurasian native performs as a short-lived perennial or biennial. Grass-green tufts of narrow, evergreen leaves are borne on lax, branching stems. Fragrant, lacy-edged, 1.5- to 2-in., single flowers, paired or solitary, range in color from pink to mauve. Prefers a rich, moist soil. Reseeds readily.

'Crimsonia' is more compact than the species with fragrant, crimson blossoms on 20-in. stems.

'Primadonna' bears bright pink, perfumed flowers with lacy-edged petals.

Diascia
Scrophulariaceae
twinspur

Despite the fast-growing popularity of these long-blooming flowers, most gardeners mistakenly believe that all diascias are annuals. In fact, though many of the 75 members of this genus are indeed annuals, others perform as perennials in the warmer regions of the United States. At least one species is reliably perennial as far north as Hartford, CT, Cincinnati, OH, and Spokane, WA.

Natives of southern Africa, where rain falls in summer, twinspurs provide fine-textured mounds or mats of glossy green foliage and a succession of vivid flowers that continues for weeks or even months on end. The 1-in. leaves are ovate and toothed; the five-lobed flowers resemble those of snapdragons, except that each twinspur blossom sports (as the common name indicates) not one but two spurs. The flowers cluster at the stem tips.

Their sprawling habit of growth makes diascias ideal for spilling out over the edges of a border, over the lip of a container, or tucked in among stones in a rock garden. Some selections are more upright. Though sensitive to cold, diascias are heat hardy, tolerating intense sun as long as they are provided with sufficient water. Soil should be fertile, humus-rich, and well drained.

Twinspurs provide abundant color in the garden especially during spring and fall when night temperatures are still cool. They mix well in containers and in the landscape, notably with late spring bulbs and early alpine perennials, including rock cress and perennial candytuft. Other good companions include heucheras and heucherellas for their foliage throughout the season, miniature hostas, bacopas, and small ferns. In window boxes they are charming with calibrachoas, verbenas, and trailing ornamental oreganos.

Cut back in late winter or early spring to promote new growth. Deadhead regularly and pinch off branch tips periodically to encourage continued flowering and bushier growth. Diascias are rarely troubled by insects or diseases, but are vulnerable to snails and slugs; deer and rabbits leave them alone.

Propagate by soft cuttings of young growth or sow seed directly into the garden one to two weeks before the local last-frost date; alternatively start indoors six to eight weeks earlier.

Diascia barberae

- pink
- midspring to fall
- 9–12 in. × 12–18 in.
- sun
- Z8–11

Twinspur. Mountains of southern Africa. Perennial where winter temperatures seldom drop below 10°F; they are grown as annuals in colder regions. Flowers, to 0.75 in., are pink with yellow throats. When bloom flags in summer heat, shear plants to promote another flush in fall.

'Genta Giant Pink' is compact with large, pink, snapdragon-like flowers. Excellent for containers and as a groundcover. The Genta Series from Israel has stronger stems and is more upright than some strains.

Diascia integerrima

syn. *D. integrifolia*

- pink
- spring to fall
- 18 in. × 30 in.
- sun, part shade
- Z6–10

Hardy twinspur. A native of southern African mountains and thus an unusually cold-hardy species. It forms an upright clump of wiry, branching stems; the narrow leaves are mostly basal, with a few smaller ones up the stems. The pink flowers, up to 0.75 in. across, are borne in terminal racemes. They open in sequence over a long season, from the bottom progressing upward with new buds continually

Diascia 'Wink Pink Imp'

forming at the stem tips. Protect from full sun in hot climates.

'**Coral Canyon**' bears coral flowers with darker pink centers. Very long blooming. Tolerates dry soil. 15 in. × 18 in.

'**Pink Adobe**' bears pale salmon-pink flowers, maroon at the throats. Appropriate for xeriscapes. 15 in. × 18 in.

Diascia rigescens
- pink
- summer to fall
- 10–12 in. × 15–20 in.
- sun, part shade
- Z7–9

Twinspur. Southern Africa. Trailing with semi-upright, branching stems clothed with heart-shaped leaves, toothed along the edges. Flowers are in various shades of pink, arranged along the stems in close erect spikes.

Other Notable Cultivars
There are numerous cultivars, with many more appearing on the market annually. Many of these have resulted from new technology applied to plant breeding, including tissue culture.

'**Blue Bonnet**' has pink flowers flushed with blue. 8 in. × 2 ft. Z8.

Flirtation Series, currently only with pink or orange flowers, promises self-cleaning plants that do not require deadheading. However, when bloom decreases in response to hot nights, a shearing keeps the plants neat and encourages a further flush of bloom when nights cool. 8–12 in. Z7–10.

Flying Colors Hybrid Series offers flowers in a range of pinks, apricot, and red on compact, heat-tolerant plants. Plants tolerate light fall frosts. Z8–9. A Proven Winners introduction.

Picadilly Series was introduced from Holland and includes blues and lilac.

'**Ruby Field**' has masses of strong salmon-pink flowers from summer to fall. 10 in. × 24 in. Z8–9.

Sun Chimes Series offers large, coral, rose, blush-pink, peach, and coppery-purple flowers on mounded plants. The rose- and red-flowered selections are trailing types; excellent for hanging baskets. Z8–9.

Wink Series blooms abundantly all season in containers and in the landscape. Flowers are sterile and self-cleaning. Cold tolerant. 10–12 in. Z5–8.

Dicentra
Fumariaceae
bleeding heart

Bleeding hearts are one of the cottage garden plants that many of us remember from the gardens of our youth, and the virtues that made them popular then are just as relevant today. Indeed, the breeders have been busy with this genus, so there are many more cultivars from which to choose.

Dicentra eximia

Several species of bleeding heart are native to North America; in the wild, they are usually found growing in partly shaded, damp spots among trees. The leaves are deeply divided and they often have a bluish cast that contrasts appealingly with the colorful flowers. The heart-shaped, mostly pink or white flowers are charmingly dainty, with inner petals protruding from the outer ones. Both flowers and leaves are carried on brittle, succulent stems.

Provide bleeding hearts with humus-rich, well-drained, moisture-retentive soil. Some selections tolerate sun well, especially in cool-summer regions, although only a few are happy in heat and humidity. As a group, they are best in light or partial shade, always with damp but not waterlogged soil.

Compatible companions for bleeding hearts include woodland natives such as bloodroot, columbines, Christmas fern, and wide blue sedge. Appropriate non-natives include spring bulbs, hellebores, lungworts, and hostas; lily-of-the-valley also mixes well. Bleeding hearts are excellent for brightening up beds and borders in spring, as a skirt around flowering shrubs, and for the edges of woodlands and paths. Compact selections are in scale in rock gardens and raised beds. Butterflies and hummingbirds often forage the flowers and foliage of bleeding hearts, making them appropriate for planting in wildlife gardens. Resistant to deer and rabbits.

Propagate by seed sown in containers as it becomes ripe or in spring. Divide named cultivars in early spring.

Dicentra eximia 'Alba'

Dicentra cucullaria

- white
- early spring
- 6–9 in. × 9 in.
- part shade
- Z3–7

Dutchman's breeches, stagger weed. Native to open clearings in the woods from Nova Scotia south to North Carolina, and west to Kansas. Small, white tubers give rise to blue- green, finely dissected leaves that disappear quickly after bloom time. Spurred, white, 0.5-in. flowers, shaped like baggy, upside-down Dutchman's trousers, are arranged on short stems along arching, pinkish stems. Needs humus-rich soil. Toxic to livestock, but formerly used as a remedy for syphilis. Squirrel corn, *Dicentra canadensis*, is similar, but has less ferny foliage and heart-shaped, white flowers. Avoid planting too deeply. Becomes dormant shortly after blooming.

Dicentra eximia

- pink
- late spring to fall
- 12–24 in. × 18 in.
- part shade
- Z4–9

Fringed bleeding heart, turkey corn. Native to rich woodlands of the eastern United States, especially in the Appalachian region. Mounds of finely dissected, 6- to 18-in.-long, gray-green leaves rise from scaly, fleshy rootstocks and persist through the season if kept moist. Each arching, pink-tinged stem bears several nodding, rosy-pink, heart-shaped flowers on short pedicels (flower stems). The 1-in.-long flowers are produced for several weeks and then sporadically till fall. Seeds about. In the garden, plant with columbines, wild gingers, lungworts, woodland phlox, and other spring shade lovers. There has been a great deal of hybridization between this species and the western or Pacific bleeding heart, *Dicentra formosa*; many selections may be hybrids, although attributed to one species or the other. Other species are also involved.

'Alba' produces mounds of bright green, cut leaves and white flowers tipped with yellow. 12–30 in. Z3–9.

'Bacchanal' has dusky red flowers in mid- to late spring. Gray-green leaves. 18 in. Z3–9.

'Dolly Sods', an introduction from Plant Delights Nursery in North Carolina, has pale pink flowers and is reputed to be the most heat tolerant of the bleeding hearts. Suitable for regions with hot, humid summers. Z3–8.

Heart Series, bred in Japan, has produced the following superior compact selections, all with lacy, bright blue-gray leaves. 'Burning Hearts' has deep rosy-red, heart-shaped flowers rimmed with white. 10 in. 'Ivory Hearts' has clean white flowers. 12 in. 'Candy Hearts' blooms with deep rose flowers. 6–12 in. All must remain damp in summer, and bloom longer with routine deadheading to the base. Z5–9.

'King of Hearts' has carmine flowers above compact, 6-in. foliage mounds in late spring. This older selection has similar genetics to the Heart Series. 9–18 in. Z3–8.

'Langtrees' is possibly the best white. Charming delicate clusters of white hearts contrast with finely dissected, gray leaves. 12 in. Z4–8.

'Luxuriant' is a popular selection for its late spring, cherry red flowers and bluish leaves. Very long blooming; sterile. Tolerates summer heat only if kept moist. 12–18 in. Z3–9.

'Stuart Boothman' ('Boothman's Variety') has wonderful dissected, 4- to 8-in.-long, strong blue-green leaves that contrast beautifully with 0.5- to 1-in., deep rose flowers. 12 in. Z3–9.

'Zestful'. Deep rose flowers above ferny, blue-green foliage. Almost nonstop blooming, even through warm weather if kept moist. 12–18 in. Z3–9.

Dicentra formosa

- pink, red
- early spring to early summer
- 15 in. × 18 in.
- sun, part shade
- Z3–8

Western bleeding heart, Pacific bleeding heart, lyreflower. Native to moist woodlands, along streambanks, and in meadows from northern California to British Columbia—but not to Formosa; the specific epithet means "beautiful." Similar to *Dicentra eximia*, spreading by underground rhizomes, this species colonizes quickly but not invasively. Rosy mauve-pink flowers hang from brittle, succulent stems; the basal foliage is finely dissected and bluish green. A nectar plant for hummingbirds and adult Clodius Parnassian (*Parnassius clodius*) butterflies and a larval plant for the caterpillars; ants spread the seeds. Valued in folk medicine in spite of all parts of the plant being toxic. Divide when dormant.

'Aurora'. More compact and possibly superior to 'Alba', with longer-blooming white flowers above mounds of ferny, blue-green leaves. Spring to summer. 12–15 in.

'Sweetheart' has white flowers. 15 in.

Dictamnus

Rutaceae
gas plant, burning bush

This genus is composed of a single species. Its common names refer to a phenomenon often described but seldom actually witnessed: reportedly, the inflammable oil that gives the foliage its lemon scent volatilizes in hot weather, and on a still summer afternoon may supposedly erupt in a flash if ignited with a lit match. Fortunately, this is the least of the plant's attractions.

Gas plant is easygoing, growing in any average, well-drained garden soil, though it prefers a moist,

Dictamnus albus

fertile, and organic-rich one. Best adapted to full sun, it also tolerates light shade, and though slow to mature—it may take several years for a seedling to reach the flowering stage—once established in the garden it is very long lived and requires little maintenance.

Planted singly or massed in a border, herb, or cottage garden it makes an imposing statement; it blends well with daylilies, campanulas, and irises. Pests, including deer, and diseases rarely afflict gas plant seriously. Contact with its foliage may cause a rash in some individuals.

Propagate by seed, planting the new seed as soon as it ripens. Once this taprooted plant is established, it resents disturbance, making division and even the transplanting of mature plants risky.

Dictamnus albus

syn. *D. fraxinella*

- white, pink, red, lilac
- late spring to early summer
- 2–3 ft. × 1.5–2.5 ft.
- sun
- Z3–8

Gas plant, burning bush. Native to southwestern Europe, and southern and central Asia to China and Korea. Upright clumps of erect, rigid stems that typically don't require staking. The foliage is light green, glossy, and pinnate with an elegant appearance, and releases a lemon scent when bruised or crushed. Showy five-petaled, 1-in. flowers have prominent wispy, upcurving stamens, and are borne in racemes at the stem tips; they may be mauve, pink, or white, etched with purple veins. Attractive star-shaped seedheads follow.

var. *purpureus* bears flowers that are pale to deep purple-pink, with darker veins.

Dierama

Iridaceae
wand flower

These natives of South African grasslands and
mountain meadows are not as widely cultivated in
the United States as they might be, although several mail-order nurseries carry some of the species.
Wand flowers follow a pattern of growth similar to
that of their relatives, the crocosmias: they form
bulb-like, underground stems called corms that on
a hospitable site multiply over the years to make
a gradually increasing group of plants. The linear,
deep green, 36-in. leaves are grassy and somewhat
stiff, and from mid- through late summer they are
topped with elegant arching flower stems. These
are furnished with spikes of funnel- or bell-shaped
flowers that hang on hair-like threads and sway in
the slightest breeze, like some exquisite catch dangling from a fishing rod—hence the other common
names: angel's fishing rod and fairies' fishing rod.

Wand flowers are most attractive as specimens tucked in between paving stones or clustered
beside ponds and pools. They also show well when
grouped or massed in sunny beds and borders.
Wand flowers grow especially well in the Pacific
Northwest. Where winters are too cold for them to
grow as perennials outdoors, they make great subjects for containers; bring the pots indoors to overwinter as for dahlias and gladioli. Wand flowers are
also good conservatory, cool greenhouse, or sunroom subjects.

Plant corms in spring when the soil has warmed,
about 3–5 in. deep. A sheltered, sunny spot where
the soil drains well but is humus rich is ideal. Keep
well watered during the growing season. Delay cutting back scruffy foliage until new growth emerges
in spring. Pests and diseases are seldom a problem.
Usually considered to be rabbit and deer resistant,
although some have reported extensive browsing
by deer.

Propagate by division in spring; these plants
resent disturbance and may take a couple of years
to bloom after division. Species may be started
from seed, sown as soon as it is ripe, and overwintered in a cold frame or other protected spot;
seedlings require as much as six to seven years of
growth before blooming.

Dierama dracomontanum

syn. *D. pumilum, D. hernia*

- coral
- midsummer
- 24–30 in. × 12–24 in.
- sun
- Z8–10

Dragon mountain wand flower, Drakensberg hairbell. From grassland regions of the Drakensberg
mountain range. This compact species has coral or
even brick-red, flaring trumpet flowers, above a tuft
of stiff grassy leaves.

Dierama pulcherrimum

- pink
- mid- to late summer
- 4–6 ft. × 3 ft.
- sun
- Z7–10

Fairy's wandflower, African hairbells. Zimbabwe,
southern Africa. Evergreen tufts of 3- to 4-ft.-long,
strappy, 0.5-in.-wide leaves rise from the ground
and, in time, develop into substantial clumps. High
above the leaves, elegant wiry stems bear delicate,
tubular, bell-shaped, 1-in. flowers of pink, magenta,
and sometimes white. Each stem may carry 12 to
15 of these flowers, each suspended by a hair-like
thread. Keep well watered during the growing season, but allow to dry off if possible during dormancy. Do not cut back foliage in winter.

'Album' has flared, pure white flowers.

'Blackbird' has dark wine-purple flowers dangling
from 3-ft., arching stems.

'Silver Dawn' has blush-pink flowers.

Slieve Donard is a mixed strain with flowers in
various shades of pink, wine, and red. 3 ft. tall.

Dietes

Iridaceae
Cape iris

These beautiful iris relatives make valuable additions to beds and borders throughout the warmer
regions of the United States. Native to open grasslands and bush, mountain cliffs, and damp forest
edges in Africa and Australia. They have rhizomatous roots from which spring erect, sword-shaped
basal leaves that are tough and leathery, arranged
in narrow fans like those of German irises. The
flowers are iris-like as well, flattened and borne on
branched stems; the lifespan of individual flowers is
short, but they open in bursts.

Cape iris tolerate a wide range of soils, even
poor, dry ones, though they grow best in soils of
average fertility. Good drainage is a must, for the
roots and crown of these plants soon rot in persistently damp soils, or even if habitually overwa-
tered. They flourish in sun or partial shade, with the
latter being better in regions of intense sunlight. In
colder climates Cape iris may be cultivated in containers in sunrooms and conservatories. Pot them
into a well-drained, soil-based mix and water freely
during bloom time; allow to dry off as the plants
become dormant.

To propagate, sow seed in spring or fall,
or divide the rhizomes with a foliage fan after
flowering.

Dietes grandiflora

- white
- spring to summer
- 3–4 ft. × 4 ft.
- sun, part shade
- Z9–11

Wild iris, fairy iris. Grows along the margins of forests in the Eastern Cape of South Africa. Forms

Dietes grandiflora

Digitalis purpurea

large clumps of stiff, sword-like leaves, up to 3 ft. in length, that rise in fans from underground stems. Slender, upright, 3-ft. stems carry lovely 4-in.-wide, white flowers that are blotched with yellow, and have lavender-flushed styles. Large seed capsules follow and split to reveal polished, brown seeds. The blooms come in flushes of flowers, each blossom lasting a day or two. Butterflies and pollinating insects are attracted to the blooms. Tolerant of urban pollution and poor growing sites close to highways and in shopping centers. Mass or use as an accent plant in containers, beds, and borders.

Dietes iridioides

syn. *Moraea iridioides, D. vegeta*
- white
- late spring to summer
- 18–24 in. × 15 in.
- sun, part shade
- Z8–11

Fortnight lily. This species from southern and east African grasslands produces its countless yellow-blotched, white flowers with lavender-flushed styles from spring into summer. The evergreen basal leaves, to 24 in. long, are dark green and remain attractive after bloom time. Do not cut back the fans of foliage except to remove shabby leaves. Tolerates light shade well.

Digitalis
Plantaginaceae
foxglove

This genus, formerly included in the Scrophulariaceae, includes both perennials and biennials—though because the biennials commonly reseed to reemerge as volunteers year after year, they too function as durable additions to the garden. Whatever their lifespan, foxgloves, with their carillons of bell-shaped blossoms, define old-fashioned charm and grace, and are stars of any cottage or wild garden that happens to host them.

Perhaps it is due to their role in folk medicine—foxgloves are a source of digitalin, a potent drug for the treatment of a variety of cardiac conditions—that the flowers were traditionally associated with fairies and the supernatural in their European, northwest African, and western Asian homelands. The presence of this drug makes the plants toxic, which in turn makes them unfit for a garden with children but also resistant to deer and rabbits.

When started from seed, foxgloves form basal rosettes of foliage during their first year of growth, sending up their tall spikes of flowers the following spring or summer. Removing the flower stalk after its blossoms fade encourages the production of side shoots and a second, smaller flowering. This treatment, however, reduces the amount of seed the plant produces and so discourages self-seeding. Rich, moist, well-drained soil is best for foxgloves, and in hot, sunny regions they prefer a site with some afternoon shade. They are sometimes susceptible to powdery mildew and leaf spot, aphids, mealybugs, slugs and Japanese beetles, and will not tolerate waterlogged conditions in winter.

Foxgloves' vertical habit of growth makes them valuable punctuation for more spreading perennials, especially those that also favor partial shade such as hostas, astilbes, heucheras, and alchemillas; planted in groups, foxgloves show up well against a backdrop of shrubs or a wall. Foxgloves are attractive to hummingbirds and pollinating insects, and make striking cut flowers.

Propagate by seed, or by division of established plants in spring or fall.

Digitalis ferruginea

- brown, white, yellow
- midspring to early summer
- 3–5 ft. × 1–1.5 ft.
- sun, part shade
- Z4–8

Rusty foxglove. A biennial or short-lived perennial, native from southern Europe to the Caucasus. Leaves are deep green, crinkled, and borne in a basal rosette; the pendulous to horizontal, tubular flowers are 0.75–1.5 in. in length, creamy yellow to honey brown with rusty veining inside. Requires a consistently moist though well-drained soil. Excellent for woodland gardens or moist meadows.

'Yellow Herald' ('Gelber Herold') reaches a height of 5 ft., and bears pale yellow flowers.

Digitalis grandiflora

syn. *D. ambigua, D. orientalis*
- yellow
- midspring to early summer
- 2–3 ft. × 1–1.5 ft.
- sun, part shade
- Z3–8

Yellow foxglove. Native to woods and stream banks from Europe to western Asia, this species thrives with a moist, organic-rich soil, but also tolerates dry shade. It produces a basal clump of fine-toothed, semi-evergreen foliage, from which emerges a tall stalk of soft yellow, 1.5- to 2-in., bell-shaped flowers that are speckled brown inside. *Digitalis lutea*, straw foxglove, also has yellow flowers but these are quite small, on 2-ft.-tall plants.

Digitalis purpurea

- pink, purple, white
- midspring to early summer
- 2–5 ft. × 1–2.5 ft.
- sun, part shade
- Z4–8

Common foxglove, Mary's thimble. Native throughout much of Europe, this species is biennial and produces a basal rosette of light green, oblong leaves in the first year's growth; the flowers are borne the second year in terminal, one-sided racemes atop leafy spires. Closely spaced, the individual flowers are pendulous, 2–3 in. long and tubular; they are colored dark rose-pink to purple, or occasionally white with purple and white spots marking the interior—like landing lights at an airport showing the way to the nectar for pollinating bees. Common foxglove reaches its peak about the same time as roses begin to bloom and provides an elegant counterpoint to those shrubs. They are also attractive with columbines, blue stars, and peonies.

'Pam's Choice' has large, white bells heavily marked with deep maroon inside the lower lip and on the throat. One-sided spikes. A special favorite of hummingbirds.

'Sutton's Apricot' has apricot-pink flowers. Comes true from seed.

Other Notable Cultivars

×*mertonensis*, the "strawberry foxglove," bears spikes of coppery rose flowers in midspring to early summer. 3–4 ft. Z4–8.

Camelot Hybrids are extra tolerant of sun and heat. They bloom the first year from seed with rose, pink, lavender, white, or cream flowers. 3–4 ft. Z3–8.

Excelsior Hybrids bear flowers all round the stems in shades of yellow, pink, apricot, purple, and white. 5 ft. Z4–8.

Foxy Hybrids are compact, to 2–3 ft., and carry flowers in pastel shades of purple, pink, red, cream,

Digitalis 'Spice Island'

yellow, and white. Blooms in five months from seed, in its first year if started early indoors. Z4–8.

Polkadot Hybrids have extra-large flowers in rose, light apricot with a yellow interior, or dark apricot. Flowers are sterile (produce no seed) so the season of bloom is prolonged and the plants are reputed to be more reliably perennial. To 3–5 ft. Z4–8.

'Spice Island' has large, apricot-peach flowers dusted with light brown. They are carried in dense spikes throughout the summer. Plants are strongly upright and branch well. Evergreen. 1–2 ft. Z4–9.

Diphylleia

Berberidaceae
umbrella leaf

This much-neglected genus is perfect for shaded woodland areas of the garden where its various species mix well with other woodlanders including white baneberry, bleeding hearts, blue cohosh, wild gingers, and primulas. Umbrella leaf is an apt name for these close relatives (and lookalikes) of May apple. Arising from stout rhizomes, umbrella leaves produce stout stems that serve as the central supports of large, peltate leaves; several clumps together look like a small army of 2-ft.-tall, green umbrellas in the woods. In spring the plants bear clusters of short-lived, small, white flowers that are followed by blue berries.

Diphylleia cymosa

Soil should be moist but not necessarily boggy, and high in humus. A sheltered location with part shade is ideal. Deer and rabbits usually—but not always—ignore this species. The two Asian species are seldom seen in the United States.

Divide in spring or start from seed; seedlings take two to three years to reach blooming size.

Diphylleia cymosa

- white
- late spring
- 2–3 ft. × 1–2 ft.
- part shade, shade
- Z4–7

American umbrella leaf. Native to damp, shaded woodlands of the southern Appalachians, this fine plant deserves a much wider audience. The stout, jointed rhizomes produce a single, cleft leaf, perhaps 24 in. across; each of the rounded, deeply lobed segments is toothed along the rim. The flower stems bear two smaller but deeply two-lobed stem leaves (to 15 in. across) and end in an upright, umbel-like flat cluster of up to ten or more 0.5-in., six-petaled, white flowers. The 0.5-in. berries that follow are bright dusty blue and quite showy on red stalks. Umbrella leaf is a great addition to shaded native plant and wild gardens, or among shade-loving shrubs, perhaps with fern companions.

Diplarrena

syn. *Diplarrhena*
Iridaceae
flag iris

This genus includes two Australian species, which, despite being popular as garden perennials in their native country, are too little used in the United States. Flag irises are lovely in sheltered borders, and benefit from being set close to the house for extra warmth, even in warm zones. Combine them with shrimp plant, justicias, and *Melianthus* (honey bush) for foliage and flower contrast. In regions where they aren't reliably hardy, grow flag irises in containers in a sunroom or greenhouse, and set them outside in summertime.

Pests and diseases are seldom serious. Deer seem to ignore these plants.

Divide clumps in spring or start from seed with protection in spring or fall.

Diplarrena latifolia

- white
- early summer
- 3 ft. × 2–3 ft.
- sun, part shade
- Z8–10

Western flag iris. This Tasmanian native is similar to but slightly more cold tolerant than *Diplarrena moraea*; reportedly hardy to 18°F. It is also taller, with wider, lance-shaped leaves and longer flower scapes (leafless stems). The flowers are white with yellow and purple splashes at the centers.

Diplarrena moraea

- white
- early summer
- 24 in. × 14 in.
- sun, part shade
- Z9–10

Butterfly flag iris, white iris, butterfly flag. Native to Tasmania and southwestern Australia. Forms clumps of slender, evergreen, iris-like foliage springing from rhizomatous roots. In season, these sprout wiry scapes that bear clusters of three to six honey-scented, 1- to 2-in., white flowers, just above the foliage. Each flower has three rounded, white outer petals and three smaller inner petals that are white and yellow, commonly marked with purple. Prefers moist but well-drained, humus-rich, sandy soil; tolerates slight frosts. A reliable and attractive addition to cottage gardens, meadows, and rock gardens; the neat, evergreen foliage makes this useful for container displays perhaps with trailing morning glory vine and 'Diamond Frost' euphorbia.

Disporum

Convallariaceae
fairy bells, Solomon's seal

This genus of Asian woodland natives offers a number of fine garden perennials. Until recently, it also included half a dozen North American natives as well, and though botanists have renamed these as *Prosartes* and reclassified them as members of the lily family, these species are still commonly sold under their former names, so we've kept them here.

These are not flamboyant plants; their attractions, though considerable, tend more to the discreetly elegant. Their bell-shaped or star-shaped blossoms are modest, but they are combined with attractive foliage and berries; their adaptation to shade makes them very useful for shady borders and woodland gardens. When selecting a site for fairy bells, dappled sunlight is ideal, but they do tolerate full shade. They prefer humus-rich, moist but well-drained soils with a somewhat acid pH—they do not tolerate drought. Thanks to their rhizomatous root systems, fairy bells tend to spread once established, although they do so at a manageable rate, making them valuable groundcovers. They are natural companions for other shade lovers such as hostas, astilbes, and ferns.

Propagation is by seed, sown in the fall and overwintered in a cold frame or other protected spot, or by division of mature plants in early spring.

Disporum cantoniense

- white
- midspring to early summer
- 4–6 ft. × 2–3 ft.
- part shade, shade
- Z5–9

Cantonese fairy bells. A highly variable Chinese species that has upright or arching stems bearing lanceolate, green, variegated, or even purple leaves, typically 5 in. long and 2 in. broad. White, pale

yellow, or even red flowers. Noted plant explorer Dan Hinkley has introduced two outstanding cultivars:

'Green Giant' produces bamboo-like shoots that emerge in shades of pink, white, and green, before maturing to deep green. Fragrant, creamy-white, bell-shaped flowers followed by black fruit in fall. 6 ft. Z7–9.

'Night Heron', whose leaves open a lustrous deep red-burgundy in spring before fading to greenish purple in summer. Creamy, bell-shaped flowers are borne in terminal clusters atop 5- to 6-ft. stems, and are followed by glistening black-purple fruit. Z5.

Disporum flavens

- yellow
- early to midspring
- 24–30 in. × 9–12 in.
- part shade, shade
- Z5–8

Fairy bells. A Korean species that forms a slowly spreading clump. Lanceolate leaves may reach 6 in. long; flower buds appear at the stem ends with the new growth in spring, opening into small clusters of tubular, 0.5- to 1-in.-long, soft yellow flowers. Berries that ripen to black in late summer follow the flowers; fall foliage color can be an attractive yellow.

Disporum flavens

Disporum lanuginosum
syn. *Prosartes lanuginosa*
- yellow
- early to late spring
- 1–3 ft. × 1 ft.
- part shade, shade
- Z4–7

Yellow fairy bells, yellow mandarin. Native from Ontario south through Appalachian region to Alabama. Forms patches of delicately branched, zigzagging stems bearing ovate, glossy green leaves to 6 in. long and 2 in. wide, with prominent veins from base to tip. Flowers, that may reach up to 0.8 in. long, are yellow-green, nodding, and bell shaped, flaring at the mouth. Bright red berries follow in fall.

Disporum sessile
- white
- early to midspring
- 2 ft. × 3 ft.
- part shade, shade
- Z5–8

Japanese fairy bells. This eastern Asian native requires an evenly moist, rich, acid soil. Where these conditions are met, growth tends to be rapid, developing into dense clumps of stemless, lanceolate, bamboo-like foliage. Showy, white, bell-shaped flowers dangle from stems. Good for the front of the

Dodecatheon meadia 'Alba'

border and edgings as well as woodland gardens.

'Variegatum' is compact, with white-and-green-striped flowers and foliage. To 16 in. tall.

Dodecatheon
Primulaceae
shooting star

This group of simply beautiful, ephemeral native plants blooms in spring, but when hot weather begins they go dormant and escape the heat underground. The best-known species is common shooting star, *Dodecatheon meadia*, a midwestern and eastern US native. Several other species are western US natives, with many from the Pacific Northwest. Tricky to grow and rarely available, these are cherished by specialist gardeners, particularly alpine plant enthusiasts. Be sure to purchase plants from reputable dealers who propagate their stock, rather than digging it from the wild, as wild populations are endangered in some states.

Typically, shooting stars produce a basal rosette of smooth, spatulate leaves, from which rises a naked stem (scape) topped with an umbel of charming pendent flowers like upside-down cyclamen. The number of flowers per stem varies, but may reach seven to ten or more. Each "shuttlecock" flower points downward with protruding, prominently pointed stamens and anthers like a beak. A spot shaded from noon and afternoon sun is best, where the soil remains moist but is not wet or waterlogged. Plant shooting stars along shaded pathways, in rock gardens, or in native and light woodland gardens. They also do well in troughs and other containers.

Propagate by division in spring, after flowering but before summer dormancy, or by seed sown as soon as it is ripe and allow it to overwinter outdoors. Seedlings require up to six years to reach blooming size.

Dodecatheon meadia
syn. *D. pauciflora*
- pink, white
- spring
- 12–24 in. × 6–12 in.
- sun, part shade
- Z4–8

Shooting star, Ohio shooting star, American cowslip. Native to glades, woodlands, and rocky bluffs from Wisconsin, east to Pennsylvania, Virginia, and further south, where they are shaded from intense sun and soil remains moist during the growing season. Tolerates alkaline soils. Thick, fleshy, and smooth basal leaves yellow and die as bloom time ends and plants enter summer dormancy. The lightly fragrant flowers range in color from white through pinks to a deep purplish pink, and are 1 in. long with strongly reflexed or swept-back petals, a yellow ring at the mouth, and exserted brown stamens. Attractive to foraging bees for their pollen. Plant in drifts or groups, but plan ahead for the foliage to disappear in summer. Christmas and other ferns, fringed bleeding hearts, partridgeberry, and maple-leaved alumroot are excellent companions. Reportedly resistant to deer and rodents.

'Alba' has pure white flowers

'Aphrodite' is a "good doer," vigorous with purplish pink flowers on 18- to 24-in. stems. Possibly a hybrid.

'Queen Victoria' is showy with larger, light purplish pink flowers on red stems. Sterile.

Doronicum
Asteraceae
leopard's bane

If you seek variety to spice up the spring garden, something to add distinction to the usual mix of bulbs and pansies, the yellow, daisy-like flowers of leopard's bane could be your answer. Leopard's banes are easy to grow, although in hot climates, they will retreat into dormancy in summer. In such areas, placing them where they are protected from the midday sun and keeping their roots moist can help to maintain a foliage presence until fall. However, it's probably easier to simply accept this tendency and fill the gap they leave with annuals, or to pair leopard's banes with later-blooming perennials.

Arising from tuberous or rhizomatous roots, leopard's bane bears alternate, heart-shaped basal leaves and oval stem leaves. The 2-in.-wide daisy flowers are solitary or several may cluster at the stem tips. Taller species and selections are excellent for cutting; some are double flowered. *Doronicum plantagineum*, at 2–4 ft., and *D. pardalianches*, at 3 ft., are appropriate for planting in informal wild gardens. Seldom browsed by deer or rabbits.

Divide when plants are dormant or start from seed. Deadhead spent blooms to prevent self-seeding.

Doronicum columnae
syn. *D. cordatum*
- yellow
- spring
- 2–3 ft. × 2 ft.
- sun, part shade
- Z4–7

Spanish leopard's bane. Spain. Tuberous roots spread quite quickly and develop large clumps of rather coarse, 6- to 8-in.-long leaves. These are kidney shaped, smooth along the edges, and borne on long petioles. Flowers, to 1–2 in. wide, top branched stems; they consist of narrow rays surrounding a bright yellow central disk. This is a fine butterfly plant, appropriate for larger gardens where space is available. To ensure vigorous plants, divide every two to three years in spring when plants are dormant.

Doronicum orientale
syn. *D. caucasicum*
- yellow
- spring
- 12–24 in. × 15 in.
- sun, part shade
- Z4–7, HS

Caucasian leopard's bane. Southeast Europe, Turkey. This species is one of the earliest of the daisy family to bloom in spring and if well grown puts on a dramatic show. Thick rhizomes produce a mound of soft, kidney-shaped, toothed leaves that usually disappear into dormancy after bloom time. Upright, sticky, unbranched stems terminate in solitary, lemon-yellow flowerheads. Slender yellow rays (petals) surround a bright yellow center of disk flowers. Good for cut flowers and in beds and borders. This species is not acclimated to regions where summers are hot and humid. Poisonous to livestock and humans if ingested.

'Finesse' has starburst daisies on 18-in. stems. Excellent for cutting and in rock gardens. One of the earliest to bloom. Good massed along stream banks or as accents in shaded borders.

Leonardo is compact with low mounds of emerald-green leaves. Abundant flowers. Excellent for spring containers or as an edging plant. Easy to force in pots in a sunroom or conservatory for winter color. A Proven Winners introduction. 6 in. tall.

'Little Leo' makes low mounds of dentate,

Doronicum orientale 'Little Leo'

triangular leaves. Free blooming with semi-double, dark yellow-centered, yellow daisies. 12 in.

'**Magnificum**' has single, 2-in. flowers a little earlier than 'Finesse'. Dark green, heart-shaped leaves. Probably a hybrid. 2–2.5 ft. tall

'**Spring Beauty**' ('Frühlingspracht') has double flowers. Susceptible to fungal diseases in warm, humid summers. 12–16 in.

Dorycnium
Fabaceae
canary clover

This genus includes a dozen or so natives of the Mediterranean region and the Canary Islands, only one of which is cultivated in ornamental gardens.

Best grown in a fertile, alkaline soil that has free drainage, this plant requires little or no irrigation once established, even in semi-arid regions. Where drainage is suspect, mix grit into the hole prior to planting; hairy canary clover does not tolerate wet feet. Winter temperatures much below 20°F damage the top growth, but the plants typically resprout from the roots even after temperatures as low as 5°F. Maintenance is low, and the flowers self-clean, avoiding the need for deadheading. Self-seeds occasionally.

Canary clovers' soft, fuzzy aspect makes this a good choice for softening the edge of a path, for sunny rock gardens, or spilling over low rocks in xeriscapes. They do best in regions where summer humidity is low.

Propagate by seed. Germination is accelerated, if the seed coats are scarified or nicked.

Dorycnium hirsutum
syn. *Lotus hirsutus*
- pinkish white
- late summer to early fall
- 12–24 in. × 36 in.
- sun
- Z8–10

Hairy canary clover, gray broom. Canary Islands. This low, evergreen subshrub—a perennial with a woody base—combines exceptional drought tolerance with an unusual, eye-catching appeal. It demands a sunny spot to thrive and it is the sun that highlights its most attractive feature: the soft, gray-white hairs that cover the clover-like, triple leaflets that glow silver when strongly illuminated. The pea-shaped, 0.75-in.-long, white flowers, veined with pinkish red, are of secondary importance. They are borne in 1- to 1.5-in. umbels of four to ten, in the leaf axils and at the branch ends. Following the flowers is a display of short, round, red-brown seedpods.

Dracocephalum
Lamiaceae
dragonhead

Many of the dragonheads are annual or dwarf shrubs and so outside the purview of this book, but the genus also includes a number of perennials that deserve a spot in sunny gardens. Their whorls of gorgeous blue flowers, aromatic foliage, adaptation to sun, and attraction for foraging butterflies, birds, and bees certainly earn them a trial. Furthermore, deer seldom browse them.

As with most members of the mint family, dragonheads' stems are square in cross section and the tubular flowers are two-lipped, grouped in whorls in the leaf axils or in terminal clusters that may reach 10 in. in length.

Plant dragonheads in a sunny or only lightly shaded spot, where the soil drains well. It does not have to be overly rich—average soil is fine, but these plants will not tolerate winter wet. If necessary, amend the soil in the planting hole to improve drainage. Protect from intense afternoon sun.

Dragonheads are easy to grow and are best propagated from soft tip cuttings or by division of

Dracocephalum argunense 'Fuji White'

established clumps in spring or fall. Seed is somewhat tricky but is usually successful if it receives a
cold spell after sowing indoors.

Dracocephalum argunense

syn. *D. ruyschiana* var. *speciosum, D. speciosum*
- blue
- early to late summer
- 12 in. × 10–12 in.
- sun, part shade
- Z4–8

Dragon's head. Native to grasslands of northeastern Asia and Siberia, this species is ideal for sunny
rock gardens, in containers, or at the front of flower
borders. It makes neat mounds of slender, deep
green, 1-in., needle-like leaves similar to those of
rosemary; stems are topped with terminal spikes of
blue, hooded flowers, similar to related sage, with
a pale blue lip. Drought tolerant and easy care, but
does not tolerate winter wet. Bees flock to the flowers in summer; fine in a wildlife garden or near
beehives.

'Fuji Blue' has brilliant blue flowers. Z5.

'Fuji White' (for Mt. Fujiyama) has snowy white
flowers with a blue-tinged lip. Z5.

Dracocephalum grandiflorum

- blue
- summer
- 10–12 in. × 6–8 in.
- sun
- Z3–8

Dragon's head. Siberia. Rising from rhizomatous
roots, 1- to 2-in., toothed leaves on long stalks form
a basal rosette. Erect flower stems are clothed in
opposite pairs of stemless (sessile), oval leaves.
Prominently hooded, 1.5-in., intensely blue flowers
are spotted with violet on the lower lip, and cluster
at the stem tips and nodes.

'Altai Blue' has pairs of softly hairy, serrated, dark
green leaves and strong dark blue flowers arranged
in whorls and at the stem tips. The lips of the flowers are whitish, decorated with dark spots. 8 in. tall.

Dracocephalum ruyschiana

- blue
- early to late summer
- 18–24 in. × 12 in.
- sun
- Z3–7

Siberian dragon's head, northern dragonhead, Nor-
dic dragonhead. Central Europe. The aromatic
foliage of Siberian dragon's head is known for its
essential oils and was used tradionally to make tea
said to imbue courage. Erect with slightly hairy
stems; typical hooded, blue flowers. Must have
free-draining soil. Ideal in rock gardens, between
patio cracks and crevices, and in xeriscapes.

'Blue Dragon' has whorled spikes of 1-in., clear
dark blue flowers on erect, sometimes hairy stems,
above the evergreen mass of aromatic, rosemary-like foliage. Good drainage is essential, but
tolerant of drought when established. 12–15 in.
Z4–7.

Dracunculus

Araceae
dragon arum

For hermits wishing to be left alone, or those really
looking to one-up a friend or neighbor, no plant is
more perfect! From tuberous roots, dragon arum
produces large, flat, Jack-in-the-pulpit-like flowers
the color of rotting meat and smelling as bad, but
only for a couple of days. The odor attracts countless flies that pollinate the flowers. These bloom in
spring and summer under the partial shade of light
woodlands. The spotted basal leaves are divided
into segments, sometimes considered to be reminiscent of a dragon's claw.

Resistant to deer, rabbits, and rodent browsing. Increase by removing offsets from the tuberous
roots in spring or fall.

Dracunculus vulgaris

- purple
- spring to summer
- 3–5 ft. × 2 ft.
- part shade, shade
- Z6–10

Dragon arum, voodoo lily, stink lily. Native to the
Balkans, Greece, Crete, and the Aegean Islands.
The red-purple spathe of this species may reach 3
in. long, with undulating edges, around an upright,
slender, blackish "Jack" (the spadix), 12–18 in. or
more in length. Coined "Viagra lily" by Tony Avent
of Plant Delights Nursery, these plants are both
erotic and exotic. Provide well-drained soil and a
site in part or even heavy shade. In cold regions, lift
the tubers and protect over winter as for elephant
ear. Slow to get started in spring. To maintain vigor
it is wise to remove offsets from the tuberous roots
every few years. The roots are toxic, so handle carefully and with gloves. Following the flower, green
berries, which mature to orange-red, appear at the
base of the spadix.

Dudleya

Crassulaceae
liveforever

These close relatives of echeverias and sedums,
mostly native to the southwestern United States
and Mexico, are valuable in desert gardens or in
summer containers in temperate zones. They also
do well and are popular as indoor plants for frost-
free sunrooms and conservatories in cold-winter
regions.

Although most species tolerate a very light frost,
they are better suited to warm climates in sun or
light shade inland; only *Dudleya arizonica* and *D.
saxosa* survive the intense sun of Arizona. Dudleyas
are well suited for xeric and rock gardens, wildlife
and native gardens, succulent gardens, or as edgings along paths of dry gardens. Excellent as companion plants for native sages, cacti, succulents,
and grasses.

Leaves may be arranged in a flattened basal rosette or may develop into tubular clumps, spreading by suckers. Flowers do not emerge from the top of the stems, as do echeverias, but rather emerge from further down the stem. Soil must drain freely; these succulents will not survive wet winter conditions. If necessary, set the crown of the plant on an angle to encourage surface rain to drain away. A mulch of gravel is also helpful. Infestations of mealybugs are sometimes serious, especially on indoor plants.

Propagate by seed in spring; seed germinates well at about 60°F. Alternatively, take stem cuttings in spring and early summer. Allow cuttings to dry for a few days to callus before inserting in a sandy rooting medium.

Dudleya brittonii
- yellow
- midwinter
- 6–24 in. × 15 in.
- sun
- Z9–11

Silver dollar plant, chalk dudleya. Baja California. Grown for its evergreen, silver foliage, silver dollar plant may sometimes be found without its gray, waxy coating, but these plants are not as popular. It makes neat, compact plants with juicy, spatulate leaves of a watery sea-green color, covered by waxy bloom. Flower stems are bright red and very showy combined with the starry, pink-bracted yellow or orange flowers above. As the plants mature, the old dead leaves hang on and form a rough "tutu" on the main stem.

Echeveria
Crassulaceae
hens-and-chicks

There are groups of plants on which collectors fixate and the genus *Echeveria* is prominent among them. It includes approximately 150 species of succulents and countless hybrids, many of which, although attractive, can seem redundant to the uninfatuated. The good news is that almost any choice will be a good one: hens-and-chicks combine striking architectural forms—typically precise, tight rosettes of fleshy leaves—with vivid colors, ease of cultivation and, for a bonus, long-lasting, Dr. Seuss-like flowers.

Echeverias originated in the high plains, mountainsides, and cliff faces of Central and South America and, although exceptionally drought tolerant, they prefer regular irrigation during periods of active growth. Let dry out between waterings and provide a gritty, very well-drained soil. Tolerant of full sun or part shade; where intense sunlight combines with high heat, protect from midday sun.

Elegant, non-invasive groundcovers for rock and gravel gardens, echeverias' tolerance for drought makes them ideal for xeriscapes. Exceptionally handsome as container plantings, which in cold-winter regions may be overwintered indoors, providing an opportunity to explore the many fine but frost-intolerant species, such as *Echeveria elegans*, *E. nodulosa*, and *E. setosa*.

Pests include aphids (especially on the flowers) and mealybugs. Sensitive to overwatering; not browsed by deer.

Propagate by removing and replanting rooted offsets or by rooting individual leaves.

Dudleya brittonii

A beautiful container with red-striped *Echeveria nodulosa*

Echeveria agavoides

- red
- spring to early summer
- 6 in. × 12 in.
- sun, part shade
- Z8–11

Red-edge echeveria. Mexico. Forms broad rosettes, often solitary, of red-edged, apple-green leaves, each tipped with a spine. Red, 0.75-in. flowers with yellow-tipped petals arranged in a one-sided spike on 20-in. stems.

'Lipstick' has leaves neatly edged with intense red.

Echeveria nodulosa

- red
- summer
- 1–2 ft. × 2–3 ft.
- sun, part shade
- Z9–11

Painted echeveria. Southern Mexico. Sprawling, branched stems, 1–2 ft., carry 5-in.-wide rosettes of pointed, chartreuse-green leaves, striped with red at mid-leaf and on the margins. Red flowers tipped with yellow borne in small sprays on erect stems shrouded with bracts the same color as the foliage.

Echeveria runyonii

- yellow-and-orange
- summer
- 1 ft. high and wide
- sun, part shade
- Z7–11

Echeveria Compact Glow

Runyon's echeveria. Mexico. Commonly sold under cultivar name 'Topsy Turvy' in reference to the growth habit of the keeled, pale blue-gray leaves that curve upward, with their tips pointing inward to the center of the rosette. Fast growing, quickly forming a mound with individual rosettes measuring as much as 1 ft. in diameter. Perhaps the cold hardiest of echeverias, reported to be hardy to 7°F by Tony Avent of Plant Delights Nursery. Grown for foliage.

Echeveria shaviana

- pink
- midspring to early summer
- 2.5 in. × 6 in.
- sun, part shade
- Z9–11

Mexican hens. Mexico. Rosettes of frilly, blue-green leaves, to 6 in., that take on a pink blush in strong light. Bears sprays of bell-shaped, pink flowers. Grown for its foliage.

'Blue Giant' is extra-large, with blue-green foliage. 6 in. × 12 in.

'Pink Frills' bears young, mauve-purple leaves at the centers of the rosettes that age to silvery blue-green.

Other Notable Cultivars

There are numerous and varied cultivars, mostly grown for their foliage. This is a sampling of what's available.

'Black Knight', very dark chocolate, pointed leaves and a long season of striking red flowers, typically in autumn and winter.

Compact Glow is slow growing with pink, crinkled, undulating leaf edges; leaf blade is bluish gray-green. 6–12 in. Z9–11.

'Jade Point' has deep green, glossy, densely packed, elongated leaves tipped with red.

'Perle von Nurnberg' displays broad leaves, green-gray around the outside of the 8-in. rosettes, deep pink toward center.

Echinacea

Asteraceae
purple coneflower

Its easy-care ways and long season of bloom has put *Echinacea* at the very top of the "essential perennials" list for many gardeners. And purple coneflowers are getting better all the time: during the past decade, plant breeders, most notably those at ItSaul Nursery, the Chicago Botanic Garden, and Terra Nova Nurseries, have been releasing all sorts of exciting new cultivars and hybrids. Now, in addition to the familiar single, purple (and sometimes white), daisy-type blossoms, a host of echinaceas with flowers in exotic colors and forms, and often fragrant, are appearing in catalogs and garden centers. Yellows and oranges have been added to the color palette, as well as outrageous double-flowered forms and some with top knots.

Purple coneflowers are vigorous plants, clothed with mostly coarse, dark green, bristly hairy foliage on strong, branching stems. Basal leaves usually have long petioles and may be toothed along their edges; stem leaves are narrower, often without petioles. The stems terminate in solitary, daisy-like flowers, good for cutting. The ray flowers (petals) surround a raised, prickly central disk that persists after flowers fade.

Purple coneflowers do best in sunny spots but tolerate light shade. They thrive in most well-drained soils, and even endure periods of drought once established; wet feet, however, especially in winter, is usually fatal. Plant in late spring or early summer so the roots have time to become established before cold weather arrives. Pollen and nectar-collecting songbirds, bees, and butterflies are frequent visitors through summer and fall. Regular deadheading results in an extended season of bloom. Allow late-season flowers to go to seed, to provide food for birds—seedeaters feast on the oil-rich seeds inside the central fruiting cone.

Purple coneflowers are versatile garden plants from the designer's perspective. Use tall selections among shrubs or at the back of the border, or mass them in informal meadows, wildlife gardens, or native plant gardens. Dwarf selections are ideal for containers, especially when combined with foliage plants such as coleus, gauras, or fountain grass. Seldom browsed by deer or rabbits, but mildew and Japanese beetles may be a problem.

Propagate species by seed sown outdoors in fall or in containers in spring and chilled for four weeks to break dormancy. Divide named cultivars and hybrids in spring.

Echinacea pallida

- purple
- summer
- 2–3 ft. × 1–1.5 ft.
- sun, part shade
- Z10–3, HT

Pale purple coneflower. Open areas along roadsides, fields, and grasslands of the eastern United States. Thrives in most soils, even poor ones, as long as they are well drained. Tolerates heat, humidity, and drought well, and is a good subject for gardens in the southeastern United States. The mound of narrow, dark green leaves contrasts well with the light purplish, sweet-scented flowerheads above. These have extremely reflexed rays, giving the heads the appearance of a shuttlecock. Ideal in meadows, native plant gardens, and wildlife gardens, or massed in open spaces where they naturalize over time. Can also be used as a temporary summer hedge, perhaps interplanted with tall ornamental grasses.

Echinacea 'Hot Papaya' and others make this garden shine

Echinacea paradoxa 'Hula Skirts Yellow'

Echinacea 'White Swan'

Echinacea paradoxa

- yellow
- summer
- 1–3 ft. × 1–1.5 ft.
- sun
- Z5–8

Yellow coneflower, Ozark coneflower, Bush's purple coneflower. Open areas of the Ozark region of Missouri and Arkansas in fertile, free-draining sites. Erect stems are topped with fragrant, showy, bright yellow, 3-in. flowerheads with swept-back rays surrounding a raised, chocolate-colored disk. Provide full sun and well-drained, even somewhat dry soil—very drought tolerant when established. Not as vigorous as *Echinacea purpurea*; may need support. If planting in fall, it is important to plant sufficiently early to give roots time to grow in well before very cold weather. New plants may not bloom the first summer. Group or mass to provide impact in meadows, or native plant and wildlife gardens. Striking at the back of the border, among shrubs such as chaste tree and butterfly bush, or *Miscanthus* and other bold ornamental grasses.

'Hula Skirts Yellow' is a particularly fine selection with larger flowers.

Echinacea purpurea

syn. *Rudbeckia purpurea*

- purple, white
- summer
- 2–4 ft. × 1.5–2 ft.
- sun, part shade
- Z4–9

Purple coneflower, eastern purple coneflower. Florida and Texas north into Ontario. These plants were a dominant species of the prairies, and in gardens are especially handsome when massed in meadows or with other natives in wild gardens. They have strong root systems and must be planted before midsummer to establish and grow deep. The flowerheads of these traditionally purple or whitish daisies may reach 6 in. or so across, with slightly drooping ray flowers. The deep brown central disk becomes cone-like as it matures. Stiff orange bracts protrude from the cone.

Other Notable Cultivars

Countless selections and cultivars of purple coneflower are in the marketplace, with more almost daily. Hybrids are mostly the results of crossing *Echinacea paradoxa*, *E. purpurea*, and *E. angustifolia*. Below is just a small sampling of what is available.

'Art's Pride' (Orange Meadowbrite) was the first orange coneflower—a color breakthrough—to appear on the market. Striking 5-in.,

Echinacea Harvest Moon

coppery-orange flowerheads; slender, reflexed rays encircle raised, dark brown cones. 2–3 ft. Z3–8.

'Coconut Lime' was the first white, double-flowered, purple coneflower; the flowers start out light green, maturing to greenish white. The full topknot of flowers, orange in the center, is long lasting above a fringe of drooping, white rays. 2–2.5 ft. Z4–9.

'Fragrant Angel' has very large, fragrant, white flowers with gold cones. Partner with tall gayfeathers and daylilies. Prefers humus-rich soil. 3 ft. Z4–9.

'Green Envy' is an unusual large-flowered novelty. The black, green-centered cones are surrounded by long ray flowers, pale green at the tips and pink toward the cone. A Mark Veeder selection. 3 ft. Z4–9.

'Green Jewel' is perfect as a cut flower for St. Patrick's Day. The fragrant, bright green, 4-in. flowerheads have jade-green rays and deep green cones. Sturdy and compact, but demands good drainage. Ideal for containers. 1.5–2 ft. Z3–8.

Harvest Moon ('Matthew Saul') belongs to the Big Sky Series from ItSaul Nursery. Single, sorbet-yellow daisies with raised, orange cones on strong, branched stems. Broad ray flowers, gently reflexed, overlap slightly. 2–2.5 ft. Z4–9.

'Hot Papaya', a double Dutch selection, has fully double, fiery-red pompon heads above a skirt of paprika-colored rays. Strong, maroon-marked stems. 2.5–3 ft. Z5–9.

'Kim's Knee High', perennial dwarf purple coneflower, has strongly reflexed, purple-pink ray flowers and prominently raised, orange cones. Ideal in limited spaces. Drought tolerant. 1–2 ft. Z3–9.

'Magnus' was the 1998 Perennial Plant Association (PPA) Plant of the Year. Its hot-pink flowerheads accented with a copper-brown cone may reach 3–4 in. across on very strong stems. The broad rays are carried horizontally. Dramatic with 'Pomegranite' yarrow. 2.5–3 ft. Z3–9.

'Milkshake' is a selection from the Dutch double-flowered Cone-factions series. It has strongly reflexed, vanilla cream ray flowers above which the usual central cone is smothered with double, vanilla-cream flowers. 3 ft. Z5–9.

'Pink Double Delight' offers "in-your-face" bright pink, double flowers. 1.5–2 ft. Z4–8.

'Razzmatazz' was the first fully double (anemone type), purple coneflower on the market. It has an eye-popping rounded topknot of bright pink, double flowers and a fringe of drooping, dark purplish pink ray flowers. Long blooming; deadhead routinely. Suitable for containers, at the front of the border, and as cut flowers. 2.5–3 ft. Z4–8.

'Rubinsturn' has carmine ray flowers that are held horizontally. Considered by some to be superior to the older 'Magnus'. Grown from seed stock. 40 in. Z4–9.

'Sunrise' (Big Sky Sunrise). Fragrant, light greenish yellow daisies accented with a green-maturing-to-orange cone make a cool color combination. 2.5–3 ft. Z4–9.

'**Tiki Torch**' is eye-catching with 3-in.-wide daisies; drooping, brilliant pumpkin to orange rays surround rounded, reddish cones. 2.5–3 ft. Z4–9.

'**Tomato Soup**' has flowers that truly are the color of real red, ripe tomatoes. Large flowerheads, 5 in. or more across, bear slightly drooping rays around brown cones. 32 in. Z4–9.

'**White Swan**'. Possibly the best white cultivar. Heat, drought, and humidity tolerant even in poor soil. Vigorous, bears plenty of flowers with slightly drooping rays on strong erect stems. 2–3 ft. Z3–8 .

Echinops
Asteraceae
globe thistle

This wide-ranging genus includes 120 or so species that are native from western Europe to central Asia, and south into the mountains of tropical Africa. None is native to North America, but most are enthusiastic self-seeders and can be weedy in US gardens if allowed to proliferate unchecked, though none as yet have proven invasive.

These are plants to use with caution then, but their spiny, silvery foliage combined with prickly, globular heads of flowers gives them an architectural quality that can be invaluable as a focal point in a sunny, dry border or bed. As specimen plantings,

Echinops ritro 'Veitch's Blue'

displayed by themselves, they have a steely, modernist elegance, yet they also blend easily into cottage gardens, perhaps because their strong presence enables them to keep their own identity within a lush, informal chaos. Globe thistles also make striking cut flowers, fresh and dried. Attractive to birds, butterflies, and bees, they are sometimes attacked by aphids, but in general have no serious insect or disease problems. Deer ignore them.

Globe thistles thrive on dry, shallow, and rocky soils as well as ordinary garden loams, as long as the soil is well drained and not overly fertile. They are taprooted, and hard to dig or transplant once established. Taller types, especially when grown on rich soils that encourage soft, lanky growth, may require staking.

Propagate by seed; divide mature clumps in spring, or root cuttings taken in early spring.

Echinops bannaticus
- blue
- early to late summer
- 4–6 ft. × 1.5–2 ft.
- sun
- Z4–9

Globe thistle. Southeastern Europe. Bears spiny, large (to 14 in.), deeply dissected leaves on stiff, fibrous, sometimes branching stems. Foliage is green above with downy-white underside. Produces showy (to 2 in.) gray-blue, globular flowerheads at stem tops over six to eight weeks in summer. Can self-seed prolifically; deadhead to keep from becoming a weed.

'**Blue Glow**' is somewhat compact and has intense steel-blue flowerheads. 4 ft. tall.

'**Star Frost**' is slightly more compact than 'Blue Glow' and bears heads of pearly white flowers. To 40 in.

Echinops gmelinii
- blue
- early to late summer
- 18–24 in. × 6–9 in.
- sun
- Z3–8

Globe thistle. Central Asia, Mongolia, China. Forms erect clumps of stiff stems with spiny-edged, oblong leaves that are green above and downy white underneath. Bears globular, white flowerheads to 1 in. across.

Echinops ritro
- blue
- mid- to late summer
- 3–4 ft. × 2–2.5 ft.
- sun
- Z3–8

Small globe thistle. Central and eastern Europe to central Asia. This species has woolly, deeply lobed, thistle-like, green foliage. Golf ball–sized, steel-blue heads, excellent for cutting. Deadhead to prevent excessive self-seeding.

'**Veitch's Blue**' has powder-blue flowers and steel-blue leaves, silvery beneath.

subsp. *ruthenicus* 'Platinum Blue' has 2-in., steel-blue flowerheads and silvery, pointed, serrated leaves.

Echinops sphaerocephalus

- white
- early summer to early fall
- 3–6 ft. × 2–3 ft.
- sun
- Z3–10

Great globe thistle. Southwestern Europe through Siberia and China. Bears silvery, slightly spiny, deeply dissected leaves, to 14-in. long, on branching, hairy stems. Globular, white, 2-in. flowerheads borne at the stem tips through summer.

'Arctic Glow' is compact with mahogany stems and white flowers. 3 ft. × 1.5 ft.

Echium
Boraginaceae
viper's bugloss

Despite the name, this genus of plants has nothing in common with poisonous snakes other than the old folk tale that one species, *Echium vulgare*, could serve as an antidote for a viper's bite. In fact, the members of this genus offer attractive foliage and vivid, funnel-shaped flowers often borne in spire-like panicles or spikes. Select specimens for the American garden carefully, however, as all these plants are of exotic origin (commonly from the Canary Islands) and several species have proven notably invasive when moved into new habitats. Washington and Tennessee both include *E. vulgare* on their official lists of invasive exotic pest plants, and *E. plantagineum* has become popularly known in Australia as "Patterson's Curse," in honor of the woman who supposedly introduced it into that continent.

The species listed below, however, are all non-invasive and tremendously attractive. The species from the Canary Islands are naturally adapted to prolonged seasonal droughts and are good material for xeriscapes in the southwestern United States. Others perform well in more temperate climates. As a group, they are magnets for hummingbirds, bees, and butterflies, and are deer resistant. They require full sun and a well-drained soil, but are generally hardy, low-maintenance plants. Many species are bristly, and contact can cause skin irritation.

Propagate by seed in summer, by stem cuttings taken in spring, or by layering.

Echium amoenum

- purple, red
- midspring to early fall
- 10–16 in. × 6–8 in.
- sun, part shade
- Z4–10

Red feathers. Northern Iran and the Caucasus Mountains. Forms a low mound of narrow, dark green, leathery leaves, above which a 16-in. spike bristling with tubular, purple flowers rises in spring.

Deadheading prolongs bloom into fall; leave a few flowers to self-seed.

'Red Feathers' has rusty-red flowers.

Echium candicans

- purple
- late spring to midsummer
- 6–8 ft. × 4–6 ft.
- sun
- Z9–10

Pride of Madeira. This Canary Island native forms a broad rosette of hairy, gray-green, evergreen leaves the first year; soaring, upward-curving branches sprout the second and succeeding springs. Branches are shrouded with lanceolate leaves and topped with stunning 12-in.-long spikes of blue-purple flowers. Excellent for coastal and seaside gardens, or a bold backing for lavender, rosemary, sages, and other silvery herbs. Flourishes on free-draining, dry, poor soils; cut back hard with the onset of winter.

Echium lusitanicum

- blue-purple
- spring to early summer
- 3 ft. × 1.5–2.5 ft.
- sun
- Z7–10

Violet-vein viper's bugloss. Southern Spain. Available in the trade as *Echium lusitanicum* subsp. *polycaulon*. One of the showiest and cold-hardiest echiums. Short lived but reseeds prolifically; bears

Echium russicum

multiple 3-ft.-tall spires of shimmering blue-purple flowers veined with violet. Outstanding as a cut flower.

Echium russicum

- red-purple
- late spring to midsummer
- 18–24 in. × 15–18 in.
- sun
- Z5–8

Russian bugloss. Russian native with basal rosettes of silvery, hirsute, lanceolate leaves, from which rise throngs of upright spikes with purple to reddish flowers. Officially classified as a biennial but perennial in most gardens on well-drained soils. A grassland species that performs well in meadow plantings.

Eomecon
Papaveraceae
snow poppy

Sometimes known as Chinese bloodroot, this charming bloodroot relative also has bright orange sap. It is useful in shaded gardens as a groundcover, but should not be introduced into formal beds and borders due to its wandering ways. Slender rhizomes spread far and wide and are brittle, making them difficult to remove if the plant gets out of hand. Grayish green leaves are arrow or heart shaped with wavy edges, to 4 in. wide on long petioles. The leaf surface is sometimes dimpled between the veins. By fall the foliage is yellow and scruffy, so interplant among ferns, hostas, coral bells, and other handsome foliage plants.

Seldom attacked by pests or diseases and ignored by deer and rabbits.

Divide or take root cuttings in spring.

Eomecon chionantha

- white
- late spring to midsummer
- 12–15 in. × 24 in.
- part shade, shade
- Z6–9

Snow poppy, Chinese bloodroot, dawn poppy. Eastern China. Snow poppies thrive in woodland or partly shaded places where soils remain moist. Vigorous growers that spread freely, they produce erect, branching, pink stems that in late spring bear pristine, 2-in. blossoms with four fluttery, white petals and a central boss of yellow stamens in late spring. Flowering at the same time as Virginia bluebells and forget-me-nots, snow poppies are also stunning when partnered with Spanish bluebells in woodland settings, but don't expect to keep them within bounds if the soil is good.

Epilobium
Onagraceae
willowherb, fireweed

Recent revisions to botanical nomenclature have transformed the genus *Epilobium* from a horticultural footnote to a real player. Formerly, the only epilobium of interest to gardeners was *E. angustifolium*, the northern wildflower "fireweed," whose wind-born seeds colonize burnt-over and bombed-out sites. But in the last decade, the genus *Zauschneria*, the "California fuchsias," were reclassified as epilobiums, endowing this genus with a host of genuine garden stars.

Epilobiums new and old are similar in their tolerance for poor, sandy soils, and their spreading rhizomes, two features that make them effective groundcovers.

California fuchsias are typically pest and disease free; fireweed is susceptible to black vine weevils, which also afflict rhododendrons, and the appearance of notches in the margins of fireweed leaves is a warning to protect the shrubbery.

Propagate by seed or divide mature plants. Take stem cuttings of named clones of California fuchsias in fall.

Epilobium angustifolium

- syn. *Chamerion angustifolium*
- pink
- early summer to early fall
- 2–6 ft. × 2 ft.
- sun, part shade
- Z2–8

Fireweed, rosebay willowherb. Northern parts of the Northern Hemisphere, including North America. Fireweed's aggressively spreading rhizomes and prolific self-seeding require restraint in the garden. Slender, lanceolate leaves, up to 8 in. long, are borne spirally around reddish, upright stems; the tubular, pink to magenta, four-petaled flowers may reach 1 in. in diameter, and gather in tapering spikes at the stem tips. Bloom span is a month or so, but routine deadheading extends flowering and reduces self-seeding. Tolerates most soils as long as they remain moist. Attractive at the back of a border, but better suited to informal wet meadows and wildflower plantings due to its aggressive roots. Attractive to butterflies, bees, and hummingbirds.

'Album' has white flowers; not quite as aggressive.

Epilobium canum

- syn. *Zauschneria* spp.
- red
- late summer to early fall
- 1–3 ft. × 4–5 ft.
- sun, part shade
- Z8–10

California fuchsia. Baja California to Oregon, eastward into New Mexico and Wyoming, a shrubby, commonly multi-branched, spreading or upright perennial with green or grayish, hairy, lanceolate to oblong, 1.5-in. leaves; evergreen in mild-winter regions. Brilliant red, trumpet-shaped, four-petaled flowers borne near branch ends, with all flowers usually oriented in the same direction. The bloom is especially impressive because it comes toward the end of California's dry season (late spring to early fall), when the prevailing landscape coloration is brown. Its nectar is an important food source for native bees and hummingbirds. Requires a well-drained soil; drought tolerant, ideal for xeriscapes or for covering a sunny bank. Combine with other coastal sage-scrub natives, icluding lemonade berry (*Rhus integrifolia*) and coffeeberry (*Rhamnus californica*). Susceptible to leaf hoppers and root mealybugs.

subsp. *canum* (*Zauschneria californica*) has orange-red to scarlet trumpets above gray or silvery, lanceolate foliage. 24 in.

'Catalina' has silver, broader leaves, and an upright habit; its orange-red blossoms bloom a little later and for a longer season.

'Dublin' has bright red flowers. 12–18 in.

subsp. *garrettii* (*Zauschneria latifolia* var. *garretti*) has reddish flowers. 7–8 in.

subsp. *latifolium* (*Zauschneria latifolia*) bears spreading grayish, lanceolate leaves and reddish flowers.

'Orange Carpet' is prostrate with orange flowers. 4–6 in. Z4–8.

Epimedium

Berberidaceae
bishop's hat, barrenwort

A large genus of hardy, shade-tolerant perennials, epimediums have long been a go-to groundcover for woodland gardens; although they prefer a moist, humus-rich soil, they are among the select group of plants that succeeds in the dry shade found under shallow-rooted trees. The introduction of new species from China in recent years and new hybrids has broadened the color palette of both flowers and

Epimedium ×perralchicum 'Frohnleiten

foliage, and many of the new types also display their blossoms more visibly, holding them higher above the foliage than older garden epimediums did.

The leaves, evergreen, semi-evergreen, or deciduous, are divided into heart-shaped, rounded, or even triangular leaflets that range in size from 0.5–6 in. long. The cup-shaped flowers are four-parted, often with petals that extend into long spurs that can lend the blossoms the look of an inverted crown (hence the common name bishop's hat).

Although persistent once established, bishop's hats are not aggressive; they form dense clumps that spread slowly by means of underground rhizomes. They make elegant edging plants and provide an effective counterpoint to other shade-tolerant foliage plants: lungworts (*Pulmonaria*), hardy gingers (*Asarum*), ferns, and sedges. Resistant to deer and rabbits, they are generally pest and disease free, though sloppy propagation in the nursery sometimes results in viral infections; plants whose leaves exhibit mosaic patterns of yellow should be discarded.

Propagate by division, in early spring or early fall for deciduous types, and in fall for evergreen ones, or by seed sown in late summer.

Epimedium alpinum

- red-and-yellow
- early spring to midspring
- 6–9 in. × 9–12 in.
- part shade, shade
- Z4–8

Bishop's hat. Southern Europe. This species spreads more rapidly than others. Foliage is deciduous to semi-evergreen (in mild climates); the heart-shaped leaflets have a pink tinge when they emerge in spring, maturing to a medium green and turning deep reddish bronze in fall. Flowers with yellow petals shrouded by red sepals are borne in racemes of 12 to 20.

Epimedium epsteinii

- white-and-purple
- midspring to early summer
- 12 in. × 18 in.
- part shade, shade
- Z5–8

Fairy wings. This recent discovery from China is an excellent evergreen groundcover that spreads 6–8 in. annually. Glossy dark-green leaflets; 10 to 30 flowers per stem, with white inner sepals and plum-purple spurs. Named for the late Harold Epstein.

Epimedium grandiflorum

syn. *E. macranthum*

- pink, purple, white, yellow
- midspring to late spring
- 12–18 in. × 9–18 in.
- part shade, shade
- Z5–8

Longspur barrenwort, horny goatweed. Native to China, Korea, and Japan. The dramatic long spurs

Epimedium ×*versicolor* 'Sulphureum'

Epimedium grandiflorum 'Lilafee'

formed by the petals of this flower are the inspiration for one common name; the other refers to a belief in Asian countries of this species' potency as an aphrodisiac. The deciduous, angel-wing leaflets are toothed along the margins, and are a red-tinged beige when young, maturing to light green and turning red in fall. There are numerous cultivars.

'Cranberry Sparkle' has young chocolate leaves and cranberry-red flowers.

'Lilafee' (Lilac Fairy) has bronze-mottled foliage and lavender-purple flowers

'Pierre's Purple' (Pierre's Purple Fairy Wings) bears wine-purple flowers.

'Red Queen' has carmine-red flowers.

'Tama-no-gempei' has white petals inset into purple outer sepals.

Epimedium pinnatum

- red, white, pink, yellow
- mid- to late spring
- 8–10 in. × 15 in.
- part shade, shade
- Z5–8

Persian epimedium, barrenwort. Japan. Spiny-edged evergreen or deciduous leaves are excellent as a slow-growing groundcover in woodlands and beneath shrubs. Bronzy pink when young, the leaves mature to green then turn bronze by fall. Airy spikes of long-lasting flowers dance above the foliage. Drought tolerant. Cut back in very early spring.

subsp. *colchicum* 'Thunderbolt' bears foliage that slowly darkens in midautumn from deep green to blackish purple beneath a pattern of green veins. Z5–8.

Other Notable Cultivars

×*cantabrigiense* is evergreen and clump forming. Long-stalked leaves of up to 17 in number have lovely fall color. Spurless, two-toned, coppery pink-and-yellow flowers held above the leaves.

×*perralchicum* 'Frohnleiten' is evergreen, 6–10 in., and spreads 6–8 in. annually. Elongated, spiny spring foliage, mottled rose-red, with bright green veins. Large, showy flowers: yellow inner sepals surround tiny, gold-and-red petals. Z5–8.

×*versicolor* 'Versicolor' is deciduous; emerging foliage is deep rose-red with green veins; matures green, then dark brownish purple in fall. Flowers are rich salmon-pink with red-flushed spurs. Z4–8. 'Cupreum' has coppery flowers; 'Sulfureum' has deep yellow flowers.

×*youngianum* is a deciduous clump former. Each stem has two to nine wavy-edged leaflets. White or pink, 0.5-in. flowers. 'Niveum' is white flowered; 'Roseum' ('Lilacinum') has grayish pink flowers.

Epipactis
Orchidaceae
helleborine

Don't let the common name confuse you: these plants have nothing to do with hellebores, but instead are terrestrial orchids that bear classically orchid-type, if modest-sized, flowers. They adapt well to waterside gardens along streams and ponds, and are especially appropriate for wet, but not boggy, wild gardens. Short, creeping rhizomes should be divided when they get overcrowded. Lance-shaped leaves conspicuously ribbed or pleated; erect, leafy stems terminate in loose racemes of flowers, among leafy bracts.

For best results provide a humus-rich, damp soil that does not dry out. A lightly sunny or partly shaded position is ideal; especially protect from hot sun. Some species seed themselves if they are happy, but others increase by their spreading rhizomes. Never dig from the wild; be sure to procure plants from reputable dealers who do not rape the landscape. Protect plants from slugs and snails. Deer resistant.

The species described below is a North American native. *Epipactis helleborine* from Europe is also worth seeking. Easier to grow than our natives, it bears dramatic spikes of up to 50 greenish flowers flushed with purple. Self-seeds to form large colonies. Watch for hybrids.

Increase by division of the rhizomatous roots.

Epipactis gigantea
- green
- summer
- 2–5 ft. × 2 ft.
- sun, part shade
- Z4–8

Giant helleborine, chatterbox, stream orchid. Western Canada to New Mexico, growing in wet places beside streams, springs, and meadows. Large (for an *Epipactis*), 0.75- to 1-in. flowers of yellowish green, veined and flushed with purple, and fragrant. Perhaps 10 to 15 of these will appear on the upper part of the flower stems among leafy bracts. The lower lip and "tongue" of the flowers move, as if chattering when the flower is touched or shaken— hence the common name chatterbox. Rhizomes sprout smooth stems with alternate, pleated, lance-shaped leaves, 2–8 in. long. Prefers alkaline soil. An attractive and vigorous grower that develops into large patches; winter dormant. Charming with maidenhair and other delicate ferns.

'Serpentine Night' has purple-black leaves. Its typical orchid flowers are yellow, marked with red at the throat. 12–18 in. Z6.

Eremurus
Asphodelaceae
foxtail lily, desert candle, king's spear

Looking for a dramatic vertical focal point for your flowerbeds and borders? Foxtail lilies never fail to attract comment with their imposing, statuesque habit and bold bloom. The flower stems rise naked from octopus-like roots to bear at their tips dense, long, "bottle-brush" racemes of starry flowers, with prominent exserted stamens. Flowers open in succession from the bottom upward, ensuring a long bloom time; they serve as butterfly attractors and are excellent when cut. Arranged in a basal rosette, the thick leaves are broadly strappy and often

Eremurus 'White Beauty' partners well with *Stachys officinalis*

become shabby, even during flowering, and retreat underground in summer; camouflage with attractive foliage of companion plants (bronze fennel works well) or plan to overplant with shallow-rooted annuals. Apply a winter mulch of leaves, compost, or straw after the ground freezes in fall to insulate from winter thaws and refreezes. Deep, rich, well-drained soil is essential for good results. It is best to plant the tubers in fall, 2–3 in. deep on a hillock or cone of soil (sand in heavy soil) with the pointed crown pointing up and the "fingers" spreading out and down 2–3 in. If the roots appear dried up upon receipt, soak them for a few hours before planting.

Foxtail lilies are ideal companions for flowering shrubs and show up well against a background of evergreens. Plant in groups between shrubby St. John's worts, hydrangeas, spireas, potentillas, or dwarf evergreens. They are also spectacular against a hedge or at the back of flowerbeds and borders, perhaps behind the bluish leaved false indigo (*Baptisia*), or silvery *Artemisia* 'Powis Castle'. Reports differ as to the deer resistance of foxtail lilies; protect from slugs that attack the new growth.

Once established, do not disturb the brittle roots, except to divide the crowns in spring or fall carefully every few years to reinvigorate the plants and increase stock. Stratify seed before sowing; seedlings may require six years to reach blooming size.

Eremurus himalaicus

- white
- late spring to early summer
- 3–8 ft. × 3 ft.
- sun
- Z3–8

Foxtail lily, Himalayan foxtail lily. Temperate regions of the Himalayas and Afghanistan. Probably the hardiest species of *Eremurus*. Grayish green foliage to 2 ft. long, and white, 1-in. flowers clustered into tapering flower spikes up to 4 in. wide and 2 ft. or more long. Plant in a wind-protected spot, in front of a dark-colored solid fence, hedge, or other sheltering background; support in windy sites.

Eremurus ×isabellinus

syn. *E. olgae* × *E. stenophyllus*

- white, yellow, pink, red
- early summer
- 6 ft. × 2 ft.
- sun
- Z5–8

This catch-all group includes many of the most sought-after and elegant flowers. Soaring above their green, 6- to 12-in.-long leaves, tall, naked stems carry 6- to 18-in.-long racemes of starry, 1-in. flowers in various colors.

'Cleopatra' has orange flowers striped with red. 4–5 ft. tall

'Isobel' is rosy pink flushed with orange. 5–6 ft.

'Pinocchio' has bright yellow flowers. 3–6 ft.

'Romance' has pale pink flowers with yellow stamens. 3–4 ft.

'White Beauty' is pure white. 4–5 ft. tall.

Eremurus robustus

- pink
- early summer
- 6–9 ft. × 3 ft.
- sun
- Z6–9

Foxtail lily, giant desert candle. Rocky alkaline hillsides of Turkestan. This huge plant demands plenty of room and commands attention wherever it is grown. Smooth gray-green foliage is about 2 in. wide and up to 4 ft. in length. Columnar, 2- to 3-ft. racemes composed of countless fragrant, 1.5-in., peachy pink flowers with orange stamens, top ramrod-like scapes in early to midsummer. Attractive to honey bees seeking pollen. Requires a cold period in winter to induce blooming. Attractive companions include hardy geraniums, euphorbias, and species roses.

Eremurus stenophyllus

syn. *E. bungei*

- yellow
- late spring to early summer
- 3–6 ft. × 3 ft.
- sun
- Z5–8

Foxtail lily. Central Asia, Iran. Tufted with grayish green, sometimes hairy leaves, to 10 in. Deep yellow, 0.75-in. flowers in dense racemes atop tall stems.

Erigeron

Asteraceae
fleabane

These unfortunately named perennials are easy to grow, tolerant of most soils and sites, good for cutting, and (reputedly) repel fleas. Furthermore, they are long blooming, bearing charming aster-like flowers, each with two or more rows of ray flowers surrounding yellow disk florets.

Found throughout the temperate zone, this genus includes many North American natives. Several, such as *Erigeron philadelphus* and *E. canadensis*, are considered weeds, although the former is sometimes included in wild, native, or meadow gardens. The showiest fleabanes are mostly hybrids with parentage that often includes orange fleabane, *E. aurantiacus*, and daisy or showy fleabane, *E. speciosus*. Though aster lookalikes, fleabanes mostly bloom prior to the aster season in spring and summer. Flowerheads may be single or semi-double, and either solitary or clustered in flat-topped inflorescences. Basal leaves are petioled, but the stem leaves are alternate and often clasping.

Well-drained soil is a must, and once established, plants tolerate dry soils well. Taller selections—which may require staking—make fine cut flowers; harvest when the flowers are fully open. Only occasionally browsed by deer, more often by rabbits.

Divide in spring or start from seed for bloom the following season.

Erigeron aurantiacus

- orange
- summer to late summer
- 12 in. high and wide
- sun
- Z4–8

Orange fleabane. Turkestan native. Basal rosettes of spatulate, softly downy, 3- to 4-in. leaves; stem leaves clasp the stem. Flowerheads are 1–2 in. across, bright orange with green disks, and borne singly atop slender, upright stems. Short lived, but easy to start from seed in spring; early seedings usually bloom the first season.

Erigeron glaucus

- mauve
- spring to summer
- 10–12 in. × 12 in.
- sun
- Z3–9

Seaside daisy, beach fleabane, beach aster. Ocean bluffs and ravines in coastal California and Oregon. Evergreen, gray-green leaves are glaucous, spoon-shaped, and blunt at the tips, to 6 in. long, sometimes rimmed with teeth. Slender-rayed, semi-double flowerheads bloom for several weeks. Excellent in free-draining sandy soils in cottage and rock gardens, as edging plants, between pavers, atop stone walls, and in containers. Salt tolerant; an important plant in seaside gardens. Attracts insects and butterflies. Deadhead to extend bloom time and cut back hard every couple of years to maintain vigor. Provide light midday shade and extra water in inland gardens.

'Bountiful' has very long-blooming, 3-in., lavender flowerheads. A compact seedling from 'Arthur Menzies'. 6–10 in.

'Cape Sebastian' has whitish foliage and violet flowerheads. 12 in.

'Roger Raiche' is upright with purple flowers. Long bloom time. To 18 in.

'Sea Breeze' produces 1.5-in.-wide, pinky-mauve blooms in abundance in midspring and continues through summer if deadheaded routinely. 8–12 in. Z7.

Erigeron karvinskianus

- white, pink
- spring to fall
- 6–24 in. × 36–60 in.
- sun
- Z7–11

Mexican daisy, bonytip fleabane, Santa Barbara daisy. Mexico to Venezuela. Excellent as a trailing groundcover, Mexican daisy is covered with small white or pink-flushed daisies all summer. Prefers sandy, free-draining soil and full, but not intense, sun. Blooms the first season if seed sown in early spring, and self-seeds abundantly. Can become invasive and is difficult to eradicate. Delightful tumbling over rocks and walls, and in containers. Tough but charming pink Santa Barbara daisy, *Erigeron ×moerheimii*, is very similar but sterile, and more compact. Both are great attractors of beneficial insects.

'Profusion' bears white flowers that fade to pink. Spreads freely. 6–8 in.

Erigeron speciosus

- lilac
- summer
- 12–30 in. × 24 in.
- sun, part shade
- Z2–7

Daisy fleabane, showy fleabane, Oregon fleabane, Aspen fleabane. Western United States. From woody rootstocks rise multiple stems clothed with clasping leaves and branching at the top. Each branch is topped with narrow-rayed but

Erigeron karvinskianus

Erigeron hybrid 'Rotes Meer'

Erodium reichardii 'Charm'

showy 2-in.-wide flowerheads . Tall selections may require staking. Best in temperate climates where summers are cool. Cut back after blooms are spent to encourage rebloom and help the new basal growth overwinter successfully. Seldom cultivated outside of native plant gardens. One of the dominant parents of the showy hybrid group (*Erigeron ×hybridus*), along with *E. alpinus*, *E. aurantiacus*, *E. speciosus* var. *macranthus*, and sometimes *E. glaucus*.

Other Notable Cultivars

Erigeron hybrids were formerly more popular in American gardens than they are today, especially the series bred by famed British plantsman Alan Bloom. These and others are still offered by mail from British nurseries. The following are available in the United States as of this writing.

'Darkest of All' is one of the best and most popular selections with deep violet flowers. 24 in.

'Pink Jewel' produces masses of semi-double, 1.5-in., orchid-pink flowers. Excellent cut flower. 24 in. Z4.

'Prosperity' is getting more difficult to find in the marketplace, but is well worth growing for its large, semi-double, lavender-blue daisies on 18-in. stems. Good cut flower.

'Rotes Meer' ('Red Sea') has several layers of shocking pink ray flowers encircling a yellow center.

Eriophyllum
Asteraceae
golden yarrow, woolly sunflower

Only one or two members of this native Western genus of 12 species are cultivated outside of native plant and wild gardens, but it seems there is always room in the garden for another yellow daisy,

especially in regions of their nativity. The genus name is derived from the Greek *erio*, meaning wool, and *phyllum*, meaning leaves.

These attractive silver-gray plants are effective in sunny beds and borders where soil drains freely or is even dry. Partner them with plants such as penstemons, sages, and agastaches.

Propagate by seed or division of the roots.

Eriophyllum lanatum
syn. *E. caespitosum*, *Actinella lanata*

- yellow
- spring to midsummer
- 12–24 in. × 12 in.
- sun
- Z5–10

Woolly sunflower, golden yarrow, Oregon sunshine. Dry open spaces and rocky slopes of the western United States as far north as Vancouver, BC. Clumping with branched stems that become covered with solitary, 1- to 2-in., yellow daisies centered with yellow disks. The stems may flop to form large mats. Lower leaves are pinnately lobed, those above mostly linear. These white plants protect themselves from intense sun and drought with a dense coat of light-reflecting and transpiration-reducing white hairs. The sunny flowerheads attract many different insects and are a nectar source for several species of butterflies and songbirds. Tolerates drought well; suitable for dry borders and xeriscapes.

var. *grandiflorum* is very similar and possibly a hybrid with other species.

Erodium
Geraniaceae
heronsbill, filaree

Most often confined to the rock garden, the genus *Erodium* also includes several excellent low-growing species suitable for lining garden paths or for the front of the border, and for inserting between pavers and stepping stones. Heronsbill's attractive and durable foliage is often divided or even dissected; the small, saucer-shaped, five-petaled flowers are arranged in loose umbels. The beak-like fruits that follow the flowers add interest as they split by twisting into tight spirals to release their seeds. Of limited application but outstanding in rock gardens or troughs and worth seeking is the so-called alpine geranium, *E. reichardii*.

Heronsbills do best in full sun or very light shade where the soil is sandy or gritty and drains freely. Apply gravel or lime chips as a mulch to assist rainwater runoff and keep the surface dry. Protect plants from intense noon and afternoon sun. Pests and diseases are seldom serious, and deer tend to avoid erodiums.

To propagate, take cuttings in early summer or divide plants in spring. Otherwise, sow seed in spring or in late summer as soon as they ripen.

Erodium absinthoides

syn. *E. olympicum*
- pink
- summer
- 8 in. × 24 in.
- sun, part shade
- Z7–10

Heronsbill, storkbill. Southern Europe, Macedonia. Forms a sprawling mound of feathery, hairy, silver-gray leaves that are cut into slender segments. Flowers are violet, pink, or white traced with darker veins, and measure 0.75 in. in diameter. Very variable.

Erodium carvifolium

- pink
- early summer to early fall
- 10–18 in. × 14 in.
- sun, part shade
- Z6–10

Heronsbill, storkbill. Spain. Pink to magenta, 0.5-in. flowers, upper petals blotched with deep red. Long, lacy, green leaves develop into low-growing rosettes of foliage. Plant this long-blooming plant in beds and borders.

Erodium reichardii

syn. *E. chamaedryoides*
- pink
- late spring to early fall
- 4–6 in. × 12 in.
- sun, part shade
- Z6–10

Alpine geranium, baby Swiss geranium. Corsica, Majorca. Forms low-growing mounds of soft, grayish, heart-shaped leaves that are scalloped along the edges. Flowers are whitish pink, to 2 in. across, etched with rose-pink veins. Protect from intense afternoon sun. Free-draining, sandy soil is ideal. This species is drought tolerant, but winter wet is sure to kill it. Charming in trough gardens or planted with low sedums, sempervivums, and creeping thymes in rock gardens.

Bishop's Form (syn. *Erodium chamaedryoides* 'Bishop's Form') has mid-pink, 0.5-in. flowers with purplish veins. 2 in. tall, but may be 10 in. across. Z8–10.

'Charm' has lavender-pink flowers, traced with hot-pink veins. Z7–9.

'Flore Pleno' has double, pink or white blooms. Z8–9.

'Roseum' has darker pink flowers with crimson veins.

Eryngium
Apiaceae
sea holly

Although popular among European gardeners, the eryngiums remain largely unknown on this side of the Atlantic. Surely it is its spiny, unfriendly aspect that has prevented this striking genus from winning the place in our gardens that it deserves. Yet the same feature that makes these plants uncomfortable to handle, the spines that armor not only leaves but also the floral bracts and petals, also make them invaluable sources of texture and contrast; nothing else so emphasizes the softness or tactile qualities of other foliages than does a strategically placed sea holly.

Eryngiums flourish in dry, well-drained, and sunny spots, making them excellent specimens for xeriscapes, or where water supply is short. Steely blue foliage makes sea hollies natural companions for blue-flowered herbs such as Russian sages (*Perovskia*) and lavenders; they also harmonize well with taller yellows such as yellow foxgloves (*Digitalis grandiflora*) and hollyhocks (preferably some single-flowered cultivar such as 'Sunshine'). Sea hollies are sophisticated and stylish as cut flowers and dry well for winter arrangements. Deer and rabbit resistant.

The deep-reaching taproots of eryngiums do not respond well to transplanting or division. Do not disturb once a plant is well established. Propagation is by seed as soon as it ripens (start in containers) or by root cuttings taken in fall. Root cuttings may be taken from pencil-thick roots in winter.

Eryngium alpinum

- blue
- early summer to late summer
- 1–2.5 ft. × 1–2.5 ft.
- sun
- Z2–8

Eryngo, alpine sea holly. Alps and mountainous parts of southern Europe. Thrives in average to poor, dry to moderately moist soils as long as they are well drained. Tolerates light shade, drought, and saline conditions—a good choice for seaside gardens. Thistle-like in appearance, with stiff stems clothed with gray-green to bluish, heart-shaped, spiny lower leaves, and palmately divided upper ones. Flowerheads are egg shaped, to 2 in. long, and framed by a collar of sharp, finely divided, blue-gray bracts. No serious insect pests or diseases, but won't tolerate wet soils in winter.

'**Blue Star**' has blue stems and foliage, and metallic blue flowerheads.

'**Superbum**' has three tiers of bracts around the base of each flowerhead, lending the blossoms a lacy look.

Eryngium amethystinum

- blue
- mid- to late summer
- 18–30 in. × 24 in.
- sun
- Z2–8

Amethyst sea holly. Balkans, Italy, Sicily. Basal rosettes of grayish, deeply cut leaves that are attractively speckled and veined with silver. Branching stems, gray-blue above, carry metallic-blue, thistle-like flowers surrounded by up-curving, long, silver bracts, armed with stiff spines. Prefers dry, poor to moderately fertile soil that drains freely.

The cold-hardiest species of the genus.

'**Sapphire Blue**' has steely blue flowers, foliage, and stems. Z5–9.

Eryngium amethystinum 'Sapphire Blue'

Eryngium bourgatii

- blue
- early summer to late summer
- 1–2 ft. high and wide
- sun
- Z5–8

Eryngo. Pyrenees. Has deeply lobed, silver-veined leaves, and vivid blue, branched stems. These bear conical, silver-blue or violet flowerheads set on collars of narrow, spiny bracts. Tolerates dry and poor soils; requires good drainage, especially in winter. No serious pests or diseases.

Eryngium maritimum

- blue
- midsummer to late summer
- 8–24 in. × 12 in.
- sun
- Z5–11

Sea holly. European native of coastal areas and sand dunes. Borne on tall stems, the evergreen foliage is showy: leathery, glaucous, and blue-gray in color, the ovate, three-lobed leaves have spiny teeth. Collars of spiny bracts frame the 1-in., thimble-shaped, light blue flowerheads.

Eryngium pandanifolium

- green
- summer
- 4–6 ft. × 2–4 ft.
- sun, part shade
- Z7–10

Pandanus leaf eryngium. Argentina and Brazil. Forms clumps of blue-gray, strap-like, sawtooth-edged, screwpine-like leaves. Tall stalks emerge from the middle bearing branched clusters of gray-green thimble flowerheads.

Eryngium planum

- blue
- early summer to late summer
- 2–3 ft. × 1–2 ft.
- sun
- Z5–9

Sea holly, flat sea holly. Central and southeastern Europe. Flourishes in dry, sandy soils; avoid overwatering and overly fertile soils that cause rank, lax growth. Basal rosettes of deeply toothed, oblong, blue-green leaves, to 4 in. long, from which sprout stiff, 3-ft. flower stems. These bear pale blue, round flowerheads collared with projecting spiny bracts. Generally pest free, but subject to leaf spot.

'**Blue Glitter**' commonly blooms in its first year from seed. Large, intensely blue flowerheads on silver-blue stems.

'**Blue Hobbit**' is dwarf, with flowerheads completely covering the foliage at the peak of its season. 8–12 in.

'**Jade Frost**' has blue leaves edged with cream, and blue flowers.

'**Silver Salentino**' has silvery-white cones sparsely ruffed with silver bracts. 2.5–3 ft. Z4.

Eryngium yuccifolium
- greenish white
- early to late summer
- 4–5 ft. × 2–3 ft.
- sun
- Z3–8

Rattlesnake master. Meadows and prairies, eastern half of the United States. Tussocks of lanceolate, 2.5 ft. × 2 in., grayish green leaves edged with spines—as the species name suggests, the foliage does resemble that of yucca. Flowerheads on stiff, upright stems that emerge from the center of the foliage rosettes; greenish white, globular heads to 1 in. across have sparse collars of long, sharp bracts at the apex of the central stem, and sometimes from the upper leaf axils. Prospers with dry to medium moisture on average soils; tolerant of clay, shallow, and rocky soils. Avoid very fertile soils that encourage soft, sprawling growth. No serious insect or disease problems. Staking may be necessary on windy sites. Equally at home in formal borders as in a meadow.

Erysimum
Brassicaceae
wallflower

Despite the name, wallflowers are guaranteed to attract admiration wherever you may plant them. Traditionally they have been used mostly as cool-season bedding plants and treated as annuals; *Erysimum cheiri* (formerly *Cheiranthus cheiri*) has been the standard choice for this purpose. A number of species, however, perform as perennials in hospitable sites, and others, while normally biennial, self-seed readily so that they function as perennials.

Most species originated in hot, sunny climates subject to seasonal drought, and so make good subjects for rock or gravel gardens, and thrive (as the common name suggests) when tucked into the crevices of wall, where they often self-sow. Wallflowers prefer alkaline soil, but tolerate most soils as long as they are well drained. Slugs and snails are often a problem; seldom troubled by deer. Mingles well with perennial herbs such as rosemary, thymes, and lavenders, whose foliages complement the *Erysimum* flowers. They are also a traditional element of cottage gardens. Several species, such as *E. cheiri* and *E. ×marshallii*, are toxic if ingested, and should not be accessible to children and pets.

Propagate by seed or by semi-hardwood cuttings of non-blooming stems taken in spring or summer.

Erysimum capitatum
syn. *Cheiranthus capitatus*
- orange, yellow
- midspring to early summer
- 1–2 ft. × 0.5–1 ft.
- sun, part shade
- Z3–7

Western wallflower, sand-dune wallflower. Western United States, as well as the upper South and Midwest. Produces evergreen basal rosettes of

These containers of *Erysimum linifolium* 'Variegata' garnished with curly parsley make quite a statement along the parapet

3-in., linear to narrowly oblong leaves. In the second spring, upright stems, 1–2 ft. tall, emerge, each topped with a dense, rounded cluster of cruciform, four-petaled flowers, 0.75 in. across. Blooms are commonly some shade of yellow or orange, but may be maroon or near white. Flourishes in average soils with moderate to low moisture; tolerates shallow, rocky soils, and drought. Naturalizes where conditions hospitable.

Erysimum cheiri
syn. *Cheiranthus cheiri*
- red, orange, yellow
- midspring to early summer
- 18–24 in. × 15–18 in.
- sun, part shade
- Z5–9, HS

Aegean wallflower, Siberian wallflower, common wallflower. Southern Europe. This species is perennial in mild climates such as those found in the US Pacific Northwest. Does not tolerate southern heat with humidity. Prefers a moderately moist but well-drained soil with mildly alkaline pH—it often colonizes the cracks in the mortar of aging masonry walls. Forms rosettes of narrow, pointed leaves to 8 in. long in the first year's growth. The second and succeeding years bring mace-like inflorescences of cruciform, four-petaled flowers borne in dense racemes on upright stems. Flowers fragrant, in shades of yellow, orange, red, mahogany, and purple. Start from seed.

Bedder Series are compact to 12 in. Individual colors of gold, primrose, orange and scarlet.

'Blood Red' has deep red flowers.

Charity Mix is compact, about 8 in., and blooms in its first year of growth, with 0.5-in., rosered, scarlet, yellow, or creamy-yellow blossoms. Fragrant.

'Harpur Crewe' (syn. *E.* ×*kewensis* 'Harpur Crewe') is a double heirloom, with very fragrant, yellow flowers. 12 in.

Sunset Mix is an F1 hybrid strain in a wide range of colors. Very fragrant. 10–12 in.

Tom Thumb Mix is compact, ideal for furnishing window boxes and planters. Subtly scented blooms range from pale yellows to strong reds. 9 in. tall.

'Wenlock Beauty' has long racemes of bronzeflushed, yellow flowers. Evergreen. 18 in.

Erysimum linifolium
- pink, purple
- early spring to late summer
- 2–2.5 ft. × 1.5–2 ft.
- sun, part shade
- Z6–9

Alpine wallflower. Native to Spain and Portugal. Vigorous, shrubby, evergreen perennial with narrowly lanceolate, gray-green leaves. Cruciform, four-petaled flowers bloom in terminal racemes over a long season.

'Bowles' Mauve' is probably a hybrid but is often assigned to *Erysimum linifolium*. It bears clusters of fragrant, mauve flowers more or less continuously, sometimes right through the winter in mild coastal areas. 2–2.5 ft.

'Variegatum' has tufts of cream-and-green variegated leaves with profuse clusters of mauve and brown flowers. Attractive foliage for winter gardens. 20 in.

Erysimum ×marshallii
syn. *Cheiranthus allionii*
- yellow, orange
- midspring to early summer
- 18–24 in. × 9–12 in.
- sun, part shade
- Z3–8

Siberian wallflower. A hybrid of garden origin. Has gray to deep green, slightly downy, lanceolate, semi-evergreen, toothed leaves. The four-petaled flowers are yellow to bright orange, and strongly perfumed. If deadheaded it continues to bloom all summer.

'Apricot Delight' bears apricot-orange flowers on compact bushy plants.

Other Notable Cultivars
There are many other cultivars, but most are bred for bedding displays and not perennial.

Rysi Strain is more reliably perennial, to 16–18 in. high and wide, with cultivars bearing golden flowers flushed with bronze ('Rysi Bronze'), coppery orange ('Rysi Copper'), chrome yellow ('Rysi Gold'), cream fading to milky white ('Rysi Moon') and primrose yellow ('Rysi Star').

Erythronium
Liliaceae
trout lily, dogtooth violet

Trout lilies are native to forests and damp meadows across temperate regions of the world and many can be found growing wild in parts of North America. They are one of the special joys of the spring garden, with gracefully nodding flowers commonly featuring swept-back petals and prominent stamens. Typically bloom time is two to three weeks long; the flowers present a pretty contrast to the tongue-shaped spotted or plain green leaves. The mottling of the leaves suggests the speckled side of a trout (hence the common name). The other traditional name for this genus, dogtooth violet, refers to the pointed, bulb-like, tuberous roots, which were imagined to resemble the shape of a dog's tooth—it's important to note that this genus is not related to violets (*Viola*).

Plant trout lilies in fall about 4 in. deep in a humus-rich soil that does not dry out. They prefer partly shaded places, and will not endure intense sun.

Seldom browsed by deer and generally pest and disease resistant. Allow to colonize in damp woodlands with ferns, primroses, summer snowflake, and other plants that enjoy shaded, damp places.

To propagate, mark the position of plants in spring, and dig in late summer to remove and replant offsets. Sow seed as soon as it ripens in late spring or early summer; seedlings are very slow growing and often require five to six years to reach flowering size.

Erythronium albidum

- white
- mid- to late spring
- 4–8 in. × 9 in.
- part shade, shade
- Z4–8

White trout lily, white fawn lily, yellow snowdrop. Moist, light woodlands of the eastern United States and Canada. Springing from a corm-like bulb, each plant has a pair of oval, 3- to 9-in.-long leaves that are irregularly mottled with silver. The solitary, 1.5-in., white flowers, flushed with yellow at the base, are borne on 6- to 12-in., leafless stems (scapes) and have reflexed petals reminiscent of cyclamen. When temperatures rise in early summer, the plants retreat underground. Spreads readily by offsets from the roots; these may take two years to bloom.

Erythronium americanum

- yellow
- early spring
- 3–8 in. × 8 in.
- part shade, shade
- Z3–8

Adder's tongue, yellow trout lily, yellow dogtooth violet. Rich, damp woods and wet meadows of the eastern seaboard of the United States. A pair of smooth, pointed, brown-and-purple-mottled leaves, 3–8 in. long, rise from a scaly bulb; immature bulbs produce only one solitary leaf. A single, 3- to 7-in. scape terminates in a nodding, yellow to brownish flower with recurved petals, brown on the underside. In the wild these plants colonize readily and some stands are reputed to be 300 years old. Summer dormant. Seeds about freely; if growing in a lawn, delay mowing until the seeds have been disseminated.

Erythronium dens-canis

- pink, white, purple
- midspring to late spring
- 8–12 in. × 6 in.
- sun, part shade
- Z3–8

Dogtooth violet. Mountain meadows of southern Europe. Flowers of this charmer are solitary, mostly rosy-purple with purple anthers and ringed with red-purple at the throat, about 2 in. long. Strongly purple-mottled, 4- to 6-in. basal leaves, in pairs are reputedly tasty in salads. Several cultivars are available:

'Lilac Wonder' has light purple flowers accented with a chocolate ring at the base. Early. 6–8 in.

'Pink Perfection' has clear bright pink flowers on 3- to 4-in. stems. Early.

'Purple King' is bright pinkish purple, sometimes rimmed with white. Vigorous, and suitable for underplanting shrubs, in rock gardens, and for lining woodland paths. 6 in.

'Rose Queen' has rosy pink flowers, with a deep brown blotch at the base. 4–8 in. tall.

'Snowflake' is clean white with a taupe base. 6 in.

'White Splendor' has white flowers, blotched with brown at the base. Early. 6–8 in.

Erythronium grandiflorum

- yellow
- late spring
- 12–20 in. × 15 in.
- part shade
- Z4–8

Yellow glacier lily, yellow avalanche lily, lambs' tongue trout lily. Clearings and open woods, often under Ponderosa pines and Gambel oaks, in the western United States, California to Alberta, Montana, and Colorado. Pairs of upright, elliptic, plain green leaves, undulating along the edges, to 8 in. in length, appear shortly after snow melt. Large, showy drifts of 2-in., bright yellow, starry flowers, several per scape, bloom for about a month.

Erythronium revolutum

- rose-pink
- early to midspring
- 12–14 in. × 10 in.
- part shade
- Z5–8

Mahogany trout lily, coast fawn lily, pink fawn lily. Coastal areas from northern California to British Columbia, especially along streams and in damp forest clearings. One to several nodding, bright

Erythronium 'Pagoda' provides early color in this hosta bed

rose flowers top pinkish scapes above basal pairs of white-marbled, broadly lance-shaped leaves to 8 in. long. Seeds about freely to form colonies.

'Pink Beauty' has reflexed, clear pink petals. Self-sows readily and is charming in drifts in light woods. 12 in.

Other Notable Cultivars

'Pagoda'. This vigorous hybrid of western US species (*Erythronium tuolumense* × *E. revolutum*) produces several 1.5-in-wide, bright yellow flowers with a reddish brown eye on each naked stem. Blooms for up to a month in mid- to late spring. Each bulb may produce several stems, in contrast to other species that bear a solitary stem per bulb. The silvery green, sometimes mottled, basal leaves emerge somewhat later than those of *E. americanum* and disappear in hot weather. An attractive companion for naturalized narcissus and Spanish squills. Often listed as a cultivar of either parent. Later-blooming 'Kondo' is similar and has the same parentage. The species *E. tuolumnense*, from the foothills of the Sierra Nevadas, is seldom grown.

Eupatoriadelphus

Asteraceae
Joe-Pye weed

This is another recently reclassified genus that has been broken away from *Eupatorium*; look there for general information.

Eupatoriadelphus dubius

syn. *Eupatorium dubium*

• pink	• 2–5 ft. × 1 ft.
• midsummer to early fall	• sun, part shade
	• Z4–8

Eastern Joe-Pye weed. East Coast of North America from Nova Scotia to South Carolina. Typically 3- to 4-ft.-tall, purple-flecked stems clothed in whorls of lanceolate, toothed leaves. Small, purplish pink flowers carried in domed heads 4–7 in. across. Prefers moist soils but tolerant of drought. A compact alternative to its better-known relatives *Eupatorium purpureum* and *Eupatoriadelphus maculatus*.

'Phantom' is extra compact, with wine-colored, sweet-scented flowers. 2–3 ft.

Eupatoriadelphus maculatus

syn. *Eutrochium maculatum, Eutrochium purpureum* subsp. *maculatum, Eupatorium maculatum*

• purple	• 4–7 ft. × 3 ft.
• midsummer to late summer	• sun, part shade
	• Z5–9

Spotted Joe-Pye weed. Manitoba south to Georgia eastward. Solid purple or purple-spotted stems bear toothed, lanceolate leaves in whorls of three to five. Small, light purple flowers borne in branched, usually flat-topped clusters to 8 in. across. Flowers are lightly scented and very showy when planted in mass. Prefers an organic-rich, moist soil; leaf edges liable to browning and crisping when subjected to

Eupatoriadelphus maculatus 'Gateway' provides a fine background for Russian sage, *Rudbeckia*, and *Artemisia* in this autumnal border

drought. Especially valuable for foraging bees.

'Atropurpureum' (syn. *Eupatoriadelphus purpureum* var. *atropurpureum*) has purplish black stems and reddish purple flowerheads to 18 in. wide.

'Gateway' is relatively compact with wine-colored stems; it bears huge, pink flowerheads, 12–18 in. across. 3–5 ft. tall.

Eupatorium
Asteraceae
boneset, Joe-Pye weed

This globe-trotting genus is found all over the Northern Hemisphere—in Europe, northern Africa, and central Asia—but it is the North American species, natives of the eastern half of the continent, that are the horticultural stars. These garden-worthy types earn their keep with their strong presence: they are large, exuberant plants that contribute foliage mass and texture, as well as flowers. Individually the flowers are small and most often subdued in color, but they are borne in substantial to huge, parasol-like heads. Furthermore, their bloom season commonly comes in late summer or fall, when the perennial garden most needs additional color. The flowers attract butterflies and other insect pollinators, and the seedheads that follow provide late-season food for a variety of birds.

The taller eupatoriums—they can stand head-high or even higher—require staking in a windswept site. Alternatively, pinch back the stems in mid- to late spring to about half their height to promote more compact, bushy growth; this treatment

Eupatorium coelestinum

also leads to a slightly later bloom season. Eupatoriums appreciate a rich, organic soil, and require moderate but regular irrigation while young, as well as for the best bloom. However, they tolerate drought once established.

Combine eupatoriums with other late bloomers such as goldenrods (*Solidago*), swamp hibiscus (*Hibiscus coccineus*), asters, and the taller ornamental grasses. The native species are ideal for native, meadow, or prairie plantings, as well as at the back of borders and among shrubs. Butterflies and bees are frequent visitors and pollinate the flowers. Typically bonesets are healthy plants, but are susceptible to leaf miners, mildew, and leaf spots. Only *Eupatorium fistulosum* is reportedly browsed by deer; other species are left alone.

Propagate by dividing mature clumps in late winter or spring, by seed, or by stem cuttings taken in spring.

Eupatorium altissimum

• white	• 3–4 ft. × 2–3 ft.
• late summer to early fall	• sun, part shade
	• Z3–9

Tall boneset. This tough and adaptable species is native throughout the eastern half of North America, inhabiting dry to mesic prairies, meadows, woodland openings, pastures, and even vacant lots. It forms a group of upright, hairy stems that branch only at their tips in the flower clusters. Dark green, pubescent leaves are opposite, lanceolate to narrowly ovate, and up to 5 in. long and 1 in. wide. Inflorescence is a flat-topped cluster of tiny, white flowers that bloom for four to six weeks. Not particularly showy, but hardy and versatile, growing equally well on loams, clays, and gravelly soils of assorted pH levels. Withstands drought well and competes successfully with most neighbors in meadow plantings or wild gardens.

'Prairie Jewel' has variegated cream-and-green, mottled foliage. More compact than the species, reaching a height of 3 ft. Z4–9.

Eupatorium capillifolium

• white	• 4–8 ft. × 3–4 ft.
• midsummer to early fall	• sun, part shade
	• Z4–10

Dogfennel. Roadsides and disturbed sites from Massachusetts to Florida, westward to Missouri and Texas, as well as Cuba and the Bahamas. Spreads by rhizomes and can be weedy; reportedly aggressive in Florida, though not further north. Forms a clump of hairy stems with aromatic, finely dissected, feathery foliage ("capillifolium" means "hair-leaf"), somewhat similar to that of fennel (*Ferula*). Individual flowers are small, but borne in large, loose plumes. A tall and striking plant, though not distinguished enough for most borders; better for meadows and native plant areas.

'Elegant Feather' is more refined, forming narrow, upright plumes of finely textured foliage. Sterile, does not self-seed as does dogfennel. Z7–10.

Eupatorium coelestinum
syn. *Conoclinium coelestinum*

- blue
- late summer to early fall
- 2–3 ft. high and wide
- sun, part shade
- Z4–9

Hardy ageratum. Eastern half of North America. Red stems bear heads of fuzzy, blue flowers that are closely similar to those of the familiar annual ageratum or floss flower. Tolerant of most soils, but best suited to clays and organic-rich ones. Prefers moist to average conditions; grows best in full sun, but tolerates light shade. Naturalizes readily, especially in warmer regions, making an attractive tall groundcover.

'Cory' is upright, with crinkled leaves and more abundant, showier blooms on purple stems.

Eupatorium purpureum
syn. *Eutrochium purpureum*

- pink, purple
- midsummer to early fall
- 5–7 ft. × 2–4 ft.
- sun, part shade
- Z3–9

Sweet-scented Joe-Pye weed. Wet meadows, stream banks, and wooded slopes throughout the eastern half of the United States and Ontario. Erect clumps of sturdy stems furnished with whorls of three to four serrated, lanceolate, dark green leaves to 12 in. long. Domed, mauve flowerheads are vanilla scented, to 8 in. across; they give way to attractive seedheads that persist into winter. Prefers a moist, fertile, richly organic soil; tolerates average soils unless subjected to drought, which causes browning of leaf edges. Plant in groups or mass at the back of borders, cottage gardens, meadows, and at the water's edge.

'Little Red' has pink-purple flowers. Compact at 3–4 ft. × 2–3 ft.

Euphorbia
Euphorbiaceae
spurge

The best-known member of this genus is the decorative holiday poinsettia, *Euphorbia pulcherrima*, but this has a number of garden-worthy, perennial relatives. Upright or trailing stems well clothed with oval, pointed leaves arranged in whorls or spirals are typical. The flowers are cup shaped with petal-like bracts ranging in color from red to yellowish green or lime. Flowers are borne in variously shaped heads or inflorescences, which are often quite large.

Best in sunny spots but appreciative of midday shade in regions with intense sunlight. Partial or light shade is acceptable, but avoid deeper shade. A

Euphorbia polychroma 'Bonfire'

moist, fertile soil, well drained and not overly rich, is ideal. The milky sap of the plants causes painful skin rashes in sensitive individuals, and in some species is actually poisonous, so avoid planting them near children's play areas. On the plus side, deer, rabbits, and most insects avoid these plants.

The larger spurges are perfect for flowerbeds and borders and for planting among shrubs, as well as for punctuating gates and entryways. Use drought-tolerant species in xeriscapes; site low-growers where they can tumble over walls and creep among pavers. Not described here but useful for xeriscapes in cooler regions (Z5–7) is *E. dulcis* 'Chameleon', which provides tight mounds of red-purple foliage. Beware of cypress spurge (*E. cyparissias*), an invasive European species. Many spurges make excellent and unusual cut flowers; flame the base or dip the base of the stems into boiling water to stop the flow of sap that will otherwise pollute the vase water.

Propagation is mainly from seed or by division of mature clumps. Leaf or stem cuttings may be taken in spring or summer to increase some species.

Euphorbia amygdaloides

- yellow
- late spring
- 12–20 in. × 15 in.
- sun
- Z5–8, HS

Wood spurge. Woodlands, meadows, and banks from Ireland, east to the Caucasus. Seeds about freely, so cut spent flower stems to the ground after bloom. Upright, reddish stems with spatulate (spoon-shaped), dark green foliage; yellow-green, bracted flowers. Seldom successful in the southeastern United States.

'Purpurea', purple wood spurge, has dramatic

Euphorbia characias subsp. *wulfenii*

Euphorbia myrsinites

deep purple or mahogany winter foliage with fluffy, wine-colored new growth in early spring. Heads of lime-green flowers bloom above a little later. Seeds freely.

'Ruby Glow' has burgundy, ruby, and bronzy foliage and chartreuse blooms. 18 in. Z6–8.

var. *robbiae* (syn. *Euphorbia robbiae*), Mrs. Robb's bonnet, spreads aggressively by rhizomes to make a dense groundcover, which may become invasive. Evergreen with showy, yellow-green flowers. Drought and shade tolerant. Suitable for woodland gardens and along wooded pathways, as well as massed in sun or shade. 1–3 ft. Z5–7.

Euphorbia characias
- yellow
- early spring to late spring
- 3–5 ft. × 3 ft.
- sun
- Z6–8, HS

Mediterranean spurge. Western Mediterranean. Strong, stout upright stems, woody at the base, crowded with spirals of pointed, blue-green leaves to 5 in. long; lower leaves may drop under stress. Large heads of greenish yellow flowers unfurl at the top. Great for winter and spring gardens. Often short lived, especially in the heat and humidity of the southeastern United States, but because it seeds freely, replacements abound. Cut back flowering stems after bloom.

subsp. *wulfenii* (syn. *Euphorbia wulfenii*) differs from the above in having larger leaves and enormous cylindrical heads of yellow-green flowers, to 6–9 in. Drought tolerant. 3–4 ft. Z7–8.

'Lambrook Gold' is bushy with narrow, gray-green foliage and chrome-yellow flowerheads from early spring to midsummer. 3.5 ft. Z7–8.

'Tasmanian Tiger' ('Variegata', 'Tassie Tiger') is a flashy variegated form of this species with slender,

blue-green leaves edged with white. Heat and drought tolerant, but resents high humidity; not good in southeastern United States. Excellent in containers. 3 ft. high and wide. Z6–9.

Euphorbia griffithii
- orange
- summer
- 24–36 in. × 24 in.
- sun, part shade
- Z5–7, HS

Griffith's spurge. Himalayas. Makes robust mounds of sturdy stems clothed with green, lanceolate leaves, pink along the midrib. Flowers have dazzling brick-red bracts. Remains attractive well after bloom time. Best in part shade in regions where sunlight is intense; elsewhere it tolerates full sun.

'Fireglow' has flame-orange floral bracts on bright red stems; green leaves take on wonderful autumn tints. 3 ft. Z6–8.

Euphorbia myrsinites
- chartreuse
- mid- to late spring
- 15–18 in. × 2 ft.
- sun
- Z5–9

Myrtle euphorbia. Eurasia. Beautiful trailer whose long prostrate stems are furnished with whorls of ice-blue leaves; looks good throughout the year. In spring, acid-yellow bracts decorate the flowerheads. Cut back hard after bloom time to avoid unwanted seedlings and promote handsome new growth, which appears at once and is particularly welcome in autumn and winter. Drought tolerant. Good between pavers, in rock gardens, and in hanging baskets. Unforgettable tumbling over a wall with *Origanum* 'Kent Beauty' in summer.

Euphorbia polychroma
syn. *E. epithymoides*
- yellow
- spring to late spring
- 18–24 in. × 18 in.
- sun, part shade
- Z4–7

Cushion spurge. Europe. Clumping with strong stems clothed with 2-in.-long, oblong leaves. In spring the tops of the stems are covered with ruffs of brilliant chartreuse-yellow bracts. Best in full sun in cooler, less sunny regions, but midday shade is necessary in areas with intense sun and heat. Perennial cornflowers and Spanish bluebells are attractive companions.

'Bonfire'. Slender, curvy-edged leaves are bluish green, purple at the tips when young. Brilliant sunny-yellow "flowers" in early spring. 12 in. Z5–7.

Other Notable Cultivars
Much breeding has taken place in recent years as euphorbias have gained in popularity. This is a sampling of what is available.

Blackbird ('Nothowlee') has bushy, very dark purple foliage that persists through the year. Chartreuse flowers. 16–18 in. Z7– 9.

'Efanthia' (syn. *Euphorbia amygdaloides* × *E. ×martinii*) is bushy and compact with evergreen, dark leaves, bright bronze when young and in cool weather. Chartreuse-yellow flowers. Drought tolerant. 12–36 in. Z4–11. Improved Efanthia

('Imprefant') is more compact at 10–14 in., but is otherwise similar.

'Glacier Blue' (sport of 'Tasmanian Tiger') is strikingly beautiful with silvery-blue leaves rimmed with white. Evergreen. Cream flower bracts striped with gray-blue. Bluer than its parent. 12–18 in. Z7–11.

Helena's Blush ('Inneuphhel', variegated form of 'Efanthia'). Rounded habit, with reddish young growth that matures to gray-green with cream variegations, with pink. Selected by Garry Grueber of Cultivaris. Resists powdery mildew. 12 in. Z4–11.

'Jade Dragon' (syn. *E. characias* subsp. *wulfenii* × *E. amygdaloides*) has huge, chartreuse flowerheads in summer. Purple when young, the blue-green foliage is later flushed with reddish pink. 1–3 ft. Z7–9.

×*martini* (syn. *E. amygdaloides* × *E. characias*). Martin's spurge, red spurge. This natural French hybrid is variable and selections may favor one parent or the other. Upright spikes of lime-green bracts with a red eye adorn stiff stems clothed with dark grayish green leaves. Short lived. Cut back to the ground after bloom time. 2–3 ft. × 2 ft. Z6–8.

'Ascot Rainbow' has bluish green foliage broadly and irregularly variegated with creamy gold; pink flushed when temperatures drop. 20 in. Z6–8.

'Shorty' is very compact with blue-green foliage that becomes bright red or purple tipped in cool weather. Chartreuse flowers in spring. Tolerates drought and heat. An introduction from ItSaul Plants in North Carolina. 15–18 in. Z7–11.

Euphorbia 'Shorty'

Euryops pectinatus

Euryops
Asteraceae
bush daisy

Bush daisies deliver outstanding value. They bloom, collectively, from late spring through late fall, mounting a continuous profusion of showy, golden flowerheads—bright yellow ray flowers and darker central disks—held on long stems above neat, bushy mounds of alternate, bright or gray-green, finely cut foliage. Young plants require regular irrigation during dry spells through their first growing season, but after that their far-reaching root systems tap deep water sources, making these plants outstandingly tolerant of xeric conditions. Not surprisingly, this genus is especially popular with Californian gardeners and in the US southwest.

Deadhead bush daisies, pruning back a couple of inches to encourage continued bloom and neatness. Where not winter hardy, bush daisies adapt very well to container culture. Be sure that soil drains freely and the pots are sited in a sunny spot. Deer resistant, but often eaten by rabbits. Otherwise mostly pest and disease free.

Propagate by seed in spring, or take softwood cuttings of soft new growth in spring; semi-ripe cuttings may be rooted in summer.

Euryops acraeus
syn. *E. evansii of gardens*
- yellow
- late spring to early summer
- 12–24 in. × 12 in.
- sun
- Z8–11

Bush daisy. Drakensberg Mountains, South Africa. Dense mounds of tip-notched, silver-gray leaves, 1 in. or more long. Flower stems 1.5 in. long carry one to three deep yellow daisies, each 1 in. across. Requires very sharp drainage.

Euryops pectinatus
- yellow
- late spring to late fall
- 4–6 ft. × 3 ft.
- sun
- Z8–11

Euryops, yellow bush daisy. South Africa. These bushy evergreen plants are subshrubby or herbaceous, with attractive, hairy, cut, gray-green leaves to 3 in. long. The reflective silvery hairs that cover the foliage equip the plants to survive harsh sun without damage. Long-stemmed, 2-in. daisies bloom singly or in small groups from midspring on. Excellent for winter bloom in mild climates or in containers in sunrooms and conservatories where not winter hardy. Can be trained as standards.

'Munchkin' is a dwarf selection, excellent for lining paths and walkways, massed in beds and borders, or as edging plants. Combine with other xeric plants in hot, dry inland sites. 3 ft. tall.

'Viridis' (green-leaved euryops, African daisy) has dark green, glossy leaves and a more rounded habit than the species. They tolerate training as standards. Very attractive to butterflies, and birds enjoy the seedheads after bloom time. 2–3 ft. tall.

Evolvulus
Convolvulaceae
evolvulus

These relatives of morning glories offer blossoms of similar form and equally intense blues without the morning glories' smothering, vining growth. Evolvulus are compact subshrubs with fluted, funnel-form flowers that recall the horns on antique phonographs. These flowers, like those of morning glories, open in the morning and close in the afternoon. Three species are in cultivation.

Propagation is from seed or cuttings.

Evolvulus arizonicus
- blue
- midspring to midfall
- 1 ft. × 1–2 ft.
- sun, part shade
- Z7–10

Arizona blue eyes. Upland areas and desert grasslands from Arizona to west Texas and south to northern Mexico. Forms low, spreading mounds of stems, each bearing narrow, lanceolate, gray-green leaves to 1 in. long. The 0.75-in. flowers range in color from sky blue to a deep azure; bloom coincides with periods of available moisture. Survives on just natural precipitation once established. Prefers a well-drained, unimproved soil—do not dig in organic matter. Excellent groundcover for xeriscapes, and displays of natives in the southwestern United States. A short-lived perennial that commonly self-seeds.

Evolvulus glomeratus 'Blue Daze'

Evolvulus glomeratus

- blue
- summer to fall
- 9–18 in. × 24–36 in.
- sun, part shade
- Z8–11

Brazilian dwarf morning glory. Brazil and Paraguay. Commonly grown as a summer annual where winters are cold, but is perennial in mild-winter regions. Forms a sprawling mound of fuzzy stems and foliage. Leaves are egg shaped, 0.5 in. wide and 1 in. long; flowers are 1 in. across, pale lavender or powder blue, with a white, star-shaped mark in the throat. Prefers full sun and sandy, well-drained soil with frequent irrigation. Excellent for providing texture and color in beds and borders, or as a groundcover; complement with yellow or pink flowering plants including petunias, low-growing sedums, and gauras. Salt tolerant and a good choice for seaside gardens. Attractive when cascading over walls, hanging baskets, or tubs.

'Blue Daze' is also the name for what is advertised as a cultivar of *Evolvulus nuttallianus*, but judging from the hardiness data (only to 32°F), this may fit better under *E. glomeratus*.

Evolvulus nuttallianus

syn. *E. argenteus*, *E. pilosus*

- blue, lavender
- spring to midsummer
- 1–1.5 ft. high and wide
- sun, part shade
- Z4–10

Shaggy dwarf morning glory. Montana and North Dakota to Texas and Arizona. Dense, hairy subshrub with sprawling stems that root at the nodes where they touch the ground; silver-green leaves oblanceolate, to 1 in. long. Lavender to pale blue, 0.5-in. flowers are centered with a five-pointed, white eye. Thrives in an organic-rich, consistently moist, well-drained soil, but also tolerates sandy ones amended with compost. Good for rock gardens, native plant displays, and xeriscapes, or where water is short.

Farfugium

Asteraceae
leopard plant

Veteran gardeners may know the leopard plants by their former botanical names as members of the genus *Ligularia*. More recently, however, the leopard plants were given their own genus, *Farfugium*, as befits such bold, intriguing perennials.

These eastern Asian plants are grown mainly for their handsome evergreen, long-stalked leaves that are held well above the crown. Valuable in wet places beside ponds and streams, or as dramatic accents in beds and shrub borders. They are good companions for astilbes, primroses, and Japanese irises. The variegated cultivars are most popular,

Farfugium japonicum 'Aureomaculatum'

particularly as dynamic container plants to decorate patios and decks, and sunrooms in cooler regions. All bear loose, long-stemmed clusters of yellow daisies late in the season; many gardeners feel these detract from the foliar display and remove them.

Leopard plants do best in average soil that is moist but not waterlogged. Most prefer morning sun, but accept light shade; some tolerate full sun. Foliage may droop or flag during midday sun, but regain its turgidity in the cool of the day. Mulch well where soil tends to dry out. Protect from slug damage; usually ignored by deer. Especially popular in warm-climate gardens.

Increase by dividing clumps in spring, or start from seed with protection in winter.

Farfugium japonicum

syn. *F. tussilagineum*, *Ligularia tussilaginea*

- yellow
- fall
- 18–24 in. × 24 in.
- sun, part shade
- Z6–11

Leopard plant. Rocky cliffs along the coasts of Japan, Taiwan, and Korea. This clumping perennial has glossy, long-stalked, 6- to 10-in.-wide leaves, kidney shaped with wavy, toothed, or entire margins. Bright yellow daisies, 2 in. or so across, cluster on long stems well above the foliage in fall and into winter. An excellent contrasting companion for fine-textured ferns. The cultivars are more often grown than the species.

'Argenteum' ('Albovariegatum', 'Variegatum'). The 10-in.-wide leaves are thick and cupped, irregularly rimmed with wide, white streaks, held on purple stems covered with woolly hairs. Yellow flowerheads. 15–24 in. Z7–8.

'Aureomaculatum' (syn. *Ligularia tussilaginea* 'Aureomaculata') has 8- to 10-in.-wide, dark green leaves, irregularly and conspicuously marked with yellow spots. Yellow, daisy-like flowers. Do not allow to dry out or become waterlogged. 20 in. Z6.

'Cristata' ('Crispatum', syn. *L. tussilaginea* 'Cristata') has bold, glossy, heart-shaped, 1-ft.-wide leaves twisted from the stem like a snail. The leaves have frilly edges and are woolly hairy beneath. Yellow flowers. 2 ft. Z6–8.

Ferula
Apiaceae
giant fennel

Although there are many species in this genus, only one—giant fennel—is perennial and suitable for ornamental gardens. This one, however, is a handsome and imposing plant worth cultivating as much for its architectural beauty as for the delicate foliage and interesting flowers. As expansive as its name suggests, giant fennel needs plenty of room in which to show off its form. It also requires full sun and a moist soil that is deep enough to accommodate its long, thick taproot.

Giant fennel is excellent in wild gardens, attracts numerous bees, small insects, and butterflies. In large perennial or mixed borders, this plant makes a stunning backdrop and mixes gracefully between shrubs. Seldom browsed by deer or rabbits, which are probably deterred by the aroma of the leaves. Aphids and slugs may be a nuisance. Do not confuse this plant with edible *Foeniculum vulgare*, also known as fennel.

Propagate by seed sown as soon as it ripens in late summer and overwinter outdoors in a cold frame or other protected spot.

Ferula communis
- yellow
- early to midsummer
- 6–10 ft. × 1.5–2 ft.
- sun
- Z6–9

Giant fennel. Dry slopes and rocky hillsides of the Mediterranean, Malta, and central Asia. This deeply rooted, robust, and dramatic cousin of celery, archangel, and parsley forms clumps of branching or simple stems that support a mound of aromatic, very finely dissected, light green basal leaves with sheathing petioles. Boldly ridged, hollow stems, sometimes as thick as a broomstick, carry alternate clasping flower stems topped with hemispherical branched umbels of tiny, five-petaled, yellow flowers. Each umbel may grow 3 in. across. Exhausted plants may die after setting copious amounts of seed that germinates readily as soon as it is ripe. Seedlings may take a few years to reach blooming size.

Ferula communis

Filipendula
Rosaceae
meadowsweet

A select genus of just 12 species, the meadowsweets offer a range of attractions: perfumed, eye-catching flowerheads and handsome foliage, combined with the ability to flourish in a variety of climates, typically without significant pest or disease problems; they are deer tolerant as well. These hardy, rewarding plants thrive in deep, organically rich, moist soils in full sun or partial shade. Summer drought may cause their leaves to scorch; cut the stems back when the dry spell breaks; fresh foliage soon replaces the old.

Depending on the stature of the species you select, meadowsweets can serve at the back or middle of a border. The taller, more robust species hold their own as part of meadow plantings, especially where soils are moist. Their airy, pastel-hued flowers and bold foliages complement the finer textures and more subdued colors of the grasses. Meadowsweets show up especially well when planted in drifts, and furnish excellent cut flowers. Propagate in spring or fall by seed or by division.

Filipendula glaberrima

- white
- mid- to late spring
- 36 in. × 24 in.
- sun, part shade
- Z5–8

Nakai Korean meadowsweet. Northeastern Asia. This underappreciated species is seldom found in the nursery trade, yet makes a fine garden perennial. In mid- to late spring, clumps of grape-like leaves give rise to stalks bearing corymbs of small white or pink flowers.

Filipendula purpurea

- pink, white
- late spring to midsummer
- 36–48 in. × 24–36 in.
- sun, part shade
- Z3–8

Japanese meadowsweet. Japan. Upright and clump forming, bears rich green, maple-like leaves that measure 4–8 in. across, and fluffy corymbs of astilbe-like flowers that are white with red stamens (appearing pink from a distance) or purple. Easily cultivated in average, well-drained garden soil, but performs best on those that are fertile, organic rich, and kept consistently moist. Benefits from some afternoon shade in hot, sunny climates. Susceptible to powdery mildew, rust, and leaf spot, but usually without serious damage.

'Alba' is white flowered.

'Elegans' is more compact, with flowers similar to those of the species, but with evident red stamens. 18–24 in. tall.

'Purpurascens' has purple-tinted foliage.

Filipendula rubra

syn. *Spiraea lobata, S. palmata, S. venusta*

- pink
- early to midsummer
- 6–8 ft. × 3–4 ft.
- sun, part shade
- Z3–8

Queen-of-the-prairie, false spirea. Wet grasslands and fens from Missouri to North Carolina, northward into Canada. This plant offers an unusual characteristic: both its flowers and foliage are fragrant. Forms an imposing, upright clump of sturdy, often reddish stems that rarely need staking. Leaves compound, to 2 ft. long, composed of one to seven bright green, deeply palmately cut leaflets as much as 6 in. long. Fluffy, sweet-scented, pink flowers are individually tiny but borne in dense, astilbe-like panicles, 6–9 in. wide. Flourishes in moist or even wet, well-drained soils, especially those that are fertile and humus rich. Does not tolerate drought, but free from serious insect or disease problems. A good planting for pond sides or stream banks, this species self-seeds freely in a hospitable site. Spectacular, especially when grown in a mass, outstanding for wild or naturalized areas, wet meadows, or the back of a border.

'Albicans' ('Magnificum Album') has white flowers and is shorter. 5–6 ft.

Filipendula purpurea

'Venusta' ('Magnifica', 'Venusta Magnifica', syn. *Filipendula venusta*) has deep pink flowers on 4 ft. stems.

Filipendula vulgaris

syn. *F. hexapetala, Spiraea filipendulina*

- white
- late spring to early summer
- 16–20 in. × 12–18 in.
- sun, part shade
- Z3–9

Fern-leaf dropwort. Pastures of Europe, much of central and northern Asia. Much more tolerant of dry soils than other members of the genus. Forms a low mound of finely cut, dark green, fern-like leaves, from which arise upright stems bearing panicles of creamy-white flowers. Useful for edging, for the front of a border, or for containers. Foliage smells of wintergreen when crushed.

'Multiplex' ('Flore Pleno') has drooping panicles of 0.25–0.40 in., double, white flowers like tiny rosebuds.

'Plena' bears double flowers; outstanding for cutting and formerly a staple of wedding bouquets.

Foeniculum vulgare contrasts daintily with *Acanthus spinosous*

Other Notable Cultivars

'Kahome' is a dwarf that attains a height and spread of just 6–12 in. Astilbe-like corymbs of tiny, fragrant, rosy pink flowers in summer to early fall. The bright green, fern-like foliage is as attractive as the blooms.

Foeniculum
Apiaceae
fennel

This genus has just a single species, but it offers a handful of reliably perennial cultivars that, in addition to the sweet, anise-like flavor of their stalks and leaves, offer decorative foliage as well. The airy foliage makes the ornamental cultivars of common fennel a great textural background in borders, herb and vegetable gardens, cottage gardens, and even meadows, and a useful addition to butterfly gardens.

The fennel used as flavoring is common fennel (*Foeniculum vulgare*). This should not be confused with edible Florence fennel or finocchio (*F. vulgare* var. *azoricum*), an annual variety that develops swollen leaf bases.

Grow in a moist, organic-rich, well-drained soil; propagation is by seed, sown directly in the garden. If started indoors, seedlings should be transplanted to their ultimate destination while still young, as they form taproots that resent disturbance. Remove spent flowering stems before seed is produced to avoid any unwanted self-seeding; common fennel has become a troublesome weed in parts of the US Pacific Northwest. Common fennel is usually trouble free but is susceptible to aphids and slugs, and may be defoliated by swallowtail caterpillars. Deer ignore it.

Francoa sonchifolia

Foeniculum vulgare

- yellow
- midsummer to late summer
- 3–5 ft. × 2–3 ft.
- sun
- Z4–9

Common fennel. This popular culinary herb is native to the lands around the Mediterranean Sea. Typically fennel forms an upright mound of feathery, compound leaves. The tiny, yellow flowers that are borne in large, flattened, compound umbels are not showy, but are very attractive to bees, butterflies, and birds.

'Purpureum' has attractive, purple-bronze foliage that contrasts vibrantly with the yellow flowers. Excellent as a camouflage for shabby basal foliage of ornamental onions and other bulbs. This cultivar seems to be identical with those sold under the names 'Bronze', 'Giant Bronze', 'Smokey', and 'Nigra'.

Francoa
Saxifragaceae
bridal wreath

Francoas are underappreciated in North American gardens, although they are generally quite easy to grow and put on a good floral display that lasts a couple of months. Their nomenclature is confusing: some experts lump all the different types together into a single species, while others distinguish many different ones.

High heat and humidity are not kind to these Chilean natives. As a result, francoas are most suitable for the western United States, especially the Pacific Northwest, or other regions with similar climates. Francoas bear closely set, 0.75-in. flowers in wand-like spikes on long, naked stems that rise above the clumps of evergreen, heuchera-like foliage. Tolerant of most soils, they thrive in moist but well-drained conditions and spread slowly by rhizomes. In cool climates treat these gems as biennials, keeping them in a cold frame or protected nursery bed through the winter and then moving them to the bed or border in spring. Seldom browsed by deer.

Francoas are fine border and cottage garden plants, mixing well with daylilies, daisies, and other perennials. They are also appropriate for rock gardens, and make fine container specimens and cut flowers.

Propagate by detaching and replanting the rhizomes. Alternatively, start from seed in spring; expect that germination may require four weeks.

Francoa sonchifolia

- pink
- summer to fall
- 2–3 ft. × 18 in.
- sun, part shade
- Z8–11, HS

Maiden's wreath, bridal wreath. Chile. Dark green, basal foliage forms clumps about 1 ft. tall. Stiff, evergreen leaves, lobed and wavy along the edges. Terminal, unbranched, densely packed flower spikes rise high above the foliage, moving in time with every breeze. Starry flowers are mid-pink with lighter centers, marked with hot pink at the base. *Francoa ramosa* (syn. *F. globrata*) is similar but with white flowers on branched stems. *Francoa appendiculata* produces looser spikes of light pink flowers. Neither is quite as cold hardy as *F. sonchifolia*.

'Rogerson's Form'. Superior to the species; bright pink flowers stained with deep magenta. Tolerates wet soils well. Excellent for cutting. 12–24 in. Z7–9.

Gaillardia

Asteraceae
blanket flower, Indian blanket

Blanket flowers are among North America's most showy native wildflowers, growing in huge sweeps across grasslands, mountain hillsides, high prairies, and meadows. Their floral hues are bold, bright, and earthy, recalling those of Native American weavings, as the common name indicates. Not surprisingly, gaillardias have in recent years attracted the attention of plant breeders, who have introduced a host of fine hybrids.

As members of the aster family, gaillardias bear their flowers in daisy-like heads consisting of deeply two- or three-lobed ray flowers (what appear to be petals) and a central button of disk flowers. The most common colors are shades of red and yellow.

Plant gaillardias in sunny spots with an average, well-drained soil; this latter quality is essential and it is critically important, especially for the hybrids, that the plants do not go into cold weather with wet feet. Deadhead for neatness and to maintain vigor, but leave a few heads if you are collecting seed, or more if you want to feed seed-eating birds. Butterflies, bees, and birds can often be seen collecting nectar and pollen from blanket flowers, adding another dimension to the garden. Lovely in native and wild gardens, in wildlife meadows, and in cottage gardens, these plants also fit in more formal applications as edgings for flowerbeds or to brighten the midsections of beds or borders. The taller sorts furnish fine, long-lasting cut flowers.

Gaillardias sometimes prove susceptible to mildews, rust, and rots. The tender young leaves are a treat for slugs and snails; however, deer and rabbits seldom browse them.

Many of the hybrids are short lived; divide established clumps in spring to maintain vigor. Propagate species by seed or division; cuttings may be difficult to root.

Gaillardia aestivalis

- yellow
- late spring to late fall
- 12–18 in. × 9–12 in.
- sun
- Z5–9

Firewheel, lance-leaf blanket flower. Southeastern United States. Yellow-rayed, 3-in. flowerheads with purplish brown, rounded centers. Some rays

Gaillardia 'Mesa Yellow'

occasionally appear to be missing, either partly or completely so; the central disk persists like an attractive purple globe after "petal" drop. Provides food for goldfinches, and butterflies are frequent visitors during the long bloom period. Lanceolate, grayish green leaves. Short lived, but self-seeds unless deadheaded.

var. *winkleri* '**Grape Sensation**' has 2-in., solid, deep lilac rays and black-currant disks. Clumps to 2 ft. × 3 ft. Long lived, with excellent drainage.

Gaillardia aristata

- purple-red, yellow
- summer
- 24–36 in. × 18 in.
- sun
- Z3–9

North Dakota south to Colorado, west to California and British Columbia. Appropriate for dry, wild, and meadow gardens. Lobed and lance-shaped, basal leaves to 10 in.; stem leaves are sessile and not lobed. Flowerheads, 3–4 in. across, are yellow rayed, purple at the base with purple disks. This rather sprawling species is seldom cultivated except as a breeding parent. Seed takes two years to reach bloom size.

'**Amber Wheels**' has vibrant, frilled, gold rays with an amber-red disk. 30 in. Z3–9.

Bijou strain. Orange-red ray flowers tipped with yellow. Self-seeds. 10–12 in. Z4–7

'**Fanfare**' has 3-in. flowerheads with fluted, yellow rays with red tubes surrounding a deep red central disk. May be listed under *Gaillardia* ×*grandiflora*. Introduced by Plant Haven. Soil must be free draining. 15 in. Z3–9.

Gaillardia ×grandiflora

syn. *G. aristata* × *G. puchella*
- red-and-yellow
- early summer to fall
- 24–36 in. × 18 in.
- sun
- Z5–9

Blanket flower. Of garden origin. This easy-to-grow cross displays hybrid vigor in its offspring, many of which have been introduced to the marketplace. Mostly erect and somewhat spreading, with hairy, soft, dark basal foliage, lanceolate and lobed along the edges; stem leaves are sessile and entire. Showy heads of flowers may reach 4 in. across. Plants tend to be short lived, often as a result of poor drainage; most resent winter wet. A few of the species shown here seed true, but uniformity is assured by propagating the named cultivars vegetatively, by division, or from cuttings.

Other Notable Cultivars

Most of the cultivars shown here are hardy to Z3. Deadhead to extend bloom time.

'**Arizona Red**' has red flowerheads. '**Arizona Sun**' has red, 3- to 4-in. flowers with yellow margins. Both are Fleuroselect Gold Medal winners. 12 in.

'**Baby Cole**' is maroon centered, with yellow-tipped, red rays. 6–8 in. '**Dazzler**' is similar but 24–30 in. tall.

'**Burgundy**' (syn. *Gaillardia aristata* '**Burgundy**') has wine-red, 3-in. daisy flowers with red-and-yellow disks. 18–24 in.

Commotion Series. These mounding selections have great vigor. Heads are fully semi-double, with fluted rays: Commotion '**Frenzy**' has red petals tipped with yellow; Commotion '**Tizzy**' has rosy red ray flowers. 18–24 in. Z5.

'**Goblin**' ('**Kobold**') has large, deep red rays, irregularly bordered with yellow. '**Golden Goblin**' is all yellow. Z3.

Monarch Strain is a seed mix of yellow and orange to dark red flowers. 2–5 ft. tall.

'**Oranges and Lemons**'. Bright cantaloupe rays tipped with lemon yellow; golden disk.

Galax
Diapensiaceae
wandflower

This native genus of but a single species deserves more attention from gardeners. Though not a fast spreader, wandflower makes a slowly expanding clump that, on hospitable sites, eventually forms large colonies of lustrous evergreen, heart-shaped foliage. Florists often use the pliable leaves of this plant to decorate Christmas wreaths and quantities of them are exported to Europe and Asia for that purpose annually.

Galax requires a moist, organic-rich, acid soil in a shaded spot. It is an excellent and unusual underplanting for acid-loving rhododendrons and azaleas, and a refined yet robust groundcover for woodland gardens, shady borders, and rock gardens.

Propagate by seed in containers (sown in acid seed mix as soon as it ripens), or by separating the rooted runners of mature clumps in spring.

Gaillardia 'Goblin'

Galax urceolata

syn. *G. rotundifolia, G. aphylla*

- white
- spring to early summer
- 3–6 in. × 24 in.
- part shade, shade
- Z4–8

Wandplant, beetleweed. Woodlands of the Appalachian mountains, and from Massachusetts and New York, southward to northern Alabama. Rounded, evergreen leaves are leathery and cordate (heart shaped), toothed around the edges and 1–3 in. across; a glossy rich green during the growing season, they turn burgundy-red or bronze in fall retaining this color through winter. The five-petaled flowers are individually tiny but are held in airy spikes atop upright, leafless stems, the whole reaching a height of 14–18 in.

Galium

Rubiaceae
sweet woodruff , bedstraw

With the exception of sweet woodruff, few species in this genus are sufficiently well mannered to grace ornamental gardens. Many are invasive and weedy, others are annual and don't warrant a place here. They are native to waste places, woodlands, and hedge bottoms across temperate Europe, Asia, and northern Africa; many of the invasive species have escaped and naturalized beyond their homeland.

The bedstraws typically have linear leaves that they bear in whorls around weak, slender stems that commonly scramble over and through their neighbors. Their flowers are tubular and flaring at the mouth, 0.25 in. in diameter, and yellow, white, or pink; typically they are borne in clusters in the leaf nodes and at stem tips.

A partly shaded spot where soil is humus rich and moisture retentive suits bedstraws best, although full sun is acceptable where summers are temperate. They are prone to mildews, rust, and leaf spots, but these are seldom serious. Deer and rabbit tolerant. Propagate by division in spring or fall. Sow seed indoors in early spring or outdoors after all danger of frost is past.

Galium odoratum

syn. *Asperula odorata*

- white
- late spring to early summer
- 6–12 in. × 12 in.
- sun, part shade
- Z4–8

Sweet woodruff, wild baby's breath, lady's bedstraw. Europe. Square, slender, smooth stems arise from rhizomes and are punctuated at nodal intervals along their length with whorls of 0.25-in.-wide and 0.5-in.-long, bright green leaves. These remain attractive throughout the season. Growth is rapid in favorable conditions, although new plants may take some time to establish. In late spring the plants are adorned with 2- to 3-in.-wide clusters of clean white, starry flowers about 0.25 in. long, which provide the spicing for the traditional German spring drink May wine. The flowers are followed by fruits that are covered with hooked bristles that adhere to animal fur, assisting in seed dispersal. Smelling of freshly mown hay, sweet woodruff has been used for generations as a deodorizer, in potpourri and fragrant sachets, and to protect clothing from moth damage. Hikers sometimes stuff their hiking boots with the dried stems to camouflage foot odor. Keep well watered during dry spells for best growth. Lovely in light woodlands, along casual pathways, and as a groundcover among shrubs. It is often grown in herb and cottage gardens too.

Gaura

Onagraceae
gaura

This genus includes only one garden-worthy perennial species. Its open structure, slender stems, and cloud of delicate, fluttering blooms makes that particular gaura an exceptional plant for leavening and enhancing the texture of a border, and a natural companion for ornamental grasses, purple coneflowers (*Echinacea*), and other taller summer bloomers. It's also well suited to native plant gardens, meadows, and wildflower gardens. This plant tolerates urban pollution well and also has exceptional heat and humidity tolerance; if given sufficient irrigation during dry spells, it will continue to bloom right through the peak of summer.

Gaura tolerates a wide range of soils, from well-drained, fertile ones to those that are dry and acid. When grown in rich soils, gaura tends to sprawl; cutting stems back by half in mid- to late spring

Galium odoratum

helps keep growth more compact and sturdy. Dead-heading the spent flowers helps to control prolific self-seeding.

Generally pest and disease free, though subject to root rot on heavy, poorly drained soils. This species is also deer resistant.

The easiest way to propagate this plant is by seed, as gaura forms taproots and is difficult to transplant once established. Start seed in containers to avoid transplant shock when planted out. Named cultivars, however, must be multiplied by division, which can be undertaken after two to three years of growth.

Gaura lindheimeri 'Whirling Butterflies'

Gaura lindheimeri

- white, pink
- late spring to early fall
- 3–5 ft. × 1–2 ft.
- sun
- Z5–9

Butterfly gaura. Texas and Louisiana. Despite its southern origins butterfly gaura is surprisingly hardy. Forms a vase-shaped, airy cluster of wiry stems from which sprout stemless, narrowly lanceolate, 1- to 3-in. leaves; the reddish stems and the foliage are occasionally spotted with maroon. The common name refers to the delicate, butterfly-like appearance of the four-petaled flowers, which are borne in long, open, terminal panicles with the blooms opening a few at a time over an extraordinarily long season.

Blushing Butterflies ('Benso') is compact, to 24 in. high and wide, with dark green foliage, and light pink-and-white flowers; 'Crimson Butterflies' has crimson new growth and hot-pink flowers: 'Sunny Butterflies' has leaves edged with white, pink flowers. 24 in. tall. 'Whirling Butterflies' has pink-tinged white flowers.

'Pink Cloud' bears unusually heavy crops of bright pink flowers over an extra-long season. 30 in.

'Siskiyou Pink' was the first strong pink cultivar. Introduced by Baldassare Mineo of Siskiyou Rare Plant Nursery.

'Snow Fountain' bears all white flowers on 18- to 24-in. plants.

Gentiana
Gentianaceae
gentian

A traditional favorite of rock gardeners, gentians have much to offer also for other horticultural applications. Indigenous to every continent except Antarctica, this genus furnishes native species no matter where you garden. Their flowers include some of the most intense blues found in the plant kingdom. They are popular as food sources, especially for native bees, butterflies, and hummingbirds. These are not aggressive plants, but their sparkling floral colors make them ideal for use as visual accents singly or in small groups. The intense dot of blue contributed by a single gentian blossom energizes any yellows in the surrounding border, and provides elegant contrast to silver foliages.

With some exceptions, gentians are native to mountain areas, and like most peak-dwelling plants they prefer moist but very well-drained soils and are notably cold hardy. Like most alpines, gentians as a group have low tolerance for heat when combined with humidity, though a few, included here, are more tolerant than most and will survive in upland areas of the southeastern United States. Gentians are outstanding in their traditional home, the rock garden, but also show up beautifully when displayed in containers, and can be quite useful in the front of a border. Deer resistant, but bothered by slugs and

Gentiana septemfida

Gentiana lutea

snails. Foliage is subject to rust and foliage spots, but is seldom a nuisance.

Propagate most species by division or use freshly ripened seed.

Gentiana andrewsii

- blue
- fall
- 1–2 ft. × 1–1.5 ft.
- sun, part shade
- Z3–7, HS

Closed-bottle gentian. Colorado, eastward to Virginia and north into Canada. Unlike other members of this genus, *Gentiana andrewsii* is a lowland plant that flourishes in moist fields and prairies, woodland edges and thickets, and low, wooded areas near streams and ponds. Its dark blue flowers never open voluntarily; borne in clusters at the top of the main stem, the flowers retain their bud form, expanding into 1.5-in.-long, pleated tubes whose tips remain closed until a bumblebee forces its way in to steal the nectar. Medium green, glossy, ovate leaves are held in opposing pairs and in a whorl beneath the floral cluster. Best in moist but well-drained, cool, organic-rich, and mildly alkaline soil, but tolerant of slightly acid, well-dug and amended clay; tolerates seasonal drought once established. A star of all woodland gardens or shady borders, as well as moist meadows or the banks of a stream or pond.

Gentiana asclepiadea

- blue
- late summer to early fall
- 24–30 in. × 24 in.
- sun, part shade
- Z5–7, HS

Willow gentian. Mountain meadows of Europe and western Asia. Its common name refers to its slender, willow-like leaves and graceful, arching growth; the 2-in. flowers are rich blue, flaring trumpets borne in pairs and sprouting from the upper leaf axils. Requires a moist but well-drained, moderately fertile, acid or neutral soil. Well suited to woodland edges where it pairs well with small ferns, heucheras, heucherellas, and variegated Solomon's seal. Does not thrive in hot, humid summers.

'Alba' is a white-flowered cultivar.

'Pink Swallow' bears intense pink flowers and dark green leaves.

Gentiana dahurica

syn. *G. gracilipes*

- purple-blue
- summer
- 6–12 in. × 12 in.
- sun, part shade
- Z4–7

Dahurian gentian. An Asian native that forms a loose mound of narrow, deep green, glossy, lanceolate leaves, from which arise lax stems bearing clusters of white-throated, deep blue, trumpet-shaped flowers. Requires moist, gritty, and well-drained soil with acid to neutral pH. Excellent for rock gardens.

Gentiana lutea

- yellow
- summer
- 3–4.5 ft. × 2 ft.
- sun
- Z6–9, HS

Great yellow gentian, bitterwort. Europe, western Asia. Erect stiff stems carry opposite pairs of glaucous, ribbed leaves to 12 in. long. Tiered clusters of yellow, starry flowers emerge from leaf axils. Seldom seen in US gardens but available as seed, and well worth seeking out. Raise container-grown plants to avoid root damage at transplanting time. Valuable medicinally and appropriate for herb gardens as well as borders.

Gentiana makinoi

- blue
- midsummer to early fall
- 18–24 in. × 6–12 in.
- sun, part shade
- Z3–7

Royal blue gentian. Mountains of Japan. Upright perennial with semi-evergreen, dark green, ovate leaves. Intensely blue, 2-in.-long flowers borne in the upper leaf axils of the stems; never fully open, retaining a close-ended tubular shape like that of a Christmas tree light bulb. Requires an acid, humus-rich, moist but well-drained soil. Generally pest and disease free, but attractive to deer.

Encourage a more compact, less sprawling habit by pruning stems back by half in late spring to early summer. This species contributes a bright note of color to late summer borders, and combines well with acid-loving shrubs such as blueberries and rhododendrons. Very attractive as a cut flower.

'Marsha' has blue-purple flowers and is compact, to 20 in.; a good choice for containers.

'Royal Blue' grows to 24 in. bearing royal violet-blue flowers.

Gentiana scabra

- blue
- late summer to early fall
- 6–8 in. × 8–12 in.
- sun, part shade
- Z4–8

Japanese gentian. Japan. Low-growing, evergreen species whose flowers, borne at the stem ends, are bell shaped and a rich, sapphire blue. Excellent for rock gardens, borders, and in open woodlands. Prefers an acid, humus-rich, moist, well-drained soil. Compatible with ericaceous shrubs such as blueberries, heaths and heathers, and rhododendrons.

'Zuikorindo' bears deep pink flowers.

Gentiana septemfida

- blue
- mid- to late summer
- 6–12 in. × 12–18 in.
- sun, part shade
- Z4–9

Summer gentian. Caucasus Mountains. Forms a trailing mound of deep green foliage that in summer glows with deep blue, trumpet-shaped blossoms, sometimes with white throats. Easier to cultivate than the fall-blooming gentians, more tolerant of the heat and humidity of the southeastern United States, where it benefits from afternoon shade.

var. *lagodechiana* has cobalt-blue trumpets. A fine rock-garden plant, suitable for edging or for planting into a retaining wall, and well suited to container cultivation. 4–8 in. Z4–7.

Geranium
Geraniaceae
cranesbill

Although cranesbills are often called "hardy geraniums," it should be noted that they do not belong to the same genus as the popular bedding plants (actually *Pelargonium*) that most people refer to as "geraniums."

Whatever you call them, the cranesbills are, typically, undemanding and long lived, requiring little maintenance in return for a vibrant floral display. They tolerate a wide range of soils, though they do not prosper in winter wet. They generally prefer sunny positions, although several species do well in part shade or direct sun for just part of the day. Alpine species and many of the hybrids grow best in full sun and a free-draining soil well enriched with compost.

Gentiana makinoi 'Marsha'

Geranium sanguineum 'Album' and *Amsonia hubrichtii* make good bedfellows

Geranium ×*cantabriense* 'Karmina'

Geranium cinereum 'Ballerina'

In general, cranesbills form low mats or mounds of foliage and flowers, although some have a more erect, if sprawling, habit. Long-stemmed basal leaves and leafy, branched, flowering stems combine to present bold masses of handsome and long-lasting foliage. Often aromatic and mostly rounded in outline, the leaves are hand shaped, divided into segments, and often further lobed and toothed along the edges. Clusters or pairs of five-petaled flowers in white, pinks, purples, blues, violets, and dark maroon mostly bloom above the foliage mass. The beak-like fruits ripen, then dry and split to release their seeds.

Rabbits and deer seldom bother cranesbills, but mildew can be a problem, especially among plants suffering from drought.

Species easily propagated by seed sown as soon as it is ripe. Hybrids and cultivars must be divided, or increased by basal cuttings in spring. Selections with thick fleshy roots strike well from root cuttings taken in fall, and protected over winter in a spot with minimal heat.

Geranium ×cantabriense

syn. *G. dalmaticum* × *G. macrorrhizum*

- pink
- late spring to early summer
- 6–12 in. × 18 in.
- sun, part shade
- Z5–8

Cambridge geranium. This sterile hybrid has bright rosy pink or sometimes white, flattened flowers with inflated calyces, on trailing stems. Glossy light green, lobed and toothed leaves, to 3.5 in. across.

'Biokovo' has white flowers flushed with pink; red calyces. A single clump may reach 3 ft. across. Red fall foliage. 6–8 in. tall.

'Cambridge Blue' ('Cambridge') has pale lavender-blue flowers. Makes an excellent groundcover to 18 in. across. 8 in. tall.

'Karmina' ('Biokova Karmina'). Vibrant rosy flowers from late spring into summer. Aromatic foliage provides red fall color. 6–10 in. tall.

Geranium cinereum

- pink
- late spring to early summer
- 4–6 in.
- sun, part shade
- Z5–9

Grayleaf cranesbill, ashy cranesbill. Pyrenees Mountains of southern Europe. Often grown in rock gardens, grayleaf cranesbill makes low, evergreen rosettes of deeply divided, grayish leaves, about 2 in. across, each of the five to seven segments further lobed. Clusters of upward facing, 1-in., white or pale pink flowers, often etched with purple. Demands free drainage. Provide light afternoon shade in hot areas; best in cooler climates.

'Ballerina' has purplish red, 2-in. flowers veined with dark pink, with a maroon eye. Grayer foliage than the species. Long blooming. 4–6 in. Similar, but smaller 'Laurence Flatman' has darker-colored flowers. 3–6 in. tall.

'Purple Pillow' has dark-veined, purplish red flowers over a mound of gray leaves. 6 in. Z3–8.

'Splendens' has screaming magenta flowers, striped and centered with purple. Dramatic in rock gardens. 8 in. Z4–8.

Geranium endressii

- pink
- early summer to early fall
- 15–18 in. × 18 in.
- sun, part shade
- Z4–7

Endress's cranesbill, French cranesbill. French Pyrenees. Mounding clumps of glossy deep green, deeply divided leaves. Long-blooming, deep pink, cup-shaped flowers; cut back hard after the first flush to encourage further bloom. Shade from intense sun. Reliable as filler in flower borders, perhaps to replace dormant spring ephemerals. Tolerates dry shade.

'Wargrave Pink' (syn. *Geranium ×oxonianum* 'Wargrave's Pink') has larger flowers, often veined with deep pink. Butterflies, bees, and birds seem to love it. Seeds about in good conditions. 18–24 in. Z3–8.

Geranium himalayense

syn. *G. grandiflorum, G. himalayense* var. *meeboldii, G. meeboldii*

- violet-blue
- late spring to late summer
- 1–2 ft. × 1.5 ft.
- sun, part shade
- Z4–10, HS

Himalayan geranium. Himalayan Mountains. Masses of 2-in.-wide, white-centered, intensely blue flowers, above dense mounds of lobed, 4-in. leaves. Appropriate for beds, borders, and beneath shrubs, or as a dense groundcover. Drought tolerant; excellent in dry and coastal climates, but not in those with summer heat and humidity.

'Baby Blue' has violet-blue, 1.5-in. flowers, white centered and veined with purple. Long blooming till midsummer. Red and gold fall color. 12 in. Z4–8.

'Birch Double' ('Plenum') has ruffled, fully double, lilac-blue, 1- to 2-in. flowers till midsummer. Good groundcover, especially on the edge of woods, and in containers. 18–24 in. Z4–7.

Geranium macrorrhizum

- cerise
- spring
- 15–18 in. × 18 in.
- sun, part shade
- Z4–8

Bigroot geranium, Bulgarian geranium. Southern Europe, particularly Bulgaria. Easy to grow, tolerates most conditions including dry shade (even under maples). Large, sticky, lobed, light green leaves, 4–8 in. across; soft to the touch, highly aromatic, vibrant red and maroon fall color. Flowers flattish, usually a deep cerise with dark red, inflated calyces, and prominent red stamens. Spreads by succulent underground stems.

'Bevan's Variety' is a superior groundcover for shaded places. Deep magenta flowers accented with red calyces bloom from spring to late summer. 12 in. Z5.

'Ingwersen's Variety'. A superior cultivar with very pale pink flowers. 12–18 in.

'White-Ness' ('Snow Sprite'), collected from the slopes of Mt. Olympus. Marble-white flowers and stamens, pale green foliage. This is worth looking for. 8–10 in.

Geranium maculatum

- pink
- spring
- 1–2 ft. × 1 ft.
- part shade, shade
- Z3–8

Spotted geranium, wild geranium, wood geranium. Woodlands and clearings of eastern North America. This slight, clump-forming woodlander bears clusters of upward-facing, saucer-shaped, 1.5-in. flowers in varying shades of pink, over pairs of deeply lobed and toothed stem leaves. Seeds may be ejected from dehiscing fruits more than 20 feet. Pest and disease free, but not the showiest of the genus. Attractive to butterflies; appropriate for native plant and wild gardens.

'Espresso' has dramatic non-fading, reddish brown leaves beneath pink flowers. Excellent as a groundcover, especially for dry places.

f. *albiflorum* is a white-flowered form.

Geranium ×magnificum

syn. *G. ibericum* × *G. platypetalum*
- violet-blue
- late spring to early summer
- 18–24 in. × 24 in.
- sun, part shade
- Z4–8

Showy geranium, purple geranium. Of garden origin. Sterile, vigorous, with abundant bloom. Soft, divided basal leaves, to 6 in. wide. Vivid 1.5-in., violet-blue flowers veined with purple. Mass along pathways and border edges, or use as a focal point in large rock gardens.

Geranium ×oxonianum

syn. *G. endressii* × *G. versicolor*
- pink
- spring
- 1–2 ft. × 2 ft.
- sun
- Z4–8

Hybrid geranium. Of garden origin.

'A. T. Johnson' has dark-veined, silvered pink flowers. Shear after bloom time to promote a possible second crop. Long blooming. Light green, lobed foliage, semi-evergreen in mild climates. 12–18 in. 'Rose Clair' and 'Claridge Druce' are similar.

'Bressingham's Delight'. Soft pink flowers from spring to fall. Deeply lobed, rounded leaves. 1–1.5 ft. Z5–8.

'Katherine Adele' has very pale pink flowers 0.75 in. across veined with purple. Leaves are marked with bronze in the centers. A seedling of 'Walter's Gift'. 15 in. tall.

Geranium phaeum

- maroon
- late spring to early summer
- 18–24 in. × 12 in.
- sun, part shade
- Z3–7

Mourning widow, dusky cranesbill. Native to damp meadows of Europe. Erect stems rise from thick roots that ensure survival during drought. Deeply divided leaves, 4–8 in., are spotted with purple at their base. The unusual pendent, almost black but variable, 0.75-in. flowers are more curious than showy, with pointed, slightly reflexed petals and strongly exserted stamens.

'Album'. Flowers are white or faintly pink blushed.

'Lily Lovell' has large, purple-mauve flowers to 1.5 in. across, and light green leaves. 'Raven' is a selection with unblotched, pale green foliage. 18 in.

'Samobor' has deep burgundy flowers above variably marked purple leaves. May self-seed. Shear after bloom for fresh foliage. 18 in. Z6–8.

Geranium pratense

- white, blue, violet
- late spring to midsummer
- 24–36 in. × 24 in.
- sun, part shade
- Z5–7

Meadow cranesbill. Northern Europe, Asia. Crowded inflorescences of blue, violet-blue, or white, saucer-shaped flowers, 1–2 in. across. Deeply divided leaves are jaggedly lobed and toothed. May need staking, especially in warm climates. Seeds freely. Prefers acid soil but tolerates lime.

'Laura' has masses of sterile, double, white flowers. Very long blooming. Mounds of cut leaves; suitable for cottage gardens or borders. 24 in.

'Midnight Reiter'. Deep burgundy foliage, non-fading, dark lilac flowers. A gem for plant collectors, selected from the Pacific Northwest. Appropriate for rock gardens and troughs. 6–8 in. × 12–16 in. Z5–7.

'Plenum Violaceum' is sterile, with rosette-like, 1-in., double, deep violet flowers, centered with dark purple. Clumps of divided, irregularly lobed, and toothed leaves rise from stout, fleshy roots. 18 in. Z3.

Geranium renardii

- white
- late spring to early summer
- 1 ft. high and wide
- sun, part shade
- Z6–8

Dwarf cranesbill. Caucasus Mountains. Low clumps of wrinkled, grayish leaves to 4 in. across. These are as soft as a kitten's ear, and are split halfway into blunt, barely lobed divisions. The white or lavender-flushed, 1-in. flowers cluster in dense umbels, but bloom is sometimes sparse. Grown for its a wonderful foliage. Lovely in rock gardens, and where soil is poor.

Geranium renardii

Geranium ×riversleaianum

syn. *G. endressei* × *G. traversii*

- pink, magenta
- summer
- 10–12 in. × 24 in.
- sun, part shade
- Z6–8, HS

Cranesbill. Of garden origin. Long, trailing, branching stems bear deeply divided, gray-green leaves 2–4 in. across. Funnel-shaped, dark-veined, bright pink or magenta flowers, 1.5 in. across, and with notched petals, bloom in summer.

'Mavis Simpson' sports 1-in.-wide, light pink flowers with cream eyes and purple veins. 18 in.

'Russell Pritchard' bears intense magenta flowers above lobed and sharply toothed, grayish green leaves. 9 in.

Geranium sanguineum

- magenta
- spring
- 9–12 in. × 12 in.
- sun, part shade
- Z4–8

Bloody cranesbill. Europe, northern Turkey. Dense, clumping perennial with far-reaching rhizomes. Few basal leaves; deeply divided into several segments, dark green, 2- to 4-in. stem leaves are seldom toothed. Good fall color in sun. Abundant upward-facing, cup-shaped, vibrant magenta, 1.5-in. flowers with notched petals, purple veining, and white eyes that face upward.

'Album' has pure white flowers; a loose billowy habit. 18 in.

'Alpenglow' displays bright reddish rose blooms on clumps 8 in. tall and to 24 in. across.

'Cedric Morris' has slightly softer deep pink, 1-in. flowers; long blooming. To 24 in.

'Max Frei'. The reddish purple flowers attract butterflies in summer. Fine groundcover with good fall color. Cut back to revitalize the plant if foliage becomes shabby. 6–9 in.

var. *striatum* (syn. *Geranium sanguineum* var. *lancastriense*, *G. sanguineum* var. *prostratum*), striped cranesbill, has light pink flowers with a deeper pink eye and darker veining. Excellent as a groundcover, edging, or a rock garden plant. 4 in. 'Splendens' is taller with similar flowers to 1.75 in. across. 18 in. Do not confuse with shorter *G. cinereum* 'Splendens'.

Geranium sylvaticum

- pink, white, violet
- mid- to late spring
- 1–2 ft. high and wide
- part shade
- Z5–8

Wood cranesbill, woodland cranesbill. Damp meadows of Europe, particularly Iceland, northern Turkey. Early blooming, with usually purple-violet (sometimes pink or white), white-eyed, 1-in. flowers appearing with tulips and late daffodils. Deeply cut, roundish leaves, 6–7 in. across.

'Mayflower'. Mats of deeply cut leaves; light blue-violet, 1.5-in. flowers, white at the base. 2–2.5 ft.

Geranium wallichianum

- pink
- early summer to early fall
- 9–12 in. × 18 in.
- sun, part shade
- Z4–8

Wallach's geranium. Northeastern Afghanistan to Kashmir. Trailing, non-rooting stems make this prostrate geranium easy to control. Scrambling and weaving through taller plants or tumbling over walls or rocks, this species and its cultivars makes a showy splash of color. Pairs of somewhat wrinkled, marbled, and coarsely divided leaves measure 2–6 in. long. White-eyed, purple-veined, flattish, 1- to 1.5-in. flowers are deep pink, purple, or blue.

'Buxton's Variety' ('Buxton's Blue'). Superior and more compact than the species. Purple-veined, brilliant blue flowers accented with a central white halo. Sprawling carpets of slightly mottled leaves. Perfect at the front of beds and borders, perhaps backed by dark coleus, *Coreopsis* 'Moonbeam', or *Salvia* 'East Friesland'.

'Crystal Lake' has glowing crystal blue flowers prominently etched with dark purple veins. Palm-shaped, marbled foliage. Long blooming and easy care. 18 in. Z5–9.

Other Notable Cultivars

'Ann Folkard'. A superior hybrid with deeply cut, yellowish green foliage on trailing stems that scramble and weave through sturdier companions. Rich magenta flowers are punctuated with a black eye. Best in cool-summer regions in part shade. 8 in. × 3–4 ft.

'Brookside' is very long blooming with bowl-shaped, white-eyed, sapphire-blue flowers from

Geranium sanguineum 'Alpenglow'

Geranium Rozanne

Close up of *Gerbera jamesonii* 'Orange DC' flowers

spring into midsummer; it repeats as weather cools. Cut back after the first flush of bloom. Heat tolerant. Good fall foliage color. 12–18 in. Z5.

'Cheryl's Shadow' develops a slowly spreading, compact mound of dark maroon foliage that remains attractive all season. Light pink flowers in spring. 6–10 in. Z7–10.

'Johnson's Blue' has 2-in.-wide, periwinkle-blue flowers. Finely cut leaves become red and gold in fall. Cut back after the first flush. Slightly sprawling (more so than 'Rozanne') but a good weaver. 18 in. Z4–10.

'Nimbus'. Possibly superior to 'Johnson's Blue'. Violet-eyed, lavender-blue flowers above mounds of dissected leaves. Good in containers, coastal gardens, and for edging beds, borders, and paths. 20 in. Z4–8.

'Orion' is a seedling of 'Brookside'. Abundant large, lilac-blue, purple-veined flowers all summer above finely dissected foliage. 18–24 in.

Rozanne ('Gerwat'; syn. *Geranium wallichianum*

'Buxtons Variety' × *G. himalayense*) is certainly among the best of the hardy geraniums for beds and borders. Very long blooming with cupped, brilliant violet-purple, white-eyed flowers, to 2.5 in. across. Good-looking foliage. Heat tolerant. PPA Perennial Plant of the Year for 2008. Strikingly similar 'Jolly Bee' may be a synonym. 18–24 in. Z5–8.

Gerbera

Asteraceae
African daisy, transvaal daisy

Their exceedingly long vase life makes these vibrantly colored daisies favorites among florists, but gerberas are far less common as garden plantings. One reason is their sensitivity to frost—in most of North America, these perennials must be used as summer annuals. Still, gerberas make superior, long-lasting pot and container plants, and are perfect for decorating decks and patios through the summer months.

African daisies require a position with full sun and well-drained soil. Keep the soil evenly moist but not wet. When grown in containers, they benefit from monthly fertilization.

Extensive breeding programs have developed for the nursery and cut flower trade, mostly derived from *Gerbera jamesonii*. This has resulted in a slew of strains and series, selected for compact growth, length of bloom time, bloom size, tolerance for cold

Geum 'Starker's Magnificum' shares a spot with *Festuca glauca* 'Elijah's Blue' and prickly pears

or inclement weather, and leaf size as well as foliage form and color intensity. The hybrids are correctly called G. ×*cantabrigiensis*.

Gerberas are susceptible to attack from aphids, leaf miners, and white flies, as well as root rot, molds, and mildews, especially where air circulation is poor. Protect from slugs and snails. Resistant to deer.

Plants can be started from seed (fresh seed germinates easily) or by basal cuttings, which root readily in summer.

Gerbera jamesonii
- all except blue
- late spring to late summer
- 12–18 in. × 24 in.
- sun
- Z8–12

Barberton daisy, transvaal daisy, gerbera daisy. Southern Africa. Solitary daisy flowers borne on naked but hairy stems rising from deep-rooted clumps of basal foliage. Petioled leaves are more or less spoon shaped, rounded at the top, and deeply lobed below, about 10 in. long. Flowers 3–5 in. across, usually with a double outer row of brightly colored, rounded or pointed ray flowers (petals) with a center of disk flowers often of a contrasting color. Fancy forms are available that have extra rows of petals, or are anemone centered, dahlia-like, or even similar to pot marigolds. Some of the flower forms are delicate and charming; others tend to be garish and even slightly vulgar. In the garden they mix well with clivias, agapanthus,

mesembryanthemums, and low grasses. Barberton daisies resent disturbance and should be planted, not too deeply, in their permanent sunny positions. Deadhead to the base of the stem, for neatness and to encourage further bloom.

Californian Giants are all single in yellow, oranges, reds, and pinks. 20–24 in.

Festival Series has compact, small-leaved plants with 3.5-in.-wide flowers in white, yellows, rosy pinks, and scarlet. 10 in.

Mega Revolution Series makes bushy plants bred for larger containers. Large flowers in pastel colors; orange, yellow, and pink flowers are dark centered, as in 'Orange DC'.

Parade Series may have single or double flowers in reds, pinks, and yellows.

Rainbow Mix. Flowers in all shades except blue, 4–5 in. across. 16–18 in. tall.

Geum
Rosaceae
avens, Grecian rose

If you are looking for a show stopper, you won't find it among the geums; what you will find, though, are reliable, low-maintenance, and consistently rewarding perennials, real workhorses that combine attractive foliage with bright and long-lasting blooms.

Geums are closely related to potentillas, and like their kin they make useful fast-growing ground-covers. The medium green leaves are fuzzy, usually lobed, and borne typically in neat, clumping mounds. The flowers are medium sized, usually 1.5 in. or so in diameter, cup shaped, and most often composed of single rounds of petals; many of the cultivars and hybrids bear showier double or semi-double flowers. The colors run to bright oranges and reds.

Due to their naturally compact, mounded habit, geums are handy for lending substance to the front of a border. Here they complement more vertical plants such as dwarf irises, delphiniums, and perennial salvias. Their bright blossoms are particularly striking when the plants are massed. Although the main period of bloom is from late spring through early summer, these plants often rebloom intermittently if deadheaded. Geums are also a good source of cut flowers.

Intolerant of the combination of heat and humidity, geums prefer a moist but well-drained soil—they adapt well to rock gardens but do not persist long on dense clays and don't tolerate wet soils in wintertime. Rarely troubled by pests and diseases; deer and rabbit resistant.

Divide established plants every three years or so in fall or spring to help maintain plant vigor and increase your stock. Plants can also be started from seed, although most species hybridize promiscuously and character of seedlings is unpredictable.

Geum coccineum

- red
- late spring to early summer
- 12–18 in. × 9–12 in.
- sun, part shade
- Z5–7, HS

Avens. Balkans. Forms a 6-in. mound of hairy, irregularly lobed leaves consisting of five to seven leaflets; evergreen in the warmer parts of their range. Five-petaled, brick-red flowers borne on wiry, branching stems that rise several inches above the basal foliage mound. Deadheading encourages rebloom in cool-summer regions; where summers are hot the plants benefit from afternoon shade. Leave some flowers on the plant to serve as a source of the attractive, fluffy seedheads that follow.

'Borisii' grows to a height and spread of 6–12 in.; orange flowers.

'Cooky' is 6–12 in. tall and spreads 6–9 in.; brilliant orange flowers with orange-yellow stamens. Foliage persists in spite of summer heat.

'Koi' has bright orange flowers above a compact, 4-in. mound of glossy green leaves. 8 in. Z4–7.

Geum quellyon

syn. *G. chiloense*

- yellow, orange, red
- late spring to early summer
- 2 ft. high and wide
- sun, part shade
- Z5–9, HS

Chilean avens. Chile. Forms a cushion of fuzzy, dark green, strawberry-like leaves that are semi-evergreen or even evergreen in the warmer parts of the plant's range. Branched stems carry the single,

1.5-in.-wide, cup-shaped flowers; those of cultivars are usually semi-double or double, and may be slightly larger. Prefers a rich, well-drained, neutral to slightly acid soil. Short lived.

'Georgenberg' has soft orange flowers with hints of apricot, peach, and salmon. Repeat bloomer. 15 in.

'Lady Stratheden' ('Goldball') has yellow, semi-double flowers. 16–24 in.

'Mrs. J. Bradshaw' ('Feuerball', 'Fireball') is a profuse bearer of large, orange-yellow, semi-double flowers. Leaves turn burgundy color in fall. 16–24 in.

'Red Dragon' bears scarlet, double flowers. 16–20 in.

'Starker's Magnificum' has double, apricot-tangerine flowers. 15–18 in.

Geum rivale

- orange, purple, white
- late spring to early summer
- 6–24 in. × 6–18 in.
- sun, part shade
- Z2–7

Purple avens, water avens, chocolate root. Bogs and wet meadows across northern North America and south into New Mexico, as well as northern Europe and central Asia. The North American population produces large plants with small flowers, whereas the European and Asian plants are more

Geum rivale

compact with much larger flowers; the blooms of both are nodding and bell shaped, pinkish apricot in color. Leaves pinnate, measuring to 8 in. long and 2 in. across; basal leaves have five to seven leaflets, the upper ones have three. Individual leaflets are coarsely serrated, slightly hairy, rough textured, and medium green; terminal leaflet is sometimes divided into three lobes. Flowers are borne in cymes on dark purple, hairy stems; individual blooms measure 0.75–1 in. across, and are composed of five dull red to pale purple petals and five dark purple sepals. Prefers a consistently moist, neutral to mildly acid soil, tolerates garden soils with more than average moisture. Best suited for growing in bog gardens or at the margins of water gardens.

Gillenia trifoliata contrasts airily with *Ligularia dentata* foliage

'Flames of Passion' bears semi-double, scarlet-red flowers from spring well into summer, followed by feathery prairie smoke–like seed pods. 12 in. × 18 in. Z5–9.

'Leonardii' ('Leonard's Variety') blooms with copper-pink flowers. 8–12 in.

'Lionel Cox' has yellow-tinged pink flowers. 12 in.

'Marika' is compact with creamy-peach flowers. 9–12 in. tall.

'Snowflake' is compact, to 9 in., with pure white flowers. Holds its flowers outward rather than nodding as in 'Album'.

Geum triflorum

syn. *Erythrocoma triflora*
- reddish pink, purple
- late spring to early summer
- 6–18 in. × 6–12 in.
- sun
- Z3–7, HS

Prairie smoke, purple avens. Prairie native, Pacific Coast inland as far as New Mexico and northward into Canada, east across the upper Midwest into New York. Hairy, rhizomatous plant with pinnately divided, fern-like, green leaves with 7 to 19 leaflets. The reddish pink to purplish, nodding, globular flowers (usually borne in clusters of three) are attractive but the distinctive beauty of this plant lies in the fruiting heads that follow: as the flowers age, the protruding styles lengthen to form a cluster of 2-in.-long, feathery, gray tails, giving the whole the look of a miniature feather duster.

Prefers a dry, well-drained soil in a sunny location, though it benefits from some afternoon shade in hot-summer regions. Tolerant of moist but well-drained soils, though likely to prove short lived in such conditions. Typically free of pests and problems. This soft-textured plant is effective at the front of a border, but is most striking when massed in a meadow or prairie setting.

Other Notable Cultivars

'Banana Daiquiri', an introduction of Illinois's Intrinsic Perennial Gardens, has semi-evergreen leaves below long-stemmed, semi-double, pale yellow flowers. Beautiful, slightly frilly blooms. 18–24 in. × 15–18 in. Z4–8.

'Blazing Sunset' grows 18–24 in. high and wide, with double, scarlet flowers 50 percent larger than those of other geums. Flowers all summer. Z5–7, HS.

'Cherry Cordial' is compact, with single, red blossoms followed by fluffy seedheads. 9–12 in. Z5–7, HS.

Gillenia

Rosaceae
Bowman's root, Indian physic

Another victim of botanical reclassification, this plant also goes by the name of *Porteranthus*; gardeners will find it listed under both names in catalogs and nurseries. Whatever you call it, Bowman's root is native to central, eastern, and southeastern North America, where it grows in open woodlands and clearings. Native Americans valued Bowman's root for its medicinal properties, especially as an emetic; hence, it is sometimes colloquially called Indian physic.

A clump-forming plant, Bowman's root has wiry, reddish stems, erect and branching. Its trifoliate leaves are wrinkled and sharply toothed, each lance-shaped leaflet measuring as much as 4 in. long. The charming, dainty panicles of white or sometimes pink flowers flutter in summer breezes to provide an element of movement in the garden. Moist soil and part shade are ideal for this unassuming plant. Seldom browsed by deer.

Good companions for Bowman's root include other woodland perennials such as ferns, heucheras, Solomon's seal, and bugbanes. *Gillenia* is perfect for native plant and woodland gardens, as well as among shrubs and in informal areas.

Divide in spring or fall or start from seed.

Gillenia trifoliata
syn. *Porteranthus trifoliatus*
- white
- early summer
- 2–4 ft. × 3 ft.
- part shade
- Z4–7

Bowman's root, mountain Indian physic, American ipecac. New York to Georgia. Long overlooked as a subject for American gardens, this wonderful native is now becoming better known. Strong, branching, mahogany-red stems gracefully carry masses of white, five-petaled, butterfly-like flowers, 1–1.5 in. across, with persistent red calyces on red petioles. Handsome foliage seldom marred by pests or diseases, ignored by deer. Turns reddish bronze in fall. Persistent seedheads provide winter interest. Best in slightly acid, well-drained, moist soils rich in organic matter. Tolerates dry shade if well mulched and planted into a few inches of compost. Prefers a partly shaded position; protect from strong midday sun. Useful as filler in beds and borders, as well as in floral arrangements. *Gillenia stipulata* (syn. *Porteranthus stipulatus*) is similar but with fewer-flowered panicles of bloom; it is better suited to hot and humid gardens.

'Pink Profusion' has clear pink flowers on stems 2–3 ft. Z4–9.

Glaucidium
Ranunculaceae
Japanese wood poppy

This genus includes but a single species, *Glaucidium palmatum*. This beautiful Asian buttercup thrives in woodland conditions in cool climates. It does not tolerate combined high temperatures with humidity and will usually fail south of zone 7 on the US East Coast. They are successful, however, in the dry heat of southern California.

Glaucidium palmatum

Glaucium flavum

For best results, give plants a moderately acid to neutral soil that drains well but is consistently moist; do not let plants dry out between watering. A gem for woodland gardens; combine with other woodland shade lovers, including cypripediums, trilliums, anemones, erythroniums, and May apples.

Glaucidium palmatum

- mauve
- late spring to early summer
- 18–24 in. × 15–18 in.
- part shade, shade
- Z3–9, HS

Japanese wood poppy. Forests and alpine meadows of northern Japan. Forms clumps of bright green, paired, maple-like leaves, that are divided into 7 to 11 irregularly toothed lobes. Exquisite large (to 3-in.-wide), cup-shaped, poppy-like flowers range in color from rose-pink to pale mauve, and are borne singly on thin stems.

var. *leucanthum* has white flowers.

Glaucium
Papaveraceae
horned poppy

This plant achieves the perennial equivalent of a hat trick, scoring in the matter of foliage and fruits as well as flowers. The flowers, borne singly in leaf axils and at stem tips, are classic poppy, with bright, tissue-paper petals. Many gardeners value the handsome, blue-green foliage more highly; the waxy covering that gives the divided leaves their glaucous sheen actually evolved as a defense against sunburn. The added late-season bonus is the intriguing curved seedheads that follow the flowers.

This plant does come with a warning, however: it has the poisonous roots and yellow sap typical of members of the poppy family. Yellow horned poppy contains an alkaloid, *glaucine*, that has the same effects as codeine; this is very potent and was used in Viking times by Scandinavians, and more recently has been employed as a cough suppressant, anti-inflammatory, and analgesic. As a result of this toxicity, deer do not browse these plants.

Grow in full sun on poor to average, well-drained soil. Horned poppies are very deep rooted and resent disturbance. Start them from seed sown in containers to minimize transplant shock.

Glaucium flavum

- yellow
- summer
- 12–36 in. × 18 in.
- sun
- Z6–9

Yellow horned poppy. Coastal regions of the Canary Islands, Britain and Europe, and the Mediterranean. Short-lived perennial often grown as a biennial. Naturalized in some areas, notably coastal regions, where it can be found growing on the beach among sand and pebbles. Rosette-forming, hairless, waxy, blue-green leaves are divided into toothed, wavy

Globularia cordifolia

lobes, the terminal one broader than the rest. In summertime oval, bristly buds open into charming bright yellow or orange flowers about 2 in. across, with four petals surrounding a central boss of stamens. They set copious amounts of tiny black seeds and self-sow freely, especially into gravel or poor, dry soils. Well adapted to dry regions. Biennial red horned poppy (*Glaucium corniculatum*) is similar but with crimson to orange flowers blotched with black at the base of each petal; it grows to 12–16 in.

Globularia
Plantaginaceae
globe daisy

Best known to rock garden aficionados, globe daisies deserve a wider application. They are excellent in troughs and can be tucked into small cracks in walls or between pavers, as well as serving as slow-growing groundcovers. In spite of their common name, they are not related to the daisy family; formerly they were given their own taxonomic family: Globulariaceae.

Mostly ground hugging, globe daisies produce mats of good-looking, leathery, evergreen leaves topped by dense, rounded heads of flowers borne on perky stems. The creeping stems, woody at their base, root where they touch soil, but this colonization is easily controlled. A sharp, well-drained soil is essential for most species, as is a sunny spot. Alkaline soil is preferable; dress with lime chips where soil tends to be acid. Tolerates droughty conditions well. Deadhead for neatness after bloom time.

Globe daisy is a larval food for some species of butterflies and moths. It is resistant to deer and gophers, but may be attacked by slugs.

Difficult to divide; heeled cuttings (softwood stems with a piece of woody tissue attached) can be separated in summer and then rooted. Seeds need a chilling for two months before they will germinate.

Globularia cordifolia
- blue
- spring
- 2–5 in. × 12 in.
- sun, part shade
- Z5–8

Heart-leaved globe daisy. Scree and rocky mountainous areas of the Mediterranean region. Makes tight rosettes of evergreen, shiny, spoon-shaped leaves 1–2 in. long and notched at the tip. Flower stems shrouded in tiny flattened leaves poke their heads above the foliage in late spring topped with 1.75-in., powder-puff heads of lavender flowers. Most attractive as a slow-growing groundcover.

Globularia meridionalis
syn. *G. bellidiflora, G. cordifolia* subsp. *bellidiflora, G. cordifolia* subsp. *meridionalis*
- blue
- summer
- 6–12 in. × 12 in.
- sun, part shade
- Z5–7

Globe daisy. Southeast Alps and Mediterranean region. Mats of lustrous evergreen, 3-in. leaves usually lance shaped and rounded at the tips. In summer upright stems clothed with smaller leaves rise to 12 in. or so, topped with showy button-like, globular heads of small flowers in varying shades of lavender-blue. Low dianthus, lewisias, and other unthirsty perennials are excellent companions.

Goniolimon
Plumbaginaceae
Tatarian statice

Of the 20 or so species of *Goniolimon*, only one has found a place in ornamental gardens. Better known as Tatarian statice or by an alternative botanical name, *Limonium tataricum*, this plant is closely related to the familiar German statice (*L. sinuatum*) used in fresh and dried flower arrangements. Formerly they were joined in the same genus but now have been separated on the basis of small botanical details.

Like its German relative, Tatarian statice produces flowers that are good for fresh or dried floral designs and wreaths. For drying, delay harvesting until the flowers are fully open. These flowers also attract butterflies.

Select a sunny place for Tatarian statice, although ideally it should include protection from the intense sun of early afternoon. It thrives in well-drained, average or sandy soils and does especially well in coastal areas where it tolerates salt spray readily. Avoid high-nitrogen fertilizers. Good air circulation is necessary for healthy growth—leave sufficient space between this plant and its neighbors.

Tatarian statice is drought tolerant when established; a combination of winter weather and water-logged soil is likely to prove fatal. In general, this is a low-maintenance, undemanding plant, and one that is seldom browsed by deer or attacked by pests and diseases.

Best propagated by dividing the fleshy roots. Take care when doing so, as the sap may irritate sensitive skin. Can be started from seed also.

Goniolimon tataricum
syn. *Limonium tataricum*
- blue, pink, purple, white
- mid- to late summer
- 12–18 in. × 24 in.
- sun
- Z2–9

Tatarian statice, German statice, Tatarian sea lavender. Steppes of South Russia, Caucasus, Europe. Basal rosettes of white-spotted, light green, leathery, lance-shaped or oblong leaves that may reach 6 in. long. Tiny, tubular, flaring flowers are borne on wiry, naked stems in wide-spreading, airy clouds 5–6 in. across. Useful as filler in beds and borders, perhaps with bright daylilies, penstemons, and blazing stars, or as tall edging plants.

Gunnera
Gunneraceae
giant rhubarb

"Bold" does not even begin to describe giant rhubarb's foliage—the individual leaves of some species can measure 6 ft. across, or even more in ideal conditions.

Gunneras require ample moisture and temperate climates. Intolerant of extreme summer heat, they perform best in Oregon, Washington, and southern British Columbia, as well as coastal regions of the Mid-Atlantic and southern New England. To satisfy their thirst for water, they are usually reserved for planting in a bog garden, or the edge of a stream or pool; they also adapt well to container culture if given an extra-large tub or barrel and kept continuously moist, or set into the marginal area of a pool or pond. Soils should be humus and nutrient rich. Evergreen where winters are mild, deciduous where frost is common. Where deciduous, gunneras benefit from a reduction in soil moisture during their period of dormancy and a heavy protective mulch of some material such as straw or pine straw. Gunneras may also be grown in containers in cold-winter regions, and moved indoors in fall for storage in a cool but frost-free location—do not water until moved outdoors again in spring.

Typically pest and disease free where conditions suit. Lends a tropical—even prehistoric—look to a pool or secluded nook. Particularly attractive thickly underplanted with assorted primulas.

Propagate by division, or by seeds soaked for 24 hours in room-temperature water; sow these in a moisture-retentive potting mix, kept slightly warm,

Gunnera manicata in flower

Gypsophila 'Franzii'

and never allowed to dry out; germination takes as much as 30 days. Alternatively, take root cuttings from leafy basal buds in spring.

Gunnera manicata

- pink
- early summer to midsummer
- 6–8 ft. × 10–12 ft.
- sun, part shade
- Z7–9

Giant rhubarb. Cloud forests in mountains of Brazil. Robust and fast growing when well established in a hospitable location. Forms a huge, spreading clump of lobed, rounded, and rough-textured leaves borne on 5- to 8-ft.-tall succulent and fibrous stems. The stems and the undersides of the leaves are spiny, and individual leaves often measure more than 6 ft. in diameter. The tiny, pinkish brown flowers are borne in conical panicles, like pinecones on steroids; these may reach to 40 in. tall and 16 in. across. Partial shade is best where sun is intense; prefers a mildly acid soil pH.

Gypsophila
Caryophyllaceae
baby's breath

Commonly used as filler by the floral industry in arrangements focused on more dramatic flowers such as roses and lilies, gypsophilas can serve a similar purpose in the perennial garden. The airy clouds of small, white flowers that they display through most of the summer furnish a delicate counterpoint to the stronger colors and forms of more assertive blossoms and foliage. Gypsophilas are also useful for filling the gaps left in the garden by early spring bulbs, wildflowers, and summer-dormant perennials, including Oriental poppies, when they retreat back into dormancy in late spring. And, of course, gypsophilas are a handy source of cut flowers.

Gypsophila means "gypsum-" or "chalk loving," and most members of this genus prefer an alkaline soil. Add lime to acid soils, and top-dress with limestone chips in rock gardens. Gypsophilas do best in sunny spots and are generally pest and disease free, although poor drainage may cause root rot. Seldom browsed by deer.

Start seed indoors in winter or outdoors in a cold frame in spring. Root cuttings may be taken from the species in late winter.

Gypsophila cerastoides
syn. *G. cerastioides*

- white
- late spring to midsummer
- 4–8 in. × 8–12 in.
- sun
- Z3–7, HS

Baby's breath. Himalayas. Forms a compact mound of small, rounded, fresh green foliage, from which emerge taller, branching stems that carry the small, pink-veined, white, starry flowers. Drought tolerant; attracts butterflies. Evergreen in mild-winter regions. Valuable for rock gardens, sunny banks, edging along pathways, and at the front of sunny borders, or in containers. Intolerant of heat combined with humidity.

Gypsophila paniculata

- white
- late spring to late summer
- 1–3 ft. high and wide
- sun
- Z3–9

Baby's breath, chalk plant. Steppes of eastern Europe. Drought tolerant, prefers dryish, well-drained, alkaline soil. Wet soil in winter is likely to prove fatal; otherwise trouble free except for some susceptibility to aster yellows. The gray-green, 4-in. leaves are opposite and lance shaped, sparsely arranged on branching, wiry stems. Cut back after initial flush of bloom in early summer to stimulate further bloom. Propagate named cultivars by rooting tip cuttings taken in spring before flowering begins. Reported as invasive in Washington, Oregon, Colorado, Wisconsin, and Michigan, and has escaped into the wild in many other states—keep an eye on this plant to prevent excessive proliferation.

'Bristol Fairy' is a traditional favorite that produces numerous long-lasting, double, white flowers up to 0.25 in. wide. Sparse, lance-shaped foliage. 2–2.5 ft.

'Rosenschleier' ('Rosy Veil') is a low-growing hybrid of this species with *Gypsophila repens*. It has pale pink, double flowers. 12–20 in.

'Viette's Dwarf' grows to a height and spread of 1–1.5 ft., with blue-green leaves and double, pink flowers that fade to white.

Gypsophila repens

- white
- early -late summer
- 4–12 in. × 18 in.
- sun
- Z3–8, HS

Creeping baby's breath. Low-growing European species, commonly 6 in. tall, forms spreading cushions of gray-green, lanceolate foliage. Smothered in early summer with tiny, white, five-petaled flowers. Beautiful groundcover for sunny, well-drained spots, also works well as edging for a path or border, or spilling over the edge of a retaining wall or container. A gem for rock gardens and containers, and for planting into crevices of a south- or west-facing retaining wall, or between flagstones on a sunny terrace. Drought tolerant, but regular irrigation during dry spells in spring and early summer is critical to the flower quality. Difficult in hot and humid gardens.

'Alba' is white flowered. 4 in. tall

'Dorothy Teacher' has a low, neat habit with soft pink flowers that darken with age. Bluish green foliage. 2 in.

'Filou Rose' has a long season of bloom from late spring to late summer. It bears large, bright pink flowers.

'Fratensis' (syn. *Gypsophila franzii* 'Nana Compacta') makes a low cushion of blue-green foliage, 2–3 in. high and 6 in. wide, from which emerge wiry stems bearing a wealth of tiny, pale pink flowers. Z4–7.

Hedychium
Zingiberaceae
ginger lily

With their bold, broadly blade-shaped, glossy foliage and flamboyant panicles of butterfly-like flowers, these relatives of culinary ginger impart a tropical lushness to the garden. Many are surprisingly cold hardy, overwintering outdoors successfully as far north as warmer parts of zone 7. Ginger lilies mix well with cannas, elephant ears, and the more cold-tolerant bananas in a faux-tropical patio or court. They also lend height, mass, and color to summertime borders, where they hold their own with dahlias, crocosmias, and daylilies. In regions too cold for them to overwinter outdoors, hedychiums may be cultivated in large containers, sturdy enough to withstand the pressures of the plant's expansive rhizomatous root system—and then moved indoors as cold weather arrives.

The native range of ginger lilies extends from southeast Asia to the foothills of the Himalayas. A region of monsoon climates, rainfall is seasonal and extended periods of wet weather alternate with periods of drought. In North American gardens, this condition is best imitated by providing plenty of moisture during the growing season and then withholding it from late fall to winter. Provide well-drained, neutral to slightly acid, moisture-retentive

Hedychium densiflorum 'Stephen'

soil, well-enriched with organic matter. Keep the soil moist, but not waterlogged when shoots emerge in spring; neglecting this stunts growth and aborts bloom. Apply balanced organic fertilizer regularly to satisfy these greedy feeders. Tolerates full sun in low-light regions; filtered light is best elsewhere.

Hedychiums may be overwintered outdoors in zones 7 and 8. After the first killing frost, cut the plants back almost to the ground, leaving stubs to mark the spot. Cover the crowns with 1–2 in. of composted manure, and top with ground bark for insulation. Specimens planted with poor drainage are unlikely to survive.

Slugs and snails attack the foliage of ginger lilies but are easily controlled; otherwise these plants are usually trouble free, and even deer avoid them. Increase stock by dividing the roots in spring, or start from seed.

Hedychium coronarium
- white
- late summer to early fall
- 4 ft. × 18–24 in.
- shade, part shade
- Z7–11

Butterfly ginger. Himalayas and tropical Asia. Dense heads of 2-in., intensely fragrant, butterfly-like, white flowers. A few buds open daily, starting from the bottom and moving gradually upward. Long blooming well into fall. Most plants sold as *Hedychium maximum* are actually this species.

Hedychium densiflorum
- orange-yellow
- early to late summer
- 4 ft. × 18–24 in.
- sun, part shade
- Z7–11

Dense ginger lily. Native to the Himalayan foothills. Crowded, 8-in., bottlebrush heads of intensely fragrant, orange-yellow flowers open from the top downward. Less expansive than many of this genus, dense ginger lily forms tightly packed clumps.

'Assam Orange'. Fragrant, deep orange flowers crowd into 18-in.-long inflorescences. 3 ft. × 4 ft. Z8–10.

'Stephen' is also perfect for limited space. Pale orange-yellow flowers, deep orange stamens. 3–4 ft. Z7–9.

Hedychium gardnerianum
- yellow
- late summer to midfall
- 5–8 ft. × 18–24 in.
- sun, part shade
- Z8–11

Kahili ginger lily is native to Nepal, but has naturalized in Hawaii, where it has proven invasive. Blue-green foliage, with giant, 1- to 1.5-ft. heads of fragrant, gold to pale yellow, 3.5-in. flowers with prominent, protruding, dark orange stigmas.

'Compactum' grows to 4–5 ft.

Other Notable Cultivars
Most of these cultivars are hardy to the warmer parts of zone 7.

'Daniel Weeks' blooms from early summer to fall; golden-yellow flowers with dark gold throats. 4 ft. tall.

'Flaming Torch' produces two flushes of orange flowers; in early to midsummer, repeating in fall. 6–7 ft. tall.

'Vanilla Ice' has white-streaked leaves, and fragrant, peach-pink flowers in late summer. 3 ft.

Tai Series, bred by Doyle Smittle, includes many large- and fragrant-flowered hybrids such as 'Tai Mammoth'. It bears 15-in. panicles of 3- to 3.5-in., fragrant, creamy-yellow flowers with darker throats, from early summer to fall. 6 ft. tall.

Hedysarum
Fabaceae
sweet vetch

Sweet vetches are typical representatives of the vetch clan: they sport pinnate leaves arranged alternately on the stem, each with an odd number of toothless leaflets; pea-type, red, purple, white, or yellow flowers cluster in racemes or spikes in the leaf axils. Each bilaterally symmetrical bloom consists of five unequal-sized petals: the biggest at the back is the "standard," the pair in front on each side are the "wings," and the pair enclosing the reproductive parts in the middle is the "keel." They are pollinated by heavyweight, nectar-seeking pollinators, including bees; when they alight on the keel it presses down to reveal the stigma and pollen-laden stamens that brush the insect's underbelly. Pod-like fruits enclose the seeds. Lateral roots have nitrogen-fixing nodules that release extra nitrogen into the soil, and thus improve the soil for other plants.

Hedysarum coronarium

Plant in average fertile soil in full sun, where drainage is good. Popular with hunters, who know that sweet vetches are a favored deer food—gardeners should take heed and protect their plantings. Young growth attracts slugs, snails, and rabbits.

Direct sow scarified seed in spring in containers, and protect seedlings from wildlife. Sweet vetches resent disturbance to the long taproots, so transplanting and division are tricky; plant initially in their permanent spot.

Hedysarum coronarium

- red
- spring
- 2–4 ft. × 18–24 in.
- sun
- Z4–9

French honeysuckle, cock's head, Italian sainfoin. Native to Algeria, Morocco, Tunisia, and Spain. This erect, bushy perennial has long been cultivated in Europe for animal feed and for honey production. The bluish green leaves have 7–15 rounded, 1.5-in. leaflets, hairy on their undersides. Blood red, 0.75-in. pea flowers cluster in dense spikes of up to 35 blooms; these are rich in nectar and very fragrant, attracting bees, butterflies, and pollinating insects like a magnet. Southern plantings need support, but plants grown in cooler climates are more sturdy if given full sun. Cut back after blooming if plants become untidy.

'Alba' is white flowered.

Helenium

Asteraceae
sneezeweed, Helen's flower

Can sneezeweeds and allergy sufferers share the same garden? Of course they can! These plants are so named not because of their allergenic pollen—sneezeweed flowers are insect pollinated (instead of by wind), and so do not cause hay fever—but rather because their dried foliage was sometimes used as a substitute for snuff tobacco in Colonial America. It should be noted, however, that sneezeweed foliage may irritate the skin of sensitive individuals, and eating any part of these plants may cause intestinal distress.

This fine, clump-forming perennial, a mainstay of summer and fall gardens, has well-branched stems that bear 4- to 12-in.-long, oval leaves. The daisy-like flowerheads are composed of a prominently raised central disk surrounded by broad, wedge-shaped ray petals in yellow, orange, and reddish tones. Bloom time is long, lasting from midsummer to midfall, depending upon the species or cultivar. All make good cut flowers, and are reliable subjects for beds and borders. Fine companions include bluebeards, monkshoods, baby's breath, catmints, and torch lilies.

Sneezeweeds thrive in average soil that drains well but does not dry out too rapidly. Apply organic

Close-up of *Helenium* Mardi Gras ('Helbro') flowerheads

mulch to retain soil moisture. Tall selections mostly require staking, especially when grown in exposed positions. Shearing them back to reduce their height by half before midsummer results in more compact, robust growth and more flowers later. Deadhead routinely to extend bloom time.

Pests and diseases are few, although they may fall prey to powdery mildew during dry seasons. Water at ground level during times of drought; thin dense clumps to improve air movement. Deer resistant.

Sow seed of species. Divide cultivars in spring or fall, or take root cuttings in spring. To maintain vigor, divide established plants every two to three years.

Helenium autumnale

- yellow, orange
- midsummer to midfall
- 2–5 ft. × 3 ft.
- sun
- Z3–8

Common sneezeweed. Native to eastern Canada and the United States. Stiffly upright, branched and winged stems clothed with 4- to 6-in.-long, toothed, oval to lance-shaped leaves. Flowerheads may reach 2 in. or more across with reflexed, yellow ray flowers, and a prominent, raised, brown disk. Avoid overfertilizing; this causes soft, floppy growth that requires staking. Appropriate for native plant and wildlife gardens.

Helenium bigelovii

- yellow
- early to midsummer
- 1–3 ft. × 1 ft.
- sun
- Z5–8

Bigelow's sneezeweed, mountain sneezeweed. Native to damp streamsides, marshes, and high meadows in California and Oregon. The lower leaves of this upright, clump-forming perennial are carried on winged petioles; those above clasp the sparse, winged stems. Solitary, 2.5-in. flowerheads, with bright golden-yellow rays and a raised spherical disk, yellow at first but maturing to dark brown, top unbranched stems. Attracts butterflies; a good honey plant. Appropriate for damp native plant and wildlife gardens; soil should not dry out.

'**The Bishop**' has deep yellow flowers with deep brown disks. Compact at 2–2.5 ft. Z6.

Helenium hoopesii
- gold
- midsummer
- 3–4 ft. × 18–24 in.
- sun
- Z3–7, HS

Western sneezeweed, orange sneezeweed. Native to the Rocky Mountain states. Robust clumps of grayish green basal leaves to 12 in. long; upper stem leaves are narrowly lance shaped and become smaller as they ascend. The strong, leafy stems carry clusters of 3-in.-wide flowerheads, with slender, slightly reflexed, golden rays around a darker central disk. Resents southern heat and humidity.

Other Notable Cultivars
There is a multitude of old and new selections and cultivars. This is just a sampling.

'**Butterpat**' has buttery yellow flowerheads, centered with a greenish disk. Erect on strong stems. 4 ft. Z4.

'**Coppelia**' has coppery red ray flowers surrounding a chocolate disk. 3 ft. Z4.

Mardi Gras ('Helbro') bears 1- to 2-in. heads of yellow daisies, splashed and speckled with red and orange; cone is tan. 3–4 ft. Z4.

'**Moerheim Beauty**'. Deep copper ray flowers surround deep chocolate central disks. Early to late summer. 36 in. Z4.

'**Red Jewel**' is relatively new with dusky red flowers, rays sometimes tipped with yellow, accented with a maroon center. Very long bloom time. 2.5–3 ft. Z4.

'**Short 'n' Sassy**' is compact with a tight habit. Brown cone, bright gold and orange rays. 12–18 in.

Helianthemum
Cistaceae
sun rose, rock rose

They aren't roses, but these perennial subshrubs thrive in sunny or partially shaded locations; they handle well-drained rocky or sandy soils with ease. Once rooted into a site, sun roses are very drought tolerant, and their ground-hugging foliage and colorful flowers qualify them as ideal groundcovers for dry sunny banks or rock gardens. They also thrive in hot, drought-prone areas along the edge of driveways or between a sidewalk and the street (sometimes called a "hell strip"). Additionally they can hold their own in more refined surroundings of a sunny border, where they mix well with lavenders, spurges, and oreganos. Beautiful draped over the edge of a retaining wall.

Helianthemum 'Hartswood Ruby' adds color to rock gardens

Opposite leaves are oblong or linear, and evergreen, to 1.5 in. long; they vary from soft downy grays to light or bright greens, sometimes with a crinkled texture. The flowers are mostly 1 in. or more across, five petaled, and in the species white, yellow, or occasionally pale pink; many hybrids on the market have extended the color palette to include a range of yellows, pinks, oranges, and reds. These flowers attract bees and butterflies, adding another kind of color to the garden.

Sow seed of species. Take tip cuttings of named cultivars in summer after bloom time. Shearing back plants at that time promotes compact growth, plus it forces out new shoots, an ideal source of cuttings.

Helianthemum alpestre
syn. *H. oelandica* subsp. *alpestre*
- yellow
- early to midsummer
- 5 in. × 8 in.
- sun
- Z6–8, HS

Alpine rock rose. Native to the mountains of southern Europe, alpine rock rose forms dense, green carpets with bright yellow flowers. Prefers a gritty soil, low in nitrogen. Not for hot and humid summer climates.

Helianthemum mutabile
syn. *H. nummularium* 'Mutabile'
- various
- late spring to early summer
- 6–12 in. × 24 in.
- sun
- Z6–8, HS

Frostweed. Native to the Mediterranean basin. Downy, gray foliage is set off by 1-in., white, pink, rose, red, or yellow flowers. Prolific bloom on suitable sites. Shear back after flowering to encourage rebloom. Provide well-drained, alkaline soil. Easily started from direct-sown seed. This is a useful and attractive cover for dry, sunny spots, and is excellent for borders or containers. Does not tolerate southern heat and humidity. Apply winter mulch in zone 5.

Helianthemum nummularium

- pink, yellow
- late spring to early summer
- 6–12 in. × 2–3 ft.
- sun
- Z5–7

Rock rose. Native to Europe and Asia Minor, the species bears evergreen, grayish green, lanceolate leaves, 1–2 in. long. Five-petaled, rose-like flowers, to 1-in. in diameter, usually bloom in shades of pastel pink or yellow; terminal clusters of flowers bloom for up to two months. Individual blossoms last only a day, but the plants are so prolific that at times flowers hide the foliage entirely. Best adapted to regions with cool summers and mild winters, this species prefers full sun and dry, alkaline, rocky or sandy, well-drained loams. Shear after flowering to promote compact growth; in zone 5, protect overwintering plants with an insulating blanket of evergreen boughs.

Other Notable Cultivars

Most cultivars are descended from *Helianthemum nummularium*, and bloom from late spring to early summer. 8–18 in. Z4–9, HS. This is a sampling.

'Ben Moore' is deep orange, with a darker eye. 5 in.

'Cheviot' has peach-colored blossoms above gray foliage.

'Hartswood Ruby' ('Hartswood') has red flowers above glossy green foliage.

'St. Mary's' bears white flowers with deep green foliage. 8 in. × 24 in.

'Wisley Pink', rose-pink flowers with silver foliage.

'Wisley Primrose' has soft yellow flowers above gray-green leaves.

Helianthus

Asteraceae
sunflower

The sunflower tribe includes many fine perennials as well as the familiar annuals. All are native to North America, indigenous to a range of habitats including prairies, meadows, roadsides, seaside dunes, and even swamps. Economically the genus is important for the production of sunflower seed oil, birdseed, and Jerusalem artichokes or "sunchokes," consumed as a starchy vegetable.

Perennial sunflowers are generally imposing and durable plants. They include some of the tallest garden perennials as well as some of the showiest blossoms. As such, they make good backdrops for sunny borders and combine well with taller ornamental grasses, especially *Panicum virgatum* 'Heavy Metal' and purple muhly grass, whose blue or purple-toned foliage complement the yellow flowerheads. For a native plant display, pair sunflowers with big bluestem grass. Purple ironweed, Russian sage, and bluebeard also make good companions. Sunflowers mix easily with other "hot"-colored summer flowers—those with red, orange, or gold flowers. Their lofty, sunset-colored blooms show particularly well when planted on the western side of a garden so that the evening sun backlights the display. The flowers attract butterflies, and the seeds are a welcome food source for songbirds. Mostly resistant to deer browsing; pests and diseases are infrequent.

Propagate by seed or division.

Helianthus 'Lemon Queen'

Helianthus angustifolius

- · yellow
- · late summer to fall
- · 8–10 ft. × 2–4 ft.
- · sun
- · Z6–9

Swamp sunflower. Native from Texas and Oklahoma, northeastward to New York, and south through Florida. This robust perennial has deep green, lance-shaped leaves, and bears a profusion of 2.5-in.-wide, bright yellow, daisy-like flowerheads with purple-brown centers, from early fall to frost. Prefers a moist soil. This species tends to spread aggressively and is best reserved for meadow or wild gardens. Salt tolerant, and a good choice for sheltered places in seaside gardens.

'First Light' forms a 4-ft.-tall, compact clump with bright yellow-orange, 2-in. flowerheads. Less aggressive than the species; a better choice for ornamental borders.

'Gold Lace' has deep green, leathery leaves and produces a fountain of golden flowerheads. 5–6 ft.

'Matanzas Creek' produces heads of light yellow flowers. 8 ft.

Helianthus debilis

- · yellow
- · early to late summer
- · 18–48 in. × 36–48 in.
- · sun
- · Z8–11

Beach sunflower, cucumber-leaved sunflower. Native to coastal regions from Texas, east through Florida and northward through North Carolina. Heart-shaped, coarse, rough-textured leaves 2–4 in. long and almost twice as wide. Slightly nodding, 2.5- to 3-in.-wide flowerheads are bright yellow with a red-purple central eye. Blooms repeatedly.

subsp. *debilis* is prostrate; makes a pretty, drought-tolerant groundcover for seaside gardens and dry spots elsewhere.

subsp. *cucumerifolius* 'Italian White' has sparse, 4-in.-wide, black-centered flowerheads with only ten pale yellow or creamy-white, petal-like rays. 4–5 ft.

Helianthus giganteus

- · yellow
- · midsummer to midfall
- · 7–12 ft. × 2–3 ft.
- · sun
- · Z5–9

Tall sunflower. Native to the eastern half of North America, north of Florida. Less aggressive than swamp sunflower; requires staking and a site protected from strong winds. Purplish, often hairy stems branch toward the top. Slender, lance-shaped leaves are medium green, toothed along the margins; rather sparse flowerheads have 10 to 20 petal-like rays surrounding a yellow, 1.75- to 3.25-in. central disk. Prefers moist to wet, sandy soils.

'Sheila's Sunshine' produces loose clusters of light, primrose-yellow flowerheads.

Helianthus maximiliani

- · yellow
- · midfall
- · 4–10 ft. × 3–4 ft.
- · sun
- · Z4–10

Prairie sunflower, Maximilian sunflower. Native to grasslands and meadows throughout the continental United States, except the extreme Southeast and the desert Southwest. Slender, erect stems bear alternate, slender, pointed, lance-shaped leaves folded down the mid-vein, and up to 12 in. long. Flowerheads, arranged in spikes rather than panicles, are 2–4 in. wide, yellow with brown-and-yellow centers, surrounded at their bases by pointed, green bracts which may stick straight out and curl at the tips. Tolerates a wide range of soils; an aggressive spreader best reserved for wildflower and prairie plantings.

Helianthus ×multiflorus

syn. *H. annuus* × *H. decapetalus*

- · yellow
- · summer to late summer
- · 4–6 ft. × 2 ft.
- · sun, part shade
- · Z3–8

Ovate leaves, 8–10 in. long. Bright yellow flowerheads may be single, semi-double, or double, from 3.5–5 in. across. Many hybrids are lumped into this classification. It is wise to buy plants by cultivar name.

'Flore Pleno' has double, bright yellow heads of flowers.

Helianthus ×*multiflorus* 'Miss Mellish'

'**Capenoch Star**' has large, single, bright yellow heads. 5–6 ft.

'**Loddon Gold**' is double flowered with gold flowerheads.

'**Miss Mellish**' is semi-double. Tends to be invasive.

'**Sunshine Daydream**' has rounded, golden, double blooms, almost 2.5 in. across. 5–6 ft. tall.

Helianthus salicifolius
syn. *H. orgyalis*
- yellow-orange
- late summer to late fall
- 4–6 ft. × 15–24 in.
- sun, part shade
- Z4–9

Willowleaf sunflower. Wisconsin, south and west to Texas, with populations in Ohio, New York, and Marylatnd. The pale green leaves are drooping and willow like, borne on rigid, whitish green stems. The flowerheads, carried in branched panicles, measure 2–2.5 in. across with bright yellow rays and dark brown central disks. Well adapted to any average, medium, well-drained soil in full sun, but also tolerates clays. Spreads by creeping rhizomes to form dense colonies; divide every three to four years to control expansion and maintain vigor. One of the brightest fall bloomers; a good source of cut flowers.

'**Low Down**' is a dwarf cultivar. 12–15 in. × 16–20 in.

Helianthus simulans
- yellow
- early to midfall
- 8–10 ft. × 3–4 ft.
- sun
- Z6–9

Tall narrow-leaved sunflower, muck sunflower. Native to the southern coastal plains from Florida to Louisiana and north into Tennessee and Arkansas. This species is similar to and was formerly considered a form of *Helianthus angustifolius*; it is however, much more robust. Alternate leaves are

hairy, slender, and willow like, with a conspicuous central vein. In fall, branched stems are spangled with a spectacular display of purplish red-centered, bright yellow, 3-in. flowers after most others are spent, even after light frost. Provides nectar for migrating butterflies. Prefers moist soil.

Other Notable Cultivars
'**Lemon Queen**' is one of the best. Pale yellow flowers, 2.5 in. across, are carried on 5- to 7-ft. stems. Can become aggressive, but ideal for wild gardens, meadows, or perhaps along a fence, as well as more formal spots.

Helichrysum
Asteraceae
everlasting flower

Everlasting flowers are so valuable in summer gardens especially for their soft, silvery gray foliage that contrasts and mixes seamlessly with colorful perennial and annual flowers. This genus of some 500 or so species has been broken up—strawflower (formerly *Helichrysum bracteatum*) is now in the genus *Bracteantha*. Many of the remaining species are evergreen woody plants; some are annuals. Those described here are tender in cold regions but are used extensively in temporary summer containers and landscapes.

Branched, white-hairy stems have mostly alternate, often aromatic leaves, also covered with woolly hairs. Flowerheads cluster at the stem tips that become tightly packed with heads resembling mini shaving brushes.

Provide lean to average, very well-drained soil with a neutral or alkaline pH; add lime to acid soils. Prune landscape plants in spring before young growth begins. Powdery mildew and rust may be a problem but are seldom serious. Be alert for caterpillars, especially those of painted lady butterflies. Deer do not care for the odor of helichrysums.

Overwinter in a warm greenhouse in cold zones.

Propagate by soft cuttings taken in summer or start seed in spring.

Helichrysum italicum
syn. *H. angustifolium*
- foliage
- late spring to summer
- 1–1.5 ft. high and wide
- sun
- Z8–10, HS

Curry plant. Southern Europe. Woody at the base, with slender, erect stems, densely clothed with white-woolly, 1.5-in., linear leaves. When bruised, the leaves and stems emit a strong odor of curry. Small flowerheads with yellow bracts cluster in terminal heads about 1–2 in. across. Grow in dry, very well-drained locations in rock gardens, gravel gardens, and along hot, sunny paths. Not suitable for regions with high summer heat and humidity.

Helichrysum petiolare

Helichrysum petiolare
syn. *H. petiolatum, Gnaphalium lanatum*
- foliage
- summer
- 2–3 ft. × 3–4 ft.
- sun
- Z9–10, HS

Licorice plant. Southern Africa. This evergreen, mounding and trailing subshrub is popular as a hanging basket annual in cold-winter areas; it is fully perennial in warm zones, except where summer humidity is high, which causes the foliage to melt. Branching stems carry oval, heart-shaped, 0.75- to 3-in. leaves, soft and woolly with white hairs, a natural protection against undue water loss through transpiration in hot climates. In summer, semi-circular, cream-bracted flowerheads gather in 1- to 2-in.-wide clusters. Drought tolerant, but will not tolerate wet feet. Mostly ignored by deer. This beautiful gray plant is superb as a foil for brighter-colored perennials and annuals. Correct nomenclature of the selections is somewhat confused.

Increase by semi-hardwood cuttings or soft cuttings with a heel in summer.

'Limelight' ('Aurea', 'Gold') has lime-green leaves. Protect from intense sun.

'Microphyllum' (syn. *Plecostachys serpyllifolia*) sports very finely textured, gray leaves. Conspicuous heads of bright yellow flowerheads. Very drought tolerant; do not plant this close to wild habitats.

'Minus' has very small, gray-green leaves. 4 in. 'Silver Mist' is reputed to be superior.

'Variegatum' has cream-variegated gray foliage.

Other Notable Cultivars
'Pink Sapphire' (syn. *Helichrysum* ×*amorginum* 'Pink Sapphire') has bright pink flower buds above white, woolly foliage. Provide lean, free-draining soil. Powdery mildew resistant. 8–10 in. Z8–10.

Ruby Cluster ('Blorub'), a parent of the above, has brilliant cherry-red flower buds above white, woolly leaves. Best in lean soil that drains well. 8–10 in. Z8–10.

'Schwefellicht' ('Sulphur Light', syn. *Anaphalis triplinervis* 'Schwefellicht'), a tried and true selection blanketed with white, woolly hairs. Minute sulfur-yellow flowers cluster in dense, congested, terminal clusters. 1–1.5 ft. Z10–11.

Heliopsis
Asteraceae
false sunflower, oxeye

Members of this genus earn their common name with the sunny, brilliant yellow flowers they bear from midsummer well into fall. Although there are several species, only *Heliopsis helianthoides* is sufficiently well behaved and refined in appearance to include in ornamental gardens. The species is seldom grown, however, and typically it is a selection or cultivar that is nurtured. Native and widespread in the eastern part of North America, Native American tribes brewed the leaves of *H. helianthoides* into a tea supposed to relieve lung congestion and fever.

In the wild, false sunflowers inhabit rough terrain with poor dry soils or scrubland, but when provided with well-drained, average garden soil in full sun they come into their own. Avoid excess fertilizer; this encourages lush growth that requires staking; indeed, taller selections often need this sort of support even if their soil is kept lean. To control the plants' height (and minimize the need for support), cut back plants by a half in late spring. Deadhead to extend bloom time.

The flowers attract nectar hunters, including hummingbirds, bees, and butterflies; seed-eating songbirds fill up on the seeds in fall and winter. Seldom browsed by deer. Powdery mildew may defoliate the plants; protect by thinning dense clumps to enhance air movement where possible. Irrigate at ground level during dry weather; do not allow foliage to remain wet overnight.

These stately plants are best grown at the back of mixed beds and borders, in native plant and wild

Heliopsis helianthoides subsp. *scabra* 'Sommersonne'

gardens, as well as other informal spots. Fiery day-lilies, globe thistles, Russian sage, and Joe-Pye weed are good border companions. Planted among tall ornamental grasses they create a naturalistic vignette. Excellent for cutting, with a long vase life. False sunflowers are useful for controlling soil erosion on difficult banks, and tolerate drought well. To maintain vigor, divide cultivars every two to three years; build stock by dividing established plants. The species and some selections come true from seed and germinate freely indoors at 70°F. False sunflowers self-seed freely.

Heliopsis helianthoides

- yellow
- late summer to early fall
- 3–6 ft. × 4 ft.
- sun
- Z3–9

False sunflower, smooth oxeye, woodland sunflower. Prairies and open woodlands of North America from Ontario to New York, west to Minnesota and to the South. Stiff, branching stems are clothed with pairs of mid-green, 5- to 6-in.-long, ovate to lance-shaped leaves, toothed along the edges. The stems terminate in solitary, yellow, 1- to 3-in., daisy-type flowerheads, similar to those of sunflowers. Pointed ray flowers are arranged in a single ring surrounding a brownish yellow disk. The species is seldom grown outside of native plant gardens, but many cultivars are in the marketplace. Those attributed to subsp. *scabra* (or *Heliopsis scabra*) are particularly well suited to garden cultivation. The leaf surfaces of this subspecies are rough like sandpaper.

subsp. *scabra* 'Light of Loddon' has large, double flowerheads. Provide staking for this 4-ft.-tall selection.

Loraine Sunshine ('Helhan') is distinguished by its eye-catching irregularly white-variegated, green foliage. Single, yellow daisies. 30–36 in. Z4–9.

'Prairie Sunset'. Single flowerheads with a reddish disk and a distinct reddish ring at the base of the ray flowers. Striking purple-veined foliage. 3–5 ft.

subsp. *scabra* 'Sommersonne' ('Summer Sun') has bright yellow, semi-double flowerheads. Very tough and forgiving. 2–3 ft. Z3–8.

'Tuscan Sun'. Single, yellow heads, 2 in. across, with an orange-gold disk. Excellent for containers. Powdery mildew seldom a problem. 12–18 in.

Heliotropium
Boraginaceae
heliotrope

Although this genus is comprised of many species, only the common heliotrope, *Heliotropium arborescens*, is widely grown. The so-called garden heliotrope, *Valeriana officinalis*, belongs to a different genus and isn't a true heliotrope. Traditionally, heliotropes have been a mainstay of cottage and fragrance gardens, though their popularity has fluctuated over time. They were especially prized by Victorian gardeners, who grew them as tall standards with trunk-like, single stems for use as punctuating "dot plants" in the elaborate bedding schemes favored in that era. Careful pinching and pruning gave these standards single stems as much as 5 ft. tall; north of zone 9, such plants were wintered under glass and then restarted into growth and planted out again in late spring.

Today's gardeners grow heliotropes as hardy perennials in zones 9 to 11, leaving them outdoors year-round to bloom in spring, with a second bloom season in fall. From zone 8 and northward they are generally cultivated as summer annuals. Wherever they are grown, heliotropes enhance beds, borders, and wildlife and fragrance gardens thanks to

Heliotropium arborescens 'Marine'

Mixed border with dark purple *Heliotropium arborescens* 'Marine'

the strong color and perfume of their flowers. The fragrance is variously described as reminiscent of vanilla, cherry pie, or baby powder. It is strongest in the early morning and late afternoon, and is a resource for the perfume industry.

Heliotropes' long-blooming flowers make good cut flowers and are included sometimes in pot-pourri. Butterflies, birds, and bees are attracted by the fragrance. All parts of the plants are poisonous to cattle and most mammals; seldom browsed by deer. White flies and rust may become a nuisance, especially indoors in the winter months.

Usually borne alternately, the simple leaves are lance-shaped, 3-in. long, and mid- to dark green (sometimes purplish). Their rough, hairy surface is wrinkled with well-pronounced veins. Tubular flowers, typically deep purple and tiny, cluster into coiled cymes that develop slightly mounded or flat-topped heads, 3–4 in. across.

Full sun is best for heliotropes in regions with low light, but part shade is preferable in regions where sunlight is intense. Soil should be sweet (alkaline), fertile, and well drained, but the plants must remain moist for best results. Mulch in summer to help retain soil moisture; where soil tends to be acid, apply a light dressing of lime.

Start from seed in spring at 70ºF with protection, and plant out after the threat of frost has past. Soft cuttings may be taken and rooted in spring and early summer.

Heliotropium arborescens
syn. *H. peruvianum, H. corymbosum*
- blue, purple, white
- late spring to midsummer
- 18–24 in. × 15 in.
- sun, part shade
- Z10–11

Garden heliotrope, common heliotrope, cherry pie. Peru. This short-lived perennial is subshrubby and may reach 4–6 ft. tall in the wild. However, young plants are usually grown in cooler climates for use in summer containers, window boxes, and bedding, and the stems seldom become woody. Lift, pot, and overwinter the plants in a sunroom or other protected spot for replanting outdoors the following spring after the danger of frost has past. If you seek strongly fragrant plants, it is probably wise to buy plants in bloom and sniff carefully, as some clones in the marketplace are not as fragrant as others. Old-fashioned varieties are usually the most fragrant.

'Fragrant Delight' has very fragrant, soft purple flowers. Purple-tinged leaves. 2–3 ft.

'Marine' has large heads of flowers to 6 in. across in deep purple, with a strong fragrance. Foliage is burgundy color. 6–12 in.

'Sweet Heaven' has lavender flowers on 2.5-ft. stems. Strongly fragrant; tolerates summer heat.

'White' is possibly the same as 'White Lady', mentioned in an 1892 seed catalog. Trusses of almond-scented, white flowers. 1.5–2 ft. tall.

Helleborus
Ranunculaceae
hellebore

"Schneerose" (snow rose) is a German name for hellebores, and it underlines one reason for these plants' surging popularity: their ability to bloom during adverse seasons when most other perennials are still hiding underground. In fact, it is quite common to find hellebores poking their flowers and foliage up through a carpet of snow. Depending on the species, they may bloom as early as midwinter in mild climates, or in very early spring where winters are harsher. This, however, is far from the only virtue of these plants. They offer beautiful long-lasting flowers and striking evergreen foliage. Though hellebores respond best to a well-watered and well-drained, rich, humus soil, once established on a site they are notably tough, withstanding both drought and neglect, and commonly surviving as last evidences of some abandoned garden. Originally cultivated for their medicinal qualities, hellebores are permeated with toxic compounds that make them notably resistant to grazing by deer and rabbits, though also less than ideal choices for a landscape with young children.

Some 20 species of hellebores inhabit various areas of Europe and Asia. Most are cultivated only by specialist collectors, but just four species, *Helleborus argutifolius*, *H. foetidus*, *H. niger*, and *H. orientalis*, together with the dozens of fine hybrids derived from them, are sufficient to satisfy the rest of us. Those who are fascinated by hellebores should consult the websites of specialist growers—be aware though, the fancy new selections and cultivars are not inexpensive. Hellebore authority Graham Rice (writing for the Royal Horticultural Society) suggests combining hellebores in the landscape with early-blooming spring bulbs, such as *Crocus tommasinianus*, *Scilla mischtschenkoana*, and snowdrops, or setting them against a backdrop of the brilliant red twigs of red stem dogwood. Hellebores also provide a handsome complement, both in foliage and flowers, to such broad-leaved evergreens as hollies and camellias.

Propagation is by seed or division; in either case, the offspring is likely to take at least two to three years to attain flowering size. Hellebores do not tolerate waterlogged soils; be sure to provide them with good drainage. Potential problems include crown rot when grown on wet or poorly drained soils, and leaf spot.

Helleborus argutifolius
syn. *H. corsicus, H. lividus* subsp. *corsicus*
- green
- late winter to early spring
- 24–48 in. × 24–36 in.
- sun, part shade
- Z6–9

Corsican hellebore. Corsica and Sardinia. Glossy, evergreen leaves are each composed of three leaflets with strongly serrate margins, light green with tints of blue and pearl. Nodding, bowl-shaped flowers, pale green in color, measure 1–2 in. across, and are borne in profusion above the foliage on stout flower stems. Sensitive to cold, though plants will survive brief dips to 0°F; tolerates a range of soils as long as they drain well.

'**Janet Starnes**' has green-and-cream variegated foliage.

'**Pacific Frost**' has foliage abundantly frosted with an overlay of cream and pale green. A favorite in the damp maritime regions.

'**Silver Lace**' has pewter-silver foliage.

Helleborus foetidus

- greenish white
- late winter to early spring
- 1–2 ft. × 1–1.5 ft.
- part shade, shade
- Z5–9

Bear's foot hellebore, stinking hellebore, stinking Benjamin. A native of western and central Europe, this species boasts dark green, evergreen leaves that are deeply lobed, divided into seven to ten narrow, lanceolate to elliptical, tooth-edged segments; the overall effect is celebrated by the nickname "bear's foot." Clusters of pale green flowerbuds appear early in the New Year; shortly thereafter, nodding, bell-shaped, greenish white flowers tipped with purple, up to 1 in. across, open. When bruised, flowers and foliage release an unpleasant skunk-like

Helleborus foetidus

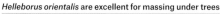
Helleborus orientalis **are excellent for massing under trees**

odor that is rather exaggerated by the names "*foeti-dus*" and "stinking."

Provide plants with a moisture-retentive, organic-rich, slightly alkaline soil that drains well. Cut back flowering stems after blooming to encourage new growth. Plants may self-seed in favorable habitats. Protect from winter winds—a blanket of evergreen boughs is recommended in zone 5.

'Gold Bullion' has bright golden young foliage. Try it with *Mukdenia* or purple bugleweed.

'Krenitsky' (Krenitsky's bear claw hellebore) has dark green, very serrate leaves; 2-ft.-tall stalks of light green flowers.

'Piccadilly' (12–18 in.) and 'Sienna' (24 in.) both have blackish green foliage.

Red Silver Strain has leaves with a silvery sheen, with reddish stems and leaf bases; chartreuse flowers, heavily rimmed with red-purple. This is a variable seed strain.

'Wester Flisk' has red-stemmed, finely divided foliage, and bell-shaped, light creamy-green flowers rimmed with purple. 2 ft. Z4.

Helleborus niger

- white, pink
- mid-winter to early spring
- 9–12 in. × 12–18 in.
- part shade, shade
- Z3–8

Christmas rose. Europe and southwest Asia. Leaves are dark green, glossy, composed of seven to nine leaflets, to 8 in. long by 2.5–3 in. across; evergreen in milder climates, but deciduous where winters are severe. The large, bowl- to cup-shaped flowers may reach 3 in. wide, with five tepals (petals) surrounding a boss of yellow stamens. They are borne singly or in threes, on thick stems, white shading to pink as they mature; bloom may begin as early as December where winters are mild, and may persist for two months. This species prefers a humus-rich, well-drained soil, and a spot protected from winter winds. Christmas roses establish slowly, generally taking several years to bloom size; they grow best if left undisturbed. May self-seed where conditions are good.

'HGC Josef Lemper' (Josef Lemper Christmas rose) grows to just 9 in. Large, white flowers over a prolonged season. Z3–8.

'Potter's Wheel' has rounded, large, white flowers accented with a green eye. A parent of several hybrids.

Helleborus orientalis

syn. *H. ×hybridus*

- white, pink, purple
- late winter to midspring
- 12–18 in. × 15–18 in.
- part shade, shade
- Z4–9

Lenten rose. Native from northeastern Greece through Turkey to the Caucasus Mountains. Large leaves are palmate, leathery, glossy green, and 8–16 in. wide, 12 in. or more in length; evergreen where

winters are mild. The large flowers are 3–4 in. in diameter, nodding or outfacing and cup shaped, ranging in color from white to pink, light pinkish purple to deep purple-black, with a contrasting boss of yellow stamens. Prefers organic-rich, well-drained soils, with a location protected from winter winds. Faster to establish and easier to grow than *Helleborus niger*; more tolerant of division. Self-seeds in hospitable sites.

Other Notable Cultivars

Hybrids and strains are numerous and growing. This is just a sampling.

×*ballardiae* (*Helleborus lividus* × *H. niger*) 'Cinnamon Snow'. Bright cinnamon-red stalks support outfacing, white blooms that age to pink in late winter to early spring. 12 in. × 18 in.

Brandywine Strain has a mix of colors, many spotted; single, semi-double, and double flowers. Bred by David Culp.

Helleborus niger

Helleborus Royal Heritage strain

×*ericsmithii* 'HGC Champion' ('Winter's Bliss'). Dark green, prickly edged leaves and rosy buds; outfacing cream flowers with pink reverse. 15 in. × 24 in. Z4–8.

Golden Lotus Strain bears large, double, yellow flowers, often with pink edging and reverse. Z4–8.

Heronswood Double Strain has double flowers in pinks and roses, cream, purple, and lilac.

×*nigersmithii* 'Walhelivor' (Ivory Prince) has burgundy-petioled, silver-veined, glossy green leaves. Reddish buds open to white flowers in midspring. To 10 in. Z5–8.

Royal Heritage Strain, introduced by John Elsley, includes vigorous growers with variously colored flowers with overlapping petals.

Hemerocallis

Xanthorrhoeaceae
daylily

This genus epitomizes one of the greatest challenges facing the perennial gardener today: how do you make choices when the menu has become so huge? Currently, there are some 60,000 hybrids registered with the American Hemerocallis Society, and more are added daily.

Fortunately, it isn't necessary to review every

alternative. Nurserymen divide hybrid daylilies into several classes based on characteristics including the size of the plant and the form, color, and blooming season of the flowers. Becoming familiar with this system enables you to identify which class will suit the aesthetics of any garden spot. Consider the cultural conditions within your garden and weed out all but those groups of hybrids adapted to your region. An abundance of choices will remain, but by applying these two sets of criteria, any selection you make will be successful.

Evergreen daylilies (cultivars that maintain foliage year-round) tend to be the best choices for hot-climate gardens. Dormant daylilies have foliage that dies down in fall prior to winter dormancy and usually are the best choices for cold-climate regions.

Hemerocallis foliage is strap shaped, long, and narrow. Leafless stems (scapes) carry the flowers; they have parts in threes. Hybridizers have added a range of new flower forms to the genus, including many doubles. There are three basic flower size categories: "dwarf" is a compact daylily that produces scapes under 12 in. tall (like 'Black-Eyed Stella'); "miniature" has flowers 3 in. in diameter or less (as in 'Peach Fairy'); and "tetraploid" describes daylilies with double the normal number of chromosomes. These tend to be more vigorous

This bed of *Hemerocallis* softens the fence and entryway to this residence

than diploids; flowers are usually larger, more intensely colored, and with heavier substance, on sturdier scapes. 'Chicago Apache' is an example.

THERE ARE MANY FLOWER TYPES AND FORMS:
Single flowers retain their original, wild type configuration. Popular cultivars include 'Hyperion' and 'Rosy Sunset'.

Double flowers have modified, petal-like stamens that create the appearance of extra petals. Examples include 'Siloam Double Classic'and 'Prester John'.

Circular flowers are rounded in outline with overlapping petals and sepals. Examples include 'Sir Francis Drake' and 'Stella De Oro'.

Triangular flowers have sepals that recurve (curve backward) more than the petals. Examples include 'Barbara Mitchell' and 'Shaka Zulu'.

Star-shaped flowers are closed at the throat; long, sometimes pinched petals, and recurving narrow sepals. Examples include 'Burgundy Star' and 'Cream Giant'.

Hemerocallis 'Rosy Sunset'

Hemerocallis 'Chicago Apache' blooms in midseason

Spider and spider variants have attenuated petals and sepals, much longer than normal in proportion to their width. Examples include 'Aabachee' and 'Tarantula'.

Typically individual flowers don't last longer than a day, but so many buds are produced that a single plant may bloom for 30 to 40 days.

Early-season daylilies typically bloom in late spring to early summer in the North; midspring in milder regions. Midseason daylies bloom in early to midsummer in the North; mid- to late spring in regions where spring arrives earlier. Late-season bloom is usually four to six weeks after peak season. There are also repeat bloomers (also known as "remontant" and "recurrent") that produce more than one flush, or bloom several times over the course of a growing season. Brassy golden 'Stella de Oro' begins flowering with the early season cultivars and continues blooming almost continuously until fall.

The color range among the hybrids is extraordinary, with hues from pale cream and yellow through gold and orange to red, pink, and purples, even near blacks; only true whites and true blues are lacking. The yellow and oranges are particularly showy when intermixed with blue delphiniums and hydrangeas, for example. White Shasta daisies provide an effective foil to colorful daylily blossoms. Massed or planted in drifts, daylilies shine against an evergreen background.

Average garden soil suits most daylilies, but they will tolerate poor, well-drained soils that retain moisture; drought tolerant when established. A site with full sun to part shade is perfect; with less than six hours of sun, daylilies survive but bloom sparsely. Daylilies have a well-deserved reputation as low-maintenance perennials, but the hybrids vary in vigor; the less vigorous often show greater susceptibility to pests. Remove spent blooms daily to maintain a neat appearance; divide congested clumps every few years to maintain vigor and enhance bloom.

Common pests include aphids, spider mites, and thrips, but they rarely pose a serious threat to healthy plants. Slugs and snails can be a problem. Rabbits are seldom troublesome, but daylilies are at the top of the gourmet menu for deer.

Divide in spring or fall; start your own seeds and see what results.

Hemerocallis citrina

- yellow
- late spring to early summer
- 3–4 ft. × 1.5–2 ft.
- sun, part shade
- Z3–9

Citron daylily. Northeastern China. Thick clumps of arching, narrow leaves to 40 in. long. Fragrant, 6-in., trumpet-shaped flowers are borne on scapes to 45 in.; blooms open at sunset and close the following morning. Tolerates a range of soil types.

Hemerocallis dumortieri

- yellow
- midspring
- 18–24 in. × 24 in.
- sun, part shade
- Z3–9

Dumortier's daylily. Japan, Korea, Manchuria, eastern Siberia. This very early bloomer may flower six to eight weeks earlier than most other daylilies. The leaves are narrowly strap-shaped; 3- to 4.5-in. flowers are lemon yellow, streaked with brown on the back. Delicately fragrant.

Hemerocallis lilioasphodelus

syn. *H. flava*

- yellow
- midspring to late spring
- 2–3 ft. × 1.5–2 ft.
- sun, part shade
- Z3–10

Lemon daylily. China. Trumpet-shaped, 4-in.-wide, lemon flowers are very fragrant; borne on erect, 3-ft.-tall scapes. One of the earliest to bloom. Similar to *Hemerocallis citrina*, this species is tough and exceptionally tolerant of poor soils and summer heat and humidity.

Hepatica

Ranunculaceae
liverleaf

Native to deciduous woodlands across eastern North America, Asia, and northern Europe, liverleafs are early to bloom and particularly welcome for that reason. Closely related to anemones, they enjoy similar conditions of humus-rich, well-drained but moist soil in partly shaded sites. Once established, however, liverleaf tolerates dry woodland conditions well. Numerous selections have been introduced into the nursery trade, but unfortunately they are not as yet widely available in North America. There are also some interesting species from eastern Asia, but these, for the most part, aren't commecially available at this time.

Liverleafs' leathery leaves appear as or just after the flowers bloom and are composed of three to five lobes, pointed or blunt tipped, depending upon the species. Solitary, bowl- or star-shaped flowers may reach 1 in. or more across, with a single or semi-double ring of showy petal-like sepals and a central boss of stamens. After bloom time, more leaves emerge; the foliage persists through winter.

Historically liverleaf has been valued for their curative properties both in Europe and North America. As early as 1653, English botanist, herbalist, and physician Nicholas Culpeper insisted that "it fortifies the liver exceedingly and makes it impregnable."

The plants themselves, unfortunately, are not impregnable. Protect young growth from slugs and snails. Some report that deer avoid these pretty plants, but others have had their plants decimated by such visitors. It is suggested that wild populations of hepaticas throughout North American woods have declined as the deer population has exploded, though overcollecting has probably also played a role. When purchasing these plants, inquire how they were produced; "nursery grown" does *not* mean the same thing as "nursery propagated"; the former label merely means that the plants have spent some time in the nursery and may well have been taken from wild populations originally.

Group in light woodland settings or in clearings, in shaded rock gardens, or plant in troughs or containers where they can be admired close-up. Avoid planting with more aggressive shade lovers, such as hay-scented ferns, that will overrun them. Mulch with composted leaves in fall.

Flowers are self-pollinating and not dependent upon insects or other pollinators. Increase stock by sowing fresh seed as soon as it ripens (it will be green), and protect the containers in a cold frame. Seedlings take several years to reach bloom size. Otherwise divide strong plants in spring, but expect these to be slow to bulk up.

Hepatica acutiloba

syn. *H. nobilis* var. *acuta*

- lavender, white
- early spring
- 3–8 in. × 4–6 in.
- part shade
- Z4–9

Sharp-leaved liverleaf. Woods and on wooded hillsides in our northeastern states. Leaves divided into deeply cut lobes that are pointed at their tips and slightly hairy beneath. Solitary, cup-shaped flowers may reach 1 in. across and are quite showy on leafless but hairy stems. This woodland gem is difficult to find in the wild, not only because of its scarcity but also because it tends to get lost beneath

Hepatica nobilis 'Rosea'

leaf litter. In gardens, group several plants together for impact; partner with other non-aggressive native spring-blooming woodlanders, including Dutchman's breeches, Christmas ferns, and wild geraniums.

Hepatica americana
syn. *H. nobilis* var. *obtusa, Anemone americana*
- purple, white
- early spring
- 4–6 in. × 12 in.
- part shade
- Z3–8

Round-leaved liverleaf. Nova Scotia west to Minnesota and Missouri, and south to Florida in rich, acid, deciduous, or evergreen woods. This species is similar to the preceding one, except that the three leaf lobes are conspicuously rounded at the ends. Fuzzy stems carry long-lasting flowers in shades of purple through lavender to white and sometimes pink. Typically the leaves, also on fuzzy stems, emerge from the base of the plant a little after bloom time, become deep red in fall, and persist through the winter. Natural hybridization occurs between this and the previous species, sometimes resulting in rare and unusual beauties.

Hepatica nobilis
syn. *H. triloba, Anemone hepatica*
- white, pink, blue
- early spring
- 4 in. × 6 in.
- part shade
- Z5–8

Common hepatica. Woodlands from the Pyrenees to western Russia. Rounded or kidney-shaped, semi-evergreen leaves are purplish and silky with hairs beneath. Bowl-shaped, 1-in. flowers on hairy stems appear just prior to the emergence of the leaves.

'Rosea' has rosy pink flowers.

Hesperaloe
Asparagaceae
hesperaloe

These southwestern natives are similar in appearance to their relatives the yuccas, and are sometimes incorrectly labeled as such. Hesperaloes provide gardeners of their region with desert-adapted, fountain-like clusters of evergreen, stemless, linear, blade-like foliage and bell-shaped flowers borne on tall, graceful spikes. A magnet for hummingbirds and deer resistant, these plants are tough, requiring little irrigation or maintenance. Attractive when massed, their neat, architectural forms make them useful as accents in dry gardens, too. Well-drained soil is essential.

Propagate by seed or by division in wintertime; growth is somewhat slow but hesperaloes are exceptionally durable.

Hesperaloe parviflora

Hesperaloe campanulata
- pink
- summer
- 3 ft. high and wide
- sun
- Z7–10

Bell-flower hesperaloe. Northeastern Mexico. More compact than the popular giant hesperaloe, but otherwise similar in appearance. Stiff, 0.5-in.-wide, lime-green leaves borne in a dense clump; pink, bell-shaped flowers borne on tall stalks in summertime.

Hesperaloe funifera
- white
- midspring to early fall
- 4 ft. high and wide
- sun
- Z6–10

Giant hesperaloe. Chihuahuan Desert, Texas, northeast New Mexico. A wonderful accent for arid-region gardens, this species forms an imposing clump of stiff, broad, lime-green leaves edged with coarse, white fibers. The inflorescence, which can last seven months, is an eye-opening 8- to 12-ft.-tall, branching stalk of creamy-white flowers infused with a pink and green blush. Virtually impervious to heat and drought.

Hesperis matronalis

Hesperaloe nocturna

- green-and-lavender
- spring to summer
- 5 ft. × 6 ft.
- part shade, shade
- Z7–10

Night-blooming hesperaloe. Mountains of northwestern Mexico. Forms a dense, 4-ft. rosette of narrow, grass-like leaves that are deeply grooved and have fine white threads along the margins. The inflorescence is striking, a 12-ft. stalk of small, greenish lavender, night-blooming flowers. Water deeply every second week during summer heat.

Hesperaloe parviflora

- red
- early spring to late summer
- 5 ft. × 3 ft.
- sun
- Z5–10

Red yucca. Northeastern Mexico and south Texas. Very popular as a landscape plant in the desert states, and also found in the gardens of coastal Florida. Evergreen, arching, grass-like leaves, borne in neat, dense rosettes, are long, narrow, and longitudinally rolled with curly threads clinging from the margins. Red to pink, bell-shaped flowers are 1.25 in. long, borne on 8-ft.-tall stalks. Exceptionally drought tolerant.

'Perpa', marketed as Brakelights, is compact, forming a clump of blue-green foliage 2–3 ft. wide and tall with 3-ft. stalks of bright red flowers. Seems to be sterile—failure to set seed prolongs its blooming season.

'Yellow' bears soft yellow flowers. 4 ft. × 3 ft.

Hesperis
Brassicaceae
dame's rocket, sweet rocket

Of this genus of 60 or so members, mostly biennial or perennial, only one or two have been deemed garden worthy, notably *Hesperis matronalis*, commonly known as Dame's rocket. With purple flowers and petals arranged in the shape of a cross, it is similar to related honesty or silver dollar plant (*Lunaria*).

Hesperis matronalis

- white, purple
- late spring to early summer
- 1–3 ft. × 1.5 ft.
- sun, part shade
- Z4–9

Dame's violet, rogue's gilliflower. Central Europe, western and central Asia. This old-fashioned cottage garden gem has collected plenty of common names over the years, testimony to its popularity in various parts of the world. Although not native to the United States, it has naturalized and made itself quite at home in most states. Be aware that it is on invasive plant lists in several states, so check with your local Cooperative Extension before including it in your garden.

Short lived, becoming slightly woody as a perennial, dame's violet is more often grown as a biennial. Plants are variable, mostly upright with branched stems clothed with dark green, 4- to 8-in.-long, oval or oblong, toothed leaves. Loose clusters of 0.5-in., cruciform, white, purple, or lavender flowers bloom for several weeks, perfuming the evening air. Encourage rebloom and prevent prolific self-seeding by deadheading as soon as blooms fade.

Lovely in natural settings and butterfly and wild gardens, where plants may seed freely. Plant in dooryard gardens close to the house or porch to enjoy the evening fragrance. For evening gardens, select white-flowering cultivars that show up better at dusk. Dame's violet is also useful along pathways in light shade and among shrubs. Good companions in beds and borders include annual larkspur, bearded iris, and peonies, followed by yarrow, tickseed, and bellflowers. In shadier places, pair with coral bells, columbines, foxgloves, and hostas.

For best results provide well-drained but moisture-retentive soil amended with lime to raise the pH. Deer resistant; pests and diseases are infrequent.

Seed, often in individual colors, is readily available; sow in late May or early June. Propagate double forms by stem or root cuttings.

'**Alba**' (var. *albiflora*) has pure white flowers and a strong fragrance.

'**Alba Plena**' is a double-flowered, white form.

'**Purpurea Plena**' has double purple or violet flowers.

Heuchera

Saxifragaceae
coral bells, alumroot

For perennial gardeners who want to plant natives but prefer a bit of flamboyance in their gardens, this genus is invaluable. *Heuchera*'s 35 or more species inhabit a wide range of habitats—woodlands, prairies, and mountain peaks—from the Gulf Coast west to California and north into southern Canada; this diversity enables heucheras to fit into a wide range of garden niches.

Heucheras form rounded mounds of leaves with woody basal rootstocks; roots are shallow and prone to winter heaving. The hairy leaves vary in shape from rounded to palmately lobed and maple-like; over the last generation, a flood of new hybrids with vibrantly colored, even gaudy foliage have appeared on the market. The flowers, which may lack petals, are borne on tall stalks well above the foliage, mostly in late spring and early summer. Although not always as showy as the foliage, the blossoms attract hummingbirds; some make fine cut flowers.

Heucheras prefer partial shade; they'll survive full sun where light intensity is low, but nothing other than morning sun where it is intense. They prefer a rich, neutral to slightly acid soil; good drainage is a must, especially in shade. Deadhead to prolong bloom.

Heucheras integrate easily into woodland and rock gardens, semi-shaded borders, and container displays. Their evergreen foliage provides an attractive groundcover, especially when intermingled with contrasting, lacy-leaved plants such as ferns or astilbes. Juxtapose colorful-leaved cultivars with

Heuchera 'Citronelle', 'Caramel', and 'Viola Frost' provide a colorful foliage foil for *Euphorbia wulfenii*

contrasting flowers or foliage—a purple-leaved heuchera, for example, alongside a yellow coreopsis or green-and-white-leaved *Carex* 'Ice Dance'.

Usually trouble free, heucheras are prone to fungal diseases if grown in damp shade. Also susceptible to black vine weevil and deer, although dark-foliaged selections appear to be browsed less often.

In cold-winter regions, cover with evergreen boughs after the ground is frozen. Start species from seed; propagate hybrids by division. Divide established plants every three to four years to prevent the centers from dying out and to reinvigorate.

Heuchera americana

- green, white
- late spring to early summer
- 12–24 in. × 12–18 in.
- sun, part shade
- Z4–9, HS

Coral bells. Rocky, open woodlands and rocky crevices throughout the eastern United States and southeastern Canada. Grown primarily for its 12- to 15-in. mounds of 3- to 5-in. leaves, heart shaped with five to seven lobes, marbled and veined with purplish brown at first, maturing to green. Airy panicles of tiny, bell-shaped flowers, greenish white tinged with red, rise atop tall, wiry stems.

'Dale's Strain' ('Dale's Variety') has silver-blue, marbled foliage accented with white flowers. 30 in. Nancy Goodwin, of the late, lamented Montrose

Heuchera 'Pink Lipstick' flowers

Nursery in North Carolina, crossed 'Dale's Strain' with 'Palace Purple' to produce 'Montrose Ruby'.

'Garnet' has bright garnet-colored new foliage that matures to green, veined with bronze. Fall and winter leaves bright garnet, with green margins. 18 in.

'Pewter Veil' has copper-pink young leaves that mature to metallic pewter. 22 in.

Heuchera cylindrica

- white
- midspring
- 0.5–3 ft. × 0.5–2 ft.
- sun, part shade
- Z4–8, HS

Roundleaf heuchera. East of the Cascade Mountains to western Montana. Mottled, dark green, slightly hairy leaves range from oval to round, with toothed and scalloped margins. Inflorescence is a tall, dense spike of 0.25-in., bell-shaped flowers, white with pink margins, that bees and butterflies enjoy.

'Greenfinch' has short, stiff panicles of green flowers. 30–36 in.

Heuchera micrantha

- white
- midspring to midsummer
- 0.5–2 ft. × 1–2 ft.
- sun, part shade
- Z4–8, HS

Crevice alumroot, small-flowered alumroot. Rocky slopes and cliffs from British Columbia to California. Evergreen, reddish green, 4-in.-wide, heart-shaped leaves with three to seven shallow lobes and toothed margins. Flowering is profuse on well-grown plants, with up to 100 reddish spikes of tiny, creamy-white blossoms. This species is more tolerant of wet soils than others. A parent of many superior selections.

var. *diversifolia* 'Palace Purple', the first purple-leaved selection, was once widely popular but now largely replaced by superior purple-leaved hybrids. 18 in.

Heuchera sanguinea

- pink, red, white
- mid- to late spring
- 12–18 in. × 9–12 in.
- sun, part shade
- Z3–9

Coral bells. New Mexico and Arizona. A parent of so many fine selections, especially those bred for floral characteristics. This species is grown for its many 6-in.-long panicles of larger flowers. Blooms profusely and holds its abundant red blossoms well, even in hot weather; bloom time is long, especially when deadheaded. Evergreen leaves are kidney shaped to round, up to 2 in. wide with scalloped edges.

'Firefly' has dark red flowers. 30 in.

'Frosty'. Dark red flowers tower over the white- to frosty-green leaves. 20 in.

'Ruby Bells' has blood-red flowers. 18 in.

'Splendens' has bright scarlet flowers. 28 in.

Heuchera villosa
- white, pink
- midsummer to early fall
- 1.5–3 ft. × 1.5–2 ft.
- sun, part shade
- Z4–8

Hairy alumroot. New York to Georgia, west to Missouri and Arkansas. Rounded basal clumps to 2 ft. high and wide of velvety, hairy leaves to 5 in. across, with seven to nine triangular, sharply toothed lobes. Flower stalks are also hairy, rusty brown, to 3 ft., bearing tiny (0.25 in.), white or pinkish blossoms in showy, airy panicles, to 18 in. long. Blooms latest of any species. Prefers a well-drained, organic-rich soil; drought tolerant and more forgiving of summer heat and humidity than other heucheras; best choice for hot, humid gardens. All the following selections (some are hybrids) have *Heuchera villosa* bloodlines.

'Autumn Bride' has light green foliage and white fall flowers. Well adapted to the hot, sticky summers of the Southeast and Midwest. To 36 in.

'Blackout' has near black leaves and creamy-white flowers. 18 in.

'Citronelle' has chartreuse foliage. Beautiful against winter snow. 2 in.

'Frosted Violet' has dark-veined, pink-purple foliage; light pink flowers in late spring. 12 in. Introduced by Charles Oliver, PA.

'Tiramisu' has chartreuse leaves tinged with red and overlaid with silver. When nights are cool, leaves turn amber-red edged with chartreuse. 8–10 in. tall.

Other Notable Cultivars
Most of the following are derived mainly from interbreeding *Heuchera americana*, *H. micrantha*, and *H. sanguinea*. These hybrids are sometimes classified as types of *H. ×brizoides*, but this label is less often applied to newer cultivars whose descent also includes other parents. Leading *Heuchera* breeders have included the late Alan Bloom of Blooms of Bressingham, Dan Heims of Terra Nova Nurseries, Charles and Martha Oliver of The Primrose Path, PA, and French breeder Tierry Delabroye. The following are hardy in Z4–9.

'Blackcurrant' is part of the Dolce series. Its frilly, deep purple leaves have a metallic overlay. 12 in.

'Caramel' has glowing apricot young growth that fades to soft amber by summer; white flowers. To 18 in.

'Electra' has golden, red-veined leaves; white flowers in late spring. 10 in.

'Key Lime Pie' has bright lime-green foliage year-round. Stunning flecked with snow, and great in containers. 10 in. 'Lime Rickey' is similar, with slightly ruffled edges. White flowers. 12–18 in.

Little Cuties Series from Terra Nova is comprised of miniature varieties bred for multiple locations. They have great year-round foliage color. 'Blondie' has caramel leaves, 5 in. × 8 in. Pink-flowered 'Peppermint' is 5 in. × 9 in.

'Obsidian'. The glossy near-black leaves hold their color well. Insignificant flowers. 10 in.

'Petite Pearl Fairy' is a miniature with deep plum leaves no larger than a quarter. Purple stems support airy spikes of pink flowers in spring. An Oliver introduction. 10–14 in. tall.

'Purple Petticoats' has well-ruffled, purple foliage, wine colored beneath. 12 in.

Heuchera 'Petite Pearl Fairy'

×*Heucherella* 'Blue Ridge' and *Phlox stolonifera* 'Blue Ridge' are compatible partners

×*Heucherella*

Saxifragaceae
foamy bells

Although the nursery industry treats ×*Heucherella* as a distinct genus of plants, in fact this is actually just a group of artificially derived hybrids, created by crossing heucheras and their close relative, the foamflowers (*Tiarella* spp.). The hope was that this mixing of genetic material would produce offspring with the colorful foliage of heucheras and the showier flowers of tiarellas.

To some extent, the jury is still out. Charles Oliver, one of the leading breeders of new heucheras, has introduced an ×heucherella—'Quicksilver'—that has generated widespread enthusiasm and won first prize from Netherland's Royal Society for Horticulture. Yet Oliver warns that he has found ×heucherellas as a group to lack the adaptability of their parents, as well as their innate vigor. According to Oliver (and others), when grown in less than ideal conditions, especially in regions with hot, humid summers, ×heucherellas may suffer from seasonal dieback, being reduced to small crowns with a dead center by late summer.

Other leading growers and breeders, such as Dan Heims of Terra Nova Nurseries and Tony Avent of Plant Delights, remain enthusiastic. To some degree, the difference in experiences with foamy bells may depend on regional factors such as climate and soil, and gardeners are urged to check with others in their area and their local Cooperative Extension before investing heavily in these plants.

One final note: like many inter-generic hybrids, heucherellas are sterile. Home gardeners must increase stock by division.

×*Heucherella*

- pink, white
- late spring to midsummer
- 1–1.5 ft. high and wide
- sun, part shade
- Z4–9

Foamy bells. Forms a compact, basal mound, usually 5–8 in. tall, of semi-evergreen, rounded to lobed, maple-like leaves, often with distinctive veining. Tiny, star-shaped flowers are borne in airy to dense panicles on stems rising well above the foliage clump. Foamy bells prefer an organically enriched, well-drained but moderately moist soil with a pH close to neutral. They tolerate full sun in cooler regions, but foliage color is best when the plants are grown in partial shade. Excellent as a groundcover or edging plant, and an attractive addition to shaded borders or woodland plantings. Good companions include other shade-tolerant plants such as lungworts, wild sweet Williams, astilbes, and Solomon's seals.

'Alabama Surprise' has large, golden leaves with sharply contrasting red veining; orange-pink in fall and winter. Small, white flowers. Heat and humidity tolerant. 12 in.

'Blue Ridge'. Deep red veins decorate the silvery green foliage; white flowers. Tolerates heat and humidity well. 6–8 in.

'Heart of Darkness' has tricolored leaves, dark maroon centers inset into silver-gray and edged with green. Showy white flowers; a Charles Oliver introduction; especially vigorous. 8 in.

'Kimono' produces young, deeply divided, crinkled, green leaves with central markings of maroon-purple; replaced in summer with larger, rounder leaves. Copper-rose fall and winter color. Cream flowers. 12 in.

'Sweet Tea' has large, maple-like leaves with cinnamon-colored stars at the centers and orange margins; foliage colors darken in summer and lighten again in fall. White flowers. 20 in.

'Stoplight' has large, bright yellow leaves with red veining and a dark red blotch at the center. White flowers. 6 in.

Hibiscus

Malvaceae
hibiscus

Hibiscus make a splash wherever they are planted. This genus contains small trees and shrubs, perennials, and annuals; here, the focus is on perennial species, all of which bring a strong tropical attitude to the garden.

Unusually large flowered, hibiscus have wide-mouthed, trumpet-shaped flowers borne singly or in clusters in the upper leaf axils. The colors are primarily reds, pinks, and white, sometimes yellow or purple, and most have a conspicuous, contrasting eye. Stamens cluster in a prominent column round the male parts (pistil), a typical characteristic of the mallow family. Foliage is large, alternately arranged on the stems, and mostly palmately lobed or maple-like.

Hibiscus 'Peppermint Schnapps'

Excellent in damp soils, hibiscus also thrive in average to rich soil in beds and borders. A natural component of waterside gardens, especially in warm parts of the country, they are valuable for rain gardens or native plant and wildlife gardens. Shorter selections work well in containers and planter beds. Good companions include cardinal flower, milkweeds, tall asters, and Indian poke (*Veratrum viride*). Interesting with ornamental grasses in containers.

Maintenance is low, except for removing the Japanese beetles that may otherwise shred the flowers and leaves. The stems may die back in winter; if so, remove them prior to the appearance of new growth. Staking may be necessary in windy places, but usually the base of the stems becomes woody, making that chore superfluous. Deadhead to avoid unwanted seedlings and to encourage further bloom.

As noted, Japanese beetles are the most serious threat, but mealybugs, scale, and white flies can also become a nuisance. Diseases include stem and root rots, viruses, rust, and fungal leaf spot. Protect from deer.

Increase stock by dividing established plants or by seed. Seeds should be scarified (nicked) or soaked overnight prior to sowing; this allows water to penetrate the seed coat and initiate germination.

Hibiscus coccineus

- red
- summer
- 5–7 ft. × 3 ft.
- sun
- Z7–9

Swamp hibiscus, scarlet rose mallow, red swamp mallow. Coastal swamps of Georgia and Florida. Sparsely clothed with maple-like leaves, tall stems become woody at the base. Bright crimson flowers 3–6 in. across with five spoon-shaped petals, borne singly in upper leaf axils. Each flower lasts just a single day, but is nevertheless eye popping. Effective in damp soils at pond sides, but also in large borders. Seldom damaged by Japanese beetles. Late to break ground in spring.

'Alba' has pure white flowers. To 10 ft. Z6–11.

Hibiscus grandiflorus

- pink
- fall
- 6–7 ft. × 6 ft.
- sun
- Z7–9

Velvet mallow. Coastal plains of southern Louisiana to Florida. This bold perennial has huge (to 10 in. across), velvety gray leaves on tall stems, woody at the base. With age, crowns increase to 2 ft. or more across. Fragrant, 7- to 8-in.-wide, soft pink flowers are marked with crimson at the base—these are the largest blossoms of any North American species, and remain open overnight. Moist but average soil; does not tolerate droughty conditions. Seldom attacked by Japanese beetles. Sometimes

hybridizes with *Hibiscus coccineus* where natural ranges overlap.

Hibiscus moscheutos

- white, pink, red
- midsummer to early fall
- 3–5 ft. × 3 ft.
- sun
- Z3–9

Rose mallow, southern rose mallow, swamp rose mallow. Texas to the eastern United States and into Canada, along streams, and beside ponds and lakes. These imposing plants, woody at the base, spread slowly to develop into large colonies that are a sight to behold. Alternate leaves are more or less heart shaped, grayish green above, white and hairy underneath. Large, open flowers accented with crimson at their bases. Brown seed capsules follow. Susceptible to Japanese beetles, although some selections reputedly less than others; deer resistant in some regions, but vulnerable in others. Hummingbird attractor. Very late to emerge in spring. Dramatic in damp places beside water features, but tolerates average garden soil well. Combine with Joe-Pye weed, tall ornamental grasses, and asters at the back of borders.

Other Notable Cultivars

Selections and cultivars abound, with more introduced annually. This is a small selection.

'Blue River II' displays pure white, 10-in. flowers on 5-ft.-tall stems; foliage a deep, slightly bluish green. Z5–10.

Disco Belle series includes 'Disco Belle', 'Disco Belle Red', and 'Disco Belle White', all compact with 9-in.-wide flowers. Japanese beetles love these. Seed propagated strain, available in separate colors. 20–24 in.

'Kopper King', bred by Nebraska's Fleming Brothers, has dinner-plate-sized, very pale pink flowers veined and centered with crimson. Copper-colored, maple-like leaves, burnt orange beneath. 3.5–4 ft. Z4–9.

'Lady Baltimore' has deep pink, slightly ruffled blooms, with a red eye. 4–6 ft. Z5–9. 'Lord Baltimore' has 10-in.-wide flowers like cherry-red dinner plates. 4 ft. Z5–10.

'Luna Red' bears bright crimson flowers to 8 in. across. Reputedly deer resistant. 3 ft. 'Luna Pink Swirl' has crimson-eyed, pale pink and red flowers. 24–36 in. Z4–9.

'Peppermint Schnapps', from the Cordials Collection, has 8- to 10-in., candy pink flowers splashed and centered with red. 4–6 ft. Z5–9.

Hosta

Asparagaceae
hosta, plantain lily

This genus regularly lists at or near the top in perennial popularity polls, and no wonder. Hostas flourish from USDA zones 3 through 8, with a few of the more heat-tolerant types performing satisfactorily in the cooler parts of zone 9. Although moisture loving, with conscientious irrigation the more resilient cultivars can survive the drought-prone summers of the prairie and Rocky Mountain states.

Hostas' chief attraction is their foliage, borne in neat circular clusters of broad leaves with parallel veins that may be colored gold or blue as well as green, and striped, edged, or splashed with white or some other contrasting color. Foliage texture varies from shiny and smooth to pleated, puckered, and waxy, and individual leaves may measure from 1–20 in. long and 0.75–12 in. wide. The flowers of most species and cultivars are unremarkable; borne in summertime in terminal racemes atop erect scapes. The blossoms are lily-like, typically pendulous, 0.75–2 in. long, with six petal-like tepals, in shades of white, lavender, or violet. One exception to the rule is *Hosta plantaginea*, whose white flowers are not only fragrant—it's the only species with this characteristic—but also measure up to 6 in. long. Plant breeders are currently focusing on hosta cultivars with more attractive and fragrant flowers.

Often categorized as a "shade plant," hostas offer some of the best choices for lower-light situations, though most prefer partial shade, and none flourish in deep, unrelieved shade, especially the dry shade found beneath conifers and shallow-rooted deciduous trees such as maples. In fact, many cultivars require a couple of hours of direct sunlight daily if they are to look their best. The best exposure for hostas is one with morning sun and afternoon shade. Noontime and early afternoon shade is particularly important where sun is intense.

For best growth, provide a nutrient-rich, organic soil that is moisture-retentive but well drained. Hostas should receive an inch of water a week, either from natural precipitation or irrigation, throughout the growing season.

Hostas are subject to a number of fungal and viral diseases; be sure to start with healthy, disease-free plants from a reliable grower. Notched leaf margins are a sign of black vine weevils. Yellowing of the leaves in June followed by chocolate-brown streaks or blotches between the veins are symptoms of foliar nematodes, and plants infested with them are best removed and disposed of off-site. Mice and voles sometimes attack the roots and crowns; slugs, snails, and deer relish hosta foliage. Cultivars with thick-textured, waxy, blue foliage appear less palatable to deer.

With their expansive foliage, hostas furnish a uniquely luxuriant effect to partially shaded beds and borders, presenting a visually soothing contrast to such brightly colored, shade-tolerant annuals as impatiens, coleus, and wax begonias. They provide an attractive edging for shade-tolerant shrubs such as azaleas, viburnums, and hollies, and under a deciduous canopy make an outstanding follow-up for snowdrops, crocus, tulips, daffodils, and

Hosta 'Francis Williams' and others play off well aginst ferns in this shade garden

other spring-blooming bulbs. Hostas mingle easily in woodland gardens, where their bold foliage provides attractive contrast to finer-leaved neighbors including ferns, hellebores, lungworts, wild gingers, and trilliums.

Propagate named cultivars by division, ideally in late summer about 30 days before the first fall frost. Hosta seed germinates readily, though the offspring of cultivars may not possess the desirable traits of their parents. Sow outdoors in fall or stratify seed in the refrigerator and start indoors in early spring.

Hosta crispula

- lavender
- early summer
- 1–1.5 ft. × 2.5 ft.
- part shade
- Z3–9

Curled-leaf hosta. Native to Japan. Traditionally treated as a species, but recent research has revealed it to be a form of *Hosta sieboldiana*. Forms cushions of long-stemmed, dull green, 5- to 7-in., ovate leaves with irregular, white margins. Racemes of 1.75-in., pale lavender flowers borne on 3-ft. scapes; as many as 40 flowers per raceme. Sensitive to hot sun; mass in shade as ground cover.

Hosta fortunei

- lilac
- summer
- 1–1.5 ft. × 2 ft.
- part shade, shade
- Z3–9

Fortune's hosta. Japan. Treated as a species by horticulturists, but recently revealed as a form of *Hosta sieboldiana*. Somewhat waxy, gray-green, ovate leaves, 6–12 in. long, borne in 2-ft. mounds. Racemes of pale lilac, 1- to 1.5-in. flowers carried on 3- to 4-ft. scapes. Genetically variable, and a parent to many selections including:

'Albopicta' ('Golden Spring'). Young leaves pale yellow with irregular, dark green margins; leaves become all green as they mature in summer.

var. *hyacinthina* (syn. *H. fortunei* 'Hyacinthina', *H.* 'Hyacinthina'). Blue-gray, greenish leaves with thin, gray rim.

'Francee' has dark green, heart-shaped leaves rimmed with a white band. Sun tolerant; a perennial favorite.

Hosta gracillima

- purple
- late summer
- 12 in. × 30 in.
- part shade
- Z3–8

Small rock hosta ("Hime Iwa Giboshi"). Native to mountain valleys in Japan's Kochi Prefecture. Narrow, glossy green leaves, 4 in. long and 2 in. wide, with wavy margins. Fast growing, a gem for troughs, rock gardens, or the fronts of borders.

Hosta lancifolia

syn. *H. japonica*
- lilac
- late summer
- 1 ft. × 1.5 ft.
- part shade, shade
- Z3–9

Narrow-leaved plantain lily. Japan. Another traditional "species" in horticulture that is probably more correctly treated as a cultivar of garden origin. Forms a mound of long-stemmed, glossy deep green, lanceolate leaves 2–6 in. long. Scapes, 2 ft. tall and spotted purple at the base, bear racemes of 1.5- to 2-in., flaring, pale flowers flushed with purple. Good for edging.

Hosta plantaginea

- white
- mid- to late summer
- 12–18 in. × 18–24 in.
- part shade, shade
- Z3–9

August lily. Native to China and Japan. Erect and spreading, this medium-sized hosta has glossy, rounded, heart-shaped, light yellow-green leaves and large, 3- to 6-in.-long, trumpet-shaped, white, heavily fragrant flowers borne on scapes up to 30 in. The common name refers to this species' late blooming season. Attracts hummingbirds. The best species for sultry climates; thrives as far south as Jacksonville, Florida.

var. *japonica* (var. *grandiflora*, 'Grandiflora') is exceptionally vigorous, to 26 in. tall and 46 in. wide.

'Royal Standard' is a cultivar of long standing with very fragrant white flowers. Tolerates full sun as long as it is not intense. Carefree and reliable.

Hosta sieboldiana

- white
- early summer
- 2–3 ft. × 3–4 ft.
- part shade, shade
- Z4–8

Siebold's hosta. The species is native to Japan, and is usually available in the nursery trade in the form of the cultivar *Hosta sieboldiana* 'Elegans' (sometimes listed as var. *elegans*; more correctly var. *sieboldiana*). Thick textured and corrugated, the large 13 in. × 10 in., blue-green leaves are heart shaped; funnel-shaped flowers, 1–1.5 in. long, are white with a violet tinge, and borne on 36-in. scapes. An exceptionally shade-tolerant hosta, but slow growing. The blue color is due to a wax on the leaf surface that rapidly degenerates in hot climates.

'Frances Williams' has large, rounded and cupped, bluish green leaves irregularly bordered with gold. White flowers.

Hosta sieboldii 'Kabitan'

Hosta 'Blue Mouse Ears' benefits from afternoon shade

Hosta sieboldii
syn. *H. albomarginata, H. lancifolia* var. *marginata*
- lilac
- late summer
- 1 ft. high and wide
- part shade, shade
- Z3–9

Seersucker's hosta. Native of Japan with undulate, lanceolate, dark green, 4- to 5-in. leaves, matte above and shiny beneath. Racemes of nodding, bell-shaped, 1.5- to 2-in., white flowers veined with purple.

'Kabitan' has pale yellow-green leaves with green margins and violet flowers.

Hosta undulata
syn. *H. lancifolia* var. *undulata, H. media-picta, H. variegata*
- lilac
- early summer
- 1.5 ft. × 1–1.5 ft.
- part shade, shade
- Z3–9

Wavy-leaf plantain lily. Of horticultural origin. Wavy, sometimes contorted leaves with elliptic to ovate, green blades 5–6 in. long, marked with a broad cream central stripe and edged with darker green.

'Albo-marginata' ('Silver Rain') has tapering, elliptic leaves, gray-green at the center, margins rimmed with cream. Fast growing, spreads, a handsome groundcover.

'Variegata' ('Undulata'), to 10 in., has smallish leaves irregularly streaked with white at the center and undulating green margins, twisted leaf tips.

Hosta ventricosa
- purple
- summer
- 4 in. × 12 in.
- part shade, shade
- Z3–9

Dark purple–flowered hosta ("Murasaki Giboshi"). Native to China and Korea. A natural dwarf with heart-shaped, glossy dark green leaves with twisted tips and vivid blue-purple flowers.

Hosta venusta
- violet
- early summer
- 4 in. × 1 ft.
- shade, part shade
- Z3–9

China, Korea. Diminutive, 1- to 2-in. leaves with long petioles; 10- to 12-in. scapes bear sparse racemes of 1–1.5 in., funnel-shaped flowers that are violet marked with darker veins.

'Variegated' has leaves with cream centers and wavy margins in various shades of green.

Other Notable Cultivars
Because hostas hybridize readily, professional and amateur breeders have created a dizzying number of cultivars—some 6000 were in commerce at last count. Within this plethora, there is considerable variation in adaptation to climate and conditions.

For starters, leaf color can provide a clue as to light requirements. In general, hostas with yellow or golden leaves (like 'Gold Regal') can stand more sun than hostas with green, blue, or white-variegated leaves. Unless they receive at least a couple of hours of full sun daily, preferably in the morning or after midafternoon, the yellow-leaved hostas take on an unattractive greenish tint. Blue-leaved hostas such as 'Blue Mouse Ears' may tolerate such sunnier sites in cooler, northern climates, but their blue color is likely to fade to green unless protected from direct afternoon sun, especially where it is very strong. White-variegated hostas also tend to prefer shadier sites, though cultivars with thicker leaves (e.g., 'Francee') are more sun tolerant. Bleached patches on the leaves that turn brown and then fall away usually indicates sunburn.

In terms of climatic adaptation, as a rule, hostas that bear fragrant flowers, like the species *Hosta plantaginea* and its hybrid descendants such as 'Fragrant Bouquet', 'Fragrant Dream', and 'Summer Fragrance', are the most tolerant of heat and humidity. Typically, fragrant-flowered hostas also share golden-leaved hostas' requirement for extra sunlight, and seem to be extra attractive to deer.

Visit the American Hosta Society's directory (www.americanhostasociety.org/DisplayGardens. html) of outstanding hosta display gardens for regionally oriented cultural information, and selections appropriate for your region.

Houttuynia cordata

Houttuynia
Saururaceae
chameleon plant

This relative of lizard's tail (*Saururus*) is just as invasive and the site on which it is planted must be carefully selected if it is not to become a nuisance. In the right location, however, chameleon plant makes a fine dense groundcover, spreading by fast-growing rhizomes that are almost impossible to eradicate.

Plant in moist, humus-rich soil, in sun or shade. Damp soil causes the plant to spread more rapidly, but dry conditions curtail invasive tendencies. It grows well in 3–4 in. of water at a pond side, but not in deeper water. Where spread must be controlled, confine to containers. Mulch deeply through the winter in cold regions. Propagate by dividing the rhizomes in spring, or start plants from seed.

Houttuynia cordata
- white
- summer
- 6–24 in. × 1.5 ft.
- sun, part shade
- Z5–11

Chameleon plant, lizard tail, fishwort. Moist, shaded woodlands and scrubland, Japan, Korea, and southeast Asia. Trailing stems root at the nodes, while the stem tips are erect. Leaves are matte bluish green, tinted with red along the rims, and about 1–3.5 in. long. They are broadly heart shaped, borne alternately on the stem. Terminal, 1-in. spikes of yellow-green flowers are decorated with four to six showy petal-like, white bracts at the base.

'Chameleon' ('Tricolor', 'Court Jester', Variegata') has brightly variegated leaves edged with cream and speckled with red. These may revert to all green especially in warm climates, and have less defined variegation in more shade.

'Flore Pleno' ('Plena') has eight or more clean white bracts producing a "double" effect. Just as aggressive as the species.

Hunnemania
Papaveraceae
Mexican tulip poppy

This genus consists of a single species, *Hunnemania fumariifolia*, popular for its sunny yellow poppy flowers and cut blue-green foliage. One explanation of the specific epithet is that it alludes to the smoky gray color of the fine-textured leaves—*fumus* meaning "smoke" in Latin. California poppy (*Eschscholtzia californica*) is a relative of *Hunnemania*, and there is an obvious resemblance in the flowers.

Tulip poppies thrive in full sun in average, well-drained soil. Once established, they tolerate droughty conditions; suitable for xeriscapes. Plant on a slope to enhance the runoff of excess water; be mindful not to overirrigate. The showy yellow flowers bloom for several months and do especially well in dry California gardens.

Propagate from seed sown in fall or early spring in situ, or in containers to avoid root disturbance at planting time. If grown as a winter-blooming sunroom specimen, sow in fall. Early bloom may occur in mild climates.

Hunnemania fumariifolia

- yellow
- early summer to late fall
- 2–3 ft. × 1–1.5 ft.
- sun
- Z9–11

Mexican tulip poppy, tulip poppy, Mexican smoke poppy. Mexican Highlands. Although considered a tender, short-lived perennial for warm areas, this bright yellow poppy is valuable in summer containers and for bedding in cooler zones. Each longstemmed, 3-in. bloom has four crinkled petals surrounding a central boss of orange stamens. The deeply cut, bluish leaves are attractive and provide a fine ferny foil for the flowers. Self-sows freely.

Hylomecon

Papaveraceae
wood poppy

Closely related to weedy greater celandine (*Chelidonium majus*), as well as better-behaved members of the poppy family, wood poppy is well suited to shaded woods, rock gardens, or wild gardens. Here, this variable genus is regarded as having but a single species, although some botanists distinguish several. If happy, wood poppy may seed about generously, but that seldom seems to be the case.

These poppies thrive in humus-rich soils that remain damp, but drain well. They dislike waterlogged, clayey soils. Sun or part shade is ideal; in warmer climates shade from intense midday sun.

Wood poppies are fine companions for native trilliums, woodland phlox, Solomon's seal, and other woodlanders, as well as ephemerals including Dutchman's breeches, Virginia bluebells, and trout lilies.

The sap of these plants is the typical yellow of most poppies and may cause a skin eruption in sensitive individuals. Deer resistant, but slugs and snails find the young plants delectable. Propagate by seed sown directly where the plants are to grow or in pots to ease the trauma of transplanting; these plants are taprooted and resent disturbance.

Hylomecon japonica

syn. *H. vernalis, Chelidonium japonicum, C. vernale*

- yellow
- late spring to early summer
- 6–12 in. × 9 in.
- sun, part shade
- Z6–9

Wood poppy, forest poppy, Japanese poppy. Far East, Manchuria to Japan. A rhizomatous perennial, wood poppy develops low clumps of odd-pinnate leaves, with usually five light green, dentate leaflets.

Hunnemania fumarifolia

Hylomecon japonica

The beautiful, clear yellow, 2-in. flowers are four petaled, carried singly or in pairs in the upper leaf axils. The flowers are short lived and bloom time is brief. This species becomes summer dormant; foliage reemerges the following midspring.

Hypericum
Hypericaceae
St. John's wort

Homeopathic healers prescribe St. John's wort for various ailments, especially for mild depression. What they administer is an extract of common St. John's wort (*Hypericum perforatum*), which can also lift spirits in the garden. A few other species of this large genus are also garden worthy. Many are shrubby or partly shrubby (subshrubby) and mix well in shrub collections. Notable among these are *H. frondosum* and its cultivar 'Sunburst', *H. prolificum* 'Hidcote', *H. ×imodorum* and its cultivars, and *H. ×moserianum* 'Tricolor'. St. John's wort flowers, which range in size from tiny to up to 3 in. across, usually have five yellow petals and conspicuously bushy central clusters of stamens. Leaves are mostly opposite or in whorls on the stems, and may be dotted with black glands.

Provide a soil enriched with compost, rotted leaves, or bagged animal manure that retains moisture but is well drained; poorly drained soils promote root rot. Most species prefer a partly shaded position; some tolerate deeper shade, but in such circumstances blooming may be compromised. Deer resistant.

Propagate by seed in containers in fall. Softwood cuttings root readily in late spring, or perennials may be divided in spring or fall. Increase shrubby species by semi-ripe cuttings taken in summer.

Hypericum androsaemum
- yellow
- midsummer
- 24–30 in. × 36 in.
- sun, part shade, shade
- Z5–8, HS

Tutsan. Western Europe, Mediterranean basin to northern Iran. A bushy, deciduous subshrub that blooms on new growth and can be cut back hard to develop a framework of branches in early spring. Tolerates drought well. The 3- to 4-in.-long leaves are sessile and entire, without black glands. Bright yellow, cup-shaped flowers may reach a diameter of 1 in., and gather in cymes of three to nine blooms. Colorful, decorative, yellow fruits follow, maturing to dark red and then deep brown; these are prized by florists. Mulch in winter in cold regions; although the top growth may be killed back, the roots usually send up new shoots in spring. Self-seeds; it has become invasive in Australia and New Zealand. Susceptible to wilt and root rot in hot, humid climates. Mass on the margins of woods, or informal banks and slopes; useful as a low hedge.

'Albury Purple' has exciting fragrant, burgundy-flushed foliage and decorative red-turning-black fruits. Interesting as a low hedge. 15–36 in. Z5–8.

'Golden Tutsan' has golden leaves. 2–3 ft. Z6–9.

Hypericum buckleyi
- yellow
- summer
- 9–12 in. × 24 in.
- sun, part shade
- Z5–8

Blue Ridge St. John's wort. Mountains of North Carolina to Georgia. Low growing with blunt, grayish leaves to 0.75 in. that turn reddish as temperatures cool. Excellent native groundcover.

Appalachian Sun is a seed strain. It has small, green leaves and 1- to 1.5-in., yellow flowers. Well-drained, moist, acid soil is best. 10 in. × 18 in.

Hypericum calycinum
- yellow
- summer
- 15–18 in. × 24 in.
- sun, part shade, shade
- Z5–8

Aaron's beard, rose of Sharon. Southeast Europe, Turkey. Excellent as an evergreen or semi-evergreen groundcover, this low, shrubby plant spreads by runners. The slightly bluish green leaves, to 4 in. long, are netted with fine veins beneath. Solitary, saucer-shaped, bright yellow flowers to 3 in. across are accented with a central boss of countless stamens. Difficult to eradicate once established. Cut back hard annually in spring or every two to three years to encourage fresh young growth. Keep irrigated in summer to avoid leaf burn. Mulch in winter in cold regions.

'Brigadoon' has striking oval, bright gold leaves, sometimes reddish when young. Protect from burning by intense sun in warmer zones. Z5–7.

Hypericum cerastoides
syn. *H. rhodoppeum*
- yellow
- late spring to early summer
- 3–9 in. × 15–18 in.
- sun
- Z6–10

Gray-leaf St. John's wort, trailing St. John's wort. Southern Europe. Ground-hugging mats of tiny, 1.25-in., silvery leaves make this beauty a charming, weed-suppressing groundcover. Deep yellow, starry flowers cover the plants from late spring on. Keep soil damp during hot weather.

'Silvana' has especially silvery foliage. Lovely in rock gardens. Z6–9.

Hypericum olympicum
- yellow
- summer
- 10 in. × 24 in.
- sun, part shade
- Z6–8

Olympic St. John's wort. Greece, Turkey. Upright and deciduous with pointed, grayish green leaves,

1.5 in. long, glaucous beneath, carried on branching, trailing stems. Golden, starry flowers bloom alone or two to three together at the ends of the stems. Lovely at the front of the border or in rock gardens, where it is well mannered. Requires very well-drained soil. Start from seed or cuttings in fall.

'Citrinum' (syn. *Hypericum olympicum* subsp. *uniflorum* 'Citrinum') has small, rounded leaves, waxy white beneath, and pale lemon, starry flowers, about 2.5 in. across. Excellent for well-drained rock gardens. 15 in. Z5–8.

Hypoestes
Acanthaceae
polka-dot plant

Best known as houseplants, polka-dot plants are tender evergreen perennials native to southern Africa, southeast Asia, and Madagascar. The most popular species is common polka-dot plant, *Hypoestes phyllostachya*. Where winters are mild it is planted extensively among shrubs, and in beds and borders; in chillier regions it is valued as a summer

Hypericum prolificum 'Hidcote'

Hypericum cerastoides 'Silvana'

Hypoestes phyllostacha 'Confetti Carmine Rose' provides a color echo for *Primula malacoides* 'Prima'

foliage plant. Common polka-dot plant is also effective in containers, window boxes, and baskets. These, of course, can be brought indoors to decorate sunrooms and conservatories through the cold months. Extensive hybridization has developed many intricately variegated leaf types.

Slightly shrubby at the base, this mounding or sprawling plant has opposite, 3-in.-long leaves that are usually ovate, often with a velvety surface. Tubular, two-lipped flowers cluster into dense racemes or are held singly at stem tips and in leaf axils. Humus-rich, well-drained soil is ideal; do not allow plants to dry out in hot weather. Although plants usually recover from a spell of drought, they often lose lower leaves as a result. Maintain a bushy habit by pinching young plants in spring, and then again sporadically through the season.

White fly and powdery mildew may need control, especially indoors; slugs may attack tender young growth, but deer seldom browse. Propagate from stem cuttings in spring or summer, or sow seed in spring.

Hypoestes phyllostachya
syn. *H. sanguinolenta* of gardens

- lavender
- late summer to fall
- 12–30 in. × 9–24 in.
- sun, part shade
- Z9–11

Polka-dot plant, freckle face, measles plant. Madagascar. Dark green leaves irregularly spotted with pink freckles or blotches; selections and cultivars are chosen for more involved leaf patterning. Tight racemes of tiny, lavender flowers bloom in the latter part of the growing season, but are visually insignificant and are often removed by gardeners.

'Carmina' has bright red leaves.

Confetti Seed Strain includes cultivars with carmine, pink, red, wine-red, and white foliages. Recommended for containers and baskets.

'Purpuriana' has plum-colored leaves.

Splash Select Series is another seed strain producing plants with foliage in individual colors: pink, red, rose, or white. 6 in.

'Wit' has dark green leaves marbled with white.

Hyssopus
Lamiaceae
hyssop

Traditionally used as an aromatic herb, hyssop is known for its antiseptic qualities and as an expectorant and cough reliever. When ingested in high concentrations it can be harmful. Often grown by beekeepers; hyssop is an excellent honey plant.

Plant in a sunny position in herb and medicinal gardens, as well as in bee and butterfly gardens. Suitable for low hedges, edgings, rock gardens, containers, and borders.

Hyssop thrives in full sun on fertile, well-drained soils, preferably with a high pH. Poor dry or sandy soils are also acceptable; winter wet can be lethal. Tolerates part shade, but this reduces the fragrance of the leaves. Harvest when the flowers have opened; chop and dry the crop for herbal use and for potpourri. Prune to shape and encourage bushiness in early spring, and after harvest for neatness.

Pests and diseases are seldom a problem; deer usually ignore the plants due to their aroma. Increase from seed sown in early spring, or root cuttings of soft young growth in spring. Plants may also be divided then.

Hyssopus officinalis
syn. *H. aristata, H. vulgaris*

- purple-blue
- midsummer to early fall
- 18–24 in. × 36 in.
- sun, part shade
- Z4–9

Hyssop. Central and southern Europe; it has become naturalized on roadsides and wasteland in some parts of the United States. This strongly aromatic, semi-evergreen herb has pairs of shiny, lance-shaped to linear leaves to 2 in. long and toothed along the edge; carried on branching, square stems that are woody at the base. Whorls of fragrant, two-lipped, tubular flowers arranged in relaxed terminal spikes; flowers, with prominently protruding stamens, are 0.5 in. across and usually purplish blue, occasionally pink or white. Chartreuse liqueur is flavored with hyssop oil.

Iberis
Brassicaceae
candytuft

Candytufts were fixtures in cottage and rock gardens of yesteryear, and endow even the most modern garden with a touch of nostalgic charm. The genus includes about 39 annual and perennial species; several of the latter are subshrubby. The name *Iberis* commemorates the fact that many candytufts hail from the Iberian Peninsula.

As the common name suggests, these plants grow in the form of tufts of dark green, alternate, linear, and entire leaves. Numerous flowers cluster into flattened corymbs or racemes above the foliage mass, sometimes hiding the leaves entirely. Each small flower is four petaled, with one pair of petals larger than the others. Seedpods are not decorative.

Plant in full sun or light shade in well-drained soil. Tolerates occasional drought. Shear plants after bloom by a third for neatness, and to prevent legginess. Every couple of years cut back the plants severely into old wood to rejuvenate them. Plants may be short lived in less than ideal conditions. Protect in cold-winter regions with evergreen boughs to mitigate winter burn from icy winds and sun.

Excellent in rock gardens, tumbling over rocks and walls, or between pavers and along pathways. Iberis can even be grown as an attractive low hedge, clipped to shape after bloom time. Choose compact selections for containers, window boxes, and planter boxes. Good companions include rock cress, pinks, basket-of-gold, and London pride saxifrage along with small, spring-blooming bulbs. Attracts butterflies; resists deer.

Propagate cultivars from cuttings; start species from seed.

Iberis saxatilis

- white
- spring
- 3–6 in. × 6 in.
- sun, part shade
- Z3–9

Rock candytuft. Native to rocky areas of southern Europe. Tight, low, almost prostrate cushions of evergreen, needle-like, 0.75-in.-long leaves become

Hyssopus officinalis

Iberis sempervirens 'Alexander's White'

covered with flattened, 1.5-in. clusters of fragrant, white flowers that fade to lilac, held at the stem tips.

'**Pygmaea**' is very compact. 4 in.

Iberis sempervirens

- white, purple
- early spring to late spring
- 9–12 in. × 18 in.
- sun
- Z3–8

Perennial candytuft. Southern Europe. Mounds of evergreen, needle-like, 1.5-in. leaves; flat, 2-in.-wide clusters of flowers borne in the leaf axils.

'**Alexander's White**' has dense clusters of chalk-white flowers. 8 in. Z4.

'**Autumn Snow**' produces white flowers in spring; repeats in fall. Keep moist during hot weather. Possibly a better repeat-bloomer than 'October Glory'. 8–10 in.

'**Little Gem**' has pure white flowers. Very compact. 6–12 in.

'**Masterpiece**' is a recent introduction with heads of white flowers, lilac-tinged buds. Mounding. 10 in. Z6.

'**Snowball**' makes mounds of white flowers; early. 10 in.

Impatiens
Balsaminaceae
balsam, busy lizzie

In recent years, market surveys have consistently found impatiens to be "America's #1 annual." In fact, most members of this species are perennial in their native habitats; they are grown as annuals in most of North America because they don't tolerate frost. There is however, one species (*Impatiens balfourii*) that offers the vigorous growth, shade tolerance, and floriferous habit typical of the genus and is winter hardy well into our colder states. This species is also resistant to the new strain of downy mildew, which has devastated *I. walleriana* types sold by the millions for annual plantings. Unfortunately, it shares the genus' susceptibility to aphids, scale, mealybugs, and slugs. Treating infested plants with insecticidal soaps is not recommended as these may be toxic to impatiens.

Mass *I. balfourii* in shady beds and borders, or group informally in woodland gardens. Valuable also in large tubs and planters.

Propagation by seed is easy. Stem cuttings root readily.

Impatiens balfourii

- lavender, pink, white
- early summer to early fall
- 2–3 ft. × 2 ft.
- part shade, shade
- Z5–11

Kashmir balsam, poor man's orchid. Native to the lower altitudes of the Himalayas, this species prefers cool, moist climates. Stems are succulent and brittle, glabrous, reddish, and much branched,

Impatiens balfourii

forming rounded mounds; the 1.5-in., alternate leaves are lanceolate, toothed along the margins. Orchid-like, spurred, 0.75-in. flowers have a white, crest-like sepal set above a lower lip of two pendulous, yellow-freckled, pink or lavender petals. An old-fashioned favorite that seems to be deer resistant; self-seeds prolifically, becoming invasive in northern Europe. Ideal for cottage gardens.

Incarvillea
Bignoniaceae
hardy gloxinia

Although the flowers of these plants resemble those of gloxinias in the African violet family, they are actually relatives of trumpet vine (*Campsis radicans*); formerly, some of the species were listed as *Amphicome*. Hardy gloxinia roots are tuberous, fleshy, and easily damaged. New growth emerges very late in spring, so mark these plants to avoid accidentally disturbing them.

The two-lipped flowers are trumpet shaped, flaring at the mouth, and carried on strong upright stems above a rosette of pinnately divided leaves. Plant the crowns 3–4 in. deep in well-drained, average to rich soil, in sun, or part shade where sun is intense. They resent winter wet that may cause root rot. Protect with mulch in cold-winter zones.

Propagate by division in spring, being careful to break the roots as little as possible. Young basal shoots may also be rooted then. Growth from seed is slow; protect young seedlings indoors over their first winter.

Incarvillea arguta
syn. *Amphicome arguta*
- pink
- early to midsummer
- 24–36 in. × 12 in.
- sun
- Z7–9

Himalayan gloxinia. Native to rocky limestone regions of the Western Himalayas to western China. Elegantly bushy with upright, branching, reddish stems, woody below, clothed with finely cut, fern-like, pinnate leaves, to 8 in. long. These are arranged alternately on arching stems and carry two to six pairs of opposite, lance-shaped, coarsely toothed leaflets. Racemes of nodding, pentemon-like flowers, 1.5 in. long, are long blooming. Deadhead to prolong bloom time. In cold regions grow as an annual, or in a container overwintered with protection. Elegant at the feet of climbing clematis or other vines.

Incarvillea delavayi
- pink
- late spring to midsummer
- 1–2 ft. × 15 in.
- sun
- Z5–10

Hardy gloxinia, Chinese trumpet. Native to China's Yunnan Province. Basal rosettes of deeply divided, dark green leaves to 12 in. long, composed of up to 11 pairs of toothed, oblong leaflets. Clusters of six or more flared trumpet flowers, yellow at the throat, and ruffled along the rim. Excellent for containers or at the front of perennial or mixed beds and borders.

'Bee's Pink' has soft pink, extra-large flowers, yellow at the throat.

'Snowtop' ('Alba') has pure white flowers.

Incarvillea mairei
- deep rose
- late spring to early summer
- 1–1.5 ft. × 6–8 in.
- sun
- Z5–9

Garden gloxinia, dwarf hardy gloxinia. Himalayas to western Nepal, southwest China. A forgiving plant tolerant of most soils with pH ranging from 5.5 to 7.5. Erect, clump-forming garden gloxinias have basal rosettes of bright green, pinnate foliage. Short, leafless stems bear several very large, deep rose to magenta trumpet flowers, with yellow throats and white flaring. Valuable in rock gardens, perennial and mixed beds and borders, and in containers. Best from seed; seedlings take several years to reach bloom size.

var. *grandiflora* bears nodding, 3- to 4-in., crimson-pink flowers on 6-in. stems. 20 in. Z4–8.

Inula ensifolia

Inula
Asteraceae
inula

If you've seen one yellow daisy, have you seen them all? Not really. Leopard's bane, arnica, and inula are superficially similar flowers, but each has its own charm, strengths, and weaknesses. Inulas offer bold, if sometimes coarse, rough foliage, typically with large basal leaves, the upper ones diminishing in size. Flowerheads are solitary or grouped, flattish, with slender, yellow ray flowers surrounding darker-colored, tubular disk flowers.

Provide a sunny site with average, well-drained soil that remains moist during dry spells. Outstandingly cold hardy, inulas commonly do not tolerate the heat and humidity of southeastern summers. The low-growing species are appropriate for rock gardens and the edges of beds and borders; mass larger species between shrubs to dramatic effect. Deadhead for a long bloom season.

Propagate by seed or division in spring

Inula ensifolia
- yellow
- late spring to early summer
- 1–2 ft. × 1 ft.
- sun
- Z3–7, HS

Swordleaf inula, elecampane, horseheal. Caucasus region of Europe. This easy, compact perennial branches freely, and is topped with solitary or groups of slender-rayed, 1- to 2-in., orange-yellow daisies. Coarse, willow-like leaves are sessile, alternate, and parallel veined, hence "*ensifolia*," which means "leaves like swords." Their bloom time may last six weeks or so; excellent cut flowers. Prone to powdery mildew.

'Compacta' grows to only 6 in.; charming in rock gardens.

'Sunray' produces its golden-yellow daisies in summer. 1.5 ft. Z3–9.

Inula helenium
- yellow
- midsummer
- 2–6 ft. × 3 ft.
- sun, part shade
- Z3–7

Elecampane, horseheal, marchalan. Britain, Europe to western Asia; naturalized in the United States. These large and rather coarse but impressive plants have huge lower leaves, 2–3 ft. in length; stem leaves are smaller and sessile. The foliage is rough-hairy on the upper surfaces, downy-soft beneath. The 2- to 3-in.-wide flowerheads may be solitary or borne in groups. Keep soil moist. Best confined to herb gardens. Valued as a medicinal herb for centuries. Sweet candy cakes were formerly made from elecampane.

Inula royleana
syn. *I. macrocephala, I. racemosa*
- yellow
- late summer
- 24–30 in. × 18 in.
- sun
- Z3–7, HS

Himalayan elecampane. Western Himalayan Mountains region, especially Kashmir. Clump forming and erect, with black flower buds that open to shaggy, orange-yellow, 5-in. blooms on unbranched stems. Basal leaves are ovate, 6–10 in. long, furry beneath and with winged petioles; upper leaves are elliptic, to 8 in., with enlarged, stem-clasping bases. Excellent cut flower. This plant has a long history of medicinal use; the roots have been used to make an expectorant, among other things.

Iris
Iridaceae
iris

Notable for its myriad of floral colors, iris is appropriately named for Iris, Greek Goddess of the Rainbow. This huge genus of about 300 species is native throughout northern temperate regions of the world, where it grows in chilly mountain areas as well as in meadows, on hillsides, and beside streams in North America, Europe, Africa, and Asia. Various forms have been cultivated for centuries and many are depicted in art (think Vincent van Gogh and George Gessart) and in emblems, particularly the 'Fleur de Lis' of French kings and of Scouting, and on the flags of St. Louis, Missouri, and Quebec, Canada.

The genus is often divided according to whether the particular species grow from bulbs, rhizomes, or fleshy rhizomatous roots. Foliage is mostly sword-shaped, narrow or broader according to type, and sometimes arranged in fans. The flowers, solitary or several per stem, have floral parts in trios;

Iris cristata 'Powder Blue Giant'

Iris ensata 'Lion King'

three inner "standards" that are generally upright, three outer "falls" that are often reflexed; the three-branched style has stigmas on the underside and covers the anthers, an adaptation to expedite pollination by flying insects and ants, or others seeking nectar. A three-part fruiting capsule follows; sometimes these are valued for dried winter floral arrangements.

Most irises require a sunny position to thrive, although some tolerate afternoon shade; crested iris do well in woodland shade. A few types such as the Louisiana irises thrive in wet soils, but most irises prefer well-drained soils of average to good fertility. Soil pH is seldom critical, except in the case of Japanese iris, which demands lime-free soil. Note that *Iris pseudacorous*, native to Europe, western Asia, and northwest Africa, though often found in nurseries, has proven invasive, although its cultivars behave better.

There is an iris for almost every spot in the garden. Tall species mix well with shrubs and other tall perennials toward the back of borders, while the slightly lower-growing bearded, Siberian, and Japanese types are colorful midborder plants, contrasting well with more rounded spurges, bleeding hearts, ornamental sages, and peonies. Bulbous netted and Danford iris are suitable for rock gardens and small spots where color is needed. They force well for early indoor displays. Bulbous Dutch iris are popular cut flowers. Japanese roof iris, *I. tectorum*, and winter iris, *I. unguicularis*, deserve mention for iris fanciers.

Deer seldom browse iris, though they occasionally nip off the blossoms of crested types, generally leaving behind the decapitated blossoms. Other pests include iris borers on rhizomatous types and thrips that attack the flowers. Both can become seriously destructive if not controlled.

Propagate by division. Start species from seed, though seedlings take a couple of years to reach blooming size. Check out specialist nurseries for the most recent introductions.

Iris cristata

- blue, purple
- spring
- 3–9 in. × 15 in.
- part shade, shade
- Z3–8

Crested iris, dwarf crested iris. Native to woodlands of the eastern United States, from Maryland to Oklahoma and Georgia. Slender, creeping, woody rhizomes spread widely along the surface, and function effectively as groundcovers. Fans of narrow, sword-shaped, 4- to 8-in.-long leaves; fragrant, almost stalkless flowers 1–1.5 in. across are held on 1.5- to 2-in. perianth tubes. Flowers may be solitary or paired, have upright monochrome standards, spreading falls decorated with a cream or yellow crest, and a large central white blotch or signal usually rimmed with purple or violet. Be alert for slugs that shred the foliage and damage the blooms too. Spectacular when allowed to naturalize in light woods or clearings, or on shaded rocky slopes and in rock gardens.

'Eco Bluebird', one of several cultivars introduced by Eco-Gardens, has dark blue flowers crested with orange and a white throat.

'Powder Blue Giant' has large, open flowers of pale lavender; purple-rimmed white blotches.

'Shenandoah Sky' has deep lilac flowers, yellow crest, and purple-rimmed white blotches on the falls.

'Tennessee White', selected by Don Shadow, is vigorous with white flowers decorated with a yellow crest. Possibly the best white.

'Vein Mountain', introduced by We-Du Nursery, has very light blue flowers, with orange crests outlined with deep purple.

Iris ensata
syn. *I. kaempferi*
- various
- summer
- 2–3 ft. × 1.5–2 ft.
- sun
- Z4–9

Japanese iris, Japanese water iris. Native to Japan, China, Korea, India, and eastern Russia. Grassy leaves to 2 ft. long, each with a conspicuous raised midrib, emerge from stout rhizomes. From two to four flowers, usually 4–6 in. across, in white, blues, purples, and reddish violet are borne on sparsely branching stems; some modern cultivars may have flowers to 10 in. across. Blooms appear flat with arching falls blotched with yellow, and slightly smaller, almost flat standards. Requires an acid, humus-rich soil, moist but not necessarily boggy. Never apply lime. Plant about 2 in. deep as soon as possible without the roots drying out. Divide in fall or just after bloom time.

Superb for rain gardens, beside water gardens, and in shallow ponds. However, Japanese irises also thrive in ordinary garden soils, and provide magnificent displays among astilbes and hostas.

There are countless cultivars; the following is a small selection:

'Dragon Tapestry' is white-splashed, dark burgundy.

'Eleanor Perry' has deep lilac flowers traced with violet.

'Great White Heron' is semi-double and pure white.

'Lion King' has frilly, purple-edged white falls flashed with yellow.

'Pink Frost' is lightly ruffled with lavender-pink flowers, yellow at the center.

Iris foetidissima
- mauve
- spring to summer
- 1.5–2.5 ft. × 1.5–2 ft.
- sun, shade
- Z6–10

Stinking iris, Gladwyn iris, foetid iris. Britain, southern and western Europe, northern Africa. This unusual iris is grown predominantly for its colorful seeds. Evergreen, 2- to 4-ft.-long, sword-like leaves have a very slight, unpleasant odor when bruised. Growing from slow-spreading rhizomes, the two- to three-times-branching flower stalks, flattened on one side and shorter than the leaves, each bear up to three, pale grayish, 2.5-in. flowers with bronzy yellow falls. Blossoms open consecutively, but many-stemmed plants may flaunt a dozen simultaneously. Seedpods similar to Brazil nuts follow; these split into three sections, each revealing two rows of round, scarlet, sometimes yellow or white ('Fructo-alba') seeds. Sow fresh seed when possible; slow to establish. Remove shabby leaves after winter. Use seedpods for dried arrangements. Tolerates coastal gardens, and almost pure sand, as well as tree roots in shaded spots.

'Citrina' has pale yellow flowers veined in purple. A superior cultivar.

'Holden Clough' (probably *Iris foetidissima* × *I. chrysographes*, or *I. pseudacorus*) is vigorous, with golden flowers overlaid with purple veining and yellow-blotched falls.

Iris ×*germanica*
- various
- early summer
- 8–36 in. × 9–24 in.
- sun
- Z3–10

Bearded hybrid iris, German iris. Of hybrid origin, probably the largest and most popular type of irises in cultivation. Named for the hairy "beard" that decorates the falls. The plants arise from thick rhizomes that lie close to the soil surface, sprouting fans of broad, sword-shaped gray-green leaves. Several flowers are borne on each stem. In addition to the bearded falls, the standards are erect, usually wide, and often frilly. Flower color varies from white through pastel pinks, blues, and yellows, to deep saturated bronzy golds, blues, and purples, with standards and beard often of contrasting hues. Some cultivars are fragrant, many repeat bloom, and most make lovely cut flowers. Spectacular additions to early summer beds and borders; low-growing cultivars are appropriate for rock gardens and the front of the border; tall ones bring grace to the back of borders and fit in well among shrubby cinquefoil, roses, weigelas, and other shrubs.

Plant in free-draining soil, with the rhizome half-buried or just at the soil surface; in very hot regions, slightly deeper. Divide every three to four years. Be alert for iris borers, which lay eggs in the rhizomes to emerge as larvae with a built-in food supply; the larvae are pinkish white with black heads. Destroy infected plants and rhizomes, which often become mushy from bacterial or fungal infections that gain entry through the borer tunnels. Traditionally the leaf fans have been cut to about 9 in. in late summer to allow sun ripening of the rhizomes.

There are innumerable cultivars; here are a few:

'Beverly Sills' is slightly ruffled with pale coral-pink flowers; apricot beard. May rebloom. 32–38 in. tall.

'Champagne Elegance' has apricot falls; very pale pink standards. Reblooms. 28–34 in.

'Immortality' ('Immortelle') has very wide, slightly ruffled, white falls; buttercup-yellow beards. Reblooms. 30–36 in.

'**Raspberry Blush**' is pale crushed-raspberry color with darker patches on the falls; orange-raspberry beards. 18–24 in.

'**Superstition**' is so deep purple as to appear almost black. 32–38 in.

Louisiana Iris

- various colors
- summer
- 3–4 ft. × 3 ft.
- sun
- Z4–9

This group of distinct species is found wild in marshes and wetlands along the Gulf Coast of Texas and Florida, and in the Mississippi basin. Species include: brick-colored *Iris fulva* (syn. *I. cuprea*), blue-flowered *I. brevicaulis* (syn. *I. foliosa*, *I. lamancei*), blue-violet *I. giganticaerulea*, purple and white-flowered *I. hexagona*, and reddish purple or yellow *I. nelsonii*. Breeding programs have produced several notable hybrids. Elegant, beardless and crestless flowers, with slender falls and floppy standards, come in an astonishing range of colors. Louisiana irises thrive in moist beds and borders, and are excellent cut flowers. Plant 2 in. deep in fall and mulch heavily. Easily divided.

Iris pallida

syn. *I. glauca, I. odorissima, I. pallido-coerulea*
- lavender
- late spring
- 2–4 ft. × 2 ft.
- sun
- Z4–9

Sweet iris, orris, Dalmatian iris. Northern Italy, Croatia. Long, fat rhizomes support sword-shaped, glaucous, almost evergreen leaves to 1.5 in. wide. Sparsely branched, leafless stems bear several flowers enclosed in papery silver spathes, well above the foliage. The pale lavender, yellow-bearded flowers smell deliciously of vanilla, orange blossom, or grape jelly depending upon your nose. All variants have excellent, good-looking foliage that persists through summer and contrasts with the rounded form of the plants. Fine in rock gardens, beds and borders, and fragrance and herb gardens.

'**Argenteo-variegata**' ('Alba-variegata') has blue-gray leaves striped longitudinally in creamy white. Powder blue flowers.

'**Variegata**' ('Zebra', 'Aurea-variagata'). The glaucous leaves are striped with yellowish cream. Similar flowers and perhaps more vigorous than the white-striped selection.

var. *dalmatica* is a superior selection with more saturated color. Yellow beards.

Iris sibirica

- blue
- late spring
- 24–36 in. × 24 in.
- sun, part shade
- Z3–9

Siberian iris. Central Europe to southern Russia, northern Asia. Easily grown, makes dense, upright

Iris pallida 'Argenteo-variegata'

Iris sibirica 'Super Ego'

Isotoma fluviatilis 'Blue Star Creeper', typically used as a skirt for heucheras

clumps of bright green, narrowly lance-shaped leaves that remain handsome through the season. Branched stems carry up to five beardless flowers, each about 3 in. across, usually well above the foliage mass. The species has blue-violet flowers with dark veining and white throats. Slow spreading but persistent. There are countless cultivars in assorted colors; a few popular ones are listed below:

'Butter and Sugar' has white standards, creamy-lemon falls. 3–3.5 ft. Z5–10.

'Caesar's Brother', an old cultivar, is very upright with deep purple flowers. 1.5–3 ft.

'Pink Haze' has soft pale lavender falls, rimmed with white, dark throat. 30 in.

'Super Ego' has soft light blue flowers; wavy falls etched with deep blue. 32 in.

'White Swirl' has white flowers, yellow at the throat. 24–30 in.

Iris tuberosa

syn. *Hermodactylus tuberosa*

- yellow-and-deep purple
- late winter to early spring
- 12–15 in. × 6 in.
- sun
- Z6–8

Snake's-head iris, black iris, Herme's fingers. Greece, Spain, Turkey. Evergreen clumps of sword-shaped, gray-green leaves, to 12–15 in. long, arranged in two ranks. Very early blooming; fragrant, 2- to 3-in. flowers with spatulate, glassy green falls, dramatically blotched with very deep purple. The erect, 1-in., pea-green standards surround a greenish yellow, conspicuously three-forked style.

Isotoma

syn. *Laurentia, Solenopsis*
Lobeliaceae
laurentia

Currently the nomenclature of this genus is somewhat confused. That said, there are a couple of species that are garden worthy, though they might be offered under synonymous names in the marketplace. Flowers are similar to related *Lobelia*, but they differ in having entire, not split, corollas. Mostly solitary, the flowers are blue, pink, or white. Provide sunny locations where soil drains well. Increase by cuttings, division, or seed.

Isotoma fluviatilis

syn. *Laurentia fluviatilis*

- blue, white
- spring
- 3 in. × 6 in.
- sun, part shade
- Z5–8

Blue star creeper, laurentia. Australia. Fast-growing, low mats of very small, rounded leaves, good for carpeting between pavers, beside woodland paths, and in rock gardens. Evergreen, where mild. Tiny, 2-in., tubular flowers bloom freely. Tolerates limited foot traffic; a star in the Stepables line of plants. Provide moist soil.

'Blue Star Creeper' has pale powder-blue flowers.

'White Star' is a white-flowered form.

Jasione

Campanulaceae
sheep's bit, shepherd's scabious

Just one species of this underappreciated genus appears in American gardens, and that one deserves far wider exposure. It is ideal for rock gardens, and also attractive in borders, lining a path, or displayed in a trough or container. Charming for posies.

Sheep's bit prefers an acid, well-drained soil. Deadhead to prolong bloom.

Divide in spring, or sow seed in autumn; over-winter outdoors in a protected spot.

Jasione laevis

syn. *Jasione perennis*

- blue
- late spring to late summer
- 10–12 in. high and wide
- sun, partial shade
- Z4–9

Shepherd's scabious. Southern Europe. Forms low tufts or mounds of gray-green, narrow and obovate, hairy leaves to 4 in. long. Wiry stems rise above bearing long-blooming, 2-in., pincushion-like heads of violet-blue flowers.

'Blaulicht' ('Blue Light') has bright blue flowers.

Kalimeris

Asteraceae
false aster

Until recently this small genus was usually included with *Aster* or sometimes *Boltonia*, and despite the botanical divorce, members of *Kalimeris* much resemble their better-known relatives. *Kalimeris* bears its compound, aster-like flowers in late summer into fall, and over time they form extensive colonies to make a splendid show in meadows or wild gardens. False aster is sufficiently refined and attractive to use as specimens in fall borders; an excellent source of cut flowers.

Kalimeris differs from many of its aster relatives in its heat and humidity tolerance, making it reliable for planting in hot, humid climates. Generally pest and problem free; deer resistant.

Propagate by seed or divide in spring or fall; cuttings of young spring growth root readily.

Kalimeris incisa
syn. *Calimeris incisa*

- white, blue
- late summer to midfall
- 3–4 ft. high and wide
- sun, partial shade
- Z5–9, HT

Blue star aster. This native of northeastern Asia bears dark, oblong-lanceolate leaves to 3–4 in. long with toothed or incised edges, and 1-in., daisy-like, white or light blue flowers with yellow centers. Unparticular about soil as long as it drains well; prefers moderate moisture but drought resistant once established. Cut back by a third or half in early summer to stimulate vigorous, compact, and bushy growth. Protect from midday sun in the southern part of its range. Cut back after first bloom flush to encourage rebloom.

'Blue Star' (syn. *Boltonia incisa* 'Blue Star') is compact, with 1-in. flowerheads with light blue rays and yellow centers. Low maintenance. 12–18 in. tall.

'Edo Murasaki' is compact with lavender flowerheads. 15 in.

Kalimeris pinnatifida
syn. *Asteromoa mongolica*, *Kalimeris mongolica*, *Aster cantoniensis*, *Boltonia cantoniensis*

- white
- early to late summer
- 2–3 ft. × 2 ft.
- sun, part shade
- Z6–9

Double Japanese aster, orphanage plant, perennial false aster. Japan. Upright and bushy arising from a basal rosette of pinnately lobed, light green leaves to 3.5 in. long. White flowerheads are semi-double, chrysanthemum-like, 1 in. across.

'Hortensis' is most often found in nursery catalogs. Upright, tough, and long lived, this is a real workhorse in the garden. It produces delicate clouds of semi-double, white daisies, that always seem fresh from midsummer through fall.

Kalimeris yomena
syn. *Aster yomena*

- white
- late summer to midfall
- 24–36 in. high and wide
- sun, part shade
- Z5–8

Japanese aster. Central and southern Japan. Serrated, oblong to elliptical leaves to 1 in. long, and white daisy-like, yellow-centered, single flowerheads.

'Aurea' has a slow, creeping habit. Pale lavender flowers with yellow centers and cut-leaf, gold-rimmed leaves. 12–18 in.

'Shogun' (syn. *Kalimeris incisa* 'Shogun', 'Variegata') makes dense clumps of medium green leaves broadly banded with creamy yellow. Best variegation in partial shade. Yellow-centered, light lavender flowers. 18 in. × 10 in.

Kalimeris incisa 'Blue Star'

Kirengeshoma palmata

Kirengeshoma
Hydrangeaceae
yellow waxbells

This genus is notably compact, including just two, closely similar species; some botanists regard them as one. However you define them, yellow waxbells offer woodland plantings with a difference: unlike so many forest dwellers, these plants wait until late summer to bloom. The yellow flowers are borne in cymes at the stem tips and upper leaf axils; individual blooms are bell shaped and waxy looking, 1–2 in. long. Out of bloom, the bold and maple-like foliage, borne on arching purplish stems, catches the eye, particularly when the leaves adopt their golden fall color. Seeds are carried in interesting, three-horned, brownish green capsules.

Kirengeshomas form slowly increasing clumps. They mingle well with shrubs and provide a fine textural contrast to astilbes, ferns, and other woodlanders. In addition, yellow waxbells provide ongoing summer and fall interest in areas planted with spring ephemerals.

Best suited to moist, acid, humus-rich, well-drained soils. No serious pests or diseases, except for deer that devour them.

Divide in spring, or sow fresh seed in a protected spot outdoors.

Kirengeshoma koreana
- yellow
- late summer to early autumn
- 3 ft. high and wide
- part shade, shade
- Z5–8

Japanese yellow waxbells. Native to Korea. Often treated as a variant of the following species, *Kirengeshoma palmata*. Flowers of *K. koreana* flare outward at the mouth of the bell.

Kirengeshoma palmata
- yellow
- late summer to early autumn
- 3–4 ft. × 2–3 ft.
- part shade, shade
- Z5–8

Yellow waxbells. Native to Japan, Korea, and perhaps northeast China. Leaves are coarsely toothed, deeply lobed, and maple-like, to 8 in. across. Typically the drooping, waxy, slender, yellow bellflowers measure 1.5 in. long, and are usually borne three per cluster (or cyme).

Knautia
Dipsacaceae
knautia

This genus of some 40 species has just one that is routinely planted in ornamental gardens. The flowers are reminiscent of those of related *Scabiosa*.

Knautia thrives in average, well-drained soil, and tolerates drought when established; if supplemental watering is required apply at the base of plants to discourage powdery mildew. Otherwise these low-maintenance plants are pest and disease free; deer seldom browse them. In flower borders, yellow or buff-colored roses make good companions, or for a more lively display, partner *Knautia* with *Coreopsis* 'Moonbeam' or *Achillea* 'Moonshine'. Mass in cottage gardens, in meadows with grasses, and in wild and wildlife gardens. The flowers are excellent for cutting, both fresh and dried.

Propagate by seed, or take cuttings from young growth.

Knautia macedonica
syn. *Scabiosa macedonica, S. rumelica*
- maroon
- summer
- 1.5–3 ft. × 2 ft.
- sun
- Z5–9, HS

Macedonian knapweed. Found growing among grasses in open meadows and light woodlands in eastern and southern Europe. In average, well-drained soil *Knautia* makes bushy tangles of slender, hairy stems topped with bright ruby or maroon heads of flowers. These consist of a dome of fertile florets surrounded by many showier, colorful sterile ones. Individual flowerheads go to seed within a couple of weeks, but plenty are always coming so that bloom persists for many weeks. Birds, hover flies, and bees are attracted to the nectar; birds and other wildlife also feed on seeds of spent

Knautia macedonica

flowerheads, so do not deadhead too assiduously. Instead, periodically prune out largest spent stems to encourage rebloom without penalizing wildlife.

'Mars Midget' is a dwarf version, with ruby-crimson, pincushion heads. Reportedly it thrives in the very hot, humid US Gulf Coast states. 12–16 in.

'Thunder and Lightning' is notable for its irregularly cream-edged, light green leaves that contrast brightly with double, brilliant cherry-red flowers. A fine container plant. 12–18 in.

Kniphofia

Asphodelaceae
torch lily, red hot poker

These flamboyant exotics won an enthusiastic following among 19th century gardeners before the tastemakers of the day branded them as vulgar, and they fell out of fashion. Today their popularity is on the rise and once again they are sought after as dramatic players for mixed and perennial beds. Extensive breeding programs, involving *Kniphofia galpinii*, *K. uvaria*, *K. praecox*, and *K. macownii*, have produced plants with more than red-and-yellow torches; cream, lime green, yellow, and varied coral flowers are not unusual; several are named below.

This genus includes natives from temperate regions around the world, but especially from southern Africa and Madagascar. Deciduous or evergreen, especially in mild climates, torch lilies are tough and long lasting. They arise from dense mats of cord-like fibrous roots that produce tufts of grassy leaves of varying widths—some quite handsome. Strong upright scapes carry usually dense "pokers" of stemless, tubular flowers, which open from the bottom up. The pokers vary in shape with the species or selection.

Plant in spring in open, sunny or partly shaded sites, in well-drained soil high in humus. The crowns should not be deeper than 2–3 in. deep. The roots require plenty of water during bloom time; if allowed to dry out, the flower buds may abort. Winter wet causes crown rot.

Torch lilies provide colorful focal points, especially among shrubs; group together to make a statement. In beds and borders, designs benefit from the addition of these vertical plants to contrast and complement rounded coneflowers, baptisia, asters, and hydrangeas. A planting of torch lilies marching down the edge of a driveway is unforgettable. Long lasting as cut flowers. Seldom browsed by deer; a nectar source for butterflies and other insects.

Leave roots undisturbed once established, except for division in springtime to relieve overcrowding or multiply stock. New plants may be started from seed, though seedling growth is slow. Outside their hardiness zones, cultivate torch lilies in containers and overwinter indoors, or lift carefully in fall and store in a cool but frost-free location. In marginal zones, traditionally the leaves have been tied up to cover and protect the crown.

Kniphofia 'Alcazar'

Kniphofia caulescens

- coral
- late summer
- 3–4 ft. × 2 ft.
- sun, part shade
- Z5–10

Blue-leaf red hot poker. High grassy slopes in South Africa's Drakensberg Mountains. This dramatic plant produces tufts of fibrous, strongly blue, strappy, 36-in. leaves, wider at the base. Fat, oblong cylinders of flowers, bright coral fading to lemon, are carried on erect, short, but sturdy stems.

Kniphofia uvaria

syn. *K. alooides*, *Tritoma uvaria*
- red
- summer
- 3–5 ft. × 4 ft.
- sun
- Z5–9

Red hot poker, common torch lily, poker plant. Cape Peninsula, South Africa. Evergreen plants are variable, developing heavy clumps of sword-shaped grayish leaves about 3 ft. long. Be careful working around them as the edges of the leaves are frequently abrasive and bloody hands result. Long pokers of 1- to 2-in. flowers, red in the bud but maturing to orange or yellow, adorn stiff scapes. Largely replaced in commerce by its hybrid offspring.

Other Notable Cultivars

'**Alcazar**' blooms early with light terra cotta flowers. 3–4 ft.

'**Earliest of All**' is among the earliest to bloom. Orange red to yellow. 2.5 ft.

'**Echo Mango**' has soft apricot flowers in late spring and summer; repeats. 3.5 ft.

'**Green Jade**' has long, icy, lime-green cylinders of flowers, paler at the tip. Midsummer. 4–5 ft.

'**Little Maid**' is excellent for containers. Long, slender spikes of creamy-white flowers. Late. A Beth Chatto introduction. 2 ft.

'**Percy's Pride**'. Very large, light yellow to lime flowers cluster tightly in oval torches. Early and repeats. Strappy, 1-in.-wide leaves. 3 ft.

Kosteletzkya
Malvaceae
seashore mallow, saltmarsh mallow

Lamium maculatum 'Anne Greenaway'

This genus includes 30 or more species worldwide, but just one commonly contributes to American gardens. Virginia saltmarsh mallow is salt tolerant and an excellent choice for seaside gardens. It is also lovely at the back of the border, in native plant gardens and wildlife gardens. A favorite of hummingbirds and butterflies.

Full sun is best for good displays of flowers. While it will grow in shallow standing water, it also thrives in regular garden soils if protected from drought by regular watering.

Propagate by seed, soaked overnight. Divide in spring or increase by cuttings in summer.

Kosteletzkya virginica
syn. *K. pentacarpos*
- pink
- midsummer to fall
- 3–5 ft. × 4 ft.
- sun, part shade
- Z6–9

Virginia saltmarsh mallow. This native mallow grows in brackish coastal wetlands from New York south and west to the Gulf Coast of Texas. It is tall and imposing with somewhat coarse, fuzzy, light green, triangular-ovate leaves with triangular lobes at the base. Over several weeks the plants are covered with five-petaled, 1- to 3-in., pink, hibiscus-like flowers with a golden central column of stamens. These may be solitary or clustered into panicles. Flowers open in the morning, but close at the end of the day to be replaced by fresh blossoms the next day.

Lamium
Lamiaceae
dead nettle

Dead nettles are among the most popular plants for ground covers for North American and Canadian gardens. Like their mint family relatives—mints, sages, and thymes—they are square stemmed with pairs of more or less evergreen leaves and two-lipped, hooded flowers. Although many of the 50 or so species of *Lamium* are weedy and unsuitable for ornamental gardens, those mentioned here are valuable, mannerly perennials.

In large part, this outstanding clan is grown for its foliage, borne on stoloniferous stems. Leaves are mostly kidney shaped or triangular, coarsely toothed, wrinkled, and often attractively marked with silver or white. Flowers are white, yellow, or pink-purple, some marked with darker speckles on the lower lip. The uppermost petal forms a protective hood over the pollen-bearing stamens.

Dead nettles are easily grown in average to fertile, moderately moist soils; the sprawling stems root at the nodes. They adapt to sun, part shade, or even shaded sites in cool regions, but further south require protection from midday sun. They are challenged by combined heat and humidity.

Space dead nettles closely as ground cover, to fill in quickly and smother weeds. Valuable at the front of borders, to face down low shrubs, in rock gardens; they also thrive in containers with other shade lovers such as Chinese astilbe 'Pumila', lungworts, and coral bells. The most showy-foliaged specimens can stand alone in interesting containers. Mostly pest and disease free, but watch for slug and snail damage. Seldom browsed by deer.

To propagate, detach rooted plantlets, or take cuttings in early summer. Some cultivars come true from seed.

Lamium galeobdolon
syn. *Lamiastrum galeobdolon, Galeobdolon luteum*
- yellow
- spring
- 9–8 in. × 18 in.
- part shade, shade
- Z4–8, HT

Yellow archangel, false lamium. Europe, western Asia. Often seen as a neglected groundcover, yellow archangel provides a handsome, weed-proof blanket only if plants are cut back hard before new growth appears in spring and after bloom; pinch back straggling shoots to encourage bushiness. This otherwise low-maintenance perennial tolerates dry and alkaline conditions well; can become invasive in rich soil. Round-toothed, mid-green, 2.5-in. leaves often marked with silver; mostly evergreen. Hairy, brown-spotted, bright yellow flowers cluster in whorls in the upper stem nodes. Heat tolerant. Mostly grown for foliage.

'Herman's Pride' makes neat mounds of dark green, metallic leaves, flecked with silver; yellow flowers.

'Variegatum' ('Florentinum'). Foliage has broad splashes of silver; yellow flowers. A fine groundcover.

Lamium maculatum

- red, pink, white
- spring to fall
- 8–12 in. × 18 in.
- sun, part shade, shade
- Z4–8

Spotted dead nettle, spotted henbit. Native to moist grasslands and light woodlands in Europe, northern Africa to Lebanon, Syria, and Turkey. Erect to sprawling stems, usually well branched at the base. Opposite, triangular or heart-shaped, toothed leaves are softly hairy, often striped or blotched with white or silver. Flowers cluster in verticillasters in the upper leaf axils; mostly pink or purplish, with darker freckles on the two lower lobes. Bloom time is extended: the first flush appears in midspring, tapers off in summer heat, but reblooms as weather cools, usually lasting until the first hard frost. Excellent planted close as an evergreen groundcover. Pinch straggling shoots to keep compact.

Other Notable Cultivars

'Anne Greenaway', a British selection, has small, green-and-silver leaves, irregularly edged with chartreuse. Mauve-pink flowers. Exciting planted solo in a black container.

'Aureum' ('Gold Leaf') has bright lemon-yellow leaves, striped with white down the middle. Pink flowers. 'Beedham's White' is similar but with white flowers.

'Beacon Silver' has green-rimmed silver leaves, red-flushed stems, and pinkish purple flowers. 'White Nancy' has white flowers, light green stems, and green-rimmed silver leaves. Supplies a cool clean look in shade. 'Red Nancy' has rosy red flowers. Intolerant of heat and humidity.

'Pink Chablis' blooms from spring until hard frost in fall. Silver leaves edged with dark green. Flowers in shades of pink. A superior selection from Garry Grueber.

'Purple Dragon'. Silver leaves edged with green; large, purple flower clusters.

Lampranthus
Aizoaceae
ice plant

This South African genus of about 180 species is native mostly to semi-arid, coastal regions, and its members, which store water in their succulent foliage, provide drought-hardy, colorful groundcovers for regions where water is limited. In the arid Southwest and southern California large swathes of land and banks along highways and other inhospitable areas are carpeted with these glistening daisies during bloom time.

Tender, succulent perennials, erect or sprawling plants carry pairs of three-angled or cylindrical, evergreen leaves, usually grayish green but possibly turning reddish in full sun. From summer through early autumn the plants are blanketed with brightly colored, daisy-like flowers. The species of *Lampranthus* are quite confused in the trade, and there has been considerable hybridization, natural and otherwise. Buy plants in bloom, to ensure that the flower colors are those you desire. Excellent subjects for xeric, succulent, and rock gardens, ice plants look spectacular tumbling down banks or over rocks and walls. Outside their hardiness zone, bring plants indoors over the winter, returning them to the garden when the weather warms. Rest plants by withholding water during winter; water occasionally but deeply. Fast growing, ice plants fill a large container rapidly from a branched, 4-in. cutting.

Well-drained soil is essential for these beauties; persistently moist soil promotes rot. Nutrient-poor, stony, sandy, or rocky soil serves ice plants well. Where sun is intense, midday shade is appreciated.

Ice plant stems root at the nodes along their length; may become invasive over time. Shear spent flowers after a flush of bloom. Deer resistant; may be attacked by aphids at bloomtime.

Propagate by rooting sections of the stem in spring or summer (allow cuttings to callus over before sticking), or start from seed in spring. Keep a supply of young rooted plants to replace older ones.

Lampranthus auriantiacus

- yellow, orange
- late spring to early fall
- 12–18 in. high and wide
- sun
- Z9–11

Cape Peninsula of South Africa. Usually spreading stems, rooting along their length, with grayish green, 1-in.-long, three-sided or cylindrical leaves, rough to the touch. Usually bright orange flowers, 1.5–2 in. across. Considered by some to be invasive in California.

'Glaucus', yellow ice plant, has vivid bright yellow blossoms. It may outshine its parent in residential gardens.

'Sunman' has bright golden flowers, with a wide, white central ring.

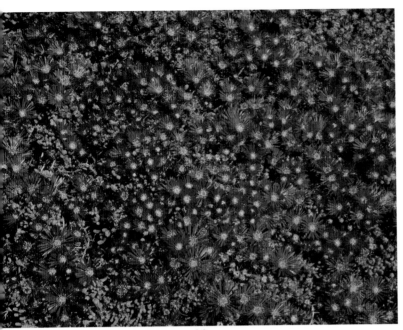
Lampranthus spectabilis

Lamprocapnos spectabilis

Lamprocapnos

Papaveraceae
bleeding heart

A genus of one species that was, until recently, classified with *Dicentra*; it is still listed mostly under its former name in nursery catalogs. Deer and rabbit resistant; mostly pest and disease free, except for aphids.

Propagated by root cuttings in winter; divide in spring or fall.

Lamprocapnos spectabilis

syn. *Dicentra spectabilis*
- pink, white
- mid- to late spring
- 24–48 in. × 18 in.
- part shade, shade
- Z3–8

Old-fashioned bleeding heart. Japan, Korea, Siberia. Clump forming. Similar to the dicentras but soft green, lobed foliage is less deeply and intricately cut. Tall, arching stems laden on one side with pendent, broadly heart-shaped, 1-in. flowers with reflexed outer rose-pink petals, and exserted inner white petals. Spectacular foliage and floral display in midspring; unfortunately usually becomes summer dormant, after an untidy interlude with scruffy yellow foliage. Excellent for cut flowers, often forced commercially for Valentine's Day; perfect for weddings. Plan to have companion plants to fill the gap after the bleeding hearts become dormant; hostas, toad lilies, astilbes, and balloon flowers are good choices.

'Alba' has pure white hearts dangling from it's arching stems.

'Gold Heart'. Pink hearts above deeply lobed golden leaves.

'Valentine' has white-tipped, cherry-red flowers on arching, deep burgundy stems. Foliage matures to dark gray-green.

Lathyrus

Fabaceae
pea

Pictures of annual sweet peas (cultivars of *Lathyrus odoratus*) decorate the pages of seed catalogs, but there is a number of useful, though lesser known, perennial species of *Lathyrus* also. These share many virtues of their annual relatives, except fragrance: all but one perennial species bears scentless flowers. The perennials offer colorful, winged, pea-type blossoms suitable for cutting, attractive pinnately compound foliage, and a climbing, mounding, or sprawling habit of growth.

Propagate by seed sown in early spring; nick seed coat and soak seeds overnight before sowing. Divide in early spring.

Lampranthus spectabilis

syn. *Mesembryanthemum spectabile*
- pink
- early summer to early fall
- 10–12 in. × 12–18 in.
- sun
- Z8–10

Trailing ice plant. Cape region of South Africa. This very variable trailing plant has succulent, red-tipped, gray-green, triangular leaves 2–3 in. long, crowded on short branches. Flowers are pink, red, rose, or purple, 2–3 in. across.

Lathyrus vernus f. *roseus*

Lavandula angustifolia 'Loddon Blue'

Lathyrus latifolius

- pink, white
- early to late summer
- 6–9 ft. × 3–6 ft.
- sun
- Z3–8

Everlasting pea, perennial sweet pea. Native to southern Europe, this long-lived, rhizomatous perennial has naturalized in many regions of North America. It is considered invasive in Michigan, Wisconsin, and Oregon, but elsewhere, though introduced in the 18th century, it has not proven overly aggressive. The winged stems bear opposing pairs of oval, 3-in., medium green leaves. Leaflets often end in tendrils that wrap any available support to clamber to 6 ft. or more, or simply scramble along the ground. The 1-in., white or pink flowers are borne singly or in racemes of six to eleven. Flattened, pea-like seeds are enclosed in pods; toxic if ingested. Provide full sun or very light shade in open, airy spots, with moisture-retaining but well-drained soil. Best adapted to regions with cool summers; high humidity and stagnant air encourages fungal diseases. No serious insect pests; slugs and snails attack young plants. Appropriate for cottage gardens and other informal places where plants can sprawl along the ground, clothe a bank, or clamber up fences and walls. In borders grow up a tuteur or rustic tepee. Good in containers.

'White Pearl' ('Pearl White') bears pure white flowers; 'Pink Pearl' ('Rosa Perle') has pale pink flowers; 'Red Pearl' bears wine-red flowers.

Lathyrus vernus

syn. *Orobus vernus*

- reddish purple
- early to midspring
- 6–12 in. high and wide
- part shade, shade
- Z5–9

Spring vetchling. This European native forms bushy clumps of unwinged stems that bear racemes of 0.75-in., pea-type flowers in the leaf axils. Reddish purple flowers are veined with red, and mature violet-blue. Pinnate, light green leaves with 1.5- to 3-in., ovate leaflets. Flourishes in average soil that drains well. In warm climates foliage may die back as temperatures rise. Slow to establish, the roots resent disturbance. Use in cottage gardens, shady borders, and wild gardens. Typically pest and disease free, but the flowers are a delicacy for deer.

'Alboroseus' has exquisite white-and-pink flowers.
'Alba' is white flowered
f. *roseus* is pink flowered.

Lavandula

Lamiaceae
lavender

Few other perennials offer such a concentration of sensual gratifications as the lavenders. With their deliciously scented, silver-hued, evergreen foliage, lavenders reward eye, nose, and touch. Not surprisingly, they find many applications in the home as well as the garden. Lavenders have a reputation among gardeners for being finicky, but if a few basic cultural needs are met, they are reliable, relatively undemanding plants. Best of all, they are rarely molested by deer or rabbits.

Nearly all species of lavender originated around the Mediterranean. To grow them successfully, match the conditions in which they evolved as closely as possible: a well-drained, lean, sweet soil, with bright sunlight in an airy location; a Mediterranean-type climate of hot, dry summers and temperate, moister winters, as found in coastal California, is ideal. However, with excellent drainage lavenders also thrive in regions with cooler summers and cold winters; summer heat and humidity are problematic for most, as are heavy, water-retentive soils. Grow lavenders in raised beds or containers if necessary to enhance drainage; a lime chip or gravel mulch creates a drier microclimate at the crown (helpful in humid regions), and aids surface runoff. Different species of lavender vary in their climatic adaption—selecting the type best suited to your conditions is particularly important with this genus. Once established, lavenders are notably drought tolerant and perform very well in xeriscapes.

Where soils are heavy, improve drainage with coarse sand or grit, along with compost before planting. Avoid an overly rich diet that encourages soft, disease-prone growth and reduces the foliage fragrance, as the essential oils do not intensify. Maintenance includes an annual barbering just after new growth has appeared: cut back by a third to encourage compact, vigorous growth. Beware of pruning too early, as soft young growth may get frosted.

Lavender is an obvious choice for herb gardens; elsewhere they are outstanding planted as low hedges along pathways or to define garden spaces perhaps in containers, to furnish color and contrast in perennial and mixed borders, in rock gardens, or in fragrance gardens, especially those for the visually impaired. Dramatic when massed, lavenders respond well to the regular severe clipping demanded by topiary. Foraging bees and butterflies flock to the flowers; lavender honey is a gourmet item. The oils are used not only in toiletries, but are important in aromatherapy. Sachets of dried lavender retain their fragrance for several years providing a pleasant aroma to clothing, and also deter clothes moths. In the kitchen, flavor scones, cookies, and ice cream with the dried flowers.

Propagate hybrids and named cultivars by spring tip cuttings, or by mound layering; start species from seed sown indoors seven to ten weeks before the last spring frost.

Lavandula angustifolia
- lavender, pink, white
- early to midsummer
- 2–3 ft. × 2–4 ft.
- sun
- Z5–8, HS

English lavender. Not of English origin but rather native to stony hillsides of the Mediterranean. Semi-woody, English lavender bears narrow, needle-like, gray-green leaves to 2.5 in. long on square stems. Tiny but abundant flowers are arranged in tight terminal spikes; corollas and calyces are frequently of contrasting hues. Both foliage and flowers are highly aromatic. Tolerates air pollution well.

There are many cultivars in the marketplace, mostly 18–24 in. This is a selection:

'Compacta' is well suited to low hedges. Extra-silver foliage; purple-and-violet flowers.

'Hidcote' ('Hidcote Blue') makes compact mounds; very dark purple-and-violet flowers. Slow growing; suitable for hedges.

'Irene Doyle' has especially fragrant, light purple-and-violet flowers; fall rebloom. Tolerates clipping well; good for hedges.

'Loddon Blue' has purple-blue flowers.

'Munstead' is compact with purple-and-violet flowers. Common in the nursery trade, but most plants sold under this name are seed propagated, and not uniform or true to type. Paler than 'Hidcote'. Popular for culinary use.

'Nana Alba' is exceptionally compact, with pure white flowers. 1 ft. × 2 ft.

Lavandula dentata
- violet-blue
- early summer to fall
- 2–3 ft. × 4 ft.
- sun
- Z8–10, HS

French lavender. Not a French native, but from southern and eastern Spain, northwestern Africa, Ethiopia, Israel, Jordan, and the Arabian Peninsula. The bright green, 1- to 1.5-in. leaves are velvety, deeply toothed along the edges. Short, fat spikes of pale lavender-blue flowers are topped with light purple bracts. Fragrance is strong and herbal, intermediate between typical lavender and rosemary. Evergreen, blooms almost year-round in the southern part of its range.

'Linda Ligon' has white-and-green variegated foliage; mauve flowers. Unusual for hedges.

var. *candicans* has more silvery foliage than the species.

Lavandula ×intermedia
- pale lavender
- early to midsummer
- 2–3 ft. high and wide
- sun
- Z5–8, HS

Lavandin. A hybrid group originating from crosses of *Lavandula angustifolia* and *L. latifolia*. These highly fragrant plants form shrubby mounds of gray-green, needle-like leaves with 3- to 4-in. spikes of flowers. Evergreen in mild regions. Some growers report a better tolerance to heat and humidity than most other lavenders.

Lavandula ×intermedia 'Grosso'

'**Alba**' is white flowered. 1–1.5 ft. × 1.5 ft.

'**Grappenhall**' has blue-purple flowers. Dries well. 3 ft. × 5 ft. Z5–11.

'**Grosso**'. Silver-green foliage in 2- to 3-ft. mounds. Large, plump spikes of exceptionally fragrant, lavender flowers bloom above the foliage. Valued for its oil. Z5–11.

'**Phenomenal**' makes uniform mounds of silvery foliage that does not die back in winter. Resists foliar diseases and drought. 24–32 in. high and wide. Z4–8.

'**Provence**' is particularly aromatic; light lavender flowers on upright stems. 24–36 in.

Lavandula latifolia

syn. *L. spica*
- blue, purple
- late spring to late summer

- 3 ft. × 4 ft.
- sun
- Z6–8, HS

Spike lavender, Portuguese lavender. Native to central and eastern Spain, southern France, northern Italy. Similar to English lavender, but with coarser foliage. Blue-gray flowers carried on long, spiky stems. Fragrance is more camphor-like. Valued in soap and perfume industries, and for aromatherapy.

Lavandula stoechas 'Madrid Blue'

Lavandula stoechas

- pink, purple, lavender
- late spring to summer

- 1–3 ft. high and wide
- sun
- Z8–9, HS

French lavender, Spanish lavender, topped lavender. Mediterranean basin, southern Europe, northern Africa. Narrow, gray-green, 0.5- to 1.5-in. leaves; short-stalked, dense, pineapple-like heads of tiny, blackish purple flowers, topped by a tuft of purple bracts. Exceptionally heat and drought tolerant.

'**Lemon Leigh**' is lemon scented; white flowers topped with showy yellow bracts. 20–28 in. × 18–36 in. Z7–9.

'**Madrid Blue**' has sky blue flowers accented with upright white bracts. Early and compact; perfect for containers. 1–2 ft.

'**Mulberry Ruffles**' is part of the Ruffles Series. Deep pink flowers. 2 ft.

Lavandula viridis

- yellow
- early to late summer
- 2–3 ft. high and wide

- sun
- Z8–10, HS

Yellow lavender. Mediterranean. Bright green foliage with a pine fragrance; flowers similar to *Lavandula stoechas* in form, but with creamy-yellow corollas and greenish yellow bracts. A striking contrast planted among other lavenders.

Lavatera

Malvaceae
tree mallow

Summertime trips to English gardens reveal an abundance of tree mallows, especially in larger landscapes that can accommodate these robust perennials. American gardeners, however, are only just starting to embrace these plants. Kissing cousins to hollyhocks, hibiscus, prairie mallows, and mallows, tree mallows bear similar five-petaled, open, funnel-shaped blossoms marked by a central column of joined stamens. The flowers are often accented with a darker-colored eye. The genus includes about 25 species, but few are garden-worthy perennials.

Lavateras thrive in light, sandy, moderately fertile, well-drained soil, in sites with full sun. Root rot may develop where soil drains poorly, and rust is sometimes a problem. Deer enjoy the soft young growth and the flowers. These plants are excellent at the back of perennial or mixed borders, and combine well with shrubs. Good for coastal gardens; protect from strong winds. Breeding programs have produced a number of hybrid cultivars, some of which are stunning, especially when sited carefully.

Propagate by seed, or take cuttings from young spring or early summer growth. Plants may be short lived; keep replacements on hand.

Lavatera thuringiaca

Lavatera cachemiriana

syn. *L. cachemirica*
- pink
- summer
- 4–8 ft. × 3–4 ft.
- sun
- Z4–9

Kashmir, India. Elegant and long blooming, this is a fine plant to back large borders and seldom needs staking. Softly hairy on top and downy beneath, heart-shaped leaves are rounded and lobed, to 3 in. long. Open, funnel-shaped, clear rosy pink flowers cluster in racemes in the upper leaf axils. The silky petals are deeply notched.

Lavatera thuringiaca

- rose pink
- summer
- 4–6 ft. × 5 ft.
- sun
- Z6–9

Tree mallow. Southeastern Europe. These plants need a large landscape, and do not show to best advantage when crowded. Erect stems, woody below and covered with fine gray hairs, carry long-stalked, 3.5-in., palmately lobed, heart-shaped leaves alternately along their length; basal leaves are entire. Purplish pink blooms to 3 in. across on long stalks are held singly in the leaf axils, or in loose spikes. Tolerates drought; appropriate for xeriscapes. A parent of many hybrids.

'Ice Cool' ('Peppermint Ice') has pure white flowers that may become pink tinged with age. Sensitive to mild, wet conditions in winter. Comes true from seed.

Other Notable Cultivars

Most hybrids are correctly known as *Lavatera* ×*clementii* but they are generally listed under *L. thuringiaca*. The other predominant parent is *L. olbia*. Mostly sterile.

'Barnsley', perhaps the best known of the hybrids, is named for Barnsley House, home of the

Leonurus cardiaca

late British garden designer and author Rosemary Verey. Flowers are 3–4 in. across, very light pink with a dark red-pink eye. 6–7 ft. 'Barnsley Baby' is probably a dwarf sport. 2 ft.

'Bredon Springs' has deep rose flowers with darker veins. 5–6 ft.

'Candy Floss' ('Cotton Candy') has grayish leaves, and bright pink, white-eyed flowers. 3–4 ft.

'Red Rum' blooms with magenta-red flowers on burgundy stems. Grayish, felted leaves. 4–6 ft.

'Shorty'. This dwarf has light pink flowers on 18- to 24-in. stems. Suitable for containers.

Leonurus

Lamiaceae
motherwort

Homeopathic healers around the world use this herb medicinally, especially for the treatment of heart problems. Reputedly, the plant should be harvested at the peak of its bloom, as that is when the active chemical components are most potent.

Motherwort tolerates most soils, except those that become waterlogged. It may become invasive on good soils, and is perhaps best reserved for colonizing poor or stony soils in difficult sunny spots. Let it grow into quite large stands to make a visual impact. Fine in wild gardens; grow in containers in herb and medicinal gardens. Siberian motherwort,

Lespedeza thunbergii 'Gibraltar'

Leonurus sibericus, is similar but usually grows as a biennial.

Not browsed by deer or other mammals; pollinated by bumblebees and others. Seeds are often spread by attachment to animal hair.

Propagate by seed or by division of the rhizomatous clumps,

Leonurus cardiaca

- purple
- summer to fall
- 3–5 ft. × 3 ft.
- sun, part shade
- Z3–9

Motherwort, lion's tail, heartwort. Europe, Mediterranean. Mostly sold as a medicinal herb, but it makes an attractive garden ornamental where space is not limited. Vigorous clumps of erect, square, purplish brown stems bear pairs of long-petioled, malodorous leaves, furry to the touch with soft hairs; the veins are conspicuously purple. Lower, deeply five-lobed leaves to 4 in. long, are further divided and toothed; smaller, coarsely toothed upper leaves are smooth, oblong to ovate. Clusters or whorls of two-lipped flowers nestle at the nodes; usually purple, pink, or white, the hairy upper lip is entire, the lower three lobed, often freckled with deep purple spots. Reseeds generously.

Leontopodium
Asteraceae
edelweiss

Edelweiss is a genus of 40 or so species, most of which grow wild in the mountains of Europe and Asia. One species, *Leontopodium alpinum*, is cultivated in gardens; it is the national emblem of Switzerland and Austria. The botanical name comes from the flowers' fancied resemblance to a lion's paw.

Propagate by seed sown as soon as it ripens in fall; overwinter in a cold frame or protected, unheated spot. Divide established plants in spring.

Leontopodium alpinum

- yellow
- midsummer to early fall
- 6–12 in. × 6–9 in.
- sun
- Z4–7, HS

Edelweiss. Alpine regions of southeastern and south-central Europe. It forms a mat of narrow, green leaves, felted with fine gray hairs. What appear to be individual flowers are in fact flowerheads, each composed of small, yellow disk flowers set into circles of showy white-woolly, fuzzy, petal-like bracts. Slow growing but gradually expands by rhizomes on hospitable sites. Provide very well-drained, sandy or gritty, neutral to alkaline soil; in the seeming contradiction exhibited by many alpine plants, the roots of edelweiss require regular moistening, but rot if consistently wet. A gravel topdressing speeds rain runoff from the crowns. Best adapted to cool-summer climates. Display this gem in rock gardens, alpine trough gardens, or containers.

Lespedeza
Fabaceae
bush clover

Bush clovers are known for their racemes of small pea flowers, and their ability (as do all the pea family) to fix nitrogen in root nodules and thus improve the soil. Furthermore their deep roots help to control erosion. Of perhaps 40 species, only two are of note: *Lespedeza bicolor* is an invasive shrub planted as a forage crop and for its seeds to attract quail, pheasant, and other game birds. *Lespedeza thunbergii*, Thunberg's bush clover, is a woody-based perennial that provides much-needed color to late summer and fall gardens.

Masses of pea-like flowers are borne in 6-in. racemes in the upper parts of the stems that bend under the weight of the flowers during bloom time. Where winters are mild, cut stems a few inches above ground level in early spring as new growth appears; in cold-winter regions (zones 4–6) most stems will die in winter, but new growth will emerge in midspring from the base.

Thunberg's bush clover is not fussy about soil conditions. It does well in average soils, and thrives where soil tends to be poor; withhold fertilizer as it is seldom necessary and produces soft, rank growth. Drought tolerant when established, the deep roots are difficult to move; the plants resent disturbance.

The elegant arching habit of bush clovers is best seen from below. Plant them where the stems can cascade over a stone or brick wall, boulders, or a bank. They are suitable for planting among shrubs or at the back of mixed and perennial borders, as well as in wildlife gardens where they attract butterflies and bees. Although *L. bicolor* is planted to attract deer and rabbits, *L. thunbergii* is listed on many deer-resistant plant lists and the authors have experienced no deer browsing on several plants over many years. Ornamental grasses, Japanese anemones, Russian sage, and garlic chives are good companions.

Propagate by seed (scarify) or by soft cuttings in summer; start both in pots so as to avoid root disturbance when planting out.

Lespedeza thunbergii
syn. *L. sieboldii*

- purple, pink
- late summer to early fall
- 4–6 ft. × 4–8 ft.
- sun, part shade
- Z4–8

Thunberg's bush clover. Japan, northern China. Fast-growing stems are clothed with alternate, trifoliate leaves, with oval, 1- to 2-in. leaflets. Young leaves are silky silver, with hairs. The axils of the upper leaves host racemes of bloom over a long period; the weight of the flowers causes the stems to bend creating an unforgettable waterfall of color. Allow the stems to remain through the winter for their architectural effect. Where the stems are too woody to be winter killed, prune in early spring. This underused plant deserves a much wider appreciation.

'Edo-Shibori' is an unusual Japanese selection. Bicolored pink-and-white flowers. Can train as a standard. 5–6 ft.

'Gibraltar' has purple-pink flowers. 4–6 ft.

'Pink Fountains' has an arching habit and soft pink flowers. 4–5 ft.

'Spilt Milk' ('Variegata'). Flowers are lavender, set against heavily cream-splashed leaves that provide long-term foliar interest. 4 ft.

'Spring Grove'. Compact and well suited to smaller spaces. Deep purple flowers. 3 ft. tall.

'White Fountains' has white flowers that bloom earlier than 'Albiflora'. Some consider it superior to the latter. 6 ft.

Leucanthemum ×superbum 'Broadway Lights'

Leucanthemum
Asteraceae
oxeye daisy

Although closely related to chrysanthemums and many formerly classified in that genus, the 70 or so species in the genus *Leucanthemum* differ from their better-known relatives, lacking the pungent odor common in chrysanthemums and the grayish white hairs that clothe the leaves of "mums." Additionly, they lack the broad palette of colors found in chrysanthemums—oxeye daisy flowers are almost universally white. However, as a reliable and prolific source of this invaluable hue (white is technically an absence of color), leucanthemums are unequalled among perennials. Their showy, gleaming blossoms help cool-summer gardens filled with hotter reds, oranges, and golds; they serve to separate or to transition between floral shades that would clash if placed side by side. White flowers show up particularly well in weaker evening light, and practically glow in nocturnal gardens.

Of all the leucanthemums worldwide, only one species and a race of hybrids derived from it have made it into American gardens. Oxeye daisy (*L. vulgare*) is a Eurasian native; it is almost unkillable and has escaped from cultivation to establish itself in the wild throughout North America. Its offspring is the much-loved Shasta daisy (*L. ×superbum*) created by prolific plant hybridizer Luther Burbank. His breeding program included *L. vulgare*, the English field or dog daisy, the Pyrenees daisy (*L. maximum*), Portuguese field daisy (*L. lacustre*), and the Japanese field or Montauk daisy (*Nipponanthemum nipponicum*, or *Chrysanthemum nipponicum*). Burbank named his new plants Shasta daisies. Many fine and diverse cultivars have since been created.

In general, leucanthemums are vigorous herbaceous perennials with daisy-like composite flowerheads, alternate leaves, and creeping root-stocks. All are fine cut flowers. Reliable, robust, and typically trouble free, oxeye and Shasta daisies are somewhat susceptible to verticillium wilt, leaf spots, and stem rots; they are occasionally targeted by aphids, mites, and leaf miners. Deer seldom browse them.

Propagate by seed or division.

Leucanthemum ×superbum

- white
- early to midsummer
- 8–48 in. × 12–24 in.
- sun, part shade
- Z5–8

Shasta daisy. Of hybrid origin. Alternate, glossy dark green leaves are oblanceolate to lanceolate, edged with coarse teeth. Typically flowerheads reach 2–5 in. across, with white rays surrounding a yellow disk. Bloom time lasts for about four weeks with intermittent bloom afterward; deadhead for further flowers. Best results are achieved in moist, rich, well-drained soil and full sun; provide partial shade on dry soils. Very prone to crown rot on wet or poorly drained soils. Mulch in winter with a loose blanket of evergreen boughs; avoid water-retentive mulch. Some cultivars may be hardier than zone 5, especially if drainage is perfect.

Leucanthemum vulgare

syn. *Chrysanthemum leucanthemum*
- white
- late spring to fall
- 1–3 ft. × 1–2 ft.
- sun
- Z3–8

Oxeye daisy. Native to meadows and fields, and in disturbed areas of Europe and Asia; naturalized throughout North America. Mostly unbranched stems rise from creeping, rhizomatous rootstocks. Dark green, long-petioled leaves are scalloped, obovate to spoon shaped toward the base; shorter, sessile, and shallowly lobed farther up the stems. Small flowerheads to 2 in. across have about 20 white, petal-like rays encircling a yellow disk. Spreading both by rhizomes and by seed, this species is considered weedy and invasive in many US states, particularly California, Montana, Arizona, Colorado, Tennessee, and Wyoming, where its cultivation is prohibited. Oxeye's aggressive personality makes it unwanted in borders, but ideal for informal landscapes such as cottage gardens, wild gardens, meadows and naturalized areas.

Oxeye daisy thrives in average, well-drained soils, and prefers a moderately moist environment; tolerant of dry soils and drought once established. Provide light shade in hot-summer regions; deadhead to prolong bloom. Attractive to butterflies; resists rabbits and deer.

'Maikonigin' ('May Queen') is compact, with typical 2-in., white daisy flowers.

Leucanthemum 'Becky' partners with *Echinacea* 'Kim's Knee-High'

Other Notable Cultivars

The following hybrids all have white, petal-like rays and yellow central disks unless otherwise noted.

'Aglaia' bears 3-in.-wide, frilled, double flowers. 2 ft. tall.

'Becky' displays 3- to 4-in. daisies on rigid stems that do not need staking. Mid- to late summer. 3–4 ft. Excellent, long-lasting cut flower. PPA Perennial Plant of the Year for 2003.

'Broadway Lights'. Single blooms open creamy yellow, mature to white. 18–24 in. Z6–9.

'Goldrausch' bears double, pale yellow flowers. 14 in.

'Little Miss Muffet' is compact, with 2-in., semi-double flowers. 1 ft.

'Thomas Killen' ('T. E. Killen') displays 3-in. flowers with a double row of white petals surrounding a crested, fluffy yellow center. Sturdy, 2.5-ft. stems.

Lewisia

Portulacaceae
lewisia, cliff maids

This North American genus of flowering succulents is named for the famed Meriwether Lewis, co-leader of the Lewis and Clark expedition. Lewisias are found in the wild in well-drained sites in the mountains of the northwest United States. They are much sought after, especially by alpine plant specialists who enjoy the challenge of nurturing them as much as for the beautiful flowers. Many species are very difficult to grow, but those outlined here are less temperamental. Wild populations of some species are under stress from overenthusiastic collectors and are now protected by law.

Typically, lewisias form basal rosettes of succulent, deciduous or evergreen leaves that arise from a fleshy taproot. The deciduous species, including *Lewisia rediviva* and *L. longipetala*, die back just after flowering and must remain dry while dormant, until the following spring.

Grow lewisias in rock gardens, between rock crevices, or, where the climate is unsuitable, in containers in alpine houses. They demand free-draining soil and a dry situation during the winter; quick to rot if roots remain wet. Gritty loam, lightly amended with coarse leaf mold or compost, is best for container-grown plants, and a similar mix is ideal for plants grown outdoors; pack the mix into vertical crevices and between rocks to ensure perfect drainage. Accelerate rain runoff with gravel mulch around the plant collars. Many do well with part shade, although a mostly sunny spot is usually fine.

Pests and diseases are few apart from stem rot; slugs, snails, and aphids may become a problem. Deer tolerant, but destroyed by voles.

Lewisia columbiana

- pink
- spring to summer
- 6–10 in. × 6 in.
- part shade
- Z4–8, HS

Columbian lewisia. Mountain regions of British Columbia, Washington, and Oregon. Evergreen and succulent, the leaves are linear to spatulate, to 3 in. long. Open sprays of pink-striped white or lavender to magenta, 0.5-in. flowers rise above the basal rosette.

'Rosea' has deep crimson-mauve flowers. Makes relatively large plants. 6–8 in.

Lewisia cotyledon

Lewisia cotyledon
syn. *L. finchae, L. purdyi*

- white, yellow, orange, pink
- spring to early summer
- 9–12 in. × 8 in.
- part shade
- Z3–9, HS

Cliff maids, Siskiyou lewisia. Siskiyou Mountains of Oregon and south to northern California coastal ranges. This is the most widely grown species for its ease of cultivation outside its natural range. It hybridizes freely and many selections are available. Evergreen basal rosettes of 1- to 5-in.-long, fleshy, spoon-shaped leaves give rise to thick, branching stems topped with compact clusters of brilliantly and variably colored, open, funnel-form flowers, to 1 in. across.

The **Cotyledon Hybrids Strain** comes in assorted colors; evergreen. 6–12 in.

'Little Plum' (*Lewisia longipetala* × *L. cotyledon*), a hybrid, has succulent, evergreen leaves that reportedly are rot and pest resistant. Deep carmine-flushed pink flowers. 3–4 in.

'Regenbogen' has salmon and pink flowers.

Other Notable Cultivars

Bright-Eyes has flowers in the usual colors, but with a conspicuous pale eye. 6–8 in.

Rainbow Dazzlers strain has white, yellow, orange, pink, or purple blooms. 8–10 in.

Sunset Strain produces 1-in. flowers in a range of colors from apricot and tangerine, through yellow to cream and pink. 6 in. tall.

Yellow Shades has flowers in various shades of pale lemon to gold. 8 in.

Liatris
Asteraceae
blazing star, gayfeather

Expect fireworks when you include blazing stars in your planting: the spikes of vivid flowers that shoot up from the clumps of whorled, narrow foliage are like slow-motion rockets. Natives of New World grasslands, liatris have evolved to raise their heads above their neighbors, making them wonderful accent plants for sunny borders, as well as ideal vertical punctuation in meadow or prairie plantings. The striking look and form of the flower spikes makes blazing stars a good source of cut flowers that open gradually; their display, whether in a vase or in the garden, is long lasting.

Flower spikes are composed of multiple, closely set, button-like buds that open to produce a fluffy effect. Unusually, these open from the top down; in floral displays the spent tops can be snapped out, allowing for a longer vase life.

Like so many prairie and grassland plants, liatris have the ability to cope with adverse conditions: their cormous roots withstand prolonged drought, as well as summer heat and humidity, and winter cold. They thrive on moderate to nutrient-poor soils, as long as drainage is good; not tolerant of poorly drained, wet soil, especially in wintertime. Liatris blooms attract butterflies and hummingbirds, and later the seeds provide fall food for a variety of birds. Taller species and cultivars may require staking. They resist deer, and suffer from no serious pests and diseases.

Propagate by seed sown in fall as soon as it ripens; overwinter outdoors. Dig and divide corm clumps in late winter before they break dormancy. Softwood cuttings root readily in spring.

Liatris aspera
- purple
- late summer to early fall
- 2–5 ft. × 1–1.5 ft.
- sun
- Z3–8

Rough gayfeather. Native to dryish soils in prairies, open woods, meadows, and along roads and railroad tracks throughout Eastern and Midwestern North America. This species produces basal tufts of rough, narrow, lanceolate leaves sometimes 12 in. long. Erect, leafy stalks rise from the base, topped

Liatris spicata

with long spikes of rounded, fluffy, rose-purple flowerheads, each up to 0.75 in. across. Tolerates shallow, rocky soils.

Liatris microcephala
- purple
- mid- to late summer
- 18–24 in. × 12–18 in.
- sun, part shade
- Z4–7

Dwarf blazing star. Native to southern Appalachians. Basal rosettes of grassy leaves from which emerge several 12- to 24-in. spikes of rosy-purple flowerheads. A good species for planting among boulders in rock gardens or in the foreground of sunny borders.

Liatris pycnostachya
- purple
- early to late summer
- 2–5 ft. × 1–2 ft.
- sun
- Z3–9

Prairie blazing star. Native to central and southeastern United States. This robust, grassland perennial produces clumps of narrow, lanceolate leaves, to 12 in. long; fluffy flowerheads are deep rose-purple, to 0.75 in. across; they are borne in dense terminal spikes to 20 in. long. Tolerates well-drained clay or poor soils, and summer heat and humidity. Prairie blazing star may be too large and vigorous for most borders, but it is an asset in wild and native plant gardens, naturalized areas, prairie plantings, and meadows.

Liatris scariosa
- purple
- late summer to midfall
- 2–4 ft. × 1–2 ft.
- sun
- Z3–8, HT

Blazing star. Native to rocky woods and slopes, grasslands, and gravelly streambanks from Maine, west to Wisconsin, and south to Mississippi and Georgia. Produces basal tufts of rough, narrow, ovate to lanceolate leaves, to 10 in. long; leaves become smaller as they ascend the stem. Fluffy, reddish purple flowerheads to 1 in. across top erect stems in columnar spikes, to 18 in. long. Prefers dry, sandy, or rocky soils; staking may be necessary if grown on more fertile soils. Intolerant of wet feet, especially in winter. May self-seed on favorable sites. Blazing stars are an excellent choice for borders, cottage gardens, meadow and prairie plantings, and naturalized landscapes.

Liatris spicata
syn. *L. callilepis* hort.
- purple
- midsummer to early fall
- 3–5 ft. × 2 ft.
- sun, part shade
- Z3–9, HT

Spike gayfeather, button snakeroot, dense blazing star. Native to low, moist sites throughout the eastern and southern United States. Grass-like leaves to 12 in. long are arranged in basal tufts; tall stems are topped with 6- to 12-in., terminal spikes of fluffy, mauve to deep purple flowerheads, to 0.75 in. in diameter. Spike gayfeather prefers moist, organic-rich soil, but ordinary garden soil suffices. It handles more moisture than other members of the genus; also tolerant of poor soil, heat, humidity, and drought. A favorite of the floral industry, a natural for cutting gardens, and as vertical accents in borders or damp meadows.

'Blue Bird' has blue-purple flowerheads

'Kobold' is compact, 2–2.5 ft., with deep purple flowerheads.

'Snow Queen' has white flowerheads.

Libertia

Iridaceae
libertia

These iris relatives are winter hardy in warmer zones; in colder regions they make excellent container plants that can overwinter indoors and be set out to decorate late spring and summer gardens. Most libertias are native to damp, grassy scrubland of New Zealand and Australasia, but some hail from Chile and other temperate parts of South America.

Arising from short rhizomatous roots, libertias' evergreen, slender, and grass-like leaves grow in two overlapping ranks or fans, forming thick clumps. The leaves are often colorful, some are exotically striped. Attractive blooms are borne in loose sprays that cluster into panicles. The saucer-like flowers consist of a double ring of three petal-like structures (tepals); sometimes the outer ring is greenish. Colorful orange, yellow, or black seeds follow.

Libertias are great additions to beds and borders, and provide a structural foil for rounded sedums, phlox, daisies, and other perennials both in and out of bloom. In containers they fill the role of "thrillers" and can be assorted with lower, more rounded "fillers"—geraniums, salvias, and osteospermum—along with trailing "spillers" such as *Origanum* 'Kent Beauty'. In rock gardens libertias bring a change of height to the usual display of low "bun" plants and creepers.

Provide a sunny or partly sunny spot for these beauties. Soil should drain well, but retain moisture, enriched with compost. Mulch in winter where marginally hardy, or bring containers indoors to a cool, frost-free spot. The woody rhizomes resent disturbance, so when planting libertias set them into what will be their permanent home. Libertias are not successful in hot gardens, except where humidity is low, as in California. Seldom browsed by deer; susceptible to slug and snail damage.

Divide clumps in spring or start from seed; seedlings take two to three years to reach blooming size.

Libertia formosa

syn. *L. chilensis*

- white
- late spring to midsummer
- 2–3 ft. × 2 ft.
- sun, part shade
- Z7–11, HS

Showy libertia, snowy mermaid. Chile. Dense tufts of stiff, wide, leathery, 0.5-in. × 12- to 18-in. leaves. Strong scapes lift 1-ft.-long inflorescences, composed of dense clusters of 0.75-in. flowers, above the foliage mass. Long blooming. Prefers acid soil. This species has escaped in the San Francisco Bay area. Attracts butterflies, bees, and birds. Good for rock gardens.

Libertia ixioides

- white
- late spring to early summer
- 1–2 ft. × 2 ft.
- sun, part shade
- Z8–11, HS

New Zealand iris, mikoikoi, tukauki. New Zealand. This clump-forming perennial provides structure and texture to gardens. The slender, grassy leaves are arranged in a fan, and are bronze, green, or chocolate-brown, paler along the midrib. Umbel-like clusters of two to nine white flowers form large substantial panicles of bloom among the foliage. Flowers may reach 1 in. across with white inner tepals and brownish green outer ones. Seedpods are yellow with orange seeds.

'Sunset Blaze' has fans of burgundy, orange, and gold leaves. Flowers held just above the foliage. 18–24 in. Z7–11.

'Taupo Blaze' is a selection of 'Taupo Sunset'. Red-and-copper-colored leaves, greenish at the base especially in summer. Flowers held just above the leaves. Yellow-orange seedpods. 18 in. Z8–11.

'Taupo Sunset' produces its white flowers in summer. Stiff, grass-like leaves are striped with green, yellow, orange, purplish red, and bronze—hence its name. Excellent beside a pool or in mixed borders. 2 ft. Z7–11.

Other Notable Cultivars

'Amazing Grace' is easy. Olive-green to bronze leaves. Airy sprays of white flowers. 30 in. Z7–11.

'Tricolor'. Olive leaves striped with cream; often turns reddish in cold weather. White flowers. 8–18 in. × 24 in. Z7–11.

Ligularia

Asteraceae
leopard plant, golden groundsel

These statuesque, dramatic plants are especially well suited to damp, partly shaded sites, such as rain gardens and watersides. They develop large clumps of rounded, heart-shaped, or arrowhead-shaped leaves, often held on dark stems. Several are grown especially for their amazing foliage; others also have attractive floral displays.

These water-loving plants demand soil that remains moist constantly, preferably enriched with humus or compost; avoid standing them in water. Ligularias are extremely sensitive to hot sun, even when the roots are damp; on sunny days, the large leaves often droop like elephant ears, only to recover at dusk. This is stressful for the plant. Select a growing spot with protection from noonday sun, ideally with light, dappled shade. Apply organic mulch to help retain moisture during the summer.

Good companions for ligularias (especially in deer country) include cinnamon and ostrich ferns, water irises, cardinal flower, and snakeroot. Boggy areas and open woodlands are ideal places for ligularias; shady north-facing beds and borders are appropriate if irrigation is available. Smaller sorts are ideal for the margins of miniature water gardens.

The conditions favored by ligularias are also ideal for slugs and snails that attack the young growth, disfiguring the foliage badly. Otherwise serious pests or diseases are few. All species resist deer browsing.

Sow seed in spring or fall; divide species and selections before bloom in spring or after flowering.

Ligularia dentata
syn. *Senecio clivorum*
- orange
- early to midsummer
- 3–4 ft. × 3 ft.
- part shade
- Z3–8

Leopard plant, big leaf ligularia. China, Japan. Basal clumps of long-stalked, leathery foliage is the main attraction of this plant. Dark green and coarsely toothed leaves, to 1 ft. long. Thick, fibrous stems carry loose clusters of untidy, yellow-orange, 3-in. daisy flowers. Largely replaced by superior cultivars.

'Britt-Marie Crawford'. Shiny, kidney-shaped leaves of blackest purple, to 7 in. long. Yellow-orange flowers rise above the foliage mass. More sun tolerant than some. 2–3 ft. Z4–8.

'Dark Beauty'. Very deep purple leaves on purple stems. Gold flowers. 3–4 ft. Z3–8.

'Desdemona'. Serrated, kidney-shaped leaves are red, but mature to green with persistent purple undersides. Purple-stemmed, ragged, yellow-orange daisies. 2–3 ft. Z3–8. 'Othello' is similar.

Ligularia przewalskii
syn. *Senecio przewalskii*
- yellow
- mid- to late summer
- 5–6 ft. × 3 ft.
- part shade
- Z4–8

Shavalski's ligularia. Northern China. Black stems clothed with triangular, palmately lobed, 12-in.-long leaves, deeply and irregularly cut. Narrow, loose racemes of yellow flowerheads rise on dark greenish purple stems.

'Dragon's Breath'. Exotic-looking clumps of very deeply cut, dark leaves. Spikes of bright yellow flowers on purple stems, early. 24–30 in. Z4–9.

Ligularia stenophylla
- yellow
- early to late summer
- 4–5 ft. × 5 ft.
- part shade
- Z5–8

Narrow-spiked ligularia. Northern China, Japan. This species is similar to *Ligularia przewalskii*, but has heart-shaped leaves and paler stems. Tall, slender racemes of few-rayed, yellow flowerheads, to 1.5 in. across.

'Chinese Dragon' has bold, deeply cut leaves, serrated along the edges. Clusters of few-rayed yellow flowers top each stem. Very attractive to butterflies. 3–4 ft. Z4–8.

Ligularia dentata 'Britt-Marie Crawford'

Ligularia stenocephala 'The Rocket'

Limonium perezii

'**Little Rocket'** is a dwarf form of 'The Rocket'. Slender racemes of yellow flowers. Late summer. 3–4 ft. Z4–8.

'**The Rocket'.** Early summer spikes 18–24 in. long held above the mass of dark green, jagged-edged leaves on black stems. 4–5 ft. Z5–8.

Other Notable Cultivars

'**Gregynog Gold'** (*Ligularia dentata* × *L. veitchiana*). Substantial green, heart-shaped leaves, rimmed with sharp teeth. Broadly conical clusters of orange daisies. 4–6 ft. Z4–9.

'**Last Dance'** is compact with bold, heart-shaped, dark green foliage beneath loose clusters of dark-centered yellow daisies. The last to bloom. 12–18 in. Z4–8.

'**Osiris Café Noir'** has thick, serrated olive, purple, or brown leaves topped by yellow daisy flowers. Introduced by Serge Fafard. Z4–8.

'**Osiris Fantaisie'.** Clumps of rubbery, dark green, heart-shaped leaves with undulating jagged edges, on purple stems; undersides are burgundy. Sturdy

branching stems hold 2- to 3-in., double, deep yellow daisies just above. Mid- to late summer. 2–3 ft. Z3–8.

Limonium
Plumbaginaceae
statice, sea lavender

Best known as a source of cut flowers, this genus is an obvious choice for cutting gardens but can also serve as a useful source of summertime color in perennial borders.

Many species of statice originated in coastal habits and their tolerance for salt, wind, and sandy soils make them well adapted to seaside gardens and other exposed sites with poor, saline, or alkaline soils.

Do not crowd plants and ensure good air circulation to minimize susceptibility to crown and root rot. Seldom attacked by pests and diseases, including deer. The flowers retain their form and color when dried.

Limonium perezii

syn. *Statice perezii*

- purple
- spring to summer
- 3 ft. × 2 ft.
- sun
- Z9–10

Perez's sea lavender. Canary Islands. Tough perennial herb arising from woody rhizomes. Oval to round leaves to 12 in. long are borne in basal rosettes; bushy panicles of white flowers with lavender sepals. Naturalized on beaches and roadside areas of coastal southern California but striking when massed in beds, on banks, or as accents among bold-leaved tropicals. Reliable for seaside plantings, and good for containers.

Limonium platyphyllum

syn. *L. latifolium, Statice latifolia*

- blue
- early to midsummer
- 2–2.5 ft. high and
  wide
- sun
- Z3–10

Sea lavender, perennial statice. Southeastern and central Europe. Basal rosettes of oblong-elliptic, leathery, deep green leaves to 10 in. long; tiny, lavender-blue flowers bloom in rounded, cloud-like panicles atop wiry stems. Flourishes on well-drained, average garden soil but tolerates droughty, rocky, and shallow soils too. May self-seed.

Linaria

Plantaginaceae
toadflax

This genus includes roughly 100 species, including a few that are garden worthy and not aggressive. On the other hand it has contributed some seriously invasive species to the North American landscape. Linarias hail from southern Europe, inhabiting chiefly dry, sunny sites often with very poor soil where they tend to seed about freely. These characteristics are problematic in enabling yellow toadflax (butter-and-eggs, *Linaria vulgaris*) to spread along roadsides and in waste places almost everywhere in North America; the yellow-flowered Dalmatian toadflax, *L. dalmatica*, has become a serious weed in Washington, Idaho, Utah, and Arizona where it crowds out native species.

Typically linaria produces upright branching stems, clothed with linear to lance-shaped, often grayish green leaves. Toadflax flowers are spurred and two-lipped, and are borne abundantly in most colors of the rainbow. Though short-lived perennials, the garden toadflaxes are easily lifted as seedlings for replanting wherever needed to fill a gap. In warmer regions they are generally treated as winter annuals.

Toadflaxes prefer sunny sites with average but sandy soil. Drainage must be good to avoid root and stem rot. Drought and deer tolerant, these charming plants are appropriate for cottage gardens, for grouping in beds and borders, or lining out along pathways. They make good filler for containers, and the flowers attract pollinating insects including bees and butterflies, so they are well suited to wildlife gardens and meadow plantings too. Combine with more substantial plants such as Shasta daisies, sneezeweed, and summer phlox.

Propagate by seed.

Linaria alpina

- violet-and-yellow
- summer
- 4–8 in. × 6 in.
- sun
- Z4–8

Alpine toadflax. Native to mountainous regions of southern and central Europe. Often grown as an annual, this species is fully perennial but may burn out in hot summer regions. The linear leaves are blue-green arranged in whorls or alternately on trailing stems. Best in well-drained rock gardens, these diminutive plants are colorful all summer long with spurred bicolored or all pink, white, or yellow blooms.

Linaria purpurea

- purple
- early summer to fall
- 1.5–3 ft. × 1 ft.
- sun, part shade
- Z5–9

Purple toadflax. Sicily, central and southern Italy. This beautiful clump-forming self-seeder is a boon to gardeners who may have holes to fill in their summer flowerbeds; transplant small plants only. Long spikes of 0.3-in., purple or lilac flowers top erect stems clothed with slender, gray-green foliage, a perfect foil for the blooms. Cut back after the first flush to reduce self-seeding and to encourage further flowers.

'Canon J. Went' has pale pink flowers. Comes true from seed.

'Springside White' is white flowered.

Linaria triornithophora

- purple, yellow
- late spring to fall
- 3–4 ft. × 1 ft.
- sun, part shade
- Z6–9

Three-birds-flying. Spain, Portugal. This toadflax, with its appealing common name, makes mounds of blue-green leaves borne in whorls on erect, branching stems. In season, the foliage mounds are crowned with flocks of bird-like, 2-in. flowers with long, tail-like spurs, grouped in threes. The blossoms vary in color and are often two toned. Best in rich, well-drained soil. Often grown as a summer annual north of its area of hardiness.

'Pink Birds' may be hard to find. It has soft pink flowers on 18-in. stems.

Linum
Linaceae
perennial flax

Common flax (*Linum usitatissimum*), the source of linen and of flax seed, is the best-known member of this genus, which also includes some garden-worthy perennial species. Perennial flax are long blooming, and supply some of the garden's most vivid blues. Individual blooms open early on sunny days but often are spent by late afternoon. Flax prefers lean, well-drained soils. They may self-seed.

Propagate by seed, by cuttings of young basal shoots in spring, or divide mature plants.

Linum flavum
- yellow
- summer
- 10–12 in. × 8–12 in.
- sun
- Z5–7

Golden flax, yellow flax. Native to central and southern Europe. Upright clumps, sometimes woody at the base, are clothed with dark, spoon-shaped foliage. Funnel-shaped, upward-facing, bright yellow flowers to 1 in. across are arranged in dense terminal cymes.

'Compactum' is only 6 in. tall.

Linum lewisii
syn. *L. perenne* subsp. *lewisii*
- blue
- late spring to early summer
- 12–24 in. × 8–12 in.
- sun
- Z3–9

Prairie flax, Lewis's blue flax, western blue flax. Native to grasslands, meadows, and disturbed soils throughout the United States west of the Mississippi River. Species named for its discoverer, Meriwether Lewis, co-leader of the Lewis and Clark Expedition. This short-lived native bears needle-like, blue-green leaves and five-petaled, 2-in.-wide, sky-blue flowers that open fully only on sunny days. Deer tolerant, but slugs, snails, and aphids may be troublesome; attracts butterflies. Susceptible to stem rot, rust, damping off, and other fungal and bacterial problems. Appropriate in dry, sunny meadows, prairie and perennial plantings, open woodlands, rock gardens, and containers.

Linum narbonense
- blue
- late spring to early summer
- 18–24 in. × 15–18 in.
- sun, part shade
- Z5–9

Spanish blue flax. Native to northern Spain. Narrow, gray-green leaves arranged in whorls around the stems, topped by cymes of about ten saucer-shaped, five-petaled, 1-in., sky blue flowers accented with white eyes. Supposedly longer lived than more common *Linum perenne*. Ideal along paths, among rocks on sunny slopes, and in dry gardens.

Linum lewisii

'Heavenly Blue' has deep blue, white-eyed flowers. 18 in.

Linum perenne
- blue
- late spring to early summer
- 1–2 ft. × 9–18 in.
- sun, part shade
- Z5–8

Perennial flax, blue flax, perennial blue flax. Europe, temperate Asia. Short-lived, tufted perennial with wiry stems and narrow, linear leaves to 1 in. long. Funnel-shaped, sky blue flowers, borne prolifically for eight weeks or more, are five-petaled, to 0.75 in. across. Tolerates dry, shallow, and rocky soils; naturalizes where conditions are suitable. Mass for best displays in rock gardens, meadows, and herb gardens.

'Appar' has outstanding vigor, a long season of bloom, and is a strong reseeder that mixes well with grasses and other wildflowers in erosion control mixes.

'Nanum Diamond' shows off clean white flowers. 10–12 in.

'Nanum Sapphire' bears bright blue flowers on 8–10 in. stalks.

Liriope muscari 'Variegata'

Liriope
Asparagaceae
lilyturf, monkey grass

Problem solvers rather than garden stars, the lily-turfs nevertheless can be attractive when used in the right spot and the right way. These low, grass-like plants from eastern Asia combine glossy foliage with grape hyacinth–like spikes of late-summer flowers in purples, blues, or white. Evergreen in hot and humid climates, but elsewhere foliage browns—refresh by mowing on a high setting in early spring.

Lilyturfs prefer moist, fertile soils in part shade but will grow in any average, well-drained soils, in full sun. Tolerates heat, humidity, and drought and air pollution; resistant to rabbits, but susceptible to slugs and snails. Deer resistance is spotty; reports stating that deer devour liriope are countered by others reporting no damage at all.

Lilyturfs have a naturally neat, almost dapper, appearance that makes them perfect for edging paths or beds in formal landscapes, as well as a handsome and durable groundcover. Has proven invasive in parts of the southeastern United States.

Propagate by division.

Liriope muscari
- lavender
- late summer
- 12–18 in. × 9–12 in.
- sun, part shade
- Z6–10

Lilyturf. China, Taiwan, Japan. Tuberous rooted, forms slowly expanding clumps of strap-like, arching, glossy dark green leaves to 1 in. wide. Erect spikes with tiered whorls of violet-purple flowers similar to those of grape hyacinths emerge above foliage in late summer. Persistent black berries follow. Survives in sheltered locations in zone 5.

'Big Blue' has 15- to 18-in.-long leaves; violet flowers.

'Monroe White' has white flowers.

'Pee Dee Gold Ingot' produces yellow young foliage that deepens to gold or chartreuse, holding color year-round. Lavender flowers.

'Silvery Sunproof' has green-and-white-striped foliage; lavender flowers. More sun tolerant than other cultivars.

'Variegata' has green-and-white-striped leaves; lavender flowers.

Liriope spicata
- blue, white
- late summer
- 9–18 in. × 1–2 ft.
- sun, part shade
- Z4–10

Lilyturf. China, Vietnam. Forms grass-like clumps of narrow, arching, glossy dark green leaves to 0.25 in. wide; erect spikes of small, pale lavender to white flowers borne among the leaves; blackish berries follow. Spreads quickly by underground rhizomes and can be aggressive. Outstanding as a groundcover under shallow-rooted trees, along streams and ponds, and for stabilizing soil on erosion-prone banks and slopes.

'Silver Dragon' has leaves striped with green-and-silver-white; pale purple flowers; whitish green berries.

Lithodora
Boraginaceae
lithodora

The brilliant blue-flowered lithodoras are somewhat fussy and do best in the mild, maritime climate of the Pacific Northwest. However, given good conditions they grace many an alpine house, raised bed, trough, or rock garden elsewhere, and they can also serve as low-maintenance groundcovers. The plants are somewhat woody subshrubs, low growing or even prostrate, sometimes trailing.

Lithodoras demand very well-drained, neutral to alkaline soil, easy to achieve with a top-dressing of lime chips around the crown. Under less than ideal conditions, branches may begin to blacken and die back; cut out damaged material. Even apparently thriving plants may die out in the center; replant with young plugs. Prune after bloom time annually to maintain vigor and control sprawling stems. The roots resent disturbance (buy container-grown plants), but if necessary should be moved during dormancy, when ground is not frozen; bare-root plants are seldom successful. Salt, deer, and drought tolerant. No serious pests and diseases.

Propagate by taking half-ripe cuttings preferably with a "heel" in summer. Seeds are slow and must be soaked or scarified prior to spring sowing.

Lithodora diffusa
syn. *Lithospermum diffusum*
- blue
- late spring to summer
- 4–8 in. × 18 in.
- sun
- Z5–7, HS

Indian plant, trailing lithodora. Southern and western Europe. An evergreen, ground-hugging subshrub, with alternate, hairy, narrowly oval leaves to 1.5 in. long. Terminal and axillary clusters of funnel-shaped, 0.5-in., brilliant blue flowers cover the plants for several weeks. Intolerant of high heat and humidity. Susceptible to freeze burn if temperatures plummet. One of only a few perennials with truly blue flowers.

'Grace Ward' has terminal clusters of azure blue flowers on trailing plants. Good for containers.

'Heavenly Blue' has deep azure flowers. Provide compost-rich, acid soil.

'White Star' has blue flowers with conspicuous white centers.

Lobelia
Campanulaceae
lobelia

Although best known for the ubiquitous annual trailing lobelia, this genus includes several outstanding perennial species and hybrids too. These North American natives are adapted to moist and wet soils, but will flourish in an average, organic-enriched garden soil, if irrigated conscientiously. These lobelias offer a combination of upright growth and bright flowers that make them very effective punctuation points in native plant gardens, mixed borders, and wild gardens; they spread to make bold statements in wet soils beside ponds and streams, or in bog gardens. Rabbit resistant but not reliably deer resistant, they attract butterflies and hummingbirds; excellent as cut flowers.

Propagate by seed, division, or cuttings taken in midsummer.

Lobelia cardinalis
- red
- mid- to late summer
- 2–4 ft. × 1–2 ft.
- sun, part shade
- Z3–9

Cardinal flower. North America, from southeastern Canada through the eastern and southwestern

Lithodora diffusa 'Grace Ward'

United States, Mexico, and Central America to northern Colombia. Clumps of upright stems clothed with dark green, finely toothed, lanceolate leaves to 4 in. long; stems are topped with spikes of bright red, 1- to 2-in.-long, tubular flowers. These are two lipped; the three lower-lip lobes are more prominent than the two lobes of the upper lip. Somewhat short lived, but reseed readily where conditions are favorable, typically along streams, wooded bottomlands, and swamps. Supply midday shade in hot and humid regions.

'Alba' has white flowers.

'Angel Song' has salmon-and-cream flowers.

'Fried Green Tomatoes' has purple young leaves that age to green with purple highlights; tomato-red flowers.

'Queen Victoria' (syn. *Lobelia fulgida* or *L. fulgens* 'Queen Victoria') has burgundy to dark purple foliage; red flowers.

'Ruby Slippers' has dark ruby-red flowers. Z4.

'Twilight Zone' is pink flowered.

Lobelia siphilitica
- blue, white
- mid- to late summer
- 12–36 in. × 12–18 in.
- sun, part shade
- Z4–9

Great blue lobelia. Wet locations and low wooded areas in Missouri. Similar to cardinal flower but with light green leaves to 5 in., and variably light to dark blue flowers. The botanical name recalls a former use of this plant as a treatment for venereal disease; it has a long history of medicinal use. Longer lived than *Lobelia cardinalis*. Self-seeds in hospitable sites.

'Alba' has white flowers.

'Lilac Candles' is compact, to 18 in., with lilac flowers.

Lobelia cardinalis

Lunaria rediviva

Other Notable Cultivars

The following all bloom in late summer. Z3–8.

'**Dark Crusader**' has deep purplish foliage; magenta-purple flowers. 3 ft.

'**Gladys Lindley**' is white flowered. To 4 ft. tall.

'**Red Beauty**' has pinkish red flowers. 2–3 ft.

×*speciosa* '**Vedrariensis**' has red-tinged foliage; bright purple flowers. 2–4 ft. tall

Lunaria

Brassicaceae

honesty, silver dollar plant

The name "lunaria" derives from "*luna*," the Latin word for moon, inspired by the glistening seedpods (or silicules) that honesty bears. Although there are three species in the genus, only biennial honesty, also known as silver dollar plant, actually has round, truly "moon-like" seedpods. When the pods ripen, the seeds are shed, leaving their papery membrane intact.

Honesty prefers an organic-rich soil that drains well, and a sunny to partly shaded position. Full sun is fine in regions with low light, but where sunlight is intense noonday shade is beneficial. Pests and diseases are infrequent although stem rot may be a problem where drainage is poor. Occasionally browsed by deer.

A useful addition to informal beds and borders, bright woodland gardens, and naturalized semi-wild areas, honesty is perhaps most valuable as a dried cut flower. It is perfect in winter arrangements and does not shatter easily. Cut when the seedpods are green.

Propagate by seed or allow existing plants to self-seed.

Lunaria annua

- purple
- spring
- 2–3 ft. × 2 ft.
- part shade
- Z4–8

Honesty. Europe. In spite of its specific epithet, "*annua*," honesty is actually biennial and seeds about so readily that it appears to be perennial. Alternate, heart-shaped, coarsely toothed leaves clothe upright stems. Flower petals, arranged in a cross, are usually in shades of purple, although they vary and often white-flowered plants appear. Circular, 2-in. seedpods follow.

'**Alba**' is white flowered.

'**Variegata**' has purple or sometimes white flowers; leaves irregularly rimmed with white.

Lunaria rediviva

- pale lilac
- late spring to early summer
- 2–3 ft. × 2 ft.
- sun, part shade
- Z5–8

Perennial honesty. Native to mountain areas of central Europe, western Siberia, the Baltic states, and Scandinavia. Erect and hairy, branching stems carry mid-green, finely serrated, triangular, 8-in.-long leaves, sometimes tinged with maroon. Fragrant, 1-in., pale lilac or whitish flowers with a lilac blush are arranged in loose racemes, sometimes 7 in. long. The flat, white, 2- to 3-in.-long seedpods that follow are elliptical and translucent; they become light tan at maturity.

Lupinus

Fabaceae
lupine, lupin

The name lupine derives from the Latin word for "wolf," recalling an old-time belief that these plants devoured the richness of a soil. In fact, the opposite is true: lupines are found mostly on poor, sandy soils, but their roots have the ability to convert atmospheric nitrogen into plant nutrients. This trait is common to pea family members.

These desirable, though often short lived, perennials, combine handsome, typically fingered, palmately divided leaves with spires of colorful, pea-type flowers. The species are best grown on loose, very well-drained, lean soils similar to those of their native habitats. The showier and somewhat longer-lived garden hybrids, however, perform best on humus-rich, moderately fertile, well-drained soils. Avoid excessive fertility, which when combined with winter wet is likely to prove fatal.

In addition to perennial species, *Lupinus* includes some annuals (notably Texas bluebonnet) and shrubs. The perennial hybrids are ideal for creating rhythms of late spring color and texture, providing a pleasant contrast to bulbs or other perennials; the dense foliage remains attractive all season. The species are better suited to meadow or prairie plantings—care should be taken, however, to keep them out of pastures as they are toxic to grazing animals. Lupines are not trouble free, though the reward is worth the extra effort. In wetter climates, they are prone to slugs and snails when young, and susceptible to powdery mildew and aphids as well; serious infestations should be dealt with by cutting plants back almost to the ground. Stake taller types. Attracts butterflies; deer resistant.

Propagation by seed is most successful: scarify seeds and soak overnight before sowing.

Lupinus arboreus

- yellow, blue
- late spring to early summer
- 3–5 ft. high and wide
- sun, part shade
- Z8–10

Bush lupine, tree lupine. Western North America. Fast-growing, semi-evergreen, shrubby perennial with palmate leaves and erect, 10-in. racemes of fragrant, yellow flowers. Drought resistant; excellent for dry and coastal gardens. A parent of many garden hybrids.

Lupinus perennis

- blue, purple
- late spring
- 1–2 ft. × 1 ft.
- sun
- Z3–8

Sundial lupine, wild lupine. Maine to Florida. Dense mounds of palmately divided leaves, each with seven to eleven leaflets, to 2 in. long. Terminal, 8-in. racemes of light blue to purplish flowers; 2-in., bean-like, seed-filled pods follow. Flourishes on sandy, nutrient-poor and drought-prone soils; dislikes clays and loams.

Lupinus polyphyllus

- blue, purple, reddish, white
- late spring to early summer
- 3–5 ft. × 2–2.5 ft.
- sun
- Z4–7, HS

Bigleaf lupine. Western North America. Robust, with bold, rich green, palmate leaves each with 5 to 18 leaflets to 6 in. long, and imposing 12- to 28-in.-long racemes of 0.5-in. flowers on mostly unbranched stems. Has escaped gardens to become a troublesome weed in pastureland in the upper midwest and northeastern United States. Best adapted to regions with cool summers. A parent of many garden hybrids.

Other Notable Cultivars

'Chandelier' has yellow flowers; repeat blooms if deadheaded. 40 in. × 18–24 in. Z4–8.

'Chatelaine' has dense racemes of bicolored, pink-and-white flowers on 3- to 4-ft. stems. Z3–7.

Gallery Strain is compact, 15–18 in., with white, blue, pink, red, and yellow flowers. Z3–7.

'My Castle' has fragrant, scarlet flowers: repeats if deadheaded. 40 in. × 18–24 in. Z4–8.

Russell Hybrids bear spikes of flowers in shades of pink, red, yellow, blue, and white, often bicolored, in early and midsummer. 2.5–3 ft. × 1–1.5 ft. Z4–8.

Tutti Fritti Mix, possibly superior to Russell hybrids, has large robust flower spikes in a range of bicolors. 3–3.25 ft.

Lychnis

Caryophyllaceae
campion, catchfly

This genus of about 20 species is closely related to *Silene* and *Agrostemma*, but over the years there has been considerable nomenclatural confusion. Nonetheless these usually short-lived perennials provide plenty of color, and are easy to grow.

Campions grow best in sun or partly sunny spots where soil is average to moderately fertile. Drainage must be excellent for gray-leaved species but otherwise a dressing of moisture-retaining compost is appreciated. Deadhead to extend bloom time. Erect and sticky, branched stems bear pairs of clammy leaves at swollen nodes. The funnel- or star-shaped flowers have five brightly colored petals, centered with five styles, and followed by five-toothed seed capsules. These are major points of difference from *Silene*. Cut stems halfway back after blooming to encourage a further crop of flowers. Deadhead to prevent self-seeding.

Lychnis has an interesting history. The name comes from *lychnos*, the Greek word for "lamp" derived from the usage of furry, felted rose campion (*L. coronaria*) leaves for lamp wicks. The popular Maltese cross (*L. chalcedonica*) was grown by Thomas Jefferson at Monticello and was popular among gardeners of the day.

Campions are susceptible to few pests and diseases, except slugs and snails, and resist rabbits and deer. They are larval food and nectar plants for several species of butterflies.

Plant small species to adorn rock gardens and crevice gardens; larger ones are suitable for wild and wildlife gardens, cutting gardens, beds and borders, and between low shrubs.

Start from seed in spring, barely covering them; early seeding may result in bloom the same year. Divide clumps in sprig or fall.

Lychnis alpina

- pink
- spring
- 4–6 in. × 6 in.
- sun, part shade
- Z4–7

Alpine campion, alpine catchfly. Sub-arctic and mountainous areas of the Northern Hemisphere. Low tufts of dark green, lanceolate, 1.5-in. leaves, from which rise short stems topped with clusters of bright pink, 0.75-in. flowers, with frilled, bi-lobed petals. Deadhead to extend bloom time. Appropriate for troughs, rock gardens, and crevices between pavers or flagstones.

Lychnis ×*arkwrightii*

syn. *L. chalcedonica* × *L. haageana*

- orange
- late spring to summer
- 15–18 in. × 12 in.
- sun
- Z5–8

Arkwright's catchfly. This short-lived hybrid has dark, hairy stems clothed with pairs of maroon-flushed green leaves. The 1.5-in., star-shaped flowers have notched petals, and are arranged in flat-topped clusters.

'Orange Dwarf' ('Orange Zwerg') has bronzy foliage that contrasts well with the brilliant orange-red flowers. 8–12 in. Z5–8.

'Vesuvius' has screaming orange flowers. 18–24 in. Z3–10.

Lychnis flos-cuculi 'Jenny'

Lychnis chalcedonica
syn. *Silene chalcedonica*
- scarlet
- summer
- 2–3.5 ft. × 1.5 ft.
- sun
- Z3–10, HS

Maltese cross, Jerusalem cross, scarlet lightning. Native to European regions of Russia, Mongolia, and northwestern China. This old-fashioned cottage garden favorite makes clumps of upright, sticky, unbranched stems that carry pairs of clasping, ovate leaves, toothed along the edges, 2–4 in. long. Dense, terminal, umbel-like heads of flowers composed of numerous star-shaped, orange-red, 0.5- to 1-in. blooms, each with deeply notched petals. Plants are long lived and very hardy, but not in high heat and humidity. Attracts butterflies and hummingbirds. If soil is rich, staking may be necessary; insert twiggy stems (pea sticks) early when shoots are about 6–8 in. Deadhead to discourage self-seeding. *Artemisia* 'Powis Castle' and silvery ornamental grasses make good companions. Mass among shrubs or in deep borders, or group in beds. Good cut flower.

'Alba' has pure white flowers.

'Alba Plena' has double, white flowers.

'Dusky Salmon' has light salmon-pink blooms. Possibly a synonym for 'Carnea' and 'Morgenrot'.

'Flore Plena' has double, scarlet flowers. May be brighter than the species, and the double flowers pack more punch.

Lychnis coronaria
syn. *Agrostemma coronaria*
- cerise
- late spring to early summer
- 1.5–2.5 ft. × 1.5 ft.
- sun, part shade
- Z3–9

Rose campion, mullein pink, dusty miller. Native to southeastern Europe, this easy and showy perennial makes spreading mats of woolly, silvery leaves. These are about 4 in. long, ovate, on short petioles; opposite stem leaves are smaller. Branched stems are topped with solitary, wheel-shaped, cerise flowers, about 1 in. across. Short lived but self-seeds freely; deadhead routinely. Demands very good drainage; root rot may result from poor drainage. Drought tolerant, and suitable for dry gardens, as well as beds, borders, and wildlife gardens. Sometimes used for edging.

'Abbotswood Rose' has 2-in.-wide, electric pink flowers over woolly, silver-gray foliage.

'Alba' is white flowered.

'Atrosanguinea' ('Bloody William') has gaudy purplish scarlet flowers above silver foliage mats. More or less sterile resulting in lack of seeds.

'Gardener's World' ('Blych', syn. *Coronaria tomentosa*) has fully double, 1.5-in., deep red flowers. Sterile, thus does not seed about. Long blooming. 2 ft. tall.

'Oculata' has white flowers centered with a spreading fuchsia eye. Z4–9.

Lychnis flos-cuculi
- pink, white
- late spring to early summer
- 12–24 in. × 12 in.
- sun, part shade
- Z3–7

Ragged robin. Damp meadows of Europe, Caucasus, Russia. Low mats of grassy, bluish green, basal foliage. Loose, branched, umbel-like clusters of star-shaped magenta or sometimes white flowers. These are 1.5 in. across and shaggy looking, with double, deeply notched petals. Attracts pollinating butterflies and bees. Drought tolerant. Deadhead to curtail self-seeding.

'Alba' produces white flowers in early summer. 12–15 in.

'Jenny' ('Nana') is double flowered with shaggy, pale lavender-pink blooms. Good for rock gardens, front of the border, for cutting, and in containers. 8–12 in. tall.

Lychnis viscaria
syn. *Viscaria vulgaris*
- magenta
- early to midsummer
- 12–18 in. × 14–16 in.
- sun, part shade
- Z3–7

German catchfly, sticky catchfly. Sandy meadows and dry clearings and roadsides from Europe to western Asia. Evergreen tufts of broadly oblong basal leaves, 3 in. long and without hairs. Stems sticky with glandular hairs rise above the foliage, and bear slender spike-like clusters of three to five bright magenta flowers with notched petals, about 0.75 in. across. Drought tolerant. Long blooming; attracts butterflies and hummingbirds. Self-seeds. Suitable for lining paths, for rock gardens, or as a groundcover; also good for cutting.

'Alba' (White Cockle) has white flowers.

'Fire' ('Feuer') has orange-pink flowers, some double. Protect from intense sun. 18 in. Z3–8.

'Passion' ('Splendens Plena', 'Flore-Plena') has double, hot-pink flowers.

Lysichiton
Araceae
skunk cabbage, swamp lantern

These remarkable plants deserve a more flattering common name; if they had one they'd undoubtedly play a larger role in our gardens. Lysichitons are botanically distinct from the skunk cabbage found in eastern North American wetlands (*Symplocarpus foetidus*), although their flowers share the bold foliage and fetid odor of that plant; the aroma attracts pollinating flies and beetles.

Lysichiton blooms resemble those of related Jack-in-the-pulpit, and consist of a central spadix, a finger-like upright stem covered with tiny flowers, partially enclosed by a spathe, or hooded bract. Both species require humus-rich, continually moist soils, and suffer no serious pest problems (including deer), except slugs. They fit well in bog gardens or planted along the margin of ponds or streams; excellent choices for rain gardens.

Propagate by seed direct sown in summer or fall, or moist-chilled and started indoors in early spring. Remove and replant small offsets from mature plants in summer. Naturalizes over time on hospitable sites.

Lysichiton americanus

- yellow
- late winter to early spring
- 1–3 ft. × 3–4 ft.
- sun, part shade
- Z4–7

Western skunk cabbage, western swamp lantern. Native to the Pacific Coast from California to Alaska, and inland through Idaho, Montana, and Wyoming. Long, thick rhizomes support leaves that may measure 4.5 ft. long and almost 3 ft. across. A yellowish green spadix is almost ensheathed by a 5-in., yellow spathe. One of spring's earliest bloomers.

Lysichiton camtschatcensis

- green, white, yellow
- early spring
- 2–3 ft. high and wide
- sun, part shade
- Z5–7

Skunk cabbage. Northeastern Asia. Before the leaves appear, flowers emerge consisting of a 12-in.-long, yellow to green spadix whose tip may extend beyond the sheath-like, white spathe. Leaves, glossy green and leathery, broadly oval to 3 ft. long, are borne in loose rosettes above rhizomatous roots. Foliage declines in summer heat. Tolerates fairly dense shade, seasonal flooding.

Lysimachia
Primulaceae
loosestrife

Notwithstanding its common name, this genus is not related to the infamous purple loosestrife (*Lythrum salicaria*) that has overrun tens of thousands of acres of North America.

Lysimachia grows mainly in damp soil, where its rhizomes can spread widely and sometimes too aggressively. Stems are usually erect with opposite pairs, or whorls of lanceolate leaves, often hairy and sometimes edged with teeth or scallops. The small white or yellow flowers are saucer or star shaped, arranged in terminal spikes or panicles, or solitary in the upper leaf axils.

This genus of about 150 species is easy to grow, especially in moisture-retentive soil amended with compost. Do not allow the plants to dry out during the summer months; browning and crisping of the leaves may result. Although most enjoy full sun, provide shade for variegated plants where midday sun is intense.

Plant larger species in perennial or mixed borders, beside ponds, lakes, and streams, or let them

Lysichiton camtschatcensis

Lysimachia ephemerum

naturalize in light woodlands, or wild gardens. Lysi-machias are seldom browsed by deer and reputedly resistant to rabbits. Rust and leaf spots may mar the foliage.

Propagate by seed or divide clumps in spring or fall.

Lysimachia ciliata
syn. *Steironema cilicum*
- yellow
- early to late summer
- 3–3.5 ft. × 2 ft.
- sun, part shade
- Z5–8

Fringed loosestrife. Native to moist woods and along streams and pond banks in much of southern Canada and the northern United States. Vigorous, rhizomatous perennial with upright, hairy stems clothed with pairs or whorls of lanceolate, hairy leaves, to 6 in. long. Nodding, 1-in., saucer-shaped, yellow flowers, accented with red eyes, are held singly or in pairs on slender stems from the upper leaf axils. Quite invasive; may be difficult to eradicate.

'Firecracker' has rich wine-red foliage; yellow flowers. 30–36 in. Z2–9.

'Purpurea' has purplish foliage. 24 in.

Lysimachia clethroides
- white
- mid- to late summer
- 2–3 ft. × 3 ft.
- sun, part shade
- Z4–9, HS

Gooseneck loosestrife. China, Japan, Korea. This aggressive exotic spreads by roaming rhizomes and rapidly covers several feet. Contain it in a large sunken trashcan or drainage pipe to stop being overrun. That said, it is excellent as a tall ground-cover especially in damp soil, and for cut flowers too. Erect stems bear alternate, narrowly lance-shaped, pointed, 5-in. leaves; mid-green with pale green undersides that turn reddish in fall. Masses of starry, 0.5-in., white flowers are packed into taper-ing spikes to 8 in. in length; the tips droop in the bud, and regain their upright habit as bloom com-mences, often leaving the flowers with a "goose-neck" or "crookneck." Attractive in wildlife gardens where butterflies harvest nectar from the flowers.

'Geisha'. The foliage of this cultivar has undulat-ing, creamy-yellow edges. Reputed to be less aggres-sive, and thus better behaved than the species.

Lysimachia congestiflora
syn. *L. procumbens*
- yellow
- spring to late summer
- 4–6 in. × 12 in.
- sun, part shade
- Z6–9

Dense-flowered loosestrife, creeping Jenny, golden globes. China. Short lived; often grown as an annual. Forms low mats of 2-in., ovate to lance-shaped leaves, arranged in whorls or pairs. Cup-shaped flowers are bright yellow, and 0.75 in.

across; they gather in congested terminal clusters. Best in full sun in cool-summer climes, but prefers midday shade in warmer regions. Lovely in summer hanging baskets, window boxes, and containers; colorful as a groundcover or at the front of the bor-der. Non-invasive.

'Eco Dark Satin' sports red-throated, yellow flow-ers, above a deep olive foliage mat. Introduced by Dr. Don Jacobs of Eco Gardens. Best in light shade.

'Outback Sunset' ('Walkabout Sunset') has gray-green leaves irregularly variegated with yellow; yel-low flowers. Demands constant moisture. 2–10 in.

Lysimachia ephemerum
- white
- mid- to late summer
- 3–4 ft. × 1.5 ft.
- sun, part shade
- Z5–9, HS

Milky loosestrife, silver loosestrife, willow-leaved loosestrife. Southwestern Europe, from Portugal west to southern France. Bushy clumps of upright stems with pairs of glaucous grey, lance-shaped leaves, 4–6 in. long, joined at their bases. Dense tapering spires of pearl-like, 0.5-in., white flowers that attract butterflies. Excellent for cutting, beside lakes and ponds, in containers and borders. Non-invasive and elegant; lovely with Japanese iris and swamp rose mallow. This fine perennial deserves a wider audience among gardeners, except in hot and humid regions where the plant will suffer.

Lysimachia nummularia
- yellow
- late spring to late summer
- 2–4 in. × 15–20 in.
- part shade, shade
- Z2–9

Creeping Jenny, creeping Charlie, moneywort. Europe and western Asia. Semi-evergreen in mild climates, this vigorous creeping plant roots at the nodes along its spreading stems. Low mats of rounded, 0.75-in. leaves; solitary, cup-shaped, upward-facing, bright yellow flowers. Grown for its foliage, and largely replaced by the golden-leaved cultivar 'Aurea'. 'Goldilocks', from Proven Winners, and 'Goldie' may be identical.

'Aurea'. Slightly glossy, bright golden leaves light up the garden. Excellent spilling from containers and window boxes, as a groundcover, and along paths. Prefers a slightly sunnier spot than the spe-cies. Can become invasive. Z3–10.

Lysimachia punctata
- yellow
- mid-late summer
- 2–3 ft. × 1–2 ft.
- sun, part shade
- Z4–8

Circle flower, yellow loosestrife, whorled loose-strife. Central and southern Europe, but naturalized in many parts of North America. Another species, quick-spreading by rhizomes particularly where soil is damp. Plant beside ponds and lakes, or in

Lythrum salicaria 'Morden Pink'

Eurasia, it has naturalized throughout North America outside of Florida to overrun and destroy native habitats in countless acres of wetlands across the continent. Although it is banned in many states, gardeners and nurseries have been reluctant to abandon this perennial, cultivating supposedly "sterile named cultivars" such as 'Morden Pink' that produce fertile pollen. These interbreed naturally with the wild-type purple loosestrife within 500 miles, becoming prolific seed producers. Check with your local Cooperative Extension office before buying plants. As an alternative, you could instead plant the native loosestrife, *L. alatum*, that offers a harmless, even beneficial, alternative.

Lythrum alatum

- pink, purple
- late spring to late summer

- 2–3 ft. × 15–18 in.
- sun
- Z3–8

Winged loosestrife. Native from US East Coast to Montana, Colorado, and Texas, in fields, wet meadows, ditches, and along ponds and streams. Requires a consistently moist soil, and tolerates wet ones. Opposite pairs of lanceolate, sessile leaves are borne on square stems, which have slight wings along the corners. The 0.5-in., six-lobed, flared, rose-lavender flowers are borne singly or paired in the axils of the leaves at the stem tips. Foliage turns orange-red in late summer. Attracts bees, butterflies, and hummingbirds.

Macleaya
Papaveraceae
plume poppy, tree celandine

Two species of plume poppies, *Macleaya cordata* and *M. microcarpa*, are commonly found in gardens. They are so similar in appearance that even nurseries that grow them may mislabel them. For gardeners, what matters is the outsized presence plume poppies furnish to any landscape. Here they are lumped together for convenience.

These rhizomatous plants are aggressive in their spread—*M. microcarpa* is supposedly more troublesome in this respect. Allow plume poppies plenty of room or be prepared to prune back the tough rootstock annually. Macleayas grow best in fertile, moist but well-drained soils. An elegant and imposing choice for the back of borders, they are dramatic behind finer-foliaged, more delicate perennials; the unassertive coloration of plume poppies complements any floral neighbors. Combine with flamboyant sunflowers, cannas, and larger ornamental grasses to create an exuberant, supersized display that makes visitors feel like tourists in a land of giants.

Divide in spring or fall. Take root cuttings during winter dormancy.

wild gardens, with astilbes, Japanese iris, and Joe-Pye weed; very attractive with calla lilies in mild climates. Upright stems with whorls of dark elliptic leaves, 1–3 in. long. Showy, cup-shaped, yellow, 1-in. flowers, red-brown at the throat, cluster in axial whorls on short stems. Increase by seed or take cuttings; may become invasive. Best in cooler climates.

'Alexander' has gray-green leaves, edged with white. Yellow flowers.

Golden Alexander ('Walgodalex') has lime-green leaves edged with deep cream. Flowers as the species. Not quite as invasive; more compact to 24 in. tall.

Lythrum
Lythraceae
loosestrife

One member of this genus, the dreaded purple loosetrife (*Lythrum salicaria*), has proven to be a particularly pernicious invasive species. A native of

Macleaya cordata

Maianthemum canadense

Maianthemum

Liliaceae
Canada mayflower, false lily-of-the-valley, false
  Solomon's seal

This cherished native has acquired numerous interesting common names over the centuries, including elf feather, deerberry, beadruby, and May lily,
attesting to its various characteristics. Botanical
classification is confusing and in a state of flux;
some authorities put it in the Convallariaceae or
Asparagaceae.

Not fussy about soil conditions, Canada mayflower is adaptable. Ideally, provide humus-rich,
moist soil, with a neutral or slightly acid pH. Best
under the partial or even full shade of trees that
keep the roots cool and protected from intense sun.
Soil must not be allowed to dry out. Best bloom in
cooler regions.

Regardless of the alternate common name deerberry, deer apparently ignore the plants; rabbits
also ignore these native gems. Plant with Christmas and lady ferns for beautiful woodland displays.
Appropriate for wild and wildlife gardens, and
damp woodlands.

Propagate by dividing rhizomes in spring; sow
seed in containers, but slow to attain bloom size.

Macleaya cordata and *M. microcarpa*

syn. *Bocconia* spp.

- white
- summer
- 5–8 ft. × 2–4 ft.
- sun, part shade
- Z3–8

Plume poppy. China, Japan. The species are distinguished chiefly by their stamen number: *Macleaya
cordata* has 24 to 30 stamens per bloom, *M. microcarpa* has 8 to 12. Tiny, petal-less, creamy-white to
pink-tinged flowers, borne in plume-like panicles in
summertime. Plume poppies are grassland plants
that stand head high when mature, forming groups
of stout stems. Handsome broad, grayish to olive-
green, lobed stem leaves to 8 in. long, downy with
hairs beneath; large plumes of tiny, creamy-white or
pink-tinged flowers top the stems.

M. microcarpa 'Spetchley Ruby' has blue-green
foliage. Reddish flowers followed by red seedheads.

M. microcarpa 'Kelway's Coral Plume' has
copper-pink flowers.

Maianthemum canadense

- white
- late spring
- 3–6 in. × 16–9 in.
- part shade, shade
- Z3–7

Canada mayflower. Native in woodlands of southern Canada and northern United States, east to
Maine and south to Georgia. A tangle of rhizomatous roots forms large colonies over time under

Maianthemum racemosum

Malva sylvestris

favorable conditions. In spring a single, deciduous, heart-shaped leaf emerges, followed by a separate zigzag flowering stem bearing one to three glossy leaves like mini lily-of-the-valley. Tiny, white starry flowers crowd ten or more into terminal racemes; pollinated by bees and flies. Pea-sized, light pink berries, each with several seeds follow; mice, chipmunks, and often ants consume them. Summer dormant.

Maianthemum racemosum

syn. *Smilacina racemosa*
- white
- mid- to late spring
- 2–3 ft. × 1.5–2 ft.
- part shade
- Z3–8, HS

False Solomon's seal. Rich woods throughout North America. Clump forming, spreads by rhizomes. Ovate, pointed, medium green leaves with prominent, parallel veins borne alternately along arching, zigzag stems. Fragrant, small, starry flowers are creamy white arranged in plume-like, terminal clusters, followed by green berries that turn red in summer. Yellow fall foliage. May form extensive colonies but resents transplanting once established. Good for woodland gardens, shady borders, and pond sides. No serious pests or diseases. Familiar to many as *Smilacina racemosa* but recently moved to this genus.

Maianthemum stellatum, starry false Solomon's seal, is similar but smaller, with 8- to 10-in. stems. Z3–7.

Malva
Malvaceae
mallow

In French "mauve" means mallow and in fact the flowers of many mallows are a soft lilac-lavender hue. This genus includes three species of perennials of special interest to gardeners.

All have alternate, palmately lobed leaves and bear five-petaled flowers in pinks or white as well as mauve. The blooms bear a strong family resemblance to those of related hollyhocks and hibiscus, and bloom over a long period. Although perhaps not as refined as tall, slender hollyhocks they are less trouble prone.

Moderately moist, well-drained soils are ideal; mallows are somewhat drought tolerant. Japanese beetles and hollyhock rust attack the foliage, but mallows seldom suffer serious damage, except in very hot, humid summers. Attracts butterflies; rarely browsed by deer.

Often short lived, mallows commonly reseed. Deadhead to encourage rebloom unless saving seed. Propagate by seed or divide in spring.

Malva alcea

- pink
- summer to early fall
- 2–4 ft. × 1.5–2 ft.
- sun, part shade
- Z4–7, HS

Greater musk-mallow, hollyhock mallow. Native to southwestern, central, and eastern Europe, and southwestern Asia; naturalized in northeastern North America. Hairy stems bear palmately lobed leaves 0.75–3 in. long and wide; basal leaves are shallowly lobed, those on the upper stems are deeply divided and fingered. Flattened clusters of flowers emerge from the upper leaf axils and stem tips; each is bright pink, 1.3–2.3 in. across; no fragrance. To control height, cut back stems in spring. Good for borders and cottage gardens.

'Fastigiata' (var. *fastigiata*) grows upright, with a narrow form. 12–18 in. wide.

Malva sylvestris

syn. *M. mauritiana, M. sylvestris* var. *mauritiana*

- mauve-and-purple
- midsummer to early fall
- 3–4 ft. × 1.5–2 ft.
- sun, part shade
- Z5–8

Tall mallow, French hollyhock. Fields and hedgerows of western Europe, northern Africa, and Asia. Erect or decumbent branching stems carry coarse, hairy, maple-like leaves with five to seven shallow lobes; foliage is deep green when young but fades and becomes ragged as the season advances. Bright mauve, 1- to 2.5-in. flowers, striped with darker purple, have notched petals. Short lived but reseeds vigorously. Tolerates heat and humidity better than most mallows or hollyhocks; good for muggy climates.

'Braveheart' has dark purple–veined, deep rose flowers.

'Primley Blue' grows to 18–24 in., with powder blue, violet-veined flowers.

'Purple Satin'. Ruffled, burgundy-violet flowers with deeper purple veins.

'Zebrina' has satiny, mauve flowers striped with dark maroon.

Malvaviscus

Malvaceae
turk's cap mallow

The brilliant red, turban-shaped blossoms borne by turk's cap mallows would have roused the envy of any old-time Ottoman dandy. Especially decorative in sultry regions, turk's cap mallows bloom through heat and humidity, and serve as magnets for hummingbirds and butterflies.

Tall turk's cap mallows are woody at the base with substantial, somewhat coarse, semi-evergreen to evergreen foliage. All tolerate shade and make fine additions to woodland gardens, where they cohabit comfortably with lyreleaf sage, holly fern,

Malvaviscus drummondii

and wood fern. Turk's caps are appropriate for informal borders or naturalized areas. Mostly trouble free, but susceptible to white flies, spider mites, mealybugs, and powdery mildew. Deer resistant.

Propagate by seed, division, or softwood cuttings.

Malvaviscus arboreus

- red
- late spring to midfall
- 4–10 ft. × 4–8 ft.
- sun, part shade
- Z8–11

Turk's cap. Native to subtropical Texas and cloud forests of Mexico and Colombia. A coarse expansive shrubby perennial with branching stems, woody at the base; three-lobed, broadly oval to heart-shaped leaves to 5 in. or more long, dark green above, paler with down beneath. Bright red, 1-in.-long flowers never open; petals remain tightly spiraled with a long pistil and protruding stamens. Red fruits are five-lobed capsules, a popular food for wildlife. Vigorous and adaptable. Cut back stem tips periodically to encourage branching and bloom.

Malvaviscus drummondii

syn. *M. arboreus* var. *drummondii*

- reddish orange
- late summer to late fall
- 5 ft. high and wide
- sun, part shade
- Z8–10

Turk's cap. Texas coastal plain east to Florida and West Indies, Cuba, and Mexico. Evergreen in the southern part of its range, but herbaceous further north; survives in zone 7 with winter protection. Upright or somewhat reclining stems bear 4- to 6-in., hairy, dull green leaves. Vermilion-red spiraling flowers are twisted into a tube showing exserted red stamens.

'Big Momma' has flowers a third larger than the species. Introduced by Texas horticulturist Greg Grant.

'White Lightning' has white flowers.

Other Notable Cultivars

'Pam Puryear' (*Malvaviscus drummondii* × *M. arboreus*) has peachy pink flowers. A Greg Grant introduction, named for the noted Texas Rose Rustler. 5 ft. high and wide. Z7 with protection.

Marrubium

Lamiaceae
horehound

Best known as a flavoring for cough drops, common horehound (or hoarhound), *Marrubium vulgare* has been used medicinally for centuries. While that species is not valuable outside herb gardens, its relative *M. incana* earns space in beds and borders with its woolly, silver-gray foliage. This provides a cooling foil for colorful companions, such as rudbeckias, veronicas, and even roses. Lovely with ornamental

forms of other Mediterranean herbs: lavenders, oreganos, thymes, and sages.

Mint-like rhizomes can become invasive, especially in fertile soil conditions. Provide poor, free-draining soil to keep under control. Drought tolerant; pest and disease free, including deer.

Divide clumps in spring or fall, or take summer cuttings.

Marrubium cylleneum

- lavender
- midsummer
- 4–12 in. × 24 in.
- sun, part shade
- Z8–10

Horehound. Greece, Albania. Upright, square, woolly stems carry opposite pairs of sage-green leaves, textured and soft, rimmed with white, undulating edges. Vertillasters of lavender-pink, two-lipped flowers crowd the leaf axils. Very tolerant of drought; thrives in hot, dry climates.

Marrubium incanum

syn. *M. candidissimum of gardens*

- white
- early summer
- 1–3 ft. × 2 ft.
- sun
- Z3–10

Woolly horehound, silver horehound. Italy, Sicily, Balkans. This silky-haired, woolly perennial presents the effect of hoar frost on the foliage. Bushy and erect, the square stems are clothed with pairs of crinkled, sage-like, 1- to 2-in. leaves, rimmed

Marrubium cylleneum

with small teeth, white-felted beneath. Insignificant white, two-lipped flowers cluster in whorls at the nodes. Prune routinely to encourage bushy growth.

Marshallia
Asteraceae
Barbara's buttons

Endangered in several areas where its favored moist riverbanks and open woods have been destroyed, this seldom-cultivated but attractive native is perfect for native plant and wild gardens; good for cutting. Partner with other damp-loving natives including beebalm, cardinal flower, and turtlehead.

Best in sun in damp soil abundantly enriched with organic matter. Seldom browsed by deer or rabbits, or attacked by pests and diseases. Attracts butterflies and birds.

Propagate by seed or divide established plants.

Marshallia grandiflora
- pink
- early to midsummer
- 1–2 ft. × 1 ft.
- sun, part shade
- Z5–9

Giant Barbara's buttons, Appalachian Barbara's buttons. Central Appalachia and eastern United States. Easy-to-grow clumps of glossy, evergreen, lanceolate leaves to 7 in. long. Solitary, 1.25-in., pinwheel-like heads of tubular mauve or pinkish florets with bluish purple anthers top 18- to 24-in. stalks. Plants seed themselves gently.

Mazus
Phrymaceae
creeping mazus

Formerly classified with snapdragons in the Scrophulariaceae, *Mazus* is now placed in the Phrymaceae with monkey flower. Just a single species is garden worthy. Creeping mazus is excellent as a groundcover. Tolerant of light foot traffic and occasional mowing, it is easy care and requires little maintenance. Evergreen in mild climates. It thrives growing in crevices between pavers on patios and pathways, in rock gardens, and is lovely underplanting weigelas, bush cinquefoils, and viburnums, and as a skirt for spring bulbs. It can be allowed to naturalize and does well in rain gardens.

Plant creeping mazus in sun or partly shaded spots in moisture-retentive soil amended with organic matter; if kept moist it tolerates summer heat and humidity but should not dry out excessively in summer. Seldom browsed by deer or rabbits, this charmer is more or less pest and disease free.

Propagate by division in spring or start from seed.

Mazus reptans 'Albus'

Mazus reptans
- purple blue
- late spring to early summer
- 2–4 in. × 24 in.
- sun, part shade
- Z5–8

Creeping mazus. Himalayan region. Prostrate, with tight, dense mats of bright green, more or less elliptic, coarsely toothed, 0.5- to 1-in. leaves. Abundant few-flowered clusters of small, five-petaled, lavender-mauve flowers blanket the foliage; these are two-lipped, the lower blotched with white, subtly dotted with red. Spreads by runners that root at the nodes. May invade lawns.

'Albus' ('Alba') has clean white flowers

Meconopsis
Papaveraceae
Himalayan poppy

A geographical puzzle, this genus includes one species native to the British Isles and almost 40 more indigenous to the Himalayas. These poppy relatives, annuals, biennials, and evergreen or herbaceous perennials all prefer cool, moist climates and seldom flourish in regions with hot, humid summers. Typically they form rosettes of hairy leaves and four-petaled, bowl-shaped flowers, reminiscent of related poppies.

Best where summers are cool, with moisture-retentive, well-drained, acid soil; they rot out in winter with wet feet. Organic mulch helps to maintain consistent soil moisture. The strong taproots resent disturbance.

All make fine additions to cottage gardens, wildflower meadows, or rock gardens; the blue poppies, for those who master their cultivation, also provide a choice ornament for sunny, well-drained borders and containers. Prone to attack by slugs and snails; deer resistant.

Propagate by fresh seed.

'Flore Pleno' bears double, yellow flowers.
'Muriel Brown' bears double, orange-red flowers.
'Rubra' has single, red flowers, 3 in. in diameter.

Meconopsis grandis

- blue
- late spring to early summer
- 2–4 ft. × 1–2 ft.
- part shade
- Z5–7, HS

Blue poppy, Asiatic poppy. Western Himalayas, northern Burma, Tibet, and Yunnan. Basal rosettes composed of bristly, entire or coarsely toothed, wedge-shaped, medium green leaves, to 12 in. long. Upright stems bear cupped, deep sky-blue flowers, 4–5 in. across. Requires climate and soil similar to those favored by *Meconopsis betonicifolia*: best adapted to mild coastal regions, or higher altitudes of mountain states. Appropriate for open woodlands or rock gardens. A heartbreaker, but a triumph for those who bring this treasure to bloom.

Other Notable Cultivars

×*sheldonii* 'Lingholm' (*Meconopsis betonicifolia* × *M. grandis*). Bristly, 6- to 10-in. leaves, rich blue, 1.25-in. flowers from late spring. Treat as *M. betonicifolia* or *M. grandis*; hybrid vigor reputedly makes 'Lingholm' easier to cultivate. 48 in. × 18 in. Z3–7.

'Slieve Donard' is vigorous with pointed, rich blue flowers. To 36 in.

Mentha

Lamiaceae
mint

Despite their seductive appeal to eye, nose, and tongue, most of the mints are simply too invasive to be released in perennial gardens. A few less-aggressive types, however, can fill the need for a self-sufficient, fast-growing groundcover, an aromatic filler for hanging baskets and containers, or even low-growing herbage to tuck into the cracks of a sunny flagstone terrace.

As a group, mints are characterized by expansive underground and aboveground stolons, erect square stems, opposite oblong to lanceolate, aromatic leaves, and small, two-lipped flowers borne in tiered whorls or verticillasters of blossoms at the upper nodes. Deer ignore them.

Mints flourish on rich, moist but well-drained soils in full sun or part shade. When grown on wet and/or excessively rich soils they are fall prey to fungal diseases. In intense sun, variegated cultivars may burn; they are somewhat less vigorous (an advantage in the case of mints). Plant mints in pots or tile drains buried almost to their rims to restrain their roving roots temporarily. Cut back top growth regularly to encourage bushy, compact new growth. Mints attract bees, butterflies, and pollinating insects but resist deer and rabbits.

Propagate cultivars by division, as mints hybridize readily, or by stem cuttings.

Meconopsis ×*sheldonii* 'Lingholm'

Meconopsis betonicifolia

- blue
- late spring to early summer
- 24–48 in. × 18–24 in.
- part shade
- Z7–8, HS

Blue poppy. Himalayas. Basal rosette of 6-in., toothed leaves covered with rusty hairs; 2- to 3-in.-wide, sky-blue flowers borne singly or in terminal cymes. Not difficult to grow in suitable climates. If soil is not sufficiently acid, colors may be muddy mauve instead. A border and rock garden gem.

'Hensol Violet' has lilac-rose flowers.

Meconopsis cambrica

- yellow, orange
- late spring to early summer
- 18 in. × 12 in.
- sun, part shade
- Z5–9, HS

Welsh poppy. Britain, Ireland, western part of northern Europe. The easiest to cultivate, this species produces basal rosettes of divided, deeply toothed, pale green leaves, from which rise upright, bristly stems that carry solitary, 2- to 3-in., bowl-shaped, yellow to orange blooms; occasionally reblooms after initial flush of flowers. Plants are short lived but reseed prolifically, even sometimes becoming invasive. Particularly attractive naturalized in open woodland settings with Virginia bluebells, forget-me-nots, or grape hyacinths. Fresh seed is essential.

Mentha spicata is corralled here in a container

Mertensia virginica

Mentha requienii

- purple
- midsummer
- 1 in. × 6–12 in.
- part shade
- Z7–9

Corsican mint. Corsica, Sardinia, France, and mainland Italy. Produces a carpet of tiny, bright green leaves with crème de menthe fragrance, and tiny, mauve flowers. Tolerates light foot traffic, suitable for planting in cracks between paving stones, or around the base of taller plants in a container.

Mentha spicata 'Crispa'

- pink-purple
- midsummer to early fall
- 1–2 ft. high and wide
- sun, part shade
- Z4–10

Curly mint. A spearmint selection of horticultural origin. Bright green leaves, highly curled along their edges, with a strong spearmint fragrance; dense spikes of pale-lilac flowers in summer. Just as invasive, curly mint is smaller than regular spearmint.

Mentha suaveolens 'Variegata'

syn. *M. rotundifolia* 'Variegata'

- cream
- summer
- 24 in. × 24–36 in.
- sun, part shade
- Z5–10

Pineapple mint. Southern and western Europe. Variegated cream-and-green leaves with a light fragrance of pineapple, scalloped edges, and crinkled texture.

Mertensia

Boraginaceae
bluebells

Blues lovers will find much to enjoy in this genus of some 50 species, 18 of which are North American natives. These herbaceous perennials vary from small alpine gems to 3-ft.-tall woodlanders. They are adapted to a remarkable range of habitats; some retreat underground and become summer dormant. The flowers, borne in nodding clusters, are typically bell shaped, and range from pale to dark violet-blues, some even open blue but mature to pink. Bluebells are available for almost any site.

Propagate by seed sown in fall; overwinter with protection. Divide mature specimens in spring, or take root cuttings in early autumn.

Mertensia ciliata

- blue
- early to midsummer
- 0.5–4 ft. high and wide
- sun
- Z4–9

Tall fringed bluebells. Native to subalpine meadows and streamsides in the United States, from the Rockies to the Pacific Coast. Groups of stems arise from branched, woody bases, and bear fleshy, blue-green, alternate, ovate to elliptic leaves, to 6 in. long, that narrow as they ascend the stems. Branched, open clusters of nodding, fragrant, tubular flowers to 0.75 in. long that flare at the mouths. Drought tolerant; a well-drained, moist, and peaty soil is ideal. In the wild they mass in mountain meadows; excellent to naturalize in gardens of the western United States.

Mertensia maritima
- blue, pink
- late spring to early summer
- 2–4 in. × 8–12 in.
- sun
- Z4–8

Oysterleaf. Beaches of northern North America, northeastern Asia, and northwestern Europe. Attractive, low mounds of blue-green, ovate leaves. Flowers cluster at stems tips; pink in the bud opening to blue. Provide a neutral to slightly alkaline, well-drained soil of average fertility and moisture. Leaves reportedly taste like oysters. Handsome in containers, rock gardens, or seaside plantings.

Mertensia virginica
syn. *M. pulmonariodes, Pulmonaria virginica*
- blue
- early spring
- 1.5–2 ft. × 1–1.5 ft.
- part shade, shade
- Z3–8

Virginia bluebells. Moist woods and river bottoms from New York and southern Ontario to eastern Minnesota, south to Kansas, Arkansas, and North Carolina. Clumps of erect stems carry smooth, oval, bluish green leaves to 4 in. long. Pendulous, trumpet-shaped, 1-in.-long flowers cluster in loose, terminal clusters; buds are pink and young flowers pinkish blue, maturing to sky blue. This popular native spring ephemeral yellows and becomes dormant as summer heat arrives. Prefers moist, rich soils, but tolerates average garden soil with irrigation. Naturalize in woodland and wildflower gardens.

Mimulus
Phrymaceae
monkey flower, musk flower

Unlike so many other perennials that demand a well-drained soil, monkey flowers thrive in damp places, especially in regions with a warm climate. Their showy snapdragon-like flowers arise from the leaf axils or gather into terminal racemes at stem tips. They appear like a gaping mouth with a two-lobed, sometimes reflexed, upper lip and a pendulous, three-lobed lower one; an open throat between them is sometimes protected by a palate. The floral hues include almost everything except blue, the lower lip often decorated with contrasting spots. Frequently toothed, the stem leaves are arranged in opposite pairs.

Monkey flowers thrive in damp, fertile soils copiously amended with organic matter; some species prefer to grow in shallow water. Sunny positions are best, but they tolerate light or dappled

Mimulus cupreus

shade, especially in hot areas. Where winters are overly harsh, monkey flowers are frequently grown as summer annuals. Keep well watered and fertilize monthly to keep bloom coming. Pests and diseases are seldom serious; tolerates deer and rabbits well.

Ideal for rain gardens, water gardens, streamsides, and bog gardens, monkey flowers also perform well in beds and borders if they are kept moist. Good companions include water iris, ligularias, meadowsweets, and other lovers of damp sites.

Increase mimulus from seed sown in fall or spring, or divide the crowns in spring. Soft cuttings root well in late spring or early summer.

Mimulus cardinalis
- red
- late spring to fall
- 2–3 ft. × 1–2 ft.
- sun, part shade, shade
- Z5–10

Scarlet monkey flower. Mountain regions surrounding deserts of California, the western United States, and Mexico. Clumps of sticky-hairy, rather weak, branched stems bear opposite pairs of evergreen, sessile, 1- to 4-in.-long, obovate, toothed leaves. Conspicuously two-lipped and tubular with exserted stamens, yellow-throated, scarlet or brick-colored, 2-in. flowers are borne on long stems. Their major pollinators, hummingbirds, frequently visit these very showy flowers, as do butterflies. Great for wildlife gardens, wildflower gardens, beside water features. Protect from intense sun. Should not dry out, especially during periods of drought. Cut back in late summer to encourage further bloom. This species sets copious amounts of seed.

'Santa Cruz Island' has yellow flowers. Originally collected on Santa Cruz Island.

Mimulus cupreus

- orange red
- late spring to summer
- 1–2 ft. × 2 ft.
- sun, part shade
- Z7–10

Flor de cobre. In the wild, this species grows at high altitudes around the timberline in Chile. Freely branching, with mostly hairless stems and conspicuously veined, coarsely toothed, oval leaves to 1.25 in. long. The 1- to 1.5-in. flowers are golden yellow when young, but quickly darken to a screaming orange with red-spotted throats. Demands constant moisture; best sited along waterways, in bog gardens, or swampy spots. Grow as an annual in colder areas.

Mimulus guttatus
syn. *M. langsdorfii*

- yellow
- early summer to fall
- 1–2 ft. × 2 ft.
- sun, part shade
- Z6–9

Common monkey flower. Native from California, north to Alaska, this vigorous, erect or spreading, fleshy plant roots at the nodes where stems touch the ground. Broadly oval, petioled, 1- to 6-in. leaves are toothed; upper leaves sessile. The typical 1- to 2-in. monkey flowers are bright yellow, frequently mottled and speckled with red on the lower lobe, and arranged in terminal racemes. This species is a parent of the ×*hybridus* group.

Mimulus ×hybridus
syn. *M. guttatus* × *M. luteus*

- various
- early summer to fall
- 1–2 ft. × 2 ft.
- sun, part shade
- Z9–11

Hybrid mimulus, of garden origin. Except in mild climates, these are mostly grown as summer annuals in containers, and beds and borders. This breeding has spawned several worthy strains including:

Calypso. A mixture in various striking color combinations of red, orange, burgundy, and pink, spotted and blotched, bicolored, or self-colored. 6–10 in.

Magic Mix. Blooms early in shades of red, orange, yellow, cream, and pink. Good for landscapes and containers. 6–8 in. tall.

Malibu Series. Yellow, red, and orange trailing plants, excellent for baskets. 6–8 in.

Mimulus luteus

- yellow
- late spring to summer
- 12 in. × 12–24 in.
- sun, part shade
- Z7–9, HS

Yellow monkey flower, small monkey flower. Chile. Vigorous creeping mats root at the nodes. Oval, 1.5-in. leaves are toothed; pairs of bright yellow, red-spotted, 1.5- to 2-in. flowers adorn the leaf axils. Self-seeds freely. An excellent groundcover; tolerates growing in up to 3 in. of water. A parent of the ×*hybridus* group.

Mimulus ringens

- purple
- early summer to fall
- 2–3 ft. × 1 ft.
- sun, part shade
- Z4–9

Allegheny monkey flower, square-stemmed monkey flower. Native to wet habitats of eastern and central United States. This smooth, hairless perennial with creeping rhizomes grows upright with watery, ridged, square stems. Lanceolate, toothed, 3- to 4-in. leaves are sessile and often clasp the stem. In the leaf axils, pairs of long-stemmed lavender-purple flowers emerge from ribbed calyces; the larger, lower, lobed lip is speckled with violet and a visible yellow palate closes the throat. Self-seeds freely, and spreads by rhizomes. Ideal for damp borders and waterside sites; tolerates growing in water to 6 in. deep.

Monarda
Lamiaceae
beebalm, bergamot

Used by indigenous peoples as a treatment for a wide variety of ailments, this genus of North American wildflowers continues to supply the antiseptic, *thymol*, employed in many modern mouthwashes. Gardeners value these hardy mint relatives for their aromatic foliage and long-lasting bloom. Like the mints, beebalms have square stems and small, tubular flowers borne in dense, mop-headed clusters.

Flourishing on a wide range of soils, beebalms prefer a moderately moist, well-drained site, but tolerate some drought once established. As their common name suggests, their nectar-rich flowers attract bees as well as butterflies and hummingbirds. The more refined hybrid selections hold their own in mixed borders; as a group however beebalms appear more at home in less formal meadows, native plant gardens, and open woods, or alongside ponds and streams. They have the rare ability to grow under black walnut trees. Good companions include black-eyed Susans, coneflowers, Shasta daisies, and gayfeathers. Little troubled by insect pests, deer, or rabbits; beebalms are, however, susceptible to powdery mildew. Search out mildew-resistant selections.

Propagate by seed; take stem cuttings or divide named cultivars in late spring.

Monarda didyma

- red
- early to late summer
- 2–4 ft. × 2–3 ft.
- sun, part shade
- Z4–9

Oswego tea, beebalm. Eastern United States and Canada. Clumps of stems clothed with aromatic, alternate, lanceolate, 3- to 5-in. leaves rimmed with teeth. Dense terminal heads of red flowers top whorls of showy red-tinged, leafy bracts. Shade from intense sun. Unlike other beebalms, this species must not dry out; a good choice for rain gardens.

'Adam' has red flowers. More drought tolerant than the species.

'Croftway Pink' is a lovely rosy pink. Susceptible to mildew.

'Grand Parade' offers lavender-purple flowers. 13–16 in. × 16–20 in. Z3–8.

'Jacob Cline' has outstandingly large, brilliant red flowers. Largely mildew resistant.

'Purple Rooster' displays large, rich purple flowers. Mildew resistant. 36 in. × 26 in.

Monarda fistulosa

- pink, lavender
- early to late summer
- 2–4 ft. × 2–3 ft.
- sun, part shade
- Z3–9

Wild bergamot. Native to prairies, dry, rocky woods, and woodland margins, and in unplanted fields and along roadsides in United States, Canada, and Mexico. Clump forming with oblong, grayish green leaves to 4 in. long. Two-lipped, lavender flowers cluster in terminal, globular heads above whorls of showy, pinkish bracts. Prefers dry to moderately moist, well-drained soil, but tolerates clay, shallow, rocky soils, and some drought. Reseeds; best for naturalized informal plantings. Prone to powdery mildew.

Monarda punctata

- yellow, purple
- early summer
- 18–24 in. × 9–12 in.
- sun, part shade
- Z3–8

Dotted beebalm, spotted horsemint. Eastern United States. Clump forming with toothed, aromatic, oblong leaves to 3 in. long. Two-lipped, tubular flowers are yellow, spotted with purple. They are borne in upper leaf axils and at stem ends in tiered, stem-encircling clusters supported on whorls of showy, pinkish bracts. Prefers dry to moderately moist, well-drained soil; tolerates poor soils and some drought. Self-seeds.

'Fantasy' is an exceptionally robust cultivar. 2–2.5 ft. × 2–3 ft.

Other Notable Cultivars

'Blue Stocking' ('Blaustrumpf') has deep lilac flowers. Quite heat and drought tolerant. 36–60 in. × 24 in. Z4–10.

'Colrain Red' has deep red flowers. Mildew resistant. 3–4 ft. Z4–9.

'Gardenview Scarlet' has bright rose-red flowers; mildew resistant. Introduced by Henry Ross, Gardenview Park, Ohio. Has largely replaced mildew-prone 'Cambridge Scarlet'. 36 in. × 24 in. Z4–10.

'Marshall's Delight'. A mildew-resistant Canadian introduction with densely packed heads of showy pink flowers. 36–48 in. × 24–36 in. Z4–9.

Monarda 'Colrain Red'

'Pardon My Purple' is dwarf with 2.5- to 3-in., fuchsia-purple flowers. 12 in. tall

'Petite Delight' is dwarf with lavender-pink flowers. Mildew resistant. 12–15 in. × 18–24 in. Z2–8.

Morina

syn. *Acanthocalyx*
Morinaceae (Dipsacaceae)
whorlflower

Few would recognize this thistle lookalike when not in bloom. Its attractive whorls of fragrant flowers borne on spikes on straight-up stems are appealing in summer, but the vicious-looking spines that decorate the leaf edges too often put off gardeners. Leaves are evergreen in mild-winter regions. Neverthless, it deserves a much wider audience.

Somewhat temperamental, whorlflower does best in full sun in highly fertile soil with very good drainage. Tolerant of drought but not of wet feet; usually heavy clay soils that drain poorly mean death. Where this fragrant plant grows well (the crushed leaves have a lemony scent), it certainly earns its place in cottage gardens, beds, and borders, preferably where it will not be in contact with people. Wear gloves to handle, not only for protection against the spines, but also because the sap can cause a rash on sensitive skins.

Propagate by seed outdoors in fall as soon as it ripens; cover very thinly with fine compost. Seedlings take two to three years to reach blooming size. Self-seeds; avoid weeding out the thistle-like seedlings by mistake.

Morina longifolia

- white
- midsummer
- 2–3 ft. × 1–1.5 ft.
- sun, part shade
- Z6–8, HS

Whorlflower, Himalayan whorlflower. Himalayas from Kashmir to Bhutan. The whole plant is covered with wickedly sharp spines, especially the basal rosette of dark green leaves, and the whorls of bracts on the stem that protect the flower clusters. Dagger-shaped, glossy, 10- to 12-in. lower leaves are equipped with stiff spines along undulating margins. Erect flower stems bear tiers or whorls of tubular, 1.25-in., white flowers ringed with spines. The flowers turn rosy pink and then red after they have been fertilized. Reportedly this change in color signals pollinating insects to visit white flowers not yet pollinated. Spent flower stems are attractive as dried flowers.

Mukdenia

Saxifragaceae
mapleleaf tickfoil

A recent addition to the perennial plant palette, mapleleaf tickfoil will surely become popular as a weed-suppressing groundcover, especially in shade.

Rhizomatous roots produce basal rosettes composed of palmately divided, maple-like leaves. Clusters of small, starry flowers reminiscent of related coral bells rise above.

This beautiful deciduous plant, native to woodlands and rocky slopes of China, Japan, and Korea, is named for Mukden, the ancient capitol of Manchuria, now known as Shenyang. They do best in regions with cool summers, where they enjoy sun or light shade; they must not dry out. If grown in warmer climes, part shade is a must. Amend soil with organic matter to improve drainage yet retain moisture; it must not waterlog. Slugs and snails may devour succulent young growth, but deer and rabbits tend to ignore them.

Mukdenias are grown primarily for their foliage, although the flowers are quite charming. An excellent and unusual plant for Asian-style gardens, for edging beds and borders, woodlands, in rock gardens, or planted close as a groundcover beneath shrubs. Combine with hellebores, coral bells, variegated Hakone grass, and others appreciative of light shade.

Divide established plants in spring before bud break, or sow seed in fall, preferably in containers.

Mukdenia rossii

syn. *Aceriphyllum rossi*
- white
- midspring
- 8–15 in. × 12–24 in.
- part shade, shade
- Z4–8

Mukdenia. Northeast Asia. Fans of asymmetrically divided, basal foliage emerge with or just after the clusters of pink buds that open to white, starry flowers on leafless, 16-in., pink stems. Each long-stalked toothed leaf is deeply divided into five to eight lobes. The young green leaves, pinkish beneath, increase in size as they mature, reaching 6 in. across, and take on a burnt red cast as the season progresses.

'Crimson Fans' ('Karasuba') is the most popular cultivar. Its dramatic, lustrous leaves are irregularly bordered with bronze. In response to cooler fall nights and perhaps shorter days, the leaves turn intense crimson burgundy from the edges inward.

Myosotis

Boraginaceae
forget-me-not

Nothing says nostalgic charm like forget-me-nots, and very few perennials are as easy to grow. If you can provide a moist, organic-rich soil in sun or part shade, forget-me-nots of one kind or another will flourish in your garden from Alaska to zone 8 in the southeastern United States and into zone 9 on the West Coast. These mid- to late spring bloomers display a range of flower colors from the namesake forget-me-not blue to pink and white. The five-lobed flowers are individually small but are borne in natural nosegays, and commonly spread seed to form

Morina longifolia

Mukdenia rossii

Myosotis sylvatica

increasing colonies. Almost mandatory for cottage gardens, forget-me-nots combine well with astilbes, bergenias, coral bells, and primroses in woodland gardens, and are naturals for moist meadows, streambanks, or pondsides. Deer resistant; attracts butterflies.

Propagate by seed or division.

Myosotis asiatica
syn. *M. alpestris*

- blue
- midspring to midsummer
- 6–12 in. × 4–6 in.
- sun, part shade
- Z3–8, HS

Mountain forget-me-not, Asian forget-me-not. Native to northern regions of the world, including from Alaska through the Pacific Northwest and the Rocky Mountains to Colorado. Commonly sold in the nursery trade as *Myosotis alpestris*, under which name it serves as the state flower of Alaska. Bloom season varies with the climate, being delayed in northern regions or at high altitudes. Leafless clusters of yellow-eyed, blue flowers to 0.3 in. Leaves oblanceolate to elliptic, to 5 in. long at base, shorter as they ascend the stems. Grows best on well-drained moist to wet soils with neutral pH. Sensitive to combined heat and humidity. Ideal for rock gardens and containers. Susceptible to red spider mites, powdery mildew, and leaf rot, especially where summers are hot.

'Ultramarine' produces prolific flushes of intensely deep blue flowers.

Victoria Series offers cultivars with blue, pink, or white flowers.

Myosotis scorpioides
syn. *M. palustris*

- blue
- late spring to midsummer
- 6–12 in. × 9–12 in.
- sun, part shade
- Z5–9

True forget-me-not, water forget-me-not. Temperate North America. Glossy, oblong to lanceolate, bright green leaves to 4 in. long; yellow-eyed, light sky-blue flowers are 0.25 in. across, borne in scorpioid cymes that uncoil as flowers open (like a scorpion extending his sting). Adapts to growing in shallow water to 3 in. deep; good for margins of water gardens, streams, and ponds, where it covers the ground (not aggressively) by creeping rhizomes. Pinch young growth to encourage bushiness. Insect and disease resistant, with the exception of mildew and rust.

var. *semperflorens* is dwarf with heavier, longer bloom than the species. Repeat blooms sporadically to frost. 6–8 in.

'Southern Blues' grows to only 6 in. but spreads vigorously. Sky-blue flowers. Exceptionally tolerant of sultry summers.

'Unforgettable' has variegated, cream-edged foliage; bright blue flowers.

Myosotis sylvatica

- blue, pink
- mid- to late spring
- 6–12 in. × 6–9 in.
- sun, part shade
- Z3–8

Forget-me-not. European native that flourishes as a garden escapee in many parts of North America. Tufts of hairy, green, oblong-lanceolate leaves 1–3 in. long; dense cymes of yellow- or white-eyed, blue flowers, to 0.4 in. in diameter. Short-lived perennial, persists through self-seeding. Provide afternoon shade where summers are hot. Refined enough for borders or beds but also appropriate when naturalized at woodland edges or pond and stream margins. Excellent and traditional interplanting for spring bulb displays, forget-me-not foliage provides cover as bulbs fade into dormancy. Susceptible to mildew and rust.

'Bluesylva', part of the Sylva Series, has bright blue flowers and a compact growth habit. 6–8 in. × 12–18 in. The series also includes bright pink, white- or light yellow-eyed 'Rosylva', and white, yellow-eyed 'Snowsylva'. These are especially good for edging.

'Royal Blue Compact' has sky-blue flowers, accented with white or yellow eyes. Compact. 6–8 in. × 4–6 in.

Myrrhis odorata

Myrrhis

Apiaceae
sweet Cicely, garden myrrh

This underused herb earns its place both in herb gardens and in borders. The attractive fern-like foliage is bright green and remains attractive throughout the season. Early summer umbels of flowers are similar to Queen Anne's lace, but since the whole plant is so aromatic they are easy to distinguish.

Sweet Cicely foliage has a light but definite fragrance of anise and is a great addition to fresh-fruit salads, to tart rhubarb and plum pies, and even to meat dishes; the chopped leaves enable less sugar to be used. Ongoing research will determine if sweet Cicely is viable as a sugar substitute for diabetics. The deep roots are also aromatic; sometimes used as a root vegetable. Add seeds ripe or green to add flavor and sweetness to fruit dishes.

Grow sweet Cicely in dappled shade in well-drained, moist, fertile soil. Deadhead to control self-seeding. For best foliage flavor, harvest prior to bloom time.

Start seed in fall in containers for spring planting. Take care not to damage the developing root system.

Myrrhis odorata

- white
- early summer
- 3–4 ft. × 2 ft.
- part shade
- Z3–7

Sweet Cicely, Spanish chervil. Mountains of central Europe. One of the prettiest aromatic herbs in the parsley family, sweet Cicely has stout, ribbed, and hollow stems. These carry delicate ferny leaves, two or three times divided into smaller, toothed leaflets. Small, white flowers arranged in compound umbels top the stems and upper leaf axils. These attract bees, butterflies, and hummingbirds. Persistent seedheads follow; useful in dried arrangements.

Nepeta

Lamiaceae
catmint

A versatile group of plants that offer subtle but elegant colors and textures, together with aromatic foliage and a remarkably trouble-free experience for the gardener. For cats, of course, catmint, especially *Nepeta cataria*, provides a truly intoxicating experience.

Close cousins to mints, catmints have aromatic, opposite leaves, square stems, and tubular,

Nepeta racemosa 'Walker's Low'

two-lipped flowers. However, their roots are seldom as invasive. Commonly catmint foliage is gray-green; the flowers blue spotted with purple. Some species have pink, white, and lilac, even pale yellow blossoms.

Though flowers are individually small, they are borne in verticillasters that produce a more substantial effect. Valuable in several garden niches, catmints range in height from 1–4 ft. for beds and borders, rock gardens, or lining a path or bed. Traditionally rosarians planted catmint to hide the "knees" or stick-like canes of rose bushes. The soft colors and textures of catmints are an attractive counterpoint to the bolder colors and foliage of roses.

Tolerant of dry soils, heat, and full sun, catmints are excellent for xeriscapes, though ordinary garden conditions suffice. They struggle and may melt in the heat and humidity of southeastern US summers; provide early afternoon shade there. Cut back plants hard after their initial flush to promote rebloom. Outstanding for attracting butterflies and bees to the garden; deer resistant, and rarely troubled by insects and diseases.

Divide in spring or fall, or take spring or summer cuttings.

Nepeta govaniana

syn. *Dracocephalum govanianum*
- yellow
- mid- to late summer
- 1.5–3 ft. × 1.5–2 ft.
- sun, part sun
- Z5–9, HS

Yellow catmint. Himalayas, Pakistan, northern India. Branching stems with velvety, aromatic, gray-green leaves; open racemes of pale yellow, tubular, lipped flowers bloom over a long period. Available in United States primarily as seed; should be more readily available.

Nepeta grandiflora

- blue
- midsummer to midfall
- 24–36 in. × 9–12 in.
- sun
- Z4–9

Caucasus catmint. Caucasus Mountains, eastern and central Europe. Velvety, aromatic, silver-gray leaves and tall, showy spikes of lavender to violet flowers. The following are commonly available as cultivars:

'Border Ballet' displays deep violet-blue, almost purple flowers. Start from seed. 18–24 in.

'Dawn to Dusk' has soft pink flowers. 24–36 in. × 18–24 in.

'Pool Bank' has rich blue flowers, with purple-blue bracts. 30–36 in. × 24 in.

'Wild Cat' sports blue-violet flowers with purplish red calyxes. 3 ft. × 2 ft. Z5.

Nepeta racemosa

syn. *N. mussinii*
- purple, lavender
- midspring to early fall
- 9–12 in. × 12–18 in.
- sun, part shade
- Z4–8, HS

Catmint. Caucasus, northern Iran. This low-growing species forms spreading clumps of decumbent stems with hairy, ovate leaves, with heart-shaped bases and crenate margins. Pale to dark violet flowers, 0.5 in. long. Shear spent blooms to encourage later rebloom. Exceptionally drought tolerant; outstanding for xeriscapes. Self-seeds; may become invasive. Useful for rock gardens, border fronts, herb gardens, for lining paths or beds, and as a groundcover.

'Little Titch' has pale blue flowers. 6 in. high and wide.

'Walker's Low' produces abundant crops of lavender-blue flowers; deadhead spent flower spikes routinely for continuous bloom from spring to fall. Sterile. Named for a place, and not its habit. 2007 PPA Plant of the Year. 2.5 ft. × 3 ft.

Nepeta sibirica

syn. *Dracocephalum sibiricum*
- purple
- early to late summer
- 30–48 in. × 12–24 in.
- sun, part shade
- Z3–8, HS

Siberian catmint. Siberia. Upright with handsome, aromatic, soft gray-green foliage, and whorled clusters of rich blue flowers. Cold-hardiest catmint, but struggles with the mugginess of the southeastern United States. Well-drained soil is essential. Fast growing, good as a low hedge, in coastal gardens, and on sunny banks. Adapts well to containers.

'Souvenir d'André Chaudron' has violet-blue flowers. Sometimes sold as 'Blue Beauty'. 12–18 in. high and wide.

Nepeta subsessilis

- blue
- midspring to early fall
- 1.5–2 ft. × 1–1.5 ft.
- sun, part shade
- Z4–8

Japanese catmint. Moist Japanese mountainsides. Mounds of aromatic, toothed, green leaves, and showy spikes of 2-in., bell-shaped, maroon-spotted, deep violet-blue flowers. Not as drought tolerant. Plant in borders, herb gardens, or naturalized plantings; outstanding for rain gardens.

'Candy Cat'. Dense clusters of pale lavender-pink flowers. 2 ft.

'Cool Cat' has white-specked, lavender-blue flowers. 2–2.5 ft.

'Sweet Dreams' bears pink flowers with burgundy bracts. 18 in.

'Washfield' carries erect branching spikes of vibrant blue-violet flowers. 1.5 ft.

Other Notable Cultivars

×*faassenii* strain, typically sterile and non-invasive, includes: 'Blue Wonder', with dark blue flowers. 1–2 ft. 'Select Blue'. Long, tapered, gray-green leaves in neat mounds; long blooming. Vigorous and drought tolerant. 15 in. × 18 in. 'Six Hills Giant' displays 9- to 12-in.-long spikes of deep purple flowers. 3–4 ft.

'Joanna Read' (*Nepeta sibirica* × *N.* ×*faassenii*) has darker violet flowers than other nepetas, to 3 ft. Named for Pennsylvania plantswoman Joanna Read. Z3–8.

Nierembergia
Solanaceae
cupflower

Although routinely cultivated as annuals, these petunia relatives perform as perennials in mild-winter climates. Winter hardiness varies, but the most cold-tolerant cupflowers overwinter successfully in protected sites as far north as zone 7, or Long Island, NY. South American in origin, cup plants offer attractive dense cushions of narrow leaves and prolific, long-blooming displays of small, cup-shaped, blue, purple, or white flowers.

Full sun, and reasonably fertile, moderately moist soil that drains well, suit these plants best; apply moisture-retaining mulch in hotter regions. Nierembergias struggle with heat and humidity, but cope well with dry heat, with irrigation. Pinch young plants for bushy, compact growth. Deadhead to prolong bloom; shear if flowering flags. Generally trouble free but susceptible to tobacco mosaic virus, slugs, and snails; deer resistant.

Mass cupflowers as a colorful groundcover, let them spill down a sunny south- or west-facing bank, tuck them into a rock garden, or use them to edge beds, borders, or paths. Nierembergias also shine as container plantings and in hanging baskets.

Propagate by seed, layering, or by stem cuttings.

Nierembergia gracilis 'Starry Eyes'
- blue
- spring to fall
- 10 in. × 18 in.
- sun
- Z8–10

A Yucca Do Nursery introduction that has proven exceptionally tolerant of heat and humidity. Tight mounds of evergreen, linear foliage covered with upward-facing, light lavender, bell-shaped flowers all season.

Nierembergia scoparia
syn. *N. frutescens*
- blue, white
- late spring to fall
- 1–2.5 ft. high and wide
- sun, part shade
- Z7–10

Cupflower. Chile. Shrubby perennial that forms a dense mound of finely cut, stiff, 0.75-in., linear to spathulate leaves. Cup-shaped, pale blue flowers, to 1 in. across, cover plants for several months.

'Blue Eyes' has blue-centered, white flowers. 8–10 in. × 24 in.

'Mont Blanc' has yellow-eyed, white flowers. 6 in. × 12 in.

'Purple Robe' has violet-blue flowers. 6 in. × 12 in.

Other Notable Cultivars

'Augusta Blue Skies' is heat and humidity resistant; lavender-blue flowers. 8–12 in. × 24 in. Z9–11.

Summer Splash cupflowers from Suntory are fast growing and heat resistant; the series includes: 'Bouquet Blue', with yellow-eyed, pale lavender flowers. 6–8 in. high and wide. Z8–11. 'Bouquet White' is white with yellow eye, 20–30 in. × 24 in. Z8–11. 'Light Blue' is pale blue with blue eyes, 20–30 in. × 24 in. Z9–11.

Nipponanthemum
Asteraceae
Nippon daisy, Montauk daisy

Another genus whose classification has been a subject of debate among botanists: in the past, Nippon daisies, which all derive from a single species, have been included in *Chrysanthemum* or *Leucanthemum*; this confusion is evident in nursery catalogs (be warned!). The current consensus is that they deserve their own genus (*Nipponanthemum*).

Japanese *N. nipponicum* has naturalized well, particularly in the Montauk region of Long Island, NY, the source of its alternate common name. It is known chiefly as a seaside plant, and its tolerance of salt spray makes it an excellent choice for coastal

Nierembergia 'Augusta Blue Skies'

Nipponanthemum nipponicum

Oenothera 'Cold Crick'

gardens. However, it also thrives inland, although Nippon daisies are grown less often there.

Nippon daisies have much in common with Shasta daisies (*Leucanthemum*), but differ mainly in their late flowering season; perfect for fall gardens often short on fresh bloom. Easy to grow.

Best in full sun, in fertile, very well-drained soil, where these daisies are largely self-sufficient. Cut the old growth in late spring, almost to ground level to force strong new growth that will produce abundant bloom later. Left uncut the plants become leggy and ungainly, demanding sedums or low grasses as companion plants to camouflage their ugly "legs." Suitable in mixed or perennial borders, among foundation plantings and to line walkways, or in dry, difficult areas where watering is impossible. They are superior additions to wildlife gardens where fall-berried shrubs are fine companions; an excellent nectar source for migrating butterflies.

Pests and diseases are seldom serious; if deer and rabbit damage occurs it is also minor.

Root cuttings of young growth, or divide older plants before spring growth commences.

Nipponanthemum nipponicum

syn. *Chrysanthemum nipponicum, Leucanthemum nipponicum*

- white
- late summer to late fall
- 1–3 ft. × 2–3 ft.
- sun
- Z5–9

Nippon daisy, Montauk daisy. Japan. Stiff branching stems, woody at the base, are clothed alternately with glossy, thick, dark green foliage, that often crowds into the upper portions; the lower leaves may drop prematurely. Toothed leaves, 3.5 in. long, are narrowly oval. The sparkling heads of white flowers may reach 3 in. across, with a central greenish yellow disk. They are held singly on unbranched stems and make fine cut flowers. Deadhead to extend bloom time.

Oenothera fruticosa 'Fyrverkeri'

Oenothera

Onagraceae
evening primrose, sundrops

Delicate though these flowers may appear, evening primroses are what ecologists describe as "pioneer plants." That is, they move in to colonize disturbed sites quickly, and may become weedy if released into gardens. In naturalized areas or patches of poor soil in need of stabilization, this vigorous growth is an asset. When planted into beds, borders, or other designed areas of the landscape, however, care must be taken that their rhizomatous roots do not strangle their neighbors. Conscientious deadheading is essential to limit seeding about, filling the surrounding areas with volunteers. Generally pest and disease free; seldom browsed by deer.

The common names refer to a characteristic of many members of this genus: the flower buds open in the evening, often unfolding in a matter of seconds, to attract night-flying pollinating insects particularly moths. Pollinated by different insects, sundrops open during the day. The four-petaled blossoms are usually yellow, but may also be white, pink, purple, or red. The stigmas are four branched, forming a prominent *X* at each bloom's center, an easy identifying mark of the genus.

Propagate by seed, or divide mature plants.

Oenothera berlandieri

syn. *O. speciosa* var. *berlandieri*

- pink, white
- spring to fall
- 8–12 in. × 3 ft.

- sun, part shade
- Z5–9

Mexican evening primrose. Texas, southern New Mexico, Mexico. The obovate, 1- to 3-in. leaves are evergreen into zone 8, deciduous farther north. Pink or white, cup-shaped flowers, to 1.5 in. across, are long blooming. Plants adapt well to infertile soils; drought tolerant and ideal as xeriscape plants. This aggressive spreader is useful as a soil stabilizer.

'Siskyou' bears prolific crops of fragrant, 2-in.-diameter flowers above small, dark green leaves, irregularly spotted purplish red.

'Twilight' has elongated, green-edged, dark bronze-purple leaves, and large, pale pink flowers.

Oenothera fruticosa

- yellow
- late spring
- 15–30 in. × 12–24 in.

- sun, part shade
- Z4–8

Sundrops. Native throughout eastern North America. Erect stems clad with 1- to 3-in. lanceolate leaves rise from basal rosettes. Terminal clusters of bright yellow flowers; individual blooms are short lived but flowers open in succession for up to two months. Seeds borne in distinctive, club-shaped capsules. Thrives on any average to moderately fertile, even poor, well-drained soil; tolerates dryish soils in hot summers.

'Fyrverkeri' ('Fireworks') sports purple, brown-tinged foliage on red stems; red flower buds open to bright yellow flowers. Superior to the species. Compact, to 18 in. tall.

Oenothera macrocarpa

syn. *O. missouriensis*

- yellow
- midspring to midsummer

- 0.75–1 ft. × 1–1.5 ft.
- sun
- Z3–7

Missouri evening primrose. Southern and central United States. Narrowly lanceolate leaves on sprawling stems. Mildly fragrant, usually upward-facing, bright yellow goblet flowers emerge from the leaf axils, followed by 2- to 3-in., winged seedpods. Adapts easily to average, well-drained soils including clays and dry, rocky ones; drought tolerant. Susceptible to root rot if poorly drained.

Oenothera speciosa

- white, pink
- early to late summer
- 0.75–2 ft. × 1–1.5 ft.

- sun
- Z4–9

White evening primrose, pink ladies. Southwestern United States, Mexico. Sprawling stems bear medium green, 1- to 3-in., narrowly lanceolate to oblanceolate leaves, sometimes lobed below. Showy, bowl-shaped, fragrant, 3-in. flowers are borne in leaf axils; they open in the evening, at first white but maturing to rosy pink. Seed capsules are oval, ridged, and 2 in. long. Self-seeding, plus spreading rhizomes can be aggressive. Tolerates light afternoon shade and drought. Cultural needs are similar to other species.

'Pink Petticoats' has yellow-centered pink blooms.

Other Notable Cultivars

'Cold Crick' seems to be a chance hybrid that is sterile and does not set seed. It is a clumping plant that does not spread. Typical bright yellow, cup-shaped flowers over a long period. Day blooming. 10–12 in. × 12 in. Z5–8.

Omphalodes

Boraginaceae
navelwort

Few woodland plants are more charming companions for spring-blooming bulbs. Navelwort's bright blue, often white-eyed flowers with spreading petals are reminiscent of related forget-me-nots and hound's tongue. Excellent shaded in wild gardens, along walkways, in rock gardens, for edging, or mass planting as groundcovers, navelworts are evergreen in mild-winter climates, semi-evergreen elsewhere. Provide humus-rich soil as might be found under deciduous trees, in part shade. Although navelworts tolerate short periods of drought, they are unsuitable for dry gardens.

Apart from slugs and snails, which dine on the young growth, pests and diseases are seldom serious. Navelworts resist deer and rabbits.

Divide carefully in spring, disturbing the roots as little as possible. Sow seed in spring.

Omphalodes cappadocia

- blue
- early spring
- 8–12 in. × 12–15 in.
- part shade, shade
- Z6–8

Navelwort. Turkey. Clumps spread slowly by rhizomes and become substantial over time. Basal tufts of 4-in., lightly hairy leaves, ovate to heart shaped and pointed at the tips; loose terminal clusters of up to ten white-eyed, azure flowers bloom above.

'Cherry Ingram' has bright blue flowers that mature to lavender. 12–18 in.

'Joy Skies' is long blooming into early summer. Arching, trailing stems with lance-shaped leaves; open, starry, azure flowers. 12 in.

'Starry Eyes' has white flowers with a sky-blue flare down the middle of each petal. 10 in.

Omphalodes verna

- blue
- spring
- 6–8 in. × 12 in.
- part shade, shade
- Z6–9

Blue-eyed Mary, creeping navelwort, creeping forget-me-not. Southern Europe. Named for Queen Marie Antoinette, this creeper spreads rapidly by underground stems. Its hairy, pointed, 1- to 3-in., oval leaves have conspicuous veins; evergreen in mild-winter regions. Useful in informal cottage gardens, in city courtyards, and on banks as well as along woodland edges.

'Alba' is white flowered.

'Grandiflora' has larger electric-blue flowers and coarse foliage. A fine groundcover under spring shrubs, especially rhododendrons. 6 in. tall.

Ophiopogon
Asparagaceae (Convallariaceae)
mondo grass

This Asian genus is valuable in the garden for its smooth, slender, grassy leaves that serve well as ground cover, as edgings along pathways, at the front of borders, or in rock gardens. Evergreen in mild climates, but becomes wind and frost damaged by severe cold. Mondo grass contrasts well with larger-leaved hostas, as well as delicately foliaged ferns and astilbes.

Ophiopogons are often confused with similar *Liriope* and share a common name, lilyturf. A singular difference is that liriope flower spikes are held

Omphalodes verna 'Alba'

Ophiopogon planiscapus 'Ebony Knight', with ferns

above the leaves, in contrast to those of mondo grass that often are almost hidden among the foliage.

Very adaptable about soil, mondo grass does best where it is fertile and drains well. In cooler climates, a sunny spot is fine, but elsewhere part or light shade is preferable. Does not tolerate drought, but handles heat and humidity well. Avoid mulching black-leaved selections with dark-colored mulch as visual impact is lost, bright ferns contrast well. Seldom bothered by deer or rabbits, but slugs and snails may shred the leaves.

Easy care, mondo grass spreads slowly. As a groundcover, set the plants 8–10 in. apart (even closer if they are small) so they knit together quickly. Cut back almost to ground level in spring as new growth commences. In colder regions, foliage often becomes shabby in cold weather, especially where it is windy; don't be afraid to cut back hard.

Propagate by dividing the roots in spring as new growth emerges, or start from seed sown as soon as it is ripe.

Ophiopogon japonicus
syn. *Mondo japonicum*
- white, lilac
- summer
- 8–15 in. × 12 in.
- sun, part shade
- Z6–11, HT

Mondo grass, dwarf lilyturf. Native in shaded woodlands of Korea and Japan. Rhizomatous and clumping with slender, grassy, 12-in.-long leaves, often curved. Short spikes of 0.25-in., bell-shaped flowers nestle among the foliage. Blue-black, 0.5-in., berry-like fruits follow. Good in coastal gardens. There are several notable cultivars:

'Compactus' is very small, reaching only about 2 in. Charming in troughs.

'Kyoto Dwarf' is also compact, about 2–4 in. tall.

'Nana Variegata' has short tufts of silver-rimmed, dark green leaves. 2–3 in.

'Silver Dragon' has leaves variegated with white. 12 in. 'Variegatus' is similar.

Ophiopogon planiscapus
- white, purple
- summer
- 8–15 in. × 12 in.
- sun, part shade
- Z6–11

Lilyturf, mondo grass. Japan, Korea. The species is seldom offered, in favor of the dramatic purplish black–leaved cultivars included here. Spreading clumps of evergreen, strap-shaped leaves rise from rhizomatous roots. Lavender-flushed white flowers in 2- to 3-in. racemes; small, deep blue-black berries follow.

'Niger' ('Nigrescens', 'Black Dragon', 'Arabicus') has near-black persistent foliage and short spikes of pinkish light purple to white flowers that nestle among the foliage. Purplish black berries. Contrast with silver- or gold-foliaged plants: wormwoods, lamb's ears, or golden creeping Jenny. Spreads slowly. 6–8 in.

Ebony Knight ('Ebknizam') has evergreen, purple-black foliage; spikes of small lavender flowers and small black berries. Slow spreading; excellent in otherwise inhospitable dry sites.

Opuntia
Cactaceae
prickly pear

Cacti are considered plants of the southwestern American deserts, but opuntias are in fact indigenous throughout the United States, except northern

Opuntia humifusa

New England. Characterized by their combination of broad, flat, fleshy pads (cladodes) and their armament of large spines, combined with smaller, easily detached, hair-like prickles (glochids), commonly prickly pears also offer large, showy flowers, and edible red or purple fruits. In ornamental landscapes they provide striking textural contrast, and a nearly impenetrable barrier when massed. Almost invulnerable to drought, prickly pears are an obvious choice for xeriscape plantings, and an effective groundcover for sandy or gravely sunny banks. Their simple, architectural form is interesting in container plantings. Be aware, however, that prickly pears shrivel in chilly regions at the onset of cold weather, and remain unsightly until they plump up again in spring. Resistant to rabbits and deer; attracts hummingbirds.

Providing very well-drained soils in an open location with full sun is critical. Opuntias are susceptible to few pests and diseases over most of their range, but persistently damp soils are lethal. In the southeastern United States, principally Florida and Louisiana, the larvae of an introduced moth, *Cactoblastis cactorum*, attacks prickly pears. This creature tunnels into the pads destroying them from the inside out; evidence of them should be immediately reported to your local Cooperative Extension.

Propagate by removing and rooting pads.

Opuntia basilaris

- pink, mauve
- mid- to late spring
- 6–12 in. × 1–6 ft.
- sun
- Z7–10

Beavertail cactus. California to Utah, south through Arizona. Gray-green pads, 1–6 in. × 2–13 in., with fancied resemblance to a beaver's tail. Almost to completely spineless pads; clad with glochids. Brilliant 2- to 3-in., red-to-lavender flowers; 1-in., brownish gray, oval fruits follow.

Opuntia cacanapa

- yellow
- early to midsummer
- 3–4 ft. × 4–6 ft.
- sun
- Z7–10

Tiger tongue. Southwestern United States, northern Mexico. Chiefly available as the spineless (and glochid-less) selection 'Ellisiana'. This forms a mound of erect, 6-in., gray-green, spineless pads. Large red fruits follow bright yellow flowers. A boon to gardeners with sensitive hands and skin.

Opuntia humifusa

syn. *O. compressa*

- yellow
- early summer
- 0.5–1 ft. × 1–3 ft.
- sun
- Z4–9

Eastern prickly pear. Eastern and central United States, north to southern Ontario. Forms jointed clusters of round-to-oval, flattened, succulent, green pads, 2–10 in. across. Showy bright yellow flowers, some with reddish eyes, are 2–3 in. in diameter with 8 to 12 yellow petals and a thick central boss of yellow stamens. Edible, red, egg-shaped fruits, to 2 in. thick, have a melon-like flavor. They ripen in late summer to fall; difficult to harvest. Well adapted to rock gardens, dry-stone walls, sandy slopes, and dry prairie plantings. *Opuntia macrorhiza* is very similar.

Origanum

Lamiaceae
oregano

If you think oregano is useful only as a culinary spice, think again, for several species can also add savor to perennial gardens. As Mediterranean region natives, these plants thrive with little water and high heat, but cannot tolerate high humidity.

Erect or spreading stems carry opposite pairs of aromatic leaves; clusters of flowers are borne in whorls around the stems. Individual blossoms are tiny, two-lipped, mostly tubular, and protected by colorful bracts that remain attractive for several

Origanum 'Kent Beauty' is a central player in this ornamental herb design

Origanum laevigatum 'Herrenhausen'

weeks. Oreganos do best in sunny spots in average or even poor soils that drain freely, preferably with an alkaline pH; dress plants with lime if soil is acid. Root rot may result from poor drainage. Little care is required, except for shearing back in early spring as new growth commences.

Ornamental oreganos are appropriate for mixed and perennial borders, in herb gardens, and as edgings in vegetable gardens; the lower growers are attractive in rock gardens and tumbling over walls. Good where water is scarce. Bees and butterflies flock to them; deer and rabbit resistant.

Propagate by seed or division in spring, or take cuttings of young basal growth in late spring.

Origanum laevigatum
- purple
- mid- to late summer
- 1–2 ft. × 2 ft.
- sun
- Z5–9

Marjoram. Turkey, Cyprus. Wiry, upright or sprawling stems, often maroon, rise from woody rootstocks. Oval, dark green leaves, about 0.5 in. long with conspicuous veins, borne in opposing pairs. Tubular, 0.5-in., purplish pink flowers with darker bracts cluster at stem tips from midsummer on. Stems may flop with the weight of the flowers; stake at 6–12 in. with pea sticks, grow among stronger stemmed companions, or allow to tumble over a retaining wall. Appropriate with roses and summer perennials, especially in fragrance gardens.

'Herrenhausen' has increasingly deep maroon foliage as nights cool. Light purple flowers. 2 ft.

'Hopley's Purple' has bright purple flowers, large, 0.5-in. bracts, and purplish foliage that greens in summer. Lovely fresh or dried cut flower. 2 ft.

'Pilgrim' is upright with bluish green leaves; bright rosy flowers. 15–18 in.

Origanum libanoticum
- pink
- midsummer
- 12–18 in. × 18–24 in.
- sun
- Z5–10

Cascading ornamental oregano, hopflower oregano. Lebanon. Trailing wiry stems are embellished at the tips by hop-like whorls of pink-tipped, pale green bracts guarding tiny, pink flowers. Smooth, rounded leaves are bluish green. A fine subject to billow over and decorate walls and terraces, and for hanging baskets and window boxes.

Origanum rotundifolium
- pink
- early to late summer
- 9–12 in. × 12 in.
- sun, part shade
- Z5–8

Round-leaved oregano. Turkey, Armenia. Low mounds of aromatic, grayish green, rounded, 0.5-in. leaves, and nodding clusters of apple-green bracts that shelter small, pink flowers.

'Kent Beauty' has largely replaced the species in gardens. This beautiful mounding plant has rounded, 1-in., blue-green leaves with prominently white-etched veins, and abundant apple-green-bracted pink flowers in hop-like clusters. The bracts are often flushed with pink especially on the undersides. Use stems in fresh floral arrangements or cut before they brown for winter decoration. Plant in hanging baskets, on top of a wall, or in raised beds or containers.

Origanum vulgare
- pink, purple
- midsummer to fall
- 12–36 in. × 15–24 in.
- sun
- Z4–9

Oregano, pot marjoram, wild marjoram. Europe. The most widely used culinary oregano. Vigorous, spreading by rhizomes. Very aromatic, 1- to 2-in. leaves are rounded and fuzzy, green in the species. Loose, whorled clusters of small flowers in light pinks to deep pinks and purples, with leaf-like, purple-flushed bracts. Cultivars include:

'Aureum' (Golden Oregano) has golden foliage; pink flowers. Not as aggressive as the species. An attractive groundcover in rock gardens, or herb garden edgings. 4–6 in. tall.

'Aureum Crispum' has curly yellow leaves crisped along the edge.

'Compactum' is 2–4 in. tall.

subsp. *hirtum* (syn. *Origanum heracleoticum*) is Greek oregano, the subspecies with the strongest flavor. White flowers, hairy leaves and bracts. Greece and Turkey.

Orostachys
Crassulaceae
hardy dunce cap

Some plants provide the big effects—others, such as *Orostachys*, provide the small but unforgettable details. A genus of 13 small but exquisite succulents, these plants form compact rosettes of fleshy, scale-like leaves. As they mature, the original rosette extends slender stems that form new rosettes at their tips, creating a slowly expanding but typically compact colony. When a rosette has fully matured, usually after a period of years, its center bulges upward, forming a conical spike (or "dunce cap") of smaller scales that finally covers itself with tiny flowers. The rosettes are monocarpic—i.e., they die after flowering just once, but a plant lives on through the younger offsets. An obvious choice for trough gardens and containers, this genus includes some of the cold hardiest of all succulents and provides gems for rock or gravel gardens too.

These designer dunce caps require very well-drained, preferably sandy soil, and prefer dry winters; cold, wet, winter soil is fatal. Water regularly, but avoid wetting the leaves. *Orostachys* tolerates light shade, but the rosettes are tightest and most attractive when grown in full sun. Mostly trouble free, except for a susceptibility to aphids and deer. Propagate by detaching and replanting offsets.

Orostachys aggregatus

syn. *Sedum aggregatum*
- white, yellow
- late summer
- 3–6 in. × 3–12 in.
- sun
- Z5–8

Dunce cap. Native to Japan. Forms tight basal rosettes of oblong to oval, grayish green, 1-in., succulent leaves. Clusters of rosettes spread over time to 12 in. or more. Leaves turn purplish in fall. Tiny, white to pale yellow flowers. As a groundcover, plant at 12-in. intervals. Naturalizes where hospitable.

Orostachys furusei

- yellow
- late summer
- 3–6 in. × 6–12 in.
- sun
- Z6–10

Dunce cap. Asia. Basal rosette, to 4 in. high and wide, of succulent, oblong, lavender-gray leaves to 1 in. long. Thin, stolon-like branchlets emerge from leaf axils to produce offsets at their tips, and develop into clusters to 12 in. across. Tiny, yellow flowers held in 6-in. spikes, appear usually during the second or third year of growth.

Oxalis

Oxalidaceae
shamrock, sorrel

It is unfortunate that so many gardeners have had to battle with self-seeding, weedy oxalis, and have become gun-shy about even looking at some of the 800 or more species, many of which are highly garden worthy. Species are native across the world, with the exception of the Poles. North and South America, South Africa, and Brazil are home to many.

Species that have become the bane of many gardeners include yellow-flowered creeping wood sorrel (*Oxalis repens*), yellow wood sorrel (*O. stricta*), and creeping, or yellow sorrel (*O. corniculata*). All release their seeds explosively and are on numerous invasive exotic lists.

Mostly, leaves are divided into three more or less triangular leaflets that fold together at night. The solitary or clustered flowers are yellow, pink, or white, and also may close at dusk. Leaves have a sharply bitter taste due to sour oxalic acid.

For best effect, group shamrocks in the landscape. Most prefer a lightly shaded place, but tolerate sun well in regions where it is not too intense. Slightly acid, well-drained, average to fertile soil is perfect; dig in compost at planting time to help retain moisture. Shamrocks make superior indoor plants where there is plenty of light but not

Orostachys furusei

Oxalis regnellii 'Jade'

necessarily direct sun: windowsills, sunrooms, or greenhouses; a pre-made container soil mix is best. Do not overwater, but these are not desert plants either, so keep the soil damp. If foliage becomes shabby from drought or too much sun, pull affected leaves out with a sharp tug and keep watered; after a light feeding, the foliage will come back fresh and new. Water sparingly through short winter days.

In the landscape oxalis can be massed on a large scale, or used to edge paths and walkways. In summer borders, they blend well with coral bells, low hardy geraniums, and *Sedum rupestre* 'Angelina'. Dark-foliaged types provide interesting foils for silver- and gold-leaved plants such as *Hosta* 'Gold Edger' or 'Piedmont Gold', *Artemisia* 'Silver Mound', or *Tradescantia* 'Blue n' Gold' ('Sweet Kate'). Interesting in large mixed containers with coleus, forced spring bulbs, or succulents. Other interesting species include *O. crassipes*, *O. bowiei*, and an adorable newcomer, *O. palmifrons*, that surely must become a winner.

Problems include rust, manifested by orange pustules on the leaves causing discoloration. Deer and rabbits rarely browse oxalis.

Increase by dividing the rhizomes or small bulb clumps as they become overcrowded.

Oxalis regnellii

- pink
- summer
- 4–8 in. × 12 in.
- sun, part shade
- Z6–11

Oxalis, purple shamrock. South Africa, South America. Often grown as a houseplant, this oxalis will also be fine outdoors within its zones; non-invasive. Small tubers multiply readily to form good-sized clumps in a couple of years. Rising from the tubers, slender, watery, 3- to 6-in. stems support green, tripartite leaves marked with a central triangular blotch. Flower stems are brittle, with two to four pink or white, funnel-shaped, 1-in. flowers. Blooms almost year-round indoors, and all summer in the landscape. Winter deciduous except indoors.

'Atropurpurea' has leaves purplish green above, but deep purple beneath.

'Jade' ('Charmed Jade', 'Jroxfroja') has olive-green leaves and white flowers.

'Silverado' (possibly a synonym for 'Silver Shadow'). Olive-green leaflets conspicuously marked with silver. White flowers.

subsp. *triangularis*. Purple-and-black false shamrock, love plant, purple shamrock. The nomenclature of this plant is confused. Easy and clumping, this subspecies has triangular, dark purple leaflets irregularly and widely bordered with velvety black. Clusters of pale pink, 1.25-in. flowers. 8–10 in. Z6–10.

The Triangularis Group has received considerable breeding attention, resulting in notable strains: The Allure series includes unpatterned foliage: Burgundy (purple with pink flowers), Ebony (black with white flowers), Lavender (mauve pink with white flowers), Mahogany (brownish with pink flowers), and Silver (metallic jade with pink flowers). The Charmed Series includes plain-leaved Velvet (very dark purple with white flowers), Jade (pale pink-flushed white flowers), and Wine (plum colored leaves, pink flowers).

Oxalis tetraphylla

syn. *O. deppei*

- pink
- late spring to summer
- 4–6 in. × 6 in.
- sun, part shade, shade
- Z7–10

Good luck plant, lucky clover. Mexico. Arising from small, scaly bulbs, the bright green leaves of this charmer are composed of four triangular leaflets each about 2 in. long with rounded edges. Each leaflet may be accented with a purple-red chevron pointing toward the tip. Clusters of funnel-shaped, five-petaled, rosy pink flowers, yellowish at the throat, open wide in sun.

'Iron Cross' is notable for the dark burgundy cross-shaped blotch that marks from the base to about halfway along each leaflet.

Pachysandra

Buxaceae
spurge

The most familiar species of this genus, Japanese pachysandra (*Pachysandra terminalis*) is a plant undone by its own popularity: it has become such a cliché of suburban American landscapes that many serious gardeners avoid it on principle. Nevertheless, it can be an invaluable problem solver. Indeed, for a shady or semi-shaded site in temperate, moist climates, Japanese pachysandra and Allegheny spurge, *P. procumbens*, have no equal when it comes to excluding weeds and providing neat, fast-spreading evergreen or semi-evergreen groundcovers. Their growth habit, the way in which they infiltrate the surface of the ground with a dense network of rhizomes, enables them to flourish on soils too shallow to support much else as long as moisture is adequate. As a result, they thrive even under shallow-rooted maples and other trees.

Japanese pachysandra won the favor of landscapers by its trouble-free nature; once established on a site, it requires almost no maintenance. Recently, however, it has fallen prey to fungal pachysandra leaf blight (*Volutella pachysandricola*), which if not addressed rapidly destroys even extensive plantings. Fortunately, the American species has so far proven immune.

Divide in spring or take softwood cuttings in early summer.

Pachysandra axillaris

- white
- early spring to midfall
- 6–10 in. × 24 in.
- part shade
- Z6–9

Spurge. Sichuan, China. Evergreen, slow growing; forms small clumps that spread by underground stolons. Leaves somewhat glabrous, triangularly lanceolate with irregular serrated edges. Inconspicuous spikes of tiny white, mildly fragrant flowers borne in the leaf axils. Prefers shady, moist site. No reports of susceptibility to leaf blight. Still uncommon but gaining popularity.

'Windcliff', a Dan Hinkley introduction, is low growing. 4–6 in. tall.

Pachysandra procumbens

- white
- early spring
- 6–10 in. × 12–24 in.
- part shade, shade
- Z5–9

Allegheny spurge. Rich woods and rocky slopes of Kentucky, West Virginia, and western North Carolina to northwestern Florida and southern Louisiana. Clump forming with procumbent stems. Evergreen (semi-evergreen in colder regions), scalloped, pewter green, ovate leaves develop pale silver mottling that fades as leaves mature. Bottlebrush-like, 2- to 4-in. spikes of small, fragrant, white flowers. Avoid poorly drained, heavy clay soils. Handsome foliage for shady beds or borders, excellent ground-cover for shaded areas, especially appropriate for woodland gardens. Less aggressive than *Pachysandra terminalis*, coexists with other woodland natives, a useful cover for spring ephemerals. No serious pest or disease problems.

'Eco Treasure' has more heavily variegated leaves.

'Forest Green' is variegated with silvery white blotches; heavier tufts of leaves on each stem. Good for gardens of the Mid-Atlantic region. 6–12 in. Z4–9.

Pachysandra terminalis

- white
- early spring
- 6–12 in. × 12–18 in.
- part shade, shade
- Z5–9

Japanese pachysandra, Japanese spurge. Japan, north-central China. Evergreen, spreads vigorously by rhizomes. Ovate, 2- to 4-in. leaves borne in whorls at stem tips. Terminal, 1- to 2-in. spikes of tiny, scentless, white to pinkish flowers. Tolerates clay and dry soils, drought, dense shade, deer, and rabbits. Good air circulation discourages leaf blight; root rot, scale, and mites may be problems.

'Green Carpet' has deep green foliage.

'Green Sheen' has extra glossy, bright green leaves.

'Variegata' has gray-green to dark green leaves with irregular creamy-white mottling along the edges. Not as vigorous.

Paeonia
Paeoniaceae
peony

As close to foolproof as any perennial can be, peonies offer spectacular, fragrant bloom combined with handsome foliage, and a lifespan that may last half a century or more. The Chinese, who brought peonies into their gardens as early as the 7th century ad, first recognized the ornamental potential

Paeonia lactiflora 'Krinkled White'

Pachysandra procumbens 'Forest Green'

of this genus. Contemporary gardeners will find peonies useful when planted singly for adding substance as well as color to mixed borders, and fine material for low, informal hedges.

Peonies are unmatched as cut flowers. Shasta daisies, flax, and bearded irises all make good companions for them. Easy and generally pest free; susceptible to foliar diseases, botrytis blight, and phytophthora blight, especially where air circulation is poor. Deer and rabbit resistant.

Peonies are another genus that offers an embarrassment of riches; there are many hundreds of cultivars from which to choose. Fortunately, identifying those that suit your conditions and taste is a relatively simple process.

Garden peonies are commonly divided into three groups:

Herbaceous peonies behave as perennials, dying back to the ground every fall. The older cultivars, which descend from Chinese garden peonies, are mostly selections of the species *Paeonia lactiflora*. Many modern breeders continue to work within that group, but in the 20th century a number of hybrid groups, descended from crosses of two or more species, appeared; hybrids represent an increasing proportion of the new introductions. Herbaceous peonies form multi-stemmed clumps, 1.5–3 ft. high and wide, with shiny green leaves that persist throughout the summer. They bloom during the transition from spring into summer, with

Japanese/anemone type *Paeonia* 'Do Tell'

each individual cultivar blooming for an average of seven to ten days. Flower colors of herbaceous peonies range from white to yellow to coral to pink to red to maroon. There are no blues, and true yellows are rare: the species *P. mlokosewitschii* bears lemon-yellow flowers, and a handful of hybrids, including 'Claire de Lune', 'Prairie Moon' and 'Goldilocks', also have pale yellow flowers.

Tree peonies, despite their name, are deciduous, woody-stemmed shrubs. A mature tree peony in full flower is one of the most dramatic sights of spring gardens, and provides a magnificent focal point in a mixed border. As shrubs, however, they are outside the scope of this guide.

Itoh peonies, or intersectional peonies, are crosses between herbaceous and tree peonies. These hybrids behave like herbaceous perennials, but exhibit the larger blossom type of their shrubby parent, with flowers 8–10 in. in diameter. They are outstandingly floriferous; mature plants may bear 30 to 50 blossoms apiece. Flower color range is similar except that the intersectionals include more bright yellows. Their height and spread is similar to that of herbaceous peonies, typically 2–3 ft. Disease-resistant foliage. Mostly hardy to zone 4.

Peonies are further categorized by their flower form:

Single. Flowers with a single ring of petals

Japanese/anemone type Flowers whose pollen-bearing stamens have become more or less transformed into staminodes or narrow petaloids, resulting in slightly fuller blossoms.

Semi-double. Flowers with more than one row of petals emerging from the crown of the flower; the central cluster of pollen-bearing anthers is visible during bloom.

Full double. Flowers with multiple rows of petals, with so many of the floral stamens and stigmas converted into petals that no trace of the flower's sexual parts are visible.

Bombs. A type of double peony; the central petals form a globular cluster that rests on a "halo" of flattened outer "guard" petals; guard petals are often differently colored from the central petals.

Growers also commonly categorize herbaceous peonies by indicating when a cultivar blooms within the four- to five-week herbaceous peony season. Intersectional peonies have a prolonged period of flowering; individual plants typically remain in bloom for three to four weeks, peaking near the end of the herbaceous peony season.

Peony flowers are famous for their intoxicating fragrances, from sweet to citrusy and spicy. Not all peonies are fragrant; the perfume intensity varies markedly even among fragrant types. Double-flowered selections tend to be more fragrant than single ones; pink- or white-flowered types have more fragrance than red-flowered ones. A light but pronounced citrus or spicy fragrance is common among the intersectionals.

Paeonia lactiflora cultivars are mostly hardy through zone 2. Other species and many hybrids may be less cold hardy, but commonly overwinter successfully through zone 3. The intersectional peonies are hardy to zone 4.

Peonies require between 500 to 1000 winter chilling hours (between 32–40°F) to flower successfully; zone 8 is the southern edge of their range. Gardeners in warm regions find that early-blooming cultivars are best adapted to their climate; the onset of very hot weather in late spring causes the buds of late-blooming cultivars to abort. Furthermore, single or Japanese types generally perform better in such areas than do doubles. The intersectional peonies cope well with the combined heat and humidity of southeastern summers.

Most peonies prefer full sun. In zone 8 where the summer sun is intense, partial shade is beneficial. Several species tolerate moderate shade, especially *P. anomala*, *P. mlokosewitschii*, and *P. obovata* (*P. japonica*).

Paeonia anomala

- red
- late spring
- 18–24 in. high and wide
- sun, part shade
- Z2–7

Anomalous peony. Native to coniferous woods, dry grasslands, rocky hillsides, northern Russia through central Asia. Striking deep green leaves, deeply divided into long, narrow leaflets, on sturdy stems; foliage turns orange-yellow in fall. Upward-facing, sweetly perfumed, single, intense rose-red flowers to 3 in. wide, with central bosses of golden anthers. Provide well-drained, moderately fertile soil. More shade tolerant than *Paeonia lactiflora* types; good for woodland edges. Usually blooms about three weeks ahead of most garden cultivars. Reportedly resistant to botrytis. Good for rock gardens, borders, and among other shrubs in woodland clearings.

Paeonia brownii

- red
- late spring to early summer
- 8–20 in. × 12–18 in.
- sun, part shade
- Z5–7

Western peony. Native to chaparral, sagebrush, and pine forests from eastern Washington, south through the northern two-thirds of California; east to Utah, western Wyoming, and Idaho. Clusters of stems bear fleshy, twice-divided leaves with oval leaflets covered with white to blue, waxy powder. Flowers solitary at stem tips, pendulous, and single, with reddish brown petals edged with greenish yellow. Drought tolerant; intolerant of wet winters. Good for rock gardens or xeriscapes.

Paeonia californica

- red
- late winter to early spring
- 12–18 in. × 12 in.
- sun, part shade
- Z8–10

California peony. Native to southern coastal range and Baja California. Leaves deeply lobed, 4 in. long, dark green on top, paler underneath. Adapted to warm, dry climates; winter rains stimulate its growth cycle; 2-in., cup-shaped, nodding, maroon flowers appear in midwinter. Summer dormant; requires very well-drained soil as summer moisture causes root rot. Best for the semi-arid regions and xeriscapes.

Paeonia mlokosewitschii

- yellow
- late spring to early summer
- 18–24 in. high and wide
- sun, part shade
- Z4–9

Golden peony, Molly-the-witch. Caucasus Mountains. Soft blue-green leaves, each with three to seven round-tipped leaflets; emerging foliage is purplish, and retains purple margins, stems, and petioles well into growing season. Early-blooming, pale yellow, shallowly cupped, 3- to 5-in. flowers are

Fruiting head of *Paeonia obovata*

single; yellow anthers cluster around central yellow-green carpels (ovaries). Mildly fragrant, shade and drought tolerant, prefers fertile, well-drained, average to moderately moist soil. When seeds ripen, the enclosing receptacle splits, exposing a shiny red or pink interior, set with scarlet and shiny blue-gray seeds. A superb accent plant in borders, cottage gardens, or at woodland edges.

Paeonia obovata

- white, red, purple
- late spring to early summer
- 1–2 ft. high and wide
- sun, part shade
- Z5–8

Woodland peony. Native to woodlands from Siberia through Manchuria, northern China and Japan. Gray-green leaves divided into oval to broad-elliptic leaflets, with terminal leaflets obovate. Single, cup-shaped flowers are rose-purple centered with yellow stamens; mildly fragrant; midseason. Receptacles split when seeds ripen in late summer, revealing red interiors studded with glossy black seeds. Blends well in bright woodland settings with hostas, astilbes, and other woodland flower and foliage perennials. Single, white-flowered *Paeonia japonica* is now considered a variant of *P. obovata*.

'Alba' has white flowers.

Papaver orientale 'Pink Ruffles'

Paeonia tenuifolia

- red
- mid- to late spring
- 12–24 in. × 9–18 in.
- sun, part shade
- Z4–8

Fernleaf peony. Southeastern Europe, Turkey, Caucasus. Persistently attractive foliage is feathery, deeply divided, and lobed. Midseason; 2- to 3-in., crimson flowers. Provide rich, moderately moist, well-drained soil. Well adapted as accent plants in perennial borders, for low hedges, and as edgings along walkways.

Papaver
Papaveraceae
poppy

A good news, bad news genus, poppies offer glorious flowers and robust growth, two qualities that have made them traditional garden favorites. First cultivated ornamentally roughly 7000 years ago in Mesopotamia, withered poppy blossoms have been found in Egyptian tombs. On the negative side, several perennial poppies, including Oriental poppies, become summer dormant. Soon after spring bloom time, the foliage becomes unsightly before disappearing altogether, leaving a gap in the border. Partner poppies with expansive, later-blooming perennials to fill the hole, or plug in summer-blooming annuals. Oriental poppies, the showiest and most popular of the perennial species, have a short season of bloom: this lasts but a week or two, though at their peak these flowers eclipse any others in the garden.

Species poppies have four to six petals, commonly red or orange, often with a black blotch at the base, encircling a knot of stamens and a compound pistil. Cultivars and garden hybrids include many double forms and a color palette of oranges, reds, yellows, lilacs, and purples, as well as white. Fertilized flowers display characteristic salt cellar–like, bulbous seed capsules; when ripe and shaken by the wind, tiny seeds escape through pores just below their circular caps. Basal clumps of alternate, commonly petioled, pinnately divided leaves, stem leaves sessile. Foliage and stems are usually hairy.

Native to open, sunny habitats on rocky hillsides and colonizers of disturbed soils, poppies thrive as agricultural weeds. In cultivation they prefer fertile, humus-rich, moderately moist, well-drained soils in full sun. Where summers are hot, provide light afternoon shade; poppies thrive in cool summer areas and struggle with southern heat and humidity. They strongly resent root disturbance and once established should not be moved.

The pharmaceutical potency of poppies varies with the species, but common sense dictates avoiding consumption. They are handsome as cut flowers; seal the stem ends with a flame immediately after harvesting.

Propagate by seed sown directly or in peat pots. Increase cultivars by root cuttings.

Papaver alpinum

- orange, white, yellow, red
- late spring to early summer
- 6–10 in. × 6–8 in.
- sun
- Z3–7, HS

Alpine poppy. Mountains of western and central Europe, Balkans. Low rosettes of fern-like, olive-green leaves; satiny, cup-shaped flowers, 1–3 in. wide carried on upright stems in assorted colors. Short lived in zone 5 to 7, but a self-seeding annual or biennial elsewhere. Best adapted to troughs, rock gardens, and cottage gardens; drought tolerant. Deadhead to prolong bloom.

Papaver atlanticum

- orange, red
- spring to fall
- 12–24 in. × 9–12 in.
- sun, part shade
- Z5–10

Atlas poppy, Atlantic poppy. Morocco. Low rosettes of hairy, 1-in.-wide, blue-green leaves to 4 in. long. Flowers to 3 in. across, followed by club-shaped seed capsules. Drought tolerant; requires well-drained soil. Reblooms, without summer dormancy; reseeds freely. Rock gardens, containers, gravel gardens, or xeriscapes.

'Flore Pleno' has semi-double apricot flowers.

Papaver nudicaule

- orange, pink, red, yellow, white
- late spring to early summer
- 12–24 in. × 9–12 in.
- sun
- Z2–7, HS

Iceland poppy, Arctic poppy. Mountains of Asia, Arctic regions. Basal clumps of pinnately lobed, blue-green leaves. Solitary flowers top naked stalks; delicately scented, saucer shaped with crinkled petals, to 4 in. across. Short lived; prefers cool summers, elsewhere best treated as winter annuals. A rock-garden gem, handsome in containers. Susceptible to powdery mildew.

Wonderland Mixture offers flowers in shades of yellow, orange, white, and red.

Papaver orientale

- red, orange
- late spring to early summer
- 40 in. × 30 in.
- sun
- Z3–8, HS

Oriental poppy. Mountain meadows and screes of Armenia, northeast Iran, Turkey. Bristly, serrate, grayish green leaves to 12 in. long are pinnately dissected into lance-shaped segments. Summer dormant shortly after bloom. Single, 4- to 6-in. flowers are orange or red blotched with blackish purple at the base of each crepy, ruffled petal; large, black seedpods follow. Drought tolerant once established. Very long lived.

Other Notable Cultivars

Many cultivars are hybrids resulting from complex crosses with other species, particularly *Papaver orientale* and very similar but slightly taller *P. bracteatum*. The following notable selections are all distinguished by dark blotches at the bases of the four petals.

'Beauty of Livermere' has 4- to 6-in., scarlet flowers. 4 ft.

'Patty's Plum' displays plum-purple flowers, 4–5 in. across.

'Pink Ruffles' has 4- to 6-in., pink flowers with deeply fringed petals. 24 in.

'Royal Wedding' bears 5- to 8-in.-wide, white flowers that sway majestically above 30- to 35-in. plants.

'Salmon Glow' displays salmon, many-petaled, almost double flowers. 30 in.

Paradisea

Liliaceae
St. Bruno's lily, paradise lily

This European genus of just two species is relatively unknown in US gardens, but tubers and seed are sometimes available through bulb specialists and bulb societies. Closely related to St. Bernard's lily (*Anthericum*), some taxonomists place it with asphodels in the Asphodelaceae, while others feel it belongs with asparagus in the Asparagaceae. Either way, St. Bruno's lilies are graceful additions to collections of bulbous plants and are unusual additions to rock gardens and flowerbeds.

Plant tubers 2 in. deep. Chill or freeze moist seed prior to sowing; be patient, germination is slow.

Paradisea liliastrum

syn. *Anthericum liliastrum*

- white
- late spring to early summer
- 1–2 ft. × 1 ft.
- sun, part shade
- Z5–8

St. Bruno's lily, paradise lily. Native to alpine meadows and grasslands of the European Alps and the Pyrenees. Regrettably seldom offered for sale, St. Bruno's lily is well worth seeking. Growing from short tubers, 1-in.-wide, linear basal leaves grow to 2 ft. or so long, making handsome clumps. Graceful, one-sided, loose terminal racemes of 15 or more delicate white flowers rise on erect scapes above the foliage. Sweetly fragrant blooms are funnel shaped with six free tepals (petal-like), 1–2 in. in length, highlighted with a green spot at their tips. Easy to grow in average fertile soil amended with compost, perhaps among shrubs or in flower borders. Maintain moist soil in sunny spots. Divide the tubers in fall or start from seed. Portugese *Paradisea lusitanica* may reach 4–5 ft., with flowers on both sides of the stem.

Paradisea luisitanica

Paris

Melianthiaceae
Paris

Unusual and fascinating, *Paris* is closely allied with trilliums and usually needs similar growing conditions. Different, though similar, species are becoming more available as they become better known. Both genera have been moved from the Liliaceae to the Melianthiaceae, but may be found in the literature under either.

Grown for their unique and curious flowers, these appear like spiders' legs or cat whiskers, yellow and radiating from the center above a whorl of leaflets. Each may last for up to three months, and if pollinated produces poisonous, blue-black or red berries. The handsome dark green leaves, arranged symmetrically in whorls, are ovate and pointed, with netted venation.

Select or order container-grown plants, rather than dried rhizomes that are sometimes offered and seldom revive. Best in woodland conditions, with moisture-retaining, humus-rich soil. These elegant plants are most suitable in light or dappled woodlands or wild gardens, massed perhaps with related trilliums, Solomon's seals, and ferns. *Paris quadrifolia* demands sweet alkaline soil, as is found in their native habitat.

Propagate from seed as soon as it ripens in fall. Divide rhizomes in fall.

Paris polyphylla

- yellow green
- summer
- 1–2.5 ft. × 1.5 ft.
- part shade, shade
- Z5–8

Multi-leaf Paris. Chinese Himalayas. Erect and smooth, unbranched stems rise with a topknot of leaflets arranged in a whorl. Short flower stalks rise above, bearing solitary flowers with a leafy collar of four to six lanceolate sepals and eight thread-like petals. Yellow stamens surround a central, knoblike, maroon stigma. Red berries follow in fall. Shorter Japanese *Paris tetraphylla* is similar, but leaves and flower parts are in multiples of four.

Patrinia

Valerianiaceae
patrinia

This genus is a close cousin of garden heliotrope or common valerian. Most patrinias are indigenous to grassy mountain habitats of eastern Asia and Japan where they thrive in cool, humus-rich soil. Several species are considered important in homeopathic medicine and have long been used for various ailments. The roots are especially valued for their antibacterial and anticoagulant properties.

Patrinias make low mounds or clumps of leaves with wide sprays of attractive small flowers above. Inflorescences rise on wiry stems, very long-lasting

Paris polyphylla

Patrinia scabiosifolia

bloom. Best in humus-rich soil; avoid overly fertilized sites that produce too much leafy growth at the expense of flowers. Drainage must be adequate; the roots rot out with wet feet in winter. Flower sprays are attractive cut, fresh or dried. Allow the spent stems to remain in the garden for winter interest. Little maintenance is necessary; easy to grow.

Butterflies and insects flock to the flowers for their nectar, but deer and rabbits seem to ignore the plants; slugs and snails may be a problem. Regrettably, it has been reported that patrinias are alternate hosts for fungal daylily rust; remove and destroy infected plants immediately.

Patrinias mix well in beds and borders with other perennials, annuals, and shrubs, and in cottage gardens. Ideal on the edge of woodlands; low species make fine groundcovers.

Increase by seed sown in containers in fall, or divide clumps in spring.

Patrinia gibbosa
- yellow
- late spring to midsummer
- 12–24 in. × 12 in.
- sun, part shade
- Z5–8, HT

Dwarf patrinia. Japan. Long blooming, with minute, acid-yellow, five-lobed flowers arranged in loose eye-catching sprays, 3–4 in. across, above the foliage mass. Broadly ovate, divided, 5- to 6-in. leaves are rimmed with jagged teeth. Deadhead to prevent self-seeding. Appropriate in cottage gardens and mixed borders.

Patrinia scabiosifolia
- yellow
- midsummer to fall
- 4–5 ft. × 2 ft.
- sun
- Z4–9, HT

Golden lace, golden valerian, camel's cover. Korea. Basal rosettes of foliage, similar to those of pincushion flower, to about 2 ft. Erect, slender, and branching stems, meagerly furnished with ovate, fern-like, divided leaves, rise way above and terminate in numerous umbel-like sprays of very small, fragrant (some say odorous) flowers. Well-drained, average soil is fine; nutrient-rich soil promotes lush, floppy growth. Tolerates dry soil, but irrigation during droughts may extend bloom time. Attracts assorted bees and other pollinating insects. The young leaves and stem tips have been used as a pot herb.

'Nagoya'. Clumps of deeply divided leaves are compact, mostly less than 15 in. Flower stems with pinnately divided, toothed leaves, rise to 2–3 ft.

Patrinia triloba
syn. *P. palmata*
- yellow
- mid- to late summer
- 8–24 in. × 6–12 in.
- sun, part shade, shade
- Z5–8

Patrinia. Grassy hills of Japan. Lobed like a hand, the fresh green leaves are irregularly cut, toothed, and 2–4 in. across, and grow into spreading mats. Panicles up to 4 in. wide, of cup-shaped, five-lobed flowers each only 0.25 in. across, perch atop wiry, branching, reddish brown stems. Not every nose finds the flowers fragrant. Prefers cool moist soils.

var. *palmata* has spurred flowers. Leaves take on reddish tones in fall.

Patrinia villosa
- white
- summer to fall
- 2–3 ft. × 1 ft.
- sun, part shade
- Z6–11, HS

White patrinia. Japan, eastern Asia. Clumping mounds of foliage arise from stoloniferous roots. Toothed, ovate leaves, simple or divided, up to 6 in. long. Loose clusters of small, white flowers are borne on erect stems. A good "see-through" plant, reminiscent of a white, tall verbena (*Verbena bonariensis*). Good for cutting, fresh and dry; persistent seedheads. Good in cottage gardens and borders; naturalizes in rich soil.

Peltoboykinia
Saxifragaceae

This genus is composed of just two very similar species. They hail from Asia and have large, handsome, palmately lobed leaves. Partly shaded sites are preferable, where soil is woodsy, humus-rich, and remains damp for most of the season. Although not widely offered in the marketplace, they are cousins to better-known saxifrages, astilbes, and coral bells.

Peltoboykinias are perfect as bold features in lightly shaded woodlands, perhaps as a textural counterpoint to large ferns. The compound leaves are shield-like ("pelte" is from the Greek for "a shield") and eye-catching wherever they are grown.

Peltoboykinia watanabei

Penstemon 'Dark Towers' with *Dianthus barbatus*

Reddish bronze at first, they mature to green as the season progresses. Considered resistant to deer browsing. Easy.

Propagate by seed or division.

Peltoboykinia tellimoides

syn. *Boykinia tellimoides*
- yellow green
- early summer
- 20–36 in. × 24 in.
- part shade
- Z6–9

Yawato-so. Native to high woodlands of eastern Asia. Fairly aggressive, short, creeping rhizomes give rise to mostly basal, umbrella-like leaves on 1- to 2-ft.-long petioles. The leaves are peltate (attached to the stem at the middle), rounded to heart-shaped, with 7–13 shallow, toothed lobes. Best in cool-summer regions. Although grown primarily for its foliage, the small, creamy yellow–green flowers, bell shaped and borne in clusters, are quite interesting. Japanese *Peltoboykinia watanabei* is similar with very deeply cleft, longer-lobed leaves, and small, yellow flowers.

Penstemon

Plantaginaceae
beardtongue

A treasure trove for gardeners who favor North American natives, the genus *Penstemon* includes over 300 species, only one of which originated outside this continent. Ranging from coast to coast, and from the Arctic tundra to the mountains of Guatemala, penstemons have achieved their greatest diversity and splendor in the western United States. Yet we owe the domestication and hybridization of these plants to the late 19th-and 20th-century European plant breeders. The recent quest for water-conserving gardens, however, has brought increased attention to drought-tolerant Western penstemons; many are available now, especially from regionally focused nurseries.

Not surprisingly, such a large group of plants offers great variety. Penstemons range in height from 1–2 in. to 7-ft. giants. Leaves are alternate; funnel-shaped or tubular flowers are borne typically in spikes. Flower color ranges from white, to blue, violet, purple, pink, magenta, red, and occasionally yellow. Individual blooms are two lipped like a gaping mouth, from which protrudes a long, frequently hairy staminode—the source of the common name, beardtongue. Attracts a variety of pollinators including butterflies and hummingbirds; deer resistant.

Most penstemons are "pioneer" plants, adapted to colonizing disturbed soils. They tolerate and favor nutrient-poor, very well-drained, even gritty soils; consistently moist conditions with poor drainage commonly cause root rot. Mulch with gravel or leave soil bare; avoid moisture-retaining, organic mulch, such as ground bark. Seldom browsed by deer or rabbits. Some species of penstemons are somewhat demanding outside their native habitats; those listed below are among the easiest to grow.

Propagate by seed, division, stem cuttings, or layer species with prostrate stems.

Penstemon barbatus

- orange-red
- late spring to early summer
- 1.5–3 ft. × 1–2 ft.
- sun
- Z4–9

Beardtongue. Rocky slopes and open woodlands from Utah to Arizona, east into Colorado. Clump forming with evergreen, oblong to ovate basal foliage, and clasping, willow-like stem leaves, 2–6 in. long. Terminal racemes of tubular, 2-in., orange-red flowers; deadhead to extend flowering. Tolerate shallow, rocky soils. Good for sunny, dry borders and rock gardens, naturalized in cottage gardens and meadows, open woods.

'Jingle Bells' (var. *coccineus* 'Jingle Bells') has scarlet flowers. Grow from seed.

'Rubycunda' has slightly fragrant, scarlet flowers with contrasting white throats.

Penstemon cardinalis

- red
- midsummer
- 24–30 in. × 24 in.
- sun
- Z5–9

Cardinal beardtongue. Southern New Mexico, west Texas. Rosettes of large, evergreen, deep green leaves; ruby-red, tubular flowers dangle from upright stems. Withstands intense sun, but tolerates very light shade. Exceptionally drought tolerant once established; will succeed in very well-drained soil in moister climates. Best for rock gardens or dry borders; a premier hummingbird plant.

Penstemon davidsonii

- blue, purple
- midsummer
- 2–5 in. × 12 in.
- sun, part shade
- Z6–8

Davidson's penstemon. Mountains of West Coast from California through British Columbia. Dense mats of creeping, woody stems with small, leathery, evergreen, oval leaves. Broad, tubular flowers, 0.75–1.5 in. long and blue-lavender to purple, rise on very short stems. Sensitive to summer drought; best where snow cover is reliable, or protect with evergreen boughs in winter (extends hardiness through zone 5). Unusual, handsome groundcover for rock gardens, sunny, sandy, or gravelly banks, or dry borders.

var. *menziesii* 'Microphyllus' is compact (2 in. × 10–12 in.) and hardier with small, more finely textured, evergreen leaves that turn burgundy color in winter. Z4.

Penstemon digitalis

- white
- midspring to early summer
- 3–5 ft. × 1.5–2 ft.
- sun
- Z3–8

Beardtongue. Native to prairies, fields, woodland edges in eastern and southeastern United States. Recommended as easy and reliable for gardens from the Midwest to the Atlantic coast and Pacific Northwest by the American Penstemon Society. Clump forming with elliptical basal leaves, becoming lanceolate to oblong higher up the stems. Panicles of white, tubular, 1- to 1.25-in. flowers. Provide average, dry to moderately moist, well-drained soil; resents wet, poorly drained ones. Striking massed in sunny borders, wild gardens, prairie plantings, or well-drained rain gardens. Generally trouble free if drainage is adequate.

'Husker Red' has non-fading, deep burgundy foliage, and white or blush-pink flowers. Compact at 2–3 ft. × 1–2 ft.

'Mystica' foliage emerges green, becoming dark maroon-red during the summer, and blazing red in the fall. Clusters of lavender-pink flowers. 30 in. × 20 in.

Penstemon digitalis 'Husker Red'

Penstemon heterophyllus
- blue
- late spring to early summer
- 12–18 in. × 12–18 in.
- sun
- Z6–10

Foothill penstemon. Grasslands, chaparral, and open woodlands of California's mountain foothills. Clump forming, with narrow, lanceolate to linear stem leaves, 2–4 in. long, and 1.5-in. tubular, gentian-blue flowers in terminal racemes on erect, spreading stems. Remove spent flowering racemes to prolong bloom time. Sunny, dry borders, rock gardens, and dry, rocky banks and slopes.

'Electric Blue' has flowers of more intense, uniform blue than the species.

Penstemon pinifolius
- red
- late spring to early summer
- 10–12 in. × 12–18 in.
- sun
- Z4–9

Pineleaf beardtongue. Arizona, New Mexico, northern Mexico. Forms low, bushy mound of needle-like foliage, evergreen where winters are mild. Constricted, tubular, orange-red flowers with fringed mouths borne over two-month season. Cut back hard as growth resumes in early spring to remove old woody growth. Glorious in rock gardens, walls, or troughs; very drought tolerant, a natural for xeriscapes.

'Magdalena Sunshine' has yellow flowers. Z5–9.

Other Notable Cultivars
Hybrids commonly offer a greatly prolonged season of bloom and a wider color range; superior in the border.

'Blackbird' bears raspberry-purple flowers; deep green leaves. 18–24 in. × 12–18 in.

'Blue Midnight' has large, deep blue-purple flowers with white, burgundy-streaked throats. 30 in. × 36 in. Z6–9.

'Dark Towers' has abundant pale pink flowers, above non-fading, deep burgundy foliage. 18–36 in. Z3–8.

'Elfin Pink'. Broad mats of glossy foliage; 12- to 18-in. spikes of salmon-pink flowers. Sun, partial shade. Z4–9.

'Prairie Dusk'. Tubular, rose-purple flowers on 20-in. stems. Deadhead for long bloom.

'Red Riding Hood' bears vivid, coral-red flowers from late spring through summer. 24–30 in. × 18–24 in. Z5–8.

Perovskia
Lamiaceae
Russian sage

One species of this genus has made its way into gardens, but this singularity has made a big impact. A premier textural plant, Russian sage's finely cut, silvery foliage glistens in the summer sun, and combined with its long-blooming clouds of tiny, blue flowers introduces an impression of lightness to the heaviest garden border. A cooling contrast to dazzling summer annuals, this plant is also remarkably tough and carefree.

Russian sage thrives on well-drained, poor soils; once established it shrugs off all except the most prolonged summer droughts. To promote compact growth, prune stems back hard into woody bases, but only after 1 in. or so of new spring growth has emerged; left uncut this plant sprawls untidily; too much fertilizer and irrigation encourages soft

Hazy blue *Perovskia atriplicifolia* shines with Shasta daisies and *Rudbeckia* in this fall garden

growth and sprawl. Like many aromatic plants, Russian sage resists deer and rabbits as well as most insect pests.

Propagate by softwood or semi-hardwood cuttings. Low-growing stems may layer themselves.

Perovskia atriplicifolia

- blue
- midsummer to midfall
- 3–5 ft. × 2–4 ft.
- sun
- Z5–9

Russian sage. Himalayas, western China. A subshrub commonly grown as an herbaceous perennial. Aromatic, deeply divided, silver-green leaves with toothed edges clothe stiffly upright, square, silver stems, woody at the bases. Light blue, tubular flowers are two lipped, borne in tiers of whorls in branched, terminal panicles 12–15 in. long.

'Blue Spire' has larger flowerheads than the species. 4 ft. tall.

'Filigran' is sturdier and more upright; especially fine, lacy foliage.

'Little Spire' is compact, 2–3 ft. tall.

'Longin' is similar to 'Little Spire' but more upright with larger, less-dissected leaves. 3–4 ft.

Persicaria

Polygonaceae
smartweed, knotweed

Because this genus includes notable invasives such as mile-a-minute weed (*Persicaria perfoliata*) many gardeners avoid persicarias altogether. Yet among the 50–80 species, a number have considerable ornamental value, and are controllable. Smartweeds usually have fleshy stems, jointed at swollen nodes, and clothed with simple, alternate, conspicuously veined leaves; the leaf bases sheath the stems. Small, long-lasting flowers collect in spikes or panicles, followed by reddish brown fruits.

Plant smartweeds in moist soil in sun or part shade. Take precautions against hungry slugs and snails. Deer and rabbits are seldom troublesome.

Divide in spring or fall, or sow seed in containers.

Persicaria affinis

syn. *Polygonum affine, Bistorta affinis*
- rose
- summer to fall
- 6–10 in. × 12–24 in.
- sun, part shade
- Z3–7

Himalayan fleece flower, Himalayan knotweed. Afghanistan to Nepal, Tibet, India. Creeping stems make wide evergreen mats of dark, 2- to 6-in., elliptic to lanceolate leaves that may display bronzy fall color. Dense, 2- to 3-in. spikes of rose-pink, 0.25-in. flowers lighten as they mature. Drought tolerant.

'Border Jewel' ('Himalayan Border Jewel'). Light pink flowers on red stems, in 2-in.-long spikes; excellent red fall color. 4 in. × 12 in. Z3–8.

'Donald Lowndes' has double, pale to dark pink flowers. 8–10 in. Z5–8.

'Superba' ('Dimity'). Upright, dense, 4-in. pokers of rosy red flowers that mature pink. 12 in. Z3–9.

Persicaria amplexicaulis

syn. *Polygonum amplexicaule, Bistorta amplexcaulis*
- red
- summer to fall
- 4–6 ft. × 3 ft.
- sun
- Z4–7

Bistort, mountain fleece. Himalayas. Vigorous but not invasive, this clumping species has clasping, slightly puckered, pointed, lance-shaped leaves to 10 in. long. The leaves have conspicuous midribs; downy with hairs beneath. Slender, bell-shaped, red-to-purple or white flowers crowd into long-stemmed, slim, 4-in.-long spikes.

'Alba' has slender tapers of white flowers on erect stems. Beautiful foliage. 3.5 ft. × 3 ft. Z6.

'Atrosangiunea' produces bottlebrush spikes of rosy flowers, well above the leaves. 4 ft. Z6.

'Firetail' ('Speciosa'). Erect, 5- to 6-in. pokers of bright red flowers. 3–4 ft. Z4–7.

'Golden Arrow'. Tassel-like crimson flower spikes contrast with 10-in., yellow-green foliage. Vigorous. 2–3 ft. Z4–7.

'Inverleith' presents stubby crimson spikes and handsome narrow foliage. Best in part shade. Compact at 18 in. Z5.

Persicaria bistorta

syn. *Polygonum bistortum*
- pink
- late spring to midsummer
- 18–30 in. × 30 in.
- sun
- Z3–8

Snakeweed, bistort. Europe, Asia. Vigorous and clumping with mostly basal leaves, undulating at the margins with a white midrib, 4–12 in. long. Dense, 2- to 3-in.-long bottlebrushes of 0.25-in., pink bells rise well above the foliage. A good cut flower; valuable in damp garden sites. Foliage sometimes used as a green vegetable. Deadhead to avoid self-seeding.

'Superba' forms clumps of dark, puckered foliage, with dense, cattail-like spikes of pink flowers. 2 ft. high and wide. Z4.

Persicaria microcephala

- white
- summer to fall
- 1.5–2 ft. high and wide
- sun, part shade
- Z6–8

Bistort. China. Non-aggressive, with beautiful heart-shaped foliage and clusters of small, white flowers at the tips of arching stems. The species is seldom grown, outshone by garden-worthy cultivars. Best in cool-summer climates; high

Persicaria amplexicaulis 'Fire Tail'

temperatures causes vibrant foliage color to fade. Moist soil for best results.

'**Red Dragon**' has dark wine-colored foliage marked with purple, silver, and green chevrons. Tiny, white flowers cluster at the tips. Clumping. 3–4 ft. Z5–9.

'**Silver Dragon**' has silvery leaves, centered and margined with red. Clusters of tiny, white flowers. 2 ft. × 3 ft. Z5–9.

Persicaria virginiana

syn. *Polygonum virginiana, Tovara virginiana*
- pink, red
- late summer
- 12–30 in. × 12 in.
- sun, part shade
- Z4–8

Tovara. Eastern and midwestern United States. Upright with short-petioled, oval, green, 3- to 10-in. leaves marked with dark green. Slender, whip-like spikes of greenish white or pink-tinged flowers that age to red, rise above the foliage. Invasive in good conditions; tolerates dry, root-ridden soil if kept watered until established.

'**Painter's Palette**' has thin-textured leaves evenly splashed and striped with creamy yellow and accented with a reddish brown chevron. Invasive, but spectacular facing down hemlocks or other evergreens in controlled sites.

'**Variegeta**' has variegated ivory-and-cream foliage.

Persicaria microcephala 'Red Dragon'

Petasites

Asteraceae
butterbur

Native to temperate and subarctic regions of the Northern Hemisphere, these robust plants typically inhabit moist, shady sites. Their bold, outsized foliage is their chief attraction, used to add a flamboyant, even tropical-looking, air to gardens in cold climates. The thick, creeping rhizomes are energetic colonizers—butterburs should be handled with care, as they prove invasive in wetlands or along stream banks; in such settings confine the plants to containers or large, sunken tubs. No pest or disease problems apart from slugs; deer resistant.

Divide, or sow seed.

Petasites japonicus

- white, yellow
- early spring to midspring
- 2–3 ft. × 2–5 ft.
- shade, part shade
- Z5–9

Butterbur, sweet coltsfoot. Korea, China, Japan. Dense clumps of slightly toothed, kidney-shaped leaves 16–32 in. across, woolly beneath. Before the foliage emerges, large, dense, bouquet-like corymbs of fragrant, yellowish white, daisy-like flowers appear on 6-in. scapes, framed by large, pale green bracts; they are showy and intriguing rather than beautiful.

'Giganteus' (var. *giganteus*) is larger in all its parts. Leaves 48 in. across. 4–7 ft. Z6–8.

'Variegatus' has dark green leaves, splashed and streaked with yellow.

Phlomis

Lamiaceae
phlomis, Jerusalem sage

Phlomis is a genus of sage-like plants grown both for their attractive foliage and eye-catching flowers. Large leaves are corrugated, and covered with white or grayish woolly hairs. The typical mint family flowers are two lipped, the upper providing a protective hood over the three-lobed lower. Lavender-pink, yellow, or white flowers are arranged in dense, several-flowered verticillasters.

Drought-resistant phlomis prefers a sunny spot where soil is fertile and drains well. They are sensitive to extreme temperature fluctuations such as those often experienced in the eastern United States, particularly in the hot, humid Southeast; they do not enjoy muggy conditions. Cut to the ground before spring growth emerges. Easy care, but leafhoppers may be troublesome. Eminently suitable for wildlife gardens, where they attract birds, butterflies, and bees; resistant to both rabbits and deer. In beds and borders phlomis provides architectural impact and color over a long season.

Divide in spring, or take soft cuttings of young growth.

Phlomis cashmeriana

- lilac pink
- midsummer
- 2–4 ft. × 2 ft.
- sun, part shade
- Z5–9

Kashmir sage. Native to drier areas of Kashmir and the Western Himalayas, this species is impressive in dry gardens where humidity is low. Upright, stately plants clothed with pairs of soft, gray-woolly leaves. Basal leaves are 4–10 in. long, stem leaves smaller. Numerous bold verticillasters of 1-in., deep lavender-lilac flowers on the upper stems. Sculptural seedheads maintain winter interest. Good as cut flowers; dried stems are attractive in winter bouquets.

Phlomis fruticosa

- yellow
- early to midsummer
- 2–4 ft. × 3 ft.
- sun
- Z6–10

Jerusalem sage. Eastern Mediterranean. Widely grown in California, this underused plant should gain acceptance elsewhere. Bushy plants, often woody below, are covered with coarse, elliptical to lanceolate, 2- to 3-in., gray-green leaves, white-woolly with hairs beneath; hairy stems appear slightly yellow. Flower buds cluster in tight, tiered whorls in the upper leaf axils and open to hooded, butter-yellow, 1- to 1.25-in. blooms. In cool climates Jerusalem sage is dormant in winter, but erupts from the base in spring. Attractive in borders with 'Big Blue' sea holly, lavender, or salvias.

Phlomis russeliana

syn. *P. viscosa* hort.

- yellow
- late spring to early fall
- 3–4 ft. × 2.5 ft.
- sun
- Z3–9

Jerusalem sage, sticky Jerusalem sage. Syria, Turkey. Evergreen, with sage-green foliage, softly fuzzy beneath. Ovate basal leaves, heart-shaped at the base, may reach 6–8 in. long. Smaller upper-stem leaves have scalloped or undulating rims. Ball-like clusters of pale yellow, hooded, 1- to 1.5-in. flowers arranged up the stem, topiary like.

Phlomis tuberosa

- pink
- early to late summer
- 2–5 ft. × 3 ft.
- sun, part shade
- Z5–8

Tuberous Jerusalem sage. Central and southeastern Europe to central Asia. Bushy, with vigorous, upright stems arising from tuberous roots. Arrow-shaped, crumpled, 8- to 10-in. leaves are variably hairy, coarsely toothed along the margin, and decrease in size as they ascend deep purple stems. Deep purple calyces contrast well with pink, 1-in. flowers.

Petasites japonicus 'Giganteus'

Bloom of *Petasites japonicus* var. *giganteus*

Phlomis tuberosa 'Amazone'

'Amazone' (Sage-leaf Mullein) has rosy-mauve flowers on burgundy stems. Mostly evergreen; toothed leaves, grayish with downy hairs. 4–5 ft. Z5.

Phlox
Polemoniaceae
phlox

"Essential" means indispensable, but it also indicates that anything labeled this way is of the essence—as a perennial for American gardens, phloxes qualify in both respects. The genus is almost entirely native to this continent, from the edge of the Alaskan tundra to the Gulf Coast of Florida.

Phlox leaves, typically entire and generally lance-olate or linear, are borne in opposing pairs; tubular, often fragrant flowers flare into five lobes at their mouths. Individual flowers, though modest in size, are abundant, grouped in large panicles or solitary in blankets that almost hide the foliage. The color palette is inclusive, lacking only yellow, unmixed oranges, and true blues to complete the spectrum.

Phlox fanciers can enjoy bloom from midspring through early fall by growing different species; summer phlox (*Phlox paniculata*) have a particularly generous bloom time that may extend over two months with assiduous deadheading. Creeping phloxes serve as groundcovers in rock gardens and on sunny banks, compact species decorate the front, and tall phloxes shine as border backdrops;

several contribute to cottage and cutting gardens. The species are appropriate in native, wild, and meadow gardens, and sometimes in open woodland gardens. Many excellent cultivars and hybrids are offered in nurseries, with more arriving annually.

The cultural requirements of phloxes vary between species, but most prefer sunny or lightly shaded sites, with six hours or so of direct sunlight daily (*P. divaricata*, described below, is the exception). Creeping and mat-forming types prefer leaner, very well-drained, even gritty soils; upright border and meadow phloxes require moderately moist, fertile, humus-rich soils. Few species thrive in high heat and humidity; timely irrigation is usually critical for good flowering.

Carefully select the phlox species suited to your climate, soil, and conditions. Fungal root rot may be a problem, but some species are resistant. In hot, dry conditions spider mites are serious; susceptibility to powdery mildew varies and it is wise to select resistant species and cultivars. Thinning to increase air circulation is also helpful. Butterflies and hummingbirds flock to phlox; deer and rabbits devour them.

Other reliable and attractive species include *P. bifida*, *P. nivalis*, *P. adsurgens*, *P. pilosa*, *P. ×procumbens*, and numerous hybrids that are well worth seeking out.

Divide cultivars in spring or early fall, or take stem cuttings in early midsummer. Start species from seed.

Phlox divaricata

Phlox carolina

- white, pink, purple
- early to midsummer
- 24–30 in. × 18–24 in.
- sun, part shade
- Z3–8

Carolina phlox, summer phlox, thickleaf phlox. Native to woodland edges and openings from North Carolina to southern Illinois, and south to the Gulf of Mexico. Groups of slender, erect, red-streaked stems with leathery, oval leaves. Loose, dome-shaped clusters of fragrant, lavender to pink flowers. Prefers moisture-retentive but well-drained soil. Powdery mildew resistant.

'Gypsy Love' (syn. *Phlox carolina* var. *angusta* 'Gypsy Love') has fragrant, bright pink flowers from late spring. Lustrous foliage. 24 in. × 18 in.

'Miss Lingard', often listed as a *P. carolina* cultivar, is probably a hybrid with *P. maculata*. Showy clusters of fragrant, white flowers in early summer with intermittent rebloom. Outstanding resistance to powdery mildew. 2–3 ft. × 2–3 ft.

'Kim' has bright pink flowers in summer to autumn. 12–18 in. × 12–24 in.

Phlox divaricata

- blue
- mid- to late spring
- 9–12 in. high and wide
- part shade, shade
- Z3–8

Woodland phlox, wild sweet William. Native to rich woods, fields, and streamsides throughout central United States northward into Quebec. Spreading mounds of sticky, hairy stems clad with 1- to 2-in., lanceolate to elliptic leaves. Sprawling stems root at the nodes to establish spreading colonies. Fragrant, 1.5-in., blue, lilac, or pink flowers in loose clusters at stem tips. Provide humus-rich, moderately moist, well-drained soil; mulch in summer. Susceptible to powdery mildew—cut back stems after flowering to force clean, healthy new growth; watch for spider mites and rabbits; mostly deer tolerant. Shallow-rooted, woodland phlox makes a good cover for early spring bulbs. Lovely in native and woodland gardens, rock gardens, and shady borders where foamy bells, hostas, and lungworts are appropriate companions.

'Chattahoochee' has fragrant, maroon-eyed, bluish lavender flowers. Probably a hybrid. Rabbit and deer resistant.

'Eco Texas Purple' has violet-purple flowers with reddish centers.

'Fuller's White' is white flowered.

'London Grove' has powder-blue flowers.

'Montrose Tricolor' has silvery-mauve flowers; foliage striped and edged white and pink.

Phlox glaberrima

- pink, purple, white
- midspring to late spring
- 2–4 ft. × 2–2.5 ft.
- sun, part shade
- Z3–8

Smooth phlox. Wet woods, meadows, and prairies throughout southeastern United States. Similar looking to *Phlox paniculata* but spring blooming and very resistant to powdery mildew. Upright stems bear thin, 5-in., lanceolate leaves. Fragrant, tubular, and five-lobed flowers, to 1 in. across, congregate in large, pyramidal clusters at stem tips. Tolerates moister soils than other species. Seldom needs staking, deadhead to prolong bloom; mulch in summer. Watch for spider mites, especially in hot, dry weather. Deer tolerant. A gem for spring borders, meadow plantings, and cutting gardens.

'Morris Berd'. White-eyed, rose-pink flowers. Long blooming. 18–24 in.

'Triple Play'. Creamy white–edged leaves; pink-lavender flowers. 1 ft. × 2 ft.

Phlox maculata

- pinkish purple
- early summer to late summer
- 2–3 ft. × 1–2 ft.
- sun, part shade
- Z3–8

Meadow phlox, wild sweet William. Moist meadows, low-lying woods and riverbanks throughout eastern United States. Rhizomatous clumps of upright, red-spotted stems with dark, thin, finely toothed, lanceolate leaves to 5 in. Sweetly scented, tubular five-lobed flowers to 0.5 in. across, carried in 10- to 12-in.-long, cylindrical panicles at stem tips. Thrives in average, moderately moist, well-drained soils in airy, open positions. Intolerant of drought; apply a

Phlox carolina 'Gypsy Love'

summertime mulch. Resists powdery mildew; spider mites attack especially in hot, dry conditions. Seldom needs staking; deadhead to prolong bloom. Spreading rhizomes and self-seeding may result in large colonies. Good for summer borders, cottage and meadow gardens, and cut flowers.

'Natascha' has bicolored pink-and-white, very fragrant flowers. Compact. 2 ft.

'Omega' is white, accented with a pale pink eye.

Phlox paniculata

- various
- midsummer to early fall
- 3–6 ft. × 1–3 ft.
- sun, part shade
- Z4–8

Summer phlox, border phlox. Open woods, meadows, and moist roadsides from central New York to Missouri and Kansas, south to North Carolina, Tennessee and Louisiana; naturalized in other regions as garden escapees. Somewhat demanding, but glorious when its needs are met. Clumps of stiff stems, unbranched below, clothed with 1-in.-wide, ovate to ovate-oblong leaves to 6 in. long; rounded, 4- to 6-in. panicles of fragrant, tubular, five-lobed flowers. Self-seeds, producing mostly magenta flowers; cultivars bloom in shades of white, coral, pink, red,

Phlox paniculata 'Robert Poore'

lavender, and violet; often bicolored with contrasting eyes.

Provide good air circulation, and protect from intense midday sun to avoid foliage yellowing. Maintain soil moisture with summer mulch; few cultivars embrace heat and humidity. Stake taller types early, at 6–8 in., to prevent flopping; extend bloom time with routine deadheading. Powdery mildew is the curse of summer phlox; seek resistant selections.

There are hundreds of cultivars; the following are resistant to powdery mildew and mites, and have notably fragrant flowers:

'Delta Snow' has 1-in.-wide, purple-eyed, white flowers. Exceptional heat tolerance; good for areas with high humidity. 2–4 ft. × 2–3 ft.

'Nora Leigh' has light green foliage irregularly margined with cream. Dark pink–eyed, white flowers. 30 in.

'Orange Perfection' has 1-in., salmon-orange flowers with magenta eyes. 36 in. × 20 in.

'Peppermint Twist' has flowers like 1.25-in.-wide pinwheels of pink and white. Very compact. 16 in. × 12–15 in.

'Robert Poore' has deep magenta flowers on 3- to 5-ft. stems.

'Shortwood' ranked most resistant to powdery mildew at Chicago Botanic Garden trials. Hot-pink flowers with darker pink eyes. 42–48 in. × 24–30 in.

Phlox stolonifera

- lavender, white
- late spring to early summer
- 6–12 in. × 9–18 in.
- sun, part shade
- Z5–9

Creeping phlox. Woodlands and stream banks of southern Appalachians. Creeping stems form 3-in.-high mats of oblong to oval, 3-in.-long leaves. Fragrant, 0.75-in. flowers are commonly lavender but sometimes white, borne in loose clusters. Tolerates light shade, deer, and some drought; vulnerable to rabbits and powdery mildew. Good groundcover for native, shade, and woodland gardens, border fronts and rock gardens, a good "cover-up" for fading spring bulbs.

'Blue Ridge' has violet-blue flowers.

'Bruce's White' is vigorous with fragrant, white flowers.

'Home Fires' has dark pink flowers.

'Sherwood Purple' has medium purple flowers.

Phlox subulata

- pink, purple, white
- early to midspring
- 3–6 in. × 1–2 ft.
- sun
- Z3–9

Moss phlox. Native to dryish, rocky soils in open woodlands and slopes from Michigan, Ontario, and New York, south to Tennessee and North Carolina. Spreading carpets of semi-evergreen, 1-in., needle-like leaves are blanketed with loose cymes of fragrant, 0.5- to 0.75-in. flowers by midspring. Provide humus-rich soil in full sun in cold climates, and dappled midday shade where sun is intense. Prone to spider mites, but powdery mildew resistant; shear after flowering to stimulate modest rebloom. Deer resistant, beware of rabbits. Showy in rock gardens and for edging, good groundcover for sandy, sunny south- or west-facing banks. Cultivars include:

'**Allegheny Smoke**' has pale, grayish blue flowers.

'**Dirigo Arbutus**' has lavender flowers with darker eyes.

'**Red Wings**' has rose-red flowers with darker red eyes.

'**Snowflake**' is compact with white flowers.

Other Notable Cultivars

×*arendsii* (*Phlox divaricata* × *P. paniculata*) is a large group of hybrids from the Arends Nursery. At their best they combine the compact habit of woodland phloxes, and the large flowerheads of summer phloxes; early to mid summer bloom. Outstanding examples with mildew resistance include: 'Ping Pong', with large clusters of mildly fragrant, red-eyed light pink flowers. 1.5–2 ft. × 1–1.5 ft. Z3–8. 'Sabine' has soft, bluish pink, fragrant flowers. 20 in. Z4–8.

Spring Pearl Series bears domed flower clusters, often but not uniformly fragrant, in white, pink, fuchsia, magenta, and bicolors; all cultivars have feminine names, e.g., 'Miss Jill,' 'Miss Karen,' 'Miss Margie,' and 'Miss Mary'. Compact at 16–24 in. × 14–18 in. Z4–8.

Phormium

Xanthorrhoeaceae
New Zealand flax

With their long and broad, colorful, sword-shaped leaves, borne in fountain-like clumps, New Zealand flaxes are popularly described as "ornamental grass on steroids." These reach head high or even more, and do have the look of a *Pennisetum* or a *Miscanthus*, albeit bigger, bolder, and more assertive. Species phormium leaves tend to a darkish green, sometimes with colored edges and central ribs; cultivars range in color from light green through pink to deep russet-bronze. Variegated selections have leaves striped in contrasting shades of green, red, bronze, pink, and yellow. Branching clusters of bright red or yellow, curving, tubular flowers top stalks that can double the height of the foliage; rich in nectar, they are a magnet for hummingbirds and other pollinators. Unfortunately, flowering is uncommon in specimens cultivated in cooler regions.

Long a fixture in Californian gardens, a host of new cultivars and hybrids of New Zealand flaxes have, in the last few decades, begun to appear in nurseries and ornamental landscapes across the country. Although long lived, these plants are cold sensitive; cultivate them in containers north of zone 8 and overwinter indoors. Display these on terraces or plunged in beds over the summer.

In cooler climates, give phormiums a spot with full sun; elsewhere, avoid intense sun and provide partial shade to prevent bleaching of the foliage. Moist, well-drained soil is ideal; wintertime wet will surely prove fatal in zone 7. In the South, phormiums embrace wetness and are good plantings for streamsides and pond edges; moderately drought tolerant once established. Successful in coastal gardens. Generally trouble free, but susceptible to mealybugs and leaf spot. Deer resistant.

Eye-catching phormiums are effective as focal points in borders or beds, where they contrast well with the lower-growing, delicate-textured foliages of hardy geraniums and coreopsis. The strong, simple form of phormiums makes them dramatic architectural elements for urns and other containers.

Propagate by division or by seed.

Phormium colensoi

syn. *P. cookianum*

- yellow, orange
- early to late summer
- 4–7 ft. × 10 ft.
- sun, part shade
- Z8–11

Mountain lily. New Zealand. Highly variable species with many heights and foliage colors. Broad,

Phormium 'Pink Stripe'

sword-shaped leaves to 7 ft. long. Orange or yellow flowers borne on 6- to 7-ft. scapes with twisted, pendulous seed capsules, to 8 in. long. Species uncommon in commerce, but represented in nurseries by many cultivars, including:

'Blondie', a weeping form with narrow, slightly twisting, creamy-yellow leaves edged with green. Protect from intense sun. 2–3 ft. × 3–4 ft.

'Cream Delight' has red-rimmed, green leaves, with a creamy-yellow mid-stripe. 2–3 ft. × 4–6 ft.

'Tricolor' displays 2.5-in.-wide, arching leaves with a broad, green, central band flanked by yellow stripes and red margins. 4 ft. × 6 ft.

Phormium tenax
- red
- summer
- 10–15 ft. × 3–6 ft.
- sun, part shade
- Z9–11

New Zealand flax. New Zealand, Norfolk Island. Upright clumps of rigid leaves to 10 ft. long; brilliant red flowers on scapes to 15 ft. Numerous cultivars include:

'Atropurpureum Compactum', burgundy-bronze leaves, red flowers. 5 ft. × 3 ft.

'Tiny Tiger' ('Aurea Nana') has gray-green leaves edged in creamy white; yellow flowers. 2 ft. × 3 ft.

'Limelight' has bright lime-green leaves; abundant bronzy flowers. 5 ft. × 6 ft.

Other Notable Cultivars
The following are of more manageable size for most residential gardens. Z8–11.

'Apricot Queen' has apricot-colored young foliage that matures to pale yellow, margined with green; red flowers. 3–4 ft. × 3–5 ft.

'Black Adder' has dark, almost black foliage. More vigorous than 'Platt's Black'. 3–4 ft. × 3 ft.

'Pink Stripe' has grayish bronze leaves edged with pink. 3 ft. × 4–6 ft.

'Rainbow Maiden' has salmon-pink to coral-red leaves flanked by narrow, bronze-green margins; red flowers. 2–3 ft. high and wide.

Phygelius
Scrophulariaceae
Cape fuchsia

Despite the common name, these plants are not actually fuchsias but, rather, relatives of foxgloves and snapdragons. Both species in the genus are fast growing, suckering perennials with shrubby bases that originated in southern Africa, where they inhabit wet slopes and streamsides. Breeders have created a number of hybrids.

Cape fuchsias have nodding, tubular flowers, flared at the mouth into five short lobes; borne in long, terminal panicles, the individual blossoms hang down like Christmas tree ornaments. The opposite (alternate above), dark green leaves are lance shaped to oval, evergreen in mild climates,

Phygelius 'Funfare Orange'

and carried on slender stems. Flowers appear in flushes over a long season, and attract butterflies and other insects as well as hummingbirds.

Provide average, well-drained but moisture-retentive soil for Cape fuchsias. Amend it with organic matter at planting time. Most do best in sun, except where it is overly intense, where a little shade is advisable. Be alert for weevils. Resists deer and rabbits.

Suitable for shrub borders, in wildlife gardens, or mixed with perennials and annuals in borders. Many make excellent subjects for hanging baskets and window boxes. Where winters are cold, grow in containers and move indoors through the cold months. Outdoors, site on a sunny south-facing wall; protect with thick, dry, organic mulch where winter hardiness is questionable. Prune in early spring; trim after flushes of bloom to keep plants bushy, compact, and floriferous.

Sow seed, or take stem or tip cuttings of young growth in spring. Detach rooted stolons.

Phygelius aequalis
- red
- early summer to fall
- 3 ft. × 1.5 ft.
- sun
- Z7–9

Riverbell. Beside streams, and among rocks in southern Africa. Evergreen, with multiple upright stems bearing ovate, undivided leaves, toothed

Physostegia virginiana

'Croftway Snow Queen' ('Croftshoque'), from the Croftway Series, is extra floriferous; dense spikes of pure white flowers from spring on. Similar 'Croftway Yellow Sovereign' ('Crofyelsov') displays creamy-yellow trumpets on strong stems. Compact, 18–36 in. Z7–9.

'Funfare Orange', from the Funfare Series. Abundant dusty orange flowers on arching stems. 24–36 in. Z7–11. 'Funfare Wine' has fuchsia-pink flowers. 16–18 in. Z7–10.

'Pink Elf' spreads slowly. Maroon stems carry thick clusters of shrimp-pink flowers, yellow at the throat. Compact 24 in. Z7–9.

'Sunshine'. Bright red at the mouth, burnt orange trumpets are set off by lime-colored foliage. Part shade in hot regions. 3–4 ft. Z7–9.

Physostegia
Lamiaceae
obedient plant, false dragonhead

These hardy perennials are "obedient" in the sense that if you twist one of the blooms on the showy flower spikes right or left, up or down, they will hold that position; this quality has endeared them to children and floral designers. Physostegias are far less obedient in the garden, however, where their tenacious, rhizomatous roots spread aggressively, often outgrowing their allotted spot. Smart gardeners site physostegias where their roaming tendencies are an asset, or with their roots confined in containers; less aggressive cultivars are available.

The genus of 12 species is native to North America. They grow wild throughout the contiguous 48 states, except in California, Arizona, Nevada, and Colorado. Outside the latter regions they flourish with little extra care in cultivation. Though they display opposite, sessile, toothed leaves and square stems common to the mints, the flowers more resemble those of snapdragons or foxgloves, borne typically in terminal spikes. Deer resistant.

Propagate by seed, division, or stem cuttings taken in spring.

along the edges. One-sided spikes of pendent, yellow-throated, red flowers with prominent red stamens. Best seen from below. Keep well watered in summer.

'Yellow Trumpet' is best known, and has pale, butter-yellow flowers and light green foliage.

Phygelius capensis
- red
- summer to fall
- 3–4 ft. × 2–3 ft.
- sun, part shade
- Z8–9

Cape fuchsia, Cape figwort. Southern Africa. Upright, ridged stems with pairs of opposite, ovate leaves rimmed with tiny teeth, to 3.5 in. long. Panicles of pendent, tubular, orange-red flowers with yellow throats are borne around the stem.

'Coccineus' is scarlet flowered.

Other Notable Cultivars
Hybrids of the two species fall under the classification of *Phygelius ×rectus*. They bear flowers all around the stems rather than on one side only; considered more tolerant of inclement summer weather. This is a sampling:

'African Queen' (*P. aequalis* × *P. capensis* 'Coccineus') has lemon-throated, apricot-orange flowers. 3 ft. Z7–9.

'Cherry Ripe' has cherry-red flowers. Great in containers. 20 in. Z6–10.

Physostegia correllii
- pink
- midsummer
- 4–6 ft. × 1.5–3 ft.
- sun
- Z7–9

Correll's false dragonhead. Wet sites in southeast Texas and Louisiana, but rare or endangered in the wild. Rhizomatous clumps of stout, tall stems with leaves that diminish in size as they ascend. Stems topped with spikes of 1-in., dark-purple-flecked, mauve-pink flowers. This water-loving perennial requires consistently moist soil; a good choice for wet meadows, streamsides, and rain gardens in mild regions.

Physostegia virginiana

syn. *Dracocephalum denticulata, D. virginiana*
- pink, white
- early to late summer
- 3–4 ft. × 2–3 ft.
- sun
- Z3–9

Obedient plant. Native to moist prairies and stream banks from Montana and New Mexico, east to the Atlantic coast, as well as Canada from Manitoba eastward. Rhizomatous clumps of erect, stiff stems with 1.5-in.-wide, lanceolate leaves, to 5 in. long. Tubular, 1-in. flowers in white, lavender, or purplish pink often accented with darker dots, stripes, or swirls; flower spikes to 10 in. long. Best in average, moderately moist, well-drained soil, but tolerates clay; staking often necessary on rich soils. Cut to 6 in. in early spring for sturdy, compact growth, less in need of support. Attracts hummingbirds. Provides late-season bloom to wildflower, prairie, meadow, and rain gardens; plant this aggressive spreader in confined gardens with caution. No serious pests, but occasionally attacked by fungal rusts.

'Miss Manners' is clumping and non-spreading; does not require staking. Pure white flowers in long, dense spikes are sterile (no viable seed). Superior to roving 'Summer Snow'. 2–2.5 ft. Similar 'Pink Manners' has white-throated, lavender-pink flowers.

'Variegata' has lovely cream-edged leaves, for long interest. Lilac-pink flowers, 2–3 ft. Z4–9.

'Vivid' has rich pink flowers. May spread. 1–2 ft.

Platycodon

Campanulaceae
balloon flower, Chinese bellflower

This single-species genus has a wealth of fine cultivars, standbys of perennial gardens. Platycodon contributes reliable color to border fronts, rock gardens, and container plantings.

Balloon flower requires well-drained, organic-rich loam; wet or poorly drained soils encourage root rot. Slow to establish but long lived. Emerges from dormancy late in spring; leave old stems through winter to prevent accidental early disturbance. In early summer, cut young stems back by half to promote compact growth and avoid the need for staking; deadhead to extend flowering. Tasty morsels for slugs, snails, and rabbits, but otherwise problems are few; deer resistant.

Propagate by seed. Division is tricky; fleshy, fragile roots are easily damaged during transplanting.

Platycodon grandiflorus

- blue
- early to late summer
- 1–2.5 ft. × 1–1.5 ft.
- sun, part shade
- Z3–8

Balloon flower. China, Manchuria, Japan. Clumps of tall stems clothed with toothed, ovate to lanceolate, blue-green leaves, to 2 in. long. Flower buds puff up like balloons before opening into upward-facing, bell-shaped flowers with five pointed lobes, 2–3 in. in diameter. Blooms all summer.

f. *apoyama* 'Fairy Snow' is compact at 10 in.; large, white, blue-veined flowers.

'Albus' has large, white flowers. 24–30 in.

'Fuji Blue' has large, deep blue flowers. Similar 'Fuji Pink' has pale pink flowers, with darker veining.

'Hakone Blue' has double, blue flowers veined with white. 'Hakone White' is a double white. 18–24 in.

'Sentimental Blue' is dwarf, forming neat, low mounds, 6–8 in. × 18–24 in., with full-sized blue flowers.

Astra Hybrid Seed Strain offers dwarf plants with 2- to 2.5-in. flowers in white, pink, or blue. 3–6 in. Z5–8.

Podophyllum

Berberidaceae
May apple

These rhizomatous woodlanders are found growing in large colonies or drifts in eastern Asia and eastern North America. They are ideal for damp shady borders and woodlands, and the fast-spreading types make splendid deciduous, seasonal groundcovers. Some are early deciduous, shedding their foliage in response to hot weather.

May apples have one or two large, peltate, palmately lobed leaves that emerge in spring, and are often decorated with dark markings. Flowers, solitary or clustered, are cup shaped with six to nine waxy petals in white or pink, but sometimes dark red. The egg-shaped fruits that follow contain lots of seeds that ripen toward the end of summer. The fruits are edible, but the rest of the plant is toxic to mammals, including deer and rabbits. Ongoing research explores if cancer-fighting drugs can be extracted from the plants, especially *Podophyllum hexandrum*.

Best in shaded or partly shaded places, may apples thrive where soil is high in moisture-retaining humus. Droughty soil promotes an early summer onset of dormancy.

Sow seed as soon as ripe; divide in spring or late summer.

Podophyllum hexandrum

syn. *Sinopodophyllum hexandrum, P. emodi*
- pink, white
- late spring to midsummer
- 18–24 in. × 24 in.
- part shade, shade
- Z5–8

Himalayan May apple. Himalayan mountains of northern India to China. Folded, umbrella-like leaves push through the soil behind the flower bud and unfurl over the next few weeks simultaneously with the bloom. Leaves are deeply lobed, about 10 in. across, with black, purple, and brown markings. Single, waxy, cup-shaped, 1- to 2-in. flowers between the leaves, open wide on sunny days and face outward rather than nodding as in other species. Fruits, 2 in. long and bright red when mature, nod on short stems. Does not have running roots; slow to spread into colonies.

Podophyllum peltatum

- white
- spring
- 8–18 in. × 18–24 in.
- part shade, shade
- Z3–9

May apple, American mandrake. Native to northeastern woodlands from Ontario and Quebec to Texas and Florida. Horizontal rhizomes spread widely and give rise to both sterile and fertile stems that emerge from the ground like unopened umbrellas. Sterile stems are 12–15 in. in height and topped by a lustrous green, 12-in.-wide, canopy-like leaf with five to nine toothed lobes. Fertile stems have a pair of similar but smaller leaves; in the crotch between them a short stem carries a solitary, slightly nodding, cup-shaped 2-in. flower. The fragrant blooms are usually white or pink, but often hidden from view by the bold leaves. Egg-shaped, edible, 2-in.-long fruits follow, green at first but maturing to yellow by late summer; these are a favorite food for box turtles and other wildlife. Fast growing and drought tolerant when established. Valuable to Native Americans as an ingredient in remedies for female complaints.

Platycodon grandiflorus

Podophyllum pleianthum

Podophyllum pleianthum

- dark red
- late spring
- 24–30 in. × 24 in.
- part shade, shade
- Z6–9

Chinese May apple. China, Taiwan. A pair of large, bold, glossy leaves with five to nine pointed but shallow lobes. Clusters of five to nine brilliant red flowers nestle between the leaves; the fruits that follow ripen to bright yellow. The flowers have a strong and putrid odor that dissipates as time passes, probably after the flowers are pollinated by flies. Seed remains viable for only a short time and should be sown quickly. Clump forming.

Other Notable Cultivars

The following hybrids are commonly known as "Asian may apples":

'Kaleidoscope' has dramatic 18-in.-wide, hexagonal leaves, boldly mottled with rings of maroon and silver. A single, burgundy-red flower appears between and below the leaves in late spring and early summer, followed by a fleshy yellow fruit. 18–24 in. Z6–8.

'Spotty Dotty' has large, lobed, umbrella-like, chartreuse leaves, dappled and mottled with

Polemonium reptans

chocolate. As the season progresses they green up but retain their lighter spots. In spring, five or more ruby-maroon flowers cluster between the leaves. Slow to spread but a wonderful accent plant in shade. 15–18 in. Z6–9.

Polemonium

Polemoniaceae
Jacob's ladder

Native to cool temperate regions of the Northern Hemisphere, the Arctic, and the Andes of South America, this genus of some 30 species includes several garden-worthy ornamentals. Jacob's ladders are especially fine in shaded, woodland areas. They produce basal clumps of distinctive, bright green, ladder-like, odd-pinnate leaves divided into broadly lanceolate or oval leaflets; stem leaves become progressively smaller as they climb the upright or decumbent stems. Flowers are clustered or solitary, borne at the stem tips and in upper leaf axils. In shape the blooms vary: cup shaped and open, bell shaped, tubular, or trumpet shaped, flaring at the mouth. Most species have blue flowers, but some are pink or yellow.

Provide a moisture-retentive, humus-rich but fast-draining soil; many types falter in heavy clay. Jacob's ladders do best in part to lightly dappled shade, in regions with cool-summer climates; full sun is acceptable only where light levels are poor. Some become summer dormant. Maintenance is low; cut back self-seeding species after flowering for neatness, to encourage rebloom later, and to discourage excessive self-seeding. Jacob's ladders are susceptible to slugs and snails, and are sometimes attacked by powdery mildew, especially if allowed to dry out. Deer and rabbits seldom browse them.

Plant polemoniums at the front of shady beds and borders and in rock gardens; the larger species are appropriate for midborder. They are popular in cottage gardens too, where they assort well with foxgloves, hardy geraniums, and spiderworts. Under deciduous trees Jacob's ladders mix well with ferns, primroses, and epimediums. Their flowers are visited regularly by bees and butterflies, and sometimes by hummingbirds; appropriate for wildlife gardens.

Increase by seed sown in spring or fall, or divide established plants in spring.

Polemonium caeruleum

- blue
- late spring to early summer
- 12–36 in. × 12–15 in.
- sun, part shade
- Z4–9, HS

Jacob's ladder, Grecian valerian, charity. Western North America, Europe, northern Asia in mountain regions. This erect clump former develops a basal mound of foliage about 24 in. high and wide. Ladder-like leaves have elliptic, odd-pinnate leaflets

0.75–1.5 in. long, which grow smaller toward the stem tips. Loose, terminal and axillary clusters of fragrant, 1.5-in., cup-shaped, deep blue flowers are carried on branched stems. Leaf tips burn if plants are allowed to dry out, and foliage typically deteriorates with onset of summer heat. Self-seeds and will naturalize.

'Brise D' Anjou' has green-and–creamy yellow variegated leaves; white-eyed, blue flowers. Short lived. 18 in.

'Lace Towers'. Lax clusters of fragrant, cobalt-blue flowers. 3–3.5 ft. Z4–8.

'Lacteum' ('Album') has elegant white flowers.

'Snow and Sapphires' has light green foliage, trimmed with a well-defined white border. Fragrant, sky-blue flowers well above the leaves. An improvement on 'Brise D'Anjou'. 24–30 in. Z3–7.

Polemonium carneum

syn. *P. amoenum*
- pink
- summer
- 18–24 in. × 18 in.
- part shade
- Z5–8, HS

Royal Jacob's ladder. Northwestern United States, west of the Cascades from Washington to San Francisco. Ferny, 3- to 7-in.-long leaves, with 12 or more leaflets. Small clusters of delicate, bell-shaped flowers, light pink touched with apricot. Not the easiest to grow, but worth the effort. Maintain moist soil; protect from hot sun.

'Apricot Delight' has apricot-colored flowers. Reported to self-seed.

Polemonium pauciflorum

- yellow
- early to late summer
- 20–24 in. × 20 in.
- sun, part shade
- Z7–9

Yellow Jacob's ladder. West Texas to Arizona, Mexico. This self-seeding but short-lived perennial has typical Jacob's ladder foliage. Terminal clusters of pendent, yellow, trumpet-shaped flowers, flushed with red at the throat both outside and in. Blooms are about 1 in. long and flare widely into five lobes, each to 0.5 in. long at the mouth.

'Sulfur Trumpets' has silvery leaves topped by 3-in.-long, pendent, pale yellow trumpet flowers. 18 in.

Polemonium reptans

- blue
- late spring to early summer
- 10–18 in. × 12 in.
- sun, part shade
- Z2–7

Creeping polemonium, Greek valerian. Native to damp woodlands from New York to Kansas and Alabama. From shallow rhizomes rise weak, sprawling stems with ladder-like leaves. Drooping, 0.75-in., light blue flowers cluster at stem tips. Reseeds readily from tan-colored fruits. Keep moist for best results. Elegant combined with sedges, woodland phlox, trilliums, and foamflowers.

'Alba' is white flowered.

'Blue Pearl' has bright blue flowers on upright, 12- to 15-in. stems. Often listed as cultivar of *Polemonium caeruleum*.

'Northern Lights' is a dwarf, sterile selection with very fragrant, periwinkle-blue flowers. Resists powdery mildew. Probably a hybrid. 12–16 in. Z4–9.

'Stairway to Heaven' has green foliage, bordered with creamy-white edges, tinged with pink in early spring. Pale lavender flowers. 12–24 in. Z5–7.

'Touch of Class' is a sport with white-rimmed, green leaflets. Pink flower buds open to very pale blue blossoms. 14 in. Z3–7.

Polemonium yezoense

- blue
- early summer
- 6–16 in. × 12 in.
- sun, part shade
- Z5–8

Jacob's ladder. Japan. Young foliage is deep purple, but becomes green with a silvery sheen as the season progresses; very fragrant, powder-blue flowers. Best in moist soil, but not fussy; sun loving. Combines well with woodland phlox, coral bells, foamflowers, and later-blooming toad lilies.

'Bressingham Purple' ('Polbress') has upright, dark purplish stems that carry dark, purplish leaves. Fragrant, lavender-blue flowers. Vigorous and heat tolerant. Probably a hybrid; from Blooms of Bressingham. 15 in. Z4–9.

Purple Rain Strain has similar foliage but dark blue flowers. 12–18 in.

Polygonatum

Asparagaceae
Solomon's seal

Combining toughness with an offbeat elegance, the polygonatums are an asset to any shady planting. Their charming bell-shaped flowers dangle in rows like miniature carillons from the arching stems. But it is the foliage effects—the alternate, lanceolate leaves that climb the stems like rungs on a ladder—that give the plant its greatest visual impact. It contributes a precise architectural note often lacking in wild and woodland plantings, and that is always welcome in perennial borders.

Although Solomon's seals prefer rich, moist but well-drained soil in partial shade, they tolerate wet or fairly dry conditions, and make do in full shade. Though not aggressive, over time their rhizomatous roots spread to form dense but compact colonies. They mix well with other woodlanders including arisaemas, ferns, and May apples. Susceptible to deer browsing.

Sow seed in containers in autumn; overwinter outdoors. Germination is slow; up to a year. Otherwise divide established plants.

Polygonatum odoratum 'Variegatum'

Polygonatum biflorum

- greenish white
- midspring
- 1–3 ft. × 1–1.5 ft.
- part shade, shade
- Z3–8

Small Solomon's seal. Eastern United States, south-central Canada. Rhizomatous; mounds of arching, unbranched stems with parallel-veined leaves to 4 in. long, that turn attractive yellow in fall. Flowers, usually borne in pairs dangling from leaf axils, are small and greenish white; blue-black berries follow. Native peoples ate the starchy rhizomes.

var. commutatum, giant Solomon's seal, regarded as a separate species by some authorities, has also been listed as *Polygonatum commutatum*, *P. canaliculatum*, and *P. giganteum*. Considerably more robust (though less heat tolerant) than *P. biflorum*, with stout, arching stems, 6- to 7-in. leaves; flowers cluster two to ten per leaf axil, followed by blue-black berries. Useful for erosion control, as well as in woodland and cottage gardens, and naturalized

areas. Needs room to show to best advantage. 3–7 ft. × 3–4 ft. Z3–7.

Polygonatum humile

- white
- late spring
- 6–12 in. × 1–3 ft.
- part shade, shade
- Z5–8

Dwarf Japanese Solomon's seal. Native to mountains in Hokkaido, Japan. A petite counterpart to American Solomon's seals. Rhizomatous, develops slowly expanding clumps of arching stems with ovate leaves. Pendent, tubular flowers dangle from leaf axils, followed by round, blue-black fruits in fall. Prefers fertile, humus-rich, moist but well-drained soil. Drought tolerant once established. Shady borders, rock gardens, or woodlands. Occasional attacks by slugs and sawfly larvae.

Polygonatum odoratum

- white
- spring to early summer
- 18–36 in. × 6–18 in.
- part shade, shade
- Z3–8

Fragrant Solomon's seal. Europe, Asia. Clusters of arching stems bear elliptic leaves with one or two fragrant, tubular, green-tipped, creamy-white flowers hanging from each axil. Spherical black fruits follow contrasting with yellow autumn foliage. Occasional problems with slugs and sawfly larvae.

'Fireworks', to 2 ft., egg-shaped, green leaves, flecked with creamy white and developing creamy-white borders as they mature.

'Variegatum' has soft green leaves tipped and rimmed with white; good fall color.

Potentilla

Rosaceae
potentilla, cinquefoil

Best known to gardeners as tough, floriferous shrubs, *Potentilla* also includes a number of fine herbaceous perennials. Typically, these share the bright, cup-shaped, five-petaled flowers and fingered leaves that are the hallmarks of their shrubby relatives. However, the perennials have a more sprawling growth habit. They are most effective as groundcovers for sunny spots, especially where soils are poor and dry, as border edgings, or for inserting into crevices in walls or stone pavements.

Potentillas are easily grown in average, moderately moist, well-drained soils and several tolerate drought well. Their foliage may be as attractive as the flowers; few other perennials are so free of pests, undemanding, and have as long a bloom season. Potentilla fanciers combine several different types, to secure bloom from midspring into late fall. Deer resistant.

Propagate hybrids and named cultivars by division (unless otherwise noted); species from seed.

Potentilla atrosanguinea 'William Rollinson'

Potentilla atrosanguinea

- red
- summer
- 1.5–2 ft. × 1–2 ft.
- sun
- Z5–9, HS

Ruby cinquefoil. Himalayas. Widely branched, leafy stems clothed with silvery gray leaves, covered with silky hairs. Sprays of blood-red, 1-in. flowers are long blooming. A parent of many superior hybrids, often listed as cultivars.

'Firedance' has red-centered, coral flowers. 10–15 in.

'William Rollinson' has semi-double, flame-colored flowers, with a yellow reverse. 15 in.

'Vulcan'. Low mounds of foliage; long-blooming, double, deep red flowers. 12–16 in. Z4–9.

'Yellow Queen' has cheerful clean-yellow flowers above silvery leaves. 12 in.

Potentilla nepalensis

syn. *P. coccinea*

- pink
- late spring to late summer
- 15–18 in. × 24 in.
- sun, part shade
- Z5–8

Nepal cinquefoil. Western Himalayas. Clump forming with branching, wiry stems bearing five-fingered, strawberry-like leaves. Foliage blanketed with purplish red flowers. Only available as cultivars in the trade. Cottage gardens, rock gardens, front of borders, containers.

'Miss Willmott' bears crimson-eyed, deep pink flowers. 12–18 in. × 12–24 in.

'Ron McBeth' has carmine-rose, 1-in. flowers, with dark red centers. Reproduces mostly true from seed. 9–12 in. × 12–18 in.

Potentilla recta

- yellow
- summer
- 12–24 in. × 15 in.
- sun
- Z3–7

Sulphur cinquefoil. Europe, but has naturalized across the United States. Upright tufts of unbranched stems bear strawberry-like, petioled leaves, usually with five to seven leaflets; light yellow flowers. Seldom cultivated but replaced by a superior cultivar 'Macrantha' (syn. *Potentilla recta* var. *warrenii*) that displays loose clusters of 1-in., brilliant yellow flowers for several weeks.

Grow in average, medium-moisture, well-drained soil in full sun to part shade. Prefers moist, cool soils in full sun. When grown as a groundcover, it can be mowed occasionally on a high setting to trim up the plants.

Potentilla thurberi

- red
- early to late summer
- 1–2.5 ft. × 1–2 ft.
- sun, part shade
- Z5–9

Scarlet cinquefoil. Coniferous forests of Arizona, New Mexico, and Mexico. Sprawling mounds of erect stems bear leaves with five to seven toothed, ovate-oblanceolate, 1- to 2-in. leaflets. Red flowers with dark blotches at the petal bases. Tolerates drought.

'Monarch's Velvet' has deep raspberry-colored flowers. Mostly true from seed.

Other Notable Cultivars

'Arc en Ciel' bears double, crimson flowers, with yellow-edged petals. 12–16 in. Z4–8.

×*hopwoodiana* (*Potentilla nepalenses* × *P. recta*). Bicolored, dark red–eyed flowers of pale salmon-pink and cream. 16–20 in. × 16–18 in. Z5–9.

×*tonguei* (*P. anglica* × *P. nepalensis*) is fast growing, evergreen in mild climates. Apricot flowers blotched with red. Resents high heat and humidity. 4–6 in. × 12–18 in. Z5–8.

Primula

Primulaceae
primrose

Although diminutive in size, primroses pack such a wallop of charm that they are beloved by gardeners everywhere. One of the earliest flowers to bloom in spring, primrose can almost be translated as "the first rose." Not even related to roses, however, more than 400 species fit into this diverse genus. It is so varied that botanists have split it into sections, grouped according to their probable relationships. Some of the most important for gardeners are the following:

Acaulis Section. Mostly derived from *Primula vulgaris*, with solitary flowers or sometimes umbels in a wide range of colors. Divide just after bloom time, or start from seed.

Auricula Section. Contains low-growing, evergreen species with flat, salverform flowers, smooth, leathery leaves. Often dusted with white farina (a mealy or granular covering like Farina cereal). *Primula auricula* belongs here. Divide after bloom time.

Candelabra Section. Flowers are held in tiers of whorls on leafless stems. *Primula japonica* and *P. pulverulenta* belong here. Moisture is critical. Divide or seed after bloom time.

Juliana Section. Solitary or umbels of flowers derived from *P. juliae* × *P. veris* or *P. juliae* × *P. vulgaris*. A wide color range, evergreen or semi-evergreen. Divide just before or just after bloom time.

Vernales Section. Includes *P. veris* (cowslip), *P. elatior* (oxslip), and *P. vulgaris* (English primrose) as well as polyantha types. Divide just after bloom time, or start from seed.

Primroses do best in climates with relatively cool summers. They do not care for southern heat and humidity, although they will sometimes tolerate but rarely thrive in the dry heat of southern California. Soil should be rich in moisture-retentive humus, well-drained, not prone to excessive drying out; many species will not survive wet feet in winter due to root rot. Provide neutral to slightly acid soil; *P. vialii* favors sweet, alkaline soil. Most prefer partly shaded sites but enjoy sunny spots in regions where light levels are low.

Primroses are lovely in woodlands and rock gardens, where the alpine species shine. For generations, assorted primroses have been planted out in blocks and patterns in public parks and gardens for colorful spring displays. Perhaps more attractive is to insert them in groups as punctuation in beds and borders, with spring-blooming tulips, daffodils, or hyacinths. Later-blooming perennials shade the primrose foliage. In woodlands, mix with ferns, violets, lungworts, and columbines for spring displays. Similar combinations are perfect for containers. Potted primroses are sold for interior decoration in late winter or very early spring; transplant to the garden when weather warms.

Seldom browsed by deer, squirrels, or rabbits. Primroses are susceptible to aphids, weevils, and spider mites (the latter particularly in greenhouses). Gray mold, rust, and viruses are sometimes a problem.

Primula auricula

syn. *P. alpina, P. balbisii, P. ciliata, P. lutea*
- yellow
- early spring
- 6–10 in. × 12 in.
- sun, part shade
- Z3–8

Auricula, mountain cowslip, bear's ears. European Mountain ranges, including the Carpathians, Alps, and Apennines. Section Auricula. Evergreen, grayish basal rosettes of 2- to 4-in., fleshy, leathery, paddle-shaped leaves often dusted with gray

farinose on both surfaces; tough, wavy margins variably equipped with teeth. A plump scape, 2–6 in. long, is topped with an umbel of up to 20 mostly fragrant, 0.5-in. flowers on 0.5-in. pedicels. Each deep yellow bloom consists of a long perianth tube that flares into a flattish corolla at the mouth. Shallow rooted; needs gritty, free-draining but moist soil.

Primula denticulata

syn. *P. cachemiriana*
- lilac, white
- early spring
- 8–12 in. × 9 in.
- part shade
- Z4–7

Drumstick primrose, Himalayan primrose. Moist, alpine regions of the Himalayas in Afghanistan to southeastern Tibet, Myanmar, and China. Section Denticulata. Robust rosettes of 3- to 6-in., spatulate leaves, finely toothed along the margins, white mealy beneath, elongate after bloom time to 12 in. or more on broadly winged petioles. As the leaves emerge in early spring, sturdy, upright, 4- to 12-in. stems appear topped with crowded 2-in. globes of funnel-shaped, 0.5-in. flowers in shades of lavender, lilac, and purple, or white, accented with a yellow eye. Supply protective winter mulch. Moderate moisture. Best from seed.

'Alba' has white flowers. 12 in.

Ronsdorf Hybrids is a seed strain of mixed colors. 18–20 in.

Primula florindae

- yellow
- early to late summer
- 2–3 ft. × 2 ft.
- part shade
- Z6–8

Florinda primrose, giant cowslip, Tibetan primrose. Native to shaded, marshy areas along streams in southeastern Tibet. Section Sikkimensis. This vigorous late bloomer has rosettes of 9-in.-long, lustrous, broadly ovate leaves, heart shaped at the base, on long, channeled, red petioles. Pendant and fragrant, tubular, bright yellow, 0.5- to 1-in. flowers gather into large umbels of 40 or more, all dusted with white farina, atop sturdy, 1- to 3-ft. scapes. Best in damp soil, or in drifts beside streams, ponds, or lakes.

Primula japonica

- pinks, reds
- late spring
- 18 in. high and wide
- part shade
- Z5–7

Japanese primrose, fairy primrose. Japan. Section Candelabra. Whorls of 8 to 12 flowers arranged in tiers, one on top of the other, topiary style. There are countless cultivars as the flowers are quite promiscuous. Plant at streamside, or beside moving ponds.

'**Miller's Crimson**' has intense rosy-red flowers. Comes true from seed. 1–2 ft. Z6.

Candelabra *Primula* hybrids

'Postford White' is a good white, possibly superior to 'Alba'.

'Rosea' has rose and pink flowers that seed true.

Primula ×*polyantha*

- various
- spring
- 8–15 in. × 9 in.

- sun, part shade
- Z3–8, HS

Polyanthus primrose. Of hybrid origin with mixed parentage of *Primula veris*, *P. vulgaris*, and *P. juliae*. Section Vernales. This fantastic group of plants have often fragrant, single or double flowers that come in all colors, plain, bicolored, or sometimes with contrasting eyes. Umbels of upfacing, tubular flowers flared and flattened at the mouth (salverform) to 1.5 in. across top stems to 12 in. Neat rosettes of wrinkled, spatulate leaves, sometimes rimmed with teeth. The polyantha hybrids have been bred extensively for bedding, for the greenhouse florists' potted-plant trade, and recently for

Primula japonica

fall landscaping displays. They prefer cool climates and struggle with heat and humidity. Moist soil. Excellent in the cool, damp northwestern parts of North America, where public parks and gardens host them widely.

Pacific Giant Strain comes in all colors with large flowers. Not as cold hardy as some.

Regal Strain. This Tasmanian strain tolerates a wide range of conditions.

Primula sieboldii
- pinks, purples
- late spring
- 4–8 in. × 8 in.
- sun, part shade
- Z4–8

Japanese star primrose, Siebold primrose. Japan. Section Cortusoides. Long petioled, wrinkled, and scalloped, the 2- to 4-in.-long, ovate leaves are hairy on both sides. Umbels of six to ten showy flowers rise on slender, hairy scapes; flattish, white, mauve, or pink blooms may have deeply notched or frilled corolla lobes, and a white eye. Often summer dormant. Excellent in moist northeastern woodlands.

'Alba' has white flowers.

Barnhaven Strain. This superior seed strain comes in a variety of colors. The history of Barnhaven is most interesting.

Primula veris
syn. *P. officinalis*
- pale yellow
- early spring
- 4–12 in. × 9 in.
- sun, part shade
- Z5–7

Cowslip. The British Isles, temperate Europe, and Asia. Section Vernales. Oblong, 2- to 3-in. leaves, wrinkled and hairy beneath, are held on winged petioles as long as the leaf blades. One-sided, several-flowered umbels of fragrant, nodding, bright yellow blooms rise on downy, upright scapes, to 8 in. long. Each lobed, bell-shaped flower is restricted at the mouth where it emerges from a pale green, slightly inflated, five-angled calyx. Moist soil.

'Katy McSparron' has double flowers.

Sunset Shades is a seed mix of orange and red flowers, with bright yellow throats. 8 in.

Primula vialii
syn. *P. littoniana*
- red violet
- late spring
- 12–15 in. × 12 in.
- part shade
- Z5–7, HS

Chinese pagoda primrose, Vial's primrose, orchid primrose. Northwest Yunnan, southwest Szechwan, China. Section Muscarioides. Short lived, with 12-in. basal leaves, pointed, lance shaped, and dentate, tapering to a winged petiole. Stiff, white, mealy stems hoist dense, conical, 3- to 6-in. spikes of bright red flower buds that open to fragrant, 0.5-in. flowers; slightly nodding with violet tubes, and

pointed, lilac-blue corolla lobes. Best massed in dappled deciduous shade in boggy ground, pond- or lakeside. Requires moist soil with high pH; add lime if soil is acid.

Primula vulgaris
syn. *P. acaulis, P. ×hybrida*
- light yellow
- midspring
- 6–9 in. × 9 in.
- sun, part shade
- Z5–8

English primrose, common primrose. British Isles, western and southern Europe. Section Vernales. Synonymous with spring in rural England, this lightly fragrant species of hedgerows and woodlands is a major player in primula breeding programs. Blunt-tipped, ovate leaves are wrinkled, softly hairy beneath, and rimmed with round teeth; they elongate to about 6 in. on short, winged petioles by bloom time. Solitary, 1- to 1.5-in. salverform flowers of primrose yellow, blotched with a darker eye, rise on slender, fuzzy, pink stems, reddish at the base. Typical of primroses, stigma and styles vary in length: when the stigma is prominent like a pinhead with shorter stamens, the flower is said to be "pin-eyed"; if the stamens are longer than the stigma, the flower is "thrum-eyed." Fertilization can only occur between pin-eyed and thrum-eyed flowers. Flowers and leaves are edible; flowers are sometimes made into primrose wine. Maybe the easiest to grow; tolerates short droughty periods.

Belarina Strain has fully double flowers in a wide color range. Long blooming.

'Blue Jeans' has grayish blue flowers, brushed with dark blue stripes.

'Jack-in-the-Green', pale yellow flowers within a loose ruff of large green sepals.

'Quaker's Bonnet' produces double, deep rose pink flowers

Spectrum Series has lacy flowers edged with white.

Prunella
Lamiaceae
self-heal

This genus is yet another in which a well-known weedy species, in this case *Prunella vulgaris*, has caused gardeners to neglect its better-behaved relatives. Aside from their supposed medicinal value— the self-heals, as the common name suggests, were formerly used to stop bleeding—a number make excellent floral groundcovers. In particular, *P. grandiflora* and its hybrids furnish handsome mats of evergreen foliage, with opposite pairs of leaves on square stems. Flowers are borne in verticillasters of six-blossom whorls interrupted by leafy bracts at stem tips. Common to mint family members, self-heal's individual flowers are two lipped, hooded, about 1 in. high; the upper lip is two lobed, the lower three lobed.

Primula vulgaris 'Belarina Buttercup'

Prunella ×*webbiana*

Self-heal thrives in moist, average soil in sunny or partly shaded spots; protect from intense sun in hot regions. It tolerates dryish soil in part shade under deciduous trees or shrubs. Probably too vigorous for rock gardens, although it looks well in such sites if kept under control. Valuable as an edging at the front of beds and borders, alongside pathways, in coastal gardens, and in wildlife gardens, where it attracts honeybees and butterflies. Resists deer and rabbits. Self-seeds freely; remove spent flower spikes immediately after bloom time.

Increase cultivars by division.

Prunella grandiflora

- violet-blue
- early to midsummer
- 6–12 in. × 12–18 in.
- sun, part shade
- Z3–8

Bigflower self-heal, large self-heal. Europe. Low-growing mats of dark green, rough-hairy leaves, 3–4 in. long, heart shaped at the base. Flower spikes to 3 in. tall.

'Alba' has white flowers

Freelander Mixture is compact, early, and very vigorous. It blooms the first season from early seeding. 2006 Fleuroselect Gold Medal winner. Currently available in single colors: blue, pink, and white. 6–8 in. Z5–8.

The Loveliness Group is probably of hybrid origin, and is correctly *Prunella* ×*webbiana*. 6–8 in. Z5. 'Loveliness' has dense spikes of deep lavender flowers; 'Pink Loveliness' is rosy pink; 'White Loveliness' has white flowers that often brown prematurely at the tips.

'Rosea' has rosy pink blooms. 6–12 in. Z4–8.

Pseudofumaria
Papaveraceae
rock fumewort

A new genus composed of two species formerly considered members of the Fumeworts, the genus *Corydalis*. Like the fumeworts, pseudofumarias have fleshy roots and finely divided leaves. The flowers are tubular and spurred, usually held in loose clusters at the stem tips. The pseudofumarias require a consistently cool, moist soil, high in organic matter; in cold climates, mulch the plants well in winter. Most species excel in the cool climate of the Pacific Northwest, and do not tolerate high summer heat and humidity. Where they flourish, they combine well with hostas, ferns, epimediums, lilyturf, and other shade lovers in woodlands, along pathways, and in rock gardens. Deer resistant; tubers are sometimes dug and devoured by squirrels and chipmunks.

Propagate by seed sown outdoors in fall, or indoors with stratification followed by bottom heat (65–75°F).

Pseudofumaria alba
syn. *Corydalis ochroleuca*

- cream
- late spring
- 12 in. × 12 in.
- part shade
- Z5–8

Native to rocky European woodlands, this species makes a mound of gray-green foliage that contrasts well with the yellow-throated, spurred, cream blooms. Sometimes repeat blooms, self-seeds freely. Create a color echo vignette with cream-edged basket-of-gold 'Dudley Neville Variegated'.

Pulmonaria saccharata 'Pierre's Pure Pink'

Pseudofumaria lutea

Pseudofumaria lutea

syn. *Corydalis lutea*

- yellow
- spring to fall
- 12–18 in. × 12–15 in.
- sun, part shade
- Z4–8

Yellow corydalis. Southern Alps. Easier to grow than *Pseudofumaria alba* or its former relatives in the genus *Corydalis*. Produces succulent mounds of light green, ferny leaves and abundant clusters of bright yellow flowers. Best in regions with temperate summers, although it can be kept going elsewhere with adequate moisture. Short lived at best. Self-seeds freely but easy to weed out. Naturalizes well with forget-me-nots and Welsh poppies for a striking spring display.

Pulmonaria

Boraginaceae
lungwort

The common name sounds like a smoker's malady, but in fact the lungworts are an invaluable, if often overlooked, group of garden perennials. They offer

Pulmonaria longifolia 'Bertram Anderson'

early season flowers—as early as late winter in mild climates—that have the intriguing habit of changing color as they mature. Their attractive, bristly, bold-textured foliage is often spotted, splashed, or painted with silver, and unlike that of many spring flowers, it remains attractive throughout summer and fall.

Natives of Europe and Asia, the slowly spreading, rhizomatous roots of pulmonarias prefer cool, moist conditions, and dappled shade. Average garden soil is fine, as long as it drains well and does not dry out; waterlogged soil is fatal. Aside from slugs, they suffer from few pests, resisting even deer. Powdery mildew can be serious, especially in dry summer conditions, but many recent introductions are resistant.

Pulmonarias bloom before or as the new foliage emerges in spring. Individual flowers are funnel shaped, divided into five shallow lobes at the mouth; some 0.25 in. across, they are held in drooping terminal clusters well above the leaf rosette. Flower color varies from purple and violet to blue, shades of pink and red, and white. Commonly, flowers are pink in bud and subsequently mature to blue or violet. After flowers fade, the basal leaves expand. Individual leaves are long, and narrowly lanceolate to oval in shape; stem leaves are smaller and usually sessile.

Lungworts combine well with early spring hellebores, lilyturfs, and crested iris; their foliage contrasts well with ferns. Elegant as a woodland groundcover, they offer a deer- and rabbit-resistant, but not woodchuck-resistant, alternative to hostas. Deadhead to the base. Amend soil with compost; mulch in summer. May prove short lived; extend lifespan by dividing plants every three to five years.

Propagate by division in fall, root cuttings taken in spring, or sow seed of species in spring. Lungworts commonly self-seed, but because they hybridize spontaneously, offspring of named cultivars rarely duplicate parents.

Pulmonaria angustifolia

- blue
- early spring
- 6–12 in. × 12–15 in.
- part shade, shade
- Z3–7

Blue lungwort, narrowleaf lungwort. Northeastern to eastern Europe. Lanceolate, dark green leaves; terminal cymes of flowers open pinkish, mature to deep, bright blue. Some authorities insist that plants in nursery trade are not botanically true *Pulmonaria angustifolia*; nevertheless, an outstanding perennial.

'Blaues Meer' bears heavier crops of bright blue flowers.

Pulmonaria longifolia

- blue
- early to midspring
- 6–16 in. × 18–36 in.
- part shade, shade
- Z3–8

Longleaf lungwort. Western Europe. Semievergreen, with long, narrow leaves, dark green with silver spots. Blue-purple to deep blue flowers. More sun tolerant than most species. Good powdery mildew resistance.

'Bertram Anderson' ('E. B. Anderson') has brilliant dark blue flowers. Somewhat slug resistant.

'Dordogne' has electric-blue flowers; silver-streaked leaves.

subsp. *cevennensis* has silver-spotted leaves to 2 ft. long; dark violet-blue flowers.

Pulmonaria mollis

- pink, blue
- early to midspring
- 2 ft. high and wide
- part shade, shade
- Z4–7

Central Europe to Asia. Largest of the species, forms robust clumps of green leaves 12–18 in. long. Deep blue flowers age to purplish pink. Among the heaviest blooming pulmonarias in a Chicago Botanic Garden trial. Exceptional sun tolerance.

'Royal Blue' has rich blue flowers.

'Samobor' has violet-red flowers that mature to a blue-purple.

Pulmonaria officinalis

- pink, violet, blue
- early spring
- 12–18 in. × 15–18 in.
- part shade, shade
- Z4–8

Common lungwort. Europe. Bristly, broad, semievergreen or deciduous, medium green leaves, spotted with greenish white. Flowers open pink, darken to violet, then fade to blue. More susceptible to powdery mildew than most other species.

'Blue Mist' has lavender-pink flowers that mature to light blue.

'White Wings' has large, white flowers; superior to older 'Sissinghurst White'.

Pulmonaria rubra

syn. *P. angustifolia* 'Rubra', *P. officinalis* var. *rubra*

- red
- early spring
- 16 in. × 24 in.
- part shade, shade
- Z4–9

Southeastern Europe. Rosettes of light green, unspotted, elliptical leaves; clusters of red, tubular flowers. One of the earliest species to bloom.

'David Ward' has white-margined, light green leaves; brick-red flowers.

'Redstart' has apple-green leaves with petunia-red flowers.

Pulmonaria saccharata

- pink, violet, blue
- early to midspring
- 1–1.5 ft. × 1.5–2 ft.
- part shade, shade
- Z3–8

Lungwort, Bethlehem sage. Europe. Bristly, 4–12 in., elliptical leaves, medium to dark green blotched or speckled with silver, persist into late fall or early winter in cold regions, semi-evergreen where milder. Pink, violet, or blue buds open to slightly nodding, blue flowers. Tolerant of deep shade, but with less vigorous growth.

'Excalibur' has nearly solid silver leaves with irregular green margins, pink buds opening to blue flowers. Mildew resistant.

'Leopard' has coral-pink flowers.

'Mrs. Moon' has leaves heavily spotted with silver; light pink buds open to bright blue flowers. Largely replaced by superior cultivars.

'Pierre's Pure Pink' has pure pink flowers that retain their color; spotted light green foliage. Somewhat slug resistant.

Other Notable Cultivars

The following are hardy in Z4–8 unless otherwise noted.

'Apple Frost' has leaves heavily splashed with silver, and green midribs; soft pink flowers mature to violet-blue. Mildew resistant. 12 in. × 18 in.

'Berries and Cream' has mostly silver leaves with slightly ruffled, mottled green margins; raspberry-pink flowers. 12 in. × 18 in.

'Bubble Gum' has mildew-resistant, silver leaves, topped with rose-pink flowers that hold their color. 14–16 in. × 12 in.

'Roy Davidson' sports silver-spotted leaves. Very tolerant of heat and humidity; among the heaviest bloomers in a Chicago Botanic Garden trial. 12 in. × 18–24 in. Z4–9.

'Silver Bouquet' combines outstanding heat and humidity tolerance with mildew resistance. Leaves mostly silver, large coral to pink to violet flowers. 7–10 in. × 20 in. Z4–9.

Pycnanthemum
Lamiaceae
American mountain mint

Wonderfully aromatic foliage is the chief attraction of this genus of North American natives; mountain mints have long been used for minty teas and for treatment of digestive ailments. They grow wild mostly in open meadows and woodlands; very easy to cultivate.

Mountain mints have running roots that may spread aggressively, especially in moist, partly shaded spots. Withholding water helps control invasive tendencies. Wiry, square stems are vertical and fibrous, clothed with opposite pairs of fragrant, softly hairy leaves, mostly narrowly lance shaped, and sessile or on short petioles. Stems branch from the upper leaf axils also. Small, 0.5-in. flowers typical of mint: two lipped, the upper lip two lobed, the lower three lobed. These crowd into dense heads accompanied by leafy bracts. The fruits are nutlets. All part of the plants smell refreshingly of mint.

Plant mountain mints in sun or part shade in loamy, consistently moist soil. Other than controlling their spreading habit, they need little maintenance. The stems are good for cutting and look especially well as filler with blousy hydrangeas; the minty aroma is pleasant indoors on a hot summer day. Although many gardeners prefer to cut most perennials to the ground, dormant mountain mints provide cover for insects, seeds for birds, and are particularly attractive dusted with snow. Rust may sometimes be a problem and need treatment. Deer and rabbits ignore these strongly aromatic plants.

Herb and kitchen gardens are improved by the addition of mountain mints for teas, potpourri, and other uses. Mix with shrubs in light woodlands where they can spread without trespassing on smaller specimens, or mass them on difficult banks.

Propagate by division in summer, or start from seed in place in spring or fall.

Pycnanthemum flexuosum

Pycnanthemum flexuosum

syn. *P. tenuifolium*

- white
- early to midsummer
- 24–36 in. × 15–18 in.
- sun, part shade
- Z5–8

Appalachian mountain mint, slender mountain mint, Savanna mountain mint. Native to the southeastern coastal plains of the United States. The tough rhizomatous clumps that this species develops are valued for soil erosion control. Upright stems clothed with pairs of fragrant leaves, often rimmed with red, are topped with fluffy, globular, silver-white heads, with white flowers and white-tipped bracts. An important larval food for caterpillars of grey hairstreak butterflies. Drought tolerant.

'Cat Springs' is a selection that is reportedly superior to the species. Masses of heads of white flowers. 36 in. Z6–8.

Pycnanthemum muticum

- pink, white
- summer to early fall
- 2–3 ft. × 15–24 in.
- sun, part shade
- Z4–8

Clustered mountain mint, short-toothed mountain mint, big leaf mountain mint. Native to damp woods and meadows from Massachusetts to Michigan, and south to Georgia, Louisiana and Texas.

Differs from *Pycnanthemum virginianum* by having broader, lustrous leaves with very showy, silvery bracts; in summer the plants appear to have been heavily dusted with silver. Excellent nectar and pollen plant for insects and butterflies; long blooming. Seldom spreads unduly. Leave the spent heads as winter cover for insects. Outstanding in native plant gardens with beebalm, coneflowers, purple coneflowers, and obedient plants. Lovely at woodland edges, perhaps with white-variegated sedges such as *Carex morrowii* 'Ice Dance'. Reputedly toxic as a tea.

Ranunculus

Ranunculaceae
buttercup

This Jekyll and Hyde genus includes a number of fine garden perennials, but also some particularly invasive species, that despite their attractive flowers, should never be planted outside their natural range.

The weedy species include creeping buttercup (*Ranunculus repens*), a European native that has naturalized on wet soils across North America, and lesser celandine (*R. ficaria*, *Ficaria verna*), native to Europe and western Asia, that has proven a very troublesome weed in the Pacific Northwest, and from Missouri east and north to Virginia and

Mixed *Ranunculus asiaticus* Bloomingdale Strain

Quebec. Cultivars of the latter species, including better-behaved 'Brazen Hussy', are fairly common in the nursery trade, but outside the species' native range should be avoided in favor of less-aggressive relatives.

In general yellow or white, occasionally orange flowers, with five lustrous petals and a central knot of stamens, characterize members of this species. The leaves are alternate, commonly or entirely basal, and often palmately compound or finely dissected; basal leaves are usually long stalked, stem leaves short stalked or sessile. Buttercups' acrid sap makes them distasteful to grazing animals, and to deer and rabbits, in particular, which enhances the plants' invasiveness. All parts should be considered toxic.

Propagate by seed or divide.

Ranunculus aconitifolius 'Flore Pleno'

- white
- late spring to early summer
- 24 in. × 18 in.
- sun, part shade
- Z5–9

White bachelor's buttons. Mountains of central and southern Europe. Vigorous, forms a neat clump of palmately divided, dark green leaves; branching stems bear 0.75-in., double, button-like, white flowers that bloom over two months. Non-spreading: roots do not run and flowers are sterile, producing no seed. Provide humus-rich, fertile, and moisture-retentive but well-drained soil. Good for cottage gardens, beds and borders, and as cut flowers.

Ranunculus asiaticus

- various
- early spring to early summer
- 1–2 ft. high and wide
- sun
- Z8–10

Persian buttercup. Southern Europe, southwestern Asia. Tuberous rooted, with finely cut, parsley-like leaves in mounds, to 12 in. high. Cup-shaped, poppy-like flowers, to 2 in. across, have purple-black anthers, and are held on 1- to 2-ft. stems. Countless hybrids, some with bicolored and double flowers, and to 4 in. across have been developed. Well adapted to mild-winter regions, long, cool springs, and dryish but not too hot summers. Plant the tubers in fall; bloom begins in early spring, and extends over a long season. Elsewhere, grow as annuals planted out around the last spring frost date, or in containers overwintered in a cool, dry, frost-free spot. Prefers moderately moist, well-drained soils; does not tolerate waterlogged soils, especially in winter. Good for beds and borders; superb cut flowers.

Bloomingdale Strain is compact, to 10 in., with pale orange, pink, red, yellow, and white, double flowers.

Tecolote Strain has mostly fully double flowers, 3–6 in. across, in bicolored picotee, gold, pastel mix,

pink, red, rose, salmon, sunset orange, white, and yellow. A visit to the the Flower Fields in Carlsbad, CA, at bloom time is unforgettable.

Ranunculus californicus

- yellow
- late winter to midspring
- 2 ft. high and wide
- sun, part shade
- Z6–10

California buttercup. British Columbia, south through California. Undemanding perennial native to chaparral, coastal scrub, and open woodlands. Dissected leaves and 0.75-in., bright yellow flowers with 7 to 22 teardrop-shaped petals on long, leafless stems. Prefers clay soils but adaptable; summer dormant without irrigation. When irrigated, cut back hard after bloom to force out new growth and second flush of flowers. Self-seeds.

Ratibida
Asteraceae
prairie coneflower, Mexican hat plant

This native prairie genus of five or six species includes two garden-worthy perennials. The genus differs from other coneflowers in having an elongated central cone or disk, usually tan colored to black; the surrounding slender ray "petals" often droop. Mexican hat plant is so named for its supposed resemblance to a sombrero, with the central flower cone forming the crown, and the ray flowers, the brim. Leaves are roughly hairy, pinnately divided into lobes.

Provide well-drained, average garden soil and a sunny spot for prairie coneflowers. These tough plants tolerate heat and humidity and thrive in inhospitable terrain. Leave spent flowerheads for seed-eating birds. Bruised leaves emit the smell of

Ratibida columnifera

anise; deer seldom browse the foliage, though they may try a flowerhead or two. Reportedly rabbits also shun these plants.

Mass prairie coneflowers in meadows, and wild or native plant gardens with grasses and other natives. Also useful in sunny beds and borders, and as cut flowers.

Mexican hats self-seed freely. Increase by seed sown in late spring.

Ratibida columnifera
syn. *R. columnaris, Rudbeckia columnifera, Lepachys columnifera*

- yellow, red-and-yellow
- mid- to late summer
- 24–36 in. × 12–24 in.
- sun
- Z3–8, HT

Upright prairie coneflower. Southwestern Canada, west and central United States to New Mexico. This prairie native has showy, butterfly-attracting daisies with three to seven slightly drooping ray flowers, and a broadly cylindrical, 2-in.-long, dark brown or purplish central cone. The hairy leaves are about 5 in. long, each lobe linear and toothless. Does not tolerate clay soils well. Short lived.

'Buttons and Bows' has frilly, double, rusty flowers with wider rays edged with gold. 18–23 in. Z6–9.

'Red Midget' sports the typical tall cone and widely reflexed ray flowers in deep auburn, orange, and yellow. Good heat tolerance. Compact at 18–24 in. Z3–8.

var. *pulcherrima* has brownish red-purple rays surrounding an ocher cone.

Ratibida pinnata
- yellow
- mid- to late summer
- 3–5 ft. × 18 in.
- sun, part shade
- Z3–8, HT

Prairie coneflower, gray-headed coneflower. Native to the US midwestern prairies. Leaves to 5 in. long with three to five lobes, each slender, ovate, pointed, and toothed. Solitary flowerheads rise on stiff, upright stems. Central cones are usually grayish, shorter than the rays, surrounded by 6 to 13 drooping, yellow ray petals, 2–3 in. long. Tolerates clay, and poor dry soils.

Rehmannia
Phrymaceae
Chinese foxglove, Beverly bells

In traditional Chinese medicine, Chinese foxgloves are used as a popular tonic for strengthening the liver and replenishing vitality, as well as treatments for various other ailments. Do-it-yourselfers should beware that all parts of this plant are poisonous if ingested without proper processing and supervision. What is less well known are the horticultural benefits of the unusual and charming flowers of Chinese foxglove. Similar in appearance to those of penstemons and foxgloves, rehmannia blooms are showier and last longer.

Chinese foxglove prefers a fertile, loose, moist soil that drains well; irrigate during dry periods. Plant in full sun in regions where sunlight is less intensive, but provide part shade elsewhere; they do not tolerate wet feet in winter, and require protection from winter winds. In harsh winter areas, treat as biennials, or pot up and overwinter with protection. Fertilize lightly in spring. Deer and rabbit resistant.

Propagate from fresh seed (collect from your own plants if possible) or take root cuttings in fall to winter. Root softwood cuttings of young spring growth, or remove and transplant runners.

Rehmannia elata
syn. *R. angulata*

- pink
- late spring to midsummer
- 24–36 in. × 20–24 in.
- sun, part sun
- Z6–10

Beverly bells. China. Underground runners form colonies of low, mat-like rosettes of hairy, oblong, gray-green leaves, usually lobed or toothed. Stem leaves are alternate with conspicuous venation. Nodding, softly hairy, pinkish purple flowers with yellow-dotted throats collect in loose spikes atop

Rehmannia elata

red stems and in leaf axils. The plants enjoy a maritime climate; bloom is best in cool-summer regions; protect from winter wet. Frequently self-seeds, or collect seeds in fall for replacements. Good for cut flowers. *Rehmannia glutinosa* is less often grown, except for medical purposes. Its flowers are yellow, flushed with purple, and the whole plant is much more hairy than Chinese foxglove.

Rheum
Polygonaceae
ornamental rhubarb

Most Americans are familiar with the culinary rhubarb that furnishes a filling for pies; fewer are aware that rhubarbs also include several bold and beautiful garden perennials. These have the outsized leaves and plume-like flowerheads of their kitchen-garden cousins, but are more refined and often more colorful. They provide a strong architectural note to beds or borders. Moreover their expansive foliage makes dramatic counterpoint to plants such as airy-foliaged meadow rues, whose dainty purplish pink flowers harmonize nicely with those of the rhubarbs. Other dramatic combinations include white-flowered penstemons, summer phloxes, and delphiniums backed by burgundy-leaved rhubarbs. For a tropical foliage effect on a grand scale, substitute rhubarbs as cold-hardy alternatives to *Gunnera*; similarly, rhubarbs thrive alongside ponds and streams. Unlike culinary rhubarb, ornamental rhubarb stems are not edible; all parts are toxic.

Provide deep, humus-rich, evenly moist soil that drains well; mulch in summer to protect against drought. Provide midday part shade where sun is intense; elsewhere, full sun is fine. Adapts poorly to combined heat and humidity. Where drainage is poor, crown rot may be a problem; occasionally attacked by rhubarb curculios. Be alert for leaf spots that mar the leaves but are seldom serious. Deer relish them.

Divide in early spring. For the patient, sow seed in fall.

Rheum alexandrae
- yellow
- late spring to midsummer
- 4 ft. × 2 ft.
- sun, part shade
- Z5–8, HS

Alexander's rhubarb. China, Tibet. Lustrous, long-petioled, white-veined, lanceolate leaves to 8 in. long arise from deep roots. Tall stalks carry insignificant flowers that are concealed by hand-sized, creamy-yellow bracts, streaked with burgundy as they mature. Foliage becomes bright wine-red and orange in autumn.

Rheum palmatum
- pink, red
- early to midsummer
- 6–8 ft. × 4–6 ft.
- sun, part shade
- Z4–7, HS

Turkish rhubarb, Chinese rhubarb. Northwestern China, Tibet. The reference to Turkey in the common name is a misnomer dating to earlier times, when this species' highly esteemed medicinal roots entered Europe through Turkey. Large domed mounds of rounded, palmately lobed, dark green leaves, each 2–3 ft. across. Pink to red flowers are individually tiny, six tepaled, and carried in 1- to 2-ft.-long, terminal panicles on stout, tall stems.

'Atrosanguineum' ('Rubrum') has bright red young leaves; only red beneath at maturity.

var. *tanguticum* (syn. *Rheum tanguticum*) has reddish bronze young leaves that mature to dark green, purplish red underneath. Soft pink flowers; red autumn foliage color.

Other Notable Cultivars
'Ace of Hearts' (*Rheum kialense* × *R. palmatum*) has spade-shaped, 3-ft. leaves, lustrous and crinkly when young, but mature dark green with prominent red veins, burgundy beneath. Deep pink flowers. 4–5 ft. × 3–4 ft. Z4–9.

Rhexia
Melastomaceae
meadow beauty, deer grass

This wonderful native genus is the most northerly member of a mostly tropical family that also includes glory bush (*Tibouchina*) and princess flower (*Centradena*). A common denominator of the family is the conspicuous, parallel veins on the leaves. Some meadow beauty species are rare, even endangered, but those described here may be spotted during a hike through the New Jersey pinebarrens or sandy swamps of the Carolinas and similar sites along the Mid-Atlantic seaboard. In gardens, meadow beauties provide a vibrant display of color toward the end of summer, when other flowers may be scarce.

The flowers have four oblique petals and four pairs of curved petals. They are pollinated by bees that buzz the flowers, shaking out the pollen from pores at the tips of the anthers. Curiously, the flowers' prominent stamens change color over the day after opening, changing from bright yellow to red. Urn-shaped fruits are tan colored.

In the wild, meadow beauties grow in acid, moist soils in open places. Grow them in damp meadows, in bog gardens beside ponds or lakes, and even in rock gardens where soil remains damp. Improve heavy or poor soils by adding generous doses of coarse, gritty sand and organic matter. Probably seldom browsed by deer or rabbits.

Propagate by division in spring or fall, or start from seed. Seeds must be dry and ripe before harvesting.

Rheum palmatum 'Atrosanguineum'

Rhodohypoxis baurii

Rhexia mariana

- pale pink, white
- summer to early fall
- 8–18 in. × 12 in.
- sun
- Z6–9

Maryland meadow beauty, dull meadow-pitchers. Native to sandy swamplands and bogs of the eastern coastal plain and south-central United States. Rhizomatous roots give rise to rounded stems bearing pairs of lanceolate, pointed leaves, 1–2 in. long, covered with stiff hairs. Pale pink or white flowers similar to those of Virginia meadow beauty are borne in 2-in.-long, terminal racemes.

Rhexia virginica

- magenta-pink
- summer to fall
- 12–20 in. × 12 in.
- sun
- Z3–9

Virginia meadow beauty, deer grass, handsome Harry. Native to sandy swamplands and bogs of the eastern coastal plain, south to Florida. Although uncommon in gardens, Virginia meadow beauty deserves wider use. Rising from tubers, square stems with prominent wings at each corner and bristles at the nodes, are furnished with pairs of sessile, pointed, ovate leaves, 2–3 in. long. These are distinctly marked with three or five parallel veins, and are rimmed with hair and tiny teeth. Loose clusters of outward-facing, bright rose-purple, 1- to 1.5-in. flowers with notched petals, crowd the top of the stems. Although moist, acid soil is ideal, this species tolerates average garden soils well.

Rhodohypoxis
Rhodohypoxidaceae
red star

To succeed with the red stars, it's essential to reproduce the dry winters and moister summers of the South African grasslands and rocky mountainsides where these plants evolved. If these conditions can be duplicated, red stars will prove valuable as edging plants at the front of rock-edged borders, along paths and walkways, or in well-drained rock gardens. They make excellent container plants. Flower colors are variable, including a wide range of reds, pinks, and white; the blossoms show off well against the grassy foliage covered with gray hairs.

These Southern Hemisphere gems do best in moderately fertile, well-drained soils where they get plenty of water during the growing season, but remain dry during their winter dormancy; some gardeners protect the plants with a piece of slate or split pot set on a slant. In containers, allow them to dry out after bloom finishes, and water only sparingly until growth recommences the following spring. Red spider mites may attack plants grown under glass. Deer and rabbit tolerant.

Increase by removing offsets or dividing clumps in fall. Start from seed in spring.

Rhodohypoxis baurii

- pink, white
- late spring to early summer
- 3–6 in. × 4 in.
- sun
- Z7–10

Spring star flower, red star, rosy posy. Native to rocky areas of the Drakensberg Mountains, South Africa. Small tubers, covered with fibers, produce basal clusters of hairy, 4-in.-long, grassy, gray-green leaves. Solitary, pink to red, or white, 0.75-in., star-shaped flowers bloom through most of the summer on 2- to 4-in. stems.

'Glitterbug' has deep rosy-pink blooms.

'Pintado' blooms with pale pink flowers tipped and centered with deep rose.

'Venetia' has vivid magenta-pink flowers.

Rodgersia

Saxifragaceae
Rodger's flower

Plants in this seriously underused genus are unmatched for making statements in moist beds or borders; furthermore they provide bold foliage effects in open woodlands, pond- and streamsides or bog gardens, where there is simply nothing more effective than these hardy eastern Asian natives.

Naturals for rain gardens. These are not plants for confined spaces, however: from rhizomatous roots rise mounds of expansive, fingered, pinnate leaves with deep-set veins; individual leaves may, depending on the species, measure 16 in. across, with the aggregate mound spanning 3–5 ft. Flower stalks as much as 4–6 ft. tall soar above in summer carrying huge sprays of tiny, pink or white flowers, somewhat like giant astilbes. Star-like seed capsules may turn red as temperatures cool, accenting the yellow hues of rodgersias' fall foliage.

In the wild, rodgersias inhabit damp sites alongside streams, ponds, or the edges of wet woods and meadows. Provide consistently moist, humus-enriched soil, and full to part sun. Select a spot protected from strong winds that damage the large leaves. Pest and disease problems are few, except for slugs and snails, and powdery mildew if plants dry out. Rabbit and deer resistant.

Propagate by division, or sow seed of species.

Rodgersia aesculifolia

- white, pink
- early to late summer
- 3–5 ft. × 3–5 ft.
- sun, part shade
- Z5–7

Native to China. Thick, black rhizomes support a clump of palmate, coarsely toothed, crinkled, dark green leaves tinted bronze, to 12 in. across. These resemble those of horse chestnut (*Aesculus*), and

Rodgersia aesculifolia

Rohdea japonica

have five to nine leaflets. Fragrant flowers, creamy white or light pink, gather in 18- to 24-in., terminal panicles atop long stems. Flower stalks, stems, and leaf margins are clad with brown hairs. Leaf margins crisp and brown if soil dries out.

Rodgersia pinnata

- pink, red
- late spring to early summer
- 3–4 ft. high and wide
- sun, part shade
- Z5–7

Southwestern China. Pinnately compound leaves with six to nine leaflets, each 6–8 in. long. Apetalous flowers, varying from creamy pink to red, borne on erect stalks in branched panicles well above foliage. Reddish bronze fall foliage. Prefers light shade.

'Alba' has bright green leaves; white flowers.

'Chocolate Wings' has deep cocoa-bronze spring foliage that matures to dark green; deep pink flowers.

'Fireworks' has cherry-red flowers and extra-large (leaflets to 10 in.) foliage with bronze spring hue.

Rodgersia sambucifolia

- pink, white
- early summer
- 2–3 ft. high and wide
- sun, part shade
- Z4–7

China. Pinnately compound, dark green leaves similar to those of elderberries (*Sambucus*); each leaflet to 8 in. long. Erect stems rise from 3- to 4-ft. foliage mounds to bear pink or creamy-white flower plumes. Vigorous and spreading; may form extensive colonies over time. Tolerates full sun only in cooler climates; provide a protective winter mulch in northern part of its range. Flourishes in boggy, wet soils.

Other Notable Cultivars

'Big Mama' bears tall plumes of fragrant, shell pink flowers in early to midsummer. Palmately compound leaves, each usually with seven leaflets. Sun, part shade. 3–5 ft. high and wide. Z5–7.

Rohdea
Asparagaceae
Nippon lily, sacred lily

If you are seeking a deer-resistant alternative to hostas, consider Nippon lilies. These Asian evergreens may not be quite as varied as hostas—the genus includes just one species—but their foliage is bold and tropical looking. Moreover, they are tough and easy to grow, thriving even beneath black walnut trees.

Nippon lilies do best in slightly moist, shaded spots, but tolerate dry shade well and manage to shine even in deep shade. Their glossy foliage remains attractive all year round; remove old, spent leaves from the outside of the plant by pulling them outward from the base. Otherwise they require little maintenance, and this, together with their ability to flourish in difficult circumstances, is winning them increasing popularity. Mass Nippon lilies under trees as a groundcover, or cultivate them in large containers; their persistent bright berries make them welcome through the holidays and beyond, even providing a brilliant counterpoint to early spring bulbs. Appropriate companions include shade-loving astilbes, ferns, hellebores, and Hakone grass. Due to their huge popularity in Japan, hundreds of selections have been made. Some of these have been introduced in this country; the species is readily available. Watch for slugs in moist shade locations. Deer do not browse.

Divide in spring or fall, or start from seed in containers in fall.

Rohdea japonica
syn. *Orontium japonicum*

- whitish yellow
- late spring to summer
- 9–24 in. × 24 in.
- part shade, shade
- Z6–10

Nippon lily, sacred lily, lily of China. China, Japan. Slow growing from fibrous roots, this evergreen perennial makes vase-shaped tufts of broad, glossy foliage that rises from the central crown. Strap shaped and slightly arching, the dark green leaves may be 12–18 in. long and 2–3 in. wide. Nestled low among them, the stubby inflorescence is pineapple-like, 1–2 in. long, with tiny, whitish yellow flowers; red fruits follow later in the season and persist through winter.

'Chirimen-boshi' ('Asian Valley') has rounded tips to overlapping leaves, irregularly edged with cream.

'Fuji No Yuki' ('Snow on Mt Fuji'). Very handsome, with 18-in.-long leaves, edged with a wide white border.

Romneya
Papaveraceae
Matilija poppy

This iconic plant of Californian gardens is also reported as far north as Vancouver, in the upper southeastern United States, and the British Isles. Arising from aggressive rhizomes, it is too assertive for borders, so only plant matilija poppies where there is space to spread. Other California natives such as flannelbush (*Fremontodendron californicum*), or drought-tolerant rosemaries, sages, and 'Coronation Gold' yarrow are appropriate companions.

Matilija poppies are useful as low-maintenance, free-flowering subshrubs, particularly in hot, dry locations. They are ideal for xeriscapes and harsh areas where other garden plants don't flourish. Outside of their native soils they require very well-drained soil, preferably light and sandy; they are

Romneya coulteri

Roscoea alpina

likely to require repeated attempts to establish in clay soils. Very heat and drought tolerant once rooted in; moderate early summer irrigation prolongs bloom in dry climates, but overwatering is fatal. Dislikes winter wet, and resents disturbance.

Propagate by seed, or by transplanting rooted suckers.

Romneya coulteri

- white
- early to midsummer
- 3–8 ft. × spreading
- sun
- Z7–10

Matilija poppy, tree poppy. Native to chaparral in southern California and Baja California. Upright, deciduous subshrub that spreads aggressively by rhizomes. Glaucus, gray-green leaves to 5 in. long, are pinnatifid with three to five lanceolate to ovate lobes. Flowers solitary, saucer-shaped to 6 in. across, with six crepe-like, white petals, and a prominent central boss of golden stamens.

var. trichocalyx (syn. *Romneya trichocalyx*) is often sold as a separate species but is almost identical, except for fuzzy calyx and slightly narrower leaves.

Roscoea

Zingiberaceae
roscoea

With their exotic, orchid-like flowers, roscoeas are much sought after, and the difficulties of their care only seem to add to their éclat. They are adapted to climates with cool summers and mild winters, which, in the United States, limits their outdoor cultivation to parts of the Pacific Coast. Elsewhere, they are best grown under glass. In the wild they grow in open woodlands and grasslands in mountain regions of eastern Asia.

Of some 17 species, only a few roscoas are offered for sale. They grow from fleshy, tuberous roots, with "pseudostems" (stems composed of the leaf bases or leaf sheaths) like other ginger family members. From the upper sheaths of stem-clasping leaves, flamboyant blossoms emerge; each sports a wide upper lip that serves as a hood, and a conspicuous, usually pendulous, lower lip.

Roscoeas do best in cool woodland gardens and moist, shaded borders, where they mix well with wild gingers, and low ferns. Provide fertile, humus-rich soil that drains well but never dries. Plant tubers at least 5–6 in. deep. Apply an organic, moisture-retaining mulch, and provide extra cold-weather protection; dormant in winter. Be alert for slug damage. Aside from the species described below, purple, yellow, pink, or white *Roscoea humeana* from China and Himalayan purple and violet *R. alpina* are worth trying, especially for rock gardens or with protection.

Increase by dividing the tubers in spring, or start ripe seed in containers in a cold frame.

Roscoea cautleoides
syn. *R. cautleyoides*
- yellow
- late spring to early summer
- 12–16 in. × 6 in.
- sun, part shade
- Z6–9

Alpine pine forests, meadows, and grasslands of Yunnan and Sichuan Province, China. Relatively easy to grow, this variable species usually has short spikes of two to five creamy-yellow, 3-in. flowers, held well above lanceolate, 5-in.-long leaves.

'Jeffry Thomas'. Pale yellow flowers with a cream lip, crumpled along the edges. 16 in. tall.

'Kew Beauty' ('Grandiflora') has large, pale yellow flowers.

Roscoea purpurea
- rosy purple
- summer
- 6–20 in. × 6 in.
- sun, part shade
- Z6–9

Himalayas. Among the easiest species to grow, usually with three or four bright purple flowers that emerge one at a time from the upper leaf sheaths. The upper petal is slender, the two-lobed lower lip is 1–2 in. long, sometimes white veined, and wrinkled along the edges. Clasping, narrowly lance-shaped leaves, 6–10 in. long.

'Cinnamon Stick'. Striking deep red stems and red-tinted foliage contrast dramatically with the large, lavender flowers.

'Spice Island' has red stems and leaf undersides, set against lavender-purple blooms.

Rudbeckia
Asteraceae
coneflower, black-eyed Susan

With their bright flowers, tolerance for drought, and prolonged bloom, these North American natives are a mainstay of midsummer and fall gardens. What they lack in subtlety, rudbeckias make up with their reliability and vigor. When massed in borders or meadows, their prolific daisy-like blooms in shades of yellow, chestnut, mahogany, or bronze are like bursts of distilled sunshine. Ranging in height from 1–7 ft., they fit many niches, and provide a generous source of showy cut flowers. Their warm floral tones make them excellent complements for the purples, mauves, and pinks of purple coneflowers and New England asters.

Rudbeckias grow from clumps of simple or branched stems, clothed with spirally arranged, somewhat coarse, hairy, entire to deeply lobed leaves, 2–10 in. long. The daisy-like flowerheads consist of gently drooping, petal-like ray florets arranged around a central cone of dark purplish brown to orange, yellow, or green disk florets. Flowerheads may be single, semi-double, or fully double.

Provide any average, dry to medium, well-drained soil; avoid overly rich ones and too generous fertilization, both of which promote soft, floppy growth. Best in full sun; tolerates hot and humid summers. Deadhead to encourage prolific bloom, leaving some seedheads to remain as winter food for seed-eating birds. Disease resistant; attracts butterflies. Deer resistant, but important rabbit food.

Other garden-worthy species not described here include cut-leaf coneflower (*Rudbeckia lacinata*).

Propagate by seed or division.

Rudbeckia fulgida
- orange, yellow
- early summer to midfall
- 2–3 ft. × 2–2.5 ft.
- sun
- Z3–9, HT

Black-eyed Susan. Southeastern United States. Upright, rhizomatous, and clump forming, with oblong to lanceolate leaves. Prolific bearer of 2.5-in.-wide, yellow-rayed, daisy-like flowereads with brownish purple central cones. Adapts to wide range of soils, including clays, dry soils, and shallow or rocky ones. Naturalizes readily. Tolerates air pollution. Mostly available in the form of cultivars.

var. *deamii* (Deam's black-eyed Susan) grows to 36 in., with slender, orange-yellow rays surrounding dark brown centers; late summer to midfall. Z4–9.

var. *sullivantii* 'City Gardens' displays golden, daisy-like flowerheads, in mid- to late summer. Suitable where space is limited. Compact at 12 in.

var. *sullivantii* 'Goldsturm' is uniform and bushy, 30–36 in., with blackish brown-centered, golden-yellow inflorescences. Seed-produced Goldsturm Strain is not uniform.

'Viette's Little Suzy' is similar but in a tidy, compact plant. 12–18 in. × 9–12 in.

Rudbeckia hirta
- yellow
- early to late summer
- 2–3 ft. × 1–2 ft.
- sun
- Z3–7

Gloriosa daisy, black-eyed Susan. Central United States. Biennial or short-lived perennial in mild regions, often grown as an annual where winters are cold. Hairy, lanceolate leaves, 3–7 in. long; 3-in.-wide inflorescences with yellow-orange rays and chocolate-brown central disks on stiff, erect stems. Prefers moist, organic-rich soils, but adapts to most well-drained ones. Tolerates heat and drought. Short lived, but self-seeds freely, supplying its own replacements.

Rudbeckia fulgida 'Viette's Little Suzy'

'Cappuccino' blooms heavily from late spring to fall; 4-in. flowerheads are orange at the margin, red toward the center. 18–20 in. × 12 in. Z5–8.

'Indian Summer' bears huge, 6- to 9-in., single and semi-double, golden yellow flowerheads with brown centers. Z3–7.

'Maya' has fully double, chrysanthemum-like, yellow flowerheads with brown centers on 18 in. × 12 in. plants. Z5–8.

'Prairie Sun' displays 4- to 5-in., single flowerheads, with yellow-tipped, orange rays surrounding a green cone.

Rudbeckia maxima
- yellow
- early summer
- 5–7 ft. × 3–4 ft.
- sun
- Z4–9

Large coneflower. Central and southern United States. Basal clumps of dramatic waxy, blue-green, cabbage-like leaves to 24 in. long and 10 in. wide; evergreen in mild-winter regions. Sturdy, sparsely leaved stalks bear 3-in.-wide inflorescences with drooping yellow rays and 2- to 6-in.-tall, dark brown central cones. Somewhat coarse but striking; good

for wildflower meadows, prairies, and larger borders. Adapts to a wide range of soils. Be alert for snails and slugs on young foliage; susceptible to powdery mildew. Self-seeds in hospitable conditions, if seeds not eaten by goldfinches.

'Golda Emanis' has bright gold young foliage that matures to chartreuse; orange-yellow flowerheads.

Rudbeckia nitida
- yellow
- late summer to early fall
- 5–6 ft. × 3 ft.
- sun, part shade
- Z4–9

Shining coneflower. Native in Georgia and Florida, west to Texas. Tall, hairy stems support 3- to 4-in. flowerheads with drooping, yellow ray flowers surrounding a greenish disk. Oval, toothed leaves are mostly basal. Rhizomes spread freely. Deadhead for further bloom.

'Herbstonne' ('Autumn Sun') is perhaps the showiest of the rudbeckias. Yellow-rayed heads centered with green disks may reach 4 in. across. Sometimes listed as a cultivar of *Rudbeckia laciniata*, or as a hybrid. 7 ft. tall.

Rudbeckia maxima

Rudbeckia nitida

Rudbeckia subtomentosa

- yellow
- early summer to midfall
- 3–4 ft. × 1–2 ft.
- sun, part shade
- Z4–8, HS

Sweet coneflower. Central United States. Toothed, gray-green leaves, downy beneath and three lobed at base of plant. Anise-scented, 3-in. flowerheads with yellow rays and dark brownish purple cones, are borne on branching stems. Thrives on average to clay soils, but intolerant of drought. Stake if necessary. Watch for snails and slugs, powdery mildew. Appropriate in borders, meadow and prairie plantings, and cottage gardens.

'**Henry Eilers**' bears bright yellow flowers with narrow, quilled rays, and reddish brown cones.

Rudbeckia triloba

- yellow
- early summer to midfall
- 2–3 ft. × 1–1.5 ft.
- sun
- Z4–8

Brown-eyed Susan. Eastern and central United States. Biennial or short-lived perennial that self-seeds freely and often naturalizes. Clumps of densely branched stems bear three- or sometimes five- or seven-lobed, rough, coarse leaves. Yellow-rayed, 1- to 1.5-in. flowerheads with purple-brown disks bloom profusely through summer and fall. Prefers moist, humus-rich soil but adapts to any well-drained soil. Tolerates light shade, heat, moderate drought. Perfect for meadow and prairie plantings, good for cottage gardens. Deadhead to control self-seeding.

'**Prairie Glow**' has chocolate-centered heads with bicolored rays of burgundy, bronze, or reddish orange shades, always tipped with gold. 5 ft. × 3 ft.

Ruellia
Acanthaceae
wild petunia

Although not related to the petunias commonly grown as summer annuals, the so-called wild petunias do have a similar-looking bloom. Many species are tropical subshrubs with large, exotic flowers mostly held in the upper leaf axils. Those described below are perennial, suitable for cottage and wild

Ruellia brittoniana 'Katie'

gardens, watersides, rock gardens, and informal borders; native species are ideal for native plant gardens. Where not hardy, they may be grown as annuals or container plants.

The foliage of ruellias is undivided, often with lightly toothed rims. The leaves, stalked or sessile, are carried in opposite pairs, and often are wrinkled, possibly with attractive, conspicuous deep veining. Trumpet-shaped flowers flare at the mouth with five petal-like lobes; typically, individual blossoms last just one day, but usually there are plenty of buds.

Ruellias prefer moist, fertile soils that drain well; some, however, tolerate much wetter conditions. They grow best in full sun, but provide some shade in intense sun regions. Several species are nectar sources or larval food for butterflies; common buckeyes, Texan crescents are frequent visitors, as are bees. Deer mostly ignore ruellias, although during dry spells, succulent young growth may be browsed by deer and rabbits. The leaves are sometimes infected with rust; waterlogged soil encourages root rot.

Sow seed in spring. Spring or early summer softwood cuttings root readily.

Ruellia brittoniana
syn. *R. tweediana*
- lavender
- summer
- 3 ft. high and wide
- sun
- Z8–10, HT

Mexican petunia. Mexico. Upright, branching stems, slightly woody at the base, are clothed with dark green, 0.5-in.-wide, linear leaves, 6–12 in. in length. Axillary clusters of 1- to 2-in., lavender to violet, trumpet-shaped flowers have broadly rounded lobes. Note that this species has escaped cultivation in parts of the southeastern United States, including Florida, where is it considered an exotic invasive, pushing out native plants, especially

in wetland areas. Check with your local Cooperative Extension office prior to planting.

The following selections are hardy in Z7–10:

'Colobe Pink' (Bonita pink) is dwarf, with pink flowers. Non-invasive. 8 in. × 24 in. 'Chi Chi' (hardy pink ruellia) has pink flowers. Good for rustic and water-wise gardens; invasive in moist, tropical and semi-tropical climates. 24 in.

'Katie' (Katie's dwarf ruellia) is a dwarf form from Texas. Blooms continuously through the summer with 1.5-in., purple trumpet flowers. Reseeds in good conditions, but is not invasive. 6 in. × 12 in. Similar 'White Katie' has clean, white flowers. 8 in. × 12 in.

Ruellia elegans
- red
- late spring to fall
- 12–24 in. × 24 in.
- sun, part shade
- Z8–10, HS

Brazilian petunia, Thai ruellia, elegant ruellia. Brazil. This tough but elegant, upright perennial attracts hummingbirds and butterflies, and is a larval food source for Texas crescent butterflies. Clusters of five to six coral-red, tubular flowers top long, slender stems. Evergreen foliage provides winter interest in cottage or woodland gardens, and beside ponds and lakes. Tolerates wet boggy sites. Spreads moderately but not invasive. Mulch heavily in zone 7; grow in containers, outside its hardiness zones.

Ruellia humilis
- lavender
- early to late summer
- 18–36 in. × 18–24 in.
- sun, part shade
- Z4–8

Wild petunia, fringeleaf wild petunia. Dry, open woods and prairies from Pennsylvania to Indiana, and south to Alabama. Erect and bushy, with bright green, sessile, oval to elliptic leaves, to 3 in. long. Solitary, lavender flowers about 2 in. across are petunia lookalikes. Pollinated by nocturnal hawk moths and bees, the plants also produce less showy, closed, self-pollinating flowers as insurance for seed production. Suitable for open wild and native plant gardens, perhaps with prairie grasses, milkweeds, purple coneflowers, and evening primroses.

Ruta
Rutaceae
rue

Traditionally grown in herb gardens for medicinal purposes, rue is exceptionally adaptable. Today, this woody-based subshrub is more likely to find a spot in contemporary gardens by virtue of its attractive foliage. It thrives in moderately fertile, moist, well-drained soils, but tolerates shallow and rocky ones, as well as drought and heat. When bruised or crushed, the foliage releases a pungent odor; the oils irritate sensitive skins. A useful foliage note in

Sagina subulata 'Aurea'

Ruta graveolens 'Blue Mound'

borders and rock gardens; the blue-green leaves make an energizing contrast to yellow-flowered neighbors.

No serious pests or diseases; susceptible to root rot where drainage is poor. Deer resistant. Tolerates light shade. Cut back to old wood in spring to promote healthy, bushy growth.

Propagate by seed or cuttings.

Ruta graveolens

- yellow
- early summer
- 2–3 ft. high and wide
- sun
- Z4–8

Common rue, herb of grace. Southeastern Europe, but naturalized as a garden escapee in parts of the United States, notably the Northeast. Feathery mounds of waxy, blue-green, 3- to 5-in. leaves, pinnately twice divided into rounded, oblong, or spatulate segments. Small, four- to five-petaled,

dull-yellow flowers appear in flattened clusters above the leaves.

'Blue Mound' has a shapely, mounding habit; deep blue-green foliage. 12–15 in.

'Jackman's Blue' has lush, metallic-blue foliage. 24 in. × 30 in.

'Variegata' has bluish green leaves splashed with white; excellent for floral arrangements.

Sagina
Caryophyllaceae
pearlwort

This moss lookalike plant can be used as a lawn substitute in cool areas as it tolerates light traffic. Excellent between pavers or flag stones, and in rock gardens, perhaps with *Mazus reptans* and woolly thyme. Taller species, including low dianthus, also make good companions.

Increase by division.

Sagina subulata
syn. *Sagina pilifera, Arenaria caespitosa*
- white
- early to late spring
- 1–4 in. × 10–12 in.
- sun, part shade
- Z4–8

Irish moss, Corsican pearlwort, health pearlwort. Mountains of Sardinia and Corsica. Tiny, white, four- or five-petaled flowers crown the bright green, evergreen carpet of 0.5-in.-long leaves. Best in acid or neutral, well-drained but evenly moist soil; protect from intense sun in hotter regions. Often confused with *Minuartia verna* (syn. *Arenaria verna* var. *caespitosa*), also commonly called Irish moss.

'Aurea' (Scotch moss, syn. *Arenaria caespitosa* 'Aurea') has slender stems that form a golden carpet. Nice as a textural contrast with golden creeping Charlie.

Salvia
Lamiaceae
sage

This enormous genus is most familiar to gardeners in the form of the ubiquitous scarlet sage (*Salvia splendens*), a frost-intolerant species with spikes of hot-red flowers, commonly grown for bedding. With some 750-plus species, however, the sages also offer many fine hardy and tender perennials. These have become mainstays of beds, borders, and cottage gardens across the country. In particular, the southwestern and central US species have become invaluable in hot, dry gardens, and a critical source of color for containers, xeriscapes, and water-wise landscapes across the country. Many make fine cut flowers.

Sages exhibit the stems, square in cross section, opposite leaves, and racemes or panicles of two-lipped flowers, typical of the mints. Flower colors include blues, pinks, and reds, or less often white or yellow. Usually foliage is entire, but sometimes pinnately divided, often toothed along the margins; the leaves may be coated with hairs that protect them from water loss, and increase drought tolerance. Leaves are often aromatic. Seldom affected by pests and diseases, although occasionally infestations of whiteflies, aphids, mealybugs, spider mites, and powdery mildew occur. Grazing deer and rabbits mostly avoid sages.

Sow seed of species in spring or early fall. Increase cultivars by softwood cuttings or divide mature clumps, both in spring.

Salvia argentea
- white
- summer
- 24–36 in. × 24 in.
- sun
- Z5–8, HS

Silver sage. Southern Europe, northern Africa. Grown mostly for its beautiful furry, silver leaves; short lived, behaves as a biennial. Basal rosettes of oblong, 7- to 8-in.-long, toothed leaves. Spikes of whitish flowers appear the second year in many-branched, terminal panicles. Self-seeds. A great accent plant.

Salvia chamaedryoides
- blue
- early summer to fall
- 18–24 in. × 24–48 in.
- sun, part shade
- Z7–10

Germander sage, blue oak sage. Mexico. Broad rhizomatous mounds of woody stems and quilted, downy, sage-green leaves. Spikes of sky-blue flowers bloom heavily in early summer, then intermittently until a fall flush. This fast-growing species thrives in

Salvia patens in a border setting with *Ipomoea battatus* 'Margarita'

sun and heat, prefers loamy, moist, well-drained soil; drought tolerant once established. Attracts hummingbirds and butterflies. Good for beds and borders, container plantings, and suitable for cottage or desert gardens, xeriscapes, and rock gardens.

Salvia farinacea

- blue
- late spring to early fall
- 1–3 ft. × 1–2 ft.
- sun, part shade
- Z7–10

Mealycup sage. Texas, Mexico. Commonly grown as a warm-weather annual, but an invaluable perennial where hardy. Shrubby, clumping with branching stems. Serrate, ovate-lanceolate, gray-green leaves, to 3 in. long. Violet-blue flowers, with white-powdered ("mealy") calyxes, are borne in 4- to 8-in., terminal and axillary racemes. Prefers evenly moist, well-drained soil, but tolerates clays, moderate drought, and dryish soils, but not winter wet. Attracts butterflies. Adaptable and valued for beds and borders, meadows, cottage and cutting gardens.

'Augusta Duelberg' blooms heavily with silvery-white flowers from late spring until frost. 2.5 ft. × 4 ft.

'Strata' is a seed strain with blue-and-white, bicolored flowers. 18 in. × 12 in.

'Victoria Blue' is compact with deep violet-blue flowers. 16 in. × 12 in.

Salvia farinacea 'Strata'

Salvia greggii

- red, pink, purple, yellow
- early spring to fall
- 1–3 ft. high and wide
- sun
- Z8–10, HT

Autumn sage. Upland areas of southwest Texas to central Mexico. Evergreen, upright or mounding with stems woody at the base; medium green leaves are glabrous, simple, and elliptical to 1 in. long. Blooms over an extended season, profusely in fall, with 0.25- to 1-in. flowers. Adapts to a wide range of well-drained conditions; quite drought tolerant but bloom is best with weekly irrigation. Thrives in the hot, humid southeastern United States and the humid Pacific Northwest. Attracts hummingbirds.

'Big Pink' has large, violet-pink flowers with dark maroon calyxes. 2.5–3.5 ft. Z7–10.

'Lowry's Peach'. Yellow-throated, reddish orange blooms with creamy-peach lower lips. Glossy foliage. 3 ft. × 3 ft. Z7–9.

'Maraschino' has bold scarlet-red flowers. Blooms almost non-stop. 3–4 ft. × 2–3 ft. Z7–10.

'Variegata' (desert blaze Texas sage) has white-edged leaves; bright red flowers. 2 ft. × 3 ft. Z8–10.

'Wild Thing' produces spectacular coral-pink flowers. Vigorous. Z5.

Salvia guaranitica

- blue
- summer to fall
- 4–6 ft. × 4.5 ft.
- sun
- Z7–10

Blue anise sage. Argentina, Brazil. Dark green, 4- to 6-in. leaves are barely hairy. Brilliant deep blue flowers in whorls of three to eight, on very long spikes. Upper flower petals appear to hover above shorter lower petals. Nectar source for hummingbirds.

'Argentine Skies' has spikes of pale blue flowers.

'Black and Blue' produces spikes to 12 in. long; flowers are deep blue, with black calyces. 3–6 ft. 'Costa Rica Blue' is very similar.

'Van Remsen' is a stunning giant selection. Spikes of cobalt-blue flowers. 6–7 ft.

Salvia officinalis

- blue
- late spring to early summer
- 12–24 in. × 24–30 in.
- sun
- Z4–8

Common sage, culinary sage. Mediterranean region. Wrinkled, strongly aromatic, 3- to 4-in., gray-green leaves on woody stems. Whorls of 0.5- to 1-in., lavender-blue flowers borne in erect spikes. This standard culinary species can be used as a hardy ornamental in borders, or cottage, herb, and kitchen gardens. Prefers average, medium-moist, well-drained soils, but tolerates dry, rocky ones.

'Aurea' has leaves variegated gold and light green. 12–18 in.

'Berggarten' has deep blue flowers; large, broad, gray-green leaves. 24 in.

'Icterina' (golden variegated sage) has foliage irregularly splashed with gold. 8–16 in.

'Purpurascens' has purplish leaves. 12–24 in. tall.

'Tricolor' has marbled gray-green, white, and purple foliage edged with pink. 12–18 in.

Salvia patens
- blue
- summer to fall
- 18–24 in. × 12 in.
- sun, part shade
- Z8–10

Gentian sage. Whorls of 1-in. flowers in the most glorious shades of gentian blue. Erect, bushy stems, clothed with aromatic, ovate leaves, rise from tuberous roots. Tolerates heat and drought. May need staking.

'Oceana Blue' ('Salsyll') has deeper blue flowers. 24–36 in.

Salvia pratensis
- lavender-blue
- late spring to late summer
- 1–3 ft. high and wide
- sun
- Z4–8

Meadow sage, meadow clary. Europe. Clump forming with mildly aromatic, 6-in., dull gray-green leaves. Upright, dense, spike-like racemes of tiny, deep lavender-blue flowers, often with sporadic rebloom through summer, if cut back as first flush fades. Thrives in average, well-drained soil. Tolerates drought and very light shade. Mostly available as cultivars.

'Eveline' produces an abundance of pink-flowered spikes from early to midsummer. Glossy foliage; compact, bushy. To 24 in.

'Rhapsody in Blue' is a prolific bearer of blue-and-violet flowered spikes. Broad, gray-green leaves; compact, bushy habit. 20–24 in.

'Swan Lake' has wrinkled, light green leaves; 20-in. spikes of pure white flowers.

Salvia ×sylvestris
syn. *S. nemorosa*
- purple, white, pink
- early summer to fall
- 3 ft. × 2 ft.
- sun
- Z4–8

Hybrid sage. Of garden origin. Clump forming with wrinkled, aromatic, green, lanceolate leaves, to 3 in. long. Spikes of showy flowers all season. Prefers moist, well-drained soil, but tolerates dry, poor ones. Available in the trade mostly as cultivars, which are many. Although European *Salvia nemerosa* is listed as a synonym, there is much taxonomic confusion; some selections are more likely to belong to the latter species than to *S. ×sylvestris*.

'Blue Hill' has true blue flowers. 18–24 in.

'Caradonna'. Abundant spikes of violet flowers, on deep purple stems. 24 in.

Salvia ×sylvestris 'Marcus'

'East Friesland' ('Ostfriesland') has bluish green foliage; narrow spikes of violet flowers in late spring to early summer, repeats in early fall. Sterile. 16–20 in.

'Marcus' ('Haeumanarc') is dwarf, long blooming with deep violet flowers. 8–10 in.

'New Dimension Rose' is dwarf, with bright rose-pink flowers from early to midsummer. 8–10 in. Z5–7.

'Snow Hill' produces white flowers in early summer; cut back for later rebloom. 18 in.

Salvia verticillata
- lilac-blue
- early summer to late summer
- 18–30 in. × 18–24 in.
- sun
- Z5–7

Lilac sage. Europe, western Asia. Clumps of erect to arching stems, with hairy, coarse, and broadly ovate-triangular, medium green leaves, to 5 in. long. Terminal racemes of small, lilac-blue flowers all summer. Prefers average, moderately moist to dry, well-drained soils. Overly fertile soils encourage soft, lax growth. Drought tolerant. Shear plants after flowering to encourage neater growth and possible fall rebloom.

'Endless Love', 14–20 in., has medium purple flowers; heavier blooming, improved form of the Piet Oudolf introduction, 'Purple Rain'.

Salvia verticillata 'Purple Rain'

Salvia hybrid 'Mystic Spires Blue'

'White Rain' has a rounded, spreading habit; pure white flowers. 20 in. × 36 in.

Other Notable Cultivars

'Indigo Spires' (*Salvia farinacea* × *S. longispicata*) is bushy, with twisting, 24- to 36-in.-long spikes of 0.5-in., purple flowers; late summer to fall. 3–4 ft. Z7–11.

'Mystic Spires Blue' ('Balsalmisp') is similar in color but on much more compact plants.

'Wendy's Wish' has dark maroon stems that bear brilliant non-fading, cherry-red flowers. Sterile, long blooming. Fine for containers. 40 in. Z9–11.

Sanguinaria
Papaveraceae
bloodroot, red puccoon

One of our most easily recognized spring-blooming natives, bloodroot identifies itself by the bright reddish orange sap that oozes out when any part of the plant is bruised. Native Americans used the sap, which is concentrated particularly in the fleshy roots, as a dye and some say war paint. Supposedly it has anti-cancer properties too.

Plant bloodroot in a partly shaded or shaded site where soil remains damp but drains well. It should also be fertile and humus rich, as under deep-rooted, deciduous trees. In sufficient shade, bloodroot also tolerates drier conditions. Unlike many spring wildflowers, bloodroot retains its leaves after flowering, so that it serves as an effective groundcover until the foliage turns shabby in late summer (earlier in dry conditions).

Where climate and soil permit, no woodland garden should be without bloodroot. Columbines, ferns, and ephemeral Virginia bluebells and Dutchman's breeches are appropriate companions in

Sanguinaria canadensis 'Multiplex'

native plant gardens. The double form is a jewel in rock gardens.

Divide the fleshy rhizomes in late summer, or start from seed. Self-seeds freely, and over time may develop large colonies.

Sanguinaria canadensis

- white
- early to midspring
- 6–8 in. × 12–15 in.
- part shade, shade
- Z4–9

Bloodroot, red puccoon, Indian paint. Native from Nova Scotia to Ontario and Manitoba, south to Florida, Alabama, and Oklahoma. In early spring each rhizome bud sprouts a single leaf with a gray-green blade rolled around the stem. These unfurl slowly to 8–12 in. across, and, though variable, are usually deeply palmately lobed, heart shaped at the base, and with irregular undulating or lobed edges. From within each rolled leaf emerges a sparkling white, 1.5- to 2-in. flower, with eight or more slender petals centered with a tiny boss of stamens; these blossoms last but a few days, but their fleeting beauty is sublime.

'Multiplex' (var. *flore pleno*, var. *plena*) has sterile, double flowers with extra petals replacing the stamens. It is longer blooming, unless shattered by inclement weather.

Sanguisorba

Rosaceae
burnet

Burnet has long been valued for its ability to stop bleeding, a characteristic commemorated in its name. *Sanguis* means blood in Latin, while *sorbere* means to absorb. Some species, primarily *S. officinalis* and salad burnet, *S. minor*, are included in salads; the young foliage is added to soups.

Burnet is winning popularity as an ornamental planting with the current trend toward prairie-style landscapes. Swept by the wind, burnets provide movement; assorted grasses, tall Culver's root, and purple coneflowers mix well in informal beds, meadows, and wild gardens. Long after the flowers are over, the faded stems with their spent blossoms retain an interesting appearance, especially when dusted with snow. Burnets make good cut flowers; compact selections are attractive in containers with grasses and summer annuals.

Moderately fertile soil that drains well but does not dry out is ideal. Burnet prefers a spot in sun or light shade; shade is especially beneficial in warmer regions. Support taller species in windswept areas. Cut down shabby foliage after bloom time. Deer and rabbits seldom browse burnets; leaf spot may be a problem.

Divide the clumps in spring or fall, or start seed in a cold frame.

Sanguisorba obtusa

syn. *Poterium obtusum*

- pink
- summer
- 2–3 ft. × 2 ft.
- sun
- Z4–9

Japanese burnet. Japan. The grayish green, lacy foliage provides a good accent in the garden and provides a handsome foil for the soft pink, bottlebrush flower spikes.

Sanguisorba officinalis

- maroon
- early summer to midfall
- 2–3.5 ft. × 1.5–2 ft.
- sun, part shade
- Z3–8

Greater burnet, European great burnet. Clumps of divided, serrated basal leaves with many leaflets. Maroon or blood-red flowers in dense, 1.5-in. spikes; no petals or protruding stamens. Naturalizes well. Self-seeds freely; deadhead routinely to prevent proliferation. Useful in herb and vegetable gardens.

'Lemon Splash' has irregularly yellow-splashed foliage. An acquired taste. 24 in. Z4–9.

'Red Thunder' has spikes of deep ruby flowers; bluish green foliage. 3–4 ft. Z4–9.

'Tanna' has wine-colored flowers. Compact; valuable where space is limited. 18 in. Z4–9.

Sanguisorba tenuifolia

syn. *Poterium tenuifolium*

- white, purple-red
- summer
- 2–4 ft. × 2 ft.
- sun
- Z4–7

China, Japan. This rhizomatous, upright species has mostly basal lacy, pinnate leaves, with numerous deeply toothed, oblong leaflets. The slender, bottlebrush flower spikes are elongated like catkins to 2–3 in. long.

'Alba' has nodding spikes of white flowers on tall, branching stems; finely divided foliage. 4–5 ft. Z4.

'Purpurea' has purple flowers. 3–4 ft. Z4–9.

Santolina

Asteraceae
lavender cotton

These dwarf, aromatic, evergreen subshrubs are invaluable for edging beds and paths. Tolerant of clipping, they lend themselves for use as compact hedges to provide garden structure. Fine-textured, entire or pinnately dissected leaves, bluish silver-gray or green, are borne densely on woody, branching stems. Button-like, yellow, 0.75-in. flowerheads on slender stems are abundant in summer, 4–10 in. above the foliage. *Santolina* foliage has a resinous, herbal scent; traditionally used as a moth and insect repellant.

Originating in the Mediterranean region, these plants prefer full sun and average to dry,

Sanguisorba tenuifolia

Santolina rosmarinifolia

well-drained soil; tolerant of alkaline and poor soils, but not of wet, rich ones. Once established the plants endure drought, but dislike hot, humid weather; in the southeastern United States a very well-drained, airy site is required. Cut back in spring to encourage compact, healthy new growth. Santolinas perform well as formal, clipped hedges, but do not flower if sheared regularly.

Insect, rabbit, and deer resistant, but vulnerable to fungal diseases in the Southeast, and root rot on damp soils. Propagate by layering or division, by half-ripe stem cuttings in summer, or by seed; germination is slow.

Santolina chamaecyparissus
syn. *S. incana*
- yellow
- early to midsummer
- 1–2 ft. × 2–3 ft.
- sun
- Z6–9

Lavender cotton. Western and central Mediterranean region. Forms dense mounds of evergreen, silver-gray foliage. Drought tolerant once established; prefers gritty or sandy soils. Vigorous but not invasive; may be grown as an annual where not hardy. An asset to herb and rock gardens, border fronts, knot gardens, xeriscapes. Good groundcover for sunny slopes.

'Pretty Carol', a hybrid with 'Nana'. Deep yellow flowers. 12 in. × 24 in. Z7–10.

'Lemon Queen' is 18 in. × 24 in., with pale, lemon-yellow flowers; silver-gray foliage.

'Weston' is a dwarf form, to 12 in.

Santolina rosmarinifolia
syn. *S. virens, S. viridis*
- yellow
- late spring to midsummer
- 1.5–2 ft. × 2–3 ft.
- sun
- Z7–9

Green lavender cotton. Dense, neat mounds of evergreen, fragrant foliage; leaves alternate, 1- to 2-in.-long, smooth, narrow, and finely divided. Long-stalked, button-shaped flowers are solitary. Uses and cultural requirements similar to those of *Santolina chamaecyparissus*.

'Lemon Fizz'. Foliage is yellow in full sun, chartreuse in part shade. 18 in. × 24 in.

'Morning Mist' is reportedly more damp tolerant than the species.

Saponaria

Caryophyllaceae
bouncing bet, soapweed

When the leaves of soapwort are wetted and rubbed together, they produce a mild, cleansing lather traditionally used to launder delicate fabrics. As recently as 1998, when the Cloisters Museum in New York cleaned its priceless series of medieval Unicorn Tapestries, it was a mixture of bouncing bet, *Saponaria officinalis*, and rock soapwort, *S. ocymoides* leaves and roots that were used.

Soapworts are native to high meadows of southern Europe and mountainous parts of southwestern Asia. Upright or creeping, typically they bear clusters of five-petaled, pink or whitish flowers. Leaves are oppositely paired at swollen nodes.

Easy to grow in sunny spots where soil is only moderately fertile or even lean, and slightly alkaline. Drainage must be good, especially for low, rock garden types that are especially attractive cascading over rocks and walls, and in rock gardens; the smaller ones are excellent for trough gardens. Taller species are only appropriate for wild or meadow gardens, but superior cultivars earn a place in beds and borders.

Snails and slugs can become a problem; a top-dressing of lime chips is a good deterrent and increases the alkalinity of the soil. Deer seldom bother soapworts probably due to the fragrance of the flowers and bitter-tasting leaves.

Divide cultivars in spring or fall, or take spring and early-summer soft cuttings. Seeds germinate readily in fall.

Saponaria ocymoides

- pink
- late spring to early summer
- 3–12 in. × 24 in.
- sun
- Z2–7, HS

Rock soapwort. Mountains of southern Europe. Semi-evergreen in most climates, rock soapwort does not care for intense heat or humidity. Vigorous with a creeping habit, it is ideal for tumbling over banks and walls, for the front of beds and borders, or as a groundcover. Shear after bloom time for neatness, and to encourage compact growth. The bright green, softly hairy leaves are paddle shaped, about 0.5 in. long. Spreading mats of foliage are covered with lax terminal clusters of fragrant, starry, 0.25-in., bright pink flowers. Drought tolerant when established. Effective in containers.

'Rubra Compacta' has dark red flowers.

'Snow Tip' (white rock soapwort) has dazzling white flowers, perhaps superior to 'Alba' (var. *albiflora*).

'Splendens' has medium to deep pink flowers.

Saponaria ×lempergii

syn. *S. cypria* × *S. haussknechtii*

- carmine
- late summer to early fall
- 10–12 in. × 12 in.
- sun
- Z5–7, HS

This Swiss hybrid grows close to the ground but does not root along the stems. Ascending, branching shoots carry soft, hairy, lance-shaped leaves to 0.5 in. long. The bright carmine, 1-in. flowers have long, pink calyxes; they are borne terminally and

Saponaria ocymoides

in the leaf axils. Largely replaced by the following cultivar:

'Max Frei' has rosy 1-in. flowers in midsummer. 12 in.

Saponaria officinalis
- pink
- summer to fall
- 15–24 in. × 24 in.
- sun
- Z2–8

Bouncing bet, common soapwort. Europe, Asia. Vigorous mats grow from fast-spreading rhizomes. The strong, unbranched stems are upright; leaves are three-veined, smooth, and without hairs, oval, 3–4 in. long. Axillary and terminal clusters of fragrant, 1-in.-wide, pink or whitish flowers. Attracts sphinx moths at dusk.

'Alba Plena' has double, pink-flushed, white flowers. Very floriferous. 24 in. Z3.

'Rosea Plena' has slightly shaggy, double, candy-pink flowers in late spring to early summer. Fragrant. 18 in. Z4.

'Rubra Plena' has fragrant, double, deep pink flowers, fading at maturity; midsummer. 24 in. Z4.

Other Notable Cultivars
'Bressingham' ('Bressingham Hybrid') is compact; dark leaves and deep pink flowers in late spring. Considered a dwarf cross between *Saponaria ocymoides*, *S. caespitosa*, and *S. pumila*. 3 in. × 8 in. Z5.

Saruma henryi

Saruma
Aristolochiaceae
wild ginger

This genus with but a single species, *Saruma henryi*, has only recently become readily available for American gardeners. Native to China, it is closely related to wild gingers (*Asarum* spp. and *Hexastylis* spp.)—indeed, its name is almost *Asarum* spelled backward. Easy to grow in partly shaded spots where soil drains well. It is charming in woodland clearings.

Saruma henryi
- yellow
- late spring
- 1–3 ft. high and wide
- part shade, shade
- Z4–8

Upright wild ginger. China. This erect, clump-forming plant has a gently silvery sheen produced by soft velvety hairs that cover the stems and foliage. Heart-shaped leaves may reach 2 in. across and as long, and remain good-looking through summer. Unusual pale yellow, three-petaled, 1-in. flowers arise from the leaf axils on 1- to 2-in.-long stems; brown seed capsules follow.

This carefree woodlander deserves a wider audience. It thrives in moist to average soils but has not shown stress in the author's garden even during periods of drought. Deer do not browse it; rabbits and chipmunks also ignore it. Upright wild ginger is a good understory plant; plant as a specimen or in drifts for maximum effect. Suitable for the edges of woodlands, for Asian-themed gardens, or in partly shaded mixed borders backed by shrubs. *Hakonechloa macra* 'Aureola' is a fine companion, along with ferns and late-spring bulbs. Allow forget-me-nots to seed themselves around this gem for a charming late-spring display. All parts of upright wild ginger are poisonous if ingested, although reportedly it was used in traditional Chinese medicine.

Saxifraga
Saxifragaceae
saxifrage

This huge and diverse genus includes many plants, often difficult to grow, that are cherished by collectors, as well as some more suitable for perennial gardens. So large is the genus that botanists have split it into 15 sections according to assorted characteristics. Most are low growing, often forming mossy cushions or rosettes encrusted with lime. Solitary, or clustered into panicles or racemes, the five-petaled flowers are white, yellow, or pink.

Most saxifrages hail from alpine regions where they survive low temperatures but thrive in extremely well-drained, alkaline soils, as can be created in rock gardens or furnished in trough gardens. Although some are from woodland habitats, they also require good drainage, but humus-rich soil. Few tolerate full sun except in the low light of the far North; most are unsuccessful in hot and humid regions. The selection below is just a sampling.

The most serious problem for saxifrages is winter wet at the roots; this is certain death. Deer and other pests are seldom a problem, although slugs and aphids can be a nuisance.

Increase by dividing or detaching individual rosettes in late spring. Seed should be sown with protection in fall.

Saxifraga ×*arendsii*
- pink, white
- spring
- 4–8 in. × 12 in.
- sun, part shade
- Z3–7, HS

Arend's saxifrage. Of garden origin. Evergreen, moss-like foliage rosettes spread slowly to form carpets. Slender, 4- to 8-in. stems each bear a single exquisite, five-petaled flower at its tip. Provide moisture-retentive soil that drains well; irrigate in hot weather.

'**Blood Carpet**' has carmine flowers that fade to pink.

'**Gaiety**' produces dainty, pink flowers early. Z5–8.

'**Purple Carpet**' bears purplish carmine flowers.

'**Snow Cap**' is pure white.

Saxifraga cochlearis
- white
- spring
- 6–12 in. × 9 in.
- sun, part shade
- Z5–7, HS

Snail saxifrage. Italian Alps. Cushions of large foliage rosettes encrusted with lime at the rims. Sprays of 0.75-in. flowers rise on slender, reddish, 9- to 12-in. stems. Dress with lime chips to maintain soil alkalinity; provide gritty, very well-drained soil that remains moist. Rock gardens or troughs.

'**Major**' has much larger rosettes.

'**Minor**' has diminutive, 6-in.-wide rosettes; red-blotched, white flowers.

Saxifraga 'Monarch' in a trough

Saxifraga stolonifera

Saxifraga fortunei

syn. *S. cortusifolia* var. *fortunei*

- white
- late summer to fall
- 12 in. high and wide
- part shade, shade
- Z6–8, HS

Japan. This semi-evergreen woodlander has seven-lobed, kidney-shaped or rounded leaves, 2.5–3.5 in. across; undersides have a purplish blush. Loose panicles of white, asymmetrical flowers, with three upper petals shorter than the two lower ones. Needs sweet, humus-rich, well-drained soil.

'**Silver Velvet**' has rounded, scalloped leaves, very dark brown or gray enlivened with veins picked out in silver. Typical white saxifrage flowers cluster at stem tips. 6–9 in.

Saxifraga stolonifera

syn. *S. sarmentosa*

- white
- summer
- 4–8 in. × 12 in.
- part shade, shade
- Z6–9

Strawberry begonia, mother of thousands. Native to shaded cliffs of China. Although more often grown in hanging baskets or as houseplants than in the garden, strawberry begonia is a fine ground-cover plant, or works well planted into a rock wall. It spreads by slender, pink runners that root at their tips. Leaves are rounded and often scalloped, traced with silver veins above, hairy and reddish beneath. Slender, branched flower stems rise to 18 in. above, bearing loose, delicate panicles of asymmetrical white, 1-in. flowers; the lower petals are several times longer that the upper.

'**Harvest Moon**' produces bright sulfur-yellow foliage.

'**Maroon Beauty**' has maroon-flushed leaves.

'**Tricolor**' ('Magic Carpet'; syn. *Saxifraga sarmentosa* 'Tricolor', 'Magic Carpet', 'Variegata') has the most beautiful pink-speckled borders on the rounded leaves.

Saxifraga ×urbium

syn. *S. spathularis* × *S. umbrosa*

- white
- spring to early summer
- 12–18 in. × 12 in.
- part shade, shade
- Z6–9, HS

London pride. Garden origin. Healthy rosettes of leathery foliage. Leaves are spatula shaped, round toothed along the margins, 1–1.5 in. across; often red tinged on their undersides and tapered to barely winged petioles. Wiry, erect branching stems to 12 in. tall are topped with loose panicles of white, starry flowers, pink at the centers.

'**Aureopunctata**' ('Variegata') has gold-variegated foliage.

'**Clarence Elliott**' ('Elliott's Variety'). Red, 6-in. stems bear small, rosy flowers above a low mat of petite, leafy rosettes.

Other Notable Cultivars

'**Monarch**' has large, 5-in. rosettes of spatulate, evergreen leaves. Dainty, white flowers bloom above. Z8.

Scabiosa

Dipsacaceae
scabious, pincushion flower

If you want to please the neighborhood butterflies and bees, make a place in your garden for these nectar-rich flowers. You'll also be assuring yourself a steady supply of intriguing, long-stemmed, and long-lived cut flowers from midspring until frost, after which you can enjoy the spent scabiosa flowers in dried arrangements.

Growing wild from Africa and Europe to Asia, this genus includes annuals and biennials as well as several outstanding, albeit short-lived, perennials. Scabiosas earn their common name of "pincushion flower" from the curious structure of their colorful, hemispherical flowers; these feature an outer

Scabiosa columbaria 'Butterfly Blue'

ring of frilly petals, surrounding a central cushion of smaller petals that bristles with protruding, pin-like stamens. Mostly blooms are in shades of blue or white, but may be pink or purplish; due to their long stalks they seem to hover above the mounds of gray-green leaves. As natives of regions subject to prolonged seasonal droughts, scabiosas require a well-drained soil; winter wet is particularly harmful, and most do not cope well with combined heat and humidity. Excellent in benign climates.

Their old-fashioned appearance makes pincushion plants ideal for cottage gardens; in borders they add texture as well as color, and are a must in butterfly and cutting gardens. No serious pests or diseases; resistant to deer.

Propagate by seed, take summer cuttings, or divide clumps in spring; extend plant life by dividing every few years.

Scabiosa caucasica

- lavender, blue, white
- late spring to early summer

- 18–24 in. × 12–18 in.
- sun
- Z3–7, HS

Caucasus mountains. Forms clumps of gray-green, lanceolate, entire or pinnately lobed basal leaves, and narrow, lobed stem leaves. Flowers are 2–3 in. across, usually lavender to blue, but sometimes white; they are borne singly on tall, stiff stems. Prefers a light soil with a neutral to sweet pH; good drainage is essential. Deadhead to prolong bloom.

'Fama' bears silvery-centered, 4-in. blossoms of intense lilac-blue on 24-in. stems. Late spring to fall. Tolerates heat and humidity. 36 in. × 18 in.

House's Hybrids is a seed-propagated strain. Lavender, light to deep blue, and silver-white, 3-in. flowers. 2–3 ft.

'Kompliment' ('Compliment'), 18–24 in., carries 2- to 3-in., lavender-blue flowers.

'Perfecta Alba' has white outer petals and an ivory center. 'Alba' is similar.

Scabiosa columbaria

- blue, pink
- early summer to early fall

- 2 ft. × 3 ft.
- sun
- Z4–10, HS

Pigeon scabious. Dry, sunny grasslands, rocky hillsides and open woods of Mediterranean region, British Isles. Clumps of much-branched stems with hairy, gray-green foliage; basal leaves are lanceolate, 2–6 in. long; stem leaves are dissected, with upper ones most finely divided. Numerous lavender-blue flowers, to 1.5 in. across. Provide neutral to slightly alkaline pH; well-drained soil is essential.

'Butterfly Blue' may be a hybrid selection. Compact, 12–15 in., prolific bearer of 2-in. flowers with lavender-blue outer petals, and paler blue central "cushion." Midspring to frost. 'Pink Mist' ('Butterfly Pink'), is similar but with frilled pink petals and a pale cushion. Z5–9.

'Mariposa Violet' is fully double, with larger heads of purple flowers on strong stems. 16–18 in. × 15 in. Z5–9.

Scabiosa japonica var. *alpina*

- lavender-blue
- early summer to early fall

- 8–12 in. high and wide
- sun
- Z4–9

Dwarf pincushion flower. Japan. Forms a 2-in.-high mound of gray-green, ferny foliage; small, soft lavender-blue flowers on stiff stalks. Prefers neutral to alkaline, well-drained, even sandy soil. Ideal for rock gardens, fronts of borders, containers.

'Pink Diamonds' has pink, 1.5-in. flowers.
'Ritz Blue' has pale, violet-blue, 2-in. flowers.

Schizostylis
Iridaceae
Kaffir lily

Late to bloom and all the more welcome for that, Kaffir lilies, like so many other bulbous plants, are natives of southern Africa. Often pot grown, they are available sometimes from perennial nurseries, or from mail-order bulb merchants.

Schizostylis coccinea

Evergreen, with slender, keeled leaves and colorful, gladiolus-like flowers. Plant the clumps of rhizomes in moist, humus-rich soil that drains well but does not dry out unduly. Add plenty of leaf mold or compost at planting time; mulch in summer to keep the roots cool. Bloom usually begins in fall and may extend into December, depending upon the cultivar, weather, and climate. Do not plant too closely—12 in. apart should be fine—as they will bulk up in a few years.

Group Kaffir lilies in sunny beds and borders, in bright clearings among trees and shrubs, or mass them along driveways, paths, and walkways. They thrive in containers, providing good late color. Excellent as cut flowers, Kaffir lilies hold up very well in a vase and are daintier than gladiolus.

Pests and diseases are seldom serious; deer may browse them but it doesn't seem to be top of their gourmet list. Rabbits seldom trouble them.

Schizostylis coccinea
syn. *Hesperantha coccinea*
- red, pink, white
- late summer to fall
- 12–24 in. × 12 in.
- sun
- Z7–10, HS

Kaffir lily, crimson flag, red river lily. Often found growing wild near streams in wet areas of southern Africa, Lesotho, and Swaziland. Swollen rhizomes develop into hearty, compact clumps of keeled, sword-shaped leaves to 16 in. long; stem leaves are shorter. Flowers are arranged in one-sided spikes, with four to ten small, gladiolus-like flowers on wiry, wand-like stems. Blooms are six tepaled and about 2.5 in. across, flattened against the stem. Divide clumps every three to four years to maintain vigor and avoid overcrowding.

'Alba' has star-like, pristine white flowers. 18 in. Z6.

'Mrs. Hegarty' has pale pink flowers. Late blooming.

'Oregon Sunset' is very long blooming; wide, coral-red petals. Z6–10.

'Sunrise'. Large, deep pink, lily-like flowers open from slender buds. Long blooming. 15 in. Z6.

'Viscountess Byng' has deep peach flowers.

Scrophularia
Scrophulariaceae
figwort

Relatives of snapdragons, penstemons, and monkey flowers, figworts include several species of ornamental value. Their application in the garden is somewhat limited, but in just the right spot, they can be invaluable. Historically, figworts were valued as sources of herbal medicines used to treat a wide variety of diseases. The five-lobed, small, tubular flowers are more interesting than showy; some provide handsome, colorful foliages.

Propagate by seed or division.

Scrophularia auriculata 'Variegata'
syn. *S. auricula*
- brownish red
- early summer
- 4 ft. × 12–23 in.
- sun, part shade
- Z5–9

Variegated water figwort. Moist meadows and shorelines of western Europe. Evergreen in mild-winter climates, with ovoid, green leaves with creamy-white margins. Small, brownish red flowers cluster in tall spikes. Prefers a rich, moist soil, ideally along streams or pond sides, or in shallow, standing water. Deadhead and cut back hard after bloom to refresh foliage. Suitable for bogs and aquatic gardens, containers. In spring gardens foliage provides a showy complement to yellow cowslips; or partner with *Carex morrowii* 'Ice Dance' or *C. elata* 'Variegata'. Deer tolerant.

Scrophularia buergeriana 'Lemon and Lime'
syn. *Teucrium viscudum* 'Lemon and Lime'
- pink
- mid- to late summer
- 24–30 in. × 24–36 in.
- sun, part shade
- Z5–9

Sticky germander. Korea, northern China, Japan. Mounds of toothed, lanceolate leaves are bright chartreuse-yellow with a splash or central stripe of lime green. Small spikes of frothy lavender-mauve flowers. Spreading but not aggressive; attractive groundcover between shrubs. Shear to 4 in. in summer to refresh foliage.

Scrophularia macrantha
- white-and-red
- early summer to fall
- 36–48 in. × 18 in.
- sun
- Z5–10

Redbirds in a tree, New Mexico figwort. Mountains of New Mexico. Darkly handsome, angular, serrated leaves to 4 in. long. Wands of white-lipped, cherry-red flowers, to 4 ft. in length, that may lean into neighbors. Long blooming; flowers attract hummingbirds. Heat, drought, and clay tolerant; prefers moderately moist but very well-drained soil; avoid overwatering. Blue pitcher's sage and *Agastache* 'Blue Fortune' make attractive partners.

Scutellaria
Lamiaceae
skullcap, helmet flower

The persistent shield-like cap on the calyx, a minor feature of these flowers, is the inspiration for the common name skullcap; "helmet flower" seems more reasonable, however, for it describes the shape of the showy two-lipped corolla. The upper lip forms a hood to protect the four stamens; the pendulous lower one commonly protrudes; both lips may be lobed. Scutellarias exhibit other mint-family features: square stems, opposite leaves, and a welcome resistance to deer and rabbits.

Provide skullcaps with well-drained, average soil and a sunny spot; overly rich or wet soil promptes lush, lanky vegetative growth. An asset to beds, borders, and rock gardens, scutellarias attract foraging butterflies; suitable for wildlife gardens. Drought tolerant, they fit well in xeriscapes. Native hoary skullcap, *Scutellaria incana*, and showy skullcap, *S. serrata*, are perfect for wild and native plant gardens.

Increase by seed overwintered outdoors. Divide established plants in spring or fall; take cuttings of young growth in spring and early summer.

Scutellaria alpina

- purple
- spring
- 4–6 in. × 12 in.
- sun, part shade
- Z5–8

Alpine scullcap, rainbow scullcap. Rocky, mountainous regions of Europe, temperate Asia. Branched, leafy stems, sometimes more or less prostrate, bear usually sessile, toothed, ovate, 0.5-in. leaves. Dense

racemes of 2- to 3-in., snapdragon-like flowers, white-marked bluish violet, all purple, or whitish yellow, are arranged around the stems.

'Arcobaleno' blooms range from pink to purple. 8 in. Z5.

'Green Court' has pale reddish purple flowers. Compact.

'Moonbeam' has scalloped leaves; light yellow flowers. 10 in. Z5.

Scutellaria baicalensis

- blue
- early to late summer
- 8–15 in. × 12 in.
- sun, part shade
- Z5–8

Baikal skullcap, goldenroot, Chinese skullcap. Korea, China, Mongolia, Siberia. The roots are used in traditional Chinese medicine. Bushy, mostly branched at the base, covered with pointed, 2- to 3-in., lanceolate leaves rimmed with fine hairs. Racemes of very hairy, 1-in., bicolored blue-purple or white flowers with long calyx tubes. Lovely along pathways, where soil is deep and dry.

Scutellaria suffrutescens

- rosy-pink
- late spring to early fall
- 8–12 in. × 12" in.
- sun, part shade
- Z6–10

Pink Texas skullcap, cherry skullcap. Texas, Mexico. Slightly woody at the base, this tough Texan requires little maintenance. Low mounds are covered with cherry-pink flowers over a very long season. Protect in cold winters in zones 5 and 6. A great addition to xeriscapes, native plant gardens, and rock gardens. Prefers sweet soil; dress with lime chips to raise pH.

'Texas Rose' has deep rose flowers that cover the plant all season. 8 in. Z7–9.

Other Notable Cultivars

'Violet' ('Violet Cloud') is sterile, with deep violet-red flowers all summer; lean soil. 6 in. × 15 in. Z5.

Sedum
Crassulaceae
stonecrop

This large genus of succulent plants flourishes throughout the Northern Hemisphere; south of the equator species are confined to mountainous Peru. There are several hundred species; roughly a third are natives of the Americas. Most sedums store water in their fleshy leaves, which makes them outstandingly drought, sun, and heat tolerant. Sedums will not endure persistent wet but many species flourish in moist climates, given excellent drainage. Sunny crevices in stone walls or sandy banks are good locations for sedums; they also sparkle in containers, and the lower growers do well as plantings for green roofs. The fine-textured and often richly

Scutellaria baicalensis

colored foliage is evergreen in mild-winter regions, semi-evergreen in colder ones, and is sedum's primary attraction; small, starry, usually five-petaled flowers cluster in showy heads, or in some cases are just a bonus.

For convenience's sake, gardeners commonly divide the sedums into two groups: the "showy" or "border" sedums are upright, clump forming, and bear their colorful blossoms in expansive cymes; the "creeping" sedums form low, spreading mats of foliage with tiny flowers borne more diffusely. The late-summer- and fall-blooming showy sedums are useful in borders, especially in regions of summer drought; the creeping types are important as groundcovers, edgings, and as lawn alternatives. Both types are ideal for rock gardens.

Easy-care sedums flourish in average, dry to moderately moist, well-drained soils of poor to medium fertility. Drainage is critical, but poor soils do not faze them; most of the creeping kinds thrive even when their roots are confined to small interstices between stones, bricks, or stepping stones. Butterflies and pollinating insects are frequent visitors. Generally pest and disease free, though snails, slugs, and scale are a nuisance, as are deer and rabbits.

Several notable species not listed here are also cultivated widely. These include low, white-flowered *Sedum nevii*, *S. makinoi* 'Ogon', *S. aizoon*, and *S. ternatum* among others. *Sedum spathulifolium* is especially noted for green roofs.

Readily increased by tip cuttings or by division (creeping types); propagate cultivars vegetatively. Species are not difficult to grow from seed, although seeds are tiny, difficult to handle, and germination is often erratic. Many sedums self-seed in hospitable sites.

Sedum acre

- yellow
- late spring to early summer
- 3 in. × 10 in.
- sun
- Z4–9

Goldmoss stonecrop. Europe, naturalized locally in North America. Creeping, with small, light green, finely textured, plump leaves. Small, yellow flowers carried above the foliage. Fast growing; may develop into large patches.

'**Aureum**' has yellow-tipped foliage.

Sedum 'Autumn Joy'

Sedum album

- white
- early to midsummer
- 3–6 in. × 12–18 in.
- sun
- Z3–8

White stonecrop. Europe and northern Africa to Siberia, western Asia. Evergreen, mat-forming, creeping, with small, succulent, linear-oblong, cylindrical to flattened, green leaves to 0.75 in. long. Prostrate stems root at the nodes. Foliage turns reddish brown in fall. Starry, white flowers cluster above the foliage. Tolerates very light shade.

'Coral Carpet' has salmon-orange young growth that matures to bright green, becoming reddish bronze in winter. White to pale pink flowers.

'Orange Ice' has red-tinted foliage that turns orange in cold weather. White to pink flowers.

Sedum cauticola

- pink
- late summer to early fall
- 4–6 in. × 18 in.
- sun
- Z5–9

Japan. Forms mounds of rounded, blue-gray leaves. Pink to rosy-red flowers. Useful as a rock garden or front-of-border specimen.

'Lidakense' has pink-tinged leaves on pink stems.

Sedum kamtschaticum

- yellow
- mid- to late summer
- 4–6 in. × 8 in.
- sun
- Z3–9

Ural Mountains to Mongolia. Dense cushions of glossy deep green, scalloped and spoon-shaped, fleshy leaves that become pinkish red in winter. Blanketed with 0.5-in., golden flowers. Extremely drought resistant; excellent groundcover for challenging spots.

'Variegata' has smart, crisply yellow-rimmed leaves. Yellow-orange flowers.

Sedum rupestre

syn. *S. reflexum*

- yellow
- early to midsummer
- 3–6 in. × 12–24 in.
- sun
- Z5–8

Central and western Europe. Creeping mats, to 2 ft. wide, of cylindrical, gray-green, 0.5- to 0.75-in. fleshy leaves flaunt vivid reddish fall color in cold regions. Yellow, 0.5-in., starry flowers. A tough, relatively fast-growing groundcover that often naturalizes.

'Angelina' has lime-green foliage; brilliant amber fall color in full sun.

'Blue Spruce' has tightly packed, needle-like leaves, the color of a blue spruce.

Sedum sieboldii

syn. *Hylotelephium sieboldii*

- pink
- late summer
- 6–12 in. × 12 in.
- sun
- Z3–9

Siebold's stonecrop, October daphne. Asia. Arching and trailing stems clothed with rounded, silvery blue, scalloped leaves, sometimes rose rimmed. Heads of dusky pink flowers. Great for containers, as well as tumbling over walls, for groundcover, and edgings.

'Mediovariegatum' ('Variegatum'). Deep pink flowerheads top mounds of blue-green leaves, centered with creamy yellow.

Sedum acre

Sedum spurium 'John Creech'

Sedum spectabile

syn. *Hylotelephium spectabile*
- pink
- late summer
- 12–24 in. × 12 in.
- sun
- Z4–8

Showy stonecrop. China, Korea. Often confused with *Sedum telephium*; these two very similar species have been hybridized extensively to produce a myriad of selections. Starry, pink flowers cluster into 2- to 4-in.-wide heads atop succulent stems clothed with alternate, fleshy blue-green or pale green, paddle-shaped leaves. The species is seldom grown, in favor of the available hybrids.

Sedum spurium

- red, pink
- early summer
- 4–6 in. × 12–18 in.
- sun, part shade
- Z3–8

Two-row stonecrop. Caucasus Mountains. Dense mats of thick and succulent, obovate, 0.5- to 1-in., green to reddish leaves, toothed near the ends. Slow to medium growth rate. Red, pink, or pinkish white flowers bloom 2 in. above the foliage for two to four weeks. Deer resistant. Outstanding cultivars include:

'Dragon's Blood' has deep purple leaves, pinkish purple flowers. Z4–9.

'John Creech' has mauve-pink flowers. Z5–9.

'Tricolor' has green-and-white variegated leaves,

Sedum 'Neon'

Sedum rupestre 'Angelina'

tinged with pink. Pink, 0.5- to 0.75-in. flowers cluster in cymes, from late spring to midsummer. Vigorous. 3–6 in. × 12–18 in.

Other Notable Cultivars

Notable hybrids abound—most border sedums fall into this category, since they are often the result of *Sedum telephium* × *S. spectabile*. Sun loving and succulent unless stated otherwise.

'Autumn Joy' ('Herbstfreude') has light green, broadly obovate, toothed leaves. Large, green, broccoli-like flowerheads from late summer on; blooms open dusty pink and mature to rich bronzy red. Chop to 6 in. in early summer to control height and flopping. Divide every two to three years. 18–24 in. high and wide. Z4–10.

'Black Jack' has purple-black leaves; clusters of bright pink flowers. Late summer to midfall. 18–23 in. high and wide. Z3–9.

'Cloud Nine' has green foliage shaded with maroon; 6- to 8-in.-wide clusters of mauve flowers in late summer. 15–17 in. × 18–24 in. Z3–9.

'Matrona' (syn. *S. telephium* 'Matrona') has thick, deep gray leaves that adorn upright purple stems. Pale pink flowerheads. Perhaps preferable to 'Autumn Joy'. Reportedly deer resistant. 24–36 in. Z3–9.

'Neon', a sport of 'Brilliant', bears brilliant rosy heads. 18–20 in.

'Vera Jameson' has smoky-blue leaves on arching stems, covered with 2- to 4-in., dusky-pink heads in late summer. 10–12 ft. × 10 in. Z3–9.

Sempervivum

Crassulaceae
hen and chicks, houseleek

Some perennials paint in broad strokes; by contrast, the sempervivums furnish jewel-like touches of architectural precision, foliage texture, and color. Native to rocky, dry habitats, these rosette-forming succulents are practically invulnerable to drought; many are surprisingly cold hardy. They thrive in poor, droughty soils and full sun; good drainage is demanded; once established, plants survive total neglect.

Their beauty is largely in their infinitely varied forms. The fleshy, scale-like leaves may be pointed or rounded, packed into tight globes or spread into something like a multi-colored artichoke. Foliage colors range from green to brown, pink and purple, and some species are covered with whisker-like hairs that produce a whitish appearance. Foliage colors vary with the season, the climate, and the degree of exposure to sun. They increase themselves vegetatively, with older rosettes typically surrounding themselves with a flock of smaller offsets—a habit that inspired the common name "hen and chicks." Flowers are rare but intriguing: each rosette blooms just once, often after several years of growth, producing a long, fleshy, scaly stalk that

looks more like an alien proboscis than an ordinary flower stem; the small head of flowers is crown-like. After flowering, the individual rosette dies.

Ideal for rock gardens, xeriscapes, and containers, sempervivums are particularly attractive when different forms are intermingled in mosaic; they are picturesque tucked into the crevices of a dry-laid retaining wall. Superb material for adding interest to green roofs: the moniker "houseleek" refers to a traditional practice of carpeting cottage roofs with sempervivums to ward off lightning. Generally pest free, though sometimes attacked by aphids and slugs; sometimes grazed by deer and rabbits in winter. Avoid overwatering. There are 40 or so species and hundreds of cultivars. We include just a sampling here.

Propagate by removing and replanting offsets, or start seed.

Sempervivum arachnoideum

- pink
- summer
- 4 in. × 4–20 in.
- sun
- Z3–8

Cobweb houseleek. Evergreen mats of tight rosettes, 0.5–1.25 in. across. Individual leaves pale green with fine white hairs stretched from tip to tip like a cobweb. Starry pink flowers 0.5 in. across in flat cymes on 5-in. stems.

'Robin' has cranberry leaves, pale green at the tips.

Sempervivum calcareum

- pink
- summer
- 2–4 in. × 4–20 in.
- sun, part shade
- Z3–8

French and Italian Alps. Striking, 3- to 4-in. rosettes of gray-green leaves, that shade to maroon at tips.

'Limelight'. Large to medium rosettes with pale, yellow-green leaves, lightly tipped with dark red.

Sempervivum tectorum

- reddish purple
- summer
- 6–12 in. × 6–18 in.
- sun
- Z3–8

Houseleek. Mountains of southern Europe. Evergreen mats of 3- to 4-in.-wide rosettes of glabrous green, sometimes purple-tipped leaves. Red-purple flowers on thick, upright stalks to 12 in. Tolerates some light shade.

'Boissieri' has bronze-tinged leaves, with rusty tips.

'Sunset' has red- or orange-flushed, bright green leaves.

'Oddity' has bright green leaves, with quilled edges and black tips.

Other Notable Cultivars

Hybrids are countless; the following is a selection. Oftentimes plants are not identified with a particular cultivar name. Mass for striking effect.

'Baronesse'. Olive-green leaves backed with dense, russet-red cobwebs.

'Dark Beauty' has bronze to blackish purple leaves. 4–8 in. × 6–12 in. Z2–9.

'Emerald Empress' has rosettes of emerald green that flush bronze in cool months. 4–8 in. × 6–12 in. Z2–9.

'Rubikon' has bright ruby-red rosettes. 2–6 in. Z4–8.

Sanford Hybrids have sharply pointed leaves in shades of red. 3–4 in. × 6–8 in. Z3–8.

Senecio

Asteraceae
senecio

This huge genus (1000-plus species) is best known for its drought resistance, although it also includes two garden-worthy perennials that prefer wet soils. Commonly known as ragworts or groundsels, most senecios produce copious amounts of seed, often equipped with parachutes similar to those of related dandelions. One of the most ubiquitous garden weeds is common groundsel, *Senecio vulgaris*.

Senecio foliage is basal or arranged alternately on the stem; the flowerheads are discoid or composed of ray petals around a central disk; they are usually anchored by a single row of bracts. Flowerheads are mostly yellow or white; where present, the central disk is yellow.

Perhaps the best-known species is the florists' cineraria (*Senecio* ×*hybridus*) grown by the million as a colorful pot plant; it has been bred extensively to produce large daisy flowers of all colors; mostly treated as an annual, but perennial in warm climates. Subshrubby, gray-leaved sea ragwort (also known as silver groundsel or dusty miller), *S. cineraria* (*S. maritima*, *Centaurea maritima*), is grown mostly as an annual but survives mild winters; typically becomes woody and leggy in its second season, bearing scruffy yellow flowers, best removed. Popular selections include 'Colchester White', 'Cirrhus', and 'Silver Dust'.

Mostly pest and disease free, senecios are seldom deer browsed; rabbits relish young growth. Propagate from seed or by division.

Senecio aureus

syn. *Packera aurea*
- yellow
- late spring
- 12–24 in. × 18 in.
- sun, part shade, shade
- Z3–9

Golden groundsel, heart-leaved groundsel, golden ragwort. Wet places in the central and eastern United States. Basal clumps of long-petioled, toothed, heart-shaped to ovate leaves. Erect, dark, smooth stems are sparsely furnished with slender, lobed leaves. Loose heads of purple buds open to deep yellow, daisy flowers with darker yellow disks, held above the leaves. Ray petals are pinked or notched at the tips. Best where soil remains moist, even wet; bog gardens. Self-seeds freely, but seldom becomes obnoxious. A fine native groundcover. Woodland phlox makes a charming companion.

Senecio smithii

- white
- summer
- 3–4 ft. × 2 ft.
- sun, part shade
- Z7–9

Southern Chile, Falkland Islands. This bold plant makes robust clumps of coarse basal leaves, initially covered with woolly hairs. These expand to 8–10 in. long, broadly paddle shaped, and puckered with wavy, crisped margins. Stiff stems hold crowded 4- to 6-in., terminal panicles of 1.5-in., yellow-centered, white daisy flowers just above the foliage; fluffy white seedheads follow. Provide deep, rich, and constantly damp soil. Protect plants from devastating slugs and snails. In bog gardens, combine with primulas, royal fern, rodgersias, and astilbes.

Senecio aureus

Setcreasea pallida

Shortia galacifolia

Setcreasea
Commelinaceae
purple heart, wandering Jew

The taxonomy of this genus is a subject of dispute, with many botanists insisting that setcreasias should be classified under *Tradescantia*. One species is of interest to gardeners. It is commonly used as a houseplant in cold-winter regions.

Setcreasia pallida
syn. *Tradescantia pallida*

- lavender
- midsummer to early fall
- 8–12 in. × 16 in.
- sun, part shade
- Z7–11

Purple heart. Mexico. Lanceolate, hairy, violet-purple leaves, to 7 in., clothe fleshy, sprawling stems; color is best in full sun. Light lavender, 0.5-in. flowers attract butterflies. Prefers damp, well-drained soil; drought tolerant once established. Pinch stem tips in spring and deadhead spent blooms to encourage dense growth. Dramatic sited behind white- or yellow-flowered perennials; popular for hanging baskets, and effective as a showy groundcover. Deer and rabbit resistant; watch for aphids and spider mites. Propagate by stem tip cuttings or by seed.

'Kartuz Giant' has larger, 2-in.-wide leaves. Extra vigorous. 1–2 ft. × 2–3 ft.

'Pale Puma' has 2.5-in. × 1.5-in. leaves, purple in sun; in part shade centers are glossy green, purple at the margins. White flowers. 1 ft. × 3 ft.

Shortia
Diapensiaceae
Oconee-bells

Underused in residential gardens, shortias are considered difficult to grow, but more accurately are tricky to propagate. Our native species grow naturally in acid, highly organic soils on steep, partly shaded sides of ravines and beside streams. Asian species enjoy similar conditions, but in somewhat more diverse habitats.

Plant Oconee-bells as rock- and woodland-garden groundcovers, especially beneath rhododendrons, mountain laurels, and Japanese andromeda. Provide moisture-retentive, humus-rich, acid, loose soil with a spongy texture. Sheltered sites with filtered sun are perfect. Mulch with organic matter. Very slow to bulk up. Deer tolerant.

Divide clumps carefully in spring or fall. Sow fresh seed when available; seed loses its viability fast.

Shortia galacifolia

- white
- spring
- 6–8 in. × 9–12 in.
- shade
- Z4–8

Oconee-bells. In wet places and beside streams in the Appalachian Mountains of North and South Carolina. Loose mats of basal foliage arise from underground runners. Evergreen, leathery leaves, on 4- to 5-in.-long petioles, similar to those of wandflower, *Galax*, are all basal and shiny; more or less paddle shaped with variably wavy or toothed margins, about 2 in. across. Leafless stems bear solitary, nodding, 0.75-in., pink-tinged white, bell-shaped flowers, with fringed or scalloped petals. Foliage colors from bright green to ruddy bronze as winter approaches.

Shortia soldanelloides

syn. *Schizocodon soldanelloides*

- pink
- late spring to early summer
- 4–12 in. × 12 in.
- shade
- Z5–8

Fringed galax, fringe-bell. Japan. Loose racemes of several, deeply fringed, rosy-pink or white, 1-in. flowers bloom 4–12 in. above the foliage mat. Toothed leaves are rounded, and heart shaped at the base. Slow spreading by underground stems.

Shortia uniflora

syn. *Schizocodon uniflorus*

- white
- spring
- 8 in. × 12 in.
- shade
- Z5–8

Nippon bells. Japan. Broadly heart-shaped, 1- to 3-in. leaves, wavy toothed along the edges. Gently fringed, solitary, white, 1-in. flowers are heavily veined with pink.

Sidalcea

Malvaceae
prairie mallow, checker bloom

Love what hollyhocks do for your garden but tired of watching them fall to rust? Try rust-resistant *Sidalcea*. These western North America natives are closely similar to related hollyhocks with tall, clustered spikes of five-petaled, star- or saucer-shaped flowers in pinks, white, or purple. Sharply toothed, deeply lobed leaves rise from basal clumps. Sidalceas commonly bloom for years without problems, even self-seeding in favorable conditions.

Full sun or partial shade, in moist but well-drained, neutral to acid soils are suitable conditions. Tall selections may require staking; cut stems back after initial flowering to promote rebloom; flowering can last all summer. Prairie mallows provide good punctuation or vertical accents for borders, with a picturesque simplicity ideal for cottage and cutting

Sidalcea oregana 'Brilliant'

gardens. Attracts bees, butterflies, and, unfortunately, Japanese beetles; deer and rabbit resistant.

Divide selections and hybrids; start species from seed.

Sidalcea malviflora

- pink
- spring to midsummer
- 36–48 in. × 18–24 in.
- sun, part shade
- Z5–9, HS

Prairie mallow, checker bloom. Moist meadows from southern Oregon to Mexican border. Dense tufts of dark green, fleshy, palmately lobed leaves rise from rhizomatous roots. Clusters of stems lined with pink to purple flowers; blooms open in the morning and twist closed at night. Reliable and easy to grow; excellent additions to grasslands or meadow plantings. Summer dormant in response to drought but thrives with moisture; tolerates moderate to low water once established.

'Elsie Heugh' has satiny, pinkish purple flowers in summer. 30–36 in. × 12–18 in. Z5–7.

'Little Princess' is compact with satiny, pink flowers in summer; cut back for later rebloom. 18–24 in. × 12 in. Z5–7.

Sidalcea oregana

- pink
- late spring to early summer
- 2–4 ft. × 1–3 ft.
- sun, part shade
- Z5–10, HS

Oregon checker mallow. British Columbia, south through California, east into Wyoming and Montana. Taprooted; rounded, toothed basal leaves are palmate and shallowly lobed; stem leaves more deeply lobed. Coarse, bristly stems with loose spike-like racemes of pink to deep rose flowers, 1–1.5 in. across.

'Brilliant' has deep rose flowers with a central white halo. 24–36 in. Z5–7.

Other Notable Cultivars

'Party Girl'. Bright green leaves, rounded below but deeply lobed on the stems. Deep pink, 2- to 3-in.-wide, hollyhock-like flowers. Prefers full sun. 2–3 ft. × 1.5–2 ft. Z5–7.

Stark's Hybrids produce flowers from pale pink to deep purple-pinks. 24–36 in.

Silene
Caryophyllaceae
campion, catchfly

According to one story, the namesake of this genus, Silenus, was a "green man," a pagan nature deity of forests and woodlands; indeed many *Silene* species do grow wild at woodland edges. Campions are also found growing in gravelly mountain screes where glaciers once melted, in meadows, and in bright woodlands across temperate parts of the Northern Hemisphere.

"Catchfly" refers to the sticky glandular hairs that often cover the stems and flower calyces. Tiny insects are often caught on these plant parts. Smooth, more or less lance-shaped leaves are basal or opposite on the stems; solitary or clustered, red, pink, or white, five-petaled flowers have clawed petals, and are often notched or cleft at the tip. Some species (e.g., *Silene uniflora*) have conspicuous inflated, bladder-like calyces often intricately veined or lined. Attracts butterflies; resists deer and rabbit browsing. Seldom attacked by pests or diseases.

Lower-growing species, including *S. acaulis*, *S. schafta*, and *S. alpestris* are eminently suitable for rock gardens, troughs, containers, and other "up close and personal" locations. Taller sorts do well in wild and cottage gardens, in front of shrubs, or in the midsection of informal beds.

Sow seed in fall and overwinter with protection. Divide offsets in late summer, or take spring basal cuttings.

Silene caroliniana

- pink
- midspring to early summer
- 9–12 in. high and wide
- sun, part shade
- Z4–9

Wild pink, Carolina campion. New Hampshire, west to Ohio, south to Alabama. Reminiscent of woodland phlox and a good substitute for dianthus, this mounding, native wildflower has lanceolate basal leaves, to 4 in. long; smaller, opposing pairs up the sticky stems. Few-flowered, terminal clusters of rosy-pink, 1-in. flowers with five spreading, pie-shaped petals, notched at the apex.

var. *wherryi* 'Short and Sweet' bears intense pink, 1-in. flowers for several weeks. Naturalizes well; adapts to containers, and spots between patio pavers or flagstones.

Silene dioica
syn. *Lychnis dioica*

- pink, red
- late spring to early summer
- 12–24 in. × 12 in.
- sun, part shade
- Z5–8

Red campion. Northern Europe and the British Isles. Rosy-pink or red flowers, with deeply divided, notched petals, and hairy, pink-flushed, slightly inflated calyces; hairy leaves. Male and female

Silene dioica 'Firefly'

flowers are on separate plants. Butterflies are frequent visitors.

'Clifford Moore' has variegated green leaves, broadly and irregularly banded with yellow. Light pink flowers in spring to fall in cool-summer climates.

'Firefly' displays its double, bright magenta flowers in early summer. Good for cutting and midborder. 12–18 in. Z4–9.

'Rosea Plena' has double, dusty-pink flowers, 1.5 in. across. 24–30 in.

Silene uniflora

syn. *S. maritima, S. vulgaris* subsp. *maritima*
- white
- early to late summer
- 6–8 in. × 8 in.
- sun
- Z2–9

Sea campion. Native to sea cliffs, sandy or shingly shores, and mountain screes of northern Europe. Semi-evergreen, low mounds of fleshy, glaucous, pointed leaves on branching, slightly succulent, pink-flushed stems. White flowers have inflated calyces traced with reddish brown markings. Deep rooted. Suitable for troughs, rock gardens, or containers.

'Compacta' (compact maiden tears). Low cushions of gray-green foliage beneath pink or pink-flushed white flowers. Attractive between flagstones and pavers. 4 in. Z3–9.

Silphium perfoliatum

'Druett's Variegated' has waxy, green leaves boldly edged with white. White flowers in early summer. Remove any green shoots that revert. A beautiful accent in rock gardens or troughs. 2–4 in. Z4–9.

'Robin Whitebreast' ('Swan Lake') has large, double, white flowers like an Elizabethan ruff, on trailing mounds of evergreen, fleshy, grayish leaves. Divide in spring. Ideal as frosting over walls and container rims.

Silene virginica
- red
- late spring to early summer
- 15–20 in. × 12–18 in.
- sun, part shade
- Z4–8

Fire pink, catchfly. Native to rocky slopes and open woods of eastern North America. Sticky, glandular hairs cover the stems. Basal rosettes of long-petioled, entire, 3- to 4-in. lanceolate to spatulate leaves. Clumps produce slender stems topped with clusters of brilliant red, 2-in. flowers, with five narrow, deeply notched petals. Ruby-throated hummingbirds are primary pollinators. Drought tolerant. Appropriate in native, cottage, coastal, and wild gardens.

Silphium
Asteraceae
rosinweed

These natives of North American prairies and woodland openings are mostly unimproved by plant breeders and retain their native toughness. Upright, sturdy stalks carry sunflower-like blooms and expansive foliage; their height ranges from modest to towering. Perhaps rather coarse for formal displays, they contribute a note of lofty exuberance to more casual summer borders, and are naturals in meadow, native plant, and wildflower gardens. Exceptionally heat tolerant, their deep taproots help protect them against drought, and anchor them so securely that they rarely need staking. Generally free of serious pests and diseases, they are unappealing to deer, no doubt because of their resinous sap; too coarse to be palatable to rabbits. Attracts butterflies, birds, and numerous pollinating insects.

Propagate by seed; these taprooted plants do not respond well to division. Slow to establish in gardens when grown from seed, but long lived; self-seeds on favorable sites.

Silphium integrifolium
- yellow
- mid- to late summer
- 2–6 ft. × 1–3 ft.
- sun
- Z4–8

Rosinweed. Eastern and central United States. Opposite pairs of rough, bristly, and sessile, medium green, toothed leaves to 6 in. long are borne on erect hairy stems. Leaves range from lanceolate to ovate or elliptic. Terminal clusters of yellow-rayed, 2- to 3-in. flowerheads with yellow central disks. Adapted to a range of soils; tolerates some light shade.

Silphium laciniatum

- yellow
- sun
- mid- to late summer
- Z3–8
- 5–9 ft. × 1.5–3 ft.

Compass plant. Central United States. Deeply pinnatifid basal leaves to 18 in. long, resemble outsized pin oak foliage; they are borne vertically in opposing pairs oriented north and south (the source of the common name) to minimize exposure to harsh midday sun. Towering, stiff, hairy stems carry loose spikes of 5-in.-wide, yellow-rayed flowers punctuated with yellow central disks. Thrives on average, moderately moist, well-drained soils; tolerates poor ones.

Silphium perfoliatum

- yellow
- sun
- mid- to late summer
- Z3–9
- 4–8 ft. × 1–3 ft.

Cup plant. Eastern and central Canada, south to Georgia, west to North Dakota and Oklahoma. Tough, erect, quadrangular stems with rough, coarsely toothed triangular to ovate leaves. Lower leaves to 14 in. long; the smaller upper ones unite at their bases around the stems to form cups that collect rainwater; a summertime water source for birds. Terminal clusters of 3-in.-wide, light yellow daisies with darker yellow disks. Prefers moist, rich soils. Occurs naturally in sandy, damp bottomlands, floodplains, and along streams; tolerates temporary flooding.

Silphium terebinthinaceum

- yellow
- sun
- mid- to late summer
- Z4–8
- 3–10 ft. × 1–3 ft.

Prairie dock. Ontario south to Georgia, Mississippi, and Arkansas. Basal clumps of 18- to 24-in., oval or heart-shaped leaves give rise to smooth stems with few or no leaves. These are topped with loose clusters of yellow, 3-in.-wide daisy flowers. Thrives in average, moderately moist, well-drained garden soils; tolerates poor soils.

Sisyrinchium
Iridaceae
blue-eyed grass

These Iris relatives are self-sufficient perennials that flourish in the wild in habitats ranging from mountainsides to meadows and coastal areas, and are equally adaptable in the garden. Their linear evergreen or semi-evergreen foliage is gray-green, and basal, often arranged in fans or clumps rising from rhizomatous roots. Flattened, winged stems bear starry, cup-shaped, or shallowly trumpet-shaped flowers encircled by bract-like spathes. Solitary or in umbel-like clusters, flower colors range from very pale blue to deep blue-purples, yellow, and white.

Grow blue-eyed grass in poor to average, well-drained soil, with a neutral or slightly alkaline pH. Plants mostly self-seed; remove seed capsules before they ripen if seedlings are a problem. Many of the smaller species are well suited to rock gardens, for edging pathways, at the front of borders, or as groundcovers; taller species are appropriate for perennial and mixed borders; meadow salvias, Shasta daisies, and hardy geraniums mix well. Attracts butterflies; resists deer and squirrels. Susceptible to aphids and spider mites; fungal rust may prove a nuisance.

Divide established plants after bloom time, or start seed in early spring or fall.

Sisyrinchium angustifolium 'Lucerne'

Sisyrinchium angustifolium
syn. *S. anceps, S. graminoides, S. bermudiana*
- blue
- spring to summer
- 8–18 in. × 12 in.
- sun, part shade
- Z3–8

Narrowleaf blue-eyed grass, Bermuda blue-eyed grass, northern blue-eyed grass. Native to the eastern United States. The national flower of Bermuda. Dense, tufted, fan-like clumps of slender, sword-like, basal leaves to 12 in. long. Broadly winged, flattened, branched flower stems, somewhat taller than the leaves, bear clusters of four to five buds that open one at time into starry, yellow-eyed, steel-blue flowers. Individual flowers usually last but a day, but are soon replaced. Long blooming; seeds about gently. Drought tolerant, but much better in damp soil. *Sisyrinchium bellum*, native to the western states, is the regional equivalent of *S. angustifolium*.

'**Lucerne**' has gold-centered, bright blue flowers. 8–10 in. Z5.

Sisyrinchium striatum
syn. *S. lutescens, S. phaiophleps*
- yellow
- late spring to summer
- 12–36 in. × 12 in.
- sun, part shade
- Z7–10

Yellow-eyed grass, Argentine blue-eyed grass, satin flower. Chile, Argentina. Evergreen clumps of 18-in.-long, gray-green leaves, to 1 in. wide, rise from creeping rhizomes. Creamy-yellow, cup-shaped flowers to 1 in. wide, accented with a deep yellow eye and striped purple on the reverse. Self-seeds, but is not invasive. Clean up spent foliage after bloom has ended, or cut back leaves by two-thirds. Ideal in beds and borders; naturalizes well.

'**Aunt May**' ('Variegata') has gray-green leaves, longitudinally striped with creamy yellow. Protect from intense sun to avoid leaf burn. Somewhat less vigorous than the species; quite beautiful. 18 in.

Other Notable Cultivars
'**Devon Skies**' has pale blue flowers with a dark blue eye and dark stripes on each perianth segment. 4–6 in. Z7–10.

'**E. K. Balls**' has satiny, small purple flowers. 6 in. Z6–8.

'**Quaint and Queer**' has unusual apricot flowers with dull maroon throats. This selection is an acquired taste. 12 in. Z6–8.

'**Rocky Point**' displays yellow-eyed, purple flowers from late spring on. Summer dormant in dry climates. 6 in. Z7–10.

'**Suwannee**' has abundant sky-blue flowers in late spring. Tolerates dry and damp soils. 8 in. Z7–9.

Solidago
Asteraceae
goldenrod

European gardeners have long esteemed native American goldenrods, but until recently they were ignored, at least horticulturally, on this side of the Atlantic, possibly due to the mistaken but enduring belief that they cause hay fever. What they actually provide is a long lasting and remarkably hardy, perennial source of late summer and fall color, as well as invaluable late-season nectar sources for butterflies and bees.

A few species of goldenrods are native to Central and South America, and Eurasia, but the overwhelming majority, more than 60 species, originated in the fields and prairies of North America. Typically, they form an aggressive network of rhizomes or woody subterranean stems (caudices). From these rise upright or sprawling stems, 6–60 in. or more tall, depending upon the species.

Solidago 'Baby Gold'

Solidago rugosa 'Fireworks'

Alternate leaves are linear to lanceolate, commonly serrated along the margins. Tiny, golden yellow (or sometimes white) flowerheads cluster into parasol-like, plume-like, or branched sprays. They bloom in late summer to fall.

Adaptable and undemanding, goldenrods thrive in lean to moderately fertile soils in full sun; some tolerate part shade. Use the aggressive species in meadows, native and prairie plantings, or at woodland edges; the hybrids shine in late-season borders, and contrast dramatically with blue and violet asters. Choose late selections to harmonize with fall fruits, berries, and ornamental grasses. Staking is seldom needed; deadhead to extend bloom. Foraging bees, butterflies, and insects flock to collect the waxy pollen and nectar; deer resistant. Rust and powdery mildew may be a nuisance.

Propagate by division in spring or fall. Sow seed of species in late fall or early spring.

Solidago caesia

- yellow
- late summer to midfall

- 18–36 in. high and wide
- sun, part shade
- Z4–8

Blue-stemmed goldenrod, wreath goldenrod. Woods and fields of central and eastern North America.

Arching, greenish purple stems bear toothed, lanceolate, 2- to 5-in. leaves. Bright yellow flowerheads cluster loosely in leaf axils along the stems. Clump forming, not an aggressive spreader. Fine cut flower.

Solidago odora

- yellow
- late summer to early fall

- 2–4 ft. × 1–2 ft.
- sun, part shade
- Z3–9

Sweet goldenrod. Dry, sandy, open woods, eastern and central United States. Sessile, anise-scented, lanceolate, 3- to 4-in., dark green leaves on smooth or downy stems. Yellow flowerheads cluster in one-sided plumes. Tolerates poor, dry soils; does not spread aggressively but may self-seed. Good for butterfly gardens, meadows, borders, fragrance, and cottage gardens.

Solidago rugosa

- yellow
- late summer to midfall

- 3–5 ft. × 1.5–2.5 ft.
- sun
- Z4–8

Rough goldenrod. Moist fields and wetlands from Newfoundland, west to Michigan, south to Texas and Georgia. Recessed veins give the 3- to 4-in.,

Solidago sphacelata 'Golden Fleece'

lanceolate leaves a wrinkled appearance. Erect, arching, hairy stems rise from low mounds with showy panicles of yellow flowerheads. Spreads slowly by rhizomes and seed; good for rain gardens, meadows, and prairies.

'**Fireworks**', introduced by North Carolina Botanical Garden. Long, arching sprays of golden-yellow flowerheads. Attractive mingled with the orange hips of *Rosa glauca*. Mass for best effect. 3–4 ft.

Solidago speciosa

- yellow
- midsummer to early fall
- 1–3 ft. high and wide
- sun, part shade
- Z3–8

Showy goldenrod. Dry soils in open woods, fields, and prairies throughout central and eastern United States. Narrowly lanceolate, 4- to 6-in., oblong-elliptic leaves become smaller as they ascend stiff, erect, reddish stems. Very showy, erect, pointed clusters of tiny, bright yellow flowerheads at stem tips. Tolerates poor, dry soils.

Solidago sphacelata

syn. *Brachychaeta sphacelata*

- yellow
- late summer to midfall
- 12–24 in. × 12–18 in.
- sun
- Z4–8

Virginia to Georgia, west to Illinois and Tennessee. Compact, with low-growing mats of heart-shaped, toothed leaves. Stiff, arching stems branch at tips with plumes of small, yellow flowerheads. Tolerates dry, rocky, and clay soils. A useful groundcover; an asset in cottage and rock gardens.

'**Golden Fleece**' produces lavish displays of bright yellow flowerheads in arching, cylindrical plumes. A Dick Lighty introduction. 15–18 in.

'**Wichita Mountains**' has gold flowers. Introduced by Steve Bieberich. 30 in.

Other Notable Cultivars

'**Baby Gold**' has large sprays of gold flowers. 2–2.5 ft.

'**Crown of Rays**'. Erect plumes of bright yellow flowers from mid- to late summer. 2–3 ft.

'**Little Lemon**'. Exceptionally compact and well branched, with racemes of pale lemon flowers. Mid- to late summer. 8–12 in. Z5–8.

'**Peter Pan**' bears extra-large, spreading clusters

of warm yellow blooms. Late summer to late fall. 24–28 in. Z3–9.

'Solar Cascade'. Abundant golden flowerheads cluster in leaf axils along reflexed stems from late summer to late fall. Not an aggressive spreader. 2–3 ft. Z3–9.

×**Solidaster**
Asteraceae
solidaster

Long considered to be a natural hybrid between Canadian goldenrod (*Solidago canadensis*) and upland white aster (*Aster ptarmicoides*). However, recent genetic studies have reclassified the aster parent as a goldenrod, despite its very aster-like appearance. Nevertheless, this marriage produced a single cultivar, described below. It is a favorite of the European cut-flower industry.

Propagate by division or take basal shoot cuttings in spring.

×*Solidaster luteus* 'Lemore'

×*Solidaster luteus* 'Lemore'
- pale yellow
- late summer to early fall
- 2–2.5 ft. high and wide
- sun
- Z4–9

Solidaster. Of garden origin, with North American parents. Slender, toothed, lanceolate leaves to 6 in. long, on stiff stems that rarely need staking. Pale yellow, aster-like flowerheads, to 0.5 in., have darker yellow disks; borne in arching, goldenrod-like sprays. Provide average, dry to moderately moist, well-drained soils. Susceptible to powdery mildew and fungal rust; benefits from an open, airy site. Good late-season color for a sunny border or cutting garden.

Sphaeralcea
Malvaceae
globe mallow

With their tough constitution and flowers like mini hollyhocks, globe mallows are certain to please. They bloom abundantly and tolerate dry, poor soil, where other species may falter, growing naturally in deserts and dry riverbeds as found in gardens of the western United States. Globe mallows may also be cultivated under glass. Some species are covered with star-shaped hairs that irritate sensitive skins; never touch your eyes after tending globe mallows.

Although they survive in poor, dry conditions, globe mallows are more vigorous when grown in average garden soils and kept thirsty. Full sun is essential. Grow in a gritty, free-draining potting soil under glass or sunroom for indoor display. Be alert for white flies. Globe mallows are food plants for some species of caterpillar, including painted ladies; checkerspots and others visit for nectar; also attractive to birds and bees. Globe mallows are an important food for deer, rabbits, and rodents. Perfect to decorate wildflower and wildlife gardens, native plant gardens, or other informal areas.

Sow seed in spring in containers, or divide plants in spring. Stem cuttings root well in spring and summer.

Sphaeralcea ambigua
- pink, orange
- late summer to fall
- 2–3 ft. × 2 ft.
- sun
- Z7–10

Desert mallow, desert hollyhock, wild hollyhock. Native to dry parts of the southwestern United States. A very variable species that hybridizes promiscuously; mostly covered with stellar, white or yellowish hairs. Clumps of stems spirally clothed with fuzzy, fleshy, 0.75- to 2.5-in., broadly ovate, three-lobed leaves; these are ruffled or scalloped around the edges. Showy, cupped, 2-in., pink or orange flowers bloom in loose spikes in the upper leaf axils almost all season. Ideal for xeric, wildflower, and desert gardens. Height dependent on rainfall; in wet seasons the plants get to 4–5 ft. or so in the wild; perhaps only 12 in. in arid sites. Tolerates alkaline soil well. Where their ranges overlap, desert mallows often hybridize with smaller, orange *Sphaeralcea fendleri*.

'Louis Hamilton' (Louis Hamilton apricot mallow) is free blooming with scarlet-coral flowers for much of the summer. 30 in. Z7–10.

Sphaeralcea munroana
- red, orange
- summer to fall
- 1–3.5 ft. × 2 ft.
- sun
- Z4–9

Munro's globe mallow. Idaho to British Columbia and California. This very tough plant adapts to inhospitable sites and tolerates poor soil and low water with aplomb. Upright, unbranched stems, grayish with hairs, are furnished with alternate, silver-green foliage. Toothed, broadly ovate leaves are shallowly three lobed (sometimes five lobed), 1–2 in. long. Long wands of 1-in.-wide, apricot-orange to red flowers bloom for several weeks in terminal and axillary clusters. Spreads by underground runners, but is seldom invasive.

Several notable cultivars have resulted from a cross of this species with *Sphaeralcea fendleri* var. *venusta*: 'Wild Blush' has pale pink flowers, 'Wild Sherbet' has orange flowers, 'Wild Pale Pink' is pale pink.

Spigelia
Loganiaceae
Indian pink, pink root, worm grass

Whether you call them pinks, roots, or even worms, you are sure to prize these glorious natives. Spigelias' brilliant red-and-yellow flowers shine like beacons when massed; plant in drifts in native plant and wildflower gardens, or along pathways in open woodlands where the flowers can be enjoyed close up. They prefer moist, fertile soils in sunny or partly shaded spots, and do not thrive in parched ones in hot sun. Striking combined with variegated Solomon's seal, wild columbine, 'Ice Dance' sedge, and golden groundsel.

Hummingbirds and butterflies flock to Indian pinks. The jury still seems to be out on whether these plants are resistant to deer and rabbits, with reports going both ways. In Westchester County, NY, at least, neither appear to find spigelias palatable—yet.

Divide in spring; allow plants to self-seed, or collect and sow seed immediately after it ripens.

Spigelia marilandica
- red
- early summer
- 1–2 ft. × 2 ft.
- sun, part shade
- Z5–9

Indian pink, Maryland pink root, worm grass. Native to moist woods and thickets of the

Spigelia marilandica

southeastern and south-central United States. Forms clumps of unbranched, upright stems with widely spaced pairs of nondescript, sessile, 2- to 4-in., undivided, ovate leaves. Terminal, one-sided cymes of upward-facing, 1- to 2-in., scarlet-red flowers; funnel to trumpet shaped, and flaring at the mouth with five bright yellow, pointed lobes. Provide light shade in hot regions.

'Little Redhead' is compact, to 12 in., with showy, yellow-lined, red flowers. Introduced by noted garden writer Pam Harper of Virginia and Bob McCartney of Woodlanders Nursery.

Spiranthes
Orchidaceae
ladies' tresses

This cosmopolitan genus includes two species native to North America. These are terrestrial, reliable, and undemanding, if your garden includes suitable habitat. In fact, they naturalize readily, spreading by stoloniferous roots and self-seeding prolifically in hospitable sites. Though charming, the late-summer- to fall-blooming flowers do not fit the popular preconception of orchids: simple and modest, they are desirable as a garden treasure but not what you might pin to a prom gown.

No serious pests (except deer), or diseases. Propagate by division or seed.

Spiranthes cernua

- white
- late summer to midfall
- 18–24 in. × 9–12 in.
- sun, part shade
- Z6–9

Nodding ladies' tresses. Wet places throughout most of eastern North America. Clumps of glossy dark green, pointed leaves to 8 in. long. Flowers are borne in dense, 6-in. spikes with two to four spiraling rows atop cylindrical stems. Individual, vanilla-scented, 0.5-in. blossoms are nodding, bell shaped, and hooded with a pendulous lower lip, ivory-white and tinged green. Adapts to clays, loams, or sands with slightly acid to neutral pH. Requires consistently moist soil; tolerates wet soils. Resents transplanting once established. Excellent for wet meadows, stream and pond sides.

Spiranthes odorata

- white
- late summer to midfall
- 9–24 in. × 9–12 in.
- part shade
- Z5–9

Common ladies' tresses. Bogs and freshwater swamps from New Jersey south to Florida, west to Texas and Oklahoma. Basal rosettes of lanceolate leaves to 12 in. long; very fragrant, 0.5-in. flowers are bell shaped and hooded with a pendulous lower lip; they are creamy or greenish white, borne in dense spiraling rows around vertical spikes. Best in moist, acid soils; ideal in damp meadows, bog

gardens, wet woodlands, and around rock garden ponds. Spreads slowly by rhizomes to form colonies where conditions suit.

'Chadd's Ford' (*Spiranthes cernua* var. *odorata* 'Chadd's Ford') grows taller than the species, with larger flowers. 18–24 in. × 6–9 in. Z5–8.

Stachys
Lamiaceae
lamb's ear, betony

A genus with a split personality, *Stachys* includes species that are valued primarily as foliage plants, and others that are cultivated for their flowers—a few even excel at both. As members of the mint family, lamb's ears and betonies have square stems, opposite leaves, and verticillasters of two-lipped flowers. The flowers come in an unusually diverse range of colors: pinks, purples, reds, yellows, and whites. Typically the lanceolate to cordate leaves are toothed or scalloped along the margins; those of lamb's ears are gray-green and woolly, with a soft texture that begs to be stroked, but their flowers are often insignificant. Betonies, by contrast, have bright flowers to 0.5 in. or more long, borne in tall, prominent spikes, often for most of the season.

Moist, well-drained soil in full sun to light shade suits most species of *Stachys*. The fuzzy leaves of lamb's ears trap moisture, resulting in rot or melting down in areas with high summer humidity or damp winters. Irrigate at ground level.

Silvery lamb's ears provide an elegant edging for beds and paths, make a striking groundcover when massed, and an attractive accent for borders, rock gardens, and cottage gardens. Problems are few, though betonies are vulnerable to slugs and powdery mildew. Cut back tired, scruffy foliage of lamb's ears to encourage fresh new growth. Resistant to deer and rabbits; tolerates sites beneath black walnut trees.

Propagate by division or seed.

Stachys byzantina
syn. *S. lanata*

- pinkish purple, white
- late spring to early summer
- 6–18 in. × 12 in.
- sun, part shade
- Z4–10

Lamb's ears. Turkey, Armenia, Iran. Dense rosettes of woolly, tongue-shaped, gray-green leaves to 4 in. long; spreads by runners to form silver foliar mats, 4–6 in. above the soil surface. Terminal spikes of tiny, purplish pink flowers rise 12 in. above the foliage. Some regard the flowers as a liability and remove them. Provide light afternoon shade where sun is intense; drought tolerant. Self-seeds prolifically and can be invasive in warm, semi-arid climates.

'Helene von Stein' ('Big Ears') is larger than the species, 0.5–1 ft. × 1–2 ft., with leaves to 8 in. long; rarely blooms.

Stachys monieri 'Hummelo'

'**Primrose Heron**' has furry, yellowish, pale green leaves.

'**Striped Phantom**' has leaves to 8 in. long, silvery gray with irregular creamy patches in the center. Rarely flowers.

Stachys discolor
syn. *S. nivea*
- yellow, white
- summer
- 18 in. high and wide
- sun
- Z5–9

Caucasus. Basal rosettes of crimp-edged, oblong-lanceolate, wrinkled leaves, 1–1.75 in., dark green above, white felted underneath. Whorls of hooded, pale yellow to white flowers.

Stachys macrantha
syn. *S. grandiflora, Betonica grandiflora*
- pinkish purple
- late spring to early summer
- 1–2 ft. × 1–1.5 ft.
- sun
- Z4–8

Big betony. Caucasus, Turkey, Iran. Basal clumps of dark green, 3.5-in., heart-shaped leaves with hairy, wrinkled surfaces and scalloped margins. Vibrant pinkish purple, 1-in. flowers in two to three whorls per stem. Spreads to make a dense groundcover; floral display is especially striking when massed. Provide light afternoon shade in hot climates.

'**Superba**' is much more floriferous. May reach 27 in. × 28 in.

Stachys monieri 'Hummelo'
- lavender
- early to midsummer
- 18–20 in. × 18 in.
- sun, part shade
- Z4–8

Kurdistan Province. Chiefly available in the nursery trade as this cultivar. Forms large, lush mounded clumps of long, narrow, wrinkled green leaves. Dense spikes of lavender-purple flowers top leafless stems. An extravagant bloomer with excellent foliage, perfect for containers, or at the front of borders. Rated best in Chicago Botanic Garden trial of 22 *Stachys* selections.

Stachys officinalis
syn. *S. betonica, Betonica officinalis*

- purple
- late spring to early summer
- 1.5–2 ft. × 1–1.5 ft.
- sun
- Z4–8

Betony, bishop's wort. Europe, Asia. Herb formerly used widely by healers, regarded as a remedy for everything from snakebite to migraines, as well as for protection against sorcery. Basal clumps of ovate to oblong, wrinkled and scallop-edged, dark green leaves to 5 in. long. Abundant reddish purple flowers, to 0.5 in. long, carried on erect stems, 10–12 in. above the foliage. Spreads to create a dense groundcover. *Stachys maxima*, sometimes found in catalogs, is similar to this species.

'Alba' has white flowers.

'Pink Cotton Candy', discovered by Richard Hawke, Chicago BG, is similar to 'Hummelo' but with soft cotton candy–pink flowers. 24 in. × 16–20 in.

'Rosea' has pink flowers.

Stanleya
Brassicaceae
prince's plume

Just a single member of this genus is in cultivation, but it does indeed have a tall, princely stature, holding its plume-like racemes of flowers proudly erect. Similar in appearance to Jacob's spear, prince's plume is a North American native. It offers an exotic flamboyance, and is especially dramatic when massed among boulders as it is often found in the wild.

This plant does best in semi-desert conditions found on our western plains. In the garden, soil should be lean and alkaline, preferably not clayey; mulch with gravel or lime chips. Prince's plume is very deep rooted, a natural adaptation to habitats short on water. Resists rabbits, but not deer browsing. Insect pollinated; attracts birds and butterflies.

Start seeds in containers to avoid damaging roots at planting time.

Stachys byzantina 'Helene von Stein'

Stanleya pinnata

Stanleya pinnata
- yellow
- summer
- 2–5 ft. × 1.5 ft.
- sun
- Z4–10

Prince's plume, desert prince's plume. From dry open plains, foothills, and prairies of South Dakota to Oregon, and south to New Mexico and Texas. Several vertical stems, woody at the base, branching in the lower part and sometimes waxy, rise to about 5 ft. Alternate, somewhat fleshy, long-petioled, gray leaves to 6 in. long; the lower ones are pinnately divided into narrow lobes. Elongating, plume-like racemes of bright yellow, 1-in., cruciform flowers with antenna-like, exserted stamens bloom for several weeks. The flowers open from the bottom; conspicuous, though slender, pod-like seed capsules (siliques) 1.5–3 in. long follow. Spent flower stems persist for a year or more.

Stokesia
Asteraceae
Stokes' aster, cornflower aster

For duration of bloom, it's hard to beat Stokes' aster. The flowers resemble those of annual China asters or bigger, bolder bachelor's buttons. As a native of the southeastern United States, however, this plant tolerates high heat and humidity well and typically blooms from late spring into fall.

Stokesias prefer a spot with full sun and fertile, well-drained, moist soil. Winter wet is lethal, but short periods of drought are acceptable. Divide plants every three to four years to maintain vigor, and extend bloom time with routine deadheading. Mulch with evergreen boughs where winters are cold. Excellent as cut flowers, the stems are sturdy and the daisy heads last well in water. Attracts butterflies. Stokes' asters are suitable for the front to midsection of beds and borders, in cottage gardens, in wildlife and native gardens, and also mix well with annuals, summer bulbs, and low shrubs. Seldom bothered by diseases or pests, including rabbits and deer.

Start seed in containers in fall for spring planting. Increase cultivars vegetatively, by root cuttings in late winter, or divide in spring.

Stokesia laevis
syn. *S. cynara*
- lavender-blue, white
- early summer to fall
- 12–24 in. × 14 in.
- sun, part shade
- Z4–9, HT

Stokes' aster, cornflower aster. South Carolina to Louisiana. Clumps of stiff, branching stems, upright or decumbent, rise from rosettes of oblong leaves (evergreen in mild climates) to 8 in. long. Stems clothed with coarse, alternate leaves terminate in shaggy, daisy-like flowerheads with five-lobed, strap-shaped ray florets surrounding small inner disk florets.

'Blue Danube' blooms abundantly for three months. 2- to 3-in.-wide, lavender-blue flowers, with white disks. 18 in. Z5–9.

'Color Wheel' produces 3-in.-wide flowers, white at first, turning lilac, then darkening to blue-purple. 18–24 in. Z4–8.

'Klaus Jelitto' has 4-in., powder-blue flowers. Great vigor. Named for Klaus Jelitto, founder of Jelitto Seeds. 14–18 in. Z5.

'Mary Gregory' has pale yellow flowers that contrast well with the dark foliage. 18–24 in. Z4–8.

'Purple Parasols'. The light blue flowers of this hybrid mature to deep purple-violet. 14 in. Z5–9.

'Silver Moon' is creamy white. 12–18 in. Z5–9.

Strobilanthes
Acanthaceae
Persian shield

Useful in late-season gardens as a contrast to the predominant colors of fall, strobilanthes is grown for its cone-shaped spikes of brilliant purple, hooded, two-lipped, five-lobed flowers, 1–2 in. in length. Foliage is undistinguished but is seldom attacked by pests and diseases; deer and rabbit tolerant.

Provide a sunny or partly sunny spot, with fertile, well-drained soil. Water freely during dry spells. Cut back as necessary; pinch for bushy, compact growth. Mulch in late fall in cold winter zones.

Although not strictly within the purview of this book, the tender, 4- to 5-ft.-tall shrub *Strobilanthes dyerianaus* deserves a mention. Widely used as a summer accent plant in containers, and beds and borders, it has long-stemmed, elliptic leaves, 6–8 in. long, that are dark purple overlaid with metallic

Stokesia laevis 'Blue Danube'

Strobilanthes dyerianus

silver; striking in combination with summer-blooming annuals and tender perennials. Z11–12.

Start strobilanthes from seed, or take spring basal or softwood cuttings.

Strobilanthes atropurpureus

- blue-purple
- late summer to fall
- 4–5 ft. × 2 ft.
- sun, part shade
- Z5–9

Hardy Persian shield, deep-blue curved bells. Northern India, Kashmir. Large, erect, clumps of branching, leafy stems. Long-petioled pairs of ovate, 3- to 4-in. coarsely toothed leaves are conspicuously veined. Tubular, purple or indigo flowers, with deeply five-cleft calyces, arranged in loose, many-flowered spikes; the arched, 1.25-in. corollas have five spreading lobes. Drought tolerant.

Strobilanthes penstemonoides var. dalhousieana

- lavender
- early to late summer
- 3–4 ft. × 3 ft.
- part shade, shade
- Z8–11

High forests of the Himalayan region. Mainly overlooked by the horticultural public, although reputedly easy to grow, this evergreen, multi-stemmed perennial quickly reaches 4–5 ft. across, rooting at the nodes of prostrate stems. Dense and bushy, with lustrous, tapering, 5-in., conspicuously veined leaves. Penstemon-like, lavender-blue flowers flare at the mouth, 1–1.5 in. long. Water routinely to prolong bloom. Uncommon in the nursery trade; sometimes available at Plant Society sales.

Stylophorum
Papaveraceae
celandine poppy

Of three species of celandine poppies, only the native *Stylophorum dipyllum* is cultivated. It is valuable for its late-spring flowers, after the early bloomers and while most summer perennials are still finding their feet. In shaded beds and woodlands it combines well with bleeding hearts, foamflowers, lungworts, and perennial forget-me-nots.

Provide moderately fertile, humus-rich soil; celandine poppies do not care to dry out, and become summer dormant during drought. Self-seeds freely; will become weedy if not controlled. Deer and rabbit resistant due to the typical toxic yellow sap of poppies. Probably pollinated by bees and other insects; seeds are distributed by ants.

Propagate from seed, or divide established clumps in spring.

Stylophorum diphyllum

Stylophorum diphyllum
- yellow
- early summer
- 10–12 in. × 12 in.
- part shade, shade
- Z4–8

Celandine poppy, flaming poppy, wood poppy.
Native to woodlands of the eastern United States.
Terminal umbels of nodding, furry buds open
to showy, yellow flowers, 1–2 in. across. Elegant
rosettes of deeply cut, velvety leaves; each of the
five to seven lobes is oval, scalloped along the
edges, and rimmed with teeth.

Symphyotrichum
syn. *Aster*
Asteraceae
aster

This genus includes several species formerly listed
as asters, but based on genetic studies, now classified separately. This move, of course, has not
changed these plants' cultural needs or aesthetic
potential.

While some species may be invasive, several others serve as stalwarts in summer and fall displays
in meadow and prairie plantings, and as sources
of cut flowers. The taller, fall-blooming types: New
England (*Symphyotrichum novae-angliae*) and
New York asters (*S. novi-belgii*), partner well with

Symphyotrichum novae-angliae 'Alma Potschke'

ornamental grasses; purple-flowered cultivars provide an especially effective complement to switch
grass cultivars such as 'Shenandoah' whose foliage becomes reddish in autumn. Symphyotrichums
offer especially fine blues—dropping one of these
into the middle of a sea of yellow flowers, or swamp
sunflowers, for example, really energizes such a
display.

Similar to asters, symphyotrichums bear composite, daisy-like flowerheads, typically in great
abundance, in shades of blue, purple, white, and
pink. The centers of each flowerhead are usually
yellow. As the common name Michaelmas daisy
(which correctly refers to New York asters but is
often applied more broadly) indicates, symphyotrichums tend to bloom late in the growing season—
the feast of St. Michael falls on 29 September, when
asters are in bloom in many regions, often persist-
ing until the arrival of a killing frost.

Symphyotrichums are susceptible to powdery

mildew and rust; search out resistant cultivars. Aphids, leafhoppers, and spider mites disfigure the plants, and serve as a source of infection for garden neighbors. Deer seldom browse asters; butterflies flock to the flowers.

Divide mature clumps in spring or fall, or take softwood stem cuttings in late spring. Start seed indoors in late winter.

Symphyotrichum dumosum

syn. *Aster dumosus*
- pale violet
- late summer to early fall
- 3–4 ft. × 1–3 ft.
- sun, part shade
- Z3–8

Rice button aster. Native throughout the eastern United States. Naturally bushy with 3-in., lanceolate leaves; unlike many asters, remains clothed with foliage to the ground throughout the growing season. Large clusters of small flowerheads congregate at the branch tips; pinch young shoots in spring to encourage more prolific flowering. Disease and pest resistant.

'Wood's Light Blue' is compact with light blue flowers. Superior rust and mildew resistance. 12–14 in.

'Wood's Pink' is similar with clear pink flowers. 12–16 in.

'Wood's Purple' has blue-violet to purple flowers. 12–18 in.

Symphyotrichum ericoides

syn. *Aster ericoides*
- white
- late summer to fall
- 1–3 ft. × 1–1.5 ft.
- sun
- Z3–10

Heath aster. Native to open, dryish sites throughout eastern and central North America. Needle-like foliage; yellow-centered, 0.5-in., white flowers are borne in profuse sprays that persist well into autumn. Disease and pest resistant; tolerates dry soils and drought; performs well in ordinary garden conditions.

'Blue Star' produces a multitude of dark blue, starry flowers. 3 ft.

'Esther' has pink-tinged, white flowers. 18–24 in.

'Snow Flurry' is prostrate, 6–8 in. tall and to 2 ft. wide. Valued as a dense groundcover with abundant white bloom. Excellent for containers.

Symphyotrichum laeve

syn. *Aster laevis*
- purple
- fall
- 2–4 ft. × 1–2 ft.
- sun
- Z3–8

Smooth aster. A native of the northeastern United States that offers disease and pest resistance, and tolerance for droughty, poor soils. Smooth green, mostly toothed, 5-in. leaves clothe unbranched

Symphyotrichum dumosum 'Wood's Pink'

stems topped with loose, 6-in.-wide clusters of yellow-centered, 0.75- to 1.25-in., violet-blue or purple flowerheads. Striking with goldenrods.

'**Bluebird**' has violet-blue flowers

Symphyotrichum lateriflorum

syn. *Aster lateriflorus, A. diffusus*

- white
- fall
- 2–3 ft. × 1 ft.
- sun, part shade
- Z3–9

Calico aster. Another disease- and pest-resistant species native to eastern North America. Clumps of branching stems clothed with lance-shaped leaves to 5 in. long, toothed or entire along the edges; 0.3-in., white flowers, with yellow centers that age to maroon.

'**Horizontalis**' (var. *horizontalis*) has horizontal branched stems, and carries tiny but abundant pinkish brown–eyed white flowers. Very bushy, with dark foliage. Full sun. 2 ft. tall.

'**Lady in Black**' makes mounds of deep purplish leaves that become blanketed with red-centered, white flowers. Foliage color is best in sites with full sun.

Symphyotrichum novae-angliae

syn. *Aster novae-angliae*

- purple
- late summer to fall
- 3–6 ft. × 2–3 ft.
- sun
- Z4–8

New England aster. Eastern United States. Robust and easily grown in average, well-drained but moist soils. Hairy, lance-shaped leaves to 4 in. long clasp the hairy stems. Generous crops of 1.5-in., yellow-centered, purple flowers. Good air circulation and full sun restrain susceptibility to mildew. Pinch back stem tips several times before midsummer to encourage compact growth and limit the need for staking. Excellent cut flowers; wear gloves to protect from the hairy stems. Cultivars abound; this is a sampling:

'**Alma Potschke**' ('Andenkan an Alma Potschke') has 1- to 2-in., bright magenta-pink flowerheads; disease-resistant foliage. Early. 4 ft.

'**Harrington's Pink**' bears 1.5-in., clear pink heads. Mildew- and rust-resistant foliage. 3–5 ft.

'**Hella Lacy**'. Plants are smothered with 2-in.-wide, blue-violet daisies. 3–4 ft. Named for garden writer Allen Lacy's wife, Hella.

Symphyotrichum oblongifolium 'October Skies'

'Purple Dome' has vibrant deep purple flowers with yellow centers. Foliage resists mildew and rust. Compact at 18–24 in.

'Wedding Lace' has pure white flowers; outstanding resistance to rust. 3–4 ft.

Symphyotrichum novi-belgii

syn. *Aster novi-belgii*
- blue, purple
- late summer to early fall
- 2–4 ft. × 3 ft.
- sun
- Z4–8

New York aster. Native to northeastern North America. Similar in habit and bloom to the New England asters but less leggy; stem-clasping leaves are smooth. Not as full flowered as the preceding species, and not as good for cutting. Provide good air circulation and consistent soil moisture to reduce vulnerability to diseases. Tall (4 ft. or more), medium (under 4 ft.), and dwarf (up to 15 in.) cultivars are available. Medium and dwarf plants are most useful, unless space is unlimited. British breeders have developed a host of cultivars offering diverse colors, as well as compact plants that need no staking. Tall cultivars are not suitable for most gardens unless they are pinched when young and are well supported.

'Professor Anton Kippenburg' has semi-double, lavender-blue flowerheads; mildew-resistant foliage. Compact. 12–18 in. tall.

'Raspberry Swirl' has a rounded form; abundant raspberry-pink flowers; mildew resistant. Compact. 18–24 in.

'Royal Opal' sports light blue flowerheads; mildew and insect resistant. 16 in. high and wide.

'Tiny Tot' is a dwarf with bright purple flowers; mildew resistant. 4–8 in.

'Winston Churchill' has bright red daisies, good for cutting. Tolerates heat and humidity. 2–3 ft. tall.

Symphyotrichum oblongifolium

syn. *Aster oblongifolius*
- blue, purple
- late summer to fall
- 1–3 ft. high and wide
- sun
- Z3–8

Aromatic aster. Native from the eastern seaboard of North America into the Rocky Mountains. This adaptable, compact, bushy plant tolerates numerous challenges including clay, rocky soils, and drought. Blue-green, 4-in., oblong leaves are aromatic; yellow-centered, violet-blue, 1-in. flowerheads. An outstanding cut flower. Plant where passersby will brush against foliage and release the minty fragrance.

'October Skies' has deep sky-blue flowers. Introduced by Primrose Path Nursery. 1.5–2 ft. high and wide.

'Raydon's Favorite' bears abundant 1.25-in., lavender flowerheads on stiff, hairy stems. Late blooming. 3 ft. × 4 ft.

Symphytum

Boraginaceae
comfrey

In addition to the contribution that their flowers and foliage furnish to perennial displays, comfreys have a long history as medicinal plants. If ingested long term in large doses, the plant can cause liver damage, but it is used safely as an ingredient of salves applied externally for healing sprains and broken bones. Comfreys can heal the garden as well: their penetrating roots draw minerals from deep within the soil, making this plant a source of rich composts and green manures. The fleshy, rhizomatous roots spread aggressively, especially in rich soils.

Somewhat coarse and usually covered with bristly hairs, comfreys have long-stalked, mostly basal, ovate-lanceolate to oval leaves with deep-set veins that give them a crinkled surface. Nodding, tubular flowers, in white, pink, yellow, or blue are borne in coiled cymes like those of related Virginia bluebells.

Where sun is not intense, comfreys flourish in sun to full shade; supply at least midday shade in regions with strong sun. Successful in dry shade; generally drought tolerant once established. Tolerates clay soils; avoid overly fertile soils to control invasive tendencies. Deadhead after first bloom to extend flowering time. Gloves recommended—comfrey's stiff hairs irritate sensitive skins. Seldom browsed by deer or rabbits, although pigs, poultry, and sheep like the fresh, high-protein foliage. Slugs and snails attack emerging leaves.

Symphytum ×*uplandicum* 'Axminster Gold'

Common comfrey is valuable in herb gardens where it provides height among lower herbs. Other species are valuable in open woodlands, at the base of hedges, in cottage gardens, or in shaded beds and borders.

Increase by division in spring, take root cuttings in winter, or start from seed in spring or fall.

Symphytum ibericum

syn. *S. grandiflorum* of gardens, *Pulmonaria lutea* hort.

- white, yellow
- late spring to early summer
- 12–18 in. × 18–24 in.
- sun, part shade, shade
- Z4–8

Comfrey, large-flowered comfrey. Turkey, Caucasus. Young, hairy, unbranched flower stems are upright with short, bristly foliage; non-blooming stems, clothed with 9- to 10-in. leaves, become decumbent. Red flower buds open to 0.5-in., cream or light yellow flowers. Excellent in dry shade at the base of hedges.

'Goldsmith' ('Jubilee'; syn. *Symphytum grandiflorum* 'Variegatum', *S. grandiflorum* 'Jubilee') has hairy, gold-rimmed and -splashed leaves; red flower buds open to 0.5 in. long, white-and-blue flowers. 12 in. Z5.

'Variegatum' has foliage marked with yellow and cream.

Symphytum officinale

- purple-violet, pink, cream
- late spring to early summer
- 4–5 ft. × 4 ft.
- sun, part shade
- Z3–9

Common comfrey, knitbone, boneset. Europe, western Asia. Coarse, but quite showy when in bloom. Whole plant covered with hairs; large, ovate lower leaves to 8 in., with the smaller, upper and middle ones leaning along the winged stems. Forked clusters of nodding, 0.75-in. flowers of purple-violet, pink, or less often cream. May need staking. Suitable for meadows, herb gardens, and informal parts of the garden.

Symphytum ×rubrum

syn. *S. officinale × S. grandiflorum*

- red
- early to midsummer
- 15–18 in. × 15 in.
- sun, part shade, shade
- Z3–8

Red comfrey. Of garden origin. Not as coarse and bristly as other comfreys. Decumbent, with dark green foliage. Drooping terminal cymes of deep crimson, 0.5 in., tubular flowers on 18-in. stems. Fine groundcover especially in dry shade; spreads slowly. Cut back after flowering. Shade from intense sun.

Symphytum ×uplandicum

- pink, purple
- late spring to late summer
- 3–4 ft. × 2–3 ft.
- sun, part shade
- Z4–8

Russian comfrey. Of garden origin (*Symphytum asperum × S. officinale*) but occurs naturally on disturbed soil in the Caucasus Mountains. Large basal leaves are 8–10 in. long and decumbent, upper ones 2–3 in. on many-branched, bristly stems that bear scorpioid cymes of 1-in., pink to purple flowers in upper leaf axils. Lovely in cottage gardens. Stake if necessary.

'Axminster Gold' has appealing green leaves banded with wide cream margins. Cut back after bloom. Moist to damp soil.

'Variegatum' has distinctive grayish green leaves edged with irregular white bands. Decorative in herb and vegetable gardens.

Other Notable Cultivars

'Hidcote Blue' is vigorous with pale blue flowers in mid- to late spring. Spreads enthusiastically. 18 in. Z4–7.

'Hidcote Pink' ('Roseum') has pink-and-white flowers. Z5–7.

Tanacetum

syn. *Balsamita, Pyrethrum*
Asteraceae
tansy

Many genera formerly classified with *Chrysanthemum* have been integrated into *Tanacetum*; nursery catalogues may list these plants under the old names or new; both are included with their descriptions here.

Tansy foliage is aromatic, sometimes strongly so. For this reason, deer usually avoid it, but rabbits unfortunately are undeterred. The alternate, finely dissected leaves give the plants a fern-like look. Blooms are grouped into flat-topped clusters; flowerheads may be daisy like with decorative ray flowers surrounding a central yellow disk, or lack rays and appear like yellow buttons.

Grow tansies in full sun, in light, well-drained soil. They thrive in coastal gardens but inland should be sheltered from strong drying winds. Wet feet in winter are lethal. Low-growing species are suitable for rock gardens, and as edgings for beds and borders. Showier, taller species can grace beds and borders, or cutting and cottage gardens. They may need staking. Divide in spring every three to four years to maintain vigor. Pests and diseases are seldom troublesome, but be alert for red spider mites in hot, droughty periods. Gloves are recommended when working around tansies; leaf contact may irritate the skin.

Sow seed in fall for spring planting, or divide established clumps. Semi-ripe cuttings taken in summer root readily.

Tanacetum parthenium

Tanacetum coccineum

syn. *Chrysanthemum coccineum, Pyrethrum coccineum, P. roseum*

- pink, red, white
- early summer
- 18–30 in. × 15–18 in.
- sun
- Z3–7

Painted daisy, pyrethrum, Persian insect flower. Iran, Caucasus. This cool-season, short-lived perennial produces tufted clumps of finely dissected, bright green leaves to 3–10 in. long, smaller above. Daisy-like, 2- to 3-in. blooms, each with a large, central yellow disk, rise on slender, wiry, usually unbranched stems. Flower forms include singles, doubles, and anemone centered, in a range of pinks, reds, and white. They are usually offered as seed mixes in mixed colors; to grow specific colors, look for plants in bloom in local nurseries. Remove spent flowers and cut stems to the ground to encourage rebloom. Best in cooler-summer climates; protect from intense sun in zone 7. Companion plants such as Shasta daisies and bearded iris can provide support for the painted daisies' rather weak stems. Excellent as cut flowers. Attracts hummingbirds and butterflies. This plant is the source of the natural insecticide "pyrethrin."

'Crimson Giant' has single, vivid cerise blooms. 3 ft. Z3–7.

Double Market is a mixed (pink, rose, red, and white) strain of large, double-flowered blooms. 18–24 in. Z3–9.

'Duro' has very large, purplish red blooms. 32 in. Z3–7.

'James Kelway' has bright, almost crimson-red flowerheads. 18–20 in. Z3–7.

Robinson's Mix includes red, deep and pale pinks, and white-flowered daisies. 24–30 in. Z3–9.

Tanacetum parthenium

syn. *Chrysanthemum parthenium, Matricaria parthenium, Pyrethrum parthenium*

- white
- early to midsummer
- 15–18 in. × 12 in.
- sun
- Z4–9

Feverfew. Caucasus, Europe. Tidy, well-branched mounds of strongly aromatic, ferny foliage. Smooth above and hairy beneath, the finely cut leaves are bright green, about 3 in. long. Small flowerheads have bright yellow disks and short, blunt, white ray flowers; these are grouped into flat-topped clusters. Self-seeds freely. Appropriate for herb gardens; the leaves are valued for homeopathic remedies. Good fillers in flower arrangements. Short lived; often treated as annuals.

'Aureum' (golden feverfew, golden feather) makes low bushes of divided, chartreuse foliage. Single, white daisy flowerheads. 12–18 in. Z3–9.

'Golden Ball' produces low mounds of fragrant, deep green leaves; double yellow button flowers. 12–18 in. Z3–9.

Tanacetum argenteum

syn. *Achillea argentea*

- white
- summer
- 6–8 in. × 12 in.
- sun
- Z5–7

Mediterranean. This beautiful, low, evergreen perennial develops mats of finely cut, silver foliage on much-branched, white-woolly stems. The leaves, like silver filigree, grow to 3 in. long with five to nine pairs of dissected leaflets. The white daisy flowerheads are relatively insignificant. Old plants become woody at the base. Pairs well with creeping thyme, 'Kent Beauty' oregano, and *Euphorbia myrsinites* planted between patio pavers and flagstones. They also mix well with colorful annuals, including trailing verbenas and calibrachoas.

'White Stars'. Compact mounds of deep green leaves topped with small, double, white-and-yellow flowerheads. 8–12 in. Z3–9.

Tanacetum vulgare
syn. *Chrysanthemum vulgare*
- yellow
- summer
- 3–6 ft. × 3 ft.
- sun
- Z4–8

Common tansy, golden buttons. Europe. Vigorous and clump forming with fibrous, upright stems clothed with bright green, ferny foliage. Finely dissected and pinnately lobed, the leaves are 7–8 in. long below, smaller above. Flat, terminal heads are crowded with rayless, bright yellow, 0.3- to 0.5-in. button flowers. Mainly for herb gardens, but foliage is interesting contrasted with daylilies, peonies, and Oriental poppies in ornamental borders.

'Crispum' (curly tansy) is the most decorative with tightly crisped, bright green foliage; yellow button flowerheads. 3 ft.

'Isla Gold' is grown for its aromatic, bright golden, dissected leaves. Makes companion plants appear to glow. 2–3 ft.

Telekia
Asteraceae
telekia

This sunny, handsome perennial is another of the sunflower-like species that provide so much summertime color. Telekias are also noted for their enormous leaves, which provide sufficient shade to almost entirely suppress weeds. However, after their long-blooming, spidery yellow flowers are spent, the plants become really shabby; cut them back to the base and fresh new leaves emerge in a few weeks.

Best in sunny places with sweet, moist soil of average fertility, where the plants will be protected from strong winds. Good in informal plantings in damp meadows and wild gardens, and at stream sides, but too coarse for most ornamental beds. Allow some seedheads to develop for seed-eating birds, such as gold- and other finches. Effective at the back of the border among shrubs. The strong-smelling foliage is not bothered by deer, rabbits, or even slugs.

Propagate from fresh seed as soon as it ripens. Divide established clumps in spring.

Telekia speciosa
syn. *Buphthalmum speciosum*
- yellow
- mid- to late summer
- 3–6 ft. × 3 ft.
- sun, part shade
- Z4–8

Telekia, heart-leaved oxeye daisy. Native at streamsides and in moist woodlands from Southern Europe into Asia and Russia. Rhizomatous roots

Telekia speciosa

produce coarse, bold clumps of upright, fibrous stems, branched at the top, bearing hairy, aromatic foliage rimmed with double rows of teeth. The petioled, heart-shaped basal leaves are imposing to 14 in. long and 10 in. across; upper stem leaves are smaller and sessile, almost clasping. Loose, branching sprays of solitary, 2- to 4 in.-wide, slightly ragged, yellow daisies bloom on long stems; yellow rays are slender and surround a flattish, yellow-orange mass of disk flowers. Self-seeds unless deadheaded. Long blooming and easy. May become invasive.

Tellima
Saxifragaceae
fringe cups

A single-species genus, *Tellima* is a native of the western United States and closely related to *Tiarella* and *Heuchera*. It is lovely as an evergreen groundcover, massed in light coniferous or deciduous woodlands, or as a foil for more colorful plants in shaded beds. The tall spikes of small, urn-shaped flowers attract butterflies and birds, especially hummingbirds, making it appropriate for wildlife gardens. It self-seeds freely in mild regions, but although classified as an invasive species in parts of western Europe, it has not proved so to date in North America.

Tolerant of poor drainage and shaded sites on the north side of buildings, fringe cups is just as happy in well-drained but moist soils in only part shade. It doesn't tolerate full sun or drought, and is poorly suited to hotter climates. Deer and rabbits do not molest fringe cups; pests and diseases are seldom significant, except for slugs.

Divide in spring, or sow seed as soon as it ripens.

Tellima grandiflora
syn. *T. breviflora, T. odorata*

- white, pink
- late spring to early summer

- 12–24 in. × 12–18 in.
- part shade, shade
- Z4–8

Fringe cup, false alumroot. Native to moist woods and rocky places of the western United States from Alaska to California. From horizontal, somewhat woody rootstocks, rise 18-in. mounds of softly hairy foliage; this consists of long-petioled, heart-shaped to kidney-shaped, five to seven lobed, green leaves accented with reddish veins, and scalloped along the edge. Upright and wiry, leafless flower stems rise well above the foliage mass and terminate in long spikes of pinkish green or white, starry flowers. Close inspection reveals that each 0.25-in. flower has five lightly fringed, reflexed petals. Long blooming.

'Forest Frost' has deep green leaves overlaid with silver, turning pinkish wine color in cold weather; flowers are chartreuse. 20 in.

'Rubra' ('Purpurea') has reddish maroon fall and winter foliage; red flushed in summer. Pink-flushed flowers. 18 in.

Teucrium
Lamiaceae
germander

In times past this herb was widely prescribed by physicians and healers as a remedy for everything from arthritis to whooping cough, but more recently it has been implicated as a cause of liver damage, hepatitis, and even death. There is no doubt, however, about its beneficial effects in perennial gardens.

These woody-based, often evergreen, perennials offer good-looking foliage and a tolerance for pruning that makes them handsome and unusual materials for compact, decorative hedges. Aside from their aromatic, broadleaved foliage, germanders also offer terminal spikes or clusters of colorful flowers, making them far more attractive than the boxwoods or dwarf hollies commonly used for that purpose. Lower-growing species make elegant groundcovers. Individual flowers are tubular and two lipped, typical of the mint family. They prefer average, dry to moderately moist, well-drained soils, but tolerate poor soils well and are drought tolerant. Deer and rabbit resistant.

Sow fresh seed in a cold frame or other protected location, or increase by softwood cuttings.

Teucrium aroanium
- purple
- late spring to early summer

- 3 in. × 3–9 in.
- sun
- Z7–10

Germander. Greece. This low-growing evergreen subshrub has stoloniferous trailing stems. Silver-green leaves are ovate to oblong, to 0.75 in. long.

Teucrium chamaedrys

Light purple, 0.75-in. flowers cluster in the leaf axils. Prefers gritty soil. Excellent as a groundcover for rock or herb gardens. No serious pests or diseases.

Teucrium chamaedrys
- pink, purple
- late spring to early summer
- 9–12 in. × 12–24 in.
- sun
- Z5–9

Wall germander. Europe, Middle East. Clump forming with woody base and ascending stems; the evergreen, aromatic leaves are shaped like miniature oak leaves. Pink to purple, occasionally white flowers are carried in terminal clusters. Pinch or clip back stems after flowering to encourage bushiness. Susceptible to mildew, leaf spot, rust, and mites, but damage is rarely serious.

Teucrium hircanium
- magenta
- late summer to fall
- 18 in. × 28 in.
- sun, part shade
- Z5–8

Caucasian germander, wood sage, purple tails. Western Asia, Caucasus Mountains. Spreads slowly by rhizomes, with loose clumps of aromatic, fuzzy, sage-like leaves; tapering 6- to 8-in. spikes of magenta to purplish flowers. Good for containers, borders, and rock gardens.

'Paradise Delight' has deep purple-red flowers; more compact, branched habit than the species.

Thalictrum
Ranunculaceae
meadow rue

"Two for one" is as appealing to gardeners as to anyone else, and meadow rues fill the bill by providing billowing masses of small but attractive flowers, and later contributing delicate, textural foliage that serves as foils for later-blooming neighbors. Thalictrums resist deer and rabbit browsing, and are generally free of other pests and most diseases; occasionally they fall prey to powdery mildew or rust.

Dainty textured leaves, recalling those of columbines or maidenhair ferns, are alternate, bipinnately compound, commonly glaucous, and blue-green in color. The flowers lack petals; in some the sepals that enclose the unopened buds are large and brightly colored, but several species have small sepals that drop when the flowers open. Visual appeal depends upon the long white, yellow, pink, or pale purple stamens. Although small, typically meadow rue flowers are borne in profusion.

In the wild, meadow rues usually inhabit damp or shady spots. In gardens, provide light, moisture-retaining, humus-rich, well-drained soil; they do not tolerate southern heat and humidity. Useful in borders, meadows, and wildflower gardens, meadow rues furnish attractive cut flowers and foliage. Native plant aficionados will appreciate the North American species for moist meadow and open woodland settings.

Propagate by seed, or divide in early spring.

Thalictrum aquilegifolium
- purple
- late spring to early summer
- 2–3 ft. high and wide
- sun, part shade
- Z5–8, HS

Europe to central Asia. "Aquilegifolium" means "columbine leaved," which accurately describes the basal clumps of blue-green foliage produced by this species. Fluffy, lilac stamens that pass for flowers are showy on male plants, less so on females; dense panicles are held on branching stems above the foliage.

'Thundercloud' has deep purple flower buds that open mauve.

Thalictrum rochbruneanum 'Lavender Mist'

Thalictrum delavayi

- lilac
- spring
- 3–5 ft. × 1.5–2 ft.
- sun, part shade
- Z4–7, HS

Western China, eastern Tibet. Dense clumps of purplish stems with lacy, medium green foliage. Large, airy, branching terminal sprays of tiny, lavender flowers with contrasting yellow stamens are carried above the leaves.

'Hewitt's Double' has pale purple, double flowers with yellow eyes.

Thalictrum dioicum

- white
- midspring
- 1–2 ft. high and wide
- sun, part shade
- Z4–7, HS

Quebec to North Dakota, south to Missouri and Georgia. Foliage is lacy and gray-green. Small, drooping flowers of greenish white, commonly with a purple tint, cluster in panicles. Provides early color for perennial borders, meadows, and wildflower gardens; foliage is a soft counterpoint for later bloomers.

Thalictrum flavum

- yellow
- early to midsummer
- 5–6 ft. × 1.5–2 ft.
- sun, part shade
- Z5–7

Yellow meadow rue. Europe. This species is the most tolerant of warm, humid summers. Lacy, green foliage and cloud-like sprays of tiny, lemon-yellow flowers. Tall and slender habit; may need staking.

subsp. *glaucum*. Flowers as for the species, but young foliage and stems are mauve, maturing to silvery blue-green.

'Illuminator' has showy chartreuse young leaves; flowers typical of species. Robust, somewhat larger than the species.

Thalictrum kiusianum

- lavender
- early summer
- 4–6 in. × 6–12 in.
- sun, part shade
- Z5–8, HS

Dwarf meadow rue. Japan. Slowly develops spreading mats of dainty, fern-like foliage, with a slightly bronze tint. Tiny lavender flowers are borne in abundance just above leaves. Ideal for troughs or rock gardens; beautiful interspersed with miniature hostas.

Thalictrum rochebruneanum

- reddish lilac
- mid- to late summer
- 4–6 ft. × 2–3 ft.
- sun, part shade
- Z4–7, HS

Japan. Slender clumps of lacy, blue-green, pinnately compound leaves. Airy 2- to 3-ft.-wide clusters of tiny, pendulous, lavender-purple flowers with yellow stamens rise above the foliage. Typically sturdy purple stems need no staking. Perfect foil for roses, striking when massed in open woodland, fine textural note for borders.

'Lavender Mist' appears to be identical with species.

Thermopsis
Fabaceae
false lupine

Close relatives of true lupines, these "false" ones provide wonderful vertical accents in beds and borders as spring moves into summer. They make fine companions for late-blooming spring bulbs such as *Camassia*, *Tritelia*, and ornamental onions. Long-lived perennials, false lupines are outstandingly drought tolerant, thanks to their deep taproots. False lupine leaves are compound, composed of three leaflets, silky hairy beneath, with a pair of

Thermopsis caroliniana

stipules at the nodes. Erect spires of canary-yellow pea flowers are mostly terminal; hairy, flat seedpods follow.

Full sun, or part shade in hot climates, is favored by false lupines, along with well-drained, deep, fertile soil. Resents division or otherwise disturbance. Staking is seldom necessary; basically easy care. Deadhead spent flower stems to their bases.

Mass false lupines in meadows and wild areas, or partner them with early summer perennials including blue star, globe thistles, and torch lilies. Blue-foliaged selections of ornamental grasses make good companions for false lupines in informal areas.

Resistant to both deer and rodents, and seldom troubled by pests or diseases.

Start from seed (fresh, if possible) in containers to avoid damaging the taproot at planting time; scarify or nick seed with a file, or soak overnight in warm water to facilitate germination.

Thermopsis caroliniana
syn. *T. villosa*

- yellow
- late spring to early summer
- 3–5 ft. × 2 ft.
- sun, part shade
- Z3–8, HT

Carolina lupine, Carolina bushpea. Native from North Carolina to Georgia. A yellow lupine that embraces the heat and humidity of southeastern

Thermopsis chinensis 'Sophia'

US summers—what a find! Its mostly unbranched, hollow, hairy stems are erect, clothed with trifoliate, gray-green leaves, silky haired beneath. Ovate leaflets are 2–3 in. long, with obvious leafy stipules. Dense, slender, 6- to 12-in., lupine-like racemes of sulfur-yellow pea flowers rise above the foliage mass; bloom lasts for one to two weeks. The attractive foliage remains good looking, and hairy seedpods develop over time; these are often removed, but their architectural structure is valuable in winter gardens, and as dried elements in floral arrangements. Provide part shade in hot regions. Mountain false lupine, *Thermopsis montana* (*T. rhombifolia*), native to the Rockies and south to New Mexico is a more or less a mountain edition of *T. caroliniana*. It differs in having shorter, less-crowded spires of flowers.

Thermopsis chinensis

- yellow
- late spring to early summer
- 18–30 in. × 24 in.
- sun
- Z3–8

Chinese false lupine, Chinese pea bush. Central and eastern China. Similar to other species, but more compact, and with gray-purple flower buds. Flowers are arranged in panicles on leafy stems.

'Sophia' is vigorous with early spikes of soft yellow pea flowers, and compound foliage all season. A North Creek introduction. 15–20 ft. Z5–8.

Thymus
Lamiaceae
thyme

These invaluable herbs are as handsome as they are savory, and are especially useful as foot-traffic-tolerant groundcovers; in fact, creeping thymes are sometimes used as a substitute for lawns. Mostly natives of the Mediterranean region, thymes thrive in poor, rocky, well-drained soils in sunny locations; they do particularly well when planted between flagstones and pavers in terraces or paths, or allowed to sprawl over stones in rock gardens.

Typical of the mint family, thymes have square stems (woody at the base), tubular, two-lipped edible flowers, and aromatic foliage, evergreen where winters are mild. Drought tolerant. No serious pests or diseases, but prone to root rot where drainage is poor; resists deer and rabbits. Attracts bees and butterflies. Shear stems periodically to encourage compact growth and refresh foliage.

Propagate by layering, division, and by stem cuttings taken with a heel. Growing from seed is possible but very slow.

Thymus ×citriodorus

- lilac pink
- summer
- 4–12 in. × 12 in.
- sun
- Z5–8

Lemon thyme. Of hybrid origin (*Thymus vulgaris ×*
T. pulegiodes). Evergreen, bushy, and woody at the
base, with very small ovate leaves, strongly fragrant
of lemon. Tiny flowers are tubular, in showy clusters at stem tips. A favorite of bees. A given for herb
gardens.

Thymus herba-barona

- pink, purple
- early to midsummer
- 3–6 in. × 9–12 in.
- sun
- Z4–8

Caraway thyme. Corsica and Sardinia. Creeping
with thin, prostrate stems supporting dense mats of
0.25-in., pointed, glossy dark green leaves, strongly
scented of caraway. Showy clusters of tiny, tubular,
deep pink or lavender-purple flowers. Naturalizes
on hospitable sites. Useful culinary herb, handsome
in containers, or as a low groundcover.

Thymus pseudolanuginosus

- pink
- early to midsummer
- 3 in. × 3–12 in.
- sun
- Z5–8

Woolly thyme. Europe. Creeping, with hairy stems
that support a mat of minute elliptical, gray leaves
with little fragrance. Tiny, pale pink flowers borne
sparsely in leaf axils.

'Hall's Variety' has soft, woolly foliage; lavender-
pink flowers.

Thymus praecox

- purple, white
- summer
- 3–6 in. high and wide
- sun
- Z5–8

Mother-of-thyme, creeping thyme. Southern, western, and central Europe. Creeping, low mats of tiny,
rounded, blue-green, aromatic leaves. Flowers are
borne in clusters.

subsp. *arcticus* is spreading, with dark green
leaves, and white, pink, or purple flowers. 2 in. × 24
in.

'Coccineus' has intense red flowers above a mat
of lustrous foliage.

Thymus praecox **subsp.** *articus*

Thymus serpyllum

- pink
- early to midsummer
- 3 in. × 3–12 in.
- sun
- Z4–8

Wild thyme. Northern Europe. Mat forming, with numerous stems bearing 0.25-in., rounded, glossy blue-green, aromatic leaves. Showy clusters of tiny, deep pink flowers. Useful as a groundcover; naturalizes in hospitable conditions.

'Aureus' has golden leaves.

'Elfin' is dwarf with neat, green foliage; purple flowers. 1–2 in. × 4–8 in.

'Goldstream' has yellow-and-green variegated foliage; lilac flowers.

'Lemon Frost' (syn. *Thymus ×citriodurus* 'Lemon Frost') is fast growing with lemon-scented foliage; white flowers. 3 in. × 18 in.

'Snowdrift' is white flowered.

Thymus vulgaris

- purple
- late spring to early summer
- 6–12 in. high and wide
- sun
- Z5–9

English thyme. Southern Europe. Culinary herb with some ornamental selections. Mounds of tiny, pointed, aromatic, gray-green leaves, rolled under at the margins. Whorls of minute flowers at stem ends.

'Argenteus' has green-and-silver variegated leaves.

'Orange Balsam' has orange-scented, elliptic to narrowly ovate, gray-green leaves; pink flowers in summer. 6–12 in. high and wide. Z5–8.

Tiarella
Saxifragaceae
foamflower

This group of extraordinary woodlanders offers outstandingly handsome foliage, ethereal bloom, and two patterns of growth—spreading and clump forming—to satisfy a diversity of needs. Most are natives of North America and require little care if given a shady site with moist, organic-rich soil. Depending on the species and type, the leaves are divided into three to nine lobes, rounded like columbine or lobed like a red maple; they are often highlighted with black or red patterning, and the foliage commonly takes on a reddish cast during cool weather. Borne in airy racemes in spring, the tiny flowers are white with very long stamens, creating the frothy effect referred to in the plants' common name.

Closely related to heucheras, with which they have been interbred to create so-called ×*Heucherella*. In recent years, breeders have also crossed different species to create a host of fine new hybrids. Whereas the species bloom for just three to six

Tiarella hybrid 'Sugar and Spice'

weeks, some hybrids may remain in flower for months. The spreading species provide shade-loving, handsome and dependable groundcovers; the clump formers provide valuable foliage interest and texture to shady borders and woodland displays.

No serious pest or disease problems, deer resistant; wet soil in winter is usually fatal. Divide hybrids in spring; sow seed of species and overwinter outdoors with protection.

Tiarella cordifolia

- white, pink
- mid- to late spring
- 9–12 in. × 12–24 in.
- part shade, shade
- Z4–9

Heartleaf foamflower. Nova Scotia and Ontario to Georgia and Mississippi, west to Minnesota. Spreads rapidly by stolons to form clumps to 2 ft. wide. Green, medium glossy, three- to five-lobed, heart-shaped leaves to 4 in. wide, red along the veins. Evergreen where winters are mild, commonly becoming reddish bronze in cold weather. Racemes of white or light pink flowers bloom for six weeks in spring on mostly leafless stems above the foliage.

Tiarella trifoliata subsp. unifoliata

syn. *T. trifoliata* var. *unifoliata*
- white
- early summer
- 4–20 in. × 8–24 in.
- part shade, shade
- Z6–10

Sugar scoop. Damp coniferous forests, Alaska south through California, east to Montana and Idaho. Broadly heart-shaped, three- to five-lobed, scallop-edged leaves, 2–4 in. wide. Small, white, starry flowers gather in spikes, followed by little, scoop-shaped pods. Removing spent flower stalks may prompt rebloom. Moderately moist, well-drained soil; irrigate every 10 to 14 days in dry weather during growing season.

Tiarella wherryi

- white
- midspring to fall
- 12–18 in. × 12 in.
- part shade, shade
- Z5–8

Foamflower. Woodlands of southeastern United States. Forms non-spreading clumps of slightly fuzzy, maple-like, lobed leaves, evergreen where winters are mild; green accented with purple, burgundy in winter. Creamy-white flowers in 1- to 6-in. spikes for six weeks, with occasional rebloom in fall.

Other Notable Cultivars

'Crow Feather'. Bright green leaves traced with purple-black turn pink, red, purple, and blackish in winter. Light pink spring flowers. 8–12 in. × 12 in. Z4–9.

'Elizabeth Oliver' is semi-spreading. Deeply cut, maroon-streaked, 2- to 3-in.-wide leaves turn purple in fall and winter. Light pink flowers. 12–15 in. × 12 in. Z4–8.

'Pink Skyrocket'. Deeply cut, medium green leaves with central black blotch, shiny black in fall. Pink flowers in 12-in.-long spikes. 6–12 in. × 12 in. Z4–9.

'Sugar and Spice' has mounds of colorful, pinnately divided foliage boldly marked with red. Bottlebrush racemes of pink flowers. 8–12 in. Z4–9.

Trachelium

syn. *Diosphaera*
Campanulaceae
throatwort

The common name of this genus comes from its supposed ability to relieve a sore throat when used as a gargle. However, the favorite Victorian species described here is more valuable as a long-lasting cut flower, or for container or border plantings.

Although *Trachelium* belongs to the bellflower family, it does not produce the showy, bell-shaped flowers typical of its relatives. Instead, throatworts have very small flowers borne singly or in multiples in flattened or domed clusters. These flower heads consist of countless blossoms with white-tipped, exserted styles, and produce an effect similar to that Jupiter's beard or bluebeard. Throatworts are popular in the cut flower trade, and several different color lines have been introduced.

In regions with strong sun, throatworts require some shade. Where the sun is more manageable, grow in full sun as an annual or biennial. Wherever they are grown, they provide long-lasting color for containers, summer beds and borders, and for cutting. Provide fertile, well-drained, and preferably slightly alkaline soil. Tolerates short periods of drought. Attracts bats, butterflies, and other pollinating insects; resists deer, rabbits, slugs, and snails. Be alert for spider mites and aphids. Foliage may irritate sensitive skins.

North of zone 7, cut plants back, pot, and overwinter with protection. However, it may be better to start new stock from seed sown indoors in very early spring. Throatwort may seed itself, but never becomes a nuisance. Take soft cuttings from young growth in spring.

Trachelium caeruleum

- violet-blue
- early to late summer
- 3–4 ft. × 1 ft.
- sun, part shade
- Z7–11

Blue throatwort, umbrella flower. Western and central Mediterranean. Clumps of slender, upright stems furnished with alternate, pointed, oval leaves, to 3 in. long, purple flushed and rimmed with a double row of teeth. Showy, long-lasting umbels of vanilla-scented, 0.25-in., tubular flowers, each with five tiny, spreading lobes; umbels may reach 3–5 in. across. Deadhead routinely to extend bloom time.

in competition with tree and shrub roots. In such areas of dry shade, let Oriental borage fight it out with lily-of-the-valley, bigroot geranium, and cinnamon and interrupted ferns.

Propagate by dividing the rhizomes in spring or fall, or take root cuttings in winter.

Trachystemon orientalis

syn. *Nordmannia cordifolia*

- blue
- spring
- 1–2 ft. × 2 ft.
- part shade, shade
- Z6–9

Oriental borage. Eastern Mediterranean, Caucasus Mountains. Thick, creeping rhizomes give rise to long-petioled, bristly basal leaves that mature to 12 in. long, wavy margined and heart shaped at the base. Foliage appears with or just after the curled clusters of blue, 0.5-in., beaked flowers; these have ringlet-like, reflexed petals and a pointed cone of black-tipped, white stamens, reminiscent of shooting star. The flowers are held on pink, leafless, branched stems.

Tradescantia

Commelinaceae
spiderwort

This popular garden plant, named for British botanists and gardeners of the 1600s John Tradescant, both father and the son, was once widely prescribed for kidney and digestive complaints; some report that the sap causes skin eruptions. Several tender species not included here, such as *Tradescantia fluminensis* and *T. spathacea*, are both grown widely as houseplants.

Spiderworts have attractive triangular flowers with parts in threes. Filaments of the six stamens are furry (possibly like a spider web) and may be brightly colored. Many flowers cluster in umbels at the top of the stems; each last but a single day. Alternate, pointed, linear leaves are olive green, slightly shiny, and clasp the stem at the node. When cut, the oozing sap is mucilaginous.

Provide average soil that drains well but does not dry out excessively. Tradescantias grow rapidly but seldom spread much. Cut back after bloom time. Deer usually leave spiderworts alone, but rabbits, and box and wood turtles enjoy the foliage.

Divide hardy cultivars in spring or fall.

Tradescantia ohioensis

- blue
- late spring to summer
- 24–36 in. × 12–18 in.
- sun
- Z4–9

Ohio spiderwort, bluejacket. Native from Minnesota, east to Massachusetts, and south from Texas to Florida. Bluish gray, grassy leaves become purplish in winter; a leafy bract partly ensheaths numerous flower buds that cluster at the stem tips.

Trachystemon orientalis

'Devotion Burgundy' has rusty burgundy flowers. Part of the Devotion series from Pan American Seed, selected for containers and bedding. 16 in.

'Hamer Pandora' has shiny, purple-black foliage and deep purple flowers. 3 ft.

'Lake Avelon' is pink flowered.

'Midnight Blue' has intense violet-blue flowers. 2–3 ft.

Trachystemon

Boraginaceae
Oriental borage

Really tough groundcovers that can tolerate dry shade are rare, but *Trachystemon orientalis* thrives in such conditions. Indeed, it can be somewhat of a thug, so be sure to plant it where its tendency to spread will be an asset. For the same reason, it shouldn't be planted in regions with mild winters and moderate summers such as the Pacific Northwest, where this plant is likely to become invasive. Reportedly, the Turks find the whole plant valuable as a nutritious vegetable, so if it gets out of hand, just eat it—deer and rabbits certainly won't.

Like its relatives in the genus *Borago*, Oriental borage has bristly hairy stems and leaves. Its large basal foliage is coarse but weed smothering. Tolerant of most soils, grows best in well-drained loam in partial or even deep shade. It thrives on neglect, and is excellent for the base of hedges,

Tradescantia virginiana 'Zwanenberg Blue'

Tradescantia hybrid 'Sweet Kate'

Lightly fragrant, pale purplish blue, 1-in. flowers open a couple at a time; long blooming. Drought tolerant and sun loving; excellent for borders, rock gardens, and meadows.

'Mrs. Loewer' has pale blue flowers above slender, gray-green leaves.

Tradescantia virginiana
syn. *T.* ×*andersoniana*
- various
- summer
- 18–24 in. × 30 in.
- sun, part shade
- Z5–9

Virginia spiderwort. Eastern United States. Strappy leaves about 18 in. long clasp the succulent stems at the nodes. Extensive breeding has resulted in numerous cultivars and hybrids for these stalwarts of perennial and cottage gardens. The following is only a small selection of hybrids and cultivars. Z3–9.

'Bilberry Ice' has white flowers flushed with lavender. Compact, long blooming. 18 in.

'Concord Grape' sports intense purple flowers. 18 in.

'Red Cloud' displays pinkish red flowers. 24 in.

'Sweet Kate' ('Blue-and-Gold') produces early, eye-popping yellow foliage, and brilliant purple flowers. 18 in.

'Zwanenberg Blue' blooms prolifically with vibrant blue flowers. Reblooms. 18–24 in. Z5–9.

Tradescantia zebrina
syn. *Zebrina pendula*
- purple
- all season
- 6–8 in. × 8 in.
- sun
- Z9–11

Wandering Jew. Southern Mexico. Trailing, succulent, hairless stems clothed with 4-in., oblong leaves, each striped longitudinally with silver, purple beneath. Pink-purple flowers nestle at stem tips. Valued in hanging baskets and as houseplants. Propagate by soft stem cuttings.

Tricyrtis
Liliaceae
toad lily

As the growing season wraps up in late summer and fall, perennial gardens often suffer from a deficiency of flowers. At that time toad lilies offer exotic,

Tricyrtis hirta 'Miyazaki'

Tricyrtis hirta
- white to lavender, purple
- late summer to early fall
- 2–3 ft. × 1.5–2 ft.
- part shade, shade
- Z4–8

Japanese toad lily. Ovate to oblong leaves, 3–6 in. long, with parallel veins and clasping bases. Flowers in small clusters of two to three, white to pale lavender with abundant purple spots. All parts of plants hairy. Requires consistently moist soil, self-seeds where conditions are hospitable. Not rhizomatous.

'Miyazaki' has pale lavender flowers, heavily spotted with deep purple. 2 ft. tall.

'Raspberry Mousse' displays its lightly spotted, deep chocolate flowers along the stems.

Other Notable Cultivars
'Eco Yellow Spangles' has red-spotted, glossy green leaves; large, yellow flowers are also red dotted. Late fall. Z5–7.

'Sinonome' bears clusters of burgundy-speckled, white flowers; late summer to fall. Good drought tolerance. 30–36 in. Z5–8.

'Taipei Silk'. White-spotted, red-purple flowers tipped with purple cluster in branching sprays. Late summer. 15–24 in. × 24 in. Z5–9.

'Tojen' bears terminal clusters of unspotted, yellow-throated, orchid-like, lavender-and-white flowers from midsummer onward. 2 ft. × 3 ft. Z5–8.

'White Towers' has unspotted, all-white, 1-in. flowers. Arching stems. May be listed under *Tricyrtis hirta*. 2 ft.

Trillium
Melianthaceae
trillium, wake robin

During a spring woodland hike it is a real thrill to come across a stand of trilliums in the wild. The best-known species is the showy snow trillium or great white trillium (*Trillium grandiflorum*), native to much of eastern North America. Of about 45 species, the bulk are North American natives, while the rest make eastern Asia home.

As one might expect from the name, trilliums have flower parts in threes. Unbranched, naked stems carry a whorl of three leaves, with the flowers borne between them, on stems or without. Some are pollinated by carrion insects—these species have flowers with the color and odor of rotting meat.

Provide humus-rich, well-drained but moist soil; prior to planting, dig in plenty of well-rotted compost or leaf mold. Maintain soil moisture with organic mulch in summer. Part to full shade is preferable for most species; the rhizomes prefer cool conditions and resent disturbance. Devoured by deer; attract early-foraging insect pollinators.

Trilliums are wonderful woodland plants, especially under tall deciduous trees. Epimediums,

flamboyant blooms with an almost orchid-like appearance to contribute color and interest. They flourish in part shade in regions where sunlight is not too intense, but otherwise require full shade.

Toad lilies are excellent companions for hostas, hellebores, erythroniums, and woodland lilies, which all share their requirement for moist, well-drained, slightly acid, organic-rich soil, and protection from the sun. Especially useful for shady borders and woodland gardens, plant toad lilies near a path, as visitors will want to examine their intriguing flowers at close range. Of the 20 or more species found across Asia, only two are common in the North American nursery trade. Both have broad, parallel-veined leaves and small (to 1 in. long) flowers; each bloom, with its six showy tepals, usually clusters in the upper leaf axils or at stem tips. Aside from the occasional slug, these plants typically are pest and problem free; deer tolerant.

Propagate by seed sown as soon as it ripens in fall, or divide plants in spring.

Tricyrtis formosana
syn. *T. stolonifera*
- red, yellow, purple, white
- late summer to early fall
- 2–3 ft. × 1.5–2 ft.
- part shade, shade
- Z4–9

Taiwan. Upright stems bear broad, lanceolate leaves with parallel veins semi-clasping at their bases. Flowers, in branching clusters, are white marked with deep, red-purple spots and yellow throats. Rhizomes spread to form colonies over time.

'Autumn Glow'. Dark-spotted, amethyst blooms; dark leaves banded with yellow.

'Gilt Edge' has deep pink, spotted blooms; large dark leaves with irregular, narrow, cream edges.

lungworts, hellebores, and ferns are good companions. Some species can be grown in rock gardens, if given amenable conditions. Most are summer dormant, so container plantings must include later-blooming companions.

Propagate by division or seed; both are slow to produce mature plants. *Never* dig plants from the wild; this threatens native populations and is too often unsuccessful. Purchase plants only from reputable dealers, who guarantee their plants are propagated from cultivated stock (not the same as nursery grown).

Trillium catesbaei

- white, pink
- spring
- 10–12 in. × 9 in.
- part shade, shade
- Z7–9

Rose trillium. Southeastern United States, especially the Piedmont Region. Somewhat nodding, pink or white, sometimes red flowers hang on slender stems, so they are largely hidden by foliage. Petals are recurved, as are the tips of the wavy-edged leaves. Slow to clump up.

Trillium cernuum

- white
- spring
- 8–10 in. × 12–18 in.
- part shade, shade
- Z5–8

Nodding trillium, northern nodding trillium. Cool woodlands of the northeastern United States. Nodding, ill-scented, white flowers with white anthers rise on stems between the leaves; their weight causes them to hang down or nod. *Trillium rugelli* is similar but has a more southerly range.

Trillium cuneatum

- maroon
- late spring to early summer
- 10–24 in. × 6–15 in.
- part shade, shade
- Z3–9

Toad trillium, toadshade. Southeastern United States. Maroon flowers are upright, without stems, and huddle between the silver-mottled, brownish green leaves that recurve downward. Likes sweet soils.

Trillium erectum

- maroon
- spring
- 12–18 in. × 12 in.
- part shade, shade
- Z3–7

Stinking Benjamin, wake-robin. Rich, damp woods along the eastern seaboard west to Alabama, Michigan, and Illinois. Malodorous purple flowers are pollinated by flies, attracted to the stench of rotting meat; white-flowered forms have no odor. Blooms are on short but erect stems. Broad leaves taper to the tip.

Trillium grandiflorum with Virginia bluebells and ferns

Trillium grandiflorum 'Flore Pleno'

Trillium grandiflorum

- white
- spring
- 18–24 in. high and wide
- part shade, shade
- Z3–7

Snow trillium, great white trillium. Showy, flaring, white flowers are carried on short, upright stems from between the foliage; blossoms mature pink. Broad leaves are stemless, wavy along the edges, and usually 3–5 in. long. Acid soil. Similar bent white trillium, *Trillium flexipipes*, has long flower stems. It may have more than a single stem per rhizome; requires alkaline soil. 18 in.

'Flore-Pleno' has double, 3-in.-wide blooms. Otherwise similar to the species.

'Quicksilver', introduced by Dr. Dick Lighty, bulks up more quickly than the species.

Trillium luteum

Trillium luteum

- yellow
- early spring
- 12–18 in. × 12 in.
- part shade, shade
- Z4–8

Yellow trillium. Deciduous woodlands of the Great Smoky Mountain region. Attractive wavy-edged 4-in. leaves, broad in the middle but with pointed tips, are mottled with silver when young; sessile, lemon-scented flowers have upright, pale yellow petals. Slow to bulk up. Aboveground parts become dormant by summer.

Trollius

Ranunculaceae
globeflower

These large buttercup relatives light up the garden with their shining globe-shaped flowers and foliage that remains attractive throughout the growing season. The blooms are usually bright yellow or orange, and may be cupped with incurved, petal-like sepals or shallower with widely spread sepals. Long stemmed and good for cutting, they open conveniently at the end of spring during the lull that comes after the spring bulbs finish. Leaves are similar to those of hardy geraniums: glossy, deeply divided, and borne in long-lasting basal clumps. Slightly poisonous if ingested, but not browsed by deer or rabbits.

Globeflowers are native to damp, open but shaded woodlands, wetlands, and swamps, and require similar conditions in gardens. Deep and fertile, slow-draining soil, or one amended with humus to increase its moisture retention, is best; although some types are less thirsty than others, in general globeflowers don't thrive without ample water. Thus, they flourish around ponds, lakes, and at stream sides where soil remains damp, in wet areas of lightly shaded woodlands, or on the edge of woods. Part shade is ideal, but globeflowers tolerate full sun if soil remains moist; protection from intense, midday sun is essential to those grown in ordinary garden soils. Louisiana and Japanese irises, tall cinnamon, royal, or interrupted ferns, and swamp rose mallow, along with other moisture lovers, combine well.

Propagate by division in spring or fall. Sow seed in fall and overwinter outdoors.

Trollius chinensis 'Golden Queen'

Trollius chinensis

syn. *T. ledebourii* hort.

- orange
- late spring
- 2–3 ft. × 2.5 ft.
- sun, part shade
- Z4–7, HS

Chinese globeflower. Northeast China. Seldom grown except as a cultivar. Not as hardy as the other species.

'Golden Queen' has large, soft orange, cupped sepals accented with a central circlet of spiky, vertical petals. Good looking, divided foliage all season. May be listed under *Trollius ×cultorum*. 2–2.5 ft.

Trollius ×cultorum

syn. *T. ×hybridus*
- yellow, orange
- late spring to early summer
- 2–3 ft. × 2.5 ft.
- sun, part shade
- Z4–6

Hybrid globeflower. Of hybrid origin (from some combination of *Trollius asiaticus*, *T. chinensis*, and *T. europeus*). Most of the reliable, well-known cultivars belong under this banner. Flowers are larger than those of the species and cupped; the handsome foliage of *T. europeus* has usually been passed on.

'**Alabaster**' has creamy-white, almost translucent, half-cupped flowers, centered with bright yellow stamens. Less vigorous than others but an unusual color. Early. Prone to powdery mildew. 1–2 ft. A sport, 'New Moon', has better vigor; bright yellowish cream, ball-shaped flowers. 2–3 ft.

'**Cheddar**'. This Dutch introduction has almost double, pale yellow, shallowly cupped flowers. Shiny, handsome, divided leaves. 2 ft. Z4.

'**Goldquelle**' ('Gold Fountain') blooms freely with cupped, lemon-juice-yellow flowers, 2.5 in. wide.

'**Lemon Queen**' has pale lemon-yellow globes. Late spring to midsummer. 24 in.

'**Orange Crest**' is compact, with open, soft orange flowers, centered with deep orange. 24 in.

Trollius europeus

- yellow
- early to late summer
- 2–2.5 ft. × 1 ft.
- sun, part shade
- Z3–9, HS

Common European globeflower. Europe and western Asia. Clumps of smooth pentagonal, 4- to 6-in. basal leaves, with three- to five-toothed, wedge-shaped lobes; smaller, three-lobed stem leaves. Composed of incurved petaloid sepals, sometimes flushed on the outside with red, 1- to 2-in. flowers, are clear, pale yellow like small light bulbs. Soil

Trollius ×cultorum '**Cheddar**'

Tulbaghia violacea

must remain damp, but tolerates drier soil better than other species. Reputedly pollinated by seed-eating flies. Resists deer and rabbits. Seeds about; control by routine deadheading.

'Pritchard's Giant' has open, 3-in.-wide flowers of dark yellow-orange. 24 in. Z5.

'Superbus' has 4-in., butter-yellow globes. 24 in.

Tulbaghia
Amaryllidaceae
society garlic

Bruise the foliage of tulbaghias and you will recognize a distinct garlic odor. This protects them from browsing by deer, rabbits, and other mammals, although they are susceptible to infestation from aphids and white flies, and root rot where drainage is poor. Provide society garlic with fertile, humus-rich soil that drains well, in full sun outdoors; indoors use a free-draining potting mix. Keep watered during droughty periods. Divide clumps in spring or start from seed in containers.

Tulbaghia violacea
- pink
- early summer
- 18–24 in. × 12 in.
- sun
- Z7–10

Society garlic, pink agapanthus. Southern Africa. Hairless, strappy, linear leaves, 12–24 in. long, with a garlicky odor, arise from corm-like rhizomes. Fragrant, 0.75-in., lavender to deep purple trumpet flowers, flaring at the mouth, are arranged in dainty umbels atop tall scapes. Where hardy, these unusual plants are suitable for rock gardens and sunny borders. Elsewhere put outdoors for summer, or grow indoors in a sunroom.

'Silver Lace' ('Variegata') has 0.75- to 1.5-in. flowers; leaves are vertically striped with cream.

Uvularia grandiflora

Uvularia
Colchicaceae
merrybells, bellwort

Who ever thought that these shy nodding flowers looked "merry"? The alternate common name, bellwort ("wort" meaning a plant), is much more apt.

Bellworts grow from rhizomatous roots and are found growing in the wild in moist, acid woodlands. All are North American natives, with upright, branched stems that lengthen further after bloom time. The alternate, smooth, hairless leaves on the upper stems are sessile and clasping, or perfoliate. Pendent yellow flowers with six apparently twisted tepals (petals and sepals are not differentiated) are borne on long stems.

These woodlanders prefer a soil high in humus that does not dry out rapidly. They do best in part to medium shade. Ideal in shaded native plant and wild gardens, and plantings under deciduous trees. Bloodroot, snowdrop anemone, pheasant's eye, and trilliums are good companions. The flowers attract foraging bees, including mason bees and bumblebees. Susceptible to slug and snail damage, and deer browsing.

Propagate by sowing seed as soon as it ripens in late summer. Divide in spring or fall.

Uvularia grandiflora
- yellow
- early to midspring
- 1.5–2.5 ft. × 1 ft.
- sun, part shade
- Z3–7

Large merrybells, bellwort, large-flower bellwort. Native to Quebec and Vermont, west to Minnesota and south to Georgia and Oklahoma. Rhizomes spread slowly but in time form nice-sized clumps. Stems carry light green, perfoliate leaves, mostly oval to lance shaped and downward facing, downy with hairs beneath, to 5 in. long. The narrowly bell-shaped, yellow flowers are also downward facing, some 2 in. in length.

Valeriana
Valerianaceae
valerian

Long grown in herb gardens for its medicinal properties and fragrance, valerian also is a useful ornamental massed along fences or walls. The roots and rhizomes are still harvested for medicinal use for ailments ranging from asthma to nausea, mental depression and stress, and insomnia, hence the medieval name of "all heal."

Provide average garden soil for valerian, preferably one that does not dry out readily. Seldom browsed by deer; acts as a sedative on rabbits, cats, and mice. Powdery mildew may be a problem.

Start seed or divide roots in spring.

Valeriana officinalis

Vancouveria hexandra

Valeriana officinalis

- white
- late spring to summer
- 3–6 ft. × 3 ft.
- sun, part shade
- Z4–7

Common valerian, garden heliotrope. Europe and Asia; naturalized in North America. From a basal rosette of foliage rise erect, tall, sturdy stems clothed with cut leaves, each divided into numerous toothed segments. Heads of white or pink-flushed, 0.25-in., salverform flowers are arranged in heads atop the tall stems. Effective in cottage gardens, borders, and herb gardens. Seeds freely; included on some state's invasive plant lists.

'Alba' has pure white flowers.

'Rubra' is red flowered; 'Coccinea' flowers are a deeper red.

Vancouveria

Berberidaceae
inside-out flower

This genus is named after the distinguished Pacific explorer, Captain George Vancouver; appropriately all three inside-out flower species are native to western North America. They are closely related to barrenworts or epimediums, and can be used in the garden in much the same way.

Delicate-foliaged vancouverias spread by fine, creeping underground stems that, in soil to their liking, can spread widely, even invasively. Graceful basal leaves are leathery and tough, divided twice or three times into mostly three-lobed leaflets, sometimes undulating along the rim. Loose panicles of pendent flowers on wiry, leafless stems, are reminiscent of shooting star with swept-back petals and a "beak" of stamens and pistil.

Provide humus-rich soil that is loose and moderately fertile, moist but well drained in part to full shade. Vancouverias do not care for full sun, and must be provided with at least part shade; they do not endure the heat and humidity of the southeast. Once established, they tolerate drought well. Good companions include other shade lovers such as May apple, coral bells, and foamflower in beds and borders, wildflower gardens and woodlands. They are excellent as shade groundcovers, or massed beneath trees. Mulch in winter. Beware of invasive tendencies. Deer and rabbit resistant.

Propagate by division or direct sow seed in fall.

Vancouveria hexandra

syn. *Epimedium hexandra, Vancouveria parvifolia, V. brevicula*

- white
- late spring to early summer
- 10–16 in. × 12 in.
- part shade, shade
- Z4–8, HS

White inside-out flower, Vancouver fern, American barrenwort. Native to mixed evergreen woods and deciduous forests of Washington, Oregon, and California. Deciduous, with bright green, smooth-textured, "duck feet" leaves, white-hairy beneath when young, that grow sufficiently thickly that they suppress weeds. Spreads rapidly. Flower panicles may contain 30 or more 0.5-in. flowers. Tolerates dry shade. Native Americans chewed the leaves of this plant for bronchial ailments; today it is still sometimes used as an ingredient in congestion and hay fever remedies.

Vancouveria planipetala

syn. *V. parviflora*

- white
- late spring to early summer
- 8–10 in. × 15 in.
- part shade, shade
- Z6–9, HS

Inside-out flower, redwood ivy, redwood inside-out flower. Native to redwood forests from Oregon south to California. The glossy, rounded leaves of this species are evergreen except in exposed places, and are divided several times with 1- to 2-in., wavy-margined leaflets. Loose, multi-flowered panicles of 0.5-in., violet-flushed, white flowers. Cut back in late winter to make room for the new flowers. Develops large patches more slowly than *Vancouveria hexandra*.

Veratrum

Melanthiaceae
false hellebore

Although handsome and in some cases native to our continent, false hellebores are rarely seen in American gardens, and this despite the fact that they have been favorites of leading British gardeners from

Veratrum viride

Gertrude Jekyll to Christopher Lloyd. Our notorious impatience may be one reason: ultimately, these plants provide elegant clusters of bold, attractive foliage, but they are slow to bulk up. Another liability is their toxicity; false hellebores contain extremely poisonous sap, especially when actively growing. Indeed, such is the potency of the sap that some Native American tribes used it to poison arrow tips, and the dried and powdered roots are a powerful insecticide. Yet false hellebore is also a traditional medicinal herb, and continues to be used by modern medicine in some critical medications.

Despite the common name, false hellebores are not related to the true hellebores (*Helleborus*) so popular today for shaded gardens. Their black rhizomes grow very slowly but produce thick, erect stems furnished with arresting, longitudinally

Verbascum 'Southern Charm'

pleated and prominently veined, broadly elliptic leaves. The leaf bases clasp the stem; leaves are arranged spirally or alternately, and may reach 12 in. long and 6 in. across at the base, smaller above. Large and dramatic, terminal, woolly, and crowded panicles of intricate, starry flowers are borne erect well above the foliage.

Plant false hellebores in moist to wet soils, high in organic matter, in a shaded site. Protect from drying winds that shred the leaf edges. They do not care for high heat combined with humidity, and are poor choices for southeastern US gardens. Suitable for massing at the edges of woodlands, in damp woods and forests, in shaded beds and borders, and even in meadows; also good as specimens or focal points along extended borders. Be sure that grazing animals and children cannot reach them. Compatible species in the garden include hellebores, globeflower, rodgersias, ferns, astilbes, and irises depending upon the location. Be alert for slug and snail damage. Resistant to deer, rabbits, and many other mammals. May be difficult to locate; native species are sometimes offered for sale at native plant garden fundraisers.

Propagate by division in fall or spring, or start seeds as soon as they ripen. Wear gloves.

Veratrum album
- white, greenish
- early to midsummer
- 2–5 ft. × 2 ft.
- sun, part shade
- Z4–7, HS

European white hellebore. Europe, northern Asia. Hairy throughout, except for the upper leaf surfaces. Upright panicles of starry, green-striped flowers, 0.5–0.75 in. across, may reach two feet long. Ants feed on nectar from the flowers.

Veratrum californicum
- white
- mid- to late summer
- 4–6 ft. × 2 ft.
- sun, part shade
- Z4–8, HS

California corn lily, skunk cabbage. Western United States in seepage areas, on meadows and hillsides, at 3500–11,000 ft. Dramatically beautiful, pleated leaves may reach 8–12 in. long and 3–6 in. across. Creamy, starry flowers cluster at the top of the single stem. Similar to *Veratrum viride*; can cause poisoning and birth defects in sheep, cattle, and goats.

Veratrum nigrum
- brown
- late summer
- 4–5 ft. × 2 ft.
- sun, part shade
- Z6–9

Black false hellebore. Europe to Siberia, China, Korea. Remarkable star-shaped, 0.3-in. flowers of deep purplish black, green striped on the reverse, held in woolly, branched terminal panicles 18 in. long. Foul smelling, probably pollinated by carrion flies. Foliage is free of hairs, pleated, broadly elliptic, and mostly basal. Great focal point in the border, where fragrance is not an issue.

Veratrum viride
- green
- early summer to midsummer
- 4–7 ft. × 2 ft.
- sun, part shade
- Z3–8

American white hellebore, Indian poke, Indian hellebore. Eastern and western North America. Broadly lanceolate, pleated basal leaves are arranged spirally on the stem, to 12 in. long, hairy beneath. Hairy, terminal panicles, to 18 in. long, with pendent lower branches, bear beautiful yellow-green, starry flowers, 0.75–1 in. across.

Verbascum
Scrophulariaceae
mullein

Old World immigrants that began arriving in North America in Colonial times, mulleins have for the most part been well behaved in their new homeland—in particular, none of the species and hybrids of interest to gardeners have proven invasive. The bulk of the 250-odd species are biennial, but those described below are perennial, though often relatively short lived and requiring replacement every three to four years. Fortunately, many cultivars and hybrids are easily started from seed.

As a group, mulleins are remarkably hardy and self-sufficient plants, flourishing even in poor, dry soils, resisting deer and insect predation, and holding their lofty flower spikes upright without need of staking. Intolerant of wet soils. Mulleins contribute dramatic vertical accents to border or meadow plantings; some species produce spikes as much as 8 ft. tall. The leaves and stems are covered with star-shaped hairs, which give them an attractive velvety texture—another common name is "Quaker rouge," because younger females of that plain-dressing sect used to rub their cheeks with a mullein leaf to give them a rosy blush.

Typically, mulleins produce a rosette of large leaves during their first year's growth, from which emerges a single flower stalk in the second and succeeding years. The upper half of this spike is densely clothed with buds of the five-petaled flowers, which open from the bottom upward over a prolonged season, up to three months. Flower colors include yellow, white, rosy-purple, and sunset oranges. Remove flower stems to the base after flowering finishes to prolong the life of the plant and curtail self-seeding.

Verbascum bombyciferum

- yellow
- summer
- 5–6 ft. × 1.5–2 ft.
- sun
- Z3–9

Giant silver mullein. Greece. Large basal rosettes of felted, silver-gray leaves. Spikes, often curling at tips, of soft yellow flowers. Notably drought tolerant; good for xeriscapes, and cottage gardens in dry regions such as the American West. Adapts to wide range of soils; self-sows.

'Arctic Summer' makes 3- to 5-ft.-wide foliage rosettes; branching, 2-ft.-wide spikes covered in white fur bear 2-in., yellow flowers.

Verbascum chaixii

- yellow
- later spring to early summer
- 2–3 ft. × 1.5–2 ft.
- sun
- Z5–8

Nettle-leaved mullein. South-central Europe to central Russia. Basal 8- to 12-in.-wide rosettes of narrow, oblong-ovate, woolly, gray-green leaves, 3–6 in. long. Yellow, 1-in.-wide flowers adorned with purple stamens on tall, straight, erect, and unbranched stems. Flourishes on any average, dry to moderately moist, well-drained soil. Self-seeds in hospitable conditions. Prone to spider mites in hot weather.

'Sixteen Candles' has golden flowers with violet stamens. 3 ft. × 2 ft.

'Wedding Candles' has white flowers with orange stamens and bright orange anthers. 3.5 ft. × 1.5 ft.

Verbascum phoeniceum

- pink, purple, white
- early summer
- 1–3 ft. high and wide
- sun, part shade
- Z5–8

Purple mullein. Central Europe, central Asia, and western China, naturalized locally in the United States and Canada. Ground-hugging rosettes of shiny dark green leaves. Precocious, 3-ft. spires of showy dark-purple, violet, pink, or white blossoms open early in the season for two weeks. Good for cottage and rock gardens, meadows. Self-sows.

'Flush of White' is compact, 2–2.5 ft. × 1.5 ft., with yellow-eyed, white flowers in late spring. Z6.

'Rosetta' is compact, 2–2.5 ft. × 1.5 ft., with golden-eyed, carmine-pink flowers from late spring to late summer. Z6.

'Violetta' has violet-purple flowers from late spring to late summer. 2–3 ft. × 1.5 ft. Z6.

Other Notable Cultivars

'Clementine' has rippled, green leaves; branching spikes of magenta-eyed, coppery-orange flowers in midsummer to early fall. 4–5 ft. × 2 ft. Z5–9.

'Gainsborough' has woolly gray leaves; produces a lavish display of primrose-yellow flowers with orange centers, on branching candelabra stems. 4–4.5 ft. × 1.5 ft. Z5–9.

'Pink Domino'. Dark green leaves; rose-pink flowers with darker eyes in early to late summer. 4–4.5 ft. × 1.5 ft. Z5–9.

'Southern Charm' has flowers in shades of buff, lavender, and soft rose from early to late summer. 30–36 in. × 24–30 in.

'White Domino'. Gray-green, fuzzy leaves; branching spires of large, white flowers in early to late summer. 3.25–4 ft. × 1.5 ft. Z5–9.

Verbena

Verbenaceae
vervain

Most gardeners have experience with verbenas as annuals, but relatively few have explored the many fine perennial members of this genus. The distinction lies in their hardiness. Those grown as annuals, categorized as *Verbena* ×*hybrida*, are in fact perennial but only as far north as zone 9; other hybrids and species are routinely hardy in colder regions.

These more cold-tolerant verbenas range in habit from upright to prostrate, but have the same clusters of small, five-petaled, tubular flowers; colors cover the spectrum from blue and purple to white, pink, and red. As a rule they are short lived, requiring replacement every three to four years, but they grow rapidly, usually blooming the first season after planting; they have an exceptionally long season of bloom—some types remain in flower from spring until first frost. Verbenas are sun lovers and heat tolerant, as well as moderately drought tolerant. They won't accept poorly drained soil. Although susceptible to aphids, whiteflies, thrips, leaf miners, and mites, they mostly remain free of serious infestations unless stressed by adverse conditions such as drought or too much shade.

Use taller types for long-lasting color in perennial or mixed borders; the trailing verbenas are particularly handsome cascading from hanging baskets, and may also serve as a flowering groundcover. Verbenas attract butterflies and hummingbirds as well as bees.

Propagate by seed sown in early spring, by division, or by stem tip cuttings taken any time during the growing season.

Verbena bipinnatifida

syn. *Glandularia bipinnatifida*

- magenta
- summer
- 4 in. × 15–18 in.
- sun, part shade
- Z3–8

Great Plains verbena. Wisconsin to Georgia, west to Wyoming and Arizona, California. Sprawling, branched stems with upward-reaching tips are covered with long, whitish hairs; opposite, deeply cut leaves 1–3.5 in. long and 1.5 in. across. Globular heads of several 0.5-in., dark-centered, tubular flowers open all summer. Tolerates extremes of heat and cold, needs a lean, well-drained soil. Colorful, hardy groundcover or edging plant.

Verbena bonariensis

syn. *V. patagonica*
- pink, purple, lavender
- midsummer to early fall
- 2–4 ft. × 1.5–3 ft.
- sun, part shade
- Z7–11

Tall verbena, Brazilian vervain. South America. Fast growing, forms clumps of lanceolate, toothed, dark green leaves, from which rise erect, wiry, and branching stems with 2-in. clusters of rose-purple flowers. Tolerates poor but well-drained soils.

Verbena bonariensis 'Buenos Aires'

Self-seeds freely; naturalized in the warmer parts of the American Southeast, and considered invasive in Georgia and Oregon.

'Buenos Aires' has deep lilac to violet flowers. 3.5–4.5 ft. Z7–9.

'Lollipop' is compact, with lavender flowers. 2 ft. high and wide.

Verbena canadensis

syn. *Glandularia canadensis*
- red, pink, purple, white
- late spring to late summer
- 6–12 in. × 24–36 in.
- sun
- Z6–10

Clump verbena, rose vervain. Virginia to Florida. Forms dense, spreading mounds of ground-hugging stems, and toothed leaves, with large clusters of fragrant flowers. Excellent as a groundcover or at the front of borders, and a perfect counterpoint to silver-leaved wormwoods or lamb's ears.

'Homestead Purple' (Purple Spreader) is vigorous. Profuse crops of medium dark purple flowers backed by clean, dark green foliage all summer.

'Homestead Red' is red flowered.

'Snowflurry' bears plentiful white flowers. Comes true from seed. To Z5.

Verbena hastata

- blue
- summer
- 2–6 ft. × 1–2.5 ft.
- sun
- Z3–8

Blue vervain. Wet meadows, bottomlands, streambanks of eastern North America. Clumps of stiff upright, branching, hairy stems clothed with large (to 6 in. long) lanceolate, toothed leaves. Tiny purplish blue flowers cluster into densely packed, 2- to 6-in., slender spikes in candelabra-like heads. Prefers medium to wet soils; self-seeds and spreads slowly by rhizomes in suitable conditions. A natural for rain gardens, moist meadows, and prairies.

'Rosea' has pink flowers.

Verbena rigida

- purple
- summer to midfall
- 1 ft. × 4 ft.
- sun
- Z7–11

Sandpaper verbena. Brazil and Argentina. Tuberous rooted with square, stiff stems and dark green, prominently toothed, lanceolate leaves 1–4 in. long. Upright and spreading, with 1-in. clusters of purple flowers at the tips of branching stems. Deadhead to prolong bloom. Vulnerable to frost damage north of zone 8, but root hardy through zone 7. Exceptionally drought tolerant.

'Polaris' blooms profusely with silver-blue flowers. 24 in. × 12 in. Z5.

'Santos' is a heavy bloomer with violet flowers. Exceptionally heat tolerant.

Vernonia glauca

Other Notable Cultivars

'Blue Princess' covers itself with large clusters of fragrant, lavender-blue flowers all season. 1–3 ft. Hardy from warmer parts of zone 7 through 10.

'Georgia's Pink' has slightly hairy, dark green foliage; bright pink flowers in clusters all summer. 12–18 in. × 18–24 in. Z7–10.

'Taylortown Red' ('L. Archer') bears large clusters of fragrant, bright red flowers from late spring to summer. Beautiful groundcover. 6–10 in. × 24–36 in. Z7–11.

'Silver Anne' has fragrant, pink flowers and lustrous silvery foliage. 8 in. Z8–10

Vernonia

Asteraceae
ironweed

Is it because we see them so commonly as roadside weeds that we rarely give ironweeds space in our gardens? Although they do not rank in the first tier of garden perennials, these plants can nevertheless provide a strong shot of purple toward the end of the bloom season, a niche for which there are few other competitors.

Erect and vigorous, ironweeds produce clusters of stems well clothed with alternate leaves, and terminal clusters of purple or violet flowerheads several inches across. The heads are composed of tubular florets that lack ray flowers, but that are surrounded by bracts. Most ironweeds are satisfied with moderately fertile, well-drained soil; they tolerate a wide range of soils, despite the fact that some inhabit wet areas and others dry. Full sun is best.

Too unrefined for formal plantings, ironweeds fit better into meadows, native plant gardens, and other informal displays that improve with infusions of fall color. Mauve and lavender native asters, dusty Joe-Pye weed, and native grasses are good companions. Ironweeds are naturals for rain gardens, combining well with swamp milkweeds, turtleheads, and cut-leaved coneflowers. Ironweeds are larval host plants for American lady and other caterpillars; nectar-collecting butterfly species including crossline skippers, sachem skippers, monarchs, and both yellow and black swallowtails flock to them.

Pests and diseases are few; deer and rabbits are seldom troublesome. Divide in spring or fall, or start seed in spring.

Vernonia lettermanii

- purple
- late summer to early fall
- 2-3 ft. × 1.5 ft.
- sun
- Z4–9

Threadleaf ironweed, slimleaf ironweed. Native to the Ozark region of Oklahoma and Arkansas. Upright stems, with attractive, fine-textured, soft, needle-like leaves, 2.5–3 in. long. Crowded terminal heads of tufted purple flowers attract plenty of monarch butterflies on their southward migration. Drought tolerant. An exciting companion for rough goldenrod 'Fireworks'.

'Iron Butterfly', a petite cultivar, 24–30 in., is reputedly superior to the species.

Vernonia novaboracensis

- violet
- late summer to early fall
- 4–6 ft. × 3 ft.
- sun
- Z4–8

New York ironweed. Native to wet places from Florida to Massachusetts, and west to West Virginia, Tennessee, and Alabama. Stiff, erect stems are purplish green and slightly rough, clothed with lanceolate leaves to 7 in. long. Flat-topped, terminal clusters of small, rayless flowerheads of deep reddish purple to violet, sometimes white, are loosely branched and develop into wide sprays. Leave spent heads to provide winter food and cover for birds and insects. Similar upland ironweed (*Vernonia glauca*), native to woodland edges from New Jersey and Pennsylvania to Georgia and Alabama, only reaches 3–4 ft. tall, a more manageable size for smaller gardens. The reverse of the leaves is pale and silvery, attractive when the wind blows. Tolerates garden soils well and is admirable in the often dry soils of wildflower and native plant gardens. Z6–8.

Veronica
Plantaginaceae
speedwell

As is the case with most large genera, *Veronica* includes the good, the bad, and the ugly. For example, greenskeepers loathe *V. arvensis*, a rampant infiltrator of shady lawns, but the genus also includes a dozen or so species that are outstanding ornamental perennials. Some of these are excellent in rock gardens, and as groundcovers; upright ones with colorful flower spikes can be mainstays of beds and borders, and are very attractive to hummingbirds and other birds, and butterflies; they are also useful as cut flowers. Shopping for these species is, unfortunately, somewhat complicated by the fact that the taxonomy of the speedwells is under revision and names are subject to change.

Veronicas are easy to grow and some provide color over several months. Clusters of saucer-shaped flowers may be arranged in the leaf axils on low mats (*V.* 'Georgia Blue'), or are star-shaped or tubular borne on dense, erect spikes (*V. spicata*). Spikes open from the base up. Colors vary from true blue to purplish blue, pink, and white. Lance-shaped leaves are often toothed around the rim; carried mostly in pairs below, but alternate or spiral on the flower stems.

Plant veronicas in full sun or part shade. Prostrate ones prefer average to poor, very well-drained soil; border species need more fertile soil that drains well; wet soil in winter is fatal. Deadhead to extend bloom time: cut spike flowers at the spike's base; shear off spent blooms of prostrate types. Some species resist deer browsing—see individual entries.

Sow seed in fall. Divide clumping sorts in spring or fall, or take cuttings of young spring growth. Divide creeping forms.

Veronica austriaca subsp. teucrium

syn. *V. teucrium, V. latifolia*
- blue
- summer
- 24–36 in. × 24–30 in.
- sun, part shade
- Z4–8

Hungarian speedwell, broadleaf speedwell. Southern Europe. Low mats of oblong, hairy, grayish green, 3-in. leaves; stem leaves mostly sessile. Terminal, 4- to 6-in. racemes of saucer-shaped flowers. Deer and rabbit resistant.

Veronica longifolia 'Eveline'

'**Blue Fountain**' has bright blue flowers on 20- to 24-in. stems.

'**Crater Lake Blue**' has lovely gentian-blue flowers. 12–18 in.

'**Royal Blue**' produces abundant royal-blue flowers. To 20 in. tall.

Veronica gentianoides
- icy blue
- late spring to early summer
- 12–24 in. × 18 in.
- sun, part shade
- Z4–7, HS

Gentian speedwell. Ukraine, north and central Turkey, Caucasus. Thick, dark green, 3-in.-long basal leaves create a glossy mat of foliage. Outward-facing, shallowly cupped, very pale blue flowers with prominent stamens congregate into terminal, 6- to 10-in.-long, loose racemes. Combines well with pink tulips, bleeding hearts, and English daisies. Not for high heat and humidity. Deer and rabbit resistant.

Veronica hybrid 'Waterperry'

Veronica prostrata

'**Pallida**' produces abundant pale blue flowers. 24 in.

'**Variegata**' has variegated, white-margined, green leaves; pale blue flowers.

Veronica incana
syn. *V. spicata* subsp. *incana*
- blue
- summer
- 12–18 in. × 18 in.
- sun, part shade
- Z3–7, HS

Woolly speedwell, silver speedwell. Russia. This species is prized almost as much for its foliage as for its bright blue flower spikes. All the leaves are tomentose, clothed with white, woolly hairs that produce an elegant, silvery effect. Above 12-in. mounds of oblong basal leaves, vegetative and flower stems are clothed with lanceolate, 1- to 3-in.-long leaves. Terminal, 3- to 6-in. racemes of densely packed, 0.25-in., blue flowers bloom for more than a month. Deadhead to encourage more flowers.

Drought tolerant; free winter-drainage essential. Not for hot, sultry gardens. Nice contrasted with hardy geraniums. Deer and rabbit resistant.

'**Rosea**' is pink flowered. 18 in.

'**Silver Sea**' has grayish leaves and medium blue flower spikes from early summer. Good for containers, edgings, and at the front of the border. 6–8 in.

Veronica longifolia
syn. *V. maritima*
- lilac-blue
- late summer to early fall
- 3–4 ft. × 12–15 in.
- sun, part shade
- Z4–8

Long-leaf Veronica. Northern Europe, Asia. Another very variable species; clumping with strong, mostly unbranched stems, excellent as cut flowers. Stem leaves are paired or in whorls of three, toothed, 3–5 in. long, and pointed-ovate. Erect, 8- to 10-in. racemes are densely packed with tubular, violet-blue, 0.25-in. flowers. Deer and rabbit resistant.

'**Blauriesin**' ('Foerster's Blue') bears dark blue flowers over a long period. 24 in.

'**Blue John**' has a long summer bloom time with spikes of pale blue flowers. A top choice at Chicago Botanic Garden trials. 12–18 in.

'**Eveline**'. Violet to reddish purple flowers in tapering spikes. 18–24 in.

'**First Love**' makes mounds of deep green foliage, beneath long spikes of deep pink flowers. 10–12 in.

'**Pink Eveline**' is a good "doer," with 15- to 18-in.-tall spikes of dark pink flowers.

Veronica pectinata

- blue
- midspring
- 3–6 in. × 18 in.
- sun, part shade
- Z2–7

Blue woolly speedwell, comb speedwell. East Balkans, Turkey. Dense, evergreen mats of gray-green, 1-in. leaves. Short racemes of saucer-shaped, white-eyed, bright blue flowers smother the foliage with bloom. Use as weed-suppressing groundcover, or between cracks on paved patios, and among rocks. Tolerates light foot traffic. Appropriate for hot and sunny areas that retain heat reflecting off concrete, walls, and bricks. Excellent in dry, sunny gardens. Resists deer and rabbits.

'Blue Reflection' is probably a hybrid with this species as one parent. Dense mats of deep green leaves are covered with myriads of lavender-blue flowers. Protect from sunburn where sun is intense. 6 in. Z4–7.

'Rosea' (var. *rosea*) has rosy pink flowers. 2–3 in. Z3–7.

Veronica prostrata

syn. *V. rupestris*

- blue
- early summer
- 3–8 in. × 12–15 in.
- sun
- Z5–8

Prostrate speedwell, harebell speedwell. Europe, northern Asia. Low mats of prostrate, sterile stems with gray-green, hairy foliage; 0.5- to 1-in. stem leaves are serrated, triangular at the base, and linear-ovate. Leaf axils host short racemes of starry, 0.5-in., dark to light blue flowers. Drought, deer, and rabbit tolerant. Good groundcover.

'Aztec Gold' makes wide mounds of golden leaves; short spikes of sky-blue flowers bloom above. 6 in. Z4–8.

'Georgia Blue' may be a cultivar of *Veronica umbrosa*. Whatever its parentage, it is a great early-blooming, gentian-blue addition to gardens. Drought tolerant. 6–8 in. Z5–8.

'Goldwell'. Gold-edged leaves make this plant sparkle. Petite spikes of bright blue flowers. 4–6 in.

'Mrs. Holt' has light pink flowers. Not as robust as the species. 6 in.

'Trehane' is noted for its chartreuse spring foliage and brilliant blue flowers. Protect from intense sun. Best used for edging or in containers. 6–8 in. Z2–9.

Veronica spicata

- blue
- summer
- 12–30 in. × 18–24 in.
- sun, part shade
- Z3–8

Spike speedwell. Europe, northern Asia. This highly variable species has upright and decumbent, rooting stems. Hairy throughout, with pairs of oblong stem leaves, rimmed with rounded teeth, 2–3 in.

long. Crowded, terminal, tapered racemes of blue, starry flowers with long, protruding purple stamens bloom for several weeks. Embraces hot, humid climates. Butterfly magnet; some species are larval hosts for grizzled skippers and others.

'Baby Doll' produces abundant pink flowers. 18 in.

'Icicle' ('White Icicle') is possibly a hybrid. Spikes of white flowers, with rich green foliage. 18–24 in.

'Minuet' has spikes of pink flowers above silvery leaves. 15 in.

'Red Fox' ('Rotfuchs') produces its spikes of deep rosy-pink flowers from early summer for several weeks. Deer resistant. 10–15 in. Z6–9.

'Ulster Blue Dwarf' displays plenty of purplish blue flowers on 12-in. stems.

Other Notable Cultivars

'Fairytale' is a heavy-blooming, upright plant with spikes of pale pink flowers. Did well in Chicago Botanic Garden trials. 32 in. × 27 in.

'Giles van Hees' has large, dark pink flower spikes. A superior upright, dwarf form. 6–8 in. Z2–9.

'Goodness Grows' is a winner, with long-lasting spikes of royal-blue flowers over grayish leaves. Deer resistant. 10–16 in. Z3–8.

'Purpleicious' bears deep purple-violet, tapered spires above mounds of shiny dark foliage from late spring for several weeks. 18–20 in. Z3–9.

'Sunny Border Blue' has sturdy spikes of long-blooming, dark violet-blue flowers; 1993 Perennial Plant of the Year from the PPA. Introduced by Robert Bennerrup of Sunny Border Nurseries, Inc. 18–20 in. Z3–8.

'Waterperry' ('Waterperry Blue') blankets its foliage mats with open, light blue flowers from spring to early summer. Effective tumbling over rocks and walls. 4–6 in.

'Whitewater' is very similar to the above, but with 0.5-in., sparkling white flowers above mats of dark green foliage; these become bronzy in cooler weather. From John Wachter at Elite Growers and the Chicagoland Grows program. 4–6 in. Z4–7.

Veronicastrum

Plantaginaceae
Culver's root

This close relative of *Veronica* is often classified with them. However, this genus has distinct whorls of leaves in contrast to the opposite-leaved *Veronica*. It is a popular perennial in eastern US gardens, but is not successful in southeastern high heat and humidity. Historically, the dried and fresh root has been used as a remedy for all sorts of complaints, including gastric and liver problems, coughs, and chills.

Soil should be of average fertility, amended with moisture-retaining humus, and with good drainage. Mulch in summer. A sunny spot is best; in part shade staking may be necessary. Flower spikes

Veronicastrum virginicum

Viola canadensis

unbranched stems bear whorls of three to seven dark leaves, pointed, lanceolate, and toothed. Pale blue, whitish, sometimes pink-tinged, tubular flowers, 0.25 in. or so across, with prominently exserted stamens, bloom in tapered, candelabra-type spires, to 9 in. long, for several weeks. These may be terminal or arise from the upper leaf axils.

'Album'. Clones of the white flowered form vary. Buy in bloom if possible to ensure the whitest flowers. 4 ft.

'Apollo' has elegant lavender candelabras of flowers. 3–4 ft. Z4–6.

'Fascination' has mauve-lavender flowers. 4–5 ft.

'Lavendelturm' ('Lavender Towers') has spikes of pale purple flowers. 4–5 ft.

Viola

Violaceae
violet, viola

These perennial relatives of the familiar biennial pansies furnish long-lasting color and nostalgic charm to the garden, and though most are short lived individually, several species reseed and naturalize to form self-sustaining colonies. Typically, the heart-shaped leaves are scalloped along the margins; many are acaulescent as well, lacking any visible stems so that the foliage appears to rise directly from the ground. These stemless species have basal rosettes of foliage; the flowers, on their individual stems, also seem to emerge directly from the soil. Other violets produce short stems, alternate leaves, and flowers that emerge from the leaf axils. Viola flowers are five petaled, with two fan-like petals on either side and one broad, lobed petal pointing downward. Colors range from violet to blue, red, orange, yellow, white, and cream, with many bicolors. The flowers of many species have a fuzzy, "bearded" throat and a nectar spur protruding from

open from the base up. Deadhead to the base of the primary spike when it is spent, to encourage further bloom. Butterflies and foraging bees of several species are attracted for the nectar. Excellent as a cut flower for large arrangements. May be attacked by mildews, and leaf spot. Deer, rabbit, and squirrel, resistant.

Plant Culver's root toward the back of the border, in rain gardens, and in damp meadows or native plant gardens. It can provide valuable height in cottage gardens and among shrubs.

Propagate from seed in fall in a warm, moist environment. Divide established plants in spring or fall; cuttings of young growth root well in spring.

Veronicastrum virginicum

syn. *Veronica virginica*
- pale blue, white
- midsummer to early fall
- 3–6 ft. × 18 in.
- sun
- Z3–8, HS

Culver's root, Bowman's root, Culver's physic. Native to moist prairies and uplands of the eastern United States from Ontario to Texas, usually in undisturbed ground. Very sturdy, upright, and the back; insects searching for a sweet treat crawl into the spur and become coated with pollen; this gets deposited in the next flower they visit. Violets are prolific bloomers, and may flower throughout much of spring and summer.

Favorites of the Victorians, violas and violets seem especially at home in cottage gardens, but also shine in borders, woodlands, and rock gardens, as well as in containers and window boxes. As a group, they perform well in either full sun or dappled shade, and prefer a moderately rich, moist but well-drained soil. Relished by deer, slugs, and snails, violas are also susceptible to foliar diseases including downy and powdery mildew; susceptibility varies with the species. Crown rot is common in poorly drained soils.

Propagate by seed in spring or divide in spring or fall.

Viola canadensis
- white
- early summer to fall
- 12–18 in. high and wide
- sun, part shade
- Z3–8

Canadian white violet. Throughout North America, except extreme Southeast and Southwest. Clumps of long-petioled, heart-shaped, deep green leaves, 2–4 in. long, borne alternately on stems 9–15 in. tall. Yellow-throated, white flowers sometimes tinged purple, perch on short, naked stalks that emerge from leaf axils. Provide moist, humus-rich soils; tolerates dense shade, resistant to deer. Self-seeds, often prolifically; too aggressive for formal displays, best where it can form colonies. Prefers cool-summer regions.

Viola cornuta
- violet
- spring to summer
- 4–8 in. × 6–8 in.
- sun, part shade
- Z4–9

Horned violet, perennial pansy. Europe. Low mounds of lanceolate, dark green leaves; abundant fragrant, long-spurred flowers to 1.25 in. across. Similar to common pansies (*Viola* ×*wittrockiana*), but hardier and more tolerant of heat and cold. Many hybrids are available in white, yellow, apricot, red, and blue to purple. Best in maritime climates; often cultivated as spring or fall annuals in the inland North, and as winter annuals in mild-winter regions.

'Columbine' bears streaked, purple-and-white flowers. 12 in. × 18 in.

'Etain' has slightly fragrant, creamy-yellow flowers with lavender-purple edges. 12 in. × 18 in.

'Rebecca' is long blooming with cream flowers blotched with purple. 9 in. × 12 in.

'Starry Night' is trailing, good for baskets and containers, with yellow-centered, dusky lavender-purple blossoms. 8 in. high and wide.

Viola cornuta 'Etain'

Viola labradorica
- purple
- mid- to late spring
- 3–6 in. high and wide
- sun, part shade
- Z3–8

Labrador violet. Moist woods in northern United States, Canada, and Greenland. Forms mats of heart-shaped, purple-tinged leaves to 1 in. across, with lavender-blue flowers in spring. In favorable locations, spreads vigorously by self-seeding and creeping stems. Good for rock gardens and woodland gardens, or even as a small-scale groundcover.

Viola odorata
- blue, purple, white
- late winter to early spring
- 4 in. × 8 in.
- sun, part shade, shade
- Z5–9

Sweet violet, English violet. Europe and Asia. Rhizomatous, forms mat of heart-shaped, dark green leaves with serrated edges, evergreen in mild climates. The sweetly scented, 0.75-in. flowers are used in perfumery. Naturalized in many regions of the United States; self-seeds and can be an aggressive spreader.

'Blue Remington' has profuse large, blue flowers from late winter through spring, sometimes repeating in fall. 6 in. × 15 in.

'Rosina' has dusky pink, sweetly fragrant flowers in spring. 2–4 in. × 6 in.

Viola pedata
- blue, purple
- early to midspring
- 3–6 in. high and wide
- sun
- Z4–8

Bird's foot violet. Eastern North America. Rhizomatous and stemless, with deeply divided, bird's-foot-like leaves, 0.75–2 in. across. Flowers variable, most commonly light blue or bicolored dark purple and light blue, 1–1.5 in. in diameter. Prefers full sun and dry to moderately moist, well-drained soil. Flourishes on sandy and rocky soils; ideal for rock gardens. More difficult that other violets, self-seeds in hospitable sites.

'Eco Artist Palette' makes a compact clump, 3 in. high and wide, that bears bicolored blue-and-white flowers in spring; often repeats in late summer to early fall.

Viola sororia

- blue, white
- early spring to late summer

- 6–9 in. high and wide
- sun, part shade
- Z3–7

Common blue violet. Eastern North America. A near ubiquitous wildflower, rhizomatous and stemless, with downy, basal, heart-shaped leaves. Flowers are blue-violet or white with purple veins, borne in early spring with sparing repeat into late summer. Prefers organic-rich, moderately moist though well-drained soil, tolerates clay. Self-seeds prolifically; too aggressive for beds or borders, but fine in open woodland, under shrubs, or in sunny meadows.

'Freckles' has white flowers speckled with blue.

Viola walteri

- violet-blue
- late spring to fall
- 3–5 in. × 10–15 in.

- part shade, shade
- Z5–8

Walter's violet. Moist deciduous woodlands of the eastern United States. Spreads freely in damp conditions by rhizomes and runners, but stays put in drier soils. Typical 1-in., violet flowers; long blooming.

'Silver Gem' has a dense mat of silvery foliage etched with purple along the veins. Deep violet flowers all season. Drought tolerant.

Other Notable Cultivars

There are many notable hybrids. The following is worth seeking:

Parma Violets, favorites of Victorian and Edwardian florists, have large, intensely fragrant, double flowers in blue, lavender, or white. Part shade, shade. Non-invasive. 6 in. high and wide. Z7–9.

Wachendorfia

Haemodoraceae
red root

A genus of perennials from South Africa whose fleshy, rhizomatous roots are permeated with a bright red sap sometimes used as a dye, as the common name indicates. One species is available in the nursery trade. Propagate by seed sown in fall or divide as soon as flowering has ended.

Wachendorfia thysiflora

- golden-orange
- late spring to midsummer

- 4–6 ft. × 2–3 ft.
- sun
- Z8–10

South Africa. Forms a basal tuft of evergreen, 24- to 40-in.-long, narrow, pleated, sword-like leaves. Dense, lofty, spike-like panicles of blossoms that open sequentially over a period of several weeks. A wetland native, it is ideally suited to bog gardens and the edges of pools or streams. This species enjoys a moist but well-drained soil. It makes a striking backdrop to a border, especially paired with *Dietes bicolor*.

Waldsteinia

Rosaceae
barren strawberry

Strawberry lookalikes, the members of this genus are "barren" only in the sense that their fruits are inedible. They do, however, provide attractive, compact groundcovers for borders and rock gardens, as well as for woodland plantings, edgings, and as a lawn substitute in low-traffic areas. Barren strawberries spread by rhizomes to form ground-hugging mats of leaves, each divided into three leaflets, or palmately lobed. This foliage is a fresh green, evergreen, or semi-evergreen. The bright yellow, five-petaled flowers are followed by red fruits.

Generally pest free, but may be attacked by slugs. They thrive in a range of soils and conditions, including dry shade. Deer resistant.

Propagate by division in spring or by tip cuttings.

Waldsteinia fragarioides

- yellow
- early to midspring
- 3–6 in. × 6–12 in.

- sun, part shade
- Z4–7, HS

Barren strawberry. Native to eastern North America as far west as Minnesota, south to Arkansas, Alabama, and Georgia. Evergreen leaves with three wedge-shaped leaflets, each 1–2 in. long, that turn bronze in winter. Yellow, 0.75-in.-wide flowers are arranged in cymes on 3- to 4-in. stems. Inedible fruits are red, similar looking to those of wild strawberries. Ideally provide organic-rich, slightly acid soil. Tolerates clay soil.

Waldsteinia ternata

- yellow
- midspring to early summer

- 3–6 in. × 6–12 in.
- sun, part shade
- Z4–8

Siberian barren strawberry. Europe, Asia, China. Thick mats of trifoliate leaves with dark green, wedge-shaped leaflets, each 0.5–1 in. long, that become bronze in fall. Buttercup-yellow flowers are sterile. Excellent as a groundcover especially where summers are cool; can be aggressive.

Waldsteinia fragarioides

Yucca
Asparagaceae
yucca

Bold, brash, and spiny, yuccas are no shrinking violets, and can be used to dramatic effect. Most species are native primarily to arid high deserts, sand dunes, and hot plains of southwestern North, South, and Central America; they tolerate extreme dry conditions with aplomb, and are thus eminently suited to xeriscapes. However, yuccas are very adaptable, with a few species growing wild even in the hot humidity of the southeastern seaboard.

These striking evergreen succulents form loose or tidy rosettes of stiff, lanceolate to linear leaves that terminate in a wicked spike. Stunning panicles of creamy-white, bell-shaped flowers rise high above the foliage. Their evening fragrance attracts pollinators, mostly night-flying yucca moths that lay eggs of their caterpillars in the blossoms.

Several other species are well worth growing, especially where water is in short supply: the narrow-leaved *Yucca glauca* (*Y. angustifolia*), or soapweed (1–3 ft., Z4–8), which in addition to its ornamental value served Native Americans as a source of soap and fiber; weeping yucca, *Y. recurvifolia*, with its strongly arching, blue-green leaves, as well as its variegated selections 'Monca' (also known as 'Banana Split') and 'Gold Ribbons'; and the very slow-growing but ultimately huge Big Bend yucca,

Yucca filamentosa 'Gold Heart'

Zantedeschia hybrid 'Gold Rush'

Y. rostrata, whose blue-gray leaves are borne in rosettes, reminiscent of giant porcupines, particularly in the selection 'Sapphire Skies'.

Few animals browse yuccas; susceptible to scale insects and cane borers; fungal leaf spots mar the leaves.

Increase by transplanting "pups" (rooted suckers) in spring, or take winter root cuttings. Sow seed of species in spring.

Yucca filamentosa

- white
- mid- to late summer
- 30–36 in. × 60 in.
- sun
- Z4–11

Adam's needle, filament yucca, century plant. Native to dry and sandy dunes of the coastal Southeast and west to Texas. Rosettes of long strap-shaped leaves, each tipped with a sharp spine and edged with curly fibrous threads. Robust flower stems may rise as much as 12 ft. or so above the leaves, carrying loose clusters of bell-shaped, white flowers, each with six tepals (undesignated petal-like structures).

'Bright Edge' forms robust clumps of spiny-tipped, stiff, curly, thread-edged leaves, widely banded with cream. Long, 8- to 10-in. spires of white flowers. Z4–11.

'Color Guard' leaves have a broad central stripe of creamy white flanked with green; sometimes coral flushed in cold weather. Vigorous, to 30 in. Similar 'Gold Heart' grows to 20 in. Suitable as architectural accents for smaller-space gardens and containers. Z5.

'Hairy' has blue-green leaves edged with white, twisted hairs. 18 in. × 36 in. Z4.

Yucca gloriosa

- white
- late summer to fall
- 6–8 ft. × 6 ft.
- sun
- Z7–11

Spanish dagger. Native from North Carolina to Florida. Dense evergreen clumps of stiff, gently arching, pointed leaves to 2 ft. in length. Large, white bell flowers sometimes flushed with purple, are arranged in stout panicles.

'Bright Star' has stiff, non-fading green leaves, edged broadly with gold. As temperatures drop in fall, leaf edges become dark pink. Pink flower buds open to white bells in summer.

'Variegata'. Variegated mound lily. Leaves, narrowly edged with cream, blush pink in winter.

Zantedeschia

Araceae
calla lily, arum lily

So fascinated was painter Georgia O'Keefe by the sensual beauty of callas that she came to be called "the lady of the lilies." In fact, they are even more ravishing in the garden than on canvas, and surprisingly easy to grow.

As natives of subtropical southern Africa, calla lilies are cold sensitive, but some hardier types overwinter outdoors in warmer parts of zone 7; a few even in zone 6. In colder regions, cultivate in containers and move indoors in winter.

Despite the common name, callas are not true lilies, but are relatives of Jack-in-the-pulpits. Large, waxy blooms consist of a finger-like, yellow spadix shrouded by a brightly colored or shining white, hood-like spathe. Leaves and flowers rise directly from rhizomatous roots; clusters of 2- to 3-ft.-tall arrowhead leaves.

Callas thrive in moist, humus-rich soil in full sun to partial shade. Consistent and generous irrigation through the summer is crucial for good bloom; mulch in fall with well-rotted compost or manure. Keep overwintering indoor plants cool; cut yellow foliage and withhold water through dormancy. Root rot results from winter wetness.

Excellent for providing exotic summer flair to terraces or borders, especially combined with elephant ears and hostas; stunning as cut flowers. Those that tolerate shallow, standing water make showy marginal plants for bog gardens. Japanese beetles relish calla lily foliage and flowers; resistant to deer and rabbits. All parts cause severe irritation of throat and mouth if eaten.

Propagate by division in spring. Seed sown in spring is slow; seedlings require two to three years to reach blooming size.

Zantedeschia aethiopica

- white
- spring to fall
- 2–3 ft. × 1.5–2 ft.
- sun, part shade
- Z7–10

White calla lily, pig lily. Southern Africa, naturalized in coastal northern California. Broad, arrow-shaped, dark green leaves to 18 in. long; flowers with 10-in.-long, white spathe and yellow, 3.5-in. spadix bloom throughout the warm season. Tolerates growing in water to 12 in. deep; good for pool edges and rain gardens.

'Crowborough' has large, creamy-white spathes; reputedly exceptionally cold hardy.

'Green Goddess' has smaller spathes, heavily splashed with green toward the margins.

'Marshmallow'. Pale pink spathes, darker toward the base.

Zantedeschia albomaculata

syn. *Z. melanoleuca, Z. oculata*

- white
- summer
- 18–24 in. × 20–36 in.
- sun, part sun
- Z7–10

Southern Africa, Zimbabwe, Kenya. White-flecked, dark green, 1- to 1.5-in.-wide leaves to 10 in. long; yellow spadix and cream-colored spathe, sometimes dark or black at throat. Requires gritty, well-drained soil.

Zantedeschia pentlandii
- yellow
- summer
- 3 ft. × 8 in.
- sun
- Z8–10

California calla. Rocky places along mountain streams in southern Africa. Leaves are broadly ovate, glaucous green, and occasionally speckled with white spots. Flowers have golden to lemon-yellow spathes, to 5 in. long, that are purple inside at the base, surrounding golden spadices. Prefers moist, sandy soil.

Other Notable Cultivars
The following are hardy to warmer parts of Z7:

Captain Series has solid or white-spotted leaves; yellow, purple, pink, orange, or red flowers. Adapts well to containers. 'Captain Camaro' is dark purple, 'Captain Murano' is bright pink with orange base. 12–24 in.

'Edge of Night'. White-spotted leaves edged with black-purple; dark, black-purple flowers. To 24 in.

'Gold Rush'. Spotted foliage, tough and long lasting. Deep yellow chalices. 18–24 in.

'Paco' has dark purple–centered spathes, bordered with mauve-pink. 15–18 in.

'Picasso' abundant purple spathes edged with wide white margins; white-spotted leaves. 30 in. × 18 in.

Zigadenus
Melanthiaceae
death camas

Take heed of a common name like this, and do not plant anywhere near a playground, sandbox, or anywhere plant parts could be ingested accidentally. All species are also toxic to livestock and deer.

Zigadenus prefers moist soils that drain well. It is excellent for replanting restoration areas of its native habitat. It should only be planted in a garden sited with great care, perhaps as a specimen or container plant that can be confined.

Propagate from seed in spring (or when ripe), or split off bulblets in spring or fall.

Zigadenus elegans
syn. *Anticlea elegans*
- white
- summer
- 2–3 ft. × 1 ft.
- sun, part shade
- Z3–9

Mountain death camas, alkali grass. Native on prairies and grasslands from Minnesota to Missouri, west to Alaska and Arizona. Thick tufts of 0.5-in.-wide, grassy, glaucous leaves to 1 ft. long arise from bulbs. Upright stems carry elegant loose racemes of up-facing starry, greenish white flowers, punctuated with green, two-pronged glands at the center.

Zigadenus elegans

Zizia
Apiaceae
golden Alexanders

Zizias are native across much of the United States where they are found growing in meadows, dry woods, and seasonally wet prairies. They host several species of butterflies, including clouded sulfers, American coppers, and the caterpillars of black swallowtails.

Provide a sunny or partly shaded spot for golden Alexanders. They thrive in humus-rich, fertile soil that remains damp. These wildflowers are well suited to native plant, wild, and wildlife gardens; unusual in floral bouquets. Pests and diseases are seldom a problem; deer ignore them.

Sow seed in fall or early winter, and overwinter outdoors for spring germination. Otherwise root cuttings of young growth or divide established plants in spring.

Zizia aptera
syn. *Taenidia*

- yellow
- late spring
- 1–3 ft. × 12–15 in.

- sun, part shade
- Z4–9

Heart-leaved golden Alexanders. Native to open woods and prairies across much of the country, especially in the Midwest. Basal leaves are handsome, bright green, oval and entire, edged with blunt teeth; they take on a ruddy hue in fall. Flat-topped umbels, 2–3 in. across, of 15 to 20 tiny, yellow flowers rise above the foliage on sturdy stems that smell of celery. Pollinating Missouri woodland swallowtail butterflies are frequent visitors. *Zizia aurea* may be a superior plant, due to its attractive twice-divided leaves that are strongly toothed along the edges. Flower clusters are similar. Seldom exhibits fall color.

Zizia aurea

Resources

PLANT HARDINESS MAPS
USDA zones of hardiness map
  http://planthardiness.ars.usda.gov/PHZMWeb

National Arbor Day Foundation zones of hardiness
map http://www.arborday.org/media/zones.cfm

Plant hardiness maps for other countries based
on the USDA system are available from the Pacific
Bulb Society website: http://www.pacificbulbsociety.
org/pbswiki/index.php/HardinessZoneMaps

COOPERATIVE EXTENSION
Nationwide educational network with divisions in
every US state and territory; provides regionally
adapted horticultural information, soil tests, etc.;
invaluable
  http://www.csrees.usda.gov/Extension

RESOURCES FOR MAIL ORDER PLANTS
Be sure to check local garden centers and nurseries for high quality plants before sending off for
the same plant by mail. Many local sources offer
fine selections. Plants received through the mail
will be smaller to save shipping costs and will have
endured the stress of transit, and thus will likely
take longer to establish in the garden and to bulk up.

United States

Ambergate Gardens
8730 County Road 43
Chaska, MN 55318-9358
www.ambergategardens.com

American Meadows
223 Avenue D, Suite 30
Williston, VT 05495
www.americanmeadows.com

Annie's Annuals
801 Chesley Ave
Richmond, CA 94801
www.anniesannuals.com

Bluestone Perennials
7211 Middle Ridge Road
Madison, OH 44057
www.bluestoneperennials.com

Brent and Becky's Bulbs
7900 Daffodil Lane
Gloucester, VA 23061
www.brentandbeckysbulbs.com

Deer-Resistant Landscape Nursery
3200 Sunstone Court
Clare, MI 48617-8600
www.deerxlandscape.com

Fairweather Gardens
PO Box 330
Greenwich, NJ 08323
www.fairweathergardens.com

Fieldstone Gardens, Inc.
55 Quaker Lane
Vassalboro, ME 04989-3816
www.FieldstoneGardens.com

Gardens Alive!
5100 Schenley Place
Lawrenceburg, IN 47025
www.gardensalive.com

Greer Gardens
1280 Goodpasture Island Road
Eugene, OR 97401
www.greergardens.com

High Country Gardens
PO Box 22398
Santa Fe, NM 87502
www.highcountrygardens.com

Joy Creek Nursery
20300 NW Watson Road
Scappoose, OR 97056
www.joycreek.com

Klehm's Song Sparrow Perennial Farm
13101 E Rye Road
Avalon, WI 53505
www.songsparrow.com

Kurt Bluemel, Inc.
2740 Greene Lane
Baldwin, MD 21013
www.kurtbluemel.com

McClure & Zimmerman
335 S High St.
Randolph, WI 53956
www.mzbulb.com

Niche Gardens
1111 Dawson Road
Chapel Hill, NC 27516
www.nichegardens.com

Plant Delights Nursery
9241 Sauls Road
Raleigh, NC 27603
www.plantdelights.com

Prairie Nursery
PO Box 306
Westfield, WI 53964
www.prairienursery.com

Select Seeds
180 Stickney Hill Road
Union, CT 06076
www.selectseeds.com

Wayside Gardens
One Garden Lane
Hodges, SC 29653
www.waysidegardens.com

Well-Sweep Herb Farm
205 Mount Bethel Road
Port Murray, NJ 07865-4147
www.wellsweep.com

White Flower Farm
PO Box 50, Route 63
Litchfield, CT 06759
www.whiteflowerfarm.com

Canada

Bluestem Nursery
16 Kingsley Road
Christina Lake, BC V0H 1E2
www.bluestem.ca

Botanus
PO Box 3184
Langley, BC V3A 4R5
www.botanus.com

Chapman Iris
8790 Wellington Road 124
Guelph, ON N1H 6H7
www.chapmaniris.com

Garden Import
135 West Beaver Creek Road
Richmond Hill, Ontario L4B 1C6
www.gardenimport.com

Fraser's Thimble Farms
175 Arbutus Road
Salt Spring Island, BC V8K1A3
www.thimblefarms.com

Whitehouse Perennials
594 Rae Road RR2
Almonte, ON K0A 1A0
www.whitehouseperennials.com

Wildflower Farm
10195 Hwy 12 West, R.R.#2
Coldwater, ON L0K 1E0
www.wildflowerfarm.com

United Kingdom

Ashwood Nurseries
Ashwood Lower Lane
Ashwood
Kingswinford, West Midlands DY6 0AE
www.ashwoodnurseries.com

Beth Chatto Gardens
Elmstead Market
Colchester, Essex CO7 7DB
www.bethchatto.co.uk

Binny's Plants
Binny Estate
Ecclesmachan, West Lothian EH52 6NL
www.binnyplants.co.uk

Broadleigh Gardens
Barr House, Bishops Hull
Taunton, Somerset TA4 1AE
www.broadleighbulbs.co.uk

Burncoose Nurseries
Gwennap
Redruth, Cornwall TR16 6BJ
www.burncoose.co.uk

Duchy of Cornwall Nursery
Cott Road
Lostwithiel, Cornwall PL22 0HW
www.duchyofcornwallnursery.co.uk

Glebe Cottage Plants
Pixie Lane
Warkleigh, Devon EX37 9DH

Guernsey Clematis Nursery
Domarie Vineries, Les Sauvagees
St Sampsons, Guernsey GY2 4FD
www.guernsey-clematis.co.uk

Iden Croft Herbs
Frittenden Road
Staplehurst, Kent TN12 0DH
www.uk-herbs.com

Knoll Gardens
Knoll Gardens
Hampreston, Wimborne BH21 7ND
www.knollgardens.co.uk

Macplants
5 Boggs Holdings
Pencaitland, East Lothian EH34 5BA
www.macplants.co.uk

Spring Reach Nursery
Long Reach
Ockham, Surrey GU23 6PG
www.springreachnursery.co.uk

Woottens of Wenhaston
Blackheath, Wenhaston
Halesworth, Suffolk IP19 9HD
www.woottensplants.co.uk

PLANT SOCIETIES

Useful sources of information about specific types and classes of plants; often offer advice on regionally adapted species and selections.

Alpine Garden Society
ags@alpinegardensociety.net
The society for anyone interested in small hardy plants and bulbs

American Hemerocallis Society
www.daylilies.org

American Iris Society
www.irises.org

American Peony Society
www.americanpeonysociety.org

Hardy Plant Society
www.hardy-plant.org.uk
Focus on hardy herbaceous plants of all sorts; based in the United Kingdom but has inspired a number of regional American groups, including:

Hardy Plant Society / Mid-Atlantic Group
www.hardyplant.org

Hardy Plant Society of New England, Connecticut Chapter
www.cthardyplantsociety.org

Hardy Plant Society of Oregon
www.hardyplantsociety.org

National Chrysanthemum Society
www.mums.org

North American Rock Garden Society
www.nargs.org

Perennial Plant Association
www.perennialplant.org
Education association of herbaceous perennial industry

Plant Heritage
info@plantheritage.org.uk
Runs the National Plant Collections Scheme with its "living libraries" of individual species, cared for by dedicated specialist growers

Society for Japanese Irises
www.socji.org

Society for Louisiana Irises
www.louisianas.org

Tall Bearded Iris Society
www.tbisonline.com

Index of Common Names

Aaron's beard   *Hypericum calycinum*
absinth   *Artemisia absinthium*
Adam's needle   *Yucca filamentosa*
adder's tongue   *Erythronium americanum*
Aegean wallflower   *Erysimum cheiri*
African daisy   *Gerbera* spp.
African hairbells   *Dierama pulcherrimum*
Alexander's rhubarb   *Rheum alexandrae*
Algerian iris   *Iris unguicularis*
alkali grass   *Zigadenus elegans*
Allegheny monkey flower   *Mimulus ringens*
Allegheny spurge   *Pachysandra procumbens*
Allwood pink   *Dianthus* ×*allwoodii*
alpine campion   *Lychnis alpina*
alpine catchfly   *Lychnis alpina*
alpine columbine   *Aquilegia alpina*
alpine geranium   *Erodium reichardii*
alpine poppy   *Papaver alpinum*
alpine rock rose   *Helianthemum alpestre*
alpine sea holly   *Eryngium alpinum*
alpine strawberry   *Fragaria vesca*
alpine toadflax   *Linaria alpina*
alpine wall cress   *Arabis procurrens*
alpine wallflower   *Erysimum linifolium*
alumroot   *Heuchera* spp.
American barrenwort   *Vancouveria hexandra*
American cowslip   *Dodecatheon meadia*
American ipecac   *Gillenia trifoliata*
American mandrake   *Podophyllum peltatum*
American mountain mint   *Pycnanthemum* spp.
American umbrella leaf   *Diphylleia cymosa*
American white hellebore   *Veratrum viride*
amethyst sea holly   *Eryngium amethystinum*
amur adonis   *Adonis amurensis*
amur pink   *Dianthus amurensis*
anomalous peony   *Paeonia anomala*
Appalachian Barbara's buttons   *Marshallia grandiflora*
Appalachian mountain mint   *Pycnanthemum flexuosum*
archangel   *Angelica archangelica*
arctic daisy   *Chrysanthemum arcticum*
arctic poppy   *Papaver nudicaule*
Arend's saxifrage   *Saxifraga* ×*arendsii*
Argentine blue-eyed grass   *Sisyrinchium striatum*
Arizona blue eyes   *Evolvulus arizonicus*
Arkansas bluestar   *Amsonia hubrichtii*
Arkwright's catchfly   *Lychnis* ×*arkwrightii*
Armenian basket flower   *Centaurea macrocephala*
Armenian geranium   *Geranium psilostemon*
aromatic aster   *Symphyotrichum oblongifolium*
arrow-leaf ginger   *Asarum arifolium*
artichoke thistle   *Cynara cardunculus*
arum lily   *Zantedeschia* spp.
asarum leaf   *Asarum asaroides*
ashy cranesbill   *Geranium cinereum*
Asian bellflower   *Codonopsis clematidea*
Asian forget-me-not   *Myosotis asiatica*

Asiatic poppy   *Meconopsis grandis*
aspen fleabane   *Erigeron speciosus*
aster   *Symphyotrichum* spp.
atlas poppy   *Papaver atlanticum*
Atlantic poppy   *Papaver atlanticum*
aubretia   *Aubrieta deltoidea*
August lily   *Hosta plantaginea*
auricula   *Primula auricula*
autumn-flowering monkshood   *Aconitum carmichaelii*
Autumn sage   *Salvia greggii*
avens   *Geum* spp.
azure monkshood   *Aconitum carmichaelii*
baby's breath   *Gypsophila cerastoides*
baby's breath   *Gypsophila paniculata*
baby swiss geranium   *Erodium reichardii*
Badger's bane   *Aconitum vulparia*
Baikal skullcap   *Scutellaria baicalensis*
Balkan bear's breech   *Acanthus hungaricus*
balloon flower   *Platycodon* spp.
Barbara's buttons   *Marshallia* spp.
Barberton daisy   *Gerbera jamesonii*
barren strawberry   *Waldsteinia* spp.
barrenwort   *Epimedium pinnatum*
barroom plant   *Aspidistra elatior*
basket-of-gold   *Aurinia saxatilis*
beach aster   *Erigeron glaucus*
beach fleabane   *Erigeron glaucus*
beach sunflower   *Helianthus debilis*
beach strawberry   *Fragaria chiloensis*
beach wormwood   *Artemisia stelleriana*
bearded hybrid iris   *Iris* ×*germanica*
beardtongue   *Penstemon* spp.
bear's breech   *Acanthus mollis*
bear's ears   *Primua auricula*
bear's foot hellebore   *Helleborus foetidus*
beavertail cactus   *Opuntia basilaris*
bedding dahlia   *Dahlia merckii*
bedstraw   *Galium* spp.
beebalm   *Monarda* spp.
beetleweed   *Galax urceolata*
belladonna delphinium   *Delphinium* ×*belladonna*
bell-flower hesperaloe   *Hesperaloe campanulata*
bellwort   *Uvularia* spp.
bergamot   *Monarda* spp.
Bermuda blue-eyed grass   *Sisyrinchium angustifolium*
Bethlehem sage   *Pulmonaria saccharata*
betony   *Stachys* spp.
Beverly bells   *Rehmannia* spp.
bicolor monkshood   *Aconitum* ×*cammarum*
big betony   *Stachys macrantha*
Bigelow's sneezeweed   *Helenium bigelovii*
bigflower self-heal   *Prunella grandiflora*
bigflower tickseed   *Coreopsis grandiflora*
big leaf ligularia   *Ligularia dentata*
bigleaf lupine   *Lupinus polyphyllus*
big leaf mountain mint   *Pycnanthemum muticum*

bigroot geranium *Geranium macrorrhizum*
bird's foot violet *Viola pedata*
bishop's hat *Epimedium* spp.
bishop's wort *Stachys officinalis*
bistort *Persicaria amplexicaulis, P. bistorta, P. microcephala*
bittercress *Cardamine* spp.
bitterwort *Gentiana lutea*
blackberry lily *Belamcanda chinensis*
black bugbane *Actaea racemosa*
black cohosh *Actaea racemosa*
black dragon *Dracunculus vulgaris*
black-eyed Susan *Rudbeckia* spp.
black false hellebore *Veratrum nigrum*
black iris *Iris tuberosa*
black snakeroot *Actaea racemosa*
blanket flower *Gaillardia* spp.
blazing star *Liatris* spp.
blood flower *Asclepias curassavica*
bloodroot *Sanguinaria canadensis*
bloody cranesbill *Geranium sanguineum*
blue anise sage *Salvia guaranitica*
blue-bead-lily *Clintonia borealis*
bluebells *Mertensia* spp.
bluebells of Scotland *Campanula rotundifolia*
blue bugleweed *Ajuga genevensis*
blue cohosh *Caulophyllum thalictroides*
blue corydalis *Corydalis elata, C. flexuosa*
blue diamond impatiens *Impatiens namchabarwensis*
blue dogbane *Amsonia tabernaemontana*
blue echeveria *Echeveria glauca*
blue-eyed grass *Sisyrinchium* spp.
blue-eyed Mary *Omphalodes verna*
blue false bleeding heart *Corydalis elata*
blue false indigo *Baptisia australis*
blue globe onion *Allium caeruleum*
blue flax *Linum perenne*
bluejacket *Tradescantia ohioensis*
blue leadwort *Ceratostigma plumbaginoides*
blue lungwort *Pulmonaria angustifolia*
blue-leaf red hot poker *Kniphofia caulescens*
blue oak sage *Salvia chamaedryoides*
blue poppy *Meconopsis betonicifolia, M. grandis*
Blue Ridge St. John's wort *Hypericum buckleyi*
blue rock bindweed *Convolvulus sabatius*
blue spiderwort *Commelina tuberosa*
blue star aster *Kalimeris incisa*
blue star creeper *Isotoma fluviatilis*
blue starflower *Amsonia tabernaemontana*
blue-stemmed goldenrod *Solidago caesia*
blue throatwort *Trachelium caeruleum*
blue vervain *Verbena hastata*
blue woolly speedwell *Veronica pectinata*
boneset *Eupatorium* spp., *Symphytum officinale*
bonnet bellflower *Codonopsis* spp.
bonytip fleabane *Erigeron karvinskianus*
border carnations *Dianthus ×allwoodii*
border phlox *Phlox paniculata*
bouncing bet *Saponaria* spp.

Bowman's root *Gillenia trifoliata, Veronicastrum virginicum*
Brazilian dwarf morning glory *Evolvulus glomeratus*
Brazilian petunia *Ruellia elegans*
Brazilian vervain *Verbena bonariensis*
bride's feathers *Aruncus dioicus*
bridal wreath *Francoa sonchifolia*
bridewort *Achillea ptarmica*
broadleaf chives *Allium senescens*
broadleaf speedwell *Veronica austriaca* subsp. *teucrium*
broad-leaved golden aster *Chrysopsis mariana*
broad-petaled geranium *Geranium platypetalum*
brook thistle *Cirsium rivulare*
brown-eyed Susan *Rudbeckia triloba*
bugbane *Actaea matsumurae, A. simplex*
Bulgarian geranium *Geranium macrorrhizum*
bunchberry *Cornus canadensis*
burnet *Sanguisorba* spp.
burning bush *Dictamnus albus*
bush clover *Lespedeza* spp.
bush clematis *Clematis heracleifolia*
bush daisy *Euryops acraeus*
bush lupine *Lupinus arboreus*
bush morning glory *Convolvulus cneorum*
Bush's poppy mallow *Callirhoe bushii*
Bush's purple coneflower *Echinacea paradoxa*
busy lizzie *Impatiens walleriana*
butterbur *Petasites* spp.
buttercup *Ranunculus* spp.
butterfly flag *Diplarrena moraea*
butterfly flag iris *Diplarrena moraea*
butterfly gaura *Gaura lindheimeri*
butterfly ginger *Hedychium coronarium*
butterfly weed *Asclepias tuberosa*
button snakeroot *Liatris spicata*
calico aster *Symphyotrichum lateriflorum*
California buttercup *Ranunculus californicus*
California calla *Zantedeschia pentlandii*
California corn lily *Veratrum californicum*
California fuchsia *Epilobium canum*
California peony *Paeonia californica*
California wormwood *Artemisia californica*
calla lily *Zantedeschia* spp.
Cambridge geranium *Geranium ×cantabriense*
camel's cover *Patrinia scabiosifolia*
campion *Lychnis* spp., *Silene* spp.
Canada mayflower *Maianthemum* spp.
Canadian columbine *Aquilegia canadensis*
Canadian wild ginger *Asarum canadense*
canary clover *Dorycnium* spp.
Cantonese fairy bells *Disporum cantoniense*
Cape figwort *Phygelius capensis*
Cape fuchsia *Phygelius* spp.
caraway thyme *Thymus herba-barona*
cardinal flower *Lobelia cardinalis*
cardinal beardtongue *Penstemon cardinalis*
cardoon *Cynara cardunculus*
Carolina bushpea *Thermopsis caroliniana*
Carolina campion *Silene caroliniana*

Culver's physic   *Veronicastrum virginicum*
Culver's root   *Veronicastrum* spp.
Cumberland rosemary   *Conradina verticillata*
cupflower   *Nierembergia* spp.
Cupid's dart   *Catananche caerulea*
cup plant   *Silphium perfoliatum*
curled-leaf hosta   *Hosta crispula*
curly mint   *Mentha spicata* 'Crispa'
curry plant   *Helichrysum italicum*
cushion spurge   *Euphorbia polychroma*
Dahurian gentian   *Gentiana dahurica*
daisy fleabane   *Erigeron speciosus*
Dalmatian bellflower   *Campanula dalmatica*
Dalmatian bellflower   *Campanula portenschlagiana*
Dalmatian cranesbill   *Geranium dalmaticum*
Dalmatian iris   *Iris pallida*
dame's rocket   *Hesperis* spp.
dame's violet   *Hesperis matronalis*
dark purple–flowered hosta   *Hosta ventricosa*
Davidson's penstemon   *Penstemon davidsonii*
daylily   *Hemerocallis* spp.
dead nettle   *Lamium* spp.
death camas   *Zigadenus* spp.
deep-blue curved bells   *Strobilanthes atropurpureus*
deer grass   *Rhexia* spp.
dense blazing star   *Liatris spicata*
dense-flowered loosestrife   *Lysimachia congestiflora*
dense ginger lily   *Hedychium densiflorum*
desert hollyhock   *Sphaeralcea ambigua*
desert mallow   *Sphaeralcea ambigua*
desert prince's plume   *Stanleya pinnata*
dogberry   *Clintonia borealis*
dogfennel   *Eupatorium capillifolium*
dogtooth violet   *Erythronium americanum*
doll's eyes   *Actaea pachypoda*
dotted beebalm   *Monarda punctata*
double Japanese aster   *Kalimeris pinnatifida*
downy amsonia   *Amsonia ciliata*
dragon arum   *Dracunculus vulgaris*
dragon mountain wand flower   *Dierama dracomontanum*
dragon's head   *Dracocephalum argunense, D. grandiflorum*
Drakensberg hairbell   *Dierama dracomontanum*
drumstick allium   *Allium sphaerocephalon*
drumstick primrose   *Primula denticulata*
dull meadow-pitchers   *Rhexia mariana*
Dumortier's daylily   *Hemerocallis dumortieri*
dunce cap   *Orostachys aggregatus, O. furusei*
dusky cranesbill   *Geranium phaeum*
dusty miller   *Artemisia stelleriana*
dusty miller   *Centaurea cineraria, Lychnis coronaria*
Dutchman's breeches   *Dicentra cucullaria*
dwarf blazing star   *Liatris microcephala*
dwarf bluestar   *Amsonia montana*
dwarf borage   *Borago pygmaea*
dwarf cranesbill   *Geranium renardii*
dwarf crested iris   *Iris cristata*
dwarf hardy gloxinia   *Incarvillea mairei*
dwarf goat's beard   *Aruncus aethusifolius*

dwarf Japanese Solomon's seal   *Polygonatum humile*
dwarf larkspur   *Delphinium tricorne*
dwarf lilyturf   *Ophiopogon japonicus*
dwarf meadow rue   *Thalictrum kiusianum*
dwarf morning glory   *Convolvulus tricolor*
dwarf patrinia   *Patrinia gibbosa*
dwarf pincushion flower   *Scabiosa japonica* var. *alpina*
dwarf scarlet larkspur   *Delphinium nudicaule*
dwarf sunwheel   *Buphthalmum salicifolium*
dwarf yarrow   *Achillea tomentosa*
dwarf yellow blackberry lily   *Belamcanda flabellata*
eastern Joe-Pye weed   *Eupatoriadelphus dubius*
Easter pasque flower   *Anemone patens*
eastern prickly pear   *Opuntia humifusa*
eastern purple coneflower   *Echinacea purpurea*
East Indies aster   *Aster tongolensis*
edelweiss   *Leontopodium alpinum*
elecampane   *Inula ensifolia, I. helenium*
elegant petunia   *Ruellia elegans*
elephant ear   *Colocasia* spp.
Endress's cranesbill   *Geranium endressii*
English lavender   *Lavandula angustifolia*
English monkshood   *Aconitum napellus*
English primrose   *Primula vulgaris*
English thyme   *Thymus vulgaris*
English violet   *Viola odorata*
eryngo   *Eryngium alpinum, E. bourgatii*
European columbine   *Aquilegia vulgaris*
European great burnet   *Sanguisorba officinalis*
European white hellebore   *Veratrum album*
European wild ginger   *Asarum europaeum*
evening primrose   *Oenothera* spp.
everlasting flower   *Helichrysum* spp.
everlasting pea   *Lathyrus latifolius*
fairies' thimbles   *Campanula cochlearifolia*
fairy bells   *Disporum flavens*
fairy iris   *Dietes grandiflora*
fairy primrose   *Primula japonica*
fairy's wandflower   *Dierama pulcherrimum*
fairy wings   *Epimedium epsteinii*
falling stars   *Crocosmia aurea*
false alumroot   *Tellima grandiflora*
false anemone   *Anemonopsis macrophylla*
false aster   *Boltonia asteroides*
false bugbane   *Beesia* spp.
false chamomile   *Boltonia asteroides*
false dragonhead   *Physostegia* spp.
false hellebore   *Veratrum* spp.
false indigo   *Baptisia* spp.
false lamium   *Lamium galeobdolon*
false lily-of-the-valley   *Maianthemum* spp.
false lupine   *Thermopsis* spp.
false rock cress   *Aubrieta deltoidea*
false rosemary   *Conradina canescens*
false sea pink   *Armeria pseudoarmeria*
false Solomon's seal   *Maianthemum racemosum*
false spirea   *Filipendula rubra*
false sunflower   *Heliopsis helianthoides*
fan columbine   *Aquilegia flabellata*

fernleaf corydalis   *Corydalis cheilanthifolia*
fern-leaf dropwort   *Filipendula vulgaris*
fernleaf peony   *Paeonia tenuifolia*
fern-leaf yarrow   *Achillea filipendulina*
feverfew   *Pyrethrum parthenium*
fig-leaf hollyhock   *Alcea ficifolia*
figwort   *Scrophularia* spp.
filament yucca   *Yucca filamentosa*
filaree   *Erodium* spp.
firecracker plant   *Echeveria setosa*
fire pink   *Silene virginica*
fireweed   *Epilobium angustifolium*
firewheel   *Gaillardia aestivalis*
fishwort   *Houttuynia cordata*
flaming poppy   *Stylophorum diphyllum*
flor de cobre   *Mimulus cupreus*
florinda primrose   *Primula florindae*
foamflower   *Tiarella* spp.
foamy bells   *×Heucherella*
foetid iris   *Iris foetidissima*
foothill penstemon   *Penstemon heterophyllus*
forget-me-not   *Myosotis* spp.
formosa bleeding heart   *Dicentra formosa*
fortnight lily   *Dietes iridioides*
fortune's hosta   *Hosta fortunei*
fox's brush   *Centranthus ruber*
foxtail lily   *Eremurus* spp.
fragrant Solomon's seal   *Polygonatum odoratum*
freckle face   *Hypoestes phyllostachya*
French cranesbill   *Geranium endressii*
French hollyhock   *Malva sylvestris*
French honeysuckle   *Hedysarum coronarium*
French lavender   *Lavandula dentata, L. stoechas*
Frickart's aster   *Aster ×frikartii*
frilly bergenia   *Bergenia ciliata*
fringe-bell   *Shortia soldanelloides*
fringe cups   *Tellima* spp.
fringed bleeding heart   *Dicentra eximia*
fringed bluestar   *Amsonia ciliata*
fringed galax   *Shortia soldanelloides*
fringed loosestrife   *Lysimachia ciliata*
fringed rock cress   *Arabis blepharophylla*
fringeleaf wild petunia   *Ruellia humilis*
frostweed   *Helianthemum mutabile*
fumewort   *Corydalis solida*
garden gloxinia   *Incarvillea mairei*
garden heliotrope   *Heliotropium arborescens*
garden heliotrope   *Valeriana officinalis*
garden myrrh   *Myrrhis* spp.
garlic chives   *Allium tuberosum*
gas plant   *Dictamnus albus*
gaudy Jack   *Arisaema sikokianum*
gayfeather   *Liatris* spp.
geneva bugleweed   *Ajuga genevensis*
gentian sage   *Salvia patens*
gentian speedwell   *Veronica gentianoides*
gerbera daisy   *Gerbera jamesonii*
German catchfly   *Lychnis viscaria*
germander   *Teucrium* spp.
germander sage   *Salvia chamaedryoides*
German garlic   *Allium senescens*

German iris   *Iris ×germanica*
German statice   *Goniolimon tataricum*
giant Barbara's buttons   *Marshallia grandiflora*
giant blue hyssop   *Agastache foeniculum*
giant cowslip   *Primula florindae*
giant desert candle   *Eremurus robustus*
giant elephant ear   *Colocasia gigantean*
giant fennel   *Ferula* spp.
giant fleeceflower   *Aconogonum* 'Johanniswolke',
    Persicaria polymorpha
giant helleborine   *Epipactis gigantea*
giant hesperaloe   *Hesperaloe funifera*
giant rhubarb   *Gunnera manicata*
giant scabious   *Cephalaria gigantea*
giant silver mullein   *Verbascum bombyciferum*
ginger-leaf false bugbane   *Beesia calthifolia*
Gladwyn iris   *Iris foetidissima*
globe centaurea   *Centaurea macrocephala*
globe daisy   *Globularia meridionalis*
globeflower   *Trollius* spp.
globe mallow   *Sphaeralcea* spp.
globe thistle   *Echinops* spp.
gloriosa daisy   *Rudbeckia hirta*
goat's beard   *Aruncus dioicus*
goat's rue   *Galega* spp.
golden Alexanders   *Zizia* spp.
golden buttons   *Tanacetum vulgare*
golden columbine   *Aquilegia chrysantha*
golden drop   *Chiastophyllum oppositifolium*
golden globes   *Lysimachia congestiflora*
golden groundsel   *Senecio aureus*
golden hawk's beard   *Crepis aurea*
golden flax   *Linum flavum*
golden lace   *Patrinia scabiosifolia*
golden lamb's tail   *Chiastophyllum oppositifolium*
golden marguerite   *Anthemis sancti-johannis, A.*
    tinctoria
golden peony   *Paeonia mlokosewitschii*
golden ragwort   *Senecio aureus*
goldenrod   *Solidago* spp.
goldenroot   *Scutellaria baicalensis*
goldenstar   *Chrysogonum virginianum*
goldentuft   *Aurinia saxatilis*
golden valerian   *Patrinia scabiosifolia*
golden yarrow   *Eriophyllum lanatum*
goldmoss stonecrop   *Sedum acre*
gold star   *Chrysogonum virginianum*
good luck plant   *Oxalis tetraphylla*
gooseneck loosestrife   *Lysimachia clethroides*
granny's bonnet   *Aquilegia vulgaris*
grape-leaf anemone   *Anemone tomentosa*
grass lily   *Anthericum liliago*
grass pink   *Dianthus plumarius*
gray broom   *Dorycnium hirsutum*
gray-headed coneflower   *Ratibida pinnata*
grayleaf cranesbill   *Geranium cinereum*
gray-leaved conradina   *Conradina canescens*
gray-leaf St. John's wort   *Hypericum cerastoides*
great blue lobelia   *Lobelia siphilitica*
greater burnet   *Sanguisorba officinalis*
greater celandine   *Chelidonium majus*

society garlic   *Tulbaghia* spp.
soldier's friend   *Achillea millefolium*
solidaster×   *Solidaster luteus* 'Lemore'
solitary clematis   *Clematis integrifolia*
Solomon's seal   *Polygonatum* spp.
sorrel   *Oxalis* spp.
southern marsh orchid   *Dactylorhiza praetermissa*
southern rose mallow   *Hibiscus moscheutos*
southernwood   *Artemisia abrotanum*
Spanish blue flax   *Linum narbonense*
Spanish chervil   *Myrrhis odorata*
Spanish dagger   *Yucca gloriosa*
Spanish lavender   *Lavandula stoechas*
Spanish leopard's bane   *Doronicum columnae*
speckled wood lily   *Clintonia umbellulata*
speedwell   *Veronica* spp.
spiderwort   *Tradescantia* spp.
spike gayfeather   *Liatris spicata*
spike lavender   *Lavandula latifolia*
spike speedwell   *Veronica spicata*
spiny alyssum   *Alyssum spinosum*
spoonleaf yucca   *Yucca filamentosa*
spotted bellflower   *Campanula punctata*
spotted dead nettle   *Lamium maculatum*
spotted geranium   *Geranium maculatum*
spotted henbit   *Lamium maculatum*
spotted horsemint   *Monarda punctata*
spotted Joe-Pye weed   *Eupatoriadelphus maculatus*
spring adonis   *Adonis vernalis*
spring beauty   *Claytonia virginica*
spring star flower   *Rhodohypoxis baurii*
spring vetchling   *Lathyrus vernus*
spurge   *Pachysandra* spp.
spurless columbine   *Aquilegia ecalcarata*
square-stemmed monkey flower   *Mimulus ringens*
squaw root   *Caulophyllum thalictroides*
stagger weed   *Dicentra cucullaria*
star astilbe   *Astilbe simplicifolia*
St. Bernard's lily   *Anthericum* spp.
St. Bruno's lily   *Paradisea liliastrum*
St. John's chamomile   *Anthemis sancti-johannis*
sticky catchfly   *Lychnis viscaria*
sticky germander   *Scrophularia buergeriana* 'Lemon and Lime'
sticky Jerusalem sage   *Phlomis russeliana*
stinking Benjamin   *Helleborus foetidus*
stinking hellebore   *Helleborus foetidus*
stinking iris   *Iris foetidissima*
stink lily   *Dracunculus vulgaris*
stinking Benjamin   *Trillium erectum*
Stokes' aster   *Stokesia* spp.
stonecrop   *Sedum* spp.
storkbill   *Erodium absinthoides, E. carvifolium*
strawberry begonia   *Saxifraga stolonifera*
stream orchid   *Epipactis gigantea*
striped cranesbill   *Geranium sanguineum* var. *striatum*
sugar scoop   *Tiarella trifoliata* subsp. *unifoliata*
sukka sweet vetch   *Hedysarum coronarium*
sulphur cinquefoil   *Potentilla recta*

summer gentian   *Gentiana septemfida* var. *lagodechiana*
summer phlox   *Phlox carolina, P. paniculata*
sundial lupine   *Lupinus perennis*
sundrops   *Oenothera* spp.
sunflower heliopsis   *Heliopsis helianthoides*
swamp hibiscus   *Hibiscus coccineus*
swamp lantern   *Lysichiton* spp.
swamp milkweed   *Asclepias incarnata*
swamp rose mallow   *Hibiscus moscheutos*
swamp sunflower   *Helianthus angustifolius*
sweet flag   *Acorus americanus*
sweet Cicely   *Myrrhis* spp.
sweet coltsfoot   *Petasites japonicus*
sweet coneflower   *Rudbeckia subtomentosa*
sweet goldenrod   *Solidago odora*
sweet iris   *Iris pallida*
sweet-scented Joe-Pye weed   *Eupatorium purpureum*
sweet violet   *Viola odorata*
sweet William   *Dianthus barbatus*
sweet woodruff   *Galium odoratum*
swordleaf inula   *Inula ensifolia*
tall boneset   *Eupatorium altissimum*
tall fringed bluebells   *Mertensia ciliata*
tall hybrid delphinium   *Delphinium ×elatum*
tall mallow   *Malva sylvestris*
tall narrow-leaved sunflower   *Helianthus simulans*
tall sunflower   *Helianthus giganteus*
tall verbena   *Verbena bonariensis*
tansy   *Tanacetum* spp.
taro   *Colocasia esculenta, C. fallax*
Tatarian cephalaria   *Cephalaria gigantea*
Tatarian daisy   *Aster tataricus*
Tatarian statice   *Goniolimon tataricum*
Tatarian sea lavender   *Goniolimon tataricum*
telekia   *Telekia* spp.
Texas hummingbird mint   *Agastache cana*
Thai petunia   *Ruellia elegans*
thickleaf phlox   *Phlox carolina*
threadleaf coreopsis   *Coreopsis verticillata*
threadleaf ironwood   *Vernonia lettermanii*
three-birds-flying   *Linaria triornithophora*
thrift   *Armeria maritima*
throatwort   *Trachelium* spp.
Thunberg's bush clover   *Lespedeza thunbergii*
thyme   *Thymus* spp.
Tibetan primrose   *Primula florindae*
tiger tongue   *Opuntia cacanapa*
toad lily   *Tricyrtis* spp.
toadshade   *Trillium cuneatum*
toad trillium   *Trillium cuneatum*
topped lavender   *Lavandula stoechas*
torch lily   *Kniphofia* spp.
tovara   *Persicaria virginiana*
trailing ice plant   *Delosperma cooperi, Lampranthus spectabilis*
trailing lithodora   *Lithodora diffusa*
trailing St. John's wort   *Hypericum cerastoides*
transvaal daisy   *Gerbera* spp.
tree celandine   *Macleaya* spp.

winter bergenia *Bergenia ciliata*
woman's tobacco *Antennaria plantaginifolia*
wood anemone *Anemone nemorosa*
woodland bluestar *Amsonia tabernaemontana* var.
  salicifolia
wood cranesbill *Geranium sylvaticum*
wood geranium *Geranium maculatum*
woodland cranesbill *Geranium sylvaticum*
wood poppy *Hunnemania fumariifolia*
wood poppy *Stylophorum diphyllum*
wood sage *Teucrium hircanium*
wood spurge *Euphorbia amygdaloides*
woodland peony *Paeonia obovata*
woodland phlox *Phlox divaricata*
woodland strawberry *Fragaria vesca*
woodland sunflower *Heliopsis helianthoides*
woolly horehound *Marrubium incanum*
woolly speedwell *Veronica incana*
woolly sunflower *Eriophyllum lanatum*
woolly thyme *Thymus pseudolanuginosus*
woolly yarrow *Achillea tomentosa*
worm grass *Spigelia* spp.
wormwood *Artemisia* spp.
wreath goldenrod *Solidago caesia*
Yawata-so *Peltoboykinia tellimoides*
yellow asphodel *Asphodeline lutea*
yellow avalanche lily *Erythronium grandiflorum*
yellow avens *Dryas drummondii*
yellow bletilla *Bletilla ochracea*

yellow bush daisy *Euryops pectinatus*
yellow catmint *Nepeta govaniana*
yellow coneflower *Echinacea paradoxa*
yellow corydalis *Pseudofumaria lutea*
yellow-eyed grass *Sisyrinchium striatum*
yellow fairy bells *Disporum lanuginosum*
yellow flax *Linum flavum*
yellow foxglove *Digitalis grandiflora*
yellow glacier lily *Erythronium grandiflorum*
yellow hardhat *Centaurea macrocephala*
yellow horned poppy *Glaucium flavum*
yellow ice plant *Delosperma nubigenum*
yellow Jacob's ladder *Polemonium pauciflorum*
yellow monkey flower *Mimulus luteus*
yellow ladyslipper *Cypripedium calceolus*
yellow lamb's tail *Chiastophyllum oppositifolium*
yellow lavender *Lavandula viridis*
yellow loosestrife *Lysimachia punctata*
yellow mandarin *Disporum lanuginosum*
yellow marsh marigold *Caltha palustris*
yellow meadow rue *Thalictrum flavum*
yellow oxeye daisy *Buphthalmum* spp.
yellow scabious *Cephalaria gigantea*
yellow snowdrop *Erythronium albidum*
yellow trout lily *Erythronium americanum*
yellow trillium *Trillium luteum*
yellow wild iris *Dietes bicolor*
yellow waxbells *Kirengeshoma* spp.
yellow wolfsbane *Aconitum vulparia*

Photo Credits

© Ruth Rogers Clausen: pages 99, 107, 116, 121, 124, 131, 143, 166, 175, 179, 181, 186, 190, 205, 227, 236, 268, 279, 288, 290, 329, 357, 364, 408.

© Nicolas H. Ekstrom / Ruth Rogers Clausen: pages 113, 153, 201, 243, 248, 252, 297, 317, 321, 326, 329, 332, 348, 368, 393.

All other photographs © Alan L. Detrick and Linda Detrick.

The photographers would also like to express their sincere appreciation for the courtesy and assistance extended to them at the following gardens:

Chanticleer Garden, Wayne, PA
Chicago Botanic Garden, Glencoe, IL
Coastal Maine Botanical Gardens, Boothbay, ME
Cornell Plantations, Ithaca, NY
Frelinghuysen Arboretum, Morristown, NJ
Goodstay Gardens, Wilmington, DE
Indianapolis Museum of Art, Indianapolis, IN
JC Raulston Arboretum, Raleigh, NC
Leonard J. Buck Garden, Far Hills, NJ
Longwood Gardens, Kennett Square, PA
Naples Botanical Garden, Naples, FL
The New York Botanical Garden, Bronx, NY
Niagara Parks' Botanical Gardens, Niagara Falls, Ontario, Canada
North Creek Nurseries, Landenberg, PA
Plant Delights Nursery, Raleigh, NC
The Royal Botanical Gardens, Burlington, Ontario, Canada
Sandy's Plants, Inc., Mechanicsville, VA
Sarah P. Duke Gardens, Durham, NC
Stonecrop Gardens, Cold Spring, NY
Sunny Border Nurseries, Kensington, CT
Wave Hill, Bronx, NY

About the Authors

ALAN L. DETRICK

Ruth Rogers Clausen, a horticulturist trained in England, has been living and working in United States for many years. Over her long career she has taught and lectured widely. Former horticulture editor for *Country Living Gardener*, she has written several books, including *Perennials for American Gardens*, co-authored with the late Nicolas H. Ekstrom. Others include *Dreamscaping* (Hearst) and *50 Beautiful Deer-Resistant Plants* (Timber Press).

SUZANNE O'CONNELL

Thomas Christopher, a graduate of the New York Botanical Garden School of Professional Horticulture, has worked for almost forty years creating gardens for clients. He is a former columnist for *Horticulture, House & Garden*, and *Country Living Gardener*, and has been a contributor to *The New York Times* and the *Journal of The Royal Horticultural Society*; this is his twelfth book.

ALAN L. AND LINDA DETRICK

Alan L. and Linda Detrick are professional photographers whose horticulture and nature images appear in media worldwide. They have lectured and conducted photography workshops at Maine Media Workshops, the New York Botanical Garden, and Chanticleer Garden, as well as for the American Horticultural Society, the Garden Club of America, and the Garden Writers Association, where they are fellows and were inducted into the GWA Hall of Fame in 2010. Alan is the author and photographer of *Macro Photography for Gardeners and Nature Lovers,* and the sole photographer for *50 Beautiful Deer-Resistant Plants*, by Ruth Rogers Clausen. Alan and Linda divide their time between Glen Rock, NJ, and Smith Mountain Lake, VA.